THOMAS
EARL OF DANBY

PUBLISHED BY

JACKSON, SON & CO., GLASGOW
Publishers to the University

———

LONDON : SIMPKIN MARSHALL, LTD.

Cambridge · · Bowes and Bowes.
Oxford · · · B. H. Blackwell, Ltd.
Edinburgh · · Douglas and Foulis.
New York · · The Macmillan Co.
Toronto · · · The Macmillan Co. of Canada.
Sydney · · · Angus and Robertson.

———

MCMXLIV

London · 16 · Apr · 1678 ·

Wee are so surpris'd here att ye obstructions given
by ye States to ye Generall treaty of Alliance betwixt
vs, the Emperor, Spaine & them, that itt has putt
things amongst vs into greater vncertainties therevpon,
but that wch amazeth most is, to find them make a
difficulty vpon ye hindring all trafficke wth France,
when Monsr Van=Beuninghen has so long insisted
to gaine itt here. & (as hee saith) by ye States order
to assure the king of theire entring into ye same
obligation, but pretends now not to have ye same
power when there is most need of itt. Wee are not
able to vnderstand ye meaning of this att a time
when my Master is so ready to goe into ye vtmost
Alliances against France wch any of ye Confederates
will come to, & to declare the warr whenever those
treatys can bee perfected; but if itt should proceed
out of an over earnest desire of a peace (wch is said
here to bee ye cause) I am sure itt is ye worst way to

FACSIMILE OF THE FIRST PAGE OF A LETTER FROM THE EARL
OF DANBY TO THE PRINCE OF ORANGE

answer from Holland as to their conjunction in this Quadruple League, and I doubt not but y^r Highness will putt your vtmost helps to itt, as I shall euer to shew my selfe,

Y^r Highness^{es}

Most truly Obedient seruant

Danby

FACSIMILE OF THE LAST PAGE OF THE SAME LETTER

THOMAS OSBORNE

EARL OF DANBY

AND DUKE OF LEEDS

1632–1712

BY

ANDREW BROWNING, M.A., D.Litt.

PROFESSOR OF HISTORY IN THE UNIVERSITY OF GLASGOW

VOLUME II

LETTERS

GLASGOW

JACKSON, SON & CO.

PUBLISHERS TO THE UNIVERSITY

1944

PRINTED IN GREAT BRITAIN BY ROBERT MACLEHOSE AND CO. LTD.,
THE UNIVERSITY PRESS, GLASGOW, FOR JACKSON, SON AND CO.
(BOOKSELLERS) LTD., PUBLISHERS TO THE UNIVERSITY, GLASGOW.

PREFACE

THE following collection of letters and papers is published with a twofold object. On the one hand it aims at providing a representative selection both of the private and of the official correspondence of the Duke of Leeds at every stage in his career, together with such of his notes and memoranda as throw real light on his policy and methods of government. On the other hand it endeavours to supply a corrected and amplified edition of the *Letters* which the Duke himself published two years before his death.

From this double object arises the somewhat arbitrary division of the whole mass of documents into two entirely separate sections, arranged on different principles and yet at various points encroaching on each other's sphere. The first section follows, on the whole, the arrangement of the preceding *Life ;* is practically confined to letters and memoranda written by the Duke of Leeds ; but naturally omits, as belonging to the second section, all the letters which he wrote in connection with foreign affairs during his period of office as Lord Treasurer. The second section follows the arrangement adopted by the Duke ; contains the letters he received as well as those he wrote ; but also omits, as belonging to the first section, a number of memoranda dealing with foreign policy which it might with propriety have included.

For the failings of the second section the blame may to some extent be laid at the door of the Duke of Leeds ; but as regards the first section no evasion of responsibility is possible. The selection and arrangement of the documents are entirely the work of the editor, who is himself only too well aware how easily criticism may be directed against them.

CONTENTS

SECTION A

LETTERS AND MEMORANDA

PART I

SIR THOMAS OSBORNE AND THE DUKE OF BUCKINGHAM

1632-73

PART II

MY LORD TREASURER THE EARL OF DANBY

1673-9

vii

PART III

A STATESMAN OUT OF OFFICE

1679-89

PART IV

CARMARTHEN AND LEEDS

1689-1712

SECTION B

THE LETTERS OF 1710

CONTENTS

ILLUSTRATIONS

SECTION A

LETTERS AND MEMORANDA

GENERAL INTRODUCTION

ALTHOUGH quite without the passion which distinguished his contemporary, Sir Joseph Williamson, for preserving every scrap of writing that came his way, the first Duke of Leeds was very methodical in dealing with his papers. When writing letters of importance it was his practice to make a draft, usually very liberally corrected, then to write out a fair version, and having dispatched the latter to endorse and preserve the former as a copy. When faced with important interviews it was his custom to draw up brief memoranda of the points he proposed to make, and occasionally to record afterwards the substance of what had been said on both sides. Letters and memorials sent to him, if of sufficient consequence, he habitually endorsed and retained, while as a result of the numerous controversies in which he was engaged he several times found it necessary to gather together and arrange large sections of the documents in his possession.

As a result he must have left behind him at his death an enormous mass of written material, the bulk of which has happily survived to the present day. A small collection, composed presumably of the papers in the hands of his faithful brother-in-law, Charles Bertie, was preserved until recently at Bertie's country seat at Uffington. It has been fairly adequately calendared by the Historical Manuscripts Commission.[1] A much larger collection, in the possession of the present Duke of Leeds, was preserved at Hornby Castle. The report of the Historical Manuscripts Commission upon it is a mere catalogue.[2]

But the largest collection of all was that sold at Sotheby's in April 1869. Fortunately the bulk of that collection was

---

[1] *Rep. XIV.*, App. 9, pp. 367-457 ; *Supplementary Report on the Manuscripts of the Earl of Lindsey.*

[2] *Rep XI.*, App. 7 pp. 1-58.

3

purchased by the British Museum, and is now arranged in the fifty-six volumes of Leeds-Godolphin Manuscripts there.[1] Another considerable portion was bought by Mr. Alfred Morrison and incorporated in his famous collection of autographs. On the sale of the Morrison collection,[2] the letters from Montagu to Danby which he possessed were secured for the British Museum,[3] but the remaining Leeds papers were hopelessly dispersed. Fortunately, however, the whole collection had already been reported upon, although in a somewhat inadequate manner, by the Historical Manuscripts Commission,[4] while the more important at least among the Leeds papers had been printed verbatim in the very elaborate catalogue of his treasures edited for Mr. Alfred Morrison by Mr. Thibaudeau.[5]

Of the documents sold in 1869 there are no doubt other small collections,[6] but only one of these merits attention. A dozen or so letters of special importance were purchased by Dr. John Webster of Aberdeen, and while in his possession were catalogued by the Historical Manuscripts Commission.[7] On the sale of the Webster collection [8] they came into the hands of Mr. J. Eliot Hodgkin, who made them the basis of the very interesting collection of Danby papers which by judicious purchases he built up. In this shape the papers were again calendared by the Historical Manuscripts Commission,[9] very fully this time, though not very accurately. Finally on the sale of the Hodgkin collection the majority of them came into the hands of the British Museum, where they can now be consulted along with Mr. Hodgkin's own very elaborate notes.[10]

When united together these various groups of documents form a remarkably complete collection of papers connected with the first Duke of Leeds. There are, however, two striking gaps. On the one hand there are practically no documents for the period previous to the Restoration, the earliest extant letter

---

[1] B.M. Add. MSS. 28040-95.   [2] At Sotheby's, December 1917-May 1919.
[3] B.M. Add. MSS. 39757.   [4] *Rep. IX.*, App. 2, pp. 406-93.
[5] *Catalogue of the Collection of Autograph Letters and Historical Documents formed by Alfred Morrison*, ed. A. W. Thibaudeau, 6 vols., 1883-92.
[6] Several documents from the Leeds sale are for instance included in B.M. Add. MSS. 34195 and 34274.
[7] *Rep. III.*, App., pp. 420-1.   [8] At Sotheby's, May 1892.
[9] *Rep. XV.*, App. 2, pp. 185-202.   [10] B.M. Add. MSS. 38849.

written by Sir Thomas Osborne being dated June 1, 1661, when he was nearly thirty years of age. On the other hand the reign of William III, from 1690 onwards, is almost a complete blank. The mass of papers which the Duke of Leeds must have gathered together during his second period of office as chief minister of the Crown has almost entirely vanished.

To fill these gaps and supplement the main collection, recourse is naturally had to letters from the Duke of Leeds preserved among the papers of his correspondents, but of these there are surprisingly few. There is, of course, the magnificent series of letters to William of Orange preserved among the Domestic State Papers,[1] in its way the most revealing set of letters which the Duke wrote. There is the less important series of letters to the Earl of Essex, while he was Lord Lieu-tenant of Ireland,[2] the group of letters to Sir John Lowther,[3] those to Lord Chesterfield,[4] and those written by Leeds towards the close of his life to the Earl of Oxford.[5] But of the more intimate letters which he must have written to the Earl of Lindsey, the Earl of Abingdon, and other relatives outside his immediate family circle, only the barest handful survive.

A collection of the Duke's letters and papers is thus neces-sarily very uneven. In the following pages, however, some attempt has been made to remedy this defect by printing as much as possible for the lean years, and only a selection from those for which the materials available are ample. To print all the Duke's papers would be impossible, and would serve no useful purpose, as a very large number are concerned with purely temporary and personal interests of his own. On the whole, the following collection is confined to important letters and documents which have not hitherto been published, but to this general rule a number of exceptions for various reasons have been made.

[1] S.P. Dom., King William's Chest. Two of the letters are among the archives of the House of Orange-Nassau.

[2] Stowe MSS. 201-212.

[3] Hist. MSS. Com., Rep. XIII., App. 7, *Lonsdale MSS.*,

[4] B.M. Add. MSS. 19253. A number are printed in *Letters of Philip, second Earl of Chesterfield.*

[5] Hist. MSS. Com., *Portland MSS.*, vol. v.

PART I

SIR THOMAS OSBORNE AND THE DUKE OF
BUCKINGHAM

1632-73

THE letters and papers of Sir Thomas Osborne for the first forty years of his life are very scanty indeed. Until his rise to fame as Lord Treasurer he rarely thought it worth while to retain copies of his own letters, while the friends to whom he wrote did not consider his communications sufficiently important to preserve them from destruction. From the last dozen years of the period, however, a few letters and papers survive, which make up to some extent in interest what unfortunately they lack in bulk.

I. FAMILY CORRESPONDENCE

EVEN when he was a married man of ten years' standing it was the practice of Sir Thomas, when he was separated from his wife, to write to her every post, or twice a week, besides sending occasional letters by special messengers when opportunity offered. In the years immediately succeeding the Restoration the care of her family practically confined Lady Osborne to Kiveton, while her husband, especially after his election to Parliament, had to pay frequent visits to London and Oxford. A fairly extensive correspondence in consequence must have passed between them, and although all Lady Osborne's letters have been lost, eight of those written by Sir Thomas still survive. It is greatly to be regretted that the number of these letters is so small, for they throw light on a side of his character which hitherto has been scarcely suspected. History has always inclined to regard him as a man in whom ambition had overborne almost every more human emotion, but it is well to remember that Sir Thomas does not really appear on the stage of history until more than forty years of age. These letters show that as a younger man he was not merely an affectionate husband and father, but a faithful friend, and even a witty and entertaining correspondent.

To Lady Osborne at Kiveton.[1]

My dearest deare heart,

I have failed you no post since I came, nor will I whilest I stay, which will bee very short, for since I have carried my councell to the Atturney they are agree'd that my businesse belongs not to the King, nor can I doe anything but force him

---

[1] Autograph letter in Leeds MSS., Packet 2. This is the earliest of Sir Thomas Osborne's letters which has been found.

to disburse the money for the use of the churches, which may perhaps induce him rather to some composition then hee will part with the whole summe to charitable uses ; so that I shall only stay to speake with him for his resolve, who I am inform'd will bee in towne upon Monday or Tuesday next.

I have not bine att Court yett, nor will I waite in expectation of anything there, though I thinke I might procure a very beneficiall bargaine in farming the Excize of Yorkshire, if I understood itt, and I am offered some good peniworths in Ireland to goe over with my Lord Ossery, which wee will consider together before I resolve. The Parliament have voted the King a benevolence for his present occasions, and have read the bill for bishops a second time. They are now moving slowly towards setling of the militia, but I perceive itt not likely to produce anything of profitt towards us officers.

Sir Francis Fane goes towards home on Monday in the coach, and so does my brother, so that I hope wee shall make a shift for godfathers, and God willing I shall bee att Keeton as soone, or soone after them. Here is vast gallantry, but I converse so litle with itt that I know no news, nor I have not yett bin att Whitehall ; but I was this day att a play, and in the box with my Lady Dorothy Savile, who cannot bee merry with the thoughts of going into the country, which Sir George talkes of in three weekes.

I am more weary then ever I was of this towne, and most impatient to bee with thy deare selfe, to whom my mother presents her service, and I my blessing to my children, who am, Dearest,

Your most intirely affectionate husband,

T. Osborne.

London, June 1st, 1661.

[To Lady Osborne] [1]

London, 8th November, 1664.

My dearest heart,

Beyond our expectation wee gott hither on Saterday night,[2] but so late that I could not write by that post. I gott so great a cold in my journey that I have not yett stir'd out of

---

[1] Autograph letter in Leeds MSS., Packet 2.   [2] November 5.

dores, but itt is only a head cold, so that I hope to bee well shortly, and intend this day to see my brother Vere. My mother is very kind to mee, and has done her best to procure mee the money, but itt is so hard to come by that I am yett upon very great uncertainty ; and Mr. Yates has not sent up the inquisition, so that I cannot proceed with my grant.

I doe not find but the Duke of Buckingham will have his commission for President, and would have had itt already but that hee is so infinitely carelesse. Hee is now att an horsematch att Newmarkett, and has left all things prepared here for his voyage to sea with the Duke of York ; but I hope hee will come too late, for his Highnesse goes to Portsmouth to-morrow to meet the fleet there. All the gallants in the towne goe along with his Highnesse, and leave many sad wifes, sisters and mistresses, and particularly my cosin Warwick for her husband.

My Lord Fitzharding has bin married this two months to Mrs. Baggot, but owned itt not till Saterday last, and was the next day sent in great hast with some private message from our King to his Majestie of France. My Lord Brackley is next weeke to marry my Lord Midlesex's neice with all consents, and I have heard of some other matrimonies of lesse importance. But I shall tell you one which will serve for all the rest, which is the Dutchesse of Richmond to northerne Tom Howard, who both owned itt yesterday.

The Dutch are not come forth with theire fleet, so that our sparks will find sea roome enough. My mother presents her service to you, and with my blessing to my poore children I remayne

Most affectionately, faithfully and intirely thine,

T. Osborne.

To Lady Osborne at Kiveton.[1]

London, 25th February, 1664 [/5].

My dearest heart,

This has bin so busy a day with mee att a comittee which concern'd the Duke of Buckingham that I am return'd home but att 9 a clock att night, so that I am still prevented in my

[1] Autograph letter in Leeds MSS., Packet 2.

intentions to write to my sister. I have got the Treasurers
certificate, and my pattent is going on att the Chancellors, but
I cannot yett have an opportunity for my other businesse ; only
the King told mee yesternight hee approved the designe and
would talke to mee of itt.   The bill in Parliament about the
Excize is only to give the farmers power as commissioners, and
I was told to-day that divers of our Parliament men were this
weeke with my Lord Treasurer to desire the farme might bee
put into gentlemens hands of the country, but could not
prevaile ; and truly I beleeve the designe (if not prevented) is to
keepe itt in the same hands itt is now.

Here is no newes but the contradiction of the tragedy att
Guiny, the intelligencer haveing confesst hee told a lie and has
this day lost his eares for itt.   The King has put out a declaration for the war, and the Duke of York intends to goe to sea
himselfe within a fortnight or three weekes.   My brother Vere
is now with mee and presents you his service.   My mother sends
you hers also, and I the most deare and faithfull affection of thy

T. Osborne.

To Lady Osborne at Kiveton.[1]

London, 11th March, 1664[/5].

My dearest heart,
       I received yours last night with my sister Campdens
inclosed, and according to your desire have burnt hers.   But by
Sir Christopher Claphams, which I sent you the last post,[2] you
will see the secrett is not so great in anything as that Mr.
Ashburnham is the solicitor.   The King is expected home but
this night, so that till I have spoke againe with his Majestie I can
putt itt into no other method then itt is, and people att your
distance see not how things stand with the Treasurer.   Besides
I have his Majesties promise that if others bid not considerably
more then I have done I shall have itt.   I hope I shall bee able
to judge more by Tuesday, or I shall grow very weary of my
expectation, since I have not your company to divert itt, and

---

[1] Autograph letter in Leeds MSS., Packet 2.

[2] Among the Leeds MSS., Packet 2, is a letter from Sir Christopher Clapham
to Sir Thomas Osborne, dated Stamford, 5 March 1664[/5], offering to join
with him in farming the Yorkshire Excise.

I have great confidence that by the end of that weeke I shall have perfected the tedious work of my pattent.

I am sorry my sister Campden has discouraged your journey to Exton, for itt is a pleasure to mee of thinking to meet you one day sooner. Here is not any news since my last but a report that the Citty will repaire the Kings losse of the *London* att theire owne charge. My mother presents you her service, and I would faine say some kinder thing then is possible to represent to thee the infinite affection of, Dearest Deare,

Thy intirely faithfull husband and lover,

T. Osborne.

[To Lady Osborne] [1]

Dearest heart,

I am so surprized with the sudden newes of my Lord Ogles sending a servant to Welbeck that I am risen out of my bed att 3 a clock in the morning to lett you know wee gott well hither yesterday, and found 1,250,000 l. voted to his Majestie to bee raised together with the next two yeares tax, but the manner not yett absolutely agreed. T'is thought wee shall not sitt above three weekes att most. I have not time to tell you the adventures of our journey, but I find all very kind here, especially the Dutchesse, who askes most kindly for you and wisht you here.

I have not seene your father, but heare hee is well, and Sir Robert Paston and I go to dine with him to-morrow. Your brother Peregrine is gone this day towards Stamford for his election, and I saw Vere, but had no discourse. Here is no newes but that itt is confidently beleeved wee shall have war with France. It is so cold I could scarse write more if I had time, so that I conclude with a present of the most faithfull and intire affection of thy

T. Osborne.

I stole this bitt of paper to write on.
My blessing to my litle ones.

Oxford, 13th October, 1665.

[1] Autograph letter in Leeds MSS., Packet 2.

To Lady Osborne at Kiveton.[1]

Oxford, 25th October, 1665.

My dearest heart,

This is the fifth letter I have writt, and have received none but by my Lord Ogles servant. In my first by the post I told you to direct them to the House of Commons, where I receive my letters very safe, from York and other places. The bill for money is now finisht, and yesterday the Parliament gave a present of an hundred and twenty thousand pounds to the Duke of York, to bee raised by one months tax att the expiration of the royall aide. Itt was moved by Sir John Goodrick, and seconded by my Lord Ogle and divers of us northerne members, which has made a great addition of the Dukes kindnesse to us, but still wee are honest Penderells.

My Lord Ogle leaves the towne this weeke, and so I hope to do the next, if I receive letters from Mr. Hill to give satisfaction about Wyvills businesse, which puts mee to a great deale of trouble. Godolphin pretends to give mee some satisfaction within a weeke about Sir Ralph Knights affaire, and Sir Robert Paston saies that so soone as hee receives letters from London hee will tell mee of a designe wherein with some paines I may bee able to do both him and myselfe good, and that hee has an assurance of the Chancellors assistance in itt already; but hee has not told mee the project, nor said anything to mee of itt these six daies, so that perhaps hee thinks of a better partner by this time.

The Dutch have made great bravadoes upon our coast, and are now with 30 sayle in the Gunfleet, but my Lord Sandwich is gone away post to see if they will stay for him. My Lord your father was here yesterday, but return'd att night, and saies hee will stay in towne all the next weeke. I writt you formerly that I can do nothing about your gowne till [I have] both your directions and measure, and I can alwaies write you truly that I am

Thy most passionately affectionate husband and lover,

T. Osborne.

[1] Autograph letter in Leeds MSS., Packet 2.

To Lady Osborne at Kiveton.[1]

London, 29 September, [16]66.

My dearest heart,

Yesterday I received yours of the 22th, with Mrs. Midletons desire to see the deed of my mothers joynture. Pray lett her know that I shall willingly lett anybody from her have a sight of itt, but I have the deed here with mee, so that shee must appointe somebody in this towne to view itt, unlesse shee can stay till my returne into the country. I had also Mr. Midletons letter, with which I am well enough satisfied, for what I askt of him I have power to do without him.

For the accounts of the officers of the navy, I writt you in my last they were already given to us, and that wee have appointed severall comittees to examine them, who begin on Monday with the particulars ; and I am very civilly treated by those gentlemen, being appointed one of theire examinors. In the meane time wee have passt the bill against Irish cattle in the comittee, and doubt not to do itt in the House, but wee are almost assured the King will not passe itt.

I thinke I have formerly acquainted you how I behaved myselfe concerning Mr. Palmer, and I will lett my brother Vere know your desires to mee about itt, but truly I thinke the best of his cause is that the place is infected, so that witnesses cannot bee brought up, and that will secure him from any disturbance of this session. I should have acquainted you if anything had bin made out of a designe in fireing the Citty, but that cannot bee found, although many are still of opinion there were some actors in the mischeife ; and for your satisfaction how the King beares itt, I assure you there is no appearance of the least alteration either in his mind or countenance. Whatever my Lord Newcastle may heare you may bee confident nothing has bin knowne of our fleets but what I have transmitted to you, and wee have no assurance where they are att present ; only they are not come to Sowld Bay as was reported the last post.

My brother Peregrine went this morning out of towne to Rycott, and goes thence to Exton to my brother Norris, who remaines there ill of the black jaundice (as I heare), and they

---

[1] Autograph letter in Leeds MSS., Packet 2.

are in apprehension of some danger. My Lord Castleton has bin here this weeke, so that you are misinformed of his being now att Sandbeck. Though you thought your queries too much to answer att once, you see I have also added all wee know here, and am pleased in nothing so much as intertaining myselfe with deare Bridgett, being

Her most constant faithfull husband,

T. Osborne.

My blessing to the children, whom I long to heare are all well ; and Robin desires mee to lett you know hee can neither tell the sort of pins you would have nor the size of the combs.

To Lady Osborne at Kiveton.[1]

London, 2nd October, [16]66.

My dearest heart,

I received no letter from you this post, and itt equally troubles mee when I do not heare or cannot write, both of them being great satisfaction to mee ; and I assure you I have not fail'd on my part, besides my letters by messingers. I have yett heard nothing how you approve of a journey hither for a while, for I do much feare the length of this session, and shall never indure itt without you, although I feare my Lord Byrons businesse will hardly bee gott on till some of the great publique difficulties bee over. Wee move deadly slow about the supply, finding many knotts in the account which wee are indeavouring to passe first, and I doubt that will prove very tedious.

I have bin this afternoon imployd in the committee of exa-mining persons suspected for fireing the Citty, but all the allegations are very frivolous, and people are generally satisfied that the fire was accidentall. Our fleet has bin in sight of the Dutch three severall daies the last weeke, but they always waved our ingaging them, and this is all wee yett know.

My Lord Frescheville talks of leaving us speedily, but leaves my cosin Frank behind him. I have bin made her solicitor to know his good intentions in future towards her, and truly can find litle more then good intentions to comfort her. In the red

[1] Autograph letter in Leeds MSS., Packet 2.

cabinett att Thorp you will find severall draughts of my mothers will, which are not signed nor sealed. Pray send mee one of them by the next post, and lett mee know how Peregrine does, and the rest of our litle ones. I most heartily wish for thy deare company, being

Thy fond as well as faithfull husband,

T. Osborne.

Besides the 100 l. in Mr. Lathums hand I find there will want 150 l. more to pay the 1000 l. to Mr. Floyd the last of this month.

To Viscountess Campden at Exton.[1]

London, 20th October, 1666.

My dearest sister,

I must beg your pardon that I have not sooner given you thanks for the favour of your letter and your kindnesse in itt, and I assure you that want of time has bin the true cause. I hope this will find you and my wife together, or otherwise I know not where to find her with a letter, for by the miscarriage of her letters I have expected her here all this last weeke till yesternight that two of hers came together ; and by one of them shee tells mee her intentions of coming from Keeton yesterday, and then I guesse shee is this night att Exton, and may possibly stay there till this post reach her.

I have not yett bin att Court, so that I am not able to give account of what modes or amours are there ; only they have begun the playes for diversion now the nights grow long. I have attended the Parliament most of this weeke, and theire time has bin for the most part taken up in considering the manner how to raise the 1,800,000 l., but are come to no resolution, nor will scarsely the next ; the designes yett on foot are the purchasing of the chimney money att eight yeares valew, and an imposition upon seal'd paper. My Lord Falconbridge does still continue his hopefull way of recovery, and is this day gott out of his bed, so that I hope hee will gett out of this danger ; and for the quarrell (which you desire to know) I protest itt is beyond mee to say certainely, hee never speaking word to mee of any, nor I desiring to know till afterwards, and that att

[1] Autograph letter in Leeds MSS., Packet 2.

second hand ; only I dare assure you there was nothing of the Duke of Buckingham in the case.

I could tell you some merry newes if I durst venture itt in a letter, but perhaps somebody else may, or however time will make itt never the worse. Pray present my humble service to my Lord and all yours, and to my brother Norris and my sister Mary. All the courtiers are in vests, and his Majestie has taken att least 200 l. of severall persons to give 100 l. for every 20 shillings when hee changes this habitt, which is intended for good husbandry, and will bee the dearest wee have had yett. I pray that some good occasion would bring you to towne this winter, because I thinke wee are preparing for a short life and a merry, and I would in that time injoy the company of my best freinds as much as I could ; and as I have the vanity to thinke that amongst those I have few better then yourselfe, so I have the confidence to affirme that to my power you have none better then, Dearest sister,

Your most faithfull brother and servant,

T. Osborne.

II. CORRESPONDENCE WITH THE DUKE OF BUCKINGHAM

It is unfortunate for the biographer of Sir Thomas Osborne that Buckingham was so incurably careless in epistolary as in other matters. During this early period Osborne's connection with him was extremely close, and a very considerable correspondence must have passed between them ; yet not one of Sir Thomas's letters has been preserved. Drafts or copies, however, were occasionally kept by the writer, and the nine which have survived are all printed. Buckingham's own letters have been more generally preserved, but the majority of them are mere notes, either insufficiently dated or not dated at all. One of them, the date of which can be identified, is included in the notes.

To the Duke of Buckingham.[1]

19 January, [16]64[/5].

I suppose by this time you may have heard of my election att York, which I have incompassed by your Graces favour, and do therefore presume to give your Grace the trouble of receiving my humblest thanks for itt. I confesse I mett with a more difficult opposition then I expected, and the rather because itt was most occasioned by some officers of your Graces regiment ; but I must do the citty that right to assure your Grace that the greatest number of the best citizens (and particularly all the aldermen but one) were very ready to give mee theire assistance upon your Graces account. I intend shortly to attend your Grace, and shall bee ready to pay my services with all the duty and respect which becomes

[T. Osborne]

To the Duke of Buckingham.[2]

Keeton, 25th December, 1665.

My Lord,

Att my returne into this country I found Sir George Savile and Sir Godfrey Copley not lesse dissatisfied then myselfe about our usage in the last businesse, insomuch that wee are all desirous to bee troubled with no affaires but our owne till wee are more capable of doing his Majesties. Yett wee dare not take that occasion to complaine, least itt should bee thought wee were afraid to have the office of finding out plotts taken out of our hands, and should indeavour to supplant others of that glorious and beneficiall employment. Your Grace will perceive by the inclosed (which I received yesterday from Sir Godfrey Copley) that wee have a call to that service, which I am forc't to excuse myselfe from because of my wifes sicknesse, and both Sir George and Sir Godfrey have some occasions which do att this time hinder them ; though for my owne part I would sett by all considerations to goe, if I could do the King or country any service by itt (which in this I know is not possible),

---

[1] From an autograph draft in Leeds MSS., Packet 2.

[2] From an autograph draft in Leeds MSS., Packet 2.

or that there were not examinors enough besides to do nothing.

Your Grace may observe what freinds of yours are prickt out to bee added to the examinors, which I heartily wish may ever bee imploy'd upon such hopefull errands ; and I confesse they are much fitter then any of us, whose opinions are that the most ignorant [1] would bee the best examinors. My Lord Frescheville in his letter saies hee understands that wee are appointed by my Lord Arlington to examine ; but haveing received no such appointment I hope our not going will bee jugded no want of duty, but that wee may first expect another kind of summons then this letter. Sir George nor myselfe have not yett heard a word from Oxford, only wee guesse att the resolves by theire haste to have the prisoners examined. I trust in your Graces favour to make your owne use of this, but not to shew itt to any other whereby itt may prove to the prejudice of, My Lord,

Your Graces [&c],

[T. Osborne]

To the Duke of Buckingham.[2]

[30th January, 1666]

May itt please your Grace,

Wee have sent your Grace the coppies of two letters, one of which wee received by an expresse upon Sonday last from Sir William Morise, and the other is our returne to itt.[3] Your Grace will find by ours that wee have sumoned the militia to appeare, and wee have appointed the severall regiments under your Graces commands to bee att the severall most convenient places for them on Tuesday next, but shall not draw them into one body till orders from his Majestie or yourselfe. In the meane time wee hope either to see or heare from your Grace, and in case of a march wee must crave your particular direction how to behave ourselves in other Leiutennancys which wee must goe through to any sea-coast. Wee must also beg your Graces order for such amunition as wee shall have need for out of Cliffords

---

[1] The words ' in this matter ' are inserted here and then struck out.

[2] From a copy in Osborne's handwriting in Leeds MSS., Packet 2.

[3] These letters have not been found.

Tower, and with all readinesse to obey your Graces comands wee remayne, My Lord,

Your Graces, &c.,

F. Fane.   T. Osborne.
Jo. Armitage.   Jo. Kaye.
God. Copley.   Jo. Dawnay.[1]

To the Duke of Buckingham.[2]

Keeton, 17th March, 1665[/6].

My Lord,

I writt to your Grace about three weekes agoe, and inclosed the coppy of a letter I received from Sir William Morice, but have received no answer ; and as I then told your Grace, so there is still nothing done upon the former orders, nor I am confident will not bee till more perfect directions from your Grace. Wee are informed that the postmaster of Doncaster is to bee removed for some miscarriages in his place, which I thinke there may bee cause enough for, and I am solicited by one Captain Benjamin Marshall, an officer of my regiment who lives in Doncaster, to recommend him to your Grace for your assistance to gett itt. Wherefore I make bold to assure your Grace that as itt is very necessary to have an honest and diligent postmaster there, so this gentleman has the generall approbation of all the persons of quality hereabouts to bee the fittest for the imployment, and therefore when hee shall apply himselfe to your Grace will I hope receive your certificate according to that character.

I am confident our enemies are att this time quiett from any designes in this country, whatever may bee pretended to the contrary ; but I beleeve Cornett Strangwaies may give some apprehensions by his intelligence to the Generall, which I find hee sends frequently by Sir Roger Langley, who conveys itt to his sonne who is ensigne in the Generalls regiment. I was in hopes to have waited on your Grace att Newmarkett to see your

---

[1] Endorsed by Osborne, 'Coppy of the deputy leiutenants letter to the Duke of Buckingham, 30th January [16]65[/6].' The signatures are in Osborne's handwriting.

[2] From an autograph draft in Leeds MSS., Packet 2.

horse match, but am prevented, so that I can only wish your Grace good successe, as I doe most heartily in all things, being, My Lord,

Your Graces, &c.,

[T. Osborne]

To the Duke of Buckingham.[1]

London, 7th October, 1668.

My Lord,

I was not able to waite upon my Lord Keeper till this day, haveing kept my bed for the most part with a very great cold. Hee fell of himselfe into the discourse of my Lord Ormond, and used the same expression hee has done formerly to mee, that itt was by no meanes fitt hee should returne any more into Ireland as Leiutenant, that hee thought this the fittest opportunity his Majestie could ever have of takeing that imployment from him, and that neither this nor the suspension of my Lord Anglesey could faile att this juncture of time, if they were presst closely and vigourously to the King by your Grace and my Lord Arlington ; but if there should bee any remissnesse in the doing of them, itt were better to lett them alone. Hee told mee further that his opinion was itt might bee best for some time att first to send justices into Ireland, whereof hee would have my Lord Ossory to bee one, for the more easy and faire parting with my Lord of Ormond. For my Lord Anglesey, hee does not only thinke itt of absolute necessity to have him suspended both his office and the Councell, but that the King ought to do itt speedily by his letter, wherein hee should also declare whom hee would have comissionated to execute the place. And hee saies hee declared this to bee his opinion the last weeke to Mr. Secretary Trevor, who tooke notes of what hee said, and was by him desired to transmitt itt to your Grace and my Lord Arlington, as also that if this opportunity were lost, there would scarse ever bee so faire an overture to settle two of the most weighty affaires, viz., the Navy and the Kingdome of Ireland.

I asked his lordship why hee did not write his judgment of these things to the King himselfe, and hee told mee because hee would not presse his opinion upon his Majestie unlesse required

[1] From an autograph copy in B.M. Add. MSS. 28053, f. 20.

to deliver itt ; but in that case hee would write itt very freely, so that your Grace sees which way you may have itt from himselfe if itt bee necessary. I have this only to adde, that his lordship desires you will impart this to none but my Lord Arlington. I am, My Lord,

Your Graces most humble and most obedient servant,

[T. Osborne]

[To the Duke of Buckingham] [1]

[8th October, 1668]

My Lord Keeper bid mee tell your Grace that if there were a necessity of his coming to Awdley End for effecting the purposes in the letter hee would bee there when your Grace should direct ; but hee would not bee putt to the trouble of the journey without such a necessity. And hee injoynd mee to tell your Grace by a note apart that hee would not have my Lord Arlington nor any other to know of his offer to goe to Awdley End, and I find him very doubtfull of my Lord Arlingtons concurrence in the businesse of my Lord of Ormond. My Lord Keeper desires you will burne this note,[2] and hee wished mee to send this expresse messinger to your Grace.

[T. Osborne] [3]

To the Duke of Buckingham.[4]

London, 8th October, 1668.

My Lord,

I sent a messinger to your Grace this day, but this will bee perhaps as soone with you by a servant of my Lord Orerys, who tells mee hee has informed you how by the post after our waiting upon the King att his house there were letters sent by my Lord of Ormond to the Councill in Ireland directing them to prepare acts for a Parliament in Ireland which would bee speedily summoned. Now your Grace knows this to bee so

[1] From an autograph draft in B.M. Add. MSS. 28053, f. 42. It is undated, but seems quite clearly to be the note carried by the messenger referred to in the following letter.

[2] Originally, ' both this note and the letter.'

[3] Endorsed by Osborne, ' A Memorandum from Lord Keeper Brigman.'

[4] From an autograph copy in B.M. Add. MSS. 28053, f. 22.

direct contrary to the Kings publique resolves that itt must either bee an act of the highest folly and insolence, or done by such underhand practises with his Majestie as must give you more then ordinary caution both in this and the rest of your affaires, and itt will most highly concerne your Grace to know the truth of itt from the King himselfe, who will need no other charge against my Lord Ormond if itt bee not true that hee had the Kings order to write to the Councill in Ireland, nor your Grace no better warning if itt bee true. My Lord Orrery and I are both of opinion that my Lord Keepers journey to Awdley End will bee most necessary, as adding more weight then anything else can do to the remove of my Lord Ormond, when the King shall understand that hee puts himselfe to the journey cheifely for that purpose ; and you need not spare him, for hee told mee hee thought hee could indure the journey very well.

I perceived by my discourse with his lordship yesterday (though hee did not say so) that the designe of makeing justices in Ireland was for an expedient of bringing my Lord Arlington to a compliance by makeing my Lord Ossory one of them, but my Lord Orrery is confident hee nor his father for him will not accept of itt, and for that cause only hee likes the expedient, because when hee has refused itt will make all the rest of the expedient vanish, and most certainely introduce a Lord Leiutenant. I must needs acquainte your Grace with my Lord Orrerys kindnesse to you in delaying to conclude that great improvement which hee only can make of the Kings revenue in Ireland that itt may appeare your Graces act ; and I do find him really and heartily concern'd in all your affaires, which I doubt not but your Grace will take notice of to his lordship.

The towne is full of that newes which the woman writt your Grace that night I last saw you, and though itt may all bee but smoake, your Grace must pardon my concludeing itt is not without good store of fire, if I shall see you not able to prevaile against this seemingly unsupported lord. What commands your Grace has for mee I beg may bee sent by this bearer and not my owne servant, because I have appointed him to goe further before hee returnes. I take your Grace to have a most criticall work upon your hands, in which as in all other things I wish your Grace the best successe, as becomes, My Lord,

Your Graces most faithfull and most obedient servant,

[T. Osborne]

Wee all thinke the speedy remove of my Lord Anglesey would much take off the disguise and facilitate the other work, and therefore that no time should bee omitted of sending for my Lord Keeper.

To the Duke of Buckingham.[1]

Saterday night, 18 December, [16]69.

My Lord,

I had one of the inclosed from my Lord Orrery to give your Grace, from which hee could not separate the cover without breakeing the seale. The other was sent mee last night by Doctor Worsley, and since that time my Lord Keeper received a letter from my Lord Leiutenant, who therein desires to bee recalled, and his lordship has shew'd itt the King this day. I have calld divers times againe to-day to have spoke to your Grace both about this and other things, which (as I writt your Grace last night) I conceived to bee of great importance ; but since I cannot have that honour, nor can possibly bring myselfe to bee of your Graces opinion, that such businesse as is now in hand will bee done with so little time given to itt as your Grace is pleased to afford, I must confesse my despaire of any future good, and therefore finding myselfe uncapable of doing your Grace any reall service in publique affaires I hope your Grace will not bee displeased that I intend to retire only to the businesse of that imployment I am charged with, and when your Grace shall have occasion to comand mee in anything which concernes your particular, I shall most faithfully approve myselfe as I am obliged, My Lord,

Your Graces most obedient and most humble servant,

T. Osborne.[2]

[1] From an autograph copy in B.M. Add. MSS. 28053, f. 28.

[2] What appears to be Buckingham's answer to this letter runs as follows :
Sunday [19 December, 1669]—Upon the receipt of your letter I got out of my bed with intention to speake with you, my Lord Keeper, and Lord Orrery ; but before I could bee ready I was forced to goe to bed againe, where I have

[To the Duke of Buckingham] [1]

[*circa* November 20, 1670]

My Lord,

Since your Graces returne from France I find myselfe so much estranged both from your trust and usuall kindnesse that I have reason to suspect some of those may have prevailed att last, who have so long designed to do mee ill offices to your Grace. For the truth of what any can say I need not to examine myselfe, haveing a perfect assurance that everything must bee false concerning mee that speakes other then my services and fidelity to your Grace, of both which I have been so happy as to give some testimonies, without the least false step or inconstancy. I know how impossible itt is for your Grace to forbid anybody (though never so uneasy to you) otherwise then by avoiding theire company as much as you can, and itt is as contrary to my nature to bee twice the occasion of such uneasinesse ; but my unwillingnesse to beleeve itt in this case has made mee trespasse more then anything else in the world could have done.

I confesse I ought not to give your Grace this trouble, but the freedome I have bin admitted to gives mee the presumption to acquainte your Grace when I thinke myselfe unkindly used. Besides I am concernd to lett your Grace know that itt is now my interest to have my Lord Anglesey restored to his place, least by mistake, and as an act of good nature to an old acquaintance, your Grace should indeavour to hinder itt, when you heare of itt from my Lord Arlington, who I suppose will move your Grace because of Sir Thomas Litletons concerne. The truth is I have agreed with my Lord Anglesey to give him no opposition, resolving, if I can gett but that compensation, to retire from all publique imployment, in which as I have never

beene in a fitt of an ague from 12 a clock till within this halfe hower, which is the cause I could not write to you sooner. I wonder why my Lord Lieftenant showld write for leave to come over, and I wonder as much why my Lord Keeper showld shew the letter to the King. I confesse I expect noe good from it. If you will meete mee to-morrow at dinner at my owne howse, and get my Lord Orrery to bee there, I showld be glad to talke with you of this whole matter. In the meane time pardon mee if I am able to say noe more at present, having a very greate paine in my head, and being very weake after the teadious fitt I have had to-day. (B.M. Add. MSS. 28053, f. 15.)

[1] From an autograph draft in B.M. Add. MSS. 28053, f. 123.

received any profitt, so have I been as far from any other satisfaction but that of doing your Grace service, which was ever performed with the greatest affection and zeale of

Your Graces most obedient servant,

[T. Osborne]

III. OFFICIAL CORRESPONDENCE

THE majority of the letters written by Osborne to Buckingham were at least semi-official in character ; but Sir Thomas, as sheriff or deputy lieutenant, was also not infrequently in direct official communication with Whitehall. A few of his letters and memorials have been recovered from among the State Papers, and a number of others are printed from drafts or copies which he retained.

Sir Thomas Osburnes paper
of the remaining part of the plot in the north.[1]

That some persons, viz., Mr. Gregory, Mr. Mountaine, Captain Linley, and others who were privy to the late intended rebellion are not brought to theire examinations.

That many prisoners not tried att the last gaole delivery because there were then but single witnesses against them will bee in no better readinesse for theire trialls att the next assizes.

That many prisoners who were tried att the last gaole delivery, and had confesst theire guilt in the late intended rebellion, were notwithstanding acquitted by the jury for want of two witnesses against them in court, and are now att liberty upon baile, so that they are still in the same readinesse for rebellion.

That there are many reasons to induce us to beleeve that the rebells in Yorkshire do still prosecute theire intended treasonable designes.

---

[1] S.P. Dom., Charles II, 93, No. 91. The document itself is in Osborne's handwriting ; the endorsement, here printed as a heading, is not. The date is certainly about February 1663/4.

That one great cause of the slow progresse in discoveries is the weekly changing the examinors.

That another as great is the informers not being att all or very inconsiderably rewarded.

[To Sir Henry Bennet] [1]

Mr. Secretary,   York, 9th Aprill, 1664.

In obedience to his Majesties commands directed by letters to us for examining and preparing the prisoners for theire trialls att the late assizes,[2] wee have done as much as lay in our power to give a good account of them to the judges ; but the effect hath falne much short of our desire, though not of our expectation, for wee have had assurance from time to time by our intelligence amongst them that itt is the cheife care of those most concern'd to keepe the rest either by profitt or perswasions from makeing any discoveries, nor is itt to bee expected otherwise, unlesse wee could make theire confessions as beneficiall as they find theire concealements.

The best progresse to bee made now, wee conceive, would bee with the Bishoprick prisoners, whom wee thought itt our duty to secure upon the informations given against them, but the way of getting them hither was so tedious that wee found itt impossible to have them in readinesse for theire trialls att this assizes, and haveing discharged the duty required of us here, wee thinke itt necessary to informe you of theire imprisonment, that they may bee continued or discharged as you shall find occasion. To that purpose wee have inclosed a list of the Bishoprick mens names who are imprisoned here and att Durham, and one Ellerington will shortly bee att London to informe you of theire guilt. If you please to afford him the freedome of discourse, you will find what opportunities have bin lost of his intelligence for want of good management, and the relation of his usage will shew you how the Kings witnesses have bin discouraged (instead of any reward), of which hee is not the single example. Wee could never gett Evan Price

[1] S.P. Dom., Charles II, 96, No. 70, in Sir Thomas Osborne's handwriting, but signed by his fellow deputy lieutenants as well.

[2] The letters referred to are presumably those calendared in Cal. S.P. Dom. 1663-4, p. 493.

hither, notwithstanding wee have divers times sent for him from Lancaster, and wee thinke great use might bee made of him if hee could bee perswaded to a confession. However itt will bee a necessary care of those you shall imploy to indeavour itt.

Haveing performed those commands laid upon us, wee shall now make bold to retire to our owne occasions, which itt concerns us very much to looke att after so long a neglect of them. But as wee have alwaies bin ready to prefer the Kings service before our owne concernes, so wee shall ever preserve the same resolutions, and are with very great respect, Sir,

Your most faithfull humble servants,

Ro. Langley.

T. Jenkyns.   Godf. Copley.   T. Osborne.

To Sir Henry Bennet.[1]
Mr. Secretary,

Since my returne home I have not heard anything which concerns the publique but by this inclosed letter from Colonel Ewbanck,[2] which I thought fitt to send you, and have marked some places where hee seemes to intimate as if I stood accomptable for Eleringtons appearance. I am sure there can bee no reason for itt, there being witnesses enough that I would have had him sent up long since, and I suppose Colonel Ewbanck himselfe is able to give you the best account of his stay. If I might presume to deliver my opinion I should thinke John Topling (now att York) much better in your custody, fearing hee has such correspondents as you will have much difficulty to find out while hee remaines there.

I crave your pardon for the trouble, which I did not thinke to have given you in this kind, but intend shortly to waite on you about my owne businesse, wherein I cannot doubt of good successe, haveing all the justice in the world and the addition of your promise for itt. I am with great respect, Sir,

Your [&c]

Keeton, 30th April, 1664.   [T. Osborne] [3]

[1] Leeds MSS., Packet 2, an autograph draft.

[2] The words ' of the 29th instant from Doncaster ' are here struck out.

[3] Endorsed by Osborne, ' Coppy of my letter to Sir Henry Bennett, 30th April 1664. From Keeton.'

Memorandum about the Excise, 1 March, [16]64[/5] [1]

Your Majesties revenue of Excize within the county of York has bin farm'd for the three yeares last past att the sume of 13,500 l. per annum, and the country has made great complaint of theire oppression by the collectors of itt, who do raise much greater summes, of which your Majestie receives no portion. It is humbly proposed to pay to your Majestie for the said Excize the yearely summe of 14,000 l., and to raise and maintaine an hundred horse with officers in pay according to the establishment of your Majesties regiment of horse under the Earle of Oxford. And that the country may also receive a benefitt by this proposall the farmer will ingage to abate them 1,000 l. yearely of what they now pay.

The lease to the present farmers expires att Michaelmas next.

March the first, 1664 [/5]

[To Sir Philip Warwick] [2]

[March, 1664/5]

Sir,

Least any mistake should arise about a paper which I presented to his Majestie concerning the farme of the Excize of Yorkshire, and being assured itt will come to your hand before anything bee concluded in itt, I beg leave to trouble you with explaning my intention, which I have already done to the King, but am afraid his Majestie may forgett itt, and therefore desire you will expresse itt for mee when there shall bee occasion. I am willing to raise and pay 60 horse, besides officers (which is the standing number of a troop in my Lord of Oxfords regiment), according to the establishment of the said regiment, which will amount to 3,700 l. per annum, and to adde 500 l. per annum besides to his Majesties present revenue, and to abate the country 1,000 l. per annum of what they now pay. But because his Majestie never spoke of any rent in money I had no occasion

[1] Leeds MSS., Packet 2, an autograph copy. The endorsement, here printed as a heading, is not in Osborne's handwriting.

[2] Leeds MSS., Packet 2, an autograph draft.

to declare my mind in that particular,[1] saving by my Lord Frescheville, who did assure his Majestie I would give 3,000 l. addition, viz., 16,500 l., which I shall performe with good security, besides the abatement of the 1,000 l. to the country.[1] If my health would have lett mee waite on you, I would have beg'd this favour from you myselfe, who am,

[T. Osborne] [2]

[To Sir William Coventry] [3]

Keeton, 17th March, 1665[/6].

Sir,

I do acknowlege the favour of yours of the 6th, and must now beg your directions concerning the inclosed. You will find by itt that some prisoners of the like nature have bin released by deputy leiutenants of the East Riding ; but being comanded by his Royal Highnesse to imprison Colonel Sawrey, wee will not release him but by his Highnesse order, wherefore I beg that you will signify his pleasure to us, by which wee may

[1] . . . [1]. This passage is not very clear. It is substituted in the draft for the following : ' but in case his Majestie shall not think itt proper to raise horse, I shall then only adde 3,000 l. per annum to the revenue, besides the abatement of the 1,000 l. to the country, since I must then loose the advantage which I should otherwise receive by the command.'

[2] Endorsed by Osborne, ' Coppy of my letter to Sir Phillip Warwick.' The answer is as follows :

Sir, Yesterday the King took into consideration the business of the Yorkshire Excise, and in the substance remembred all the parts of the proposition you have bin pleased now to comunicat to me. There were severall other proposalls which were paralell in point of revenew and good intention to the country. The reasons were principally that swaid with his Majesty to the determination he made that the old farmers should continue for one three yeare longer, these, that he would not discourage men that had bin instrumental in setling it, by being too soon changed, since they offered 16,000 l., and 16,500 l. was that which was offered him by others, and since they stood much upon their justification, that in their carriage towards the country, though many complaints had bin made against them, yet still (and cheifly at last sizes) they had cleered themselves and agents. And because his Majesty beleived that such gentlemen as yourselfe, whose interest in the country was his advantage, would rather loose with the cominalty then improve that interest by being farmors of this duty, and there being some gentlemen having appeared for Major Greathead, who offered 16,500 l., others as Sir Thomas Gow[er] and Jerdan Crosland, who offered lesse, and Sir Thomas Dacres and others, who offered 16,000 l. and abatments to the lesser alhows keepers, the resolve was for the old farmors, which since I cannot wait on you and that you have not heard of otherwise you will please to receive, Sir, from Your most humble servant, P. Warwick.—Aprill 22, 1665. (Leeds MSS., Packet 2.)

[3] Leeds MSS., Packet 2, an autograph draft.

give answer to Colonel Sawrey, and in whatsoever you shall lay
your owne commands upon mee you shall find mee as ready to
approve myselfe, Sir,

Your most faithfull humble servant,

T. Osborne.

IV. MEMORANDUM

FROM this early period one solitary memorandum survives,
which has been frequently quoted or printed in part, but is
now for the first time printed in full.

King Charles 2nd his discours to mee about the Duke of
Buckingham.[1]

8th June, 1667.

That hee observed strangenesse in mee when hee spoke
to mee in the drawing-roome, and upon that inquired and
heard I went with ill men in the House.

That hee beleeved the Duke of Buckingham might have
possest mee with some things falsely, for that itt was his
custome to do so. That hee had dealt very ill with him in many
things. That hee must have very ill intentions. That hee had
tampered with his spies, had writt divers letters to Headon,
and alwaies call'd him brother in them. That although hee had
acted so closely that perhaps the law might not reach him, hee
was never the honester but rather the more dangerous.

That in the House hee said publiquely the King paid 50 in the
100 to the bankers, and how could the war bee managed att that
rate, and that hee contradicted the Duke of York when hee
affirmd the contrary. That when hee was in the Tower hee
brag'd hee was sent thither only because hee spoke for the
seamens haveing theire pay. That Headon did move the seamen
to mutiny, and hee had great reason to beleeve itt was by the
Dukes meanes.

[1] B.M. Add. MSS. 28042, f. 1, autograph memorandum, thus endorsed.

[1] I told him I had never heard the Duke speake anything to the prejudice either of his person or government, and if I had I should have informed him.[1] I told him I was not to answer for other men, nor was itt fitt, without his Majesties leave, to aske what particulars hee meantt of myselfe.

Hee answered hee would tell mee freely (for hee might speake freely of his Commissioners) that I joyned against him with those who would throw by his commission under pretence of want of power, when indeed the designe was only to take away that branch of his power by bringing itt into an Act, and so divesting him for the future of so much power in himselfe as to take an accompt of his own money.

I answered that was never my designe, nor of divers others, I was confident, for that they desired as well as myselfe that wee were sufficiently impowred by this commission ; but I hop't his Majestie knew there was no power to examine anybody but produc't by the accountant, and that only in his behalfe but not against him.

Hee said hee desired not wee should make brick without straw, and when wee brought itt so far as to examine anybody against them hee would supply that defect, but hee was sure there was no will to examine att all, and that hee was confident there would no fault appeare in his great officers, but perhaps might in the pursers or those meaner people ; but now hee had made itt bee begun hee was resolved itt should bee gone through.

Hee then told mee I had joynd also with those who had delayd the giving of the money (whom the Dutch were att this day beholding to), which I denied, saying that if what both myselfe and others now Commissioners propounded had not bin obstructed the money had bin given three months sooner ; but I confesstt myselfe one of those whose judgement was against a generall Excise, and was still so in my owne opinion, and gave my reasons, to which the King replied itt had bin the best and easiest tax, but hee presently quitted itt when hee saw the Parliament did not approve itt ; but how could hee thinke anybody served him well that did not leave him judge which was the best way.

---

[1] . . . [1] This sentence appears to have been added after the memorandum was drawn up.

I replied that men could not know his Majesties mind unlesse hee acquainted them with itt. Hee said that was not possible for him to tell to 400 men, and if any were so much his freinds they might easily come to him and know how hee would have things done, but under pretence of being led by theire judgements they did but obstruct his safety and the kingdomes.

I told him I feared that as itt was certainely prejudiciall to them, so itt was of some ill consequence to him too to make the same construction of all those who agreed in those votes which sometimes displeased him, for I was confident some of them had very different ends from others, and had no other designe then promoting his service.

Hee said that was all one if they used the same meanes which promoted the others ill designes, and yett hee had that charity to beleeve that some of them did not intend ill ; but for A,[1] hee was confident hee had mischeivous intentions, and B [1] was an errand villaine.

I replied I never heard A expresse anything like itt, and I was very well assured that none living wisht him better, or would venture both life and fortune more freely for him then C and D,[1] and had upon occasions said to mee, Wee must take heed that some of these people have not ill ends of theirs promoted by us whose designes are quite contrary.

Hee said, For C, I beleeve hee intends very well, and I beleeve D would neither cutt my throat nor subvert my governement. I know hee has servd the King my father, but hee complies too much with those which are very ill people, and I beleeve hee is some way personally dissatisfied.

In his discourse hee said that wee might thanke those men for the Dutch fleet liyng now upon our coast, for had the money bin given in time wee had had a fleet in readinesse, and they could have gott none, the people refusing to contribute any longer till they heard of our backwardnesse ; insomuch that att first they were sending embassadors for a peace, then but an agent, then but a letter, and that only because they had promised the Swedish ambassador. Yett hee said they would

---

[1] It seems hopeless to attempt the identification of these letters. The fact that the first four letters of the alphabet are used makes it practically certain that they are not initials.

not gett by this vapour, for in the meane time hee had sixty sayles in severall places, divers of which were now gone to the coast of Holland to intercept theire trade, which would bee worse for them then this bravado would profitt them.

Hee said hee had refused divers who would have spoke to him, but had more kindnesse for mee ; and if hee found mee to remaine of that temper which formerly I had bin, and would leave him judge in his owne businesse, I should find him my freind as much as ever.

PART II

MY LORD TREASURER THE EARL OF DANBY

1673-9

APArt from Danby's foreign correspondence, which is dealt with elsewhere,[1] the letters and papers which have survived from his period of power as Lord Treasurer are not nearly so numerous as might have been anticipated. There are suggestions that a considerable number of documents which the Earl would not have liked his enemies to see were deliberately burnt. It seems probable also that while he was rearranging his foreign papers in the Tower, and writing his various pamphlets in defence of his administration, he destroyed many of the less important of his domestic papers. Only a few scattered letters and documents in consequence remain, and these have had to be pieced together as well as possible in order to convey some idea of his activities at home.

[1] *Infra*, p. 239.

I. FAMILY CORRESPONDENCE

Of the many letters which Danby must have written during these years, not merely to his wife but to his sons and daughters, only the barest handful remain. Fortunately the majority belong to much the same period and are to a certain extent connected with each other. Six which have not hitherto been published, together with one which has previously appeared, are printed as illustrating a side of Danby's life for which only too little evidence survives.

[To the Countess of Danby] [1]

London, 5th February, 1675[/6].

My dearest heart,

I thanke you for your letters, and I have been very glad to find by Monsieur de la Motte that hee is confident, if my son make not too much hast to rise, that hee will recover very perfectly and without any lamenesse. My son Coke, I suppose, is returned to you before now, and I have been more laborious in his businesse then my owne since hee went ; but wee thinke so much will depend upon setling the businesse betwixt him and the executors that wee have resolved this day to gett respitt of judgment till next tearme if wee can, purposely to have some determination of the other businesse in the meane time. This I would have you informe my son, and withall that some impediment has hapned by Mr. Gwavas being gone out of towne, which they say is upon his wifes being in danger of death, but I hope that in some time of the next weeke both hee and Captain Coke will bee here.

Wee have no sort of publique newes, and the private is only that my Lord Duras is going to marry a daughter of Sir George

[1] Leeds MSS., Packet 6. Autograph letter.

Sands, and that there will bee a great ball att court on Monday, where your daughter Katherine was sumoned, but my sister Herbert carries her that day to Kingsey, where shee will stay a month without your Ladiships order to the contrary. Remember mee kindly to my daughter Coke, and give my blessing to them all. I have sent you the inclosed [1] to shew you the good inclinations of Sir Ch[arles] Wheeler, and I have nothing more to say but that my Lady Annes comands to Dunbar are obeyed, and so shall your Ladyships when you please to honour with them, Madam,

Your Ladyships most truly affectionate

Danby.

Pray lett mee know when I may hope to see you againe, and present my service to my son Coke and the Captaine.

To the Countess of Danby at Wallingford House.[2]

[8th April, 16]76. [3]

. . . in them and if . . . returned you I would not [have] been so long without doing itt ; but here is nothing spoke of but horse matches, saveing great indeavours to gett the King to Ewston, where hee goes this night and returnes to-morrow. I have taken the same time to see my daughter, and returne hither on Tuesday.[4] My Lord Great Chamberlaine and my Lord Frescheville goe with mee, and I have stolen from hence without any warning to avoide a crowd which lay in waite for mee both here and on the rode.

The King dined yesterday with my Lady Portsmouth att Culford, and seemed more kind then of late, but hee has nothing here to divert itt. His Majestie saies hee will go from hence on Friday [5] to New Hall and on Saterday to London, when I hope to bee with my deare Bridgett, who am her most faithfully affectionate

Danby.

---

[1] This cannot be identified.

[2] Leeds MSS., Packet 7. Autograph letter, damaged.

[3] The date can be identified exactly from letters in *Cal. S.P. Dom.*, 1676-7, pp. 65, 69.

[4] April 11.   [5] April 14.

To the Countess of Danby at Holkham.[1]

Wytham, 16th September, [16]76.

My dearest heart,

I have not had any opportunity before now of writeing to you since I came into these parts, nor have I much to intertaine you withall more then the narrative of my proceedings. I have been att Rycott till yesterday, where I was visited by my Lord Privy Seale two daies agoe, and in returne my Lord Norris and I dined with him yesterday. Itt hapned to bee the day for the plate att Wodstock, and being so neare the place wee staid to see that sport, and came from thence hither, where wee intend to stay two or three daies and then back to Rycott, where I thinke to passe two or three daies more, and so to London ; and I hope so to order my affaires there as to bee able to attend or bee quickly after his Majestie att Newmarkett.

I am here become as errand a Nimrod as ever you knew mee, and your brother Norris and I so in love with one another that wee are both unwilling to thinke of parting. And I do assure you I find him heartily to endeavour both the Kings interest and mine amongst the gentlemen in this country. My Lady Anglesey and I intertained one another yesterday very pleasently, and with great freedome of discourse, there being no women to spoile our mirth, nor take exception att our liberty. But I shall not have that satisfaction I perceive you thought of seeing Mrs. Bennett, nor did I ever intend itt, however you come by the intelligence.

I am very glad to find you are so well satisfied with my son Coke, and that everything pleases you so well there. I am sure nothing can please mee better then to see poore Nan happy, and whatever I can contribute to the makeing her so shall not bee wanting ; and by what steps soever itt is to bee attained, I know nothing is to bee done without a new modell of the whole family and all att once, so as not to corrupt new men with old manners. Pray present my service to my son Coke and my blessing to all our flock. Tell Bridgett that I acknowlege myselfe indebted to her for her letters, and but that they bring mee word of supper comd up I intended to have thankt her

---

[1] Leeds MSS., Packet 7. Autograph letter.

myselfe. I was att Kingsey, where Kate was both much comended and longd for, and my sister Herbert went to London on Monday last for advice about a sore brest, and intended to bee back as this night.

Your brother Norris desires mee to present you his humble service, and I present thee with the truest, most faithfull and affectionate heart of

Your Danby.

To the Countess of Danby.[1]

Rycott, 23 September, [16]76.

My dearest heart,

I was surprized to find by a letter of yours yesterday that you designed to bee att London as last night, when I never expected other then your stay att Holkham till I had fetch't you thence. However I am glad to bee deceived of that side that brings us one minute the sooner together, and though I intended not for London before the middle of the next weeke I will now bee there (God willing) on Monday night,[2] and desire you will send your coach horses to meete mee att Beconsfeild on Sonday night. I will trouble you with nothing before that time, which I long for to have thee in the armes of

Your faithfull and most intirely affectionate

Danby.

To Viscount Latimer at Rycote or elsewhere. [3]

Wallingford House, Christmas day att noone, [1676].

Son,

I know not whither to blame your carelesnesse, your ill manners, or your ill nature, but there is such a mixture of them all in staying from your wife till her labour, and att a time when I beleeve you scarse know what else to do with yourselfe, that I am truly asshamed of you for itt, and do most condemne myselfe, who suffer you to do so much you ought not, and so litle you should, that I now find I have not educated you to that comon civility which scarse anybody wants. I suppose this will bring you to towne, by which time your wife may either bee a dead woman, or not beholding to you if shee bee not ; and

---

[1] Leeds MSS., Packet 7. Autograph letter.   [2] September 25.
[3] Leeds MSS., Packet 7. Autograph letter.

women of lesse kindnesse to an husband then shee has to you
does not use to want that satisfaction. Present my humble
service to my Lord Norris, where I heare this is most likely to
find you.

Danby.

[To the Countess of Danby] [1]

Newmarkett, 28 September, 1677.

My dearest heart,

     You must excuse mee to my brother because I have
scarse time to write this to you, the King being just going abroad,
and I making myself as good a waiter as Posling himselfe. You
may lett him know that the King has consented to his being
a Comissioner when Sir William Lowther shall die or bee
removed, but will gratify some other with his place.

     Your brother Lindsey and my Lord Rosse are here and have
complained of Sir Robert Car to the King, from whom they
have received very good satisfaction ; and my Lord Arlington
looks so dejected here that even all wee do pitty him. Sir
Robert Howard is also com'd, and the King does not speake to
him, so that I am here lookt upon as a much greater conqueror
then I am. The Duke of Albemarle arrived last night, and saies
the Prince of Orange will be here very speedily. I am, Dearest,

Thy own Danby.

     Remember to send to see my Lord Burford without any
message to Nelly, and when Mrs. Turner is with you bid her tell
Nelly you wonder shee should bee your Lords enemy that has
alwaies been so kind to her, but you wonder much more to find
her supporting only those who are known to bee the Kings
enemies, for in that you are sure she does very ill.

To the Countess of Danby at the Cockpit in Whitehall.[2]

Newmarkett, 11th October, 1677.

My dearest heart,

     You shall see I will not faile you with letters, and this is
not only to advertize you of the Prince of Orange his being

---

[1] From the autograph letter among the Lindsey MSS., printed in *Lindsey
MSS.*, p. 386.

[2] Leeds MSS., Packet 8. Autograph letter.

arrived, but also of his going this night to Ewston, and the King with him, and yett without any of those consequences which I know you will bee ready to make upon the newes of itt. They returne hither to-morrow to dinner, and his Majestie keeps his resolution of being att London on Saterday,[1] where I hope you will welcome, Dearest,

Your owne Danby.

II. GENERAL POLITICAL CORRESPONDENCE

WHILE a large number of Danby's letters on financial affairs are preserved among the Treasury records, surprisingly few of those which he wrote in his capacity as a principal minister of the Crown are among the domestic state papers. It has therefore been considered worth while to print the two letters to the Corporation of York which nearly involved him in trouble with the House of Commons, together with a solitary letter to Lord Chancellor Finch and one to the Duke of Lauderdale. Danby was very careful to avoid even the appearance of interfering in Scottish affairs. His letters to Lauderdale do not seem to have been numerous, and with two exceptions all that survive have already been printed.

[To the Mayor and Corporation of York] [2]

Whitehall, 6th September, 1673.

My Lord and Gentlemen,

His Majestie haveing been pleased to remove mee out of the House of Comons, I thinke myselfe to remaine under an obligation to give you thanks for the honour you did mee in promoteing mee to serve you there, and I cannot but remember that your choice was with so much kindnesse and affection as

---

[1] October 13.

[2] B.M. Add. MSS. 28051, f. 21, an autograph draft. Great care was apparently spent on the composition of this letter. The notes on which it is based, scribbled on a blank sheet of a letter from Robert Benson giving advice on the point, are *ibid.*, f. 18.

obliges mee to assure you that since my remove is not by death, but to a station more capable of doing you service, you may depend upon a returne of gratitude from mee suitable to the obligation you have laid upon mee. I acknowlege to have many severall ties of freindship to the Citty of York, as the place not only of my education, but whose kindnesse was ever extended as well to my father as myselfe, and the consideration of those ties has bred in mee so naturall an inclination both to wish and act anything that might bee to the good of itt that I never received any of your commands but I applied myselfe with as much delight to effect them as any of those could take whose concerne itt was to obtaine theire desires. And I thank God my successes have been suitable, for I know not anything directed to mee in behalfe of the Citty wherein I have not speeded according to my wishes.

I could enumerate divers particulars, if that were fitt to bee my part, but I would mention none were itt not that I am informed there are some who would rob mee of all the reward I expect, which is that you may but know I served you in those things which are very unjustly claimed by any other that can pretend to them. I say this because I am told that somebody else would pretend to bee the instrument of closeing the difference betwixt the Citty and some of the churchmen att Shrovetide, in which businesse I doe assure you there were very eminent men of the Councill against you, and not one advocate there for you but myselfe. Itt was also my fortune to have some disputes with the Archbishop about the seates in the Minster. I suppose you have also received the good effects of my solicitations with the Duke of York about the wine lycences, and I hope the hindring a towne-clerke to bee imposed upon you (contrary to your charter) may have had itts convenience. But I will not say any more of this kind then is necessary to justify myselfe that I have never been wanting in the performance of what you desired att my hands.

Haveing been thus happy, not only myselfe but in my family by the services which have been likewise paid you by my father, I confesse I am ambitious of haveing one linke more added to the chaine of our freindship by admitting my son to the same honour of serveing you in Parliament, by which as you will give

mee occasion to valew myselfe upon the continued favour and
kindnesse of so noble and antient a citty, so you will have two
obliged and constant attendants in both Houses to take care of
your concernes there, and promote any comands you have for
them ; and whatever you may have with his Majestie I shall
alwaies bee ready to charge myselfe withall preferably to any
businesse of my owne. I know there has been application made
by some others for the same honour I desire to my son, but I
have good reason to beleeve they will cease the competition.
However I do so litle doubt the affection of the Citty, and do so
much presume upon my capacity of doing them as acceptable
services as any other, that I intend to make a triall of itt by
sending my son to waite upon you himselfe.

I have desired to have this comunicated to the Comon
Councell and free burgers, because I must owne the particular
kindnesse I received from them att my owne election, and I
would not have them thinke mee forgetfull of itt. I have only
to adde, or rather repeate, that any commands I receive which
may bee to the advantage of the Citty are so many obligations
laid upon, My Lord and Gentlemen,

Your most affectionate and most humble servant,

Latimer.[1]

[To the Mayor and Corporation of York.] [2]

16 September, [16]73.

My Lord and Gentlemen,

I have received a letter from some of you dated the 12th
instant [3] in answer to mine concerning my sonns election to bee
your burgess, and I cannot but make this observation upon itt,
that whither my son deserve that honour or no I have deserved
better from the Citty myselfe then to have itt made an argument to exclude any man from your service by saying hee is not
of your body, for that is plainly to tell mee that your affaires
have been prejudiced under my management, and to adde to
the aggravation of itt you tell mee further that you had pur-

---

[1] Endorsed by Latimer, ' Coppy of my letter to the Citty of York about my
sons election, sent 9th September 1673.'

[2] B.M. Add. MSS. 28051, f. 28, an autograph draft; *Kenyon MSS.*, p. 97.

[3] This letter is in B.M. Add. MSS. 28051, f. 23.

posed itt long before my promotion. I confesse in a letter from Sir Henry Thompson of Escrick, in answer to one of mine before I knew of his pretensions, hee told mee hee was ingaged long before my letter, and seemed to bee sorry for itt, but I imputed that to a defect which I expected not to find ; and certainely those which know the respect that is due betwixt gentlemen of any quality to one another would not have been wanting in giveing notice att least to a predecessor promoted to a better station, nor can I imagine there are many of the Citty pre-ingaged without the least sort of intimation to one who had served them so faithfully and was now more capable either of doing or obstructing itt.

In another part of your letter you speake of two gentlemen whom I said my son should not oppose if either of them would stand, which is most true, and had Sir Henry Thompson mentioned any such desire to mee hee had been the third to whom I should have made the same declaration ; but I must acknowlege I cannot but distinguish betwixt those who use mee civilly and those who do not, as I dare appeale whither hee has done, and therefore I cannot hinder myselfe from giveing him opposition, and if in the successe I should find my measures wrong taken in one kind, others would att least find theires not much better. I heare that many suggestions have been made as if the Duke of Buckingham were for promoteing the interest of Sir Henry, the truth of which you will find by his Graces letter to the Citty by this post, and I beleeve you will find most of the insinuations grounded upon like bottomes. But I am sorry to heare (which truly I did not know before) that 150 l. of the arreares of the wine lycences is not yett paid, which is certainely yett very recoverable, and perhaps by Sir Henry Thompsons solicitations. I heare also that itt is made a great inducement to the election of Sir Henry because hee will bee so great a promoter of the trade of the Citty, but certainely itt is the first time that any mans interest was thought equall to the Lord Treasurers in promoting of trade in England.

I cannot but complaine also that when your Lordship had adjourn'd the reading of my letter to a longer day for giveing notice to all the freemen, and to a larger place for theire con-veniency of hearing, you should send mee a letter to which I

have reason to beleeve the tenth part of the Citty has not been
privy, and therefore I now desire your justice to lett all who are
concern'd have due notice and time to consider what they
conceave may bee best for theire service, and then I doubt not
but upon triall I shall find the continuance of the citizens
affections to mee by theire approbation of my son to serve them,
and I do assure them of no lesse zeale on my part, who am,
My Lord and Gentlemen,

Your most humble servant,

[Latimer] [1]

[To Lord Chancellor Finch] [2]

Newmarkett, 4th April, [16]76.

My Lord,
    I received your Lordships of the 31th March, and am as
desirous as any man in the world can bee to oblige my Lord
Cheife Justice North in anything. I have constantly for a good
while past kept the King in mind of preferring Mr. North, and
have alwaies found great willingnesse in his Majestie to do itt,
and hee has now as fully expresst itt upon this occasion of your
Lordships letter ; but hee will yett declare nothing how the
removes shall bee upon the Bishop of Norwich his death more
then the translateing of Exceter thither, but my Lord Cheif
Justice may rest assured of my dilligence in that matter. His
Majestie was extreame well pleased with the account my Lord
Cheif Justice gives of his observations in his circuit, and wherever you can give the like account from any other of the judges
itt ought not to bee omitted, being both very agreable to his
Majestie, and his resolutions being every day more fixt to shew
his steadinesse to the Church of England and his perseverance
in the councills hee has taken.

    His Majestie saies hee will certainly write to the Queene to
lett her know his mind concerning Mr. Sawyer, but I find itt not
ground enough to speake to him, because the King will first
receive the Queenes answer, and itt will not bee amisse (unlesse
your Lordship know itt already) to learne Mr. Sawyers inclina-

---

[1] Endorsed by Latimer, 'Coppy of my letter to the Citty of York, 16
September 1673.'

[2] Leeds MSS., Packet 7, an autograph copy.

tions, because I was told but a litle before I left London as if
Mr. Sawyer did not desire the place. His Majestie leaves itt to
your Lordship to lett Kenrick Eyton succeed Sir Thomas Jones,
only hee would have you to consider whither there bee none of
the House of Comons and of the long robe that ought to bee
obliged, and I have informed him that by my intelligence Mr.
Walcott is of the principles of his brother-in-law, Sir Thomas
Litleton, which hee thinkes ought to bee well advised of before
such dispositions bee made of places if itt should prove so.

Here is not one word of anything but horse matches, so that
I am able to furnish your Lordship with nothing of newes, not
so much as when the King intends to leave this place. I am,
My Lord,

Your Lordships, &c.,

[Danby] [1]

I desire your Lordship will not deliver out the grant to the
Irish farmers untill your Lordship have other satisfaction then
by theire words that theire 30,000 l. is ready to bee paid, which
I have great reason to doubt, they haveing already broke
promise with mee for 12,000 l. above a fortnight.

[To the Duke of Lauderdale] [2]

Wimbledon, 15 September, 1677.

My Lord,

I do with great thanks acknowlege the honour of two of
your Graces letters.[3] The last was brought mee by your
Secretary, with whom (according to your Graces desires) I went
imediately to the King, and hee delivered your Graces letter
wherein were the four declarations. After his Majestie had read
itt and the declarations (with which hee was very well pleased),
I shew'd him my letter, which had very litle but what was in
his, saveing the businesse of Murray, concerning whom the
King declared his resolution that so soone as hee should receive

---

[1] Unsigned. Endorsed in an unknown handwriting, ' Copy of a letter of the
Lord Treasurer to the Lord Chancellor, April 4, 1676.'

[2] B.M. Add. MSS. 23138, f. 63. Autograph letter. The draft is B.M.
Add. MSS. 28053, f. 112.

[3] Probably those of August 28 and September 4, printed in *Lauderdale
Papers*, iii. 86, and *Morrison Catalogue*, iii. 99.

the next letter from the Councill, hee would imediately make him bee apprehended and sent for Scotland, without bringing that businesse any more in debate, and hee has already in my heareing comanded Mr. Secretary Coventry to write to my Lord of Ormond to send such a party into the North of Ireland as was there the last yeare.

Here is not the least newes worth sending your Grace, nor shall wee much thinke of businesse untill his Majestie returnes from Newmarkett, where hee intends to bee on the 24th instant, and I designe to waite upon his Majestie there. In the meane time hee is diverting himselfe att Windsor, and returnes to London to-morrow. Hee seemes to bee very sensible of the great services your Grace does him in all the affaires of that kingdome, and truly hee does you but justice in itt, there being nothing more apparent then that the peace of Scotland is oweing wholly to your Graces care and prudence.

For prevention of any misreports (because I have heard some) about my haveing forbid a building which is begun in New Park, I thinke itt fitt to lett your Grace know that upon an information brought mee of Mr. Delmahoys going to build upon Sheene Laund, I comanded that the workmen should not proceed till I had spoke with Mr. Delmahoy, to know what itt was to bee, and whither the Kings pleasure was knowne as to the place of setting itt. But before I could see Mr. Delmahoy, my Lord Maynard told mee itt was by your Graces directions, whereupon I imediately asked the King if hee had no dislike to the place, and haveing received his approbation, I told my Lord Maynard they might proceed if they pleased. And if any other story have been made of this matter, I hope your Grace will beleeve I should bee far in this or any other thing from doing otherwise then is suitable to the profession I make of being with perfect truth and reallity, My Lord,

Your Graces most humble and most obedient servant,

Danby.

My wife and I beg leave to present our most humble services to the Dutchesse.

III. IRISH CORRESPONDENCE

OF the really significant part of Danby's Irish correspondence not a trace has been found. All the letters which he wrote to Orrery and Ranelagh have vanished, and even of the replies comparatively few survive. A number of his letters to Conway are preserved among the domestic state papers, but these are concerned almost entirely with English affairs. On the other hand his official correspondence with the Lords Lieutenants who held office during this period has been very fully preserved. Of his many letters to Essex those which have some general or personal interest are printed, while a single letter to Ormonde is included which has become divorced from the great collection of Ormonde Manuscripts at Kilkenny Castle and so has not been calendared by the Historical Manuscripts Commission.

[To the Earl of Essex] [1]

London, 18th April, [16]73.

My Lord,

This gentleman, Mr. Hedges, is tennant to all the estate of the Duke of Buckingham in Ireland, and because hee may perhaps bee necessitated att some time to give your Excellency trouble by reason of his concernes in that kingdome, hee has desired my recomendation of him to your Excellencies protection. I am not ignorant how litle ground I have to intitle myselfe to this presumption, but I hope the request will bee attended with small inconvenience, and I am very willing to putt myselfe under obligations to a person of your Excellencies great worth, being with high respect, My Lord,

Your Excellencies most humble and most obedient servant,

T. Osborne. [2]

[1] Stowe MSS. 201, f. 357. Autograph letter. Although it does not strictly belong to this period it has been included here for the sake of completeness.

[2] Endorsed, ' Sir Thomas Osborne, received Aprill 28.'

[To the Earl of Essex] [1]

London, 19 August, [16]73.

My Lord,

I had long agoe acknowledged the honour of your Excellencies letter,[2] but that this is the first time I have been able to write by my owne hand this six weekes, for I do assure your Excellency that nothing has given mee greater content then to find myselfe in your good opinion, and there is nothing I shall endeavour more then to keepe myselfe in itt. I perceive your Excellency has an intire friend of my Lord Conway, of whose worth I have so great experience that I am sure your Excellency is happy in itt, and I account itt no small good fortune that one who deserves to have so much creditt with your Excellency will beare mee witnesse how great a valew and esteeme I have both for your person and abilities.

I must beg your Excellency will give yourselfe the trouble of excusing mee for a post or two to his Lordship, and I am desired by my Lord Buckingham to present his service to your Excellency, and to desire that if one Mr. Hilliard (who was imploy'd by him about collecting some rents and arrears) shall not give a satisfactory account to this bearer (who is sent by his Grace about the same affaire) your Excellency will please not to give him any protection in that businesse, as also that you will please to give countenance to this bearer if hee shall have occasion to apply to your Excellency in his Graces concernes. I have only to adde that I am with the greatest respect imaginable, My Lord,

Your Excellencies most humble and most obedient servant,

Latimer.[3]

[To the Earl of Essex] [4]

Wallingford House, 4th December, 1673.

My Lord,

I received a letter from your Excellency by my Lord Conway,[5] and another by the gentleman who was in Ireland

---

[1] Stowe MSS. 202, f. 303. Autograph letter.

[2] Presumably Essex's letter dated Dublin Castle, June 21, 1673 (*ibid.* 213, f. 230), written in reply to Osborne's letter of April 18.

[3] Endorsed, ' Lord Treasurer. Received September 2.'

[4] Stowe MSS. 203, f. 223. Autograph letter.

[5] This letter, dated Dublin Castle, 2 November 1673, is B.M. Add. MSS. 28053, f. 78.

upon the Duke of Buckingham's businesse,[1] and I return your Excellency my humble thanks for the honour of them both. I am extreame glad to find the continuance of your Excellencys kindnesse to my Lord Conway, and I do him but right in assuring you he deserves from your Excellency that character you allow him of a just and worthy friend. I know not yett how successful wee shall bee in our endeavours for his being Master of the Ordinance in Ireland, Sir Thomas Chichley haveing already made great advances towards the annexing that office to this in England, but wee have obtained a stop of Sir Thomas Chichleys grant untill the matter may bee debated before his Majestie, which I suppose will bee very speedily.

Your Excellency is pleas'd to incourage mee with hopes of receiving some information in matters relateing to the revenue of that kingdome, which I must owne as a very great obligation, and shall endeavour to deserve by studying how to improve my knowledge in itt to the service of his Majestie and your Excellency. I have not yett gott time to discourse fully with my Lord Conway upon that subject, but I find his Lordship of opinion that his Majestie might have severall considerable advantages hee does not receive att present.

I suppose your Excellency has a constant account how all affairs stand here, and there has been no late alterations of any kind, saving a quarrel betwixt the Duke of Buckingham and Mr. Ralph Montague in the Kings presence, for which Mr. Montague was this morning comitted to the Tower. The Parliament will certainely meete att the time appointed, and then wee are in great expectations to see what humor they will bee in.

I humbly beg your Excellencys pardon for detaining you so long, being loth to give your Excellency the least trouble, but on the contrary haveing an ambition more then ordinary to become serviceable to your Excellency, as, My Lord,

Your Excellencys most obedient and most faithfull servant,

Latimer.[2]

---

[1] This letter, dated Dublin Castle, October 23, 1673, is Stowe MSS. 213, f. 317.

[2] Endorsed, ' Lord Treasurer. Received December 28, [16]73.'

To the Earl of Essex.[1]

Wallingford House, 12th December, 1673.

My Lord,

I received both your Lordships of the 22 and 29 of November,[2] and am glad to find the character of the farmers fair deportment confirmed by your Excellency. They have thereby intitled themselves the more to his Majesties grace and favour, and to all due encouragement from his ministers, which I agree with your Lordship ought to bee extended to them so far as is consistent with his Majesties service. In order whereunto I have discourst some of the farmers to understand their sense in this matter, and am of opinion that the best way and most agreeable to his Majesties service and their covenants, and for discovering a true state of their losses susteined by the warr, will be for your Excellency to commissionate some persons to go to the several outports to view their books, with power to administer an oath to the collectors and other officers of the farmers, thereby to find whether they have received any more mony for the Customes then what they have certified and returned to the commissioners at Corke House, and the persons so employed are also to examine and take notice whether the said bookes be fairly kept without interlineations. And I humbly propose to your Lordship to proceed in the same method for these last six months, to end at Christmas, as well as for the other six months ended at midsomer last. I am, My Lord,

Your Excellencys most humble and most faithfull servant,

Latimer.

To the Earl of Essex.[3]

My Lord,

Sir John Peyton being suddainly to go for Ireland is importunate for my recommendation of him to your Lordships favour, wherein I am willing to gratifye him, being a very deserving person and my neere kinsman, which forbids mee to speake what I might in his commendation. He is at present a

---

[1] Stowe MSS. 203, f. 249.   Original letter, in a clerk's handwriting.
[2] *Ibid.* 213, ff. 351, 354.
[3] Stowe MSS. 204, f. 314.   Original letter, in a clerk's handwriting.

lieuetenant in one of the companyes that lately belonged to the
Duke of Buckinghams regiment, and when your Lordship has
an opportunity of preferring him to a better station, by doing
it your Lordship will very much oblige, My Lord,

Your Lordships most obedient humble servant,

Wallingford House,   Latimer.[1]
21 March, 1673/4.

[To the Earl of Essex] [2]

Windsor, 30th July, [16]74.

My Lord,

I have received many favours from your Excellency,
which tis fitt I should acknowledge ; but the great assurance
of your kindnesse and friendship which Sir Arthur Forbes has
given me by your Excellencys comand is an obligation of so
high a nature as will ever tie me to the service of your Excellency, and it gives mee great hopes that you will beleeve this
profession, because I am sure your Excellency would not have
given that incouragement to any but where you did expect to
meete with a returne suitable to such an honour. Upon this
foundation your Excellency may depend that all faithfull
services will bee performed on my part, and I shall esteeme
nothing a greater happinesse then to improve your Excellencies
good opinion of mee by proofes of my sincerity. It is a very
great addition to my satisfaction to see two such worthy men
in your Excellencies esteeme as my Lord Conway and Sir Arthur
Forbes, who as I am assured they will doe mee all good offices
neare your Excellency, so I have no lesse confidence of theire
being admirable instruments to your Excellency both in the
Kings concernes and your owne.

Your Excellency will receive this by my Lord Ranelagh, who
has hitherto given the King so good satisfaction that hee is very
considerably in his good opinion, and I should be extreame glad
to heare from your Excellency what prospect you have of his
undertaking. I beg also att your leasure to receive your
Excellencies opinion concerning a future farme of that revenue,
as also whither you judge a Parliament there necessary, and

---

[1] Endorsed, ' Lord Treasurer. Received Aprill 15th.'
[2] Stowe MSS. 205, f. 369. Autograph letter.

when. I have lately received some papers from your Excellency concerning quit rents, but I will not mix this letter with anything but my thanks to your Excellency, and a faithfull assurance of my being, My Lord,

Your Excellencys most obedient and most humble servant,

Danby.[1]

[To the Earl of Essex] [2]

My Lord,   London, 14th August, [16]74.

I doubt not but your Excellency has had some account of a warrant which by my meanes his Majestie signed for a commission to my Lord Orrery, and suppose you may have likewise heard by what mistakes itt had some progresse. Your Excellency will receive a full narrative of itt from Sir Arthur Forbes, who is hastning into Ireland within a few daies, so that I shall now only informe your Excellency that the contents of itt importing more then I knew, I durst not doe lesse then acquainte his Majestie with the mistake before itt proceeded any further after I was informed of itt. Upon discourse of this matter with his Majestie, itt was his pleasure that by a private inquiry from your Excellency hee might bee informed whither itt would be any prejudice to his service, or any injury to your power, to grant his Lordship the like comission for severall counties (that is to say so many as are within the Province of Munster) as hee has done to severall governours of single counties, because if itt may be done without any great inconvenience hee would bee glad to gratify my Lord in itt, and especially because his Lordship did surrender that pattent of Governour of the Province of Munster without being demanded of him, and which he might have kept with very extraordinary powers, whereas he desires now no other then what is given to divers already.

Itt must needs be agreed that his Lordships eminent comands in that country distinguish his pretensions strongly from any others, and yett both Sir Arthur Forbes and Sir Henry Capell will witnesse that I was against anything new (though in his case) without your Excellencys approbation first to itt, in

---

[1] Endorsed, ' Lord Treasurer. Received August 10.'
[2] Stowe MSS. 205, f. 388. Autograph letter.

order to which I did move for his Majesties letter to your
Excellency, till I found by Sir Henry Capell that hee thought
itt might putt too great a difficulty upon your Excellency in
point of civility to my Lord Orrery, and for that reason I proposed the giveing your Excellency this trouble, to the end his
Majestie may receive your Excellencys advice by such way as
you shall thinke most agreable to yourselfe. I have inlarged
more upon this matter then perhaps was needfull, because I was
desirous your Excellency should know what part I had acted
in itt ; and your Excellency may rest assured that I shall never
behave myselfe in any kind towards your Excellency, but as
becomes the profession I have made of being with great reallity,
My Lord,

Your Excellencys most obedient and most faithfull servant,

Danby.

I should be glad to receive an answer from your Excellency so
soone as might bee.[1]

[To the Earl of Essex] [2]

My Lord, London, 28 January, [16]74/5.

I hope your Excellency is pleased to forgive my not
paying my respects to you so often as I desire, and as I acknowledge I ought to do, were I more master of my time ; but I trust
to my Lord Ranelagh to beare witnesse that the fault is not so
much mine as it might reasonably bee supposed, and I doubt
not but both his Lordship and Mr. Harberd does me that justice
to confirme your Excellency in the assurance that no man can
be more truly and more concern'dly your servant then I am.
Amongst the many idle reports here, your Excellency cannot
but have heard of severall named to be your successor in the
goverment of Ireland, which though in ittselfe is ridiculous
enough to be laught att, and could have no other effect with
your Excellency, yett it cannot be unwelcome to you to know
that when such discourses came att any time to his Majesties
knowledge, hee was alwaies ready to make them occasions of
his expressing the valew and esteeme he had both of your person

---

[1] Endorsed, ' Lord Treasurer. Received August 21.'
[2] Stowe MSS. 207, f. 106. Autograph letter.

and service, and of declaring that he had niver intertaind one thought of removeing your Excellency from the post you are in.

My Lord Ranelagh tells mee hee has given your Excellency an account att large of our discourses with his Majestie about the affaires of Ireland, by which you may see how willingly he concurres with any advices coming from your Excellency, and I dare bee confident they will alwaies bee prevalent against any of your opposers. As to a new farme of the revenew, I have yett received no proposalls, but when I do will certainely transmitt them to your Excellency before I conclude anything ; and in the meane time I beg your opinion whither itt might not bee better to see what will bee done by your Parliament, before any absolute agreement were made in that affaire. I have many particular obligations to owne to your Excellency, both relating to my friends and to myselfe, which you could not have bestow'd upon any whose remembrance of them will bee more gratefull, and I shall thinke myselfe very uneasy while I am without some fitt opportunity of shewing the sense I have of your favours.

His Majestie is takeing most effectuall courses to cure the suspicions which many had received here of the incouragement or att least connivance which was given to popery, haveing requir'd the bishops to acquainte him with what they judge necessary to be done for suppressing the growth of itt, which they have done accordingly, and his Majestie is resolved to putt effectually in execution ; so that when the Parliament meets next itt will take off all disguises, and shew them bare fac't who made religion a pretence to their other designes. I have obey'd your Excellencies commands in giveing my best assistance to Mr. Harberds pretensions, in whose behalfe I must needs testify that hee behaves himselfe here as becomes an excellent servant to your Excellency, and I am obliged to him for the trouble hee has given himselfe in some businesse of mine. I beg your Excellencies pardon for this tedious letter, and have to express the great content I have in being, My Lord,

Your Excellencies most obedient and most humble servant,

Danby.[1]

---

[1] Endorsed, ' Lord Treasurer. Received February 13th.'

[To the Earl of Essex] [1]

London, 15th February, 1674/5.

My Lord,

Though I have nothing of importance to trouble your Lordship withall, I cannot lett passe so good an occasion as by Mr. Harberd to present both my humble service and acknowledgements to your Excellency, which I find by my Lord Conway I owe your Excellency in so extraordinary a manner as deserves all the returns I can ever be capable to make. I confesse it suites perfectly with my inclination to pay your Excellency all imaginable services, and I dare very confidently assure you that my taske is not att all hard, there being nothing more agreable to our master then the giveing your Excellency any marks of his favour and kindnesse.

I take itt now to be past all doubt that the Parliament will sitt in Aprill, and therefore I hope your Excellency will not only spare my Lord Conway, but prevaile with him to lett us have his company att that time. The King has laid his comands upon Mr. Harberd, and I must gett your Excellency to helpe mee to thanke him enough for his favours to mee here. If your Excellency and my Lord Conway will in the meane time by your letters influence as many of your friends as you can which are of the Parliament to assist the makeing this next session a quiett and calme one, itt will be a very acceptable work, and that which I am sure all good men ought to contribute to.

I obey'd your Excellency in the matter of Deane Ward, as I shall do most readily in all things wherein you shall please to lay the honour of your comands upon, My Lord,

Your Excellencies most faithfull and most obedient servant,

Danby.[2]

[To the Earl of Essex] [3]

London, 11th May, 1675.

My Lord,

I am sure your Excellency will forgive my not haveing troubled you with a letter, since I know you cannot bee ignorant

[1] Stowe MSS. 207, f. 171. Autograph letter.
[2] Endorsed, ' Lord Treasurer. Received February 27.'
[3] Stowe MSS. 207, f. 384. Autograph letter, printed in *Essex Papers*, ii. 12.

how I have had my time taken up here. Though I hoped theire
malice had terminated in this kingdome, yett I find they have
pursued it into Ireland, and with the like falsehood also they
have done here ; but instead of hurting me, they have shew'd
they did not stick to have suborned false witnesses, no more
then I heare they have stuck to write falsehoods to your
Excellency.

I have not yett time to unfold att large all the transactions
which are necessary for your Excellency to know, and which I
intend to write in a particular narrative for your information
(I meane those things which relate to Ireland singly) ; but I
resolved to take this first minute of leasure to give itt you under
my hand that if anything may have been represented to your
Excellency concerning those Instructions of 29th July [16]74
as instructions that I received from your Excellency, itt is
utterly false that I ever made any such pretence, either in
Councell or elsewhere ; but I did owne in Councell that both by
divers letters from your Excellency and severall complaints
from my Lord Ranelagh I had been informed of the great
prejudice to his Majestie both in the giveing away money and
quitt rents by letters obtained without due examination, and
that your Excellency had severall times desired that some course
might be taken for preventing of itt. I did further say that I
had received from your Excellency a letter acknowledging the
receipt of those Instructions, which your Excellency did approve
as very conducing to hinder those many irregular grants which
were not otherwise to bee resisted ; and for the Instructions
themselves, my Lord Ranelagh doth owne the drawing of them,
and by the coppy of those former Instructions to the Lords
Leiutenants which were brought over by my Lord Conway, they
appeare to be agreable to those ancient formes ; and by what
appears of defalcations due to my Lord Ranelagh upon letters
obtained before those Instructions, itt will be found that they
have been of vast advantage in saveing the Kings treasure.

I am sorry I have not time to inlarge more upon this subject,
but I hope this may arme your Excellency against the practices
of your enemies as well as mine in this matter, who would first
divide us, and then destroy both, and haveing done their worst
to mee would now wound your Excellency if they could by

makeing you privy and instrumentall to the recruiteing the
forces in France. As I doubt not but all this will vanish, so I
assure your Excellency I am not lesse firme either in my owne
services to your Excellency or in the representing of your
enemies as well as my owne to his Majestie, and within a post
or two your Excellency shall find I have done itt with considerable effect to the securing of your power where you are (I meane
by prevaileing with his Majestie to make those about you
depend more imediately upon your Excellency then yett they
do). I hope your Excellency will pardon this abrupte letter,
which is so merely for want of time, which will only give mee
leave to subscribe myselfe, My Lord,

Your Excellencies most humble and most faithfull servant,

Danby.[1]

[To the Earl of Essex] [2]

My Lord,

London, 1st June, 1675.

    I acknowledge the great honour and favour of your
Excellencys letter by Mr. Godolphin,[3] and concurre with you
that itt would bee of great use to have your Excellency here
to conferre with his Majestie upon those important matters
mentioned therein. I have nothing to object against itt, if your
Excellency have not ; but on the contrary, as I beleeve his
Majestie will receive advantage by itt, so I should take itt
for an happy occasion to give your Excellency a confirmation
of my readinesse to pay you all manner of service and respect.

Your Excellency is so well knowing to the present constitution
of our Court, that nobody can give you better measures of itt
then your Excellency is able to give yourselfe, and though itt
be very difficult to steere amongst so many rocks of faction
without strikeing upon some, I doubt not but your Excellency
by your great prudence may bee so happy as to do itt. The
newes of your Excellencies intentions to come for England
arrived here two or three daies before Mr. Godolphin, and I have
heard that some who hope in time to be your successors were
glad of itt ; but I conceave your Excellency is so well assured

[1] Endorsed, ' Lord Treasurer. Received May 16.'
[2] Stowe MSS. 208, f. 5. Autograph letter, printed in *Essex Papers*, ii. 21.
[3] *Letters of the Earl of Essex in 1675*, p. 277.

of all our services to you, how little soever wee afford of good ones to one another, that you can bee in no danger of that kind, although in a matter so nice as this your Excellency must needs be the best judge.

I beleeve the Parliament is like to sitt longer then was expected, for the differences between the Houses are so widened and yett itt is so necessary they should come to some composure before they part, that itt lookes as if theire sitting would yett be of a months continuance att least. The King has directed mee to attend him to-morrow about the matters of your Excellencies last letter,[1] and I shall not bee wanting to acquainte you with his Majesties pleasure so soone as I know itt, and in the meane time I desire your Excellency will continue to mee the happinesse of being esteemed, My Lord,

Your Excellencies most faithfull and most humble servant,

Danby.[2]

[To the Earl of Essex][3]

My Lord,   London, 8th June, 1675.

I should not have troubled your Excellency with a letter till I could have given you some account in answer to your Excellencys by Mr. Godolphin, but that I am requested by Mr. Bolton to joyne in recommending him to your Excellencies favour for the place of adjutant to the horse. I doubt not but your Excellency receives many addresses in his behalfe, and truly I should be very unjust if I did not assure your Excellency that by the experience of divers yeares acquaintance I know him to bee a very deserveing gentleman and a good officer, and should thinke myselfe very happy in doing both him and your Excellency a good service in promoting him to yours.

I have nothing more att present to trouble your Excellency withall but the tender of my most humble service, who am, My Lord,

Your Excellencies most faithfull humble servant,

Danby.[4]

---

[1] *Letters of the Earl of Essex in 1675*, p. 274.
[2] Endorsed, ' Lord Treasurer. Received June 9th.'
[3] Stowe MSS. 208, f. 34. Autograph letter.
[4] Endorsed, ' Lord Treasurer. Received June 17th.'

To the Earl of Essex.[1]

My Lord,

December 4th, [1675]

I am sorry I did not know of your Excellencies being here, because I would have waited upon your Excellency, though I have denied myselfe to others by reason of haveing taken phisick and being desirous to observe my phisitions directions in not mixing businesse with itt. I did last night according to my promise to Sir James Shaen gett the warrant for the comission signed by the King, and countersigned itt at the same time, and appointed Sir Phillip Floyd to acquainte him that itt was ready so soone as I had notice that theire money was paid into the Navy Office according to Sir James his promise last night. But instead thereof Sir Phillip brought mee word that they said itt was in Mr. Kents hand, and upon inquiry of Mr. Kent, hee said that hee had 11,000 l. and notes upon Bartlett, Duncomb and Kirwood, goldsmiths, in Lumbard Street, for 9,000 l. more, which he thought were good, but under the present disturbance they were there hee durst not answer for itt ; so that I find the money is att this time no otherwise ready, and I have reason to beleeve that were the whole in Mr. Kents hands, itt would rather bee so much upon accounts betwixt Mr. Kent and the goldsmiths (which may bee paid upon reckonings to Major Huntingdon and the rest named in the warrant to receive it) then so much that could bee deposited in cleare money in the Speakers hands.

This being the state of the matter on one hand, and on the other there being that great necessity of dispatching a commission into Ireland for the Kings service, I confesse itt is hard for mee to judge which is the greater danger ; but in the meane time I see no inconvenience in your Excellencies declareing the present farmers collectors to bee his Majesties officers, and to proceed from Christmas forwards till further order. If I durst have stir'd abroad I would have spared your Excellency this trouble by waiting on you myselfe, who am, My Lord,

Your Excellencies most faithfull humble servant,

Danby.[2]

[1] Stowe MSS. 208, f. 413. Autograph letter.
[2] Endorsed, ' Lord Treasurer. Received 4th December 1675.'

To the Earl of Essex.[1]

London, 9th March, 1676/7.

My Lord,

I have had the honour of two letters from your Excellency, both which I am to acknowledge. The one I received by Mr. Weld, who I am glad to find has given your Excellency so good satisfaction in his employment ; the other I had by Sir Cyrill Wiche, of whom your Excellency cannot possibly have a better opinion then I have. Since his arrivall here my time has been so taken up by reason of the Parliament and the preparations for itt that I have not yett been able to gett time to discourse so much with him as I desire, but I am very glad to find by both these gentlemen that I retaine the honour of your Excellencies good opinion, and I hope your Excellency will alwaies give mee leave to preserve itt, by being, My Lord,

Your Excellencies most faithfull humble servant,

Danby.[2]

[To the Duke of Ormonde] [3]

London, 4th December, 1677.

My Lord,

This post will bring you the newes of the Parliaments being adjourned only to 15th of January next, and the reason of itt proceedes from my Lord Fevershams being returned from the King of France with such a sort of answer as gives the King reason to beeleve that King will not content himselfe to make peace without a greater share of Flanders then is fitt for us hee should have ; and therefore hee will not have itt out of his power to call the Parliament to assist him in doing what shall bee best for us. In the meane time Mr. Montagu is to returne to-morrow towards Paris, to try the French King once more upon the propositions discoursed here betwixt the King and the Prince of Orange, and when wee have gott the answer to

---

[1] Stowe MSS. 211, f. 184. Autograph letter.

[2] Endorsed, ' Lord Treasurer. Received March 16.'

[3] B.M. Add. MSS. 28103, f. 58. Autograph letter.

this message, itt will appeare whither wee are like to keepe our good correspondence with France, the King and Duke being both of opinion that without such a fronteer left to Flanders as is now proposed itt must needs bee the designe of the French King to have itt all, and that wee ought by all meanes possible to prevent itt.

I dare not write more particularly, haveing no cipher with your Grace, but truly things appeare to mee more like a war with France then otherwise, and what influence that may have upon your country, or what provisions you ought to make there if that should fall out, you would do very well to bee thinking of in time. Upon this occasion of sooner calling the Parliament I asked the King if hee would command your attendance att that time, to which hee answered that your service would bee more usefull where you are, and that hee would send you orders if hee should change his mind. I had not time to enter upon the subject of a letter from your Grace to my Lord Maynard, but intend to take the first opportunity of doing itt, the scruple raised by those lords being in my opinion of as factious a nature as anything can bee that is not rebellion ittselfe. Wee have no newes yett whither St. Ghillin bee taken, but the beseigeing of itt has much added to our apprehensions, as beleeving that Mons cannot bee long after itt. I will beg leave to present my wifes most humble service and my owne to the Dutchesse, and am, My Lord,

Your Graces most humble and most obedient servant,

Danby.

IV. MEMORANDA

A NUMBER of memoranda survive from this period which are of the very greatest value as exhibiting Danby's attitude to the principal problems confronting the Government. Several unfortunately are undated, but internal evidence has enabled each of these to be assigned with some confidence to a particular month. Only the more important are printed.

[October, 1673] [1]

In all things to promote the Protestant interest both att home and abroad.

To keepe firme to the Triple Alliance, and to indeavour to bring all Protestant princes into itt.

To suffer no diminution nor imbezelment of the revenue either in England or Ireland.

To suffer no money assigned either for land or sea service to bee diverted to any other use, nor any gratuities to bee given but by the Kings owne appointment.

A comittee of the Councill to bee joynd with the Admirall for manageing the economicall part of the navy, and all officers relateing to that part to bee appointed by the King himselfe, and no officer of a ship being of the degree of a captain and upwards to bee appointed but with his Majesties approbation.

Concerning the Kings old officers.

Concerning the Parliament to bee governed by the rules sett downe in a paper apart for that purpose.

State of the present condition of the Crowne,
which cannot bee amended but by force or by compliance.[2]

[December, 1673]

If by compliance, then itt must bee by Parliament or infinite reducement of expence.

If by Parliament, by this or a new one.

If by this, they must bee gratified by executing the laws both against popery and nonconformity, and withdrawing apparently from the French interest.

If by a new one, they will either desire comprehension or toleration of all religions but popery, and as to France the inclinations will bee the same, only the new one will in all likelyhood presse the Crowne to itt with lesse respect.

And as to money, itt is probably to bee feared that neither the one nor the other will give anything proportionable to the wants of the Crowne till satisfied in theire feares as to France.

[1] B.M. Add. MSS. 28042, f. 15. Notes in Danby's handwriting, undated and unendorsed.
[2] B.M. Add. MSS. 28042, f. 17. Notes in Danby's handwriting, endorsed in another hand, ' N.B. Memorandums for the King.'

Only itt is certaine a new one will not, unlesse by sale of the Church lands, and that only for the cause of destroying the Church thereby.

And if money bee given by this, itt must bee by takeing a time when the House will bee empty, and consequently bee esteemed such a surprise of the Parliament as will render those members liable to such censures as they are loth to undergoe.

From all which itt seemes as if the compliance must necessarily conclude in a resolution to give satisfaction in the point of France.

If otherwise, and that the expedient should bee force, then that must bee either forreigne or domestique or mixt.

If forreigne, itt must bee a totall conquest.

If mixt with either French or papist, itt must bee the like, and then the whole nation against both as a totall subversion of property.

If domestique, itt depends upon the constancy of the officers who comand, and the certainty of good pay to the souldier, which cannot last long by alwaies forceing contribution from the people, and in any of the cases there must bee a large provision of money to begin with.

Memorandums to speake with the King.

17 March, [16]73/4.[1]

In [16]67 all payments for three quarters of a yeare were stopt, even to the Gentlemen and Groomes of the Bedchamber.

In [16]69 an Order of Councill for retrenchments, which were made accordingly in paper, but in fact so much otherwise that although that yeare was the lowest expence yett itt amounted to above 1,700,000 l.

That itt is with confidence depended upon that againe itt will bee in words but not in deeds, and this will certainly bee the last triall.

That this money for the seamen must bee taken out of this yeares income, or bee such a debt as must make the necessity

---

[1] B.M. Add. MSS. 28042, f. 3. Memoranda in Danby's handwriting thus endorsed by him. The endorsement continues, ' To consider what may bee had out of these papers which may bee usefull.' This, however, presumably applies to a bundle of papers of which this document was one.

as great when the Parliament meets againe as itt was before, and though I gitt creditt to find the money still the revenue must pay itt.

That att the end of three yeares betwixt 3 and 400,000 l. of the revenue ceases, which may bee lengthened by a Parliament if you can live without needing them and by no other meanes, so that the sinewes of the monarchy are to bee recovered in these three yeares or niver ; and whereas by good husbandry the revenue is to bee improved considerably beyond what itt is, itt will bee impossible to do anything of that kind under necessity.

Consider that all the miscarriages have been wrong measures in your revenue, and by which all your undertakeings have still falne for want of money, and all this for want of forecast, or sometimes that your officers have been under the dilemma that if they did not lett you undoe yourselfe they were to bee undone by makeing themselves uneasy to you, whereas truly nothing under heaven can ever make your life easy but undergoing at any rate the being once beforehand in your revenue.

Such a number of pensions is established to which men have a right of law, and such an habituated course of payments out of severall offices more then your service does require, that itt amounts to much more then the revenue can beare, so that of course you walke into an inevitable ruine though nothing extraordinary should happen, and out of the power of a Lord Treasurer to helpe without your steddy and unalterable resolutions to assist him in itt.

An Association of Lords to defend the just rights of the Crowne and of the Church of England.[1]

In order to which they desire :

1st. That inquiry bee made into the due execution of the Act of Corporations made [13] Car. II, to the end that all who have not been admitted according to the qualifications of the said Act may bee excluded and others put in theire places according to law.

2nd. That inquiry bee also made into the execution of the Act of the 17th Car. II concerning the nonconformist ministers resideing in corporations, &c.

[1] Leeds MSS., Packet 16. Notes in Danby's handwriting, undated, but probably drawn up late in 1674 or early in 1675.

E

3rd. That his Majestie bee addresst to that hee would bee pleased to consider and review his commissions of leiutennancy, deputy leiutennancy, and justices of the peace, to the end that none ill affected may bee continued in any of the said imployments, and that preference in all counties may bee given to those within the said counties who have actually been in armes or sufferers for your Majestie or royall father, and to the sons of such, and that in the choice of justices of the peace the Lords Leiutennants of each county may bee informed and required to give theire opinion of such person to his Majestie and Lord Keeper before hee bee admitted into the commission of the peace.

4th. That none may bee continued judges in any of his Majesties courts of Westminster who have either been judges under any of the late usurped powers or acted as standing councell to any of the said powers.

5th. That for defraying the charges of sheriffs, justices of the peace and officers of the militia, by which they may bee made offices of benefitt as well as trust, consideration may bee had of some way out of the moneys which shall arise by the forfeiture of recusants, and for the makeing itt the more easy that some expedient might bee found of a certaine tax upon such in every county instead of the rigid penalties now in being.

Memorandums to the King.

April 4th, 1677.[1]

That his affaires are in a more hopefull condition then could have been expected.

That I feare I am in the right when I say that the quietnesse of this session has not proceeded from money only,[2] but a creditt to which I [3] thinke myselfe to [3] have been to a good degree instrumentall, in [4] makeing men beleeve [4] not only [5] your sincerity to the Protestant religion, but that your concernes

---

[1] B.M. Add. MSS. 28042, f. 9. Notes in Danby's handwriting, of which this is his endorsement. Printed in *Campana de Cavelli*, i. 193-6.

[2] In the shaky handwriting which the Duke of Leeds developed late in life ' money only ' is struck out and ' money ' substituted.

[3] . . . [3] Altered by Leeds to ' hope I.'

[4] . . . [4] Altered by Leeds to ' giveing men good assurance.'

[5] The word ' of ' is inserted by the Duke of Leeds.

for France were no other then as they might bee most usefull to the interests of your owne people, and that you would never suffer its greatnesse to goe beyond those due bounds which might consist with the safety of England.

That when mens feares are growne both so generall and so great as now they are by the successes of France, neither his Majestie nor any of his ministers shall have any longer creditt if acts do not speedily appeare some way or other to theire satisfaction.

That upon this will not only depend all the good which can bee expected from another session (in which my hopes are to make a good future establishment or never), but I dare with confidence affirme that the next session (without something done in the meane time) will not only bee the worst that wee ever yett saw, but that the hearts of the people will bee so alienated from the government that there will bee few concernd for the change of itt to whatever offers ittselfe. Whereas on the contrary there appeares to mee the greatest conjunction of honour, wisedome, glory and nationall advantages that ever offered ittselfe in any age to any prince or nation.

1st. In being the redeemer of all Christendome from an universall calamity if not thraldome.

2. In being the restorer of so many kings and princes to theire just rights.

3. In makeing yourselfe not only safe att home but great, and haveing by itt an opportunity of setling yourselfe for the future both in the hearts of your people and in those establishments of revenues which nothing but such an opportunity could ever make us hope for.

4. In haveing what reasonable advantages both of trade and treaties could bee desired both from Spaine and Holland, and such places either in these seas or the Mediterranean as might bee of use to us.

Memorandum that perhaps the conjuncture may never bee so proper to attaine all these ends as att this instant if the time bee not lost.

But itt may bee objected that

1. This may putt you into danger of the power of France, which is the only one that can hurt you.

2. Or, which indeed is the only great thing to bee feared, that you may bee deserted here by your Parliament, and consequently the Crowne left poorer and in worse condition then when the war began.

To the first t'is to bee answered (supposeing, as I alwaies meane through my whole discourse, that the King should bee inabled over and above his present revenue to fitt out his present fleet) that 40 or 50 ships being att sea, hee can do us no other harme then by his privateers, which tis true will for some time hurt trade and consequently Customes, but those also must bee supplied by Parliament, and so explained by them before entrance into the war.

To the second, tis not likely you will bee deserted when you have not only the ingagement of the Parliament to assist you from time to time, but the concurrence of all the people of the kingdome, and certainely to such a degree as would bee on your side to punish anybody even in Parliament that should refuse you fitt aides in that case. And because I would suppose the worst, you will bee putt into such a condition of armes both by sea and land as might incourage you to speake boldly if they should deny you, and att last, if the nation saw that to disband that force you desired nothing but to bee left free from your debts and in a condition to subsist with a fitting maintenance for the future, the people would helpe you destroy that Parliament which should refuse itt.

Consider also how fixt that resolution seemes to bee even in this Parliament (then which I never hope to see a better) that they ought to meete often, and that (though they are convinced the revenue is too narrow for the necessary expence) the Crowne ought from time to time to bee beholding to them for those additions which may bee wanting att the yeares end. And then how uneasy itt must bee to any king to live so precariously, and thereby depend rather upon his subjects then they upon him, is too apparent, insomuch that whether some small insurrection might not rather have been desireable (provided itt had not gone too far) then such an uncertaine state of government may bee a question ; and since the good of that could only have been the getting into some condition of armes and money by the consent of the people, who would otherwise

not give the one and bee jealous of the other, is not this a much
better occasion for the same purpose, which may bee continued
as long or suppresst as soone as you shall find itt most convenient [1] for your purposes,[1] and which gives you a strength
by sea as well as land ?

If itt shall bee objected, how shall money bee had beforehand
to make preparations, tis answered, by the Kings telling the
House of Commons that hee has considered theire last addresse,
but unlesse they furnish him with a good summe to putt
himselfe into a condition for war in case itt should happen by
reason of such alliances as hee might judge necessary, itt is
neither wise nor safe for him to make any of his neighbours his
enemies.

Itt would certainely either have the effect I have said of
putting him into a condition of armes, or itt would leave the ill
accidents which may happen by the French power att the dore
of the House of Commons, which they would bee as litle able to
answer to the people as I feare wee shall bee to the Parliament
if the fault bee thought to bee yours, which the generall opinion
even of honest men is you will not bee able to avoide, and
consequently (which is the maine scope of this discourse) meete
your Parliament the next time in ill humor and perhaps never
more to bee recovered.

Memorandums in June [16]77
for the King.[2]

The necessity of officers to assist mee, haveing neither time
to labour as I ought to do in his Majesties other concernes, nor
to thinke of improveing his revenue ; nor dare I trust that
anything I would do for his service shall not bee exposed to
publique knowlege.[3]

That nothing is more necessary then to lett the world see hee
will reward and punish, and that no longer time must bee lost

[1] . . . [1] These three words have been crossed out, probably by the Duke of
Leeds.

[2] B.M. Add. MSS. 28042, f. 13. Notes in Danby's handwriting, of which
this is his endorsement.

[3] Opposite this paragraph Danby has noted :
       Sir P[hilip] W[arwick] in Sir R[obert] H[oward]
       Lord Co[nway] in Sir Jo[hn] D[uncombe]

theirin, for that people begin already to thinke hee will do neither.[1]

That nothing can spoyle his affaires att home but unsteadinesse of resolution in those steps hee has begun, and want of vigor to discountenance all such as pretend to others,

Note here the variety of opposition this must meete,

As the perswasive arguments of the dissentors,

Theire conjunction with others,

The no possibility of convinceing some, and the discouragement that gives.

Memorandum : Bishop Duresme, Colonel Norton, the Test. F. Munson, Coleman, Talbott.

Till hee can fall into the humour of the people hee can never bee great nor rich, and while differences continue prerogative must suffer, unlesse hee can live without Parliament.

That the condition of his revenue will not permitt that.

As to forreigne affaires, I cannot as a Councellor but consider them in the first place as they stand with the interest of England, and then I am for concerting the peace with the Prince of Orange to his satisfaction, and makeing the alliance strict with him, by which many advantages may accrew to us, as the flag from Spayne, great advantages in trade from them, &c. Whereas I know none from France, but on the contrary itt must bee a fatall blow to the Prince of Orange to have the States force him to a disadvantageous peace, the displeasure of which may make him, though unwillingly, joyne into the interest of France, and att best leave both Spayne and the States jealous of your parting from them upon any occasion.

But to what may bee said in point of decency, I can only say that being under no obligation of state to France I shall only boldly affirme that were the King of France in the place of the King of England his actions have shewne hee would not forgoe so many of his greatest concernes both att home and abroad for ten times as many good words as wee have received, especially when a peace made in favour of him shall maintaine

---

[1] Opposite this paragraph Danby has noted:

Sir Ed[ward] D[ering] in Sir R[ichard] T[emple]

Mr. Ch[eyney] in Sir W[illiam] L[owther]

in Bir[ch]

in Tib [? Titus]

our ill humour here ; and I could never see what usefull helpe wee can receive from him when the peace shall be made.

But against this also there will bee strong opposition from mistaken opinions, and whilst the King will remaine almost single in his opinion against all others in his kingdome itt will also bee necessary to shew upon what foundations hee will build or maintaine himselfe.

To consider the pursuance of the provisoe and its consequences.

Memorandum in [16]79
about Edward Seymour, Esquire, being chosen Speaker.[1]

[March, 1679]

This man the most odious to the House till hee disturbed your Majesties affaires.

Hee promoted the difference betwixt the Houses.

Hee was the promoter of the most desperate addresses and proceedings of the House of Commons the last sessions.

Hee would now bee Speaker whither you would or not, or otherwise hee would create the dispute now in being.

When hee had declared both to your Majestie and myselfe that hee would freely submitt to your pleasure, hee (contrary to that promise, and against the ordinary course of Speakers, that you might bee forc't to the choice) makes no excuse, but declares his acceptance, and in so impudent a manner and words that most of the Lords were of opinion that his behaviour would have produced his imediate being turnd out of the Councill att least.

Hee then imediately takes the confidence to come to your Majestie himselfe, and instead of the great correction hee deserved hee getts not only good words but (as hee saies) an approbation for himselfe against an undoubted right of your Majesties.

Hee tells that private discourse of your Majesties to an hundred of the House of Comons, and from thence is the dispute made much stronger against your Majestie.

After all this, when hee heard that the House would call him to the chaire, and make him act without your approbation, hee was so sensible of that danger to himselfe that his freinds perswaded him by all meanes to gett off for his owne sake.

[1] B.M. Add. MSS. 28042, f. 21.   Notes in Danby's handwriting.   The endorsement, here used as a heading, is not written by him.

Thereupon hee brags that hee has been againe with your Majestie, that hee has given you satisfaction, that hee is as well as ever hee was in his life with your Majestie, that itt has apparently been only the malice of the Treasurer against him, that hee valews not the Treasurers power of a fidlestick, for that hee has more powerfull freinds then myselfe att Court, and I shall find my businesse done very speedily both in Court and Parliament.

V. ARTICLES OF IMPEACHMENT

THE articles which the House of Commons rejected in 1675 are printed, together with those which they adopted in 1678.

A charge or impeachment against Thomas Earl of Danby, Lord High Treasurer of England, containing several offences, crimes and misdemeanors of a very high nature.[1]

[Introduced in the House of Commons, April 26, 1675]

I. That the said Earl hath overthrown and violated the ancient course and constitution of the Exchequer, by perverting the method of receipts, payments and accounts contrary to law, whereby the King's revenue is put into confusion and a wasteful way of expence, to the destruction of his Majesty's credit, and exposing his Majesty's treasure and revenue to private bargains and corruptions ; and hath ingrossed into his own hands the sole power of disposing almost all the King's revenue, laying aside the Chancellor and Under-Treasurer of the Exchequer and other officers, whereby the usual and safe government of his Majesty's affairs relating to his revenue and all checks and comptrolls are avoided.

II. That a suit of law being intended about the marriage of the daughter of Sir Thomas Hyde, the said Earl caused one Mr. Brandly, a principal witness in the said case, to be arrested by an extraordinary warrant from one of the Secretaries of State, and to be kept for some time in close custody, during which

------

[1] C.J., ix. 324.

time the agents of the said Earl did labour the said Mr. Brandly by threatnings and promises of reward not to declare the truth ; and at midnight he was brought and examined before his Majesty upon oath, where the said Earl was present and assisting, whereupon the said Mr. Brandly did by the means aforesaid deliver in a testimony contrary to his own knowledge and against his conscience, he being then in duress ; by which illegal practices his Majesty was highly abused, the parties concerned in the said law suit greatly prejudiced, and the truth suppressed, to the manifest obstruction of justice ; and all this was done with an intent to procure the said heiress to be married to the second son of the said Earl.

III. That the Earl hath received very great sums of money besides the ordinary revenue, which have been wastfully spent, and far greater sums than ever issued fo : secret service without account, the King's debts remaining unpaid, the stores unfurnished, and the navy unrepaired, to the discredit and hazard of the King and kingdom.

IV. That the said Earl hath violated the rights and properties of the people, by stopping without authority their legal payments due in the Exchequer.

V. That though the office of Lord High Treasurer of England is always very full of great and necessary employments, yet the said Earl hath also assumed to himself the management of the Irish affairs, which were in precedent times dispatched always by the Secretaries and passed in Council, thereby interrupting the said Secretary's office and neglecting his own, and subtily enabling himself the better to convert a very great sum of money out of the Irish revenues to his own private advantage.

VI. That the said Earl hath procured great gifts and grants from the Crown, whilst under great debts, by warrants countersigned by himself.

VII. That about the 4th of December 1674, at the hearing of a cause in the Treasury Chamber, some Acts of Parliament now in force were urged against a proclamation and contrary to what his lordship aimed at, whereupon the said Earl, in contempt of the law, uttered this arbitrary expression, ' that a new proclamation is better than an old Act,' several of his Majesty's subjects being present ; and upon his lordship's report to the Privy Council the person in question, being a foreigner and not obeying such proclamation but pursuing his right at law, was banished the kingdom.

Articles of impeachment of high treason, and other high crimes, misdemeanors and offences, against Thomas Earl of Danby, Lord High Treasurer of England.[1]

[Introduced in the House of Commons, December 21, 1678]

I. That he hath traiterously encroached to himself regal power, by treating in matters of peace and war with foreign princes and ambassadors, and giving instructions to his Majesty's ambassadors abroad, without communicating the same to the Secretaries of State and the rest of his Majesty's Council, and against the express declaration of his Majesty and his Parliament, thereby intending to defeat and overthrow the provisions which had been deliberately made by his Majesty and his Parliament for the safety and preservation of his Majesty's kingdoms and dominions.

II. That he hath traiterously endeavoured to subvert the ancient and well-established form of government in this kingdom, and instead thereof to introduce an arbitrary and tyrannical way of government ; and the better to effect this his purpose he did design the raising of an army upon pretence of a war against the French King, and then to continue the same as a standing army within this kingdom ; and an army being so raised, and no war ensuing, an Act of Parliament having passed to pay off and disband the same, and a great sum of money being granted for that end, he did continue this army contrary to the said Act, and misemployed the said money, given for disbanding, to the continuance thereof ; and issued out of his Majesty's revenue divers great sums of money for the said purpose, and wilfully neglected to take security from the Paymaster of the Army as the said Act required, whereby the said law is eluded and the army is yet continued, to the great danger and unnecessary charge of his Majesty and the whole kingdom.

[1] C.J., ix. 561.

III. That he, traiterously intending and designing to alienate the hearts and affections of his Majesty's good subjects from his royal person and government, and to hinder the meeting of Parliaments, and to deprive his sacred Majesty of their safe and wholesome councils, and thereby to alter the constitution of the government of this kingdom, did propose and negotiate a peace for the French King upon terms disadvantageous to the interest of his Majesty and his kingdoms, for the doing whereof he did endeavour to procure a great sum of money from the French King, for enabling of him to carry on and maintain his said traiterous designs and purposes to the hazard of his Majesty's person and government.

IV. That he is popishly affected, and hath traiterously concealed, after he had notice, the late horrid and bloody plot and conspiracy contrived by the papists against his Majesty's person and government, and hath suppressed the evidence and reproachfully discountenanced the King's witnesses in the discovery of it, in favour of popery, immediately tending to the destruction of the King's sacred person and the subversion of the Protestant religion.

V. That he hath wasted the King's treasure by issuing out of his Majesty's Exchequer and several branches of his revenue, for unnecessary pensions and secret services, to the value of two hundred thirty-one thousand six hundred and two pounds within two years, and that he hath wholly diverted out of the known method and government of the Exchequer one whole branch of his Majesty's revenue to private uses, without any account to be made of it to his Majesty in the Exchequer, contrary to the express Act of Parliament which granted the same ; and he hath removed two of his Majesty's commissioners of that part of the revenue for refusing to consent to such his unwarrantable actings therein and to advance money upon that branch of the revenue for private uses.

VI. That he hath by indirect means procured from his Majesty for himself divers considerable gifts and grants of inheritance of the ancient revenue of the Crown, even contrary to Acts of Parliament.

VI. CORRESPONDENCE WHILE IN HIDING

THE letters which Danby wrote in the three weeks between March 23 and April 15, 1679, when he lay concealed from the wrath of Parliament, have a special interest of their own. One of the most important, that of March 28, in which he summoned to his assistance his friends among the peers who had not yet come up to Westminster, has already several times been printed.[1] It has consequently been considered unnecessary to publish it again ; but four other letters are printed, together with some notes which Danby supplied to Lord Bath for an interview with the King at the very moment when he was preparing to go into hiding.

Notes upon which my Lord Bathe spoke to the King,
23 March, 1678/9.[2]

The laying downe the staffe.

The passing a bill of incapacities before other bills when the session may end with that bill and no other thing done this session.

That the bill intends to take away all grants already passt as well as to passe, by which all but my paternall estate is taken away.

Itt takes away my seat in Parliament.

And all this to bee consented to by the King for faults that I could not have comitted but that his Majestie sent the businesse of the Plott to mee and comanded mee to write the letters.

That in no case a minister ought to bee made a sacrifice of state to the will of the people.

But when itt is for haveing obey'd the King that I am to bee a state sacrifice itt is without example, and beyond the case of my Lord Strafford.

---

[1] *Hatton Correspondence*, i. 184 ; *Portland MSS.*, ii. 153 ; *Letters of Lord Chesterfield*, p. 194. The original draft is B.M. Add. MSS. 28049, f. 18.

[2] B.M. Add. MSS. 28043, f. 11. Notes in Danby's handwriting, of which this is the endorsement.

And if the King suffer them to go beyond what hee has said in his speech itt is downeright desertion, and I will trust God only.

That if his Majestie do not stand by his speech strictly without doing anything more hee has given mee the most mortall wound by itt, whereas itt was his owne offer to do itt in kindnesse to mee.

[To the King] [1]
                                                    [24th March, 1678/9]

I have just now received a message by Sir Charles Wheeler from my Lord of Bathe that your Majestie is made beleeve itt will bee for your quiett and my safety to have a bill passt to incapacitate mee from bearing any office or coming neare your Majestie for ever. I beleeve both your Majestie and myselfe undone by itt, and especially your Majestie, for departing from this days speech, if that did not content them, being but an assurance to your enemies that noise and clamour will make you depart from anything or anybody, which was the true cause of your fathers ruine. I shall pray for your Majestie to divert the fatality coming upon you, whatever becomes of the most faithfull that ever served a master.

                                                    Danby.[2]

[To the Duke of Lauderdale] [3]

                                                    2nd April, 1679.
My Lord,

I returne your Grace my humblest thanks for your favour and kindnesse to mee yesterday in the House, and your willingnesse to have brought the bill to a question. I heare the King was perswaded against bringing itt to a question yesterday, when I am sure my freinds were very well sett for mee, and I can no way imagine how itt can bee hoped to bee better for mee this day. I beg your Grace will argue this with his Majestie, and lett the bill have its fate to-day, unlesse you receive some satisfactory reason to the contrary ; for either the bill will bee throwne out (which will putt an end to what they can do in Parliament this session), or I am sure the whole world would

[1] B.M. Add. MSS. 28049, f. 12, an autograph draft.
[2] Endorsed, ' Coppy of my letter to the King, 24th March 1678/9.'
[3] Stowe MSS. 199, f. 16. Autograph letter.

justify the King to refuse this bill, which perhaps they would not a more moderate one. And for banishment, itt cannot now bee done by Act of Parliament this session, because an Act for that purpose has been already throwne out of the House of Comons. Since banishment and incapacitys are both out of dores this session (by reason of that bill for both which is flung out) I thinke itt my happinesse that there is such a bill of severity as I hope the Lords will not passe, and the King would bee condemn'd in the opinion of all the world if hee should passe, so that those who speake for moderateing the bill advise the greatest prejudice to mee that is possible as the case stands. Itt will bee the greatest favour your Grace can ever do mee to make the King enough sensible of this, for I am assured hee does not only intend mee justice but all kindnesse imaginable. I am

> Your Graces most faithfull and obedient servant,
>
> Danby.

Besides my owne concerne in this matter, I cannot but with sadnesse reflect upon the condition of our master, if I should any way suffer for the letters to Montagu, for hee must to the worlds end never blame nor expect from Secretary (or any other) to do or write anything but what must first bee considered how itt will bee approved by the Parliament.

[To Viscount Latimer] [1]

11th April, 1679.

Deare Son,

I thanke you for your letter this day, and I cannot but bee glad to see you so sensible of my misfortunes. The greatest of them is that I should make my wife and children miserable, and especially yourselfe, who is like to beare the greatest share of the cruelty, if his Majestie please not to have some mercy for you. Whatever happen, bee not too much afflicted, but keepe your spiritt above itt, and trust in Gods mercys when mans faile. My innocence towards God (as to the crimes charged against mee), and my assurance that I have deserved better usage from the King then to passe the bill, makes mee past all concernes but that of my family, and therefore if I can find any way to avoide the bill (though with my life) I am resolved to do itt. The

---

[1] B.M. Add. MSS. 28049, f. 42. Autograph letter or draft.

teares of your mother are the only present trouble I am under, with whom I cannot prevaile to lett mee stand my triall, but if I could bee satisfied that my estate would bee safe after itt, I will rather give her that one sharp affliction then live to see her and you under a perpetuall one of want, haveing none of those treasures to releeve you with which my malitious enemies would make the world beleeve, though they themselves know the contrary. In case the present bill passe both Houses, I intend to present a petition to his Majestie by your hands, and att the delivery of itt I will not have you trouble him more then to say that your father has comanded you to deliver that petition to his Majestie, and hopes for a gracious answer, being no lesse then the concerne of his whole family.

The bearer has acquainted mee with the informations which two men pretend a willingnesse to sweare against Oates and Bedloe, and I agree that the evidence would bee of great use to mee in case of my triall, if itt were sworne to ; but I understand them to bee or have been clarks to Oates or Bedloe, and doubt whither one of them bee not the man that once swore that Nox had endeavoured to bribe him to give him informations of what his master did do, and particularly if hee had anything against the Queene or mee. This being false (and yett I thinke was then sworne against Nox), I dare never advise any conversation with such a fellow, and hee may perhaps have gott a companion for better proofe against Nox, which may then bee brought to mee, as the last was indeavoured to have been. Besides Nox (though hee may meane well) is very silly and impertinent, and hee has taken poore Bladen to his assistance, who I thinke is very honest, but will bee easily deceived by such knaves. All I can advise is that the King may bee made acquainted with itt, to the end that there may nothing bee said hereafter of secrett acting in itt, nor indeavour to procure testimony against Oates and Bedloe by any private meanes, which will otherwise certainely bee pretended, though never so falsely. I thinke your best way is to carry itt to my Lord Sunderland, and tell him how you come by itt, and desire hee will know the Kings pleasure what shall bee done in itt, to avoide att least future danger.

If these fellows should refuse to go before either the Secretaries or the Comittee of the Councill for Examinations, I should have great suspicion of theire knavish intentions, and indeed should bee assured of itt. Therefore lett that bee putt to triall as soone as may bee. Do not owne you have these directions from mee, nor tell Nox anything of what you do, till you have acquainted my Lord Sunderland and the King with itt, whose directions you must observe. In the meane time lett Bladen have 5 l. as money you lend him, but tell him you dare give no directions till you heare from mee, which yett you cannot, and advise him that both hee and Nox bee very cautious that these fellows do not att last play them some trick, which you cannot but bee in feare of till you see theire proofes fixt somewhere.

I will direct my wife to send you the five pounds, and you may tell Bladen and Nox you hope every day to heare from mee. Present my service to your wife, and I pray God blesse you both and make your fortune happier then

Your most truly affectionate fathers,

Danby.

To Viscount Latimer [1]

Deare Son,   April 12th, [1679], att 3 a clock.

I would much rather my freinds should adhere to the bill of attainder (in case the House devide upon the question) then agree to this bill of confiscation and banishment, and would have you lett them know this to bee your fathers mind. But if theire justice or kindnesse to mee will not lett them vote for attainder, I desire they would withdraw from the question (as itt will bee fittest for you to do). Itt will bee dangerous to lett my freinds know my desire in this till the question is going to bee putt, for feare my enemies gett notice of itt, nor are you to give my freinds any other reason, but that you know itt to bee my desire. Yett for your owne satisfaction, my reason is that I know the King will never passe the bill of attainder, but will passe any other bill they shall bring to him. Lett mee heare what you have done upon my letter yesterday, and bee assured I am

A most truly affectionate father,

Danby.

---

[1] B.M. Add. MSS. 28049, f. 44. Autograph letter.

PART III

A STATESMAN OUT OF OFFICE

1679-89

Danby's activities during the ten years when he was out of office were of so varied a character that it has been found impossible to treat the documents belonging to these years as one unit. Three entirely distinct periods present themselves, that during which the Earl was still in the Tower, that during which he was living peacefully and at liberty under Charles II and James II, and that during which he was engaged in the Revolution. The papers illustrating these three periods have been grouped in separate sections.

I. IN THE TOWER, 1679-84

For the period of his incarceration in the Tower the mass of Danby's papers is enormous. Time must have hung heavy on his hands, and he devoted much of his too abundant leisure to drafting and redrafting letters, petitions, legal arguments, and pamphlets, all with the object of securing his release from confinement or explaining away the causes which had brought about his fall. These papers he religiously preserved, and along with them the greater number of the letters he received. From this vast mass a few illustrative documents have been selected and are printed together. In separate sections are added a number of more personal letters, which throw light on the fortunes of Danby's family at this time, and on the matrimonial tangle in which his son Dumblane had become involved.

A. POLITICAL PAPERS

[To the King] [1]

21 May, 1679.

I suppose your Majestie is not without the knowlege that there are industrious endeavours to promote a petition of thanks from the Citty to the Parliament for theire great care in suppressing of popery, and to lett them know that they will stand by them with theire lives and fortunes. By some itt is endeavoured that they might bee thank't also for theire proceedings against the Duke ; and that has been promoted by the meanes of one Charlton (an engine of my Lord Shatsburys), Sir Thomas Player, and one Pilkington, but meetes not with great incouragement. I have gott one to make the Lord Maior sensible of the danger of such petitions, and that nothing relateing to the

---

[1] From the autograph draft in B.M. Add. MSS. 28049, f. 48.

State ought to bee admitted amongst them without your Majesties knowlege of itt first ; but least such an admonition should not bee sufficient, itt would certainely bee necessary the Lord Maior should have such a positive order from your Majesties owne mouth. Young Gerrard busies himselfe very pragmatically in these matters with some members of Parliament, and hee and Sir Thomas Armstrong take great paines to cry up Sir Nicolas Carew and his associates in all places, by reason of theire great earnestnesse to have a successor named, for the worthiest and best subjects your Majestie has.

I hope your Majestie is not unsensible of what the whole world does see so plainely aimed att by the villany of my Lord Shaftsbury and the weakenesse of those hee makes his instruments, who although they faile of theire owne end will carry things beyond a possibility of being retrived. In short nothing is more evident then that this House of Commons is so treacherously managed, and so ill disposed, that itt must either bee shortly dismiss't or your Majestie and your kingdomes must bee undone by them. If they shall refuse to proceed to the triall of the popish lords att the time sett by the Lords, your Majestie can never have a more just pretence to the kingdome to send them home, for men do so generally complaine of them for theire delays in that particular that your Majestie will not againe have so great an advantage to render them odious to the nation if you lett slip that opportunity.

I am sorry to find that your Commissioners of the Treasury do take the ways of putting your Majestie out of Mr. Kent and other mens debts, instead of applying the present incomes of the revenue to your use, which I know to bee true ; but besides the present losse which your Majestie sustaines by Sir Robert Howards ignorance (which guides them), I am the more troubled for the prejudice which your affaires will suffer by itt when the Parliament shall rise without supply, as most certainely itt will. The evident ruine of the Government makes most men (who were not so heretofore) now willing to make any shift without calling to your Majestie if they can see that you will resolve to overcome these difficulties ; and I will suffer death if I do not demonstrate to your Majestie the way of doing itt if you shall please to take up such resolutions as are necessary for itt. I pray God your Majestie may take a true state of your condition, and that you may not bee carried into wrong hopes by timourous, ignorant, or false councells, and I call God to witnesse that I cannot imagine how you can expect others from the much greatest part of those now about your Majestie.

Since I had writt this letter my brother Charles Bertie writt to mee that hee heard hee should bee examined about four score thousand pounds hee received from France (I suppose by Mr. Montagus information to the Secrett Comittee) ; but your Majestie knows hee never received any but from Mr. Chiffinch, so that hee desires (in case hee shall bee examined) to know what answer hee shall give, and begs your Majesties directions in itt. I conceave itt ought to bee the same as in the former, that if they shall aske particularly as to Mr. Chiffinch hee may owne to have received bills from him, but as to the sumes or laying out itt was by your Majesties directions, and that the accounts are given to your Majestie. I do not mention this particular to my Lord Bathe (because itt concernes the French money), but if your Majestie approve this method I desire my Lord may lett mee know that your Majestie would have Mr. Bertie follow those directions you have given mee, and I will acquainte him with your Majesties pleasure.

[Danby] [1]

[To the Earl of Bath] [2]

3rd June, 1679.

I have consulted divers councill in my owne case, and they all agree that his Majestie haveing given mee a pardon, and I haveing pleaded itt, and haveing been att the Lords House in order to my triall att the time appointed, and prevented thereof only because I could not have councell, I ought certainly to bee bailed by the Kings order att the Councill Board. They tell mee no other court can take notice of itt, because itt is not before them, but they beleeve that my Lord Chancellor and the Atturney General will not for theire owne safetys approve itt there, though the law will admitt itt, nor for the same reason that my councell durst not appeare for mee in Westminster

---

[1] Endorsed, ' Letter to the King, 21 May 1679.'

[2] From the autograph draft in B.M. Add. MSS. 28049, f. 56.

Hall they dare not appeare to say this att Councell table. Some of my lawyers were with mee this day againe, and say that by what they have seene att the Kings Bench in the cases of Mr. Pepys and Sir Anthony Deane they know not what they have to do more either with law or prerogative but to study the Journalls of the House of Comons, which though the law does not allow to bee a record yett all records are made but pamphlets in comparison of them.

This gave mee occasion to blame them and the judges for theire timorousnesse in declareing the law, but to that they answered that till the King would take upon him to rebuke such proceedings in Parliament, and both assert his owne authority better and see to bring both Houses into the due bounds of theire respective jurisdictions, the Comons would certainely bee obey'd in Westminster Hall, and they said but that they knew the King to bee in London they should not beleeve hee was in England. I confesse itt has made mee very mellancholly to heare theire judgments upon the condition of the monarchy, and (though they spoke with better intentions) I find they conclude with my Lord Shaftsburys maxime that things must bee worse before they will bee better. But by the exposition of theire meaning I found itt was not theire opinion that necessarily they must bee so, but they concluded they would bee suffered to bee so, and att last they would mend themselves as to the nation, whatever became of the Crowne.

Itt is wondred that there is no news of a declaration, when there is so much need of one and so good grounds for the King to make one upon. Itt is thought a fitt work for somebody to view the Journalls of this last session in the House of Comons, and to consider theire proceedings, which have not only outdone all limits of theire owne power but have far exceeded all that the Long Parliament did attempt till the King was gone from them. In short these gentlemen said this last Parliament had denied the Kings most necessary and most unquestioned prerogative, which was his power of pardoning; had taken upon them a joynt power with the Lords in judicature; had not only questioned the right of the bishops seates in Parliament, but taken upon them to determine itt; had imprisoned men contrary to law, and contrary both to justice and law had refused to admitt councell in point of law to plead for men accused by them ; and after all this had putt an abstract of most of these things in print under the name of reasons, but indeed a remonstrance against the King, Lords and bishops, and observed that nothing was done to controll these things nor to putt anything into the world to informe or undeceive the people.

They said I was not to wonder therefore when all the wheeles of government were thus broken, and nothing done to repaire them, if they did truckle to those who were suffered to assume soveraignity att this rate, and one of them with great earnestnesse advised mee, and said itt should bee his advice to his owne son (if in my case) that if the King would not release mee by his owne power I should make my escape if I could, for that as the torrent runs they should not bee able to defend mee, and they could not thinke itt prudent to depend upon the King for protection, who did not make one step they saw whereby hee would bee able to protect himselfe. In conclusion the same gentleman, who is my freind as well as councell, advised mee alone when the rest were gone to gett the Kings leave from time to time to go abroad [1] and to returne att a certaine time, as was allow'd to my Lord Wharton, Lord Salisbury and others before theire inlargement, rather then move for any baile, because both the Chanceller, &c., would bee tender in itt, and that baile was some diminution to my pardon.

I wish I could any way learne what the King intends as to the time of the Parliaments sitting, and whither hee will call the same Parliament, because I could thereby guide my owne measures much the better ; but for his Majesties I professe by what appeares to publique view I have lost all my poore skill, and do live now only in hope that his Majestie has some secrett designe which will miraculously deliver himselfe and his kingdomes. I confesse that in my owne opinion as things now stand I thinke itt would bee best both for the King and mee that his Majestie should take occasion, upon my petition for such a liberty as I have mentioned, to say in Councill that when the Parliament meets againe hee expects to find the same difficulties which have been made already about mee, that hee is resolved

---

[1] The following words are here struck out, 'with a keeper as a prisoner to Wimbledon or elsewhere into the country.'

never to depart from his pardon nor to suffer anything more against mee then hee has already declared to both Houses, and that therefore hee thinkes itt the best expedient to comand mee to go beyond sea for two or three yeares, and if the Parliament should desire to have mee recalled to my triall his Majestie would send for mee over.

I conceave that this expedient would both satisfy the present men in power, who thinke I would hinder theire designes by staying in England, and that the Parliament would bee rather contented to lett mee alone when abroad then send for mee to enter a contest againe about the Kings pardon, which can never bee laid aside but by an Act of Parliament, nor that obtained but by the Kings consent, which must bee the highest misery to himselfe and greatest injustice to mee. I shall bee like to suffer great inconvenience by this expedient should itt bee taken, but I would bee content to beare itt for his Majesties ease, and that itt might thereby bee tried whither my absence will accomodate the Kings businesse, as my enemies do as falsely pretend, as they did that my laying downe the staffe would do itt. But my feare in this case will bee that in my absence his Majestie may bee prevailed upon by my false freinds to consent to some Act of Parliament against mee under a pretence of being for my good (as hee is made beleeve that these councells are for his owne) ; but unlesse I can first bee assured against that danger I would by no meanes have this expedient thought on, but rather leave gott for mee as was for the lords before named. I beg your Lordship will take the paines to discourse those severall ways to his Majestie, and to do itt so that I may know his pleasure before his going to Windsor, where I shall want your Lordship and the opportunity of any good applications to his Majestie. I thanke your Lordship for your letter yesterday by my Lady, and the comfortable hopes your Lordship gives mee in itt, but I confesse mine are almost as low as the rest of the Kings freinds, and I find nothing to bee glad of but that they say these Commissioners of [the] Treasury will prevaile to cutt off those expences I never could do.

I wonder the King gives no better incouragement to my Lord Roberts, who hee may keepe as a bridle upon my Lord Shaftsbury, if hee pleases. That noble President makes all his freinds in the Citty declare that hee stays att Court only to bee a tribune for the people there, and truly I beleeve hee will bee a successfull one. I am unalterably, as I ought to bee,

Yours,

[Danby] [1]

Memorandums about the Duke of York, &c. [2]
[September, 1679]
[I]

As the French interest was chiefly supported by my Lady Portsmouth, so itt was infinitely incouraged by Mr. Montagus indeavours both to procure money for the King, and by makeing a match betwixt the Dauphin and the Kings neice (now Queene of Spaine), [3] and by indeavouring to gett the King consent to the relinquishing some townes to France which the Confederates would not consent to.

Itt was also much countenanced by my Lord Sunderland, whose businesse itt was with my Lady Portsmouth to perswade mee to go into that interest of France, and to joyne heartily with that King in everything by which I might make myselfe both great and rich, and secure the King from all those insolences hee was every day subject to from his Parliament, who would never bee good but for feare of a power over them.

Both my Lord Sunderland and Mr. Montagu were frequently att mass in the time of theire severall embassies in France, and were the first English embassadors who did ever dishonour this Crowne by giving place to the princes of the blood in that country.

Memorandum, the Prince of Orange his desire of privacy from the Duke of his marriage or the transactions in relation to France.

[1] Endorsed, ' To Lord B[ath], 3rd June [16]79.'

[2] This heading or endorsement, in Danby's handwriting on B.M. Add. MSS. 28042, f. 28, seems to apply to the three sets of autograph notes which follow on ff. 29, 30 and 32. These notes are obviously connected, they were probably drawn up at much the same time, and they are accordingly printed as a series, those on f. 32, however, before those on f. 30. *Campana de Cavelli*, i. 289-95.

[3] Maria Louisa, daughter of Philip Duke of Orleans, the brother of Louis XIV, married Charles II of Spain in August 1679.

Memorandum, the Dukes letter from Newmarkett to the King of France to assure him that should never bee a match, and the rupture betwixt the King of France and him upon that letter.

The Kings makeing that match against the Dukes will.

[II]

1. That although I am a stranger to you there is no man but yourselfe of the House of Commons whom I would have trusted with those things which I intend to say to you. But I must desire to bee answered to some things previous to the matter, as first,

2. That I expect your faith and honour to bee ingaged that what I say shall not bee mentioned to any other man in the world, the Duke of Munmouth haveing assured mee that the rest of your freinds will acquiesce in your opinion of the matter if you shall declare yourselfe to have received satisfaction.

3. That I desire to know, in case you shall bee satisfied, how I shall bee assured that your House will addresse in my behalfe for another pardon, so as all disputes about the present pardon may bee removed.

4. How the motion for another pardon shall arise in your House, for that I will never bee brought as an informer whatever becomes of mee, but that what I shall say may bee in my place in Parliament, where I shall deliver what I say as my duty to the King and my country, and which I had done long since if my pardon had been confirmed, and was resolved to do whenever I could speake under the protection of a pardon, which I desire more for feare of my enemies in Court then in Parliament.

These things premised, then to enter upon the matter ittselfe by telling him :

How much the world has been mistaken in theire opinions of my being ingaged either in the popish or French interests, and how on the contrary I am hated to such a degree by both those parties that I know my persecutions have arisen from both those interests, and that I am sure I could not bee safe in any place of the world that were under either popish or French govern-

ment ; and though other men have been accused by false
witnesses yett I am the first that was ever accused for things
to which I am the most opposite enemy in the nation.

How much they are also mistaken in theire beleife of my being
in the Dukes interests, who will never forgive mee neither the
seizing Colemans papers nor being the cause of his being sent
away the first time from the King, which my Lord Sunderland
knows to bee true, as the whole Councill does that the letters
had not been seized but for mee, which are the greatest evidences
yett knowne against the Duke.

To relate the particular animosities of Montagu, Harbord,
Titus, Winnington, Capell, Powle, Hyde, Car, Clarges.

That whenever I am free and under the protection of a pardon
I thinke itt my duty to tell the House what paines the Duke has
taken and with what threats to myselfe to have had the businesse of the Plott to have been kept from the Parliament, and
to have been proceeded in only by the King and Councill, and
the Parliament to have been putt off till all persons accused
about the Plott should have been tried by the Kings comission
out of Parliament. And hee told mee hee had gained all about
the King to itt but myselfe, and bid mee looke to itt if ever itt
was brought to the Parliament.

When the Duke found the King resolved to bring itt to Parliament, and the King thereupon thinkeing itt necessary for the
Duke to withdraw himselfe, the Duke attempted by all meanes
possible to divert the King from that resolution of his withdrawing ; but the King useing many arguments to convince the
Duke how impossible itt would bee for his Majestie to protect
him from that storme of the Parliament which was like to come
upon him, the Duke answered that his Majestie had enough of
the army which was not yett disbanded to protect him if hee
pleased, and if his Majestie did not make use of that protection
for himselfe the Parliament would not suffer him long to bee
King. Upon which some debate arose, wherein I show'd the
unreasonablenesse of the Dukes proposition, and the King
totally rejected to heare any more of itt, upon which the Duke
said, nay, then hee did agree with his Majestie that itt was time
for him to provide for his safety, and asked the King when hee
would have him go.

There were many former occasions upon which the Duke had indeavoured to perswade the King to governe by force, upon which I have divers times told his Majestie that itt was plaine the Duke would faine ingage his Majestie to a war in his owne lifetime, doubting whither his Highness should find so many freinds as to make one for him, being of another religion, after his Majesties death. To which his Majestie has as often answered that hee saw itt plainely enough, but should never bee drawne into such councills ; and upon this last motion of the Dukes of useing open force the King said his brother had now shew'd barefac'd what hee would bee att, and seemed to bee much displeased with him for itt.

To assure that no man will go farther for the Protestant interest and against the French then myselfe.

[III]

1. Shall bee no informer, but to speake freely in my place in Parliament what I know to have been the cheife causes of the misfortunes of the kingdome as to popery and the French interest amongst us.

2. That the Duke has been a principall cause of both, but that hee had been drawne from the French upon the marriage of the Lady Mary to the Prince of Orange had itt not been for the Dutchesse of Portsmouth, who for greedinesse of money from France did hold the King to them, and keepe his Majestie from declareing the war against them.

3. One instance of this was his incessant agitation for the declaration for liberty of conscience, which was designed only in behalfe of the papists, as my Lord Clifford has confesst to mee.

5.[1] Another was his constant indeavour to have had an army of English and Irish alwaies in France, to have been comanded wholly by popish officers, and to have had this clause in theire respective capitulations with the King of France, that they should alwaies bee in the Kings power to bee recalled into his owne service, and not to bee forced to march above such a distance from the sea-cost next adjoyning to England ; and my

---

[1] The numbering suggests that Danby intended to reverse the order of this paragraph and the next.

knowlege of this was first from old Monsieur Ruvigny, who (beleeveing I had knowne this project) told mee one day [1] (speakeing about some agreements which had been made for French
money in my Lord Cliffords time) that the King could not
reasonably both expect the continuance of those payments and
have his master obliged to pay an army of the King of Englands
subjects, who must quarter upon our coasts, and must do his
master service only within such a distance of England as might
perhaps bee of no very great use to him, and that the Duke was
so much of this opinion that his Highnesse had told him the
army would bee of ten times the use of that money to our King,
and Monsieur Ruvigny said hee hoped I would not bee against
itt. I pretended to Monsieur Ruvigny that I would speake
further with the King and Duke about itt (although in truth I
had never spoke with either of them of any such thing), but I
asked Monsieur Ruvigny what good that army could do us, for
I thought the money was much better. To which hee answered
that the Parliament would never do the King good, and hee
must throw off that bondage, and hee was sure the Duke was of
the same opinion. I told this to the King, who seemed to take
very little notice of itt ; and afterwards I spoke of itt to the
Duke of Buckingham, who swore Ruvigny was in the right, and
that there was no way of governing the Parliament but as
Cromwell did governe them.

4. When the Duke of Buckingham was sent to the French
King to breake the Triple League and to adjust the war against
Holland and to make the agreement of what parts of the conquest wee were to share, I advised him against takeing that
journey or medling with that businesse, and said itt would bee
his ruine. To which hee answered hee must venture that, for if
itt did ruine him yett itt might save him two or three yeares,
whereas if hee should refuse to go with that errand the Duke and
my Lord Arlington would certainely ruine him in three months,
besides that matters were so laid that wee must now come to the
French government or nothing, and swore hee would not bee
without his share in itt.

Was once discoursed by the Duke why I would not alter my
religion, for that my freind the Duke of Buckingham had

[1] The words ' in the gallery att Walingford ' are here struck out.

reconciled himselfe to the Church of Rome. To which I answered that possibly hee might to the Court of Rome (according to my Lord Bristolls distinction), but I did beleeve hee would scarce bee reconciled truly to any Church, and that his Grace would bee no example to mee about religion. To which the Duke answered I might have the example of a greater man, if that would serve ; but I answered that was not a thing to bee done by example, and then the Duke said no more.

The Duke told mee also that Mr. Montagu was reconciled to theire Church, but I afterwards heard him speake very often against him for a false and perfidious man.

Instructions [to Viscount Latimer] [1]

17 March, 1680/1.

You have a list of the lords ranged into four columes, viz., the first and second are those which I thinke will bee for mee, the third those which I imagine will bee against mee, and the fourth those which I suppose will either bee neuters or for my baile.

Your first care must bee to bee certaine what lords are com'd to Oxford before my businesse bee moved, and in order to that you are to count the lords in the House dayly by the list aforesaid, and particularly to see the Clarks booke every day att the riseing of the House to find what lords have been sworne that day, and especially the first and second daies, and from time to time to give an account thereof to my freinds.

If itt shall appeare att any time that there are more of those lords in the House who are noted to bee for mee then of those who are supposed to bee against mee (I meane of temporall lords), I desire in that case that no time might bee lost in presenting my petition to the House as soone as is possible.

When my petition has been read itt will probably bee indeavoured to bee obstructed

1st. By insisting to have the petition sent to the House of Commons.

2dly. By objecting that I am not there to tender my owne baile.

1 B.M. Add. MSS. 28043, f. 25. In Danby's handwriting. The date is taken from his endorsement on f. 29.

3dly. Itt may bee objected that the Comons perhaps are ready to proceed to my triall, and my adversaries may make that a pretence that itt is more reasonable I should bee some way delivered from my imprisonment, rather then bailed, haveing been so long confined.

To all which objections may bee answered

1st. That if I had petitioned either to bee tried or discharged itt had been necessary to have sent notice to the Commons, but haveing only pray'd for baile I am still to remayne a prisoner, and theire lordships only are judges whither itt bee proper to take baile for any prisoner or not, for that otherwise itt would bee to lett the Comons into a principall part of theire judicature, which they have not thought fitt to do in the Lord Cheife Justice Scroggs his case (although a comoner), and much lesse sure will they apply to the Comons in the case of a peer.

2dly. That although I am not there myselfe, itt will bee all one as to my forthcomming if theire lordships bee satisfied with such baile as will bee offered for my appearance ; but if itt shall bee strongly insisted on to have mee there in person to tender baile, then to move that an order may bee imediately made for my being bailed when I come thither, and another order obtained att the same time directed to the Leiutenant of the Tower for bringing mee to the House for that purpose.

3dly. That if the Commons should bee willing to bring mee first to bee tried, yett itt is most certaine that all things are yett so unprepared for the triall of any peers att Oxford that itt will bee unreasonable to deny a lord the liberty of fresh aire in the meane time who has been so long restrained and hath such bad health, especially when theire lordships have not only bailed but not thought fitt to putt an houres confinement upon others who are no peers, and yett theire crimes said to bee greater then mine.

Note that the judges which were comitted by Parliament for high treason in the time of the last King were bayled. And note hereupon that my confinement has been within a fortnight of two yeares, and has in truth been made a greivous punishment, instead of being only a safe custody in order to a triall, which is what the law intends.

As to the time of delivering my petition :

My opinion is to have itt delivered before the House of Commons have passt all theire ceremonies of swearing, chusing theire Speaker, nameing theire comittees, &c. But if itt shall happen that no such time can bee taken, and that the Commons should send a message to the Lords for the preventing or delaying of my baile, I desire that my freinds will however bring itt to a question upon the reasons aforesaid, and such other as they will bee better able to give in my behalfe. Your care must bee also to putt them in mind (in case itt shall bee agreed that I shall bee bayled) that the order bee so fully worded for my bayle that there bee no roome left for future disputes after I shall bee brought to Oxford whither I shall bee bayled or no. You must also desire that care may bee taken in telling the House, if itt shall come to a division of the House, and you are to take care to mind itt yourselfe.

I desire also that the debate of my businesse (whenever entred upon) may not bee adjourned to another day without a question, nor can there bee any danger in putting itt to that triall, if the cautions aforesaid bee observed of not entring upon the debate without haveing the greater number of my freinds present att that time.

If I bee ordered to bee bailed, you must remember to gett mee an order att the same time for the Leiutenant of the Tower to bring mee forthwith to Oxford, unlesse the Lords shall bee pleased to bayle mee without my owne appearance att theire bar.

I am informed that a fourth objection will bee made, viz., that no peer shall bee my baile, as becoming thereby both judge and party.

But that will bee easily overruled by precedents, as also because the suggestion is untrue, for that by the appearance of the prisoner the baile is discharged, and consequently the lords who were the baile are then no more concerned then any other lords in the House.

Unlesse I alone am to have an usage contrary to all other men, as I have had already, in haveing been denied councill and haveing laid two yeares in prison without an inquiry whither the crimes charged against mee bee treason or not, &c.

Private Instructions [to Viscount Latimer] [1]

17 March, 1680/1.

You are to waite upon all my freinds if you can att theire lodgings, with my humble service to them and request of theire favour to my petition when itt is presented to the House.

For the guidance of my businesse you are to apply yourselfe more particularly to my Lord Lindsey, Lord Norreys, Lord Bathe, Lord Arundell of Trerice, Lord Culpeper, Lord Alesbury and Lord Berckley ; and to those only I would have you show my other paper of instructions. But you may comunicate the contents of them (as comands to yourselfe) to what other lords you thinke convenient, and especially to my Lord Newcastle and Lord Rutland.

You may shew the list of the lords to any of the lords above named, but to no others ; and I would have you keepe the list yourselfe.

You are to acquainte my Lord Great Chamberlaine that I desire his lordship would do mee the favour to present my petition to the House ; but in case hee shall either not bee att Oxford, or bee desirous that itt should rather bee presented by some other person, then I would have you attend my Lord Norreys with the same request.

I would have you present my letters yourselfe to the lords who are desird to bee my baile, viz., Duke Newcastle, Earl Lindsey, Earl Rutland, Lord Norreys, Earl Chesterfeild, Earl Alesbury, and Lord Noell, and to send Griffin with the letters to Salisbury, Bridgwater, Huntington and Clare, and with directions to present my humble service to each lord, and to give them the letters himselfe if hee can.

In case the Lords shall order mee to bee bayled you are imediately to send mee a coppy of that order, and att the same time also to gett and send away by my servant an order to the Leiutenant of the Tower for bringing mee forthwith to Oxford, unlesse the Lords shall please to order my being bayled without my appearance, and in that case you are notwithstanding to send away my servants with notice

[1] B.M. Add. MSS. 28043, f. 27. In Danby's handwriting. The date is taken from his endorsement on f. 28.

of what is done, and the coppies of any orders or votes pass't in my businesse.

Upon any occasion wherein itt may bee necessary to apply to the King, you must have recourse to my Lord Conway and Lord Bathe, but principally to the first.

You must make my complements to the bishops, and bespeake theire kindnesse in my businesse, and you must imploy your brother Dumblan in all the parts of your instructions which you thinke convenient.

Whenever the House goes upon my businesse, bee sure that my servant have his horse in readinesse to come away so soone as the House has com'd to any definitive resolution concerning mee, whatever itt bee.

If there bee order for my baile and for my appearance, beg my Lord Norreys to send his coach imediately to Tetsworth, because I will lay coaches to bee att Oxford as soone as can bee possible.

And gett a post warrant of my Lord Conway for my servant, that hee may take post when hee has rid his horse as far as may bee convenient without hurting him.

Say nothing to the King of any comission you have about my businesse, unlesse hee aske you ; and in that case say you are ordered to solicite my freinds and to send mee an account of theire appearance, upon which you expect my further orders. And bid your brother say nothing, but that hee is com'd with you to helpe to solicite my freinds if there bee occasion. But when my petition is delivered to the House I would have you tell his Majestie that I present my most humble duty to him, and hope I shall have his assistance effectually.

Speake to my Lord Maynard to see if hee can make Earl Kent for my baile or to bee absent.

B. FAMILY CORRESPONDENCE

To the Countess of Danby.[1]

My dearest,   12 August, 1679.

Haveing yett received no letter from you makes mee doubt they may miscarry, which is more probable also if you

[1] Autograph letter among the Lindsey MSS. Partly printed in *Lindsey MSS.*, p. 413.

direct them to mee. For this reason I send this, and so shall do the rest, under cover to John Langwith, and I desire to know whither mine of the 9th have com'd safe to you.

Here is now a man named Jenison, who I am told has sworne that Fenich the priest (who is executed) did tell him that I was ingaged in the Plott att last, but that itt was long before they could gett mee into itt ; and if they could, there are some of my good friends who would fain improve this hearsay from a dead witnesse, just as they would have done my escape by my sons pistolls, which was found so ridiculous a story att Councill that my son was ordered to have his pistolls againe, and so that matter ended. I know not this Jenison, nor they say hee pretends not to know mee, but I heere he is a loose rascall ; and the man who married the Marques Dowager of Worcester is accused to bee one of the four ruffians who should have killd the King att Windsor.

My son Latimer is com'd from Buckingham, elected with Sir Richard Temple, but Sir Peter Tirrell intends to dispute the election with my son att the House. My son Herbert goes to-morrow with the writt to Quinborough, and 'tis said will meete another competitor, but hee is yett namelesse to us. I have nothing more to send you but all our duities and affections, which you have most intirely from

Your faithfull husband,

Danby.

To the Countess of Danby at Wimbledon.[1]

14 July, 1681.

My dearest heart,

I have herewith sent you one of our young men ; but for my own son, hee has been gone two or three daies with my Lord Grafton without my knowlege, and when hee will think fitt to return I know not.

The custom of finding a dinner ready att the Tower is grown so habituall, and to so many, that I find itt onpracticable to continue itt but with the same expence as when the rest of my family was here ; so that I begin on Saterday next to putt my

[1] Autograph letter among the Lindsey MSS. Partly printed in *Lindsey MSS.*, p. 436.

whole family to board wages, and bespeake only what you and I have a mind to ourselves.

I desire that whatever is yett to finish att Wimbleton may be done, that all sorts of workmen may bee gott out of the house. I have nothing more but my blessing to my daughters and dear Ned, and there is no other newes but that the Protestant Joyner is to bee sent to bee tried att Oxford. I am

Thy most truly affectionate husband,

Danby.

[To the Countess of Danby] [1]

6th August, 1681.

My dearest heart,

I have received your letter, and do not thinke fitt to acquainte my daughter with itt, because itt would bee to fright her without cause ; but if you should find the least suspition of the childs haveing the small pox, itt is fitt his mother should bee with him, and I am sure your care will bee beyond any phisitian in that disease. I have bid Mrs. Fleet send those things you write for, but shee dares not acquainte her lady for feare of putting her into too great an apprehension.

I have been writt to by my Lord Conway about takeing my house att the Cockpitt, for which hee would give mee 300 l. a yeare, but I writt him word that my daughter Plymouth had a part of itt, which I would not remove her from, but that the rest should bee att his service if hee pleased ; and hee has thereupon writt againe this day to desire that I would appointe one to meete a servant of his, to adjust what part shall bee reserved for my daughters use. I desire therefore that my daughter will step over hither about Monday or Tuesday, that I may agree with her what part shee shall reserve ; and itt must bee considered where my owne goods must bee putt, or that they bee carried to Wimbleton. Itt would bee necessary that you bee here when wee settle this affaire of the Cockpitt. I am most intirely yours,

Danby.

Mrs. Fleet is also gone to speake with the docter, but unlesse hee give other directions I thinke the lesse hee is tampered

---

[1] Autograph letter in B.M. Add. MSS. 28050, f. 35.

withall whilst hee is very well will bee the better ; but above all things bee sure you keepe him to a spare diett, which I am sure his nurse will never do without a watchfull eye over her, and cooleing things are best for him so hee have not too much of them. Pray lett him bee kept from the company of all children if you can during this sickly season.

To Viscount Latimer at Kiveton.[1]

17th August, 1682.

Deare Son,

Yesterday I received yours of the 14th,[2] and am glad to find you were so kindly received by our neighbours. I perceive you intended a visitt to Welbeck yesterday, by which you will have some guesse what grounds have been for the things of which you received those informations you writt mee word of. I can give you no advice as to particulars, in which yourselfe must bee the best judge when you see partys ; but in generall I should bee glad of that relation if everything else will correspond, and I would have you satisfied in the first place.

I hope you received the cipher the last post,[3] in which I did sett downe ' Marquis of Winchester ' because of a discourse I had with ' Lord Bathe ' that ' Marquis of Winchester ' would give 15,000 l. a peice with his daughters, and hee thought (but said hee had no comission) a proposal from us might bee accepted if made in time, for that hee was sure that upon this declaration of 15,000 l. a peice good matches would bee speedily offered. However, I would say nothing to itt till I heard your owne mind in all those matters. I heare ' Lord Chesterfeild ' will bee in towne about ten daies hence, and if wee have any thoughts there I beleeve time must not bee lost as to our resolution longer then theire arrivall ; but wee must bee carefull that nothing interfere upon one another.

[1] Autograph letter in Leeds MSS., Packet 11.

[2] This letter, dated Kiveton, August 14, 1682, is also preserved in Leeds MSS., Packet 11. It gives an account of Latimer's arrival in Yorkshire, his reception there, and the negotiations for his marriage to a daughter of the Duke of Newcastle.

[3] Enclosed in a letter from Danby to Latimer dated August 15, 1682, which is preserved in Leeds MSS., Packet 11. The names printed within quotation marks in this and the following letter have been deciphered with its assistance

Here is nothing new since my last, only it's reported that my
Lord Hallifax indeavours to have the privy seale himselfe, and
my Lord of Ormond did yesterday declare his staying in England till the next spring by the Kings comand ; by which some
will conjecture the call of a Parliament in the winter, but I feare
itt is too good newes to bee true. Secretary Jenkyns is very
backwards in doing anything about the warrant for the Dele-
gates, but I hope wee shall gett itt signed, though with much
trouble and solicitation, and thanke God wee are not pinched in
point of time. Tell your brother that hee bee sure to bee constant in writeing to his wife, and I hope my Lord Ormonds
stay may bee of use to his businesse ; but I find Sir Robert
Vyner has great influence upon Secretary Jenkyns.

I thought itt convenient to adde the following cipher,[1] and
then conclude,

Your most truly affectionate father,

Danby.

My blessing to your brother.

[To Viscount Latimer] [2]

26 August, 1682.

Deare Son,

I have not heard from you the two last posts, and therefore durst make no use of the opportunity I have had of sounding
' Lord Chesterfeild,' who is in towne, but goes into the country
againe on Tuesday next.[3] Thomas Thanett (my Lord Thanetts
brother) was to see mee this day, from whom I had two stories
worth the knowing ; one that his brother had offered himselfe
to my Lord Brooks his daughter, but that itt is broken, because
a joynture was demanded of 2,500 l. a yeare by way of rent
charge and 700 l. a yeare for pockett money. Another offer was
made by him to ' Duke of Newcastle ' for one of his ; but hee
would make no kind of assurance of anything but 10,000 l. to
bee paid as a portion, and declared hee would marry them in the

---

[1] At the close of the letter some additional names are given with cipher
equivalents.

[2] Autograph letter in Leeds MSS., Packet 11.

[3] August 29.

course of theire ages and not otherwise, whereupon that broke for want of competent beauty, unlesse hee might have broke the rule for some other of the sisters, which would not bee permitted.

When this was done in that lords case you may take itt for the best you can hope for, and therefore I would by all meanes have you consider very well beforehand what you resolve to do, least instead of continuing freindship itt should prove an occasion of dislike betwixt our families. And to prevent that danger itt will bee absolutely necessary to avoide the opportunities of discourseing upon that matter att all, unlesse you resolve to proceed if the overture bee made to you. I perceive also that ' Lord Bathe ' was mistaken (and hee now thinks so himselfe) when hee told mee that hee beleeved ' Lord Latimer ' would bee well received by ' Marquis of Winchester,' for ' Marquis of Winchester ' expects much greater things then ' Lord Latimer ' is able to performe, and I must confesse that for any prospect I have round about I see nothing neare so well as that of ' Lord Chesterfeild ' if itt can bee had, which will every day bee more doubtfull.

' Lord Bathe ' has desired his interest due att midsummer last, and would have the principall att Christmas next or att farthest att Lady day, which must bee thought on accordingly, and in the meane time I will see the interest paid to him. I am this day informed (and beleeve itt is true) that Duke Lauderdaile is dead att Tunbridge Wells.[1]

To Viscount Latimer at Kiveton.[2]

28th August, 1682.

Deare Son,

I have not heard from you in three posts, and I had not now writt but that I have just received the newes from Wycliffe that your father Bennett is dead. I have not time to write more, the gates going to shutt up, nor do I know whither you have any expectations upon his death. I heare hee has made a will, and they have sent for Jack Bennett, who is att Lancaster Assizes.[3]

---

[1] Unsigned, but certainly from Danby.
[2] Autograph letter in Leeds MSS., Packet 11.
[3] Unsigned, but certainly from Danby.

[To Viscount Latimer] [1]

23th September, 1682.

Deare Son,

Wee are in great wonder to have heard nothing from you nor your brother in so many posts, and I am in some paine when these inclosed may come to your hands, because you will find by the nature of them that they will both require your consideration and your speedy attendance on the Duke of Newcastle so soone as you are returned to Keeton ; for they do att least deserve very great acknowlegments of the honour done you, and if you can bee satisfied I can have no objection to that alliance, but on the contrary shall desire itt for all considerations whatsoever, unlesse (which I find most doubt) by reason of my Lady Frances her ill constitution of health shee should not bring children, which I should not for any fortune whatever consent to have you married to any such if itt were justly to bee suspected, besides that I beleeve your future hopes in this match would depend wholly upon that.

I have sent you the Dukes originall letter because I have not time to coppy itt, but you must bee carefull not to loose itt ; and I have inclosed a coppy of my answer to his Grace by this post, whereby you will see how I have left the matter either for your proceeding or not as you please. And if you can have Jack Knight with you to Nottingham hee will bee the best meanes of discloseing your great likeing of my Lady Margarett (for you must not thinke of Lady Kathrine) to the Duke, whereby you will either have admittance there or att least thereby civilly gett off from my Lady Frances, if you shall not like her, as by my remembrance of her I am sure I should not.

I cannot now stand to say any more to you, but must leave itt to yourselfe. The Duke of Munmouth wee are told is taken into custody by a sarjeant-att-armes, but for what I do not heare, and they say my Lord Hallifax is made President of the Councill. I would have your brother to come up with the first conveniency, and if hee bee not tied to a stage coach I would have him visitt as by our comands att Belvoir, Grimsthorpe,

[1] Autograph letter in Leeds MSS., Packet 11.

and Exton ; but if you can do itt, and intend to come that road yourselfe, itt will bee better, and hee may lett itt alone. I am
Your most affectionate father,
Danby.

C. Correspondence with Bridget Hyde

[To the Honourable Mrs. Hyde] [1]

2nd August, 1679.

Madam,

I have hopes given mee by Sir Robert Vyner that your Ladyship retaines the same favourable intentions for my son which you have formerly incouraged both him and mee to beleeve ; and therefore I thinke I am obliged on my owne part as well as his to owne both your goodnesse and generosity with all due acknowlegements. As I thinke him and myselfe most happy in itt, so I beg your leave to promote our happinesse by all the meanes that lies in my power, and particularly by makeing the acquaintance better betwixt your Ladyship and my son. His impatience would have troubled you often att Swakeley, but I find Sir Robert so fearefull (and not without just cause) of his visitts there being too publiquely taken notice of, to the prejudice of your cause, that I make itt my humble request to your Ladyship my son may have the honour of waiting upon you in towne, and that you would please to give yourselfe the trouble of a journey thither so soone as your conveniency will permitt ; and I have by this messinger requested Sir Roberts favour and consent, who did assure mee of his willingnesse when I saw him last.

As I have not been wanting in all those services which have concernd yourselfe (and which your Ladyship has highly deserved from mee), so I hope still to bee an usefull instrument in them, especially since I heare the reason why they will not now accept the ten thousand pounds they would have done formerly is because they say the bishops dare no more appeare in that cause, which I make no doubt will deceive them. The cheife thing now to bee pursued is to gett a certaine day sett for heareing, and as soone as may bee, in which I doubt not but Sir

---

[1] Autograph letter in B.M. Add. MSS. 28050, f. 11.

Robert will do all that is possible, and I beleeve I may bee able
in a good measure to contribute to itt. I hope your Ladyship
will not deny my request, and if you will afford mee a line in
answer to itt I shall esteeme itt a very great additionall obligation to, Madam,

Your Ladyships most humble and faithfull servant,

Danby.

To the Honourable Mrs. Hyde.[1]

21 November, 1679.

Madam,

I have of late seene so plainely into the condition of your
Ladyships affaires, as well as into my sons concernes in that
greatest one of being made happy by your Ladyship, that I had
troubled you before this time with a letter if my health had
permitted mee ; and yett I must confesse my indisposition is
this day greater then itt has been, but Sir Robert Vyner (who I
could not see) has himselfe been the messinger of so base a
practice of his owne, both against you and mee, that I could not
forbeare to send your Ladyship my sense of itt, and how
unawares hee betrayd his treachery to my wife, the narrative
whereof would bee too long to sett downe, and I have therefore
left to my sons relation.

In short this hath only rendred more barefac't that designe
which I have long expected if Sir Robert could incompasse itt,
which is to sell you to Emerton unlesse hee can find a better
markett, and for prevention of which I have thought, and am
still more confirmd, there is no other way but a contract, which
will both give mee a liberty of acting more freely with Sir
Robert, and (being private) will give him such a security of not
being in any present danger of my son that hee will not hasten
his bargaine with Emerton, as otherwise hee will do. For as the
case is, hee will not only adde every day to his articles with mee
(which already betwixt your Ladyship and mee is brought to
neare 30,000 l.), but though hee should adde nothing, hee will
expect such collaterall securitys from mee about his releases,
and about the moneys hee expects out of your rents and woods,

---

[1] Autograph letter in B.M. Add. MSS. 28050, f. 13.

as are not reasonable, nor will any councill advise mee to give ; and then after all will turne to Emerton, who I heare will bee of age to give him such releases and to make such payments without any need of collaterall securitys, and I do assure your Ladyship that Sir Robert is not takeing one minutes care for your concernes in the match, but only of his owne.

If your Ladyship shall thinke fitt to proceed this way, itt will require more time then my health will now give mee leave to explane what is after to bee done ; only in generall, when I shall scruple the doing some things which councill will not advise, your Ladyship (upon his representing those things to you) must say you were not willing the match should breake on your side, but if my Lord Danby shall scruple to do what is reasonable, then the fault is not yours but ours, and will justify your not proceeding in itt. Upon which Sir Robert will perhaps hope to bring on his kinsman againe (which your Ladyship must not discourage), but att least hee will hope to gett still better tearmes from Emerton, and in that time your cause in the spirituall court will bee brought to some period, whither Sir Robert will or no ; and itt may bee so ordered (supposeing secresy) that all jealousys concerning my son may bee laid asleepe.

Your Ladyship must forgive the disorder of this letter, both being under a disturbance with Sir Roberts new action about the letter and being scarse able to hold up my head, but being unfeignedly, Madam,

Your Ladyships most truly faithfull servant,

Danby.

[To the Honourable Mrs. Hyde] [1]

12th June, 1680.

Madam,

I have received a letter by Sir Robert Vyner which I suppose is from your Ladyship, though not under your hand as I thinke ; but if itt bee, I am sorry that my obedience to your Ladyship has only produced an exception to my part of the articles, although I must confesse I was told itt would rather have

---

[1] Autograph letter in B.M. Add. MSS. 28050, f. 19.

that effect then any other. In case your Ladyship bee satisfied
in all the points which relate to Sir Robert Vyner, and that you
expect to have my sons estate charged with 8,000 l. more then
Sir Robert desired, itt will deserve some time of consideration,
because unlesse there bee some assurance on your part that your
Ladyships estate shall bee setled on your eldest son, itt may so
happen that hee may only have the remainder of his fathers
1,000 l. a yeare charged with 8,000 l., which I suppose is not
your intention.

I hope also that in case you should comand this to bee done
you will give mee the satisfaction of secureing my son by a contract in case you shall bee free from Mr. Emerton, to the end
there may not bee that use made of my articles which your
Ladyship knows I have been informed has been spoken of not
long since, viz., that you were not att all obliged by those
articles, but might make any other choice afterwards ; and then
my articles are only to bee a property for the security of others,
without being serviceable either to your Ladyship or my son.
My son should have waited upon your Ladyship with this, but
that hee went out of towne this morning, and is not yett
returned. I am, Madam,

Your most faithfull humble servant,

Danby.

I told Sir Robert I would write an answer to your Ladyship
this night, and that I did suppose you would comunicate itt to
him.

[To Viscountess Dumblane] [1]

10th August, 1682.

Deare Daughter,

Although I do not thinke itt att all improper to your
service (but the contrary) that your husband should rather bee
absent for some time then bee here to hazard that which may
bee a certaine ruine to your cause, yett I had not comanded him
out of towne on such a sudden warning but that I had notice
given mee of a malitious contrivance against him, which (knowing his temper) I have reason to beleeve might have succeeded

---

[1] Autograph letter in B.M. Add. MSS. 28050, f. 38.

according to the wishes of the contrivors, if they might have had opportunity for itt. To prevent this I was sure the safe way was to send him out of towne till I find the bottome of the designe, according to which I shall governe the time of his returne, and I am certaine you would not wish mee to do otherwise.

In the meane time there shall bee nothing wanting in which I can serve you, but if you expect my services you must (whilst you remayne under these great difficulties) suffer yourselfe to bee directed by my advices, for I must bee excused not to suffer my name to bee made liable to other peoples conduct, nor to have any mixture (if you thinke mine of use) of such councills as either by folly or falsehood have hitherto spoiled your businesse. And therefore you must pardon this plainesse from one who can have no designe upon you but to gett you putt into a capacity of being my sons wife in such a manner as may justify your being so to all the world ; for the makeing you to fall to Emarton, or the putting your affaires into such a posture as must unavoidably make those your heires who are in the intaile after your life, cannot bee my interest, though itt may bee others ; and therefore as my interest cannot (if I would) bee any but yours, so I do assure you upon my faith and honour that my inclinations and affections are to serve you to the utmost degree I am able, nor will I bee wanting in itt if you give mee leave.

I doubt not but your consideration of mee will also move something with you to what I desire, since I hope you do beleeve that my experience must have given mee a litle more knowlege of what is fitt to bee done then anybodys can do with whom you have now opportunity to converse. And in the next place, what shall now bee done in your affaires will in a great measure reflect upon mee, as many things have done already which should not have been done, if my opinion had been taken in them ; and as I take my honour to bee in some degree concern'd in what you now do, so there are not a few eyes watching every step of our actions. If I have any regard with you, I hope you will both take this as kindly as I intend itt and give mee leave to shew myselfe as I am most sincerely, Deare Daughter,

Your most truly affectionate father and humble servant,

Danby.

II. IN RETIREMENT, 1684-88

From the day of his enlargement from the Tower to that on which the invitation was despatched to William of Orange Danby was largely in the background, and his activities, so far as they were important, were mainly secret. As a result little correspondence of any great significance survives from this period, but chance has happily preserved one or two documents which are of special value :

A. The relations of the Earl with the Government are well illustrated by the three memorials which he successively presented to Charles II, to the Earl of Rochester, and to James II, with the object of securing some adequate recompense for his past services and sufferings, if not actual reinstatement in office.

B. His relations with the presumptive successors to the throne are similarly illustrated, and the development of his political outlook is partly elucidated, by four letters to William of Orange, which in all probability are the only survivors from a considerably greater number. One of William's replies is still preserved, and this is printed, along with a solitary letter from Mary, in the notes.

C. Several of Danby's private letters have been summarised by the Historical Manuscripts Commission in the *Lindsey Manuscripts*. Four of these are now printed in full, while from similar letters found elsewhere five have been selected as illustrating the Earl's political activities, his private life, and his difficulties with his son Dumblane.

D. One solitary speech survives, which was almost certainly intended for use in the House of Lords, but which in all probability was never delivered.

A. Memorials to the Government

To the King.[1]

27th March, 1684.

That which made mee submitt without regrett to my unjust imprisonment was not only my innocence but because itt was so plainely visible to all the world that my crime was only for my obedience to your Majesties comands. And that which inabled mee to undergo that imprisonment with patience so many yeares was the frequent testimonies of your Majesties favour and constant good intentions towards mee, though hindred by those pretences which your Majestie has since found to bee as illegall as they were false.

I cannot doubt but common justice does suggest to your Majestie that if I had deserved anything before my sufferings, those sufferings cannot have lessened but must have made my claime to your favour much the stronger, unlesse some act during or since my imprisonment had forfeited my pretensions ; and as your Majestie hath been so gracious as scarse ever to dismisse any of your servants (unlesse such as were under your displeasure) without a recompense or leave to sell theire places, so itt was your goodnesse to give mee an addition of title, together with a pension for my life, in recompense of that great imployment with which I was honoured by your Majestie ; and I am confident your Majestie did not intend mee to bee the only example who should reap no benefitt for quitting such a station att your Majesties comand and with your favour.

Your Majestie also knows that the bounties given mee were confirmed to mee by your Majestie, not only by promise but att least by warrant under your signe manuall, and some of them by great seale ; and if your Majestie please to reflect upon your goodnesse to all others, I beleeve your Majestie will not find an example since your restauration where any man hath had your Majesties warrant for any title of honour of which hee hath not

---

[1] The original of this petition has not been found, but two autograph drafts have been preserved, one of which is printed in *Morrison Catalogue*, iii. 118, the other in *Lindsey MSS.*, p. 442. The latter of these drafts is here followed, but it shows no substantial divergence from the former. It is endorsed, ' Coppy of the paper given to the King by myselfe, 27th March 1684.'

had the effects, although they have not served your Majestie in
such places of trust as I have had the happinesse to do, and
which to the best of my skill I discharged with that zeale which
your Majestie knows was the principall ground of creating the
number of those enemies I mett with in Parliament.

By some words which fell from your Majestie to mee I
observed an objection to have been raised, that although I was
very innocent, yett I was but under baile. But I suppose that
argument will need little answer, because itt will appeare to bee
both against reason and against your Majesties constant
practise, as in the cases of Mr. Seymour and Sir William Scroggs,
the first not only having leave to sell his place for 15,000 l., but
being then made one of your Cabinett Councill during his impeachment, which hee never was before ; and the other had his
pension continued to him till his death. Nor has your Majestie
been diverted by the extravagant votes of Parliament from
placeing those men in the greatest employments, who were
renderd as black to the people by those votes as they could be
by impeachment. And with great reason has your Majestie
done so, because itt was suitable to your justice to give the world
publick testimony how scandalous and false you thought the
accusations against them, and itt was no lesse suitable to your
prudence to lett the world see that those who serve you should
be both protected and rewarded, notwithstanding the malice or
greatnesse of their enemies.

I hope therefore that your Majestie will not suffer mee to bee
distinguished from all others for such a man as must either have
deserved very ill from your Majestie or should certainly have
found equall favour under the same circumstances.

As to the warrant of the Rolls, although the alterations
mentioned will lessen the value of the place from being worth
10,000 l. not to be worth 2,000 l., and although I have received
none of the compensations granted me by your Majestie instead
of my place, yett whatever your Majesties pleasure is shall be
obeyd with willingnesse. Only I beg leave to remind your
Majestie that having had a grant therof for life already in one
mans name, [1] and a warrant since for life in another mans name,[1]
itt is but the continuance of an old grant to a new name, and

[1] . . . [1] This clause is given only by the draft in the LindseyMSS.

consequently not under your late rule of not granting for life, being att first intended for my life before that rule was made ; and for what is said by my Lord Keeper against a deputy is as much without law as what has been said by him against baile.

But I submitt all to your Majesties good pleasure, being able to undergo anything but the thoughts of your Majesties unkindnesse, which can bee recompenst with nothing in this world, and without which I would desire nothing which can bee given to mee. I must acknowlege that after my long sufferings I should have been to the greatest degree ambitious to have carried some publick mark of your Majesties favour with mee into my country ; but if the time bee not suitable to your Majesties pleasure I shall not now move your Majestie either about the title or pention, which your Majestie has been pleased to grant mee under your sign manuall and privy seale, but hope your Majestie will give mee leave to putt you in mind of them hereafter, when your Majestie shall thinke the time more seasonable. And in the meane time I only pray to know what your pleasure shall be concerning the draught [1]of the warrant[1] which is now with the Secretary concerning the Rolls.

And above all I pray I may never be rendred uneasy to your Majestie, there being nothing further from my intentions, nor nothing I covett so much in this world as to retain your Majesties favourable opinion towards mee.

To the Lord Treasurer.[2]

28th February, 1684/5.

Upon an assurance given to the late King by the Duke of Munmouth, that the then Parliament would give him money without any condition to bee made with him, but only to remove mee from the place of Lord Treasurer, his Majestie was pleased to acquaint mee with the proposall, and to tell mee that the Duke of Munmouth did bring itt to him from the chief leaders of the House of Comons, so as he did not doubt of the successe of itt, but yett that hee would not putt such an hardship upon mee without my consent, but hee thought itt would bee for his

---

[1] . . . [1] These three words are given only by the draft in the Lindsey MSS.

[2] *Morrison Catalogue*, iii. 119.

service att that conjuncture, and hee would take care that I should be no loser by itt.

I answered his Majestie that I did not only consent to itt, but that I would not for all the world keepe that staffe any longer ; for though I did not beleeve my parting with itt would gett him anything from the Parliament, yett I was sure my keepeing itt would bee said to bee the cause both of the continuation of theire ill humor and of theire giveing no money, which should not bee laid att my door.

The King thereupon said hee would give mee a pension of 5,000 l. a yeare for my life, and would make me a marquiss. And for the first hee gave immediate order to the then Lord Chancellor to see itt done, who accordingly assur'd both the King and mee that itt was done, although hee had only putt the recepi to itt, but not the great seale.   And for the second, of marquiss, his Majestie gave mee his warrant with his own hands att the Cabinett Councell, and I then kiss't his hand for itt before all those Lords of the Councell, and my family thereupon had both congratulations and places given them accordingly for severall daies before my comitment to the Tower.

Since my release I putt the King in mind of those bounties, and beg'd to know his pleasure concerning them, as also concerning my grant of the Rolls ; to which hee answered that for the pension hee was not yett in a condition to confirm that to mee, but for the other two things I might proceed with my grants when I would.

My Lady Portsmouth, heareing this, gott stops put to them both, and in lieu of the Rolls I had only two Six Clarks places granted after one to Lord Culpeper, for both which I would bee glad to take 3,000 l., and for the confirmation of which I do own myself obliged to the Kings bounty.   But upon the King's putting the place of the Rolls into the hands of a lawyer (which his Majestie told mee was the only reason why I had itt not), I reminded his Majestie of the title granted, and hee was pleased to answer that I must have patience a while longer, but I might depend upon him that itt should not bee long before I should both have that title confirmed and bee restored to his Councill, but hee must take his own time for itt.   And hee was pleased to repeat the same againe to me the next day but one after my

H   D.L. II

Lord Culpeper and I had been heard before his Majestie att the Cabinett Councill, when he likewise told mee that hee had promised to the present King that my Lord Culpeper should have the next vacancy of a Six Clarks' place, and therefore hee could not break his word with his brother.

I have likewise a reversion of the farme of exported coales for twenty-one yeares after the present lease to the Lord Townsend; but both his lease and mine do cease by the death of the late King.

My humble request is that I may passe my pattent of marquis (which is already pass't the signett and Attorney-Generall, and whereof there is not one instance of any title being stopt after its having proceeded so far), and that haveing had none of the compensations intended mee for my places, nor thinking itt seasonable att this time to desire any pension from his Majestie, hee would bee pleased to grant mee a confirmation of my pattent for exported coals, in case the Parliament shall continue the customes to his Majestie, which as itt will bee then easy to his Majestie to grant, so there is not an example besides myselfe of any great officer who has left any employment with the King's favour but who has had either leave to sell his places or hath received some compensation for itt, besides that his late Majesties intention of compensation to mee appeares by the grant, which hath the late Lord Chancellor's recepi to itt, and is now remaining in the Lord Treasurer's company.

[To the King] [1]

May itt please your Majestie,   [6th July, 1685]

Your Majestie was pleas'd att the beginning of the late sessions of Parliament to tell mee that I should receive your comands from yourselfe if you had any occasion for my service, and you gave mee leave att the same time to apply myselfe on all occasions to your Majestie. I received those gracious expressions of your Majestie with very great comfort and satisfaction, and I waited your Majesties comands during the session with no lesse duty and readinesse to have obey'd them. But haveing received none,

---

[1] From the autograph draft in B.M. Add. MSS. 28053, f. 343, endorsed, ' Coppy of the paper presented by mee to his Majestie concerning my pretentions the 6th day of July 1685.'

and the session being now ended, I humbly presume to lay before your Majestie some state of my condition and pretences, and to submitt both myselfe and them to your Majesties pleasure and goodnesse, and should thinke I were doubly gratified to owe my obligations (if I shall bee thought worthy of any) to your Majestie only, for whose person and meritts I have as great esteeme as I have duty to you as my soveraigne.

Your Majestie knows that I was not dismist by the late Kings approbation from his service, but was forced from him and from the place of Lord Treasurer by a Parliament which would have forced his Majestie from his crowne if they could, and your Majestie from the succession. I doubt not but your Majestie has also been inform'd that in compensation of my place his Majestie was pleased to grant mee a pension of 5,000 l. a yeare for my life, and to grant me the title of a marquis, the first of which was passt all the seales but the great seale and has the Chancellors recepi to itt, and for the second I have the Kings warrant countersigned by my Lord Sunderland, and did not only kiss his Majesties hand upon itt before my Lord Sunderland and divers other Lords of his Councill, but my wife and children had place given them accordingly for some time [1] untill my imprisonment ; and that having been for obeying his Majesties orders does I hope not lessen my claime to your Majesties favour.

Since my inlargement all his Majesties bounties to mee were suspended by the Dutchesse of Portsmouths power and her displeasure against mee ; notwithstanding which his Majestie did to the last [2] give mee assurances of performing all things to mee for which I had his hand, only hee said that itt would not be proper to lett the grant for my title passe any further whilst I lay under my impeachment, and for the pention hee said hee was not yett in a condition to confirme that to mee, but would see in the meane time if hee could comply with my request about a pension of 2,000 a yeare in Ireland formerly granted mee, the story of which is too long to trouble your Majestie withall in paper, but I hope your Majestie will give mee leave to do itt myselfe. And the last time I ever spoke with his Majestie upon the occasion of the dispute betwixt my Lord Culpeper and mee,

[1] Originally ' tooke theire places for some daies accordingly.'
[2] Originally ' to his dying day.'

and telling him that I had reason from thence to feare I was under his displeasure, hee told mee I was not, but that hee was ingaged to your Majestie to make his word good to my Lord Culpeper ; and to satisfy mee of the contrary he said I should have but a little longer patience and hee intended to restore mee to his Councill with a particular mark of his kindnesse when hee did itt.

Things standing thus with mee att his Majesties death, itt hath since hapned that by his death a reversion is also become void which I had of the farme of exported coales att the determination of the Lord Townsends lease, unlesse your Majestie will bee so gracious as to renew itt, which I should thankfully receive (if your Majestie were so pleas'd) instead of the pension intended mee by his late Majestie.

Haveing had your Majesties permission to speake myselfe, I have taken this presumption to make my case knowne to your Majestie without the mediation of any intercessor on my behalfe ; and if in these, or in such of them as your Majestie shall thinke fitt, your Majestie will vouchsafe your bounty to mee, the valew of them will not bee a greater obligation of my gratitude then the mark of your favour by them will bee a comfort to mee, who will do the utmost in my power to deserve itt, if I may bee so happy as to know wherein I may bee serviceable to your Majesties comands, which I am sure will never require any other sort of obedience but what is suitable to the duty of an honest subject.

B. CORRESPONDENCE WITH THE PRINCE AND PRINCESS OF ORANGE

[To the Prince of Orange] [1]

London, 30th May, 1687.

Att the arrivall of Monsieur Dykevelt in this place I did by him receive the honour of being remembered by your Highnesse. Hee also then told mee that your Highnesse had been pleased to name mee amongst some others with whom itt was your pleasure hee should confer on such occasions as hee should thinke were for the service of your Highnesse. I am therefore in the first place obliged to returne your Highnesse my humble

---

[1] From the autograph letter in S.P. Dom., King William's Chest, vol. i., printed in *Dalrymple*, App., i. 194.

thanks for so great an honour, and next to do that justice to
Monsieur Dykevelt to assure your Highnesse that as you could
have employ'd nobody here who would have been more agreeable to your well-wishers in this country, so I am confident that
nobody could have discharged themselves better then hee has
done, both in his deportments to the King, and with all the
satisfaction that could have been wished to those with whom
hee has conversed concerning your Highnesse (of which both
the numbers and qualities has been very considerable), his cheife
businesse haveing been to give assurances of your Highnesses
great firmnesse in the Protestant religion, and to make knowne
not only your wishes but endeavours that no alterations may
bee made amongst us otherwise then by Parliaments and as our
laws direct. By his prudent management of these discourses hee
has done your Highnesse great service, and in all other things
your Highnesses worth and meritts were so well knowne before
that there needed nothing to sett them forth more then your
owne actions have already declared them to the world.

I am sorry hee is able to bring your Highnesse no better an
account of our services during his stay here, but you know that
our present stations do render most of us but litle capable of
doing anything which can deserve to bee thought considerable.
I confesse that could there bee a convenient opportunity for
some of us to have a personall conference with your Highnesse,
itt is not only my opinion but the opinion of others who have
the honour of corresponding with your Highnesse that some
overtures might bee made which would bee of use to your service, and I hope that from those hands your Highnesse is well
inform'd of theire thoughts who are devoted to your service.
For my owne part I am so tied to bee of that number by what I
have done already (besides my continued inclinations to bee so),
that if I were disposed to alter that character, I should not bee
able to make myselfe beleeved, unless your Highnesse would
contribute to itt by some proofe of your displeasure towards
mee, which I can never feare, because I am equally assured of
your justice, as I am of my owne integrity to your service, and of
the satisfaction I have received by those happy successes I have
had in itt, to which I am sure no competitor can pretend an equall
share. And therefore if in this I presume to say more then I ought,

I hope I may bee pardoned a litle vanity, haveing been the happy instrument of so great a publick good as I doubt not but itt will att last prove, as well as a particular one to your Highnesse.

I am glad to find that Monsieur Dykevelt, who is so able to serve your Highness, is so well establish't in your confidence as I understand by my Lord Hallifax, to whom you gave him such credentialls as made mee willing to speake much more freely to him then otherwise I should have done. But yett I must confesse to your Highnesse (which I rely upon your justice to keepe to yourselfe) that finding his lordship who received those credentialls not willing to impart some things to him, which are not very proper to bee written, I thought itt lesse prudent for mee to say to him all that I could wish your Highnesse were truly informed of. I say not this with the least reflection upon my Lord Hallifax (who I am confident is truly zealous in your service), but to shew our unhappinesse who dare not by second hands speake what were necessary for your knowlege.

I have only to adde that if I can in any kind bee serviceable to your Highnesse your commands will meete with so great obedience and faithfulnesse that I shall not consider myselfe, if your Highnesse shall thinke mee worthy of the continuance of that favour I have formerly received, and which I am sure I have not justly forfeited. In the meane time I will beg the honour of being presented by your Highnesse with all duty to the Princess's memory, and that I may remayne in your Highnesses opinion, as I truly am,

Your Highnesses most obedient and devoted servant,
Danby.

[To the Prince of Orange] [1]

Wimbledon, 4th September, 1687.

I was very proud to receive by Monsieur Zuylesteyn the honour of a letter from your Highnesse,[2] and to find in itt so great a condescention as to remember the services of one who is now so litle able to pay any. The character your Highnesse gives of Monsieur Zuylestein would give mee confidence to say anything to him which I would venture to say to anybody but

[1] From the autograph letter in S. P. Dom., King William's Chest, vol. i., printed in *Dalrymple*, App., i. 206.
[2] This letter has not been found.

yourselfe ; nor would I forbeare upon that recomendation to say to him anything which were so materiall to your Highnesses service as might receive any prejudice by the delay. But I can say nothing which is so pressing in point of time, nor would I comitt to writing what is the thoughts of other men besides my owne, without theire consent, for which I have had no opportunity since I received your Highnesses letter, which was but on the 2nd instant. I am sure your Highnesse will receive all necessary accounts of things from hence as the occasions require, and Monsieur Zuylesteyn will informe you of the present posture of all things amongst us.

I confesse I could wish that the understanding both on your Highnesses part and ours were more perfect in relation to such future events as may probably happen (and which are too long to bee express't by letters) ; but I have toucht some things of that kind to Monsieur Zuylesteyn, as questions which I have been asked by others, and hee made mee such answers as I was glad to heare, and which hee said hee was instructed to give, in case any such inquiries were made, of which hee will give your Highnesse an account. I made some open attempts the last summer and some private ones in this to have seene if I could have gained leave to go into Holland with the same indifferency that itt is permitted to many others ; but I still found designes were laid to do mee more prejudice by that journey then I could have done service to your Highnesse. I must therefore deny myselfe the honour of waiting upon your Highnesse till my attendance may bee as usefull as such an occasion would bee agreable to mee, and then nothing shall bee an hindrance to

Your Highnesses most obedient and faithfull servant,

Danby.

[To the Prince of Orange] [1]

London, 27th March, 1688.

I have presumed to give the Princesse the trouble of a letter [2] att the earnest request of my daughter Plymouth, who is so infinitely ambitious to devote herselfe to the service of her

[1] From the autograph letter in S.P. Dom., King William's Chest, vol. i., partly printed in *Dalrymple*, App., i. 216.

[2] This letter has not been found. The letter which the Princess wrote in reply to it and to Danby's letter of March 29 is printed *infra*, p. 122.

Highness that shee makes itt her humble suite to become one of her domesticks in the quality of a lady of her bedchamber. I can only say in her behalfe that if her Highness shall please to accept of her I beleeve her diligent observance of the Princesse will bee suitable to the duty shee will owe her, and how shee is qualified for the honour of itt I have rather desired that her Highness should receive from the Bishop of London then myselfe. If the Princesse shall please to approve of our request I hope your Highnesse will bee so favourable as to give your consent to itt, and as I have reason to hope that upon a better acquaintance the Princesse will not bee displeased with her service, so I am sure I shall have a much better opportunity of doing your Highnesse such services as may fall within my power.

My son Dumblan is the carrier of this letter; but I thought your Highness might like better to have itt delivered to you by Dr. Stanley, because I am confident my sons motions will bee so strictly observ'd that there will bee particular notice taken whither hee delivers any letters to your Highness. Hee will this day aske the Kings leave to go beyond sea, and I doubt not but the King will aske him if hee intends to go into Holland, upon which order will certainely bee given to observe his actions. I hope that will not prevent your Highnesses goodnesse towards him, in allowing him a favourable accesse to present my humble duty and his owne to the Princesse and your Highness. I am able to inform your Highness of very litle here more then what appeares in publick, only I am certaine that the Cabinett Councill gives the King firme assurances that the States will not bee provoked to a war by any usage his Majestie can do towards them, and I dare as confidently affirme to your Highness that wee cannot make a war att sea if wee would.

Many of our ladies say that the Queens great belly seemes to grow faster then they have observed theire owne to do; and because itt is fitt her Majestie should alwaies have the greatest persons neare her in this condition I hope the Princesse will take care that the Princesse Ann may bee alwaies within call, and especially to see (when the time is neare) that the midwife discharge her duty with that care which ought to bee had in a case of so great concerne. Our zeale here for the Protestant religion does apparently increase every day in all parts of the nation, and the examination of the minds of the nobility and gentry has made such an union for the defence of itt through the kingdome that I verily beleeve they begin to despaire of supplanting itt by violent meanes, and itt is certaine they can do itt no other way. The constancy and firmnesse which both the Princesses have shew'd in theire religion, and your Highnesses mind in relation to things here (which was so prudently made knowne by Monsieur Fagels letter) has so contributed also to adde courage to that union that I looke upon our security to bee much strengthened by itt, as well as both your Highnesses interests raised here beyond your owne expectations, insomuch that I am confident there wants only an opportunity to the greatest part of the nation to shew theire zeale for your services.

I must beg your Highnesses excuse for so tedious a letter, and yett I am desirous to have said much more, but that without some discourse to explaine myselfe I might bee liable either to have my meaning mistaken, or not fully understood, which would only bee to give your Highness an uselesse trouble. I have one thing only to lament, that although our union in generall bee very great, yett particular distrusts are so great also as render many good intentions very ineffectuall. I am with all that duty and respect I ought to bee,

Your Highnesses most faithfull and obedient servant,

Danby.

[To the Prince of Orange] [1]

London, 29th March, 1688.

I am forced to give your Highnesse the trouble of this second letter, to informe you that upon my sons askeing the Kings leave to go beyond sea his Majestie granted the leave, but said with some heat, Provided itt bee not into Holland, for I will suffer nobody to go thither. My son answering that hee had no designe of anything but to see a country hee had not seene, the King answered, Perhaps so, but hee had relations who had other designes there, and hee knew there were those in Holland who gave themselves hopes of seeing some English lords att the head of some of theire squadrons ; but hee would take care to prevent itt. After this discourse to my son, which was in a

[1] From the autograph letter in S.P. Dom., King William's Chest, vol. i., partly printed in *Dalrymple*, App., i. 217.

roome next to the bedchamber, hee came out into the bedchamber, and my Lord Dumbarton and Lord Leichfeild being
only there the King said to my Lord Dumbarton, I find they are
much surprised in Holland with my raising three new regiments;
to which my Lord Dumbarton answering that hee wondred why
they should bee so, the King replied, They would bee surprised
much more before hee had done with them. This was on the
27th att night, and on the 28th my son went to court to gett his
pass from one of the Secretaries of State, and the King, hapning
to see him, called him to one side of the roome and said, My
Lord, I had newly received some newes last night when you
spoke to mee which had disturbed mee, and made mee speake to
you in some disorder, therefore I would not have you take notice
of anything I then said to you, for I dare trust you to go where
you will ; but said, If you go only for curiosity you might as
well satisfy that elsewhere as in Holland.

I thought itt not wholly impertinent to give you this account,
and my son being yett too young to bee imploy'd with any larger
commission to your Highnesse then the carriage of the letters, I
have chosen rather to lett him go into Flanders, and have sent a
trusty gentleman with him thither, who shall from thence carry
these letters to Dr. Stanley, and receive what answers your
Highness or the Princesse shall please to returne by him. By
what the King has said to my son I conceave hee would not att
this time consent to my daughter Plymouth's going into the
Princesses service, but shee is so very desirous to devote herselfe
to her Highnesse, that she hopes her goodnesse will bee such as
to receive her whenever shee can find an opportunity of gaining
the Kings consent. Whatever the issue of her request bee, shee
most humbly begs that nothing may bee said of her haveing
made application about itt, untill itt bee seasonable for her to
acquainte the King with her desires. I have only to adde, that
I shall alwaies bee, as I ever have been,

Your Highnesses most obedient and devoted servant,

[Danby] [1]

[1] Unsigned, but in Danby's handwriting throughout. Answers to this and
the preceding letter were received from both Mary and William :

Loo, Aprill the 29th—By a letter of yours, my Lord Danby, I find myself very
much obliged both to you and your daughter, the Countesse of Plymouth, for
the ofer you make. The Bishop of London gives her an extream good carecter,

C. FAMILY CORRESPONDENCE

To the Countess of Danby at Wimbledon.[1]

31th July, [16]84, att 4 a clock afternoon.

My dearest heart,

I did att this minute receive yours by James, and am just going into the coach for Rycott. The King is just as formerly, very kind in words, but nothing more, and the Duke very civill in appearance, who is gone this morning to the Dutchesse to Tunbridge ; the Queen extreame kind, and I excused you not waiting on her upon pretense of indisposition in the health.

I have taken care to place the musquetoons so as cannot possibly do any prejudice, but I thank you for your dear care,

and all I have ever heard agrees so well with what he says that I belive I shou'd like her extreamly. But by your second leter I see you think this an unfit time to make any such propositions to the King, and I belive you are in the right. I am sure I shou'd be very sory you shoud expose yourself to any inconvenience upon my account, or meet with any unpleasing ansere, which makes me think we might refere this busines to anothere opertunity that may prove beter. But this ocasion, my Lord, I must let you know that you have laid an obligation upon me I can never forget. I need not tell you 'tis my being heer I mean. I find myself so well that I shall have cause to thank you for it as long as I live, and you may be sure it shall be returned you whenever there is any opertunity in the power of Marie. (*Morrison Catalogue*, iv. 168.)

[From William of Orange, dated Loo, April 30th, 1688.] Je receu hier les deus lettres qu'il vous a pleu m'escrire du 27e et 29e de Mars. Je suis bien marri que la fatalite du temps m'empesche d'avoir la satisfaction de vous voir, et mesme M. vostre fils, my Lord Dumblain. Je ne m'estonne point que l'on n'a pas voulu qu'il vien en ce paiis ; l'on est si mal satisfait de moy que l'on ne s'en cache presque plus, quoyque je ne sache pas d'avoir donne auqu'un juste subjet ; car l'on a tousjours bien sceu que je ne pourois jamais entre en des mesures qui fussent prejuditiables a la religion dont je fais profession, et que ma conscience et mon honneur m'obligoient a faire tout ce que je pourois pour le bien de cette religion protestante, que je suis persuade estre la seule bonne et vraie religion, et m'opposer autant qu'il seroit en mon pouvoir a ce qui la peut ruiner et destruire. C'est avec une joye extreme que j'aprens la bonne union qu'il y a en toutte la nation sur ce point ; il seroit a souhaiter que des mefiances et des petittes misintelligences particulieres ne fit auqu'un prejudice a ce grand interest commun, a quoy chachun de son coste doit con-tribuer le plus qu'il peut. J'ay parle a la princesse au reguardt de la proposi-tion que vous luy faites de la part de Madame la Contesse de Plymouth, vostre fillie. Elle m'a temoigne fort souhaiter que la chose se puisse faire, dont elle vous escrira elle-mesme. Pour moy, j'en aurois beaucoup de joye, et de tous les occasions ou je vous poures temoigner et a toutte vostre famillie avec quelle recognoissance je seres toutte ma vie. (*Ibid.*, vi. 419.)

[1] Autograph letter among the Lindsey MSS. Partly printed in *Lindsey MSS.*, p. 444.

which has never been wanting, and you have a return of love suitable to itt. Wee are so late that I am in great hast. My son Latimer is not com'd, and son Dumblan presents you his duty, and love to his wife. I am intirely yours,

Danby.

[To the Countess of Danby] [1]

Kevton, 6th September, [16]84.

My dearest heart,

I have received yours of the 2nd, and should have been very sorry to have had you take a journey hither when I am indeavouring all I can to gett away. I thank God I am well but for my cold, which has proceded from the sudden change of weather wee have had here, and I am much better of that then I have been. All you write of taking away pipes on Putney Common and laying them down since I came away is newes to mee, nor till I come to see itt can I imagine what itt meanes, if itt bee any thing betwixt Wimbledon and the great roade which crosses betwixt Wandsworth and Kingston. But whatever itt bee I am sure nothing shall bee done to the prejudice of Wimbledon which the law can prevent.

I have been visited by all the country to a very great distance, except my Lord Castleton, from whom I have not heard, though he bee att Sandbeck ; and amongst others I have had Mr. Montague with mee (my Lord Sandwich his son), who lives att Wortley and calls himselfe by that name, and is really a very fine gentleman, and told mee he was sorry that any of his relations (much more of his name) should have carried themselves so unjustly towards mee, and he hoped I woud not have the worse opinion of him for their ill behaviour.

I have not spoken to nurse Turner myselfe, but her answers to Langwith have been that her daughter is married, and that for herselfe shee is old and onwilling to remove out of her native country, and her son is young, and she not able to live without him. I will speake with her myselfe, and see whither

---

[1] Autograph letter among the Lindsey MSS. Partly printed in *Lindsey MSS.*, p. 444.

they will bee tempted with proposalls you make them, but
I beleeve they will hardly bee perswaded to remove theire
present station. I received a letter out of Norfolk from my
daughter Plymouth, by which I suppose she may by this time
be return'd to London. If she be, remember me kindly to her,
and I will write to her in a post or two. Present my service
also to my Lady Monings, and be assurd that I am most
affectionately yours,

Danby.

[To Viscount Latimer] [1]

Wimbledon, October 23th, 1684.

Dear Son,
        I desire you would waite upon my Lord Cheif Justice
Jefferyes, and lett him know that itt is by my command that
you came to present my humble service to him, and to excuse
my not waiting on him myselfe, having been so very ill and
being still so weake that I am not yett able to make visitts ; but
that I am very sencible of his favours, and shall bee allwayes
ready to acknowlege them to the best of my power. I would
have you take Mr. Headley along with you when you goe (which
hee desires may bee as speedily as you can), and acquaint his
Lordship how steddy and active hee has been to serve the King
in the Corporation of Leedes, and how much good hee has
wrought amongst them by that strict hand which hee has held
over the fanaticks there ; but that unlesse hee bee very well
supported that Corporation will speedily relaps to its old distemper, and therefore, although the Kings service alone bee
recommendation enough of any man to his Lordship, that you
could not (knowing the truth of this matter) but bee willing to
present him to his Lordship, that hee might bee known to him
when hee shall have occasion to attend him in his busynesse.
        If you come not hither this night or to-morrow morning, pray
send mee full directions about the farcy horse, for itt is much
increased within this three last dayes, and will bee spoiled if
somthing bee not done speedily.[2]

------

[1] From a copy in B.M. Add. MSS. 28050, f. 45.

[2] Unsigned, but endorsed by Latimer, 'My fathers letters.'

To Viscount Latimer.[1]

Wimbledon, 14th April, 1685, 2 a clock afternoone.

I have just now received a letter from you sent hither by the porter which is comonly imploy'd att Soho.[2] The letter is both without date and place, so that though you therein desire to have a speedy answer I cannot tell whither this bee so or not. Only I can tell you that itt is answered as soone as received, and directed according to the instruction on the backside of the letter.

For what relates therein to the lord you attended att Newport,[3] nothing more needs to bee said till wee meete, and for what relates to yourselfe, may bee very liable to mistake unlesse one were upon the place ; but as your relation makes itt appeare to mee, itt seemes as if the foresaid lord you were with att Newport does not concerne himselfe att all for you in the matter, and I do from thence conjecture that you are not like to meete with any assistance from that side in the House any more then you do upon the place, insomuch that I cannot advise your struggling to make six more then seven in the House, unlesse you had some better pretence to support your title there.

The best of your case (which by your representation of itt seemes litle better then desperate) is in my opinion to stand, because itt will otherwise bee said here to bee deserted by you, and that you might have carried itt if you had stood, and to declare that you will stand because you will not bee thought to decline the service either of the King or of the towne, and that the blame shall not bee laid by the towne upon you, if itt shall hereafter meete with any disappointments to theire advantage, upon which may bee insinuated by others the danger of looseing both theire towne-house and assizes. And for matter of the returne, I would say nothing till the election were over, and then if they would returne you without any engagement about building the towne-house (unlesse you were continued in Parlia-

[1] From the autograph letter in B.M. Add. MSS. 28053, f. 318, addressed to Latimer at the Post House at Stony Stratford.

[2] This letter is probably B.M. Add. MSS. 28087, f. 3, the date of which is about April 10. If it was addressed to Danby at Soho and sent on to Wimbledon it might well take four days.

[3] Newport Pagnell. Other letters make it clear that the reference is to Jeffreys.

ment to bee theire burgesse, in which case you ought to bee
obliged), I would advise you to accept the returne (though by
the six) ; but I would by no meanes have you obliged to build
the house upon an uncertainty of being turn'd out of the House
afterwards, for that would certainely render you ridiculous.

Had the lord I before mentioned been zealous for your service, hee would have done for you what has been done already
in divers places, viz., have changed some electors whilst the
matter was held in so long suspence as this election hath been.
And that argument will bee no ill one (amongst the rest) to bee
used by your freinds, that they may perhaps find the same usage
which some other townes have done in like cases, and particularly att Sudbury, as well as in some other burrows, where
aldermen have been changed for promoting those who are not
approved by the King ; but this is language which must not bee
used either by yourselfe or your brother. I can give no advice
to incourage your election by the populace, because I am of your
opinion that itt will not bee well taken ; but itt had been proper
to have knowne the foresaid lords advice in that matter, and to
have putt the complement of being ruled by him in itt. But yett
in that matter I do not see any just fault can bee found here, if
you should take theire election only conditionally, that if the
King will give you leave to try theire right you will bee att the
charge of doing itt for them in Parliament ; and this to bee done
only in case you find certainly that seven will bee against you.

I am able att this distance to give you no better councill, but
unlesse your businesse bee speedily over I must needs desire my
coach to bee returned, for the coronation being so neare, and
your mother haveing so much businesse in London, shee is forc't
to use hackney coaches, with very great inconvenience to her.
I will write no name, and so farewell.[1]

To the Countess of Danby at Wimbledon.[2]
                                        13th May, [16]85.

My Lord Chief Justice (who is now Lord Wems) did
yesterday invite himselfe to dine with me on Thursday,[3] which

---

[1] Unsigned, but certainly written by Danby.

[2] Autograph letter among the Lindsey MSS. Partly printed in *Lindsey
MSS.*, p. 446.

[3] May 14.

does not only kepe mee this day in towne, but has made me send
for the cooks from you. After we have din'd that day I intend
to come to Wimbledon, having done all I can here till Monday
next. I find the King and ministers outwardly very civill, and
there will be no danger of my going to our old quarter. My
Lord and Lady Rutland design you a visitt about Friday or
Saterday next, unlesse you contrive how to avoide itt till you
are better prepared for their reception. I am, Dearest,

Yours most affectionately,

Danby.

To the Countess of Danby.[1]

22 June, [16]85.

For the satisfaction of your folly I have done so foolishly
myselfe as to comand Dunbar away from my son Dumblan,
although he bee the only man with him that knows what to
do in an army. I have had the opportunity of doing itt by an
expresse from my Lord Sunderlands office, which goes away
this night at ten a clock, and goes through Salisbury where your
son staies. I am assured that they give no passes, and that
there needs none, the way being clear from all enemies betwixt
Salisbury and Chard, where the King's forces lie, who disturb
nobody, unlesse upon examination they find them going to
Munmouth.

I have sent you this to satisfy you (if any thing can) that what
you have desired (though very unreasonable) is done ; but for
my own quietnesse I intend not to lodge att Soho this night, and
since I can never be a moment in peace where you are I must be
content to gett itt as well as I can elsewhere, that being all that
is aimed att in this world by your unfortunate husband,

Danby.

To Viscountess Dumblane at Mimms.[2]

London, 27 October, [16]86.

Deare Daughter,

I am sorry to have no better account of my son then his
leaveing you att such a time as hee hath taken for itt, and though

---

[1] Autograph letter among the Lindsey MSS. Printed in *Lindsey MSS.*,
p. 446.

[2] Autograph letter in B.M. Add. MSS. 28050, f. 52.

hee hath shew'd as litle duty to his mother and mee as hee has done of good manners to you, yett I could more easily forgive his part to mee then you. I have sent you an hundred pounds by this bearer, and so soone as you are in condition to travell to towne I shall desire to speake with you to settle things for your conveniency, for which only I shall bee concern'd, being

Your very affectionate father and servant,

Danby.

Pray lett mee know what hee has writt to you by one of his lewd companions, Cressett.

[To Viscountess Dumblane] [1]

22th November, 1686.

Deare Daughter,

I am sorry to heare you are so ill, and that I cannot gett to see you ; but understanding by my wife that you feare I may have writt so unkindly to your husband as may discourage him from comeing back to you, I have thought fitt for your satis-faction to lett you know the substance of what I have writt.

Tis true that I have not forborne to shew him that sense which (unlesse hee takes mee for an errand foole, as I have reason to beleeve hee does by my being so often deceived by him) I ought to have of his complicated folly and falsenesse both to you and mee ; but I did att the same time tell him that his ill example of a son should not make mee forgett the duty of a father so far as not to contribute by my advice in anything which might tend to saveing of a fortune so shattered by him, and to the withdrawing him from such courses as must tend to his destruction. For this purpose I told him that if I knew where to send one to him instructed to discourse him upon those subjects, I would speedily send one ; but I also writt him that instead of haveing any remedy applied I had reason to beeleve by his concealeing himselfe from mee (whilst hee thought fitt to intrust an ordinary seaman by whom I must answer his letters

---

[1] Autograph letter in B.M. Add. MSS. 28050, f. 56.

or not att all) that hee must either remayne still mad himself, or thinke mee so, to imagine that such an application to a father was like to putt us upon better tearmes, for any sober man would have concluded that itt must add to his crimes to tell a father, I will not trust you, but however pray do what I desire. I concluded that if hee thought fitt to putt things into such a way as I had then directed I should not bee wanting to do what was fitt on my part, but I would not bee treated with upon his tearmes, but my owne, which hee knew best whither hee would bee governd by or not ; but if hee would not, hee was to expect no other answer from mee.

This is the substance of what I then writt ; and as I did then beleeve, so I am now confirm'd by your last letter from him, that his letters to mee were but essays to try if hee could continue his old custome of cheating mee in words and himselfe in deeds, for you see that although yourselfe and others have since received letters from him I have not been thought worthy of a line from him, since hee sees I will bee no longer deceived by him. And I must own to you that I shall not trouble myselfe with his name, unlesse as itt may relate to your concernes, who has laid obligations upon him of which hee has been very unworthy ; and yett you must forgive mee if your supplies bee not yett what you deserve, because I am resolved to keepe all the dores shutt I can against his being supported to live under his obstinate and disobedient courses.

I confesse that, could I wonder att any actions of his, I cannot comprehend why hee should run away beyond sea, when hee knew that I was for his going out of England ; and I am as much still of the same opinion, thinkeing itt a place att present no way fitt for him, besides the small satisfaction I should take in seeing him. But I would have been glad some things might have had some course taken in them before his going, which might have hindred a considerable charge to the estate, and as I writt to him, so I should bee glad to contribute my advice for the saveing of that as much as I could.

I cannot blame your kindnesse to your husband in desireing that his debts might bee paid ; but I were much to bee blamed if I did suffer your estate to bee so much diminished by payment of debts so contracted as most of his have been, if that were in my power. But as the case stands, there is not roome in the estate to pay such summes as his reckonings do now amount to, and keepe the due payments of the other interest moneys, anuitys, and other certaine charges which go anually out of the estate ; so that if I were never so willing to lett you hurt yourselfe, I can see no possibility of doing anything now but by a considerable part of the 1,500 l. a yeare being assigned for payment of debts yearely, which was for your and his present maintenance. And how that is to bee hoped for from one who knows no bounds but his owne will and pleasure will not enter into my thoughts or beleife, whatever pretences hee should say or sweare to.

I have troubled you too long in your condition, but my wife told mee you desired to have a knowlege of what I had writt to him, and of what my mind was, which I could not expresse in fower words, to which I can truly add that I am for your sake only concern'd to trouble myselfe in his affaires, being

Your very affectionate father and servant,

Danby.

To the Countess of Danby at Wimbledon.[1]

20th February, 1687/8.

My deare,

There is nobody that more easily then myselfe beleeves that I am abused by my servants. Nay, I am so much of that opinion that I beleeve there is no master who is not, insomuch that I am confident all wee have to looke to is to bee as litle abused as wee can. I shall therefore bee very thankfull to anybody who helpes mee in that kind, and your servant Bullivant may bee assurd of being rewarded for any service of that nature. Pray therefore lett him bee incouraged both by yourselfe and from mee, and what you writt about shall certainely bee very private. I am

Your very affectionate husband,

Danby.

---

[1] From the autograph letter in Leeds MSS., Packet 13 c.

D. SPEECH

[November 23, 1685] [1]

I am sure that no man liveing can speake with more reluctancy then myselfe to anything which may but seeme to bee contradictory to his Majesties pleasure, as those may bee thought to do who shall except to any part of his Majesties late speech. Nor would I open my mouth on that subject did I thinke I could bee silent without abandoning my duty both to God and to the King. Itt is a matter wherein not only our laws but our religion is concernd, and wherein both the King's honour and our safeties are involved, and is consequently a matter of the greatest importance that ever did or ever can come before your Lordships.

I say this with the greater confidence, being a son of the Church of England, whose principles will not give leave to make that hipocriticall use of those words religion and property which I have but too lately heard done by others, who under those specious names did only promote a faction whilst in reallity they had almost destroy'd what they pretended to support.

As I say I shall never go about to make those words stalkeing horses to ill designes, so the rule by which I shall go will bee a publick witnesse for or against mee whither what I say can bee capable of any ill or sinister intention (the rule I meane is the laws as they are now established in this kingdome both in Church and State) ; and as all who make that rule the measure of theire words and actions can bee guilty of no errors towards the government, so they cannot but bee safe from giveing any just offence to his Majestie, because his word is sacred, and hee has not given itt superficially to us, but has repeated his gracious promises att the last session in words which ought forever to bee remembrd with thankfulness. His Majestie tells us that hee speakes the same words hee did att his first coming to the Crowne purposely that wee may see they were not spoken by

---

[1] B.M. Add. MSS. 28091, f. 110. Autograph draft, much corrected. The changes, however, are almost entirely verbal in character, and are not worth noting.

chance, and consequently that wee may the more firmely rely upon a promise so solemnely made.

Now my Lord[s], haveing this sheat ancre (for I can putt no lesse a valew upon his Majesties word), if that maine cable should once breake I am sure our ship is not only adrift, but there is no more prospect of security then left us, there being in my opinion nothing in nature to bee proposed which can secure us if that do not.

I am therefore the last man in the world that will intertain a thought so derogateing from the Kings honour as to thinke that his Majestie intends any violation of the laws by that expression in his Majesties late speech concerning the Roman Catholick officers, but do truly beleeve that his Majestie may have some opinion that hee may by his prerogative dispence with that law, and if that bee so itt were unreasonable to expect but that his Majestie should imploy them in his service as well as other men.

In my opinion, therefore, our first businesse in this debate should bee to heare what the Judges will say to the Kings power of dispenceing in this case, because both the nature of your debates here and of your addresse (if you shall make any) will bee very different according as the Kings power in that matter shall bee made appeare to your Lordships. My humble motion therefore is (before any progresse bee made in this matter) that the Judges may bee asked theire opinions whither as the Act concerning the Test is penn'd his Majestie can dispence with any man to hold an employment contrary to the letter of the said Act.

III. REVOLUTION AND SETTLEMENT, 1688/9

The mass of correspondence dealing with the seven or eight months which followed the despatch of the invitation to William, considerable though it undoubtedly is, forms in all probability but a small part of what originally passed. The most disappointing feature about it is the almost complete absence of letters illustrating the activities of July, August and September. Presumably the intrigues of the malcontents were carried on largely by word of mouth, but the very remarkable letter written to Lord Chesterfield, probably towards the close of September, can scarcely have stood absolutely alone. Many letters no doubt were burnt ; others have been lost ; and the result is a paucity of information regarding the actual identity, plans and ultimate intentions of the conspirators which one cannot but deplore.

A similar gap exists at the other end. The negotiations which resulted in the elevation of William and Mary to the throne were carried on mainly by private conversations in London, and there is little documentary evidence to show what Danby's attitude was. The correspondence of November and December, however, has been very fully preserved, and enables an almost complete picture to be drawn of the rising which the Earl organised in the north.

So thoroughly is the whole period dominated by the one main development that it has been considered best to print letters and memoranda in strictly chronological order. Associated letters have also frequently been printed in the notes, attached either to the letters to which they are replies or to letters in which they are mentioned.

To Viscount Latimer.[1]

Deare Son, 7th July, [16]88.

I am gone to Wimbledon till Monday evening,[2] and desire that in the meane time care may bee taken some way or other for getting Sir Edward Hales his hand provd. Your unckle Osborne has Sir Edwards letter, which you will do well to take into your keepeing if hee has done with itt. I am

Your most affectionate father,

Danby.

To the Countess of Danby at Kingsey.[3]

My dearest heart, London, 10th July, 1688.

Wee found the journey so long, and the way so bad that way wee came, that wee gott not hither till past 11 a clock, and

---

[1] From the autograph letter in Leeds MSS., Packet 13 c.   [2] July 9.
[3] From the autograph letter in Leeds MSS., Packet 13 c.

my horses so quite tired with theire two daies work that I have
been forced to hire horses to my owne coach.   I have sent the
coach to Amersomme, itt beeing the better as well as much
shorter way, but you must take care to go as softly as foot can
fall for the first four miles to Kimball Warren, and for that
reason my daughter must bee in the coach as early in the
morning as is possible, or shee will not gett hither that day.

When wee arrived here wee mett the newes of my Lord Cheife
Justice haveing putt off the cause againe for eight daies longer,
in which time I should have been glad to have been att Wimbledon.   But I have sent for my cook and butler hither, because of
haveing something ready for my daughter and her servants
when they come ; but I hope you will order itt so, that itt may
not continue att my charge, but that wee may bee gone to
Wimbledon with our family.   Mall has had a better night (as
Wyborne tells mee) then ever shee had yett, and burnes not so
much as shee did, and I intend to advise to-day what will bee
best to do with her.   I am with great truth

   Your most affectionate and faithfull husband,

               Danby.

To the Earl of Chesterfield.[1]

          Lecester, [September] 1688.
My Lord,

   The long acquaintance I have had with your Lordship,
and the confidence I have of your honour and worth, makes me
venture to impart to your Lordship the great design that is now
on foot.   The Prince of Orange, if the wind serves, will land in
England with twelve thousand men within this fortnight ; Hull
will be delivered to him, and the greatest part of the Kings army,
with many of the nobility, will revolt.   I confess as to my own
part I had rather lose my life in the field then live under an
arbitrary power, and see our laws and religion changed, which
is now visibly the Kings intention.   But I doe not know what
your Lordships thoughts may be of this matter, and therefore I
will stay at Lecester till you send mee word.   If you doe approve

---

[1] From a copy in B.M. Add. MSS. 19253, f. 167, printed in *Letters of Lord
Chesterfield*, p. 336.   Chesterfield's reply refusing Danby's offer, dated strangely
enough 1689, is printed *ibid.*, p. 338.

of our undertaking, I will come over to Bretby, and after the having acquainted you with all the particulars of our whole designe take my measures with your Lordship ; but if you dislike our proceedings I will not doe you so great a prejudice. However, I thought it might be a service to you to let your Lordship know what is now transacting, that you may sute your occasions, and prepare yourself for so great a change as is speedily like to happen. I am, my Lord,

Your, &c.,

[Danby]

Pray send me your answer immediately by this bearer, for I doe onely stay in this place to receive it.

To the Countess of Danby at Kiveton.[1]

Ribston, 2nd October, 1688.
My dearest heart,

The King's proclamation (which I send you here inclosed) has given us an happy opportunity of armeing for defence of our country, and upon itt the gentlemen of this county have resolved a meeting att York to consider how to do itt in the best manner. When they have appointed their day (which will bee known this afternoon) I intend to be there amongst my countrymen, who have many of them desird my assistance amongst them ; and this prevents my present returne to Kevton, which otherwise I had designd with my brother Charles to-morrow morning, and had all things prepared for itt. I have sent Woodnott to bring my horses and chasse mares to mee to bee here on Friday night,[2] and I have appointed him to bring my charriott hither (my coach beeing too heavy for the ill ways) ; but I cannot send back the coach because I shall have use for all the horses. I have directed Woodnott what servants to bring with him, and I am sorry to leave you so slenderly attended; but I know you will dispense with the greatnesse of the occasion.

I have also sent you my will, in which you are my sole executrix ; but I hope to come and open itt myselfe att Kevton,

[1] From the autograph letter among the Lindsey MSS. Printed in *Lindsey MSS.*, p. 447.
[2] October 5.

where I have thoughts to winter if there bee no Parliament, which itt lookes as if there would not.   I doubt not but you will take care to make everything as safe as you can, and I desire you will use some meanes (and if you have no other that you will send a man purposely upon pretence of seeing your brother Lindsey or Lady Rutland) to bring you notice when any horse or dragoons passe by Newarke, and what number they are, and by whom commanded, and to inquire what more are following them, and att what distance ; and I thinke Mr. Gutterige would be best for this purpose, whose charges I desire you will defray, and call for money to Robinett.   Pray bid Robinett call for what money hee can gett from my Lord Darcy, and although the summe bee not so considerable as I could wish, lett him take for the present what they will pay for your owne use.

My Lord Devonshire came to Wetherby on Satirday,[1] and goes to Rippon to-morrow ; hee was here yesterday,[2] and I hear Mr. Wharton (my cosin Whartons husband) came to him last night.   Divers of the Yorkshire gentlemen have been so civill as to give mee visitts, and my Lord Fairfax has sent mee word that he intends mee a visitt this night.   You shall constantly hear from me by all opportunities, and your brother Charles intends to see you to-morrow ; but now and att all times, so long I live, bee assurd that I am most truly, and will live and die so, My dearest creature,

Your most intirely affectionate husband,

Danby.

Give my blessing and kind remembrance to Lansdowne.

Wee have no certaine newes, but all conclude the Prince of Orange has been att sea this three daies.

---

[1] September 29.

[2] Devonshire announced his coming in the following letter, the earliest extant of those which he wrote at this time to Danby :

October the 1st [1688]—My Lord, Hearing last night that your Lordship was at Sir Henry Goodrickes I resolv'd to have kist your hands this morning, but some indisposition after a long journey obliges me to defer it till the afternoon, and then you shall not fayl to be attended by, My Lord, Your Lordships most obedient and humble servant, Devonshire.

The letter is endorsed by Danby, ' Lord Devonshire, 1st October [16]88. From Wetherby in Yorkshire.' (Leeds MSS., Packet 13 b.)

To Viscount Latimer in Soho Square.[1]

Keeton, 31th October, 1688.

Deare Son,

You will receive this by Wycliffe, who although hee does not go up by my order but his owne choice, yett I should not have kept him much longer neare mee, his humor being much too insolent for a servant, and his behaviour such towards your mother as was insufferable. Your brother Dumblans passion made him correct him more severely for itt then I wish hee had done, or should have done if I had seene itt ; but hee had the confidence a litle before that to refuse to obey my orders, when I comanded him to waite upon my wife to Welbeck, for which alone (if there had been no other reason) I should have parted with him.

I suppose you have received my draught of a letter to excuse your not accepting a commission for collonell in the militia,[2] but I have since found that itt will not bee so difficult as I then thought to gett officers for the regiment ; but itt must certaine-ly bee an occasion of calling you downe to itt att this time, and therefore in my opinion itt is still best to decline itt. Your mother is very earnest to make a triall herselfe of that matter

---

[1] From the autograph letter in Leeds MSS., Packet 13 c.

[2] The draft referred to, or more probably a draft of the draft, is preserved in Leeds MSS., Packet 13 c. Intended as a letter from Latimer to the Duke of Newcastle, it runs as follows :

London, October [16]88.—My Lord, I understand from my father that your Grace has been pleased to honour mee with being both a deputy leiutennant and a collonell under your Graces comand in the militia of the West Riding ; and itt is so great a pleasure to mee to bee anything under your Grace that I am infinitely greived not to bee able (by reason of the great concernes att law which I am under att present) to attend the duty of a collonell as I ought to do att this conjuncture, and I would bee very loth to have such an employment as would att this time bee justly a reproach if I should make itt bee executed by a deputy. Itt is yett a greater misfortune that I am not now att liberty to attend the Kings and your Graces service, because I perceive this honour was bestow'd upon mee on my fathers motion to your Grace ; but since I am so unhappy that my affaires do make itt impracticable, I hope your Grace will please still to continue mee as one of your deputy leiutenants, and that you will beleeve mee so ambitious of any favour from your Grace that I would lett go none of them that I could possibly retaine, either with satisfaction to your Grace, or preservation of my owne honour att such a time as reports and alarmes speakes this to bee. I am with all respect and gratitude, My Lord, Your Graces most obliged and most humble servant.

which Mr. Hutton assisted you in formerly, and has an opinion of succeeding ; but I will not give any encouragement without your owne approbation, and therefore pray write as soone as you can what you desire should bee done in that matter. All your freinds are well here, and remember them kindly to you, and I am

Your most truly affectionate father,

Danby.

[For the Prince of Orange] [1]

[20 November, 1688]

To give the ciphers of the names for credentialls.

To acquainte him with the disappointment of haveing neither armes, officers, nor money sent, as was expected to bee sent into which part soever hee did not land with the maine body.

That two or three ships are still expected with armes and officers and some money.

That notwithstanding all those disadvantages itt was resolved by divers lords and gentlemen that on Wednesday, the 21th of November, they would secure York (where there would then bee 500 horse of the militia and two regiments of foot of the militia), and seize the Duke of Newcastle and the Governor of York, and that they doubted not but to make most of that militia act for the Prince.

That on the same day divers other lords and gentlemen would meete att Nottingham, and that in both places att the same time they would publish such a declaration as would bee then agreed upon, shewing theire resolutions to assist the Prince in this undertakeing and theire reasons for doing so.[2]

---

[1] Leeds MSS., Packet 13 b. A draft in Danby's handwriting presumably of instructions for a messenger to William. The messenger, probably Peregrine Bertie, set out about November 20 with the Earl's first letter to the Prince.

[2] The only surviving part of the correspondence which must at this time have passed between the conspirators in Yorkshire and those to the south is the following letter from Devonshire to Danby, written probably in response to an intimation that the seizure of York had been postponed to November 22 :

Nottingham, Tuesday night, 7 a clock [20 November, 1688]—At my arrivall here I mett your Lordships servant, whom I would not detaine, having no expectation of news till wee hear what you do in Yorkshire. Here is a pretty good appearance of the gentry of these parts. I expect some more out of

That they are able to raise a great body of foot if they could arme and pay them when raised, but that till they know how to do both they dare suffer no great number of foot to come to them.

That some course must necessarily bee taken in the meane time to gett some officers sent to them, and especially some one generall officer under whom men of such quality will bee willing to serve.

That there will bee an infinite discouragement in a litle time, unlesse somebody bee sent from the Prince to give them some directions what hee desires they should do, considering the condition of things as they are now represented, viz., whither hee would have them endeavour to joyne him with these bodys of undisciplined horse, which may bee about 2,000, or whither they should remayne in the north and raise what foot they can. And if hee desires foot should bee raised (which is not doubted but would bee 10,000 in fourteen daies), care must bee taken to send both armes, officers and money as aforesaid.

That an intelligence and correspondence bee duly kept betwixt the Prince and this body of men already raised, for the preventing of mens deserting his service, who are already but too apt to thinke they have been too much neglected.

To tell my Lord Shrewsbury (whose counterfeit name is Stephens) that I rely cheifely upon him and Mr. Russell (whose counterfeit name is Adams) to gett a dispatch of these things as they ought to bee, and to make them sensible how great a neglect the gentlemen of this country thinke there has been of them already, in sending them no manner of intelligence, when they had putt themselves in so great hazard and readinesse to have joyned his forces.

Darbyshire too-morrow. My Lord Delamere lyes at Darby too-night, and will be here too-morrow, well accompany'd as I hear. My Lord Stanford (who is here) tells me my Lord Manchester and my Lord Grey, with some others, expect an advice from him of what we in these parts intend to do. So a gentleman is dispatch't to them to tell them we desire them to hasten hither, where we are to resolve what is best to be done. I heard upon the road that 5,000 were landed in the north. If that be, your Lordship has certainly heard it by this. I long to hear of my kindred, and how they behave themselves upon so surprising a turn of fortune as they are in danger of. I am Your Lordships most obedient servant, Devonshire.—I hope the messenger I sent westward will be here by the latter end of the week. (Leeds MSS., Packet 13 b.)

To acquainte my Lord Abingdon with all the instructions, and unlesse hee can gett to the Prince with safety to desire him to come with all the forces hee can to Nottingham, and to bring my Lord Northampton and his freinds along with him as soone as he can, there being nobody to interrupt them.

The cipher of names is

The Prince	Barebones.
Shrewsbury	Stephens.
Abingdon	Richards.
Mr. Russell	Adams.
Mr. Sydney	Lloyd.
Mr. Bentinck	Wilson.
Northampton	Cary.
Humphreys	The messenger to be credited.

Memorandum about Oxford.[1]

[To Viscount Latimer] [2]

York, 21 November, [16]88.

Deare Son,

I have nothing to write from hence but that all is quiett here, and the Duke of Newcastle going from hence this day to returne to Welbecke. Hee sent mee this morning a comission for your being deputy leiutenant in the North as well as West Rideing, for which you must thanke him. I have not time this post to write either to my brother Charles Bertie or Mr. Bates. Pray make my excuse to them, and gett my brother to send imediately to Mr. Childs shop to receive what money of mine is in theire hands, according to the note inclosed, which I desire you to give him as soone as you receive itt. Mr. Staniland desires you will lett his wife have money in his absence, which hee saies hee will repay you, and I will bee security for his doing so. I am most affectionately yours.

Remember mee to your sisters.[3]

[1] Endorsed in an unknown handwriting, ' Memorandums about the cipher.'
[2] From a draft in Leeds MSS., Packet 13 c.
[3] Unsigned, but in Danby's handwriting.

To Sir John Hanmer at Hull.[1]

Sir,

York, 30th November, 1688.

As I have heretofore paid you all the services which were in my power, so I should be glad you would embrace the opportunity I can now put into your hands, of doing yourself an infinite greater kindness in point of advantage to your fortune than can probably ever offer itself again whilst you live, if you let slip this occasion ; and besides your personal advantage, it is to doe but what divers of the best quality have newly set you the example, as particularly the Earl of Bathe, who has declared for the Prince at Plymouth, the Duke of Grafton, the Lord Churchill, and twenty others, men of the first ranke.

My proposal is that you would give both your advice and assistance to our surprize of Hull, and if that you wil be instrumentall in it, you wil let me know as wel what officer besides yourself wil be assisting to us in it, as by what meanes you think the thing may be best effected. I am sure most of both seamen and townsmen of the place wil be ready to give their help, and I am as sure that many of the poor soldiers themselvs that are in the garrison are so sensible the Protestants wil be destroyed, if the Prince should now be beaten, that they stay amongst you more for subsistance than any kindnesse.

Were there any visible hopes under heaven of saving the Protestant religion in England but by this oppertunity that God has given us, I think you know me wel enuf to beleive that I am the last man in the kingdome that woud attempt to have it rescued by force ; but it has bin made so plain to us what we are to expect from a power in the papists hands that, whatever any may pretend, noe man can in his heart beleive that any man shal be able to finde protection that wil persist in the Protestant religion ; and I take the greater confidence in writeing all this to you, because I know your principle to be truly Protestant. I

---

[1] From a copy in a clerk's handwriting in B.M. Add. MSS. 28053, f. 365. There is another copy, also in a clerk's handwriting, in Leeds MSS., Packet 13. Partly printed in *Campana de Cavelli*, ii. 352.

have reason to hope, upon the strong grounds by the last letters which are come to us, that there wil not be a blow struck by the armyes, but that the matter wil be decided by a Parliament, his Majesty having putt off all his Roman Catholick Privy Councillors and advised with most of those bishops and lords who did first petition for a Parliament ; and in truth it is so plain that his army wil desert him, that he wil imediatly be under a necessity of complying with the just requests of his subjects.

If you are willing and can help us in this designe, so far as to make us masters of Hull, I do hereby enguage that five thousand pounds shal be paid to you in a month after it is done, besides the just merits you wil deserve from the Prince, which shal not want my recomendation of it as it deserves ; and you shal not want 1,000 men to your assistance, if other things be all prepard for it. I have employed so trusty a messinger to carry this, and to bring an answer from you (if you please to send any), that although he knows nothing of the contents of this letter, I am sure he wil be as careful in the safe delivery of whatever is comitted to him as if he was knowing to the particulars ; and I trust so much to your honour (having known you intimately so long as I have done) that I do not question but you wil dismiss the bearer (who is totally ignorant of what he brings) whatever your resolutions shal be in the matter. If the messinger be not dismissed by you in six hours after he has delivered this into your hands, I shal take it as the signe of your not accepting the proposall, which I shal be sorry for, not only for your religion and countrey's sake, but in reallety for your own, being with a true kindnesse,

Your most faithful humble servant,

Danby.

You may know this to be from me by the token that the last time I saw you was at Lyndsey House, where you and Sir Richard Wiseman came together to visitt me ; but I beleive you know my hand. Although I have named six hours for the dismissing the messinger, I must desire it may not be above three hours at most.

To the Prince of Orange.[1]

York, 1st December, 1688.

I congratulate your Highnesses happy arrivall in England, and should have been very sorry itt was not in the north, but that I hear you are very successfull in the march you have made. I was ready to have attended your Highnesses landing in these parts with many very considerable persons who are with me, and I have had the good fortune to seize this citty for your service, where I have taken prisoners three companies of foot, and have since seized upon the castle of Scarborough, where I have taken a very good magizine both of cannon and ammunition, and have putt a garison in the place to secure itt. I am in some hopes of making myselfe master of Hull, but dare not assure myselfe of itt.

These successes and hopes of more makes mee delay marching to your Highness with my Lord Devonshire and those lords who are att Nottingham ; but my Lord Haughton, Mr. Vane and severall others who were with mee here will attend your Highness with those lords from Nottingham. My son Dumblan, my Lord Lumley, my Lord Willughby, and Lord Fairfax stay with me here att my request till I have made triall of my designe against Hull, and if your Highness shall thinke fitt rather to have me with my friends to march to you rather then to prosecute anything further in these parts, I will upon receipt of your orders imediately obey them.

I have been so unfortunate as not to receive any comands from your Highness since your landing, but hope I may now by the meanes of my nephew Phillip Bertie, to whom I beg your Highness's favour. I sent an expresse to your Highness ten daies ago to receive your orders, but have not heard whither hee has arrived with you. I am with the same constant duty as ever,

Your Highnesses most obedient servant,

[Danby] [2]

[1] From the autograph draft among the Lindsey MSS., printed in *Lindsey MSS.*, p. 449. Danby's third letter to the Prince.

[2] Endorsed by Danby, ' Coppy of my letter to the Prince of Orange, 1st December 1688. By cosin Phillip Bertie.'

To the Bishop of London.[1]

My Lord, Yorke, December the 4th, [16]88.

I should have been extreame glad to have waited imediately upon the Princess (who I am overjoy'd is brought safe out of their hands by your Lordships prudent conduct) ; but it is impossible for me to leave this place till all move. I heartily wish her Highness amongst us here, both for her security and the great addition it would give to our interest in these parts, which would be noe less then the secureing the whole north ; but I doubt not but your Lordships conduct and councills will advise her what is best. Your Lordship knows me soe well that I hope you will give her Highness an assureance of my readyness to pay her the uttmost of my service, and I am most entirely, My Lord,

Your Lordships most faithfull humble servant,

D[anby]

I can't close this without letting your Lordship know with how great joy and acclamations this citty has received the news of her Highness being com'd soe far northwards, and what hopes they give themselves of their being honoured with her presence, where she will finde soe unanimous a concurrence to her service both from city and countrey that she may depend upon haveing the whole north under her protection.

[1] From a copy in Leeds MSS., Packet 13 b. This and the following letter appear to have been written about the same time, the one as a private note to the Bishop and the other as an official communication to the leaders of the rising at Nottingham. Of the letters to which they are answers, the Bishop's, dated December 2, is printed in *Hist. MSS. Com.*, ix. 2, p. 461, while Devonshire's is as follows :

Nottingham, December the 3rd—My Lord, I suppose your Lordship will learn by the inclos'd from my Lord Bishop of London more then I can possibly inform you of from hence, onely I am afraid your Lordship mistooke one part of my last letter as if I had prest you to come away yourself, when I am not ignorant how important to the service your remaining at York is ; but I was and am still of opinion (especially if the Princess think of going toward the Prince of Orange) that it were to be wish't we had a greater force to guard her. We expect every houre to hear of the surrender of Hull, which would be very welcom newes. I sent a party to wayt on my Lord Dunblain to Welbeck, of which I doubt not but he has given you a good account. The Princess being here, great numbers come in every day ; but I am sure the most serviceable and welcom would be those your Lordship could spare us from York. I am, My Lord, Your Lordships most faithfull humble servant, Devonshire. (Leeds MSS., Packet 13b.)

To the Earl of Devonshire and the Bishop of London.[1]

Yorke, 4th December, 1688.   11 a clock att noone.

My Lords,

Your expresse is just now arrived, and haveing brought us the good newes of the Princesse being safely com'd to Nottingham wee would have march't imediately, had itt not been for the prospect wee have of makeing ourselves masters of Hull in three or four daies more. Wee have therefore sent an officer with this expresse to lett you know itt, but that wee will lay all other considerations aside for the safety of the Princesse (although the takeing of Hull bee of so vast importance) if her Highnesse shall comand itt, and wee are not strong enough to divide forces without laying aside the thoughts of Hull.

I am desired also by the lords and gentlemen here to informe your Lordships that haveing secured the strong castle of Scarborough (whereing is great store of armes and amunition, and into which wee have putt a sufficient garison to defend itt) wee can most certainely secure her Highnesse from all danger which can possibly happen to her, if shee should thinke itt for her service to come to this citty, for if anything should appeare too strong for this place (which wee do in no sort apprehend) there will bee a certaine retreat for her Highnèss to Scarborough, and from thence by sea wherever she pleases. But wee say all this only by way of information, being resolved to obey whatever her Highnesse shall comand, and with all the expedition wee are able after the returne of this officer.

Wee hope this small delay can bee no prejudice to her Highnesse, to whom wee are all ready to pay our obedience, and most particularly, My Lords,

Your Lordships most faithfull humble servant,

[Danby]

I beg your Lordships will present my most humble duty to her Highness.[2]

---

[1] From the autograph draft in Leeds MSS., Packet 13 b.

[2] This letter evoked the following replies :

Nottingham, December 5—My Lord, I am heartily glad to hear you are in so good a posture, and wish myself with you for many reasons. We are here a considerable body of men, and there are dayly coming in from all parts. But we want officers extreamly, which you may easily beleeve when I make so great

To Sir John Hanmer at Hull.[1]

York, December 5th, 1688.

Sir,

I humbly thank you for the favour of your letter [2] by Mr. Idle, and more for the contents of it, being so important a service as deserves a most considerable regard to be had of it. I perceive your zeale for the service of the publick was as forward as my wishes, and went into action before my desires for so good a work coud reach you ; but it makes your meritt so much the greater, by your having contributed so effectually to the service, without being prompted to it. I beleive it wil not be long before I shal have the oppertunity of waiting upon the Prince of Orange, where I shal not fail to represent your services in this particular as the merits of them have deserved ; and I

a part of the councel of war. We have sent an express to the Prince, so that we can take no resolutions till we hear from him. However the Princess is extreamly sensible of the readiness of your parts to give her assistance. We shall certainly take our resolutions one way or other before Saturday. I do not find here any preparation to give an account wherefore we are met, or what resolution to take in reference to the prudential part of being in a posture to convince the world that we have a share in standing by and seing the nation have right. I am, My Lord, Your Lordships most obedient servant, H. London. (Leeds MSS., Packet 13 b.)

My Lord, As soon as I receav'd your Lordships directed to the Bishop of London and myself I carry'd it to him ; and Mr. Pullen had not been detaynd so long, but that we wayted till the Princess was stirring, who receav'd your Lordships and the rest of the gentlemen's complements with great civility and kindnes, but commanded us to return this answer, that she can take no resolution till the return of the express that was sent on Sunday night last to the Prince. I hope he will be here too-morrow, and as soon as he comes your Lordship shall not fayl of having an account of it from, My Lord, Your Lordships most faithfull humble servant, Devonshire.—Nottingham, December the 5th. (Ibid.)

[1] From a copy in a clerk's handwriting in B.M. Add. MSS. 28053, f. 366.

[2] The letter referred to is as follows :

Hull, the 4th of December, 1688.—My Lord, In answer to your Lordships letter I can onely tell you that wee have thought itt fitt to secure the Lord Langdale, the Lord Montgommery, the major of our regiment and the major of the Duke of Newcastles, with all such officers and souldiers as are knowne papists, and to take the governement of the towne into the Lieutenant Governors hands, who heartily joynd with mee. Wee have don itt without effusion of blood, and to the satisfaction of the towne. My Lord, I intend suddenly to kisse your hands at York, or else to send an officer on purpose iff I can nott be spared, and leave this place with security. This is returnd by your owne messenger with the submissions of, My Lord, Your most humbly devoted servant, John Hanmer. Our Governor, Captain Copley, presents his most humble service. (B.M. Add. MSS. 28053, f. 369.)

hope his Highnesse wil not think them the lesse for the forwardness you have shewn in it. At least there shal be nothing wanting of my parte to make all things succeed to your advantage, as they ought to doe, being with great truth and reallety, Sir,

Your most faithful humble servant,

Danby.

[To the Countess of Danby] [1]

Yorke, December the 5th, 1688.

I send this by my daughter Dumblaine's footeman to lett you know the good news that on Munday night Colonel Copley, Deputy Governour of Hull, and Sir John Hanmer, Lieutenant-Colonel to the Earle of Montgomery, with some other Protestant officers belonging to the garrison, did seize upon the Governour, the Lord Langdale, the Earle of Montgomery, and all the popish officers, and declared for the Prince of Orange ; and I have this night received a letter from Sir John Hanmer of his coming hither to give me an account of the particular.

I received letters yesterday from the Earl of Devonshire and Byshop of London, which brought me an account of the Princess being at Nottingham, and to desire we would send them some horse to help to guard her towards the Prince of Orange ; but I sent an express imediately to excuse it by reason of our designes upon Hull (which we did not know then to be taken), and to show our reasons why we thought it both more safe for her Highness and more for the Princes service that her Highness would please to come to this place. But the express is not yet returned, therefore we know not what her Highness's commands will be ; but whatever they are they will be obey'd upon the returne of the express.

Remember me to my children, and particularly to my daughter Herbert, whose excuse I must aske for not writeing to her, as I must doe yours for not useing my owne hand, being both soe full of bussiness and soe sleepy that I can scarse indite

---

[1] From the original letter, in a clerk's handwriting, among the Lindsey MSS. Partly printed in *Lindsey MSS.*, p. 449.

this. Tell my daughter Herbert that I will be more carefull of her husband than of myselfe, and that I desire she will not leave Kiveton till I can gett to see her there. I am, Dearest,

Most intirely and affectionately yours,

Danby.

To the Prince of Orange.[1]

York, 7th December, [16]88.

I have sent so many expresses to your Highness without an answer that I know not to what to impute the miscarriage of them. I have now sent one of my lieutenants (Pullen) of horse, who I hope will gett to your Highness ; and I desire you will be kind to him, for he deserves itt. Hee will give you an account of the seizeing of Hull by the Protestant officers in that garison; but they have lett go both the Lord Langdale, who was Governour, and the Lord Mongomery, who comanded one of the regiments, and all the rest of the popish officers, and are not so free in their declaration as I could wish. I thinke itt for your Highnesses service if you would please to send me a commission with all speed to be Governor of Hull, and if you would honour mee with another commission to be Lieutenant-Generall over the five northern counties, viz., Yorkshire, Northumberland, Cumberland, Westmorland, and the Bishoprick of Durham, which is what my father had many years ago. I am sure I shall be able to adde considerably to the service I have already had the good fortune to do in these parts, of which this bearer will give you a true account. I desire I may also have blank comissions sent me both for horse and foot regiments to be disposed as I shall find necessary, and comissions also for commissioners to manage the revenues in the said five counties and Berwick-upon-Tweed (which is a single place distinct from the five counties), with a power to them to depute receivers and collectors and other officers under them for that service.

When Lieutenant Pullen shall have given you an account of this place I shall expect your orders by him what you think fittest for us to do who are in this place ; that is whether you

[1] From the autograph draft among the Lindsey MSS. Printed in *Lindsey MSS.*, p. 450. Danby's fourth letter to the Prince.

thinke itt more for your service that we secure the whole north (which I shall do by staying here), or that wee shall attend you and joyn the army, because whatever your orders are shall be obeyed by, [&c]

[Danby] [1]

To the Prince of Orange.[2]

Yorke, December the 11th, [16]88.

This is the fifth letter which I have presumed to write to your Highness since I appeared in armes, which was the 20th of November, and I possessed myselfe of this city on the 22nd and of Scarborough Castle the 28th, where I gott some store of armes and ammunition, by which we have been enabled to arme most of those which are now with me. My first letters was by my nephew Peregrine Bertie, my second by a messenger I sent habited like a countrey fellow, my third by my nephew Philip Bertie (who has the honour to be one of your domestick servants), my fourth by a lieutenant of horse who cannot yet be gott to your Highness, and this fifth by my Lord Lumley ; but I have never heard one word in answer to these.

I have writt soe at large by my lieutenant (who I hope is with your Highness long before this will come to your hands)

[1] Endorsed by Danby, ' Coppy of a letter to the Prince of Orange by Leiutenant Pullen, 7th December [16]88. There is some alteration from this in the originall sent to the Prince.' This letter evoked the following reply, the postscript to which presumably refers to the letter of the same date printed *infra*, p. 152 :

Abbington, ce 12/22 Decembre, 1688.—J'ay receu hier au soir celle qu'il vous a pleu m'escrire du 7/17 de ce mois de Yorck, qui est la premiere que j'ay receu de vous depuis mon arrivée en ce paiis et mesme auqu'une de vos nouvelles qu'au commencement par Monsieur de Bartie. Je vous suis infiniment oblige de tous les soins et pienes que vous avez pris en cette grande affaire, et comme la nouvelle que j'ay receu hier et a ce matin que le Roy c'est retire change extremement les choses de face, je vous prie de me venir trouver pour vostre personne le plustost qu'il vous sera possible, ayent besoin de vos bons consiels en une conjuncture si importante, vous asseurent que je n'oblires jamais les obligations que je vous ay, et que vous me trouveres tousjours entierement a vous, G.H. Prince d'Orange. Au reguardt du reste je me refere a la lettre angloise que je vous escris. (*Morrison Catalogue*, vi. plate 165.)

[2] From a copy in a clerk's handwriting among the Lindsey MSS., printed in *Lindsey MSS.*, p. 453.

that I shall now onely trouble you with knowing that I had
a letter this day from the Byshop of London,[2] who writes me
word that he is sure your Highness would have me come to
you with what horse I can spare soe as to leave these partes
in some security ; whereupon I have order'd 600 horse to be
in readyness to march in two dayes, and will not faile to
attende your Highness with them as soone as we can. I shall
have three dayes march from hence to Nottingham, and five
dayes march from thence to Oxford, designeing to quarter
at the same places the Princess of Denmark has done if there
be occasion. I hope your Highness will order some party to
meet us in the last dayes march, or if you shall not approve
of our comeing to you your Highness will please to send

[2] Danby received at this time, probably by the same messenger, two letters
from the Bishop of London and one from the Earl of Devonshire :

Nottingham, December 8.—My Lord, If I had not heard from the Prince
before Munday, I had certainly carryed the Princess to York. But now we
have received orders from the Prince to come to Oxford, and shall therefore
march to Leicester to-morrow. He wonders he has not heard from you. I send
you his letter as the best information where you shall find him. Your answer
by this express will do well to follow us—Munday at Leicester, Tuesday there
still or at Lutterworth, next to Daventry, next to Banbury, and so to Oxford.
I pray God send us a happy meeting, which I hope is not far off. I am most
sincerely, My Lord, Your Lordships most faithfull humble servant, H. London.
(Leeds MSS., Packet 13 b.)

Nottingham, December 8.—My Lord, The inclosed will give you the reason
why it is impossible for us now to meet. I am sorry for it with all my heart,
because I could have unburdned myself to you. But there is now no help, we
must be gone early to-morrow morning. The Prince wants horse, and would
therefore be glad if you would send any that you have to spare. I once more
pray God to send us a happy meeting, and am most heartily, My Lord, Your
Lordships faithfull and obedient servant, H. London. (B.M. Add. MSS. 28053,
f. 373.)

Nottingham, December the 8th.—My Lord, Upon the return of the express
I sent on Munday last to the Prince of Orange the Princess resolves to move
too-morrow towards Oxford. The Prince was on Thursday last at Salisbury,
and was to march that day towards Hungerford, from thence to Newbery, and
from thence to Redding, where the Kings horse are quarterd, if they think fitt
to stay for him. Our orders are to march directly to Oxford. We are about
1,500 horse (the gentlemen comprehended), and we have two companyes of foot
very well arm'd. We intercepted the last pacquett that went southward,
which gave an account of the garrison of Hull seising the Governor and declaring for the Prince of Orange. This account coming from Hull itself, I venter'd
to send the Prince word of it by the express that went from hence this morning,
and hope it is true, tho we have not had the confirmation of it from your Lordship. I am, My Lord, Your Lordships most faithfull humble servant, Devonshire. (Leeds MSS., Packet 13 b.)

somebody to meet us with your orders, which shall alwayes be obeyed by

Your Highnesses most obedient servant,

Danby.[1]

To the Countess of Danby at Kiveton.[2]

York, 12th December, [16]88.

My dearest,

Having an opportunity of sending this by Mr. Clayton, I would not omitt the occasion, and though I have litle to write yett itt is of no lesse importance than to acquaint you that your brother Charles is comeing to York, sent by the King with a message to me and the gentlemen here. I know not yett what his comission imports, but expect him here to-morrow or next day att farthest.

The writts for electing Parliament men came to my hands last night, and my son Dumblan's election for this citty will be on Monday next,[3] but those for the county not till Monday seven-night. The knights of the shire will be Lord Fairfax and Colonel Darcy, and I know not whither these elections may not retard my march three or four daies, in which time I expect to hear againe from the Prince.

[1] Endorsed, ' Copie of a letter to the Prince of Orange of the 11th of December by Lord Lumley.' The reply, however, refers to the letter as dated a day earlier :

My Lord, I receaved yours from York of the 10th of December, for which I give you many thanks, as also for all the service that you have done me. The affaires being now altered by the Kings retirement, I thinck it is not necessary to keep those gentlemen that have been so much my friends any longer together, being that it would be a charge to the country and a trouble to them-selfs. Therefore I desire you to give them my hearty thanks for their zeale to the cause and for my service, and to let them know that it is best for them, and that they can doe me no better service for the present, then to go back for their respective dwellings, and stand for to be chosen Parliament men in their counties, and keeping their inclinations for me, of which they have given such evident proves in this occasions that they shall be alwaies aknoledged by me ; and that you will discharge all the foot you have togither, keeping onely just so many as is absolutely required to keep the town of Yorck in peace and good order. I am, Your most affectionate friend, G. Prince d'Orange.—Abbington, the 12th December, 1688. (B.M. Add. MSS. 28053, f. 375.)

[2] From the autograph letter among the Lindsey MSS., partly printed in Lindsey MSS., p. 453.

[3] December 17.

The generall pardon is expected to follow the writts in a post or two ; but without a cessation of armes wee cannot see what either writts or pardon will signify, and there is yett no appearance of a cessation, the Prince advancing daily nearer the King's army, and having refused all treaty untill the King shall have dismissed all his Catholick officers and souldiers, which is not likely he will do. You will hear from me almost every day till we go, and alwaies that I am with a true heart,

Your most intirely affectionate husband,

Danby.

My blessing and kind remembrances to all my dear children. Pray lett my horse coullors and trumpett banner bee lookt out, and sent to me when anybody comes, but not to send any for that only.

[To the Countess of Danby] [1]

Yorke, December the 14th, [1688],
halfe an houre past six in the morneing.

The post is but newly arrived here with the newes [2] that the King, Queen and Prince of Wales have all taken shiping and are gone beyond seas either to Calis or Dunkirk as the winde shall serve them. The Lord Chancellour, the Lord Peterborough, and severall both of the judges and others are gone away with them. The Prince of Orange was expected to be in London at last night. The Lords Spirituall and Temporall mett a Guild Hall on Tuesday morneing [3] together with the Lord Mayor, and made an address of invitation to the Prince to come to London. They at the same time remooved Mr. Skelton and all the popish officers out of the Tower, and have placed the command thereof in the hands of the Lord Lucas untill further order.

These extraordinary changes will make me march with coaches instead of troopes, and I designe to sett forward from

---

[1] Leeds MSS., Packet 13 b. Not written by Danby but signed by him.

[2] Presumably this post brought the letter of December 10 (really December 11) from Charles Bertie to Danby, which is printed in *Lindsey MSS.*, p. 451.

[3] December 11.

hence on Tuesday morneing, not being able to remoove sooner both by reason of my son Dunblain's election, which will be on Munday, and for the settling of those forces which are to remaine here. In the meane time I desire you will put all things in order for the most speedy remove of my family and plate to London, and care shall be taken of the pressing of what carryages shall be necessary for that purpose. When I have had time to consider things a little further I will send Langwith to you with such directions as I thinke necessary, and will alsoe send you a coachman and six horses for your coach there. I question whether it will be more convenient for me to come to Keeton or to appoint a time for meeting you att Newarke, because it will be impossible for me without disobligeing many gentlemen of quality to be rid of much more company then can be received at Keeton, and it will be taken unkindely if I should not invite them along with me. But of this you shall know more certainly by Langwith, and in the meane while lett noe time be lost in getting things carefully pack't up for your remoove.

I intend this day to send some gentleman of quality post to London to the Prince of Orange, which should have been my son Dunblaine but that his election prevents, and therefore I thinke to send my son Herbert ; but he haveing satt up all night in expectation of the news by this post I am not yet willing to awake him, and shall doe in it onely what shall suite with his own inclination ; but all the lords are soliciting to be the messenger, and I am rather willing my son Herbert should have the honour of it. You will heare frome me every day till the time of my moveing, and when we meet it will be to the true satisfaction of

Your most entirely affectionate husband,

Danby.

My blessing and kinde remembrance to all my daughters.

I desire you will send a letter to the post at Bautre to-morrow for Acherly to put the house at Lindsey House in order for our comeing, and imediately to gett the best beer she can to be lay'd in there and what else you shall thinke fitt to give her directions in ; and pray omitt not to give these directions by to-morrows post.

To the Mayor of Pontefract.[1]

Yorke, Sunday, December the 16th, 1688.

Sir,

I have just now received yours of this morning,[2] and haveing received the same alarm from divers other places I am doeing all I can for the security of this county. I have already sent a troope of horse to Ferybrige, and two troopes more to Wakefield. There are three troops more upon their march to Leeds, and I intend to march with five troops more to-morrow towards the west of Yorkeshire as I shall finde by my intelligence to be most necessary.

If all the gentlemen of this county had been as forward to serve the interest of their countrey and nation as they ought to have been, and as some have done (who will deserve to be distinguished), we had not now wanted forces both to have preserved our own countrey and to have reveng'd ourselves upon those bloody villaines ; and I hope you will make such distinction in the elections of Parliament men to serve for your borough that you will not chuse any who have onely lookt on whilest others have ventured their all to preserve you, or if you doe I am sure you will not have deserved your preservation. I cannot but say this to you for the honour of your corporation as well as for the encouragemente of the deserving countrey men on like occasions, and I can speake it with the greater freedome, haveing noe designe to preferr any but such in generall as have showed you that they deserve it.

Your honourable resolutions in that affair (if I can understand them) will much encourage me to pay you my more particular services. However, as I have had the honour to begin in this countrey, soe I will persevere to the end for the safety and preservation of itt, and remaine, Sir,

Your very affectionate servant,

D[anby]

[1] From a copy among the Lindsey MSS., printed in *Lindsey MSS.*, p. 454.

[2] This letter, dated Sunday morning [December 16], is preserved in Leeds MSS., Packet 13 b, and is calendared in *Leeds MSS.*, p. 28, where ' Chester ' is a mistake for ' Chesterfield.'

To Viscount Latimer.[1]

York, 17 December, 1688.

I have very little time [to] write, being just upon a march. The occasion of it, and for all the news here, I must refer you to my brother Charles Bertie's letter ;[2] but since that was written I understand by an express from Sir John Lowther of Lowther that he has intercepted an express from the Lord Tirconnell to the King, wherein he presses most earnestly to have arms sent immediately to him from Carlisle, by which it appears they are doing all they can to defend themselves against the Prince in that kingdom ; and it seems my Lord Feversham took what care he could to send them formed troops, by disbanding all the Irish with their arms, which is the occasion that gives us also our present trouble. If the Prince of Orange be come to London, be sure you attend him to give him an account of this matter, and let him know that I writ by the last post [3] to acquaint his Highness with the consternations which these Irish have put these countries into, which is the cause I am not able to obey his commands in attending him at London as soon as I would have done.

[Danby]

[To the Princess of Orange] [4]

[4th January, 1688/9]

As I have pay'd the utmost of my services to the Prince in this country (where by the wonderfull providence of God, and the prudent conduct of his Highnesse, things have been brought to an happy issue), so I do not only congratulate your Highnesses share in these blessings, but I presume to give your Highnesse an assurance that no man in this kingdome shall bee more strictly devoted to your personall intrests. I take the greater confidence to say this, because there will bee various trialls of mens minds and humors amongst us, and although I may bee one of the least considerable, there is none but what may bee of

---

[1] *Lindsey MSS.*, p. 454.

[2] *i.e.* a letter from Danby to Charles Bertie, which has not been found.

[3] This letter has not been found.

[4] From an autograph draft in Leeds MSS., Packet 14.

use in this conjuncture. I presume also to renew my owne and my daughter Plymouths humble request to your Highnesse, that shee may have the honour of attending your Highnesse in your bedchamber, and I asked the Princes leave to write to your Highnesse on her behalfe. But wee shall desire to receive that obligation (if your Highness shall thinke her worthy of itt) only from yourselfe, and if you shall please to accept of her service shee will imediatly pay her attendance in Holland, or where ever shee shall receive your comands to do itt.

I hope your Highnesse will speedily afford us the happinesse of your presence in this kingdome, and I beg leave to tell your Highness (because I am sure itt is a certaine truth) that itt is absolutely necessary for the Princes interest as well as your owne (and above all for the nations sake) that your Highness should make what hast you can hither. I am with all that duty which becomes mee

[Danby] [1]

[1] Endorsed by Danby, ' Coppy of my letter to the Princesse of Orange, 4th January, 1688/9.'

PART IV

CARMARTHEN AND LEEDS
1689-1712

For some reason which has not been ascertained the papers of the Duke of Leeds from the close of 1689 onwards have almost entirely vanished. The result is a deplorable lack of information not merely for his later years, but for one of the most important epochs in his career. The total mass of correspondence for the period during which he was Lord President, when compared with that for the period during which he was Lord Treasurer, is almost ludicrously small.

I. CORRESPONDENCE WITH WILLIAM III

Of the letters which the Lord President wrote to the King during his repeated absences from England a large number have been preserved, although there are indications that William worked upon a systematic plan, and retained only those which he considered specially important. All of these have been summarised in the *Calendar of State Papers, Domestic*, but so inaccurately as well as inadequately that it has been considered advisable to print them in their entirety.[1] A series of memoranda and two drafts of letters belonging to the year 1689 have also been found, and these are printed in their place at the beginning.

Memorandums att my first coming out of the North to the Prince att St. James.[2]

I found the matter then negotiateing about the getting Ireland secured, and that whole transaction carried on with such secresy as to mee that I found care taken that I should not know what measures were taken about itt ; and when I spoke against what I heard of Colonel Richard Hamilton being to bee sent about itt, and would have had a squadron of ships to have been sent thither, I was answered by the Prince that hee durst not trust the fleet, but had putt that businesse into a very good way, and would enter no further into the consideration of itt with mee.

---

[1] Illustrations of the many inaccuracies are, ' main regiments ' instead of ' marine regiments ' (p. 167) ; ' evening ' instead of ' morning ' (p. 169) ; ' four great ships ' instead of ' ten great ships ' (pp. 173-4) ; ' submit to your government ' instead of ' subvert your government ' (p. 213) ; and the astounding error of attributing the last letter to ' Sir P. Leeds ' (p. 217).

[2] B.M. Add. MSS. 28042, f. 34. Notes in Carmarthen's handwriting. The heading obviously refers to the date of the events mentioned in the notes rather than to the date at which the notes themselves were drawn up.

I found my Lord Hallifax then in much greater creditt then myselfe with him, notwithstanding what I had done and that I was forbid by Mr. Russell from the Prince from trusting him with the Princes designe of coming into England, and that the Prince knew that hee had laught att us for medling in that undertakeing.

Hee refused to make mee a duke, and itt was with difficulty that hee agreed to make mee marquis, although I had a warrant for that three yeares before Lord Hallifax.

Notwithstanding so many gentlemen of note had been ingaged under mee for his service in the north, yett I was not able to gett one man prefer'd either into the Treasury, Customes, Excize nor Admiralty, except Sir John Lowther, whereas Lord Hallifax and divers others who had done nothing prevailed to prefer men into every one of those stations, and some who were denied when I spoke for them did gett into employments att the request of others, as Mr. Roberts, Sir Robert Cotton, Sir Jonathan Jennins, &c.

My owne brother was a Commissioner of Customes in King Charles his time, and putt out by King James ; yett I could not gett him restored, although my Lord Warrington and others gott in theire younger brothers who had never knowne anything of the businesse.

Hee then promised my brother should have the sallery of the riding surveighors place (in which my brother had been formerly), viz., 630 l. a yeare, and this promise was made in March 1688/9, but hee never yett had one shilling.

Hee refused to make my eldest son Latimer to bee a Gentleman of his Bedchamber, although hee had been so some yeares to King Charles, and that hee had made my son his atturney to receive and discharge the Exchequer of the money paid to him by King Charles upon the treaty of peace with the Dutch, and that hee had never gott that money without my promoteing the treaty for itt.

Hee gave my son Danby the office of Postmaster Generall by warrant under his signe manuall, and without any notice to mee hee granted itt away to others. And instead of this hee gave him one of the regiments of marines, wherein hee never gott a farthing pay, and has been an occasion of great expence to him.

Hee gave him also the comand of a ship, which has been another occasion of great expence to him, and have occasioned a great debt upon him, besides that hee has not mett with the countenance nor incouragement which has been given to many private sea captaines.

When I beg'd him to have given some countenance to my daughter Landsdowne (who was then liveing) by makeing somebody interpose so as to see if my Lord Lansdowne had anything to say against her, and if hee had not that hee would speake [1]

To the King. [2]

18th February, [16]88/9.

Haveing been able to do nothing which can bee called considerable for any of those gentlemen who were in armes with mee in the north, the weight of itt is growne no lesse burdensome to mee by the reproches I lie under as if I had been carelesse of theire concernes then itt is greivous to mee to bee troublesome to your Majestie in anything.   Itt is yett the harder upon mee because they will not beleeve itt to bee my want of interest to serve them, but whatever difficulties I undergo I will make itt as litle uneasy to your Majestie as I can.   Only I must assure your Majestie that if I am not able to procure something of consideration for Sir Henry Goodrick I can have no reason to expect any longer interest amongst the gentlemen of my country, having alwaies declared that I would use my utmost endeavours to serve him with your Majestie.   Hee is a gentleman capable of dischargeing any employment in the kingdome, but since I heare most other places are disposed, I would presume to beg a Commissioner of the Customes place for him, if your Majestie please to bee so gracious to us both.

I likewise beg leave to informe your Majestie that a brother of my owne, Mr. Charles Osborne, has been fifteen yeares an officer in the Customes, first in the office of a Rideing Surveighor, and then as a Commissioner of the Customes, and that hee was putt back from being a Commissioner to bee againe Rideing Surveighor when I was putt from the Treasury, and was afterwards

---

[1] The document ends abruptly here at the foot of a sheet.

[2] From an autograph draft in Leeds MSS., Packet 14, endorsed, ' Coppy of my letter to King William, 18th February, [16]88/9. About Sir Goodrick, &c.'

putt from that also by the late King for refuseing to take off the Test. I hope therefore your Majestie will thinke itt but justice to restore him to his Rideing Surveighors place, and no extra-ordinary favour to restore him to his place of Commissioner of the Customes. There is also Mr. Watly Montagu (brother to the Earle of Sandwich) and Mr. Vane, who highly deserve your Majesties consideration both for theire parts, estates, and inter-est in theire countrys ; and I hope your Majestie will please to forgive this presumption to one who I hope has been as litle troublesome to your Majestie as any that pretends to have servd you, and who is according to his duty, [&c]

[Danby]

To the King.[1]

5th April, [16]89.

Haveing troubled your Majestie so lately I could not now presume to do itt againe, but that if your Majestie thinkes mee worthy of any such marke of your favour as shall remayne to my family I hope you will please to do itt as soone as you intend the like to any other ; and since I understand your Majestie designs itt to some lords before the coronation, I presume to informe your Majestie that upon any alteration of title itt will require a weeks time to prepare those things which are necessary to such alteration. If your Majestie designes mee any honour of this kind, I hope you will please to make itt suitable to whatever your owne thoughts are of my service ; and since the Marquis of Winchester hath (as hee saies) your warrant already to bee a duke, I am sure my Lord Hallifax can take no just exception to my precedence of his lordship, because I was created both earle and marquis before him, and may with modesty pretend to have done your Majestie more service then his lordship. But what-ever your Majestie shall please to do with mee shall bee thank-fully received or submitted to, as becomes your Majesties most dutifull and most obedient subject and servant,

[Danby]

[1] From an autograph draft in Leeds MSS., Packet 14, endorsed, ' Coppy of my letter to the King, 5th April, 1689.'

[To the King] [1]

London, 13 June, 1690.

Sir,

Yesterday I received the honour of your Majesties letter of the 10th,[2] and this day wee had the newes of your Majesties being embarqued on the 11th with so good a wind that I doubt not but your Majestie arrived in Ireland on the 12th, where I hope you will find your victories as easy as your passage.

The wind has stood so well ever since the 10th that I hope itt will have remedied the mistake of those ships which are gone to Kircubright, and itt may have carried the fleet wherever they would go, only they will bee retarded a while by staying to take my Lord Pembroks regiment on board att Portsmouth.   I imparted your Majesties commands to the Queene concerning the Parliament, about which I found you had given her some intimation, but itt will bee necessary before the time of its meeting to lett her have your expresse direction in that matter to the end her Majestie may deliver itt as such to the great Councill.

Itt hath been expected that before this time some informations would have com'd from Scotland by which Sir John Cokram and Mr. Ferguson might have been detain'd in custody.   There hath litle appeared by theire papers, saveing a constant correspondence betwixt them and some of the Club, and Sir Johns haveing been ordered to buy some serviceable horses for my Lord Ross in Aprill last, in which month itt appeares by severall letters which have been taken in other hands that something was expected to have been then done which failed.

All things here seeme to bee in a very peaceable posture, and the Deane of Pauls and I do intend to attempt the makeing of some reconciliations in the Citty amongst such as are best able to contribute to your service there, if they can bee brought to agree with one another.

I do not perfectly understand your Majesties pleasure as to mine and my sons private affaires, but understand itt to bee that your Majestie will have them both to remayne in the posture they are till your Majesties returne from Ireland.

---

[1] From the autograph letter in S.P. Dom., King William's Chest, 7, No. 50, summarised in *Cal. S.P. Dom.*, 1690-1, p. 31 ; *Dalrymple*, App., ii. 106.

[2] This letter has not been found.

I acknowlege your Majesties great goodnesse and condescention in haveing been pleased to afford mee expressions so far beyond what is possible for mee to deserve, and I am sure that if I had not been already devoted to your Majesties service with such an intire resignation as is not possible to bee greater, I must necessarily have been so from the date of that letter, which comes from an hand so sacred both for truth and greatnesse of mind.

I am sorry that my sons interest seeming to interfere with Major Wildmans makes itt lesse fitt for mee to reflect upon his actings ; butt there are divers passages which make itt highly probable that Major Wildman is privy to whatever has been acting against the government in Scotland, and particularly his burning very many of his papers, as hee did certainly the same night after Ferguson and his papers were seized, with whom I find hee used to bee constantly in private twice or thrice every weeke. His proceedings also with Sir Samuel Moreland, which are too tedious to trouble your Majestie withall, and about which hee gave Sir Samuell a particular strict charge that I should know nothing. Upon that whole matter I do truly beleeve him to bee a very dangerous man to the government, and that neither your Majesties nor the Queens letters do escape his search if hee can gett to them, insomuch that I am in my conscience of opinion that of all the hands in England the Post Office ought least to bee trusted in his, and especially att this time.

I beg leave to conclude with this assurance to your Majestie, that I am both by obligation, inclination, and duty, Sir,

Your Majesties most obedient and most faithfull subject

and servant,

Carmarthen, P.

[To the King] [1]

London, 16th June, 1690.

Sir,

My former of the 13th did not go as I expected, because I understood itt would have no other conveyance then by the ordinary post, by which not only myselfe dare not write, but

---

[1] From the autograph letter in S.P. Dom., King William's Chest, 7, No. 52, summarised in *Cal. S.P. Dom.*, 1690-1, p. 33 ; *Dalrymple*, App., ii. 174.

my Lord Malborow and others (who know lesse then I do of that matter) have declared publickly that they will not write but by expresses, haveing reason to beleeve that Major Wildman has exact impressions of most peoples seales, and that hee makes use of his art.

Hee does now produce letters which hee pretends to intercept every post, which are interlined in white ink with the best intelligence which can bee given of your Majesties councills and affaires. They are alwaies directed to Monsieur Coutenay a Amsterdam, and I remember my Lord Munmouth told mee of such a direction above two months ago ; but wee never saw any of these till one about four daies before your Majesties departure, and they are so much of one straine that I cannot hinder myselfe from suspecting them to bee sham letters, either to bring some of your Councill under suspicion of betraying secretts, or to putt a valew upon Major Wildmans great diligence in your service att this time.

I cannot but also acquainte your Majestie with a private dis-course of my Lord Munmouths to mee on the 14th, which did much surprize mee ; but although I now beleeve there is no such danger yett itt is fitt for your Majesties knowlege. Itt was that hee did then beleeve wee should in a few houres from that time heare that 5,000 French foot were landed in Scotland, to which a great number of Scoth were joyned by that time. I told him if hee knew itt to bee true hee ought to acquainte the Queene with itt, which hee said hee would have done if hee had been very sure of the truth of itt ; but hee was confident itt would bee found true in a few houres longer. But heareing nothing of itt the next day I asked him why he had said so before. To which hee answered that the newes had been brought by a man who came post out of Scotland in forty-eight houres, and had rid himselfe almost dead ; but said hee did not know the man, nor how to inquire after him. And upon further discourse hee said hee had told your Majestie that hee would endeavour to gett what intelligence hee could out of Scotland for your service, and that hee would endeavour to prevent all things there which might tend to your disservice, but that hee would bee torne to peices before hee would name any persons, and that you were contented to give him that liberty.

In short, although I hope hee intends well to your Majestie I beleeve him to bee abused by Wildman, and hee was in as much disorder as I ever saw when Fergusons papers were searched, and went above a dozen times to his lodging, where Wildman was all that time. I say not this with any reflection upon my Lord (who I do in my conscience beleeve meanes well to your interest), but I beleeve hee has been privy to more of the Scoth designes then hee now wishes hee had knowne.

My Lords of the Cabinett Councill seeme to thinke itt very convenient that the five regiments when they come from Holland (with what other force is hereabouts) might incampe in Hyde Park or some other neare place, and the charge will not bee above 6,000 l. more to the officers, which must also bee paid in some time after. But I say not this by any order, but for your Majesties consideration of itt. I am

Your Majesties most obedient and dutifull servant,

Carmarthen, P.

[To the King] [1]

London, 23 June, 1690.

Sir,

I had the honour of your Majesties of the 16th,[2] and besides the good newes of your health (which will ever bee the most welcome) itt was very comfortable to heare that your Majestie found most things in so good a condition. By the accounts from the Transport Commissioners wee have reason to hope that all the horse will bee arrived in Ireland as soone as this letter, and yett forgive mee to say I should not bee sorry to heare they had com'd too late for the first engagement, because I confesse I can feare nothing there but the hazarding of your person further then may bee necessary, and therefore I hope you will pardon my presumption to putt you in mind how much depends upon your preservation.

My Lord Nottingham assures mee that hee gives your Majestie a full account of all matters which pass att Councills and are

[1] From the autograph letter in S.P. Dom., King William's Chest, 7, No. 61, summarised in *Cal. S.P. Dom.*, 1690-1, p. 37.

[2] This letter has not been found.

worth your knowlege, so as all things of that kind would bee only to trouble your Majestie with repetitions. I shall therefore only presume to say that in my opinion all possible incouragement should bee given to the businesse of Savoy, and that I hope your Majestie will approve of the method wee have proposed for prepareing a state of the accounts against the next sitting of the Parliament.

I know itt will not bee needfull to putt your Majestie in mind of the Marine Regiments, if any use can bee made of them by a discent in the south parts of Ireland, in case the French do not appeare att sea, or, if they should, wee are inform'd by the Admiralty that the fleet is now so well supplied with seamen that I hope they would not bee much misst on shipboard.

Itt is wondred by everybody that Scotland holds no sort of correspondence with us. I wish your Majestie would give some directions to your Commissioner in that matter, and that besides what hee sends imediately to your Majestie some account might bee sent weekly to the Queene. Her Majestie is very diligent att Cabinett Councills, and whenever anything concernes your Majestie either personally (as some late transactions att Somersett House have seem'd to do) or in haveing your orders obey'd, shee is not only very active but very strict, and lets us see that shee will not bee served superficially, insomuch that wee shall bee without all excuses, but want of money, if your Majestie bee not served in your absence as you ought to bee.

When I had writt thus far newes came about 11 a clock att night that the French fleet appeared off of Falmouth, being computed about 100 sayle, and by another letter early this morning that itt was seene from the Isle of Portland about 120 sayle.[1] The Queene did hereupon call the Cabinett Councill and gave severall orders, of which your Majestie will receive the particulars from my Lord Nottingham.

Besides the misfortune of our fleet not being together (nine of them being att Plymouth, and some of them in the Irish seas, and seaven of the Dutch not yett com'd) wee have also intelli-

---

[1] This sentence seems to cast some doubt on the precise date of the whole letter. A comparison with other sources of information makes it clear that the first part of the letter was written late on June 22 and the remainder on June 23.

gence that the Toulon squadron has passt by Killigrew, and therefore wee may bee sure that upon joyning theire fleet att Brest they have made this hast to fight before Killigrew could arrive. Notwithstanding all these disadvantages, Mr. Russell, Captain Preistman, &c., are of opinion that your Majesties fleet now with my Lord Torrington will bee strong enough ; and to helpe us itt hath pleased God that last night about 12 a clock the wind changed from west to north-east, which wee have reason to beleeve did save your fleet att St. Helens from being surprized att an anchor, as well as itt has given itt the wind in case of engagement, of which wee must necessarily have some speedy account. And whatever the intentions of the French are this is certainely one of the boldest attempts they ever yett made either by sea or land.

Itt is not impossible but they might designe a diversion to our fleet in the Channell, while they with some small convoy might send men into Scotland by the west of Ireland in transport ships. Your Majestie knows best whither they have any such men to spare, for itt must bee certaine, either that they have positive orders to ingage our fleet, or that they are designed to give countenance to some landing or insurrection in Scotland ; and my private opinion is, that if the men-of-war in the Irish seas bee not already sayled to joyne my Lord Torrington, they might prevent landing of men on the west of Scotland, and will bee too late to signify anything in the Channell.

I shall only adde my prayers for your Majesties happinesse, and remaine as becomes mee, Sir,

Your Majesties most dutifull and most obedient
subject and servant,

Carmarthen, P.

[To the King] [1]

26th June, 1690.

Sir,

I am almost ashamed to send the inclosed letters of the older date, the state of divers matters in them being chang'd

[1] From the autograph letter in S.P. Dom., King William's Chest, 7, No. 66, summarised in *Cal. S.P. Dom.*, 1690-1, p. 40. *Cf.* Lord Nottingham's letter of the same date in *Finch MSS.*, ii. 317.

since ; but itt hath not been my fault, because no expresse hath been sent since till this day. Wee thought last night that the fleets had been ingaged yesterday (Sir Robert Holmes haveing writt so by an expresse dated from the Isle of Wight att 6 in the morning), but by letters from Portsmouth att 3 in the afternoone yesterday wee find that no other engagement had been then but betwixt scout ships, and by the last account wee understand that the wind being then north both the fleets were upon a stretch southwards, indeavoureing to gaine the wind, and itt is supposed that whichsoever could gett the wind would begin the attack. Wee have hopes also that most of the Dutch ships are joyn'd your fleet, and wee hope that every houre will bring us newes of a generall engagement.

The Councill has thought fitt att this time to issue warrants for the comitment of divers suspected persons, of whom my Lord Nottingham sends a list, as also an account of what Crone has confesst, which is not much, but I beleeve is all hee knows. I thinke itt fitt also to acquainte your Majestie that my Lord Munmouth told mee yesterday that by a letter hee had newly received from Scotland hee understood that my Lord Atholl, my Lord Arran and Lord Anondall had absconded, and that hee feared they were imediately ready to go into an insurrection. But however this may bee true or not, there is this remarkable, that no man is knowne to have received a letter from Scotland this twelve daies, but this letter to Lord Munmouth, from whence everybody concludes Wildmans foule play, and beleeves that both hee and Ferguson can give account, if they would, of all the transactions of the Club, who appeare to bee ingaged with the late King by Crones confession, who names Montgomery and saies hee has forgott the names of the other two, who had writt to the late Queene.

There will bee an occasion of sending againe so speedily to your Majestie that I will now only presume to subscribe myselfe, Sir,

Your Majesties most dutifull servant,

Carmarthen, P.

[To the King] [1]

London, 28 June, [16]90.
Sir,

I have this day received your Majesties of the 22th from Loughbrikling.[2] Itt was given mee att the Cabinett Councill when the Queene was present, and upon her reading itt the newes of your Majesties being in probability of a battle so speedily did putt her into some disorder, and her mind will not bee in ease till shee heares something from you that is more comfortable.

I am sure your Majestie will bee surprised when you read my Lord Torringtons letter.[3] Hee is condem'd by everybody here to no small degree, and your Majestie will see what orders have been thought fitt to send him from hence,[4] upon which wee hope hee will no more loose the advantage of the wind, which hath been favourable to him all this day, and wee compute that hee must have received those orders this day by noone. Sir William Lockhart arrived here yesterday from Scotland, where hee saies all things are quiett att present ; but I finde they thinke there is a numerous party of disaffected men amongst them, if they have an opportunity of shewing themselves, and my Lord Ross is com'd privately to give the Queene an account of the plotters there and theire designes.

Wee are wanting in no endeavours to gett more ships ready and man'd, and hope to gett out four of the great ones in eight daies, and two of them in four daies, one of which my Lord Munmouth has desired to comand, and is gone to Portsmouth this day for that purpose. Wee are also as diligent as wee can in all kinds for our security att land, and I must do Mr. Shadrack Vincent that justice as to lett you know that the care and paines hee has taken in Cornwall amongst the tinners has done your Majestie so good service there (in which place wee had no small apprehensions) that hee has made them signe a very loyall address, and they have offered to secure that country under him against any invasion or insurrection, which is a service for which

---

[1] From the autograph letter in S.P. Dom., King William's Chest, 7, No. 68, summarised in *Cal. S.P. Dom.*, 1690-1, p. 43.

[2] Loughbrickland. This letter has not been found.

[3] Printed in *Finch MSS.*, ii. 315.   [4] *Ibid.*, p. 318.

I hope your Majestie will consider him hereafter. The Leiu-tennancy of London did also make a very good and dutifull addresse this day, and I am confident will acquitt themselves as they ought to do if there bee occasion.

When I had writt thus far, I understood by my Lord Notting-ham (who came from the Queene) that her Majestie had newly spoke with my Lord Ross, but that hee thought by the manner of his discourse, and haveing said nothing but in generalls, that hee was rather com'd hither as a spy to concert things with theire confederates in the Citty then for any good end. And att the close of his discourse hee said hee should bee able to say more to the Queene (refuseing to speake with anybody else) when hee had discoursed with Mr. Ferguson, who hee said was the manager of all the conspiracies betwixt this Citty and Scotland. In short, notwithstanding the best of our endeavours, all will depend upon your Majesties successes, and our im-patience till wee heare againe will bee equall to the concerne wee have for the safety of your person, which that God may keepe under His particular protection is the zealous prayer of, Sir,

Your Majesties most dutifull servant,

Carmarthen. P.

[To the King] [1]

2nd July, 1690.

Sir,

You will find that this morning has brought an ill account from the fleet, and wee are able to say nothing more then what your Majestie will read in my Lord Torringtons letter,[2] which in my opinion speakes not much in his justification, for thereby there seemes to have been but two houres of his being ingaged, and the Dutch to have borne the hardship of that time without

---

[1] From the autograph letter in S.P. Dom., King William's Chest, 7, No. 74, summarised in *Cal. S.P. Dom.*, 1690-1, p. 46.

[2] This letter is S.P. Dom., King William's Chest, 7, No. 71, and is printed in *Dalrymple*, App., ii. 112-3. For the statement made by Dalrymple and repeated in *Cal. S.P. Dom.*, 1690-1, p. 44, that the letter was written to Carmarthen, there is no authority whatever beyond the fact that Carmarthen mentions it. Presumably it was written to Nottingham, and sent on by Nottingham to the King in his letter of July 2, printed in *Finch MSS.*, ii. 331.

haveing been assisted as they ought. I thinke the greatest misfortune from first to last has been the imploying of that man, and I shall hope for no good whilst the comand remaines in his hand ; but itt is yett too soone to give a perfect judgment, only I thinke itt might bee well to consider who shall supply his roome if itt shall appeare necessary after examination of the conduct.

Wee cannot yett apprehend the English fleet to bee in any so ill condition but that itt might bee out againe in ten daies ; but the difficulty is how to gett those ships together which wee have. My Lord Torrington saies nothing whither the nine ships which were sailed from Plymouth seven daies ago to joyne him were com'd to him, nor have wee heard of Killegrew, who wee have reason to suspect has staid to convoy marchant ships for his private profitt instead of hastning to the fleet according to his orders. All wee have been able to do as to those ships has been to send them advice to secure themselves in the first safe ports they can make.

The great distresse will bee from want of money, which will fall short either to the occasions of the navy or to those supplys which should bee sent into Ireland, and itt happens that the assistance wee should have had from the fund of the hereditary revenue does faile, by that pretence of the bankers debt upon itt, which is now under the suspence of a triall in Westminster Hall. These things considered have made mee of an opinion for the sitting of the Parliament, and so I find severall others ; but Sir Thomas Lee is so positively of opinion that a Parliament would quarrell, instead of doing good, that itt hath not been yett proposed, but will bee I suppose att the great Councill, which is to sitt this afternoone of course, and where her Majestie will acquainte them with your pleasure to have the Parliament prorogued on Monday next, but will debate att the Councill to what time the prorogation shall bee, which must necessarily bee but very short.

Here are various discourses about land men. Some speake of 7 or 8,000 aboard this fleet, and others say they are on board lesser vessells which are gone or to go into the Irish seas, but there is no foundation for any of these discourses. A letter from Captain Elmore, which came with my Lord Torringtons from the fleet, speaks as if the French did stand after our fleet (as hee saies) to try to pick up some lame ships, so that wee cannot say yett they are quite parted, and the wind being full east itt is impossible to gett into this river, so that all accounts to your Majestie must yett bee very imperfect. I thinke itt might not bee amiss for mee to take out the commission for that regiment of volonteer horse in the Citty, and to make use of itt only as there may bee occasion ; but I will not speake of itt till I heare your Majesties pleasure. I am with all duty, Sir,

Your Majesties most obedient subject and servant,

Carmarthen, P.

Your Majestie will please to pardon the scribling in this letter, being writt in hast to go with the expresse, and I beg leave to speake my opinion that Haddock would bee your best admirall, and besides other reasons because I find the world hereabouts does generally thinke so, which is of no small importance.

[To the King] [1]

Sir,   London, 6th July, 1690.

My Lord Devonshire and Lord Pembrok are returned from the fleet this afternoone, and informe us of its being out of danger of any further prejudice from the French, itt being probably arrived by this time att the Gunfleet, and the French off of Rye. My Lord Nottingham tells mee hee sends your Majestie the coppies of all our intelligences, by which your Majestie will find that since the last account from hence the Dutch have been forced to sett fire to four more of theire ships, as our men did also yesterday to the *Ann*, a third-rate of your Majesties, neare Rye, into which place three fireships of your Majesties are also gone, and I feare will bee forced to bee burnt by our owne men, the whole French fleet being now att anchor before the towne, and haveing been sounding before the harbour most of this afternoone.

All diligence is useing to gett ships in readinesse for men to bee turn'd into out of the same ships, and wee shall have ten

---

[1] From the autograph letter in S.P. Dom., King William's Chest, 7, No. 82, summarised in *Cal. S.P. Dom.*, 1690-1, p. 51.

great ships ready in Chatham and Portsmouth in fourteen daies, but wee shall find great difficulties to gett them man'd as they ought to bee. Your Majestie will also understand from my Lord Nottingham that Mr. Harbord is to go to-morrow for Holland to negotiate there for more ships, and all the instructions are given him which wee can thinke necessary, and the Queene has writt to some persons there, as I doubt not but shee informes you. But your Majesties owne letters thither (added to theire interest, which is comon with ours, not to suffer the French to bee masters att sea) would prevaile most if you will please to write or send to them.

Your Majestie will heare also what information is given from France of twenty-eight frigatts almost ready att Brest to go into the Irish seas, of which none are said to exceed 36 guns, and against this itt is thought adviseable to send Shovell and Sandersons squadron (which my Lord Torrington left att Plymouth) to cruize about the mouth of St. George's Channell, and they will also bee in the way to joyne Killegrews squadron, of which (to our admiration) wee heare nothing as yett. They will also convoy eighteen ships of Pereras provisions from Plymouth to the mouth of St. George's Channell, from whence they will go with security into Ireland under small convoy.

Although this may secure the Irish seas and the transport ships att present from any insult from Brest, yett if the French should thinke itt of more importance to send the gross of theire fleet that way then to keepe itt here, there would bee no possibility of saveing a boat in the Irish seas. And then itt would not only take away all meanes of sending anything to your army from England (or almost any intelligence), but your Majestie would not bee able to gett hither were the necessity never so great, or att least you could bring no force with you, when itt is certaine that if any riseing were intended either in England or Scotland the successe of theire fleet will make itt bee putt in execution, and if itt should bee apparent that neither your Majestie nor any of your troops could gett hither, itt would tempt those to appeare against you who perhaps do not now thinke of itt, and would embolden your enemies to make some attempt which might incourage them to rise.

The Queene will give your Majestie an account of my Lord Ross his behaviour, and about Sir James Montgomery, who I beleeve were both designeing to have made theire peace ; but I am of opinion the newes of the fleet has diverted my Lord Ross his intentions, and itt will I suppose Montgomeries, and if an insurrection should happen in Scotland I feare your enemies there would bee so numerous that your comeing that way would bee too much hazard.

All this considered, and that itt is very possible to bee the case, I submitt to your Majesties consideration whither any time should bee lost in your returne hither, and with such troopes as you should thinke necessary and may bee spared from Ireland, where your Majestie will now leave things in a much better posture then they would have been if you had not gone there to see them putt into order. Sir, this being only a thought of my owne (and which I have not dared to speake to anybody but the Queene) I acknowlege is too great a presumption in mee to offer to your Majestie ; but since itt is manifestly in the power of the French fleet to putt your Majestie under these dangerous circumstances, I do rather admire not to heare this councill offered by others then retract my owne opinion in this matter, after two daies serious deliberation without being able to give myselfe much rest for the disquiett of itt till I had disburthen'd my mind to the Queen and had both her consent and approbation to move itt to your Majestie.

If your Majestie should take this resolution (as I hope you will, and in time), I suppose you will bring Duke Schomberg with you, there being so good a reason to bee given for itt as the need you may have of a generall towards Scotland as well as in the south parts of England, and haveing nobody here fitt for that comand. In that case itt will also bee necessary that the transport ships you shall use bee imediately ordered where they shall go, and unlesse you comand them on that service I should thinke itt might bee safest for them, as well as most convenient for your service, that they should go into Scotland, where (in case of necessity to save themselves) they might go up the river of Grenock, or some such place where itt would bee too hazardous for the French to follow them.

I perceive by my Lord Pembrok that hee thinkes my Lord Torrington (who has desired to waite upon the Queene when the fleet shall bee in some safe station) will desire to give up his commission, or however itt will bee so fitt hee should that itt will bee necessary for your Majestie to consider who shall comand your fleet. Mr. Russell, I beleeve, will wholly decline the thought of itt, and ownes the charge is too great for him, nor will hee like to bee in a joynt comission. Sir Richard Haddock will not undertake itt alone, but will bee contented to bee joyned in a comission ; and the choice can only bee amongst Sir Richard Haddock, Sir John Ashby, Sir Clowdsley Shovell, Mr. Killigrew, and Mr. Davis, unlesse your Majestie will imploy my Lord Grafton, who everybody agrees has behaved himselfe very honourably in your service.

The great Councill did yesterday advise her Majestie that the prorogation of the Parliament might bee to Monday the 28th instant, and to defer for a weeke longer the giveing any intimation whither itt shall then sitt or nott, in which also wee hope to have your Majesties pleasure signified to us. Itt is requisite also to know your pleasure about a lord leiutenant for Leceistirshire, which my Lord Rutland does still decline, although I am now told that, seeing the present occasion requires one, hee will accept itt ;[1] but if hee does not before the arrivall of your letter I desire to receive your comands who shall have itt, and am desired by my Lord Sherrard to lett you know that if you will do him that honour (itt being formerly in one leiutennancy with Rutlandshire) hee will keepe itt only till my Lord Rutland will have itt, and will raise a regiment of volonteers in itt besides the militia.

Wee have for the present ordered a regiment of militia into Portsmouth, where the dock and ships are said to bee too much exposed, and wee have made bold with the habeas corpus in secureing divers persons, and have ordered severall more to bee secured. The letters are just now arrived which bring us the newes of your Majesties great deliverance, and wee cannot bee thankfull enough for itt ; but forgive mee to say that if your Majestie will consider in what condition your death would have

[1] Carmarthen's letter to the Earl of Rutland on this subject is calendared in *Rutland MSS.*, ii. 129.

putt the Queen and this kingdome att this time I cannot thinke but your Majesties regard for such great concernes would prevaile with you not to hazard your person upon such occasions as wee understand this to have been.

I hope your Majestie will forgive my great presumptions, since I can faithfully protest they proceed intirely from my infinite zeale for your service, being as I ought, Sir,

Your Majesties most dutifull and obedient subject
and servant,

Carmarthen, P.

[To the King] [1]

London, 7th July, 1690.

Sir,

I writt so att large to your Majestie yesterday that J ought not to trouble you so soone againe were itt not to congratulate your Majesties victory over your enemies att Drogheda, which I hope I need not go about to perswade your Majestie of my rejoyceing in as truly as any of your subjects. Itt is pitty that so much bravery and greatnesse as your Majestie shews in all kinds should meet with any such repulse as you have done att sea ; but I hope that may bee repaired if those will do theire dutys to whom itt belongs.

However, as the present case is, without your Majesties speedy returne (besides many inconveniencies here which would bee prevented by itt) I do to the utmost degree apprehend its being made impracticable in some litle time hence for you to returne this summer if you would, especially with any force, of which I thinke there is appearance enough that there will bee need here ; and yett how great soever that need bee, itt seemes unreasonable to desire troopes from you whilst your person is there. Your great Councill do generally hope that haveing lessened your enemies army you will send back some troops, the feares here being very great, especially whilst the French fleet are about the Downs, where itt is expected they will anchor this night. I will presume to trouble your Majestie no further,

[1] From the autograph letter in S.P. Dom., King William's Chest, 7, No. 84, summarised in *Cal. S.P. Dom.*, 1690-1, p. 53 ; *Dalrymple*, App., ii. 175.

but to beseech you to consider the importance of your returne whilst itt is in your power. I am with all duty and esteeme, Sir,
Your Majesties most faithfull and most obedient
subject and servant,
Carmarthen, P.

Since I had writt this letter, the Cabinett Councill being mett to consider about the fleet, and that debate giveing occasion to speake of the generall state of our affaires, itt was thought of absolute necessity by them to desire that some troopes might bee sent back out of Ireland imediately, and upon the whole itt was agreed unanimously that as far as itt could bee done with good manners your Majestie should bee presst to returne with all imaginable speed, all agreeing that itt would otherwise bee impracticable in a litle time longer, and very unsafe both to your Majesties person and the nation if you did not comply with our desires. Your Majestie will accordingly receive our humble request by my Lord Nottingham,[1] with the state of our condition and motives for our request, which I hope will prevaile with you. Your Majestie will also find that in hopes of your Majesties being of our opinion in this matter wee have ordered the squadron under Shovell to a station where hee should not bee, but that wee take itt to bee of the first importance to secure your Majesties passage to us. Wee have sworne one another to secresy in this matter, and the Admiralty thinkes wee have ordered Shovels squadron only to prevent the designe of the twenty-eight Brest ships burning our transport vessells. Your Majestie will bee pleased to send us the most speedy answer to this that is possible, and to keepe itt private as long as may bee.

[To the King] [2]

Sir,   London, 9th July, 1690.

I did with great joy receive your Majesties of the 4th instant from Bellharry,[3] and do heartily pray God you may never have occasion to write but of your successes. I have

---

[1] The letter referred to, signed by Carmarthen, Devonshire, Dorset, Nottingham, Monmouth and Marlborough, is summarised in *Finch MSS.*, ii. 347-8.

[2] From the autograph letter in S.P. Dom., King William's Chest, 7, No. 88, summarised in *Cal. S.P. Dom.*, 1690-1, p. 57.

[3] This letter has not been found.

nothing to adde to my last, but that the want of small armes everywhere is so very great that wee shall bee as much exposed by that want as any other, unlesse itt can bee some way supplied. I should hope that with the armes you have gott from the enemy and the 10,000 spare armes you carried, which came from Leige, your Majestie might now bee able to spare some of them, for I do assure your Majestie from Sir Henry Goodrick that there are not an hundred musketts more in the Tower, nor to bee gott in any reasonable time.

My Lord Torrington is expected here from the fleet this night, which is now att the buoy in the Nore ; and the French fleet sayld yesterday from our coast towards theire owne, towards Haver de Grace, and on Monday fifteen gallies passt neare the island of Guernsey, standing eastwards, which points also towards Havre de Grace.

I cannot forbeare by every opportunity to bee very importunate in my humble desires to have your Majestie returne to us with all speed, and I hope your haveing seene by a letter under the late Queens hand theire intentions to send vessells into the Irish seas will have made your Majestie already sensible with what speed itt will bee necessary to transport forces hither before itt bee rendred impracticable. I am most dutifully

> Your Majesties faithfull and most obedient subject
> and servant,
>
> Carmarthen, P.

I would not send your Majestie such blotted letters but that I have not time to make coppys of them.[1]

[To the King] [2]

Sir,   London, 13th July, [16]90.

I know your time is too pretious to bee troubled unnecessarily, and therefore I had said nothing now but that I

---

[1] It is obvious from the letters themselves that Carmarthen at this time was sending out the first draft of his letters instead of following his usual practice of making a fair copy for dispatch and keeping the draft for reference. *Cf.* Nottingham's statement in his letter to Southwell of July 8 (*Finch MSS.*, i. 350) that he had been ' scarce ever in bed till three or four o'clock in the morning.'

[2] From the autograph letter in S.P. Dom., King William's Chest, 7, No. 95, summarised in *Cal. S.P. Dom.*, 1690-1, p. 64.

perceive, by your letter to the Queene this day,[1] your Majestie
does not thinke your returne yett necessary, because you do not
thinke there will bee any considerable landing in England. I
confesse I cannot but differ from your Majestie in that opinion,
first because severall letters as well as discourses have mentioned
that to bee theire intentions in case they had successe with
theire fleet ; secondly because they would not have made such
an expencefull sea preparation only for the advantage of a sea
victory which they know wee can repaire in another yeare, if
they should not imediately pursue theire blow further ; and
lastly because they must bee assured that if they do not this
yeare give you such a diversion you will bee att leisure from
Ireland the next yeare to give them considerable disturbance.
Besides in my opinion they may have time for such an attempt
yett for a month, because I neither thinke that diligence used
here which should bee for dispatch of the English ships, and if
there was, yett I feare the Dutch will bee more then a month in
theire preparations of what ships are repaireable, and I do not
expect any more from them in time for this yeares service.

Your Majestie will receive from the Admiralty the orders sent
to Shovell, and from my Lord Nottingham the resolutions of
the States upon my Lord Dursleys memoriall concerning the
fleet ; so that I shall only humbly subscribe myselfe, Sir,

Your Majesties most dutifull and faithfull subject
and servant,

Carmarthen, P.

[To the King] [2]

London, 15th July, 1690.

Sir,

Wee are very unfortunate in haveing but ill intelligence
of our enemies designs on the other side of the water ; but by all
wee can gett, and by what wee see by our advice boates of a
great number of transport vessells which lie ready all along
theire coast, wee have all the reason in the world to beleeve there
is a landing intended with a strong force, and that very speedily

---

[1] This letter has not been found.

[2] From the autograph letter in S.P. Dom., King William's Chest, 7, No. 96
summarised in *Cal. S.P. Dom.*, 1690-1, p. 65.

To prevent which wee are doing all wee can with the assistance of the Citty, which seemes very well disposed to helpe with men ; but our want of armes is so great that wee must bee destroy'd through that defect alone, allthough all other things were supplied to us, if any such force should land as is pretended to bee designed out of Monsieur d'Humiers army, and from Dunkirk, towards which place they have detached a part of theire fleet. I beg your Majestie will not despise this alarme, but that both troops and spare armes may bee sent over with all speed ; and I hope your Majestie will bee pleased to returne yourselfe with them, or if you will not bee prevailed with to do so, your Majestie must necessarily send somebody more able then our present generall to conduct our military affaires.[1]

The Citty has besides theire militia agreed to raise 6,000 auxiliaries, 400 horse, and 1,000 dragoons, and to pay the said horse and dragoons, which the Queene has directed to bee comanded by my Lord Winchester for the horse and my son for the dragoons ; but they expect the auxiliaries to bee armed by your Majestie, which is utterly impossible. The militias of all England are ordered to bee in armes, and there will bee about 2,000 of that horse so quartered as may bee drawne together in a litle time. Orders are also given out for secureing of horses as much as may bee through all counties, so that all is done that lies in our power ; but with all this our force will bee very inconsiderable against any old troops.

Wee had the good newes this day of Killigrews being arrived att Plymouth with his squadron, and I hope that in three weekes (but not sooner) wee may bee in a condition to attempt the joyning of our disperst ships ; and betwixt this time and that must bee theire attempt if they make any, which everybody beleeves they will.

I am not willing to lay blame anywhere, but itt is fitt for your Majestie to know that to adde to our want of armes they have left behind them betwixt 3 and 4,000 new armes which belong to the five regiments which came last from Flanders, and theire old armes are not halfe of them serviceable, nor have wee any armes for 5 or 600 men which belong to the yard att Portsmouth. Your Majestie will by all this see our condition for war, and I

[1] The ' present generall ' was the Earl of Marlborough.

doubt not but will give your orders accordingly ; and I confesse that I hope but litle from the Citty succors. Monsieur Evertse is just now arrived here, by whom I find itt will bee three weeks att least before the Dutch squadron can bee ready, and then there will bee twelve of them, whereof six above 60 guns. I am with all duty

Your Majesties most obedient servant,

Carmarthen, P.

[To the King] [1]

Sir,
London, 16th July, 1690.

I have nothing to trouble your Majestie withall, but that I would not omitt any opportunity of paying my duty. Only Sir Robert Holmes pretends to have certaine intelligence that the French intend to attempt the Isle of Wight, and I have alwaies delivered itt as my opinion that theire attempt will bee upon Portsmouth. Something of this kind is apprehended by them in those parts this day, from whence wee have had letters of the French fleet appeareing in sight of the Isle of Wight, and standing under an easy sayle towards theire coast. Wee have already sent what wee dare spare that way, and have ordered both horse and foot of the neighbouring militia thither.

I hope your Majestie will spare us some armes with speed, and I have said so much already about men with them that I shall not presume to say any more upon that subject. I am with all duty, Sir,

Your Majesties most obedient and most faithfull
subject and servant,

Carmarthen, P.

[To the King] [2]

Sir,
London, 2nd August, 1690.

I had the honour of your Majesties of the 29th July this day,[3] and must confesse I am not sorry to heare of your

[1] From the autograph letter in S.P. Dom., King William's Chest, 7, No. 100, summarised in *Cal. S.P. Dom.*, 1690-1, p. 68.

[2] From the autograph letter in S.P. Dom., King William's Chest, 7, No. 124, summarised in *Cal. S.P. Dom.*, 1690-1, p. 86.

[3] This letter has not been found.

Majesties stay a while longer in Ireland, especially since you give us hopes of seeing your Majestie amongst us againe in so short a time as you mention. I hope wee shall preserve ourselves in safety in the meane time, and I should not have the least doubt of itt if those who pretend to bee your freinds could but agree amongst themselves against the comon enemy ; but as faction is very naturall amongst us, so itt is as artificially and industriously improved as is possible, and alwaies by the same hands.

I find your Majestie has been pleased to name Mr. Killigrew to bee the third man to command the fleet, and hee is undoubtedly very fitt for itt ; but there happens to fall out two difficulties in that nomination—first a dispute about prœcedence, how they shall bee ranked in the commission, and secondly itt happens that about three daies ago itt was moved by the Duke of Bolton, my Lord Devonshire and others in the great Councill that hee should bee questioned for his ill conduct in the Streights, and for not returning sooner into England ; and the marchants do make so great a clamour against him in the Citty as hath given a pretence for theire motion. But upon a due examination of his case itt appeares not only by his owne relation but by his Journalls that the complaint against him is without any just cause. However justice does not alwaies passe amongst us for reason, and itt will take some time to satisfy men who have taken up so prejudic't an opinion against him, and for the more speedy takeing off of that prejudice his Journalls are ordered to bee brought to the great Councill on Monday next.

If this point should bee then setled, yett I feare the first point of prœcedence will make Sir Richard Haddocks going impracticable, for although hee bee a man who has shew'd by his former submissions to bee a captaine, first to my Lord Sandwich and then to Prince Ruperts ship (although hee was both times offered a Flag), that hee would rather do the Crowne service (as they desired) then insist upon his right, yett hee being then entred into Flags pay to preserve his right, and haveing alwaies continued so, and being comanded ever since to do service on shore as a Commissioner of the Navy, whilst all the present Flags in the fleet have been advanc't from being but leiutenants of ships, hee hopes itt will not now bee thought reasonable to have all those Flags putt before him, which must either bee a right to them all or to none. And hee lookes upon itt as such an insupportable diminution of him as would make him bee despised if hee should submitt to itt, and hee has therefore this day desired my Lord Nottingham and mee to make his humble excuses to your Majestie and the Queene, and to beg that itt may not bee expected from him to give the procedence to either of them. And hee does solemnely protest that hee beleeves nothing can qualify the present divisions amongst the comanders in the fleet but one of the three to bee a man of greater quality then any of those now named, and thinkes itt the only possible expedient to make the fleet serviceable att this time.

I am sorry I am not capable of doing your Majestie the service I desire in that matter, although I am the better contented with your Majesties spareing mee because I am now almost confident that the disagreements about commands, the backwardnesse of the Dutch ships, and the sicklinesse of the seamen (which happens to bee very much) will make the season to bee so far spent before the fleet bee in a condition to fight that there will then bee but litle time longer for the great ships to stay out, nor for the French to stay in these seas, and consequently no probability of any more action att sea this yeare, insomuch that I feare the businesse will bee more how to keepe peace amongst your owne captaines then how to bring them to fight with your enemies. As the case stands I wish your Majestie would lay your comands upon Mr. Russell to take the management of the fleet upon himselfe, by which att least the present divisions might bee allay'd ; or that otherwise my Lord Pembrok might do you that service in commission with Mr. Killigrew and Sir John Ashby, which I am confident hee would not refuse if your Majestie shall desire itt ; and as these matters appeare to mee I confesse I see no other expedient but one of these.

I shall long to heare of your Majesties successe against Lymerick, the whole fate of Ireland, I thinke, depending upon itt, and your affaires here being likely to bee much the more easy or harder according to your successe there. If I were able to contribute to itt any other way then by my prayers, I am sure nothing in my power should bee wanting, being with as much zeale as duty, Sir,

Your Majesties most obedient and faithfull subject
and servant,

Carmarthen, P.

[To the King] [1]

London, 12th August, 1690.

Sir,

I was not so well as to bee able to write to your Majestie by the last expresse, nor had I then anything to have writt but what was sent by my Lord Nottingham. The French are gone from our coast, and the militias are everywhere dismisst, and I beleeve itt will bee ordered to-morrow in Councill that all the prisoners shall bee bayled, unlesse such against whom any materiall evidence can bee produced.

The Queene received a letter from your Majestie last night, and tells us shee hopes you will bee speedily att Dublin, by which I give myselfe the satisfaction to beleeve that your Majestie expects Lymerick to give you very litle interruption, the French being gone to Galloway, which I suppose they designe rather for a place of embarcation then of defence.

Your Majesties fleet is most of itt sayled to the Downes, where all the ships from Portsmouth are com'd to them except the *Ossory*, which will bee also there in three daies. None of the ships from Holland are yett arrived, but are expected with this wind, which is very faire for them ; nor are those they have in this river yett ready, by reason of Monsieur Evertse his delay before hee would make use of any materialls from your Majesties yards. I confesse I do not looke for much use of them in the Channell this yeare ; but I am in some paine for the marchant ships in the Streights, whither I expect to heare the French will have sent a squadron of theires, and if wee find no probability of theire appeareing againe att sea with theire fleet this summer itt would bee a great saveing of money to lay up your first rates and some of your seconds as soone as might bee, and to provide

---

[1] From the autograph letter in S.P. Dom., King William's Chest, 7, No. 139, summarised in *Cal. S.P. Dom.*, 1690-1, p. 95 ; *Dalrymple*, App., ii. 110.

early for a good winter guard ; but I hope to see your Majestie here time enough to settle that matter.

I suppose your Majestie is informed by others what scruples some of the Admiralty raise upon all occasions, and that as some of them have refused to signe the commission for the present admiralls (though contrary to your expresse orders to have itt done), so they now raise numbers of doubts about formeing a commission for triall of my Lord Torrington, and are designeing to bring that matter into a Parliament, and to bee tried there by a faction, if they can incompasse theire designes in that as they hope to do in other things.

I know not whither the Queene does give your Majestie any account of my Lord Anendales confession to her this day[1] concerning the transactions which have been since December last betwixt the late King and Sir James Montgomery, my Lord Ross, and himselfe. Hee saies hee shall recollect more then hee has yett said ; but hee does acknowlege theire haveing treated with the late King and received comissions from him, and that one Sir Robert Clark, Captain Williamson, Nevile Paine, and one Sympson have been theire cheife agents and messingers ; that Ferguson was privy to itt, and others in England whom hee does not know ; that they did first designe to have carried itt on in Scotland by a Parliament, but finding that to faile theire businesse was then to interrupt the progresse of all affaires in Parliament. Hee saies Sir James Montgomery is now in towne, notwithstanding his haveing newly promised the Commissioner in Scotland that hee would come directly to the Queene, insomuch that the Commissioner writt but ten daies ago to the Queene that hee had promised Sir James hee should bee safe from any restraint, and besought the Queene that his promise might bee kept with him. But itt now appeares that hee hath only cheated the Commissioner, thereby to secure himselfe from being taken whilst hee negotiates with his confederates here, who have made some of themselves appeare by refuseing to signe my Lord Ross his commitment.

[1] A copy of this confession in Carmarthen's own handwriting is S.P. Dom., William and Mary, 3, No. 25. It is fully summarised in *Cal. S.P. Dom.*, 1690-1, pp. 92-4.

I feare your Majestie will find a great many such freinds amongst us, and I beleeve you have not found the difficulties so great in the conquest of your adversaries abroad as you will do how to deale with a people att home who are as fearefull of your being too prosperous as any of your enemies can bee, and who have laid as many stratagems in your way as they can to prevent itt. And if by your prudent conduct your Majestie can surmount theire designes I shall not doubt of your being as great a king, and wee as happy subjects, as I wish both, and will contribute towards, as far as can bee in my small power.

I have the good fortune to have a grandson borne to my family, who I shall never desire may inheritt my fortune if hee does not also inheritt my zeale to the service of your Majestie and your posterity ; and that hee may have the greater obligation to do so I beg your Majestie will bee pleased to afford him the honour of your name, and of being his godfather by a deputy. I hope your Majestie will pardon this presumption, being from one who is resolved to make all the returne that is possible to a king, by being intirely and without reserve, Sir,

Your Majesties most dutifull and most obedient
subject and servant,

Carmarthen, P.

If wee receive no comands to the contrary itt is intended on Monday next to prorogue the Parliament to the 8th of September, which is three weeks further.

[To the King] [1]

London, 19th August, 1690.

Sir,

I thanke God all things are so quiett here that I have nothing to trouble your Majestie withall but to congratulate your happy progresse, which the letters of the 10th bring us an account of this day. I am glad your Majestie has been pleas'd to delay your returne to this time, of which I hope you will find the good effects here as well as in Ireland, unlesse wee can bee brazen faced in our ingratitude, which I hope the very mobile

[1] From the autograph letter in S.P. Dom., King William's Chest, 7, No. 150, summarised in *Cal. S.P. Dom.*, 1690-1, p. 99 ; *Dalrymple*, App., ii. 176.

will not suffer us to bee, whatever our naturall inclinations might otherwise dispose us to.

Wee have ordered an additionall provision to bee made and sent both from Chester and Bristoll, of ten daies provisions for the army from each place, for feare of any want, which is the only thing I can now apprehend in Ireland ; for wee dare not depend upon the Plymouth provisions comeing in time, being liable to so many accidents to prevent itt. And amongst the many other miscarriages of the Board of Admiralty one hath been the not sending those provision ships from Plymouth to Ireland with Sir Cloudsley Shovell, wee haveing given them orders for itt in due time, and was omitted through perfect neglect.

Itt is pitty to take up any of your Majesties time impertinently, and therefore with my prayers for your prosperity I beg to bee estimed, as I most truly am, Sir,

> Your Majesties most dutifull and intirely devoted
> subject and servant,
>
> Carmarthen, P.

[To the King] [1]

London, 29 August, 1690.

Sir,

This expresse is occasioned by the French letters which were taken and are sent to your Majestie by my Lord Nottingham.[2] The intelligence which those give us, together with the bad weather wee have had for four or five daies past, has made us adventure to stay all the first and second rate ships from going with my Lord Marleborough, not doubting but hee will have ships enough and too many for that service.

I must make great excuses to your Majestie for divers things I writt in my last, and indeed I dare hardly write anything of which I am not certaine myselfe. I have seene letters this day from Sir Clowdsley Shovell, by which I perceive hee was not gone from Plymouth the 27th, and therefore am afraid those provision ships were then there. This hath hapned by the

---

[1] From the autograph letter in S.P. Dom., King William's Chest, 7, No. 167, summarised in *Cal. S.P. Dom.*, 1690-1, p. 108.

[2] *Cf. Finch MSS.*, ii. 400-4, 436.

Admiraltys information of the 22th, that some of those ships which were to joyne Shovells squadron were sayled out of the Downes towards him, which did not go out of the Downes in five daies after ; so that I feare those provisions will not bee with your Majestie so soone as I hoped, though I beleeve they are sayled by this time.

I writt also according to my Lord Marleboroughs information that his men would bee on board the ships att Spithead on Tuesday and Wednesday last ; but by his letter this day I perceive they have not yett begun to ship them, and that hee finds the regiments from Ireland very weake, insomuch that hee writt to have a batallion of the guards from hence, and Beaumonts regiment to come hither to recruite, which wee have rather chosen to bee done by takeing what hee shall need from the garrison att Portsmouth, where there can bee no present danger.

The Dutch ships have appeared very backward in all places, and those five which were with Killigrew did want victualls, so that they have not joyn'd the fleet ; nor will ten which are with Calemberg bee ready for this expedition.

I long to heare of your Majesties progresse att Lymerick. So very much does depend upon itt, and your Majestie is wanted for so many things here, although (thanks bee to God) itt is more for the takeing of timely measures forward then that there is either any present danger or want but that of money.

Mr. Paston, to whom your Majestie has formerly been willing to shew kindnesse, has putt himselfe to some expence in your service since you left England, and begs your favour to succeed one Car who is dead and was Marshall in the Leeward Islands. Hee prevailed with mee to give your Majestie this trouble about itt, which I hope you will forgive, Sir,

Your Majesties most dutifull subject and servant,

Carmarthen, P.

[To the King] [1]

Sir,

London, 23 January, 1690/1.

Since your Majesties departure I have had my health so ill that I have been able to waite upon the Queene but once, and

---

[1] From the autograph letter in S.P. Dom., King William's Chest, 8, No. 77, summarised in *Cal. S.P. Dom.*, 1690-1, p. 229.

can therefore say litle of any affaires but as your Majestie left them. My Lord Sydney saies hee gives your Majestie an account of the transactions about my Lord Preston and Mr. Ashton, and sends you my Lord Prestons paper, which has been given since his condemnation. Tis hard to say whither in that hee does wilfully conceale anything, or whither his memory bee deficient ; butt tis certaine that his owne notes (of which hee has desired a coppy, which is not yett sent him) must refresh his memory in many particulars which are not yett in his paper (viz., that Seymour said King James is betray'd by J[ames] Porter, &c.), of which his lordship will bee reminded ; and the Queene has thought fitt to lett him bee reprieved for three weekes, on purpose that hee may both have time to recollect himselfe, and that your Majesties pleasure may bee fully knowne concerning him when you have seene all that is to bee hoped for from him. And in the meane time her Majestie has not thought fitt to defer Mr. Ashtons execution beyond Monday or Wednesday next.

I have long seene by private letters that the affaires of Ireland have been thought to bee in a deplorable condition ; but I never had so ill an apprehension of them till I saw the letter from the Justices of the 16th instant (a coppy whereof my Lord Sydney sends your Majestie),[1] which (together with the Protestants being reduced in some places to take shelter amongst the Reparees for subsistance) must needs bespeake the most dangerous circumstances a nation can fall under. And unlesse the Treasury can provide certaine payments for the army there, according to the late regulations and abatements, I expect all your affaires there to recoyle instead of makeing any advances the next summer ; nor (whatever your Majestie may bee made beleeve) will you gett halfe the recruites necessary without a greater allowance for levy money then 20s. a man. But all this depending upon your Treasury, and I being wholly ignorant of the methods taken there, I can only foretell the consequences if the provisions bee not made in due time to prevent them.

I am sorry wee have heard nothing yett of your Majesties safe arrivall in Holland, only I satisfy myselfe that your Majestie has mett with no ill adventure, because ill newes would not have

---

[1] This letter, from the Lords Justices to Sidney, is summarised in *Cal. S.P. Dom.*, 1690-1, pp. 226-7.

failed to have made more hast. I hope your Majestie whilst you are on that side the water will provide for some better intelligence from the French coast then wee have had hitherto, and particularly from Brest and St. Malo's and from Dunkirk. And that your conference with your Allies may prove to your satisfaction is the zealous prayer of, Sir,

Your Majesties most dutifull subject and servant,

Carmarthen, P.

Pray, Sir, bee pleased to send Mr. Jepson your order about Mr. Pastons 200 l.

[To the King] [1]

London, 3rd February, 1690/1.

Sir,

I had the honour this day to receive your Majesties comands by your letter of the 30th January,[2] but I should bee very sorry that such important affaires as your Majestie hath upon your hands att this time, in this place, should bee expected to lie upon mee any more then upon the rest of my associates. Only I could wish that some of them would shew a litle more warmth in your service by theire diligence, which my Lord Sydney can tell you is not done ; for when my health does not permitt my attendance (which for a weeke past itt has nott) I can gett no Comittee for Irish Affaires to meete, and this day (which is the second time I have been able to go myselfe) I had much adoe to gett a comittee, whereas the backwardnesse of all things relateing to Ireland requires a dayly attendance.

Butt what is yett worse is the ill state of the Treasury, as my Lord Godolphin represents itt to mee,[3] insomuch that hee seemes to despond of makeing the necessary payments to the army att due times, unlesse your Majestie can procure from the States the loane of the 200,000 l. (which is yett unpaid) to bee continued in course upon the same fund next after the said 200,000 l., which I should hope they would not refuse, because they would receive

[1] From the autograph letter in S.P. Dom., King William's Chest, 8, No. 85, summarised in *Cal. S.P. Dom.*, 1690-1, p. 243 ; *Dalrymple*, App., ii. 184.

[2] This letter has not been found.

[3] *Cf.* Godolphin's letter to the King, dated February 2, in *Cal. S.P. Dom.*, 1690-1, p. 241.

8 per cent. for that summe, which they can borrow for the same time att a much lower interest. And therefore since the proposall hath no unkindnesse in itt, butt rather an advantage to them, I hope your Majestie will thinke fitt to use your interest in a matter of such concerne to yourselfe.

My Lord Preston hath since his last paper made some addition to his confession, though not very considerable, viz. : That Sir Edward Seymour told him that King James was betray'd by James Porter, and that Lord Nottingham had said a peace would bee made with France exclusive of King James. That Lord Weymouth was with him, together with Sir Edward Seymour, and that both of them knew of his going into France. That Lord Annendale and Sir James Montgomery had been att his house in theire way to Scotland, where they spoke very discontentedly against your government. That hee mett Nevile Paine in his way to Scotland, who told him hee had comissions for divers persons in that kingdome from King James. The said Paine told him that Ferguson had his pardon, and managed things for them att London, and that Wildman was a well-wisher to theire cause. That Duke Hamilton had his pardon, and Lord Argyle was theire freind, and I thinke said hee had his pardon, but I am not certaine, haveing not yett seene his last confession in writing.

This being what my Lord has said already, and that perhaps hee may yett recollect more, I submitt to your Majestie whither itt may not bee more for your service to continue him (as hee now is) till further order, without any repreive, till the meeting of a Parliament, where his declaration of these matters will breake the teeth not only of Sir Edward Seymour, but of that whole party, from doing your businesse any harme in Parliament. Itt will also bee an ingredient to putt a Parliament into an humor for your service. Itt will also shew the designes intended in Scotland, and Paines negotiations there, and you may reserve what part of that matter you shall thinke fitt. Hee is also the only witnesse both against my Lord Clarendon, the Bishop of Ely, and Pen, whereas by his execution you disappointe all these ends ; and in my opinion itt will not bee to your Majesties disadvantage if you should thinke fitt to shew your clemency rather then draw any more blood on this occasion.

I hope your Majestie will speedily resolve who shall comand your army in Ireland the next summer, and if Lieutenant-Generall Ginkle shall bee thought fitt for itt I beleeve Mackay might bee very usefull to comand under him ; and in that case itt would much expedite the service if hee were sent hither to take care of all things before his going thither.   My zeale prompts mee to say more then I ought on this subject, but proceeding from that error, I hope your Majestie will forgive, Sir,

Your Majesties most dutifull subject and servant,

Carmarthen, P.

[To the King] [1]

10th February, 1690/1.

Sir,

As I thinke itt of greatest concerne for your service to have the businesse of Ireland putt into a good condition, so wee apply ourselves all wee can to itt, butt wee find very litle effect of our paines ; for the want of Pereras being here (who wee have been told to bee comeing above sixteen daies) nothing is done about the waggons, and the fund for moneys upon the bread contract being not yett agreed, wee are not only without prospect how the future provisions will bee made, but wee are in dayly feare whither the army may not want in some places. I am also unable to make any conjecture about the recruites, for I suppose my Lord Marleborow has inform'd your Majestie that whereas you thought there would want 6,000, the officers demands are but 1,600, and yett itt is certaine they want above double that number, and there will now want more, since your letters this day have directed those regiments not to bee broke in Ireland which you intended.   And in short, the officers do as litle mind the getting of recruites here as they do how to governe them when they are in Ireland, and without some remedy att the head of your army there all things that relate to itt will bee but weakly performed.

Wee have a great desire to have a squadron in readinesse to intercept the French ships att Dunkirk from getting to joyne

---

[1] From the autograph letter in S.P. Dom., King William's Chest, 8, No. 89, summarised in *Cal. S.P. Dom.*, 1690-1, p. 251.

theire fleet att Brest, and if they are not in readinesse to gett out of Dunkirk the next spring tide (which will bee the 18th instant) wee doubt not but to bee ready for them before the next spring, which will bee the 4th of March. And in the meane time itt would bee of great use if wee could have advice from thence of the time of theire being ready, and of theire number, and force of each ship, which perhaps your Majestie may procure better then I find us provided for itt.

I am glad to heare your Majestie keeps your health, and for the preservation of itt you must bee as carefull to defend your-selfe against the strong batteries of those potent allies now with you as against any assaults of your Irish enemies. I hope your Majestie will find some meanes of giveing the French some con-siderable diversion by the way of Savoy, from whence (next to the absolute recovery of Ireland) I should hope for a successe more advantagious to your affaires in England then any other would prove that is probably to bee hoped for. I am sorry I am able to contribute so litle to any as I find myselfe to bee ; but nobody can bee with more zeale, Sir,

Your Majesties most dutifull subject and servant,

Carmarthen, P.

[To the King] [1]

13 February, 1690/1.

Sir,

I have so very litle to say, that I should not have troubled your Majestie this post were itt not that the Queene told mee this day that the Commissioners of the Treasury have desired of her Majestie not [to] signe my warrant for my pension upon the Post Office till shee knows your further pleasure, and that shee had consented to the request, but would write to your Majestie this night about itt. I hope I shall not need to say anything to your Majestie concerning itt, your pleasure haveing been so fully declared already, and I am sure I need not tell your Majestie how few my freinds are in the Treasury, insomuch that I doubt not but the best of theire endeavours will bee used to prevent your Majesties favour.

[1] From the autograph letter in S.P. Dom., King William's Chest, 8, No. 91, summarised in *Cal. S.P. Dom.*, 1690-1, p. 259.

Since your Majestie continues your resolution to breake Colonel Russells regiment, I hope you will thinke of disposeing of him in some kind that may make him easy, because (although I know nothing against his honesty), yett being as most say a good officer, itt would bee inconvenient to have him under a temptation of being against you in a country which hee knows so well as hee does Ireland.

I send your Majestie inclosed an account which is just now arrived from the Isle of Wight and I beleeve is true, and I wish that all newes that is so may bee to your advantage. I am, Sir,

Your Majesties most dutifull and faithfull subject
and servant,
Carmarthen, P.

[To the King] [1]

London, 20 February, 1690/1.
Sir,

I can say nothing of matters here but what your Majestie is informed of att large by my Lord Sydney ; but your affaires in Ireland do seeme to mee to bee in so ill a posture, and so likely to bee worse rather then better (unlesse some other course bee taken then is now), and itt is so certaine that your businesse in the next Parliament will go better or worse according to your successe the next summer there, that I presume to give your Majestie my opinion of the necessity of your sending somebody thither as Lord Lieutenant, with the accustomed powers of that place, whose quality as well as authority may give a countenance to his actings, and may make him bee more willingly obey'd then these Lords Justices are or will bee. I confesse the cure is difficult, because your Majestie has no English subject who is fitly qualified for the employment, and yett you can imploy no other. But I do truly beleeve your affaires would do better in an indifferent hand of such quality, assisted with good councellors and some good military assistants

---

[1] From the autograph letter in S.P. Dom., King William's Chest, 8, No. 97, summarised in *Cal. S.P. Dom.*, 1690-1, p. 270 ; *Dalrymple*, App., ii. 178.

(although those were forreigners), then they can do by any comission of Justices as the present state of things are in that kingdome.

Now as I am of this opinion, so I thinke my Lord Shrewsbury, my Lord Chesterfeild, my Lord Pembrok, my Lord Moulgrave, or my Lord Godolphin are capable of doing your Majestie this service, if your Majestie should approve any of them and that they would undertake itt. Nay, so absolutely necessary I thinke itt is that something of this kind should bee done, that rather then itt should not I do offer myselfe to your Majestie for that service, although I am lesse fitt then any of those I have named. Your Majestie will easily beleeve that, my circumstances considered, I should not have named myselfe, but that I would rather perish in endeavouring to save this government then live to perish with itt, which (as infirme as I am) I may probably do if Ireland should cost another yeares war ; and another reason why I offer myselfe is because I thinke itt yett to bee prevented by an industrious care and such provision made for itt as is within your Majesties power. What would certainely prevent this danger is your Majesties going thither in person, but I feare your other affaires (being wanted everywhere) will not permitt you to do itt this yeare, and no more time must bee lost (the yeare being so far advanc't) in fixing your resolutions about this matter. But if your Majestie should approve of this method, your orders must bee imediately sent to whoever you shall imploy in that service.

I beseech your Majestie to take this affaire of Ireland throughly into your consideration, being what the whole prosperity of your government depends upon in these kingdomes. And forgive mee for telling your Majestie so bold a truth as itt is, that mens affections to the government do apparently decrease amongst all parties, and nothing but a more vigorous conduct of affaires can retreive itt, the effects of which must appeare this next summer either att sea or in Ireland or both ; and a miscarriage in either will bee probably fatall to the cheife comanders (how innocent soever they bee) and deeply prejudiciall to your Majestie.

Although I have writt all this to your Majestie as my owne opinion, I find itt to bee also the opinion of all the thinkeing men that I converse with, and itt is such a dayly discourse (even amongst us who are of the Comittee for Irish Affaires) how impossible itt is for things to succeed in Ireland under the present conduct of them, that I beleeve itt to bee the reason why wee can so seldome gett a number sufficient to make a Comittee, of which my Lord Sydney and I are alwaies two, and comonly Sir Henry Goodrick the third ; but (which is yett worse) if any others do chance to come, they seeme to act like pyoneers for pay rather then by inclination.

If your Majestie shall thinke all this impertinent, I hope you will take no notice itt was ever writt, but forgive, Sir,

> Your Majesties most dutifull and faithfull subject
> and servant,
>
> > > Carmarthen, P.

[To the King] [1]

27 February, 1690/1.

Sir,

I am glad I have but litle to trouble your Majestie withall from hence, all things going on very well as to the fleet, which is our principall concerne. The Citty loane also of 200,000 l. (which wee were sent to borrow) is in a good forwardnesse, notwithstanding the discouragement given them by Mr. Hampden in Parliament, who there said that those had lent your Majestie least who had lent you most upon former loanes. Butt the Comon Councill did only take notice of itt with a declaration that itt should not hinder this loane, and that they would not for the future bee obliged to pay theire money to the Chamberlaine of the Citty, but that everyone would lend in what manner they pleased, and did desire to have a list out of the Chamberlaines books who had been the former lenders upon each fund, and what sumes every man had lent ; to which my Lord Maior gave them no answer.

As to the affaires of Ireland, your Majestie will have received a large pacquett by the last post from the Lords Justices and

---

[1] From the autograph letter in S.P. Dom., King William's Chest, 8, No. 101, summarised in *Cal. S.P. Dom.*, 1690-1, p. 281 ; *Dalrymple*, App., ii. 180, 191.

Leiutenant-Generall Ginckle, and wee are doing all wee can to send over oates and other provisions ; but all creditt being lost, and nothing to bee bought but with ready money, the want of that delays things very much. And I find that your Majesties clothing of the army yourselfe will turne but to an ill account to your Majestie as well as to the souldiers, both being much abused as itt is now done.

I hope your Majestie has true informations of things from Scotland, and if you have I doubt not but you will give speedy directions to putt a stop to the giddy proceedings of the Commissioners of the Assembly against all the Episcopall clergy of Scotland att one blow, who are to bee turn'd out of dores with theire familys, unlesse they will renounce prelacy, to which they are sworne ; so that they are not to keepe theire liveings unlesse they will preserve them by perjury. I have given my Lord Sydney a memoriall which I have received from two Scots ministers who were sent to your Majestie by a great number of the Episcopall clergy, but they came here after your departure, by which your Majestie will see that the Commissioners were to begin theire progresse the first of March, guarded with two troops of horse. But they cannot bee gone so far in theire work before your Majesties orders may reach them, but that if you please they may bee ordered not to proceed further in that matter till your Majesties pleasure bee knowne. And truly I beleeve that the speedy doing of this may bee of no lesse consequence then the preventing a rebellion, and att a time when nothing but the folly of clergymen would have putt itt to a venture.

I wish the States fleet may bee in as good a readinesse as your Majesties, and that they would send some of theire lighter ships into the Downes to waite for the Dunkirk squadron, of which wee do not heare the least intelligence ; and I wish that your Majestie would order 20,000 armes to bee bought and sent over, which is the fewest you will need besides what can bee made in England. I am with all duty, Sir,

Your Majesties most obedient and most faithfull
subject and servant,

Carmarthen, P.

[To the King] [1]

London, 13 March, [16]90/1.

Sir,

I would not have troubled your Majestie now but to have acknowleged the honour I received by your Majesties of the 3rd instant,[2] and I do assure your Majestie that whilst I have the happinesse to bee imploy'd in your service I have resolved to lett nothing rebute mee from performeing itt in the best manner I am able.

I doubt not but the fleet will bee in a very good condition as to men as well as all other things, and as early as is necessary, but wee want ships of lesser size to provide for all the stations which would bee convenient. I feare wee shall also bee wanting of such a number of small armes as is necessary to supply both the army and militias of Ireland, and to have any left here ; but I hope your Majestie gives order to buy what can bee gott on that side of the water, and for all other things relateing to Ireland wee are not failing to do as much as the money will permitt. But Perera being so lately com'd hither, and insisting upon such high tearmes about the bread waggons, wee have thought best to defer any conclusion with him for so short a time as wee hope itt will bee before wee have the happinesse of seeing your Majestie.

One of your judges called Ventrice is said to bee in danger of dying, and if hee dies I would humbly presume to recomend to your Majestie one Mr. Ettrick to bee a Baron of the Exchequer. Hee is a very able lawyer, and long practised in that court ; hee is a Parliament man, and has constantly served you well there ; and as I have not yett recomended any to your service that were not fitt for theire places, so I assure your Majestie this gentleman is for what I request on his behalfe. I am, Sir,

Your Majesties most dutifull subject and servant,

Carmarthen, P.

---

[1] From the autograph letter in S.P. Dom., King William's Chest, 8, No. 118, summarised in *Cal. S.P. Dom.*, 1695, p. 168.

[2] This letter has not been found.

[To the King] [1]

London, 22 May, 1691.

Sir,

I am not willing to trouble your Majestie with writing when I have nothing but to repeate what you receive from other hands, especially being unwilling to intertaine you with complaints of the slack and cold attendance of your service in towne, and the difficulties of getting any orders observed abroad.

I doubt not but your Majestie is informed of the late going away of the ships which carried the armes and pontoons to Ireland, and the unwillingnesse there hath been to sayle with the whole fleet, which is not yett gone from the Downes, and which had been gone long since had those orders been followed which were given above three weeks ago, and which were approved by Mr. Russell after the losse of a journey hither, though disapproved by him when hee received them att the fleet. Wee have yett no intelligence of the French ships being arrived in Ireland, by which appeares almost a certainty of our haveing intercepted them, had the fleet then sayled, upon which a principall part of your successe there would have depended, and consequently of all that a Parliament would account a successe anywhere ; besides that itt would have sett your armes att liberty in due time for other services. But if yett they shall faile of those provisions they expect from France, itt is certaine that kingdome is in so ill a condition that itt must take what tearmes you will please to give them within six weekes from this time.

Secretary Staires will informe your Majestie of the different schœmes made here by the severall parties as to Scotland, about which I shall only presume to speake my opinion, that if there bee any speedy disturbance there no alteration ought yett to bee made, but if there bee none (which will appeare within one month) there should bee some alterations made by removes of some few, and an addition of some of a different opinion from most of those in present power, concerning whom (as to the persons fittest for such removes) Mr. Secretary will best informe

---

[1] From the autograph letter in S.P. Dom., King William's Chest, 9, No. 99, summarised in *Cal. S.P. Dom.*, 1690-1, p. 385 ; *Dalrymple*, App., ii. 182.

your Majestie, as also of what the Queene has thought fitt to do for prevention of any present disorders there.

Whilst your Majestie is contriveing schœmes how to save us, and exposeing your person for us, some are no lesse busy here in drawing theire schœmes to putt all things in disorder when a Parliament shall meet, and theire principall designes are to lessen your power and increase theire owne, insomuch that without such a successe as will bee valewed here itt is already apparent that our condition will bee very deplorable. But I hope the same providence which hath conducted your Majestie through so many great actions will help you to surmount all difficulties, and make you as happy and great as is most truly wish't by, Sir,

Your Majesties most dutifull subject and servant,

Carmarthen, P.

[To the King] [1]

London, 14 July, 1691.

Sir,

The account of the good successe att Athlone and the arrivall of the Smyrna fleet att Kingsale hath begott a very good humor amongst us for the present, and there is no doubt but itt will increase with the reduction of that kingdome in a litle time more.

I beleeve also there will bee no danger of any commotions in Scotland, unlesse they bee caused by the insolence of the clergy, and folly or knavery of some of your Councill there, who seeme both to make and allow of broad attacks upon your Majesties power, as they have done particularly in a matter relateing to the people of Aberdeen, wherein some of your Privy Councill have signed warrants for certaine suites to bee raised as well in the name of the Agent for the Kirk as in the name of your Majesties Advocate, which is not only a thing never done before to the councill of a king, but is with plaine intent to give the Kirk a joynt power with your Majestie in your owne courts, which they will not allow you in theires.

[1] From the autograph letter in S.P. Dom., King William's Chest, 9, No. 130, summarised in *Cal. S.P. Dom.*, 1690-1, p. 446.

There hath also been as strange a proceeding about the election of a Provost of Edenburgh, where contrary to all former methods of proceeding they have voted one Archibald More into that chaire, who was deeply charged in Sir James Montgomerys plott ; and itt will have divers ill consequences if itt bee not timely prevented. The particulars are too long to relate ; besides I doubt not but all these things are transmitted to your secretary, and your Majestie will see (when you are fully informed) the necessity of giveing your timely orders for the redresse of them.

I hope your Majestie will have your thoughts of what troops you will draw out of Ireland, and whither, because I cannot doubt but that very shortly 10,000 men will bee enough to bee left there ; and the transport ships must bee thought on accordingly, for itt will otherwise bee too late to gett anything of that kind done this sumer, and itt will bee hard to gett so great an army the next. I am glad to see so good a likelyhood of a peace with the Turk, and most things seeme to have so good an aspect, that if itt would please God to give your Majestie any good successe in Flanders, I should give myselfe hopes both of seeing your Majesties affaires in a good condition here, and the French King very willing to have a peace on reasonable tearmes. And I thinke so much of this depends upon your Majesties life that I hope God will preserve itt for the universall good of Christendome. I am with all duty, Sir,

Your Majesties most obedient and most faithfull
subject and servant,

Carmarthen, P.

[To the King] [1]

London, 18 July, 1691.

Sir,

  This is to wish your Majestie joy of the happy newes you will receive by this expresse,[2] and which I hope will give you liberty to make use of some of that army elswhere. The great

[1] From the autograph letter in S.P. Dom., King William's Chest, 9, No. 133, summarised in *Cal. S.P. Dom.*, 1690-1, p. 450.

[2] News of the battle of Aughrim, which was fought on July 12. *Cf.* Ginkel's dispatch to William in *Cal. S.P. Dom.*, 1690-1, pp. 444-5.

question will bee where they may bee most usefully imploy'd, and in that question itt must in my opinion bee as much considered what will please the humor of those who are to support the next yeares war as what might bee best in ittselfe, unlesse that best could appeare to bee so before the meeting of Parliament.

Your Majestie knows very well that a litle thing done upon France ittselfe will not only please better then a very great one done in Flanders, and might perhaps force the French to send some of theire troops out of Flanders, but the Parliament would certainely continue any support for that service, which I feare they will hardly do to maintaine them in Flanders, where they do already grumble att the charge. And although theire grumbling bee unreasonable, and perhaps the carriyng of troops into Flanders would in the end have better effects then in any other place, yett as to your Majestie and with regard to your affaires att home in order to further supplies I cannot but deliver my opinion, which I feare your Majestie will find to bee too well grounded.

As to what could bee done by a descent in France I am no competent judge, but by discourse with the Duke of Leinster and two or three French officers (besides what I have talked heretofore with Monsieur Ruvigny) all agree itt would bee done with greatest effect about the river of Burdeaux, to which the passage would bee best from Galloway, which in this discourse I must suppose to bee yours and your army now ready for shipping in those parts. But if itt were thought better to give a diversion to the French in Flanders, itt would then bee best done in Normandy by burning theire corne and laying wast a great part of that country, which the Duke of Leinster thinks to bee very feasible with 10,000 foot and 2,500 horse and dragoons, and for such an army there might bee a trayne of artillery and bread and transport ships enough had in time.

If your Majestie shall thinke of anything of this kind no time must bee lost, and itt ought to bee very secrett ; but if you will have any troops carried into Flanders I thinke itt would bee best to alarme them with an intention of landing in France, which they will have reason to beleeve true by the preparations which must bee made for sending them into Flanders.

I hope your Majestie will pardon these thoughts of mine, which proceed from sincere intentions for your service, being as I ought, Sir,

Your Majesties most dutifull and obedient subject
and servant,

Carmarthen, P.

I had forgott one argument for landing in France, which is the drawing theire fleet by that meanes to a battle.

[To the King] [1]

London, 28 August, 1691.

Sir,

I am sorry that your Majesties affaires in Ireland are not so far advanced as I was in hopes they would have been when I was so pressing to have had all things in a readinesse for a transportation of men from thence. But I thought the large-nesse of the conditions granted att Galloway would have invited them att Lymerick to have readily imbrac't the same, whereas on the contrary your Majestie will bee informed that by the foolish conduct of Colonel Michelburne before Slego hee hath incouraged that place to defend ittselfe, and O'Donnell to play one of his Irish tricks, instead of submitting as hee pretended.

Yesterday I received a letter of the 20th from Monsieur Ginckle [2] (then five miles from Lymerick), wherein hee desires mee to lay before the Queene the absolute necessity of a squadron of ships to guard the Shannon when the maine fleet goes away, without which hee thinkes hee cannot block the river ; and hee saies they are incouraged to persist in the defence of Lymerick by the assurances given them of new supplies of all kinds from France, and that they will have them in a very litle time. This matter of the squadron in the Shannon hath been under her Majesties consideration a good while, and shee hath heard both the Admiralty and sea officers of the Navy Board two or three times upon that subject, who are all possi-tive that that squadron must bee drawne from thence whenever

[1] From the autograph letter in S.P. Dom., King William's Chest, 9, No. 161, summarised in *Cal. S.P. Dom.*, 1690-1, p. 501.
[2] This letter has not been found.

the maine fleet leaves that coast, and Mr. Russell hath writt his opinion to bee the same.

For avoiding of repetition I say nothing of the orders given to Mr. Russell both as to that and other matters, because I am sure your Majestie receives them from my Lord Nottingham, by which you will see that that squadron will bee called from the Shannon before the end of September ; but the Generall is writt to this night to consider of some other methods which have been proposed for secureing the passage of that river. I hope that squadron will have received no prejudice in the meane time, the whole fleet haveing staid eighteen or twenty daies in Torbay upon nothing but Spanish formallities for what I understand ; whilst two of the biggest Virginia marchantmen have been taken in the Soundings, which would have paid 12 or 14,000 l. Customes, besides other losses which have been. But wee hope itt is sayled by this time.

I received an order from my Lord Sydney to stay all hearings att Councill of the differences which are amongst themselves in the Hambrough Company ; but itt was putt off before by the Councill till the 15th of October, though not upon the reasons laid before your Majestie by Mr. Atturneys report, which was not brought before the Councill as itt ought first to have been (being refer'd from thence to him), but was reported ex parte to your Majestie, contrary to all proceedings att the Councill table, from whence only itt should have been reported to your Majestie with theire opinions. But there have been other private actings in that matter, of which your Majestie shall bee informed, and obedience given in the meane time to your order, which I hope wee shall bee so happy as to receive from your owne mouth before the 15th of October ; but itt was my duty to acquainte your Majestie with the irregularity of that proceeding.

There was also an order some time ago to the Chancellor of the Dutchy to incert the names of seven or eight persons into the comission of the peace for the county of Lancaster att the motion of my Lord Brandon, and there being two or three of those named by him who were obnoxious to the best gentlemen and Parliament men of that county, some whereof did declare they would not sitt upon the bench with them, I did thereupon represent the same to my Lord Sydney to know your Majesties

pleasure about itt, and did receive answer only that the Lord
Leiutenant was to bee answerable if hee did recomend unfitt
justices. But I had no direct answer, and thereupon haveing
returned to the Chancellor of the Dutchy the said answer as itt
was from my Lord Sydney, some of the Parliament men have
againe declared that they will not act as justices if one Patten
and Clayton (two of the men recomended by my Lord Brandon)
bee putt into that comission. I have laid the same before the
Queene as itt now stands, who comands mee to receive your
Majesties pleasure about itt.

I am desired also by Sir John Morgan, Governor of Chester,
to pray your Majesties favour to him in granting him the
Auditors place of Wales, which hee saies hee had some incouragement to hope for when itt was granted to Colonel Herbert,
and hee hopes hee has now a better claime to your favour by the
dilligence and expence hee hath been att both in seeing the
recruites, &c., speeded from thence into Ireland all the last yeare,
and in keepeing a table by order to intertaine the officers when
they have been there about the transportations, and for which
hee hath had no allowance as hath been given to others.

Mr. Peregrine Bertie, my Lord Lindsey's son, hath received
newes from sea that his brother Norris Bertie, who was guidon
in the troop of guards comanded by my Lord Ormond, is passt
all hopes of recovery. Hee hopes in case his brother die that
your Majestie will bee pleased to lett him succeed his brother in
that employment. Hee has the Queens consent and leave to
apply to your Majestie about itt, which hee desired mee to do in
his behalfe.

Here are many things which want your Majesties presence to
direct them, and your Majestie will easily beleeve itt will bee
especially pleaseing to some of us who are more particularly
exposed to censures, whilst most of our number are takeing
theire pleasures for more then months att a time, and there are
but three of us now to advise in these difficult matters now
depending, and especially which concerne the fleet. But if your
Majestie bee satisfied with what wee do, I shall bee very indifferent for the rest, being only concerned to approve myselfe

Your Majesties most dutifull servant,

Carmarthen.

[To the King] [1]

London, 11th September, 1691.

Sir,

I am sorry to find your Majestie cannot draw the French to an engagement ; but the good I hope for from itt is that itt will bring your Majestie shortly to us. I doubt not but your Majestie has in your thoughts the meeting of the Parliament, which I perceive the Lords of the Treasury desire may bee as soone as will consist with your Majesties conveniency ; but to have the Parliament full, the Term and meeting of itt must bee neare one another, which begins the 23th October.

I am sorry to find such difference as there is in the opinions of the generall officers about the blocking or attacking of Lymerick. I wish your Majestie would interpose with your directions in that matter, haveing all theire opinions before you in writing, as I am informed, for itt will bee of ill consequence if that place bee not reduced before the French can have an opportunity of sending fresh succors.

I suppose my Lord Nottingham gives your Majestie an account of some intercepted letters, which shew what tampering there is betwixt some Scothmen and some English for promoteing the late Kings interest, by which itt is to bee seene that some men are not to bee made honest by obligations. Great noise is made of the losse of ships in the late storme, but, thank God, itt is not considerable further then the losse of the *Coronation* and *Harwich* which last will bee only as of a ship being broken up, all things being saved which were in her ; and most of her timber will bee usefull againe in the building a new one.

Sir Edmond Jennins (who was a Commissioner of Prizes) is newly dead, and I know my Lord Abingdon would take itt as a favour to himselfe if your Majestie would bestow that employment upon his brother, Mr. Henry Bertie, who was att considerable expence in raiseing a troop of horse att your Majesties comeing into England ; and nothing can bee done more cheaply for him, since itt takes nothing out of your Majesties Exchequer, but itt would bee better for him if your Majestie would please to give him Mr. Fergusons place, who I suppose you will not thinke

---

[1] From the autograph letter in S.P. Dom., King William's Chest, 10, No. 14, summarised in *Cal. S.P. Dom.*, 1690-1, p. 516; *Dalrymple*, App., ii. 187.

fitt to continue longer in your service, after so many informations concerning him. I am desired also by my Lord Pembrok to remind your Majestie that upon his speakeing to you in my heareing for one Mr. Pocock to succeed his father in the place of Hebrew Professor att Oxford, your Majestie was pleased to approve of him, and his father being now dead, my Lord hopes your Majestie will confirme your good intentions towards him for that place.[1] I am with all duty, Sir,

Your Majesties most obedient and most faithfull subject
and servant,
Carmarthen, P.

[To the King] [2]

London, 14th June, 1692.

Sir,

I thinke the subject upon which I now write to your Majestie is of the greatest importance that ever can happen in relation both to your person, your government and the future happinesse of this kingdome, and I find itt in everybodys expectation to have something more done in pursuance of your late victory att sea, the opportunities for itt seeming to bee so very obvious. I find also the greatest part of your Cabinett Councill both zealous in theire wishes and unanimous in theire opinions that there is now an opportunity to destroy a great part of the French navall force, insomuch that I cannot but both joyne in what my Lord Nottingham hath writt more att large on this matter to my Lord Portland, and further add that, as I beleeve, a sufficient land force would certainely incompasse what wee propose to do either att St. Malos, or Brest, or both, so that the omitting to endeavour itt with such a force as may bee likely to effect itt will bee lookt upon as an unpardonable crime in us not to advise, and will have the worst of consequences with a Parliament if itt should faile for want of a due prosecution; and

---

[1] Edward, eldest son of Edward Pococke, the orientalist, was chaplain to the Earl of Pembroke. In spite of this recommendation he was not appointed in place of his father.

[2] The main part of this letter is S.P. Dom., King William's Chest, 12, No. 99, summarised in *Cal. S.P. Dom.*, 1691-2, p. 326. The remainder is S.P. Dom., King William's Chest, 7, No. 70, calendared, under date June-September 1690, in *Cal. S.P. Dom.*, 1690-1, p. 44.

amongst many other ill humors which itt will create itt will most certainely and unavoidably make them never give more for the support of any troops beyond seas. I should hope that 7 or 8,000 men, added to what is here already, might bee sufficient for this work, and pardon my presumption to say that as to your Majesties interest, and the advantage itt would bring to this nation, itt is impossible that your Majesties spareing that number can bee of equall prejudice to your affaires abroad.

I acknowlege that my zeale makes mee liable to your Majesties censure unlesse your goodnesse will forgive itt; but I hope your Majestie will consider how criticall the time is for itt, and that there is not a probability of ever liveing to see the like opportunity. I am glad (besides the concurrence of the generall and flag officers) to find by Mr. Russell's letter this day such warme expressions as hee uses upon this subject, and wee seemed to bee so inflamd upon itt in the Cabinett that most of us have offered to the Queene to give our personall securities to borrow what money shall bee necessary for this expedition, as for my owne part I am ready to do to the utmost of my ability. In short there needs nothing but your Majesties concurrence in this matter, and I hope God will putt itt into your heart to add this blessing to those in which you have been so happy an instrument to these nations, and which will give you an establishment never to bee shaken.

As no time must bee lost to putt this affaire in execution (nor will anything bee left undone on this side the water), so if your Majestie shall thinke fitt to promote itt by sending more troopes, I hope you will also send hither some generall officer that may bee an assistant to the Duke of Leinster, who (although I bee but a small judge in these matters) I can see hath not that compasse of conduct which will bee necessary in an action so much depending upon foot service. I wish that in this I were capable of acting any usefull part, I am sure I would do itt in the meanest capacity; but if not, I hope your Majestie will forgive my perhaps over forward zeale for the service of your Majestie and my country, being as I ought, Sir,

Your Majesties most dutifull subject and obedient servant,

Carmarthen, P.

[To the King] [1]

London, 14th July, 1692.

Sir,

I am alwaies loth to give your Majestie any trouble, when I have nothing to write concerning your service which may excuse itt ; but I hope you will give mee leave to acknowlege the great honour your Majestie hath been pleas'd to do mee in your letter of the 7th instant ; [2] and as in your goodnesse you are pleasd to wish mee health, so if itt shall please God to give itt mee I am sure itt shall bee imployd to do your Majestie the best service I am able.

I am sorry to find your Majestie has so small hopes of doing anything considerable in Flanders, and the slownesse of our proceedings here makes mee as hopeless of anything which may bee expected from this side of the water. But itt is apparent that the untimely finding of money for the severall services which call necessarily for itt is the principall cause of this backwardnesse, and in the meane time the enemy hath been makeing all those defences for theire security which were heretofore wholly wanting ; and I have seene two private letters from Paris, which say that the King has given orders for the imediate fortifiyng both Brest and St. Malo's as strongly as they are capable of being made. My owne feares, I confesse, are that not being strong enough to undertake a seige att either of those places, our successe will bee very doubtfull if not hazardous, and I find wee shall go about wee do not know what if wee shall attempt anything att Rochfort, besides that the sea officers thinke itt will bee too late of the yeare to go so far with the great ships.

These considerations, together with the probable ill consequences in Parliament of haveing done nothing after such a successe, make mee apt to move anything (though never so much att randome) rather then to do nothing. And therefore I presume to putt into your thoughts whither itt might not bee possible to take Dunkirk, there being not the least suspicion of an enemy by land there, and theire expectations being wholly

[1] From the autograph letter in S.P. Dom., King William's Chest, 12, No. 114, summarised in *Cal. S.P. Dom.*, 1691-2, p. 369.

[2] This letter has not been found.

taken up of finding us att St. Malo's or Brest, insomuch that itt would bee a surprize to them ; and I suppose the garrison to bee but very weake, and wee are able to bring 17,000 foot against itt, with a sufficient traine of artillery, so that if your Majestie could cover the seige with your army I should thinke this to bee feizable.   But because I know not how wild this notion may bee (not knowing the posture of your affaires), I have not said a word of itt but to the Queene herselfe, who gives mee leave to name itt to your Majestie as a peice only of my zeale for your service, because itt would bee a work highly acceptable to the nation and Parliament if itt could bee done.   And if itt can bee made practicable, your orders for itt must bee given without delay, and with greater privacy then to the whole Cabinett att first, for I am assured you are not served with secresy there.

I feare the gentleman, who my Lord Portland knows pretended to make some good discoveries concerning the late plott against the government, will not bee able to do much in that matter.   I beleeve him to bee well intentioned, but that hee did not know very much ; and hee has not yett given any written information, although hee promised to do itt in three or four daies after my Lord Portland's departure.   And instead of improveing the intelligence by the way I hoped, I find my principall correspondent falne under the suspicion of theire freinds, and that words have been repeated which I have spoken to very few persons, and (which is yett a greater obstruction to our intelligence and an encouragement to theire obstinacy and secresy) they have daily experience of our laws being too weake to do them any greater prejudice then such a short confinement as rather gives them opportunity to understand one anothers minds more exactly and to take truer measures by itt of what they ought to do ; insomuch that I am confident theire hopes were never greater then they continue to bee att this time, some promiseing themselves a winter assistance from France, but most depending upon an ill humor in the Parliament (in which they have the concurrence of the republican party), and thereby a kind of certainety of not finding the necessary supplies for another yeare.   If therefore such a project as I have mentioned could bee incompassed, I should hope itt would blow away a great part of the storme. However I doubt not but your Majestie has goodnesse enough to pardon the zealous wishes of, Sir,

Your Majesties most dutifull and most obedient subject

and servant,

Carmarthen, P.

I have heard as if the Duke of Leinster and Lord Galloway had writt that they thinke the troopes designed for the discent were sufficient for that undertakeing, and yett they are daily complaining here of the contrary, and pressing for more horse then can either bee spared or transported.

After I had writt this letter my Lord Montjoy told mee hee was going to attend your Majestie, and desired hee might deliver itt. I doubt not but his sufferings and great forwardnesse to serve your Majestie will recomend him to your good opinion, and I verily beleeve hee will deserve itt if your Majestie have any occasion to make a triall of him.

[To the King] [1]

London, 9th September, 1692.

Sir,

The Queene hath been pleased to lett mee bee absent for fourteen daies, in which time I find some of the Lords of the Committee did write something of theire thoughts concerning the Parliament att theire next meeting.[2] I confesse I should not willingly have writt anything of that kind which could have had witnesses to itt, nor would I have presumed to have written on that subject now, but that itt is by her Majesties comand, because nobody can say anything upon itt but with very great uncertainety.

I suppose my Lords did rather write theire feares then theire opinions, it being impossible for any man of understanding not

---

[1] From the autograph letter in S.P. Dom., King William's Chest, 12, No. 127, summarised in *Cal. S.P. Dom.*, 1691-2, p. 443.

[2] The reference is to Rochester's letter of August 16 in *Dalrymple*, App., ii. 240 ; *Cal. S.P. Dom.*, 1691-2, p. 410. This letter was later submitted to and annotated by Carmarthen.

to think itt necessary to have as great a land force the next yeare as itt was this; and the necessity for itt seemes to bee so obvious that I cannot but hope the greater part of so many gentlemen as are of the House of Commons must bee sensible that theire comon safety will bee concerned in itt. That which seemes rather to bee like to bee the question is where those men should bee imploy'd, the generall opinion which hath gained amongst most being that the sending an army into Flanders is not the way to putt an end to the war. But that which is far more prevalent amongst the country gentlemen is that the war there exhausts the species of the money out of the kingdome, which they account worse then payment of the tax, and which they thinke itt would not do in any degree so much if the war were carried into France, where the army would either subsist upon the country, or all things must bee provided from England to them, so that the species would still remaine here.

I doubt not but your Majestie will att the opening of the Parliament say those things which will make much stronger impressions upon theire minds then anything else can do, and I hope there will bee that defference shew'd by them which is due to your Majesties more discerning judgments. And indeed I should not thinke the difficulty would bee so great as is imagined were the country gentlemen left to theire owne thoughts ; but the caballs are already form'd with so much malice betwixt those who would subvert your government and those who would governe your Majestie in itt, and who thinke this will bee a faire opportunity for incompassing theire designe, that I feare more from that spiritt of division and opposition which they hope will begett disagreements betwixt you and the Parliament, then I do from anything else, there being in truth no other way for your enemies on either hand to attaine theire ends.

The prevention of these contrivances will depend cheifely upon your Majesties owne prudent conduct and interest with persons, there being now no such thing as any particular interest that is considerable enough to do good, and itt is almost in every mans power to obstruct itt. But yett if those who ought to serve your Majestie faithfully, and who have tasted liberally of your favours, would do so, I should not despaire but that there might bee a good issue of theire next meeting ; and I assure your Majestie that nothing of that kind shall bee wanting that can bee in the power of, Sir,

Your Majesties most dutifull and faithfull servant

and subject,

Carmarthen, P.

[To the King] [1]

London, 28 April, 1693.

Sir,

My Lord Galloway will informe your Majestie of the conferences which have been had with him about what is thought probable to bee attempted att Brest, St. Malos, or Rochefort, which are all the places can bee thought on with probability of doing anything upon them. And the two latter being to bee attempted by land, and that the ships will only bee of use to protect theire transport, my Lord Galloway will lett your Majestie know what his thoughts are about both, and hee will receive your Majesties owne orders concerning them, when hee has laid downe before you the same objections which hee hath done to the Queene, and in which I acknowlege for my owne part that I do intirely agree with him.

As to Brest (which I thinke to bee the only place where there can bee hopes of effecting anything this summer), that is also reduced in my opinion within a very narrow compass, as to what is advisable to bee tried there, according to the opinions of the three admirals who are to comand the fleet, which is, that if a fleet (not under sixty-five sayle of men-of-war) can bee gott to sea in time, so as to bee att Brest before the Brest ships bee gone out, and before the Toulon squadron bee gott to joyne them, in that case your fleet should attempt to destroy them in Brest Water, notwithstanding the batteries in theire passage up to Brest Water, and notwithstanding any preparations of fire-ships or other defences which the enemy can have made to oppose them. But as itt will bee to no purpose to go into Brest Water if theire fleet bee gone out, so also itt must by no meanes bee ventured to attack the enemies whole fleet in Brest Water if the Toulon squadron should bee com'd to them there, itt being

---

[1] From the autograph letter in S.P. Dom., King William's Chest, 14, No. 10, summarised in *Cal. S.P. Dom.*, 1693, p. 111.

the unanimous opinion of your Admiralty that whenever your fleet shall make that attempt in Brest Water they must either bee intire conquerors over all the enemies ships they find there, or that all the ships which make the attempt must bee destroyed, insomuch that they say the undertakeing is of no lesse concerne then the whole fleet of England.

This is what the said three admiralls have only said to mee in private, and seeme not willing to speake so freely to your Councill, for which I know not theire reason. And they did tell mee att the same time that they had reason to beleeve, unlesse some very positive and particular order shall bee given to the Dutch about this undertaking, the Dutch would not hazard to make the attempt with them, notwithstanding theire generall orders to obey the English admiralls. I must also informe your Majestie (although I doubt not but my Lord Portland has already done itt) that when the three admiralls were gone from mee, Sir Clowdsley Shovell returned back, and told mee that as hee beleeved the Dutch would not make that attempt with them unlesse they had positive orders for itt, so hee was confident excuses would also bee made by the English themselves, if itt should bee left to the discretion of a councill of war to attempt itt or not as they should thinke fitt ; and therefore hee wish't that if they should proceed with that designe the orders to your fleet may bee positive to attempt itt, unlesse they can give very good reasons why they ought not to putt itt in execution.

If your Majestie shall resolve to attempt anything of this kind att Brest, there will bee no use of horse there, nor of more then 5 or 6,000 foot, a good number of which the admiralls would desire to have on board the men-of-war, as well for haveing good store of small shott on board when they go into Brest Water as to endeavour to take some of the batteries in theire passage, if they shall find itt practicable. In order to this the Queene has already comanded five regiments to bee quartered as neare to Portsmouth as they can conveniently, and I wish your Majestie would bee pleased to appointe three or four regiments more to bee laid so as to bee ready for the same use, if itt shall bee thought convenient ; for secresy is so necessary, and wee are in such reserves to one another, that wee do not speake out enough to bee understood amongst ourselves, insomuch that your

Majestie will bee forced to send us your owne orders for whatever you think fitt to have done of this kind. In short, if anything can bee done that is considerable, itt depends upon expedition and secresy, and itt is so difficult to find either that I much feare our successe. And one cause why I find there are not those dispatches made which ought to bee is because some amongst us do declare itt to bee so much in vaine to thinke of attempting anything that they find fault with going about itt.

Another thing desired by the admiralls is that Monsieur Meesters may go along with them with his machines, in case they go to Brest ; and all his materialls are in such readinesse that the addition of charge will not bee much more then is laid out already.

Whatever your Majesties comands shall bee, the execution of them will so wholly depend upon dispatch, that I hope your Majestie will write something to bee comunicated to your Councill to quicken them in makeing that dispatch ; and I hope you will lett us know who shall comand those land forces which shall bee putt on board the ships for the purposes aforesaid, in case you shall give order for no more then what will bee necessary for the expedition to Brest. I am with all duty, Sir,

Your Majesties most obedient and faithfull subject
and servant,
Carmarthen, P.

[To the King] [1]

London, 30th September, 1693.

Sir,

My Lord Lovelace being now dead, your Majestie will give mee leave to putt you in mind of your formerly intended favour to my Lord Abingdon for the office of Justice in Eyre south Trent ; and I hope you will forgive my presumption to request his place of Captain of the Pensioners for my son Danby, your Majestie haveing formerly intended him a place of benefitt in the grant of the Post Office ; and those in which hee has served your Majestie haveing been imployments of very great expence to him, your Majestie (if you please) may bestow the

---

[1] From the autograph letter in S.P. Dom., King William's Chest, 14, No. 59, summarised in *Cal. S.P. Dom.*, 1693, p. 348.

comand of his regiment of marines upon somebody who will looke upon itt as a great favour. If your Majestie were informed of the sumes hee hath expended in your service, both att sea and amongst those poore marine officers who are starveing, I am sure your Majestie would have a consideration of that alone, and I am sure hee is not so ambitious of anything in this world as to signalize himselfe in something for your service.

There being now foure mailes wanting, so that wee can heare nothing from your Majestie, makes us all very uneasy ; but I am willing to flatter myselfe with hopes that wee may now bee so happy as to see your Majestie as soone as the letters, and that itt may bee both with speed and safety are the prayers of, Sir,

Your Majesties most dutifull and obedient subject

and servant,

Carmarthen, P.

[To the King] [1]

Sir,   London, 26 May, 1694.

I can say nothing that is worth the giveing your Majestie the trouble of a letter, but I think itt becomes mee to informe you that the Council hath made so good a progresse in the commission and draught of the letters patents for establishing the corporation for a banck, that itt is hoped there will need but one sitting more of the Councill for what they can do towards itt ; but so many difficulties have appeared therein that itt is not easy to say how the consequences may answer our desires.

As to the matters of the fleet, and the land forces which are aboard itt, I feare that the delays which have hapned will prove not only to have lost the opportunities of the easterly winds, but of those designes for which (as I suppose) the land forces were att first intended, and hath no lesse retarded the service principally aimed att in the Mediterranean, unlesse the winds serve very speedily to carry them away. And as things do stand now, I beleeve that had there been a Cabinett Councill acting as heretofore, and which would have taken upon them to offer theire advices to her Majestie upon these matters, the majority of them would have proposed the stopping of the land forces,

[1] From the autograph letter in S.P. Dom., King William's Chest, 15, No. 19, printed in *Cal. S.P. Dom.*, 1694-5, p. 152, as ' Sir P. Leeds to the King.'

rather then theire going so late upon an expedition which has not that prospect of successe which itt had a month ago. As itt is, they waite only for a good wind, but I confesse as to my owne part I could now wish that that part of the fleet which is not to go with Mr. Russell might rather have been imployd with the machine and bomb vessells to have spoiled the mole of Dunkirk, which Monsieur Meesters and others have alwaies thought practicable, and which would have brought the land forces nearer your Majestie and have preserved them from great inconveniencies which they are like to undergo by being so long on shipboard.

I beleeve your Majestie may remember that some time ago I acquainted you with Sir Henry Goodricks desire to bee sent into Holland to succeed my Lord Dursley, and now that my Lord Falkland is dead hee has repeated his request, and desired mee to mention itt againe to your Majestie, which is all I shall presume to do, your Majestie knowing so well his fitnesse for the employment and his zeale for your service. And I shall only add my hopes that your Majestie beleeves mee to bee as I am, Sir,

Your Majesties most dutifull subject and servant,

Leeds, P.

II. MISCELLANEOUS CORRESPONDENCE

From the small number of miscellaneous letters which survive from this period a few have been selected as illustrating mainly the private life of the Duke of Leeds. These are printed in chronological order.

To the Countess of Danby.[1]

2nd April, 1689.

My dearest heart,

I intended to have been in towne this day, but there hapned a businesse att Hampton Court yesterday which occasions my going thither againe this day, of which I will give you

[1] Autograph letter in Leeds MSS., Packet 14.

a relation when I see you. Your son Dumblan and I did both thinke that wee were not so well look't upon att Court as wee us'd to bee, and wee intend to try that a litle further to-day. I have sent Cooper to make my excuse to the Irish Comittee, haveing chosen this time of speakeing to the King purposely when his Councill was not so neare him. I am, Dearest,

Your most intirely affectionate husband,

Danby, P.

[To William Robinson, Sheriff of Yorkshire] [1]

Wimbledon, May the 16th, 1689.

Sir,

I had returnd an answer sooner to yours of the 4th instant (which was also signd by Sir Thomas Gower and Colonel Holt) [2] but that upon shewing it to the King his Majestie thought fitt to take some time to consider of it. And as to the papists he thinkes it onely necessary that a carefull eye be had over their motions so as to finde out if any of them be acting anything against the Government of which any particular proofs can be made out, and he will be willing to reimburse any expence you shall be at in makeing discoveries of that kind amongst them. He would gladly alsoe be inform'd of any particular discourses which were talk't against the Government by any of Sir John Lanier's officers or soldiers, that some example might be made amongst them ; and as to the places you name for haveing forces sent to them, his Majesty thinkes not at all necessary, the danger (if there be any) being like to be on the west and not the east side of England. It will not be long before Yorke and the places adjacent be eased of the burthen of the soldiers quarter'd thereabouts, and if I could have prevail'd they should have been removed before now, being sencible how great the trouble has been to them.

The many accidents which have happned here has occasion'd greater delays in the comissions both of lieutenancy and of the peace then could have been imagin'd, but I hope will now be

---

[1] From a copy in a clerk's handwriting in Leeds MSS., Packet 14.

[2] This letter is also preserved in Leeds MSS., Packet 14, and calendared in Leeds MSS., p. 37.

both speedily dispacht, and I begg the favour of you that you would cause a list to be drawn and transmitted to me of all such Roman Catholic gentlemen in the three severall rideings as are look't upon to be active men and fitt to bear armes, and to enquire how those are provided with armes and horses fitt for service. Your care in this will be very acceptable to the King and thankfully acknowledgd by me, who am with great truth, Sir,

Your most affectionate and humble servant,

[Carmarthen]

[To the Marchioness of Carmarthen] [1]

3rd December, 1689.

Dearest heart,

I can hardly expect to be beleeved that itt is so great a truth as itt is that I have not written for want of time ; and now I write att 11 a clock att night because I will defer itt no longer, although I have litle to say newe then to tell you that I am sorry to bee so long without your company, and to acquainte you that your brother Lindsey has ben a weke in town, and would also bee glad to see you. For news, here is none ; but I feare a litle time more may produce too much, from the ill humors which seme daily to increase in the body politick.

Your brother Abingdon has this day asked leave of the House to go into the country. He neither takes leave of the King nor comes att Court, but is in great favour with the Princesse of Denmark, where I and my whole family find as litle. My daughter Herbert is very well, but I never saw her bigger in my life, and she saies she looks within a fortnight ; and if she could alwaies bring such boys as her eldest she could not have too many, for I never saw a finer. My daughter Obrien is ill with a sore throat, or else she and her sister Plymouth had made you a visitt this day att Wimbledon. I do not know when I shall be able to gett thither myselfe, and therefore pray bestow a visitt upon

Your most truly affectionate husband,

Carmarthen.

[1] Autograph letter among the Lindsey MSS., partly printed in *Lindsey MSS.*, p. 456.

[To the Countess of Danby] [1]

3rd September, [16]90.

Deare Daughter,

I have this day received a letter from the King,[2] but hee takes no notice of my request about his being a godfather. I suppose the reason to bee because hee is too much concern'd about other businesse, haveing been so unfortunate as to have been repuls't in an attack hee made upon Lymerick on the 27th past with the loss of five or six hundred men and severall officers. One Colonel Hamilton, Colonel Margotson, three captains, &c., have been killed, besides severall wounded, but none of our acquaintance. I feare this, together with the great raines, will force him to raise the seige, but wee shall not know that certainely till the next courier ; and there being severall letters by the comon posts, which were wind bound att Dublin and are not yett arrived, wherein the King may have writt about the christning, itt will bee best to stay for those letters. But if those shall say nothing of itt (which wee shall know in two or three daies) my advice will bee to have the child christned without waiting any longer for a royall gossip.

Pray remember mee to your sisters with you, who you will lett partake of the newes, as I hope to do shortly of the groaning cake, who am, Deare Daughter,

Your truly affectionate father and servant,

Carmarthen, P.

[To the Countess of Danby] [3]

3rd September [1690], past 5 a clock.

Since I writt my other letter (which was att noone) I received another letter from the King of the 22th August,[4] by which hee does us the honour of being godfather to your son, and leaves the nomination of a deputy to mee. I desire therefore you will by this bearer lett mee know what gossips you would have. My wife would have her brother Lindsey to bee

---

[1] Autograph letter in B.M. Add. MSS. 28050, f. 75.
[2] This letter has not been found.
[3] Autograph letter in B.M. Add. MSS. 28050, f. 77.
[4] This letter has not been found.

one, and in that case I must write to him by the post to-morrow, and must stand for the King myselfe. I would bee glad also to know your time, which would bee most convenient on a Sonday, but I can gett leave for any day but a Wednesday. I am

Your very affectionate father to serve you,

Carmarthen.

To the Countess of Danby at Mimms.[1]

27 February, [16]92/3, att 6 a clock att night.

Deare Daughter,

I have sent you my coach to bring you to towne early to-morrow morning. Itt is in order to your going to your husband, who is sick att Upner Castle. They write word that the phisitian there saies there is no great danger. However my wife is gone to him this night, and I know you will bee desirous to do so too, which makes mee send you this who am, Deare Daughter,

Your most affectionate father,

Carmarthen.

To John Ellis, one of the Commissioners for Transport.[2]

March the 31th, 1693, at St. Jams.

Sir,

I have sent this by my servant John Roberts, whose name is intended to be made use of as owner of the ship *Queen of Poland*, which I yesterday desired might be taken into the transport service upon the same terme and conditions which are granted to other persons for such ships as are taken up in this river. The master, Richard Kennett, informs me that she is well fitted with all things necessary, and is ready to take in her victualls and lading when you please, and my servant not being experienc'd in these matters I must rely upon you to favour my wife so farr as to instruct him in all things which are necessary to be done in order to the making the bargain as it

---

[1] Autograph letter in B.M. Add. MSS. 28050, f. 80.

[2] Original letter, signed but not written by Carmarthen, in B.M. Add. MSS. 28878, f. 69.

ought to be betwixt the King and the owner, and I find my wife is willing to lett the ship be hired into the service for as long a time as you please. Your kindness herein will oblige, Sir,

Your very humble servant,

Carmarthen, P.

[To William Blathwayt] [1]

London, 8th August, 1693.

Sir,

You have been so very obligeing to mee with your letters and intelligence that I cannot acknowlege itt enough, and if att any time itt shall lie in my power to make any reall returnes of your favour you may depend that I shall not bee wanting in itt. I must also returne you my thanks for the civility you offered mee of venison from your park, and I would have made use of your kindnesse but that I was so plentifully provided during my stay att Bath ; but I was in hopes of seeing both your house and divers others thereabouts, and I was prevented of that satisfaction by my sudden coming away upon the newes of the last battle, which was represented much worse att the beginning then thank God itt proves to bee.

This place affords no newes att present, but is prepareing to make a great deale against our winter camp bee form'd, and if you can then defend yourselves as well as you have done att Landen your conduct will deserve no lesse comendation then itt has justly gained by that action. I am with great truth, Sir,

Your most faithfull and humble servant,

Carmarthen, P.

[To the Countess of Danby] [2]

London, 15th August, 1693.

Deare Daughter,

I am extreame sorry to heare you have been so very ill, and itt troubles mee that I am not able to gett time to see you. But besides the ties which I have upon mee att Court, I have been and am yett under trouble for my daughter Lempster, who is so dangerously ill that I have sent Doctor Gibbon to her, and

---

[1] Autograph letter in B.M. Add. MSS. 34351, f. 5.
[2] Autograph letter in B.M. Add. MSS. 28050, f. 82.

your mother and sister Plymouth are gone in great hast and affliction to Easton. I expect to heare by expresse by this night how shee is, and if shee do not mend I intend to go to her myselfe.

My last letter from your husband is of the 23th July, att which time hee was very well, and itt will not bee above a month longer before his ship must come home, and then you will bee sure to see him. My blessing to all the little ones, and I do assure you that I am most truly, Deare Daughter,

Your most affectionate father,

Carmarthen.

[To the Countess of Danby] [1]

Wimbledon, 19 August, [16]93.

Deare Daughter,

Mr. Daggett is com'd with letters from your husband, who is now att Torbay, and I suppose may have letters for you ; but I forgott to aske him, being com'd out of towne in some hast. But the errand of this letter is to lett you know that I understand by my wife that shee thinkes you run some hasard both to your owne life and your sucking childs, unlesse you both give over being nurse to the child and come to towne for better help then you can have in the country. If this bee the case I desire you will not too much trust to your country advisers, but that you will hasten to towne, where you shall bee very welcome to, Deare Daughter,

Your most affectionate father,

Carmarthen.

My blessing to all the little ones.

[To the Earl of Abingdon] [2]

London, 7th November, 1693.

My Lord,

This day the Parliament mett, but the Kings speech is not yett printed, so that I am not able to informe you of the matters recomended to them by itt. I can only acquainte you

---

[1] Autograph letter in B.M. Add. MSS. 28050, f. 84.
[2] Autograph letter in Egerton MSS. 1525, f. 68.

that the contents of itt are of so great importance as hath given occasion to the House of Commons to defer the consideration of itt to Monday next,[1] till which time they are adjourn'd, as the House of Lords is also till Friday next, haveing some private businesse before them which they can intertaine themselves withall till Monday.

I did presume to remind the King of your Lordship by a letter into Holland upon the death of my Lord Lovelace,[2] but finding the King to take no notice of that letter I asked his Majestie yesterday whither hee had received such a letter from mee, which hee owned hee had, and had only forgott to speake of itt, and to lett me know that hee had reserved the place of Justice in Eyre for your Lordship, and gave mee leave to write you word of itt. I asked what disposition hee had made of the place of Captain of the Pensioners, to which hee was not pleased to give mee any answer ; but the report is that my Lord Westmoreland will have itt.

This post will spread the newes of my Lord Nottinghams being out of his place of Secretary, and itt was taken for granted that my Lord Shrewsbury would have succeeded him ; and the comon report is also that my Lord Nottingham did resigne his place. But the truth of that matter is that my Lord refused to resigne volontarily, and hee delivered the seales by the Kings positive comand ; and itt is as true that my Lord Shrewsbury hath not accepted the place as yett upon some scruples which tis said hee makes about itt, so that the seales are not yett disposed of to anybody.

The King did last night declare Mr. Russell to comand the fleet the next yeare, and they say a few daies more will produce more changes ; but I thinke these are enough for one post, and I hope you will not lett many more pass before wee have the honour to see you here. In the meane time I suppose you will send directions to somebody to take out the warrants for Justice in Eyre, and I will tire you no longer then to subscribe myselfe, My Lord,

Your Lordships most faithfull servant and affectionate brother,

Carmarthen.

[1] November 13.   [2] *Supra*, p. 216.

[To the Marchioness of Carmarthen] [1]

London, 1st April, 1701.

Deare Daughter,

I have given order about takeing the best course I can for secureing your arreares of rent due from Taylor, Keene, and Seabrook, but must bee particularly inform'd what theire severall yearely rents are, and what arreare is severally due from each of them, which I desire you to send mee as soone as you can. I have reason to fear that Mr. Kemp absconds himself, for he has made three severall appointments of coming to me, but hath keept never one of them, nor sent any excuse for three or four days last past, which gives me more than an ordinary cause to suspect that wee shall see him no more.

I will trouble you with no more at this time, it being uneasy to write with mine own hand, with which I began this letter, but could not write out the remainder; [2] and I will therefore conclude this with telling you that this day the House of Commons hath brought up an impeachment to the House of Lords against the Earle of Portland for high crimes and misdemeanors, which I fear will be carryed with some violence against his lordshipp, and I have nothing more to say but that I am, Dear Daughter,

Your most affectionate father,

Leeds.

[To the Marchioness of Carmarthen] [3]

Wimbledon, 23 July, 1701.

Deare Daughter,

I did once designe to have com'd to Myms before my going into Yorkshire, but I have been so delay'd in my businesse here that I cannot do itt till my returne. In the meane time itt is necessary for you to bee informed (although perhaps they may lay aside theire designe) that some of my son your husbands creditors have been consulting (now that Parliament privilege

---

[1] Original letter in B.M. Add. MSS. 28050, f. 102.

[2] Only the first sentence is in the handwriting of the Duke of Leeds.

[3] Autograph letter in B.M. Add. MSS. 38849, f. 204.

is taken away by Act of Parliament) how they may gett execution upon severall judgments which your husband has given to severall of his creditors ; and finding that the morgage I have upon all the lands will hinder theire extents upon the lands, some of them are advised to execute theire judgments upon his personall estate, which will reach all your houshold goods, or plate, or jewells, or anything they can find either in your house or your cabinetts or in your grounds or stables. The intent therefore of this letter is both to give you a caution of all persons who desire admittance into your house, and to prevent your being surprized with this accident if itt should so happen that any bayliffes should bee sent, and also to lett you know that you may oppose theire entrance into your house unlesse they should have my Lord Cheife Justice Holts warrant. And itt is cheifely to advise you to putt everything out of the way that is of any value, and which in my opinion may bee left more safely att my grandson Cokes att Tittenhanger [1] then in your owne house, which may bee done without theire knowing why itt is done. But of that you will bee the best judge yourselfe, and I hope nothing of this disorder will bee putt in execution. However, itt is wisest to provide against itt.

I shall go from hence on Monday next,[2] and I have taken the best care I can to gett you notice if anything of this kind will bee attempted, but that must not bee relied on. My blessing to yourselfe and all yours, who am, Deare Daughter,

Your most affectionate father,

Leeds.

If my son had been in England I should have hoped to have prevented this danger by makeing him have given mee a judgment upon all his personall estate, which I could have extended upon his goods before any of theire judgments had been executed ; and I will endeavour to gett such an one prepared against his returne if I can, and I will leave you notice what order is left about itt.

[1] In Hertfordshire, not far from Mimms. Edward Coke had taken the mansion of Sir Thomas Pope Blount there, probably on the death of Sir Thomas in 1697.

[2] July 28.

[To Lord Godolphin] [1]

Wimbledon, 23th June, 1702.

My Lord,

Both Mr. Atturney and all the councill retained for my son Carmarthen in his suite about the Auditors office do say now that my son must necessarily bee both admitted and sworne by your Lordship into the said office, and that an admittance by the Lord Hallifax his consent would signify nothing in court, insomuch that itt is to no purpose to aske him. Since therefore this is the only way by which my son must proceed to bee made capable of trying his title, and itt being agreeable to the Atturney Generalls opinion as well as the other councill that hee should bee so admitted, my son will attend your Lordship himselfe to desire that favour, and hee being necessarily to go speedily to sea, and the Term on the equity side of the Exchequer being neare an end, I hope your Lordship will please to give him your dispatch, so that neither the Queens service nor his owne businesse may bee neglected by him.

In this your Lordship will very much oblige, My Lord,

Your Lordships most humble and obedient servant,

Leeds.[2]

[To George Clarke] [3]

21 August, 1702.

Sir,

I spoke to the Prince the other day about one Captain Chasseloup (who is now a leutenant in Colonel Holts regiment in the company of Captain Louis de Sediere), for whom I desired that hee might have had leave to have parted with his comission to one Scott (who had been a lieutenant in the Lord Portmores regiment) ; but the Prince would not grant that, but was pleas'd to allow that his pay should bee continued to him without his doing duty, hee being not in a condition able to performe his service as hee ought ; and his Highnesse gave mee leave to

[1] From an autograph draft in B.M. Add. MSS. 28086, f. 69.

[2] Endorsed by Leeds, ' Coppy of my letter to Lord Treasurer Godolphin about my son Carmarthen's place of Auditor, 23 June 1702. This day my son received this letter from mee att Wimbledon.'

[3] Egerton MSS. 2618, f. 188, autograph letter. Addressed to Clarke as Secretary to the Admiralty.

lett Monsieur Chasseloup know his pleasure therein, which I did accordingly, and thereupon hee has desired hee may have the Princes order to his colonel or captain signifiyng his Highnesses pleasure therein.

I have accordingly writt to his Highnesse in the inclosed letter to request such an order in his behalfe, and I desire you would please to favour him in itt. Hee will either come him-selfe if hee can, or send somebody to waite upon you for the said order, when you have received his Highnesses directions about itt ; and I pray you to deliver my letter to the Prince yourselfe, because itt containes other matters besides what relates to Captain Chasseloup. This gives mee also an opportunity to assure you that I am with great truth, Sir,

Your most humble and faithfull servant,

Leeds.[1]

To Dr. Hans Sloane.[2]

Wimbledon, January 15th, 1704/5.

Sir,

I have sent this letter on purpose to give you an account of the state of my health, which is, that the next day after I came hither from London I had a severe fitt of my pain, and had another in a day or two after, but since that (which is above a fortnight) I have had no fitt and but seldome any pain, but my water is constantly very browne and with a good deale of sedi-ment, but scarce any gravell or very little appears to be in it. I have all this while been troubled with an ill cold, and can hardly stirr out of my own apartment without renewing it, which has made me very tender ; but that which makes me principally give you this trouble is that I am for the most part very sickish after meales, and I find a little hecktick heat upon me which hinders me from sleeping till six or seven a clock in the morning, and I find myself more then ordinary weak, all which last complaints I fancie does proce[ed from] that feavour-ish distemper.

I desire therefore to know what you think adviseable to be

---

[1] Endorsed, ' Shewn the Prince. Monsieur Chasseloup to have leave to be absent for recovery of his health and then returne to his duty.'

[2] Sloane MSS. 4078, f. 200. In a clerk's handwriting, but signed by Leeds.

done, and were it not for the badness of my nerves I would have adventured to have taken one of Matthews's pills to have procured more sleep ; but I would not do that or anything else without your opinion, which I rely much upon, who am, Sir,

Your most humble servant,

Leeds.

To the Marchioness of Carmarthen at Mimms.[1]

Wimbledon, 21 October, 1706.

Deare Daughter,

I do not blame you for endeavouring to dispose of your son so happily as to the Lady Elizabeth Hastings, of whom the world gives so worthy a character, but I cannot but blame both your overforwardnesse in makeing such a proposall without any incouragement for doing so, and much more for not preventing your son in time from being so far ingaged in his affections as you speake him to bee. And since by yours I find shee takes so small an objection as the inequality of age for an excuse, itt is by no meanes proper for mee after knowlege thereof to trouble her ladyship with an offer which I know beforehand is more likely to bee refused then accepted. I call the excuse a small one, because itt was my owne case, who was the happiest man liveing notwithstanding the like inequality, and so have many others been whom I have knowne. I therefore rather beleeve that shee either does not like him well enough to bee her husband, or his father being alive shee may reasonably think they must waite his life before theire fortune can bee considerable, of which you know the contrary, and that after my death your son will have a greater part of my estate in his fathers lifetime then his father will have from mee. Nor do I beleeve shee takes the whole estate to bee so considerable as itt will bee when both yours and mine are joyn'd, as they will bee in him and his children.

I would not have you to use this last argument to her, because itt would look as if wee thought her only to bee perswaded by interest, but I am acquainted with none of her freinds or relations to whom shee might think itt fitt to have anything said

[1] B.M. Add. MSS. 28050, f. 110. Autograph letter.

of this kind, so that if you ladies can carry this matter no farther betwixt yourselves itt must bee att an end, and in that case I must lay my commands upon you not to delay the sending both him and his brother hither to mee to bee out of her way before his affections bee so intirely fixt as to take up his thoughts from all other necessary improvements.

I thought I should have had as litle inclinations to his marrying anybody till hee was older as shee can have for him, nor would I now consent to his haveing any other woman that I know. But I can give you no further advice in this affaire, only that whatever the issue bee itt may not bee defer'd for feare of those ill consequences which I have mentioned ; and so with my blessing I remayne, Deare Daughter,

Your most affectionate father,

Leeds.

Lett mee heare from you and when you intend to bee in towne.

To Dr. Hans Sloane.[1]

Wimbledon, January 10th, 1706/7.

Sir,

My servant that brings you this will give you a larger account of my condition then I can write, but the short of my case is that I have been five or six months troubled with a pain in my right shoulder every day, but especially in the night time. It frequently goes quite away, sometimes for an hour or two, and sometimes much longer, without any pain, and sometimes removes to my elbow and to my wrist, but lets me not sleep above two or three hours, and then continues for the most part more or less till the morning, but is alwaies better after I have been an hour out of my bed. My servant will acquaint you how I have anointed it with severall things, and how long I wore a plaister that was recomended to me, but with no benefitt by any of them. But that which makes me send now is my being alarmd with very great twitchings in both my feet, and especially this last night, which are such violent cramps as makes me fear they may go to convulsions unless something can be done

---

[1] Sloane MSS. 4078, f. 198. In a clerk's handwriting, but signed by Leeds.

to prevent it, and I have a little of those swimings in my head which I had in Yorkeshire, and I am confident that all these proceeds from the same cause.

My servant will also acquaint you with a powder which I am advised to lay to my shoulder, concerning which I desire your opinion, and I will come to town if you think it necessary to apply anything which cannot be done as conveniently here. Some also advise my going into the bagnio, but I shall very much rely upon your opinion in all these matters, being, Sir,

Your very humble servant,

Leeds.

To the Marchioness of Carmarthen at North Mimms.[1]

Wimbledon, November 16th, 1710.

Dear Daughter,

I could not send you word before this day that my son Carmarthen appeared on Tuesday last [2] before the Judges in the Queens Bench, accompanyed with the Duke of Beaufort, the Earle of Scarsdale, the Earle of Plymouth, and Lord North, when he was required to give bayle for his good behavior for twelve months, and my brother Osborne and one Mr. Ward were his baile, but the Court did it in so slight a manner that they required but 200 l. baile from himselfe and 100 l. apeice on the other two.

Upon this occasion my sons councell would have entered upon proofs both that there could be no legall marriage with that infamous woman who pretended to it, but would have shewed a paper under her own hand in 1694 where shee herself has disclaimed any such marriage, which was a paper which I did put into their hands of an examination taken before Mr. John Duval, a then justice of peace, and which I had kept since that time in my custody. But the Judges said that they had no power in that Court to examine any matter concerning marriages, but whatever concerned that must be examined in the Doctors Commons, and so that matter ended there. But my son did thereupon take occasion to make a short speech to the

[1] B.M. Add. MSS. 28050, f. 116. In a clerk's handwriting.
[2] November 14.

Court, wherein hee declared the greatness of his misfortune to have been so long seduced by so base and infamous a woman, and how unworthy he had been in his behaviour to one of the best of wifes and the best of fathers, and that he was glad of the occasion of declareing his sorrow for it.

This matter having been carryed so happily thus farr, it is now thought proper that there should be a further prosecution against the woman, by which there may be a finall conclusion of her claime to any marriage to my son, and that action can be only brought against her by you, for which an instrument shall be drawne by which you are to commence that action, and it is what my son now desires, as well as myself, that you may do, so that you may now come to towne as soon as you please, and things will be prepared in the meantime for your prosecution of that action. I hope God in his mercy has made this infamous woman both an instrument to whipp herselfe, and to prevent all future inconveniences which might have given disturbance to my family after my death, and I hope will continue his blessings both to you and yours, as I do who am, Dear Daughter,

Your most affectionate father,

Leeds.

[To the Earl of Strafford] [1]

London, January 18th, 1711/12.

My Lord,

I am related to a gentleman whose name is Peregrine Bertie, and who I recomended to my Lord Privy Seale to attend him in his journey to Utreckt, being one who is very fittly quallifyd to improve himselfe in anything fitting for a gentleman to learne ; and since his being at Utreckt hee requested my recomendation of him to your Lordship that hee may have the honour of being knowne to you, and to offerr himselfe to do you any service in which you may think him capable upon any tryall which your Lordship shall think fitt to take of him.

Wee are here in a longing expectation of hearing good news from the congresse, and I wish it may prove such as may bring us to a better agreement amongst ourselves at home, which

---

[1] B.M. Add. MSS. 22222, f. 22. In a clerk's handwriting.

seems at present to be at a great distance ; but her Majesties message to both Houses yesterday seems to have brought some angry men into a better temper, and which I hope will be improvd by your Lordships and your colleagues wise conducts, and I will take this oppertunity to assure your Lordship that I am with the greatest respect, My Lord,

Your Lordships most obedient and most humble servant,

Leeds.

III. CORRESPONDENCE WITH HANOVER

Four letters to the Elector of Hanover and the Electress Sophia illustrate the relations of the Duke of Leeds with the Hanoverian Court and his determined championship of the Protestant succession.

[To the Elector] [1]

[November, 1710]

I hope your Electorall Highness will pardon my acknowledgeing in this manner the extraordinary favours which I understand your Highnesse hath beene pleased to shew to my grandsons, Danby and his brother ; and I am sorry my years will not allow me to go and do it myselfe. Whilst I was able I was an actor to the best of my power to incompass those alterations which were necessary for the security of our religion and laws, and [as] those alterations have justly brought the succession to the crowne of these kingdomes into your illustrious family, so I doubt not but they will be preserved by it whenever they shall come to be under its protection. And although I may not live to pay my personall services, I hope I shall leave a family both as well principled in loyalty and as dutyfull to your

[1] From a copy in a clerk's handwriting in B.M. Add. MSS. 28054, f. 213.

person and family as they ought to bee, and with that esteeme
which is due to your Highness from all the world, and particularly from

[Leeds] [1]

[To the Electress Sophia] [2]

[November, 1710]

I durst not presume to give your Electorall Highnesse the
trouble of a letter were itt not that I should bee guilty of a greater
crime if I should not make my humblest acknowlegements for
those infinite graces and favours which I am informd by my
grandsons that your Highnesse hath been pleased to confer upon
them.   As I had the blessing to bee a principall instrument in
procureing that happy match betwixt our late King William and
his Queene, so the consequence of itt has procured us the prospect
of comeing to bee hereafter under the government of your
Electorall Highnesse and your illustrious family, by whose
knowne goodness and wise conduct wee have all humane grounds
to hope that our nation will bee secured to our posterity both in
our religion and laws.   And as I have been a constant assister of
both through many perillous times in which they have beene
attackt, so whilst God spares mee life I will bee no lesse zealous
to pay my loyall duty to your Highnesse, as the true successor to
the crowne and sovereignety of these kingdomes.   And as your
Highnesse has been pleasd to give my grandsons an earnest of
your favour to them, so they will never have my blessing longer
then they shall returne itt to your Highnesse by the utmost of
theire services and obedience to your comands, for no man
liveing can bee with more profound zeale then I am, Madam,

Your Electorall Highnesses most dutifull and most
obedient servant,

[Leeds] [3]

[1] Endorsed by Leeds, ' Coppy of my letter to the Elector of Hanover,
November 1710.'   The Elector's reply is partly printed, under date December
10, in *Morrison Catalogue*, ii. 169, and under date December 22 in *Hist. MSS.
Com.*, ix. 2, p. 470.

[2] From the autograph draft in B.M. Add. MSS. 28054, f. 215.

[3] Endorsed by Leeds, ' Coppy of my letter to the Princess Sophia, November
1710.'

To the Elector.[1]

London, April 4th, 1711.[2]

Sire,

Your Highnesse has been pleased to bestow so many marks of your favour on my grandsons during theire stay in your Court, that I make bold rather to transgresse in presumeing to give your Highnesse the trouble of a letter then not expresse my acknowlegment of your grace and favour to them ; and haveing no other way of doing itt, and being now unable to attend your Highnesse myselfe, I hope you will not only pardon this presumption, but give mee leave to renew my assurances that you have not in this nation a man more devoted to your service and interest then, Sire,

Your Highnesses most dutifull and obedient servant,

[Leeds] [3]

To the Electress Sophia.[4]

[4th May, 1711]

Madam,

The great indulgence which both your Highnesses have been pleased to shew to my grandsons has made mee willing to comply with theire desires to stay longer in your Court then I intended ; but as I have gratified them in the injoyment of so much pleasure and satisfaction, so I am obliged to make the greatest acknowlegements both in theire behalfes and my owne

---

[1] From the autograph draft in B.M. Add. MSS. 28054, f. 217.

[2] Place and date are inserted in another handwriting.

[3] Endorsed by Leeds, ' Coppy of my letter to the Elector of Hannover, 4th May 1711.' That this date is incorrect, however, is suggested by the Elector's reply, which is as follows :

A Hernhausen, ce 5 de Juin 1711—Mylord, Je suis ravi de voir par vôtre lettre du 4 d'Avril passé que vous avez quelque satisfaction de l'acceuïl que Mylords Danby et Peregrin reçoivent icy, et je vous fais de sinceres remercimens des expressions obligeantes par lesquelles il vous a plû de me le temoigner. Leur conduite a été telle depuis qu'ils sont en ce pays, qu'ils se seroient acquis une estime generale quand même ils n'auroient pas l'honneur d'être petits-fils d'une persone dont les merites sont si distinguez. J'embrasseray avec un plaisir singulier toutes les occasions qui se presenteront de faire voir que je suis parfaitement, Mylord, Vôtre trés affectioné à vous servir, George Louis, Electeur. (B.M. Add. MSS. 28054, f. 221.)

[4] From the autograph draft in B.M. Add. MSS. 28054, f. 219.

for the grace and favour your Highnesse hath been pleased to shew them during theire stay there, and I hope they may live to pay that duty to your Highnesse which they will bee obliged to by theire personall as well as publick obligations. And if in my old age I could hope to bee of any use to your Highnesse, none should serve you with greater sincerity, nor could anything bee more agreable to the inclination as well as duty of

Your Highnesses most dutifull and most faithfull
servant,

[Leeds] [1]

IV. ARTICLES OF IMPEACHMENT

A natural conclusion is provided by the articles of impeachment drawn up against the Duke of Leeds in 1695, the introduction of which practically meant the end of his political career.

Articles of impeachment exhibited by the knights, citizens and burgesses, in Parliament assembled, in the name of themselves and of all the Commons of England, against Thomas Duke of Leeds, President of his Majesty's most honourable Privy Council, for high crimes and misdemeanors. [2]

[Introduced in the House of Commons, April 29, 1695]
  1. That certain merchants trading to the East Indies having either forfeited their charter, or being under an apprehension that they had forfeited the same, and having made their humble applications to their Majesties in Council for obtaining a charter of confirmation, the said Duke of Leeds, being then President of their Majesties most honourable Privy Council, and sworn to give their Majesties true and faithful advice, did, contrary to

---

[1] Endorsed by Leeds, ' Coppy of my letter to the Princesse Sophia, 4th May 1711.' This may also be a mistake for 4th April.

[2] C.J., xi. 328.

his oath, office, and duty to their Majesties, and in breach of the great trust reposed in him, by himself, his agents or servants, corruptly and illegally treat, contract, and agree with the said merchants or their agents for five thousand five hundred guineas to procure the said charter of confirmation and also a charter of regulations, or to use his endeavours to obtain the same.

2dly. That in pursuance of such corrupt contract and agreement the said Duke of Leeds did, by himself, his agents or servants, receive or accept from the said merchants or their agents certain notes or securities, whereby he or they were impowered to receive the said 5,500 guineas upon the passing of the said charters.

3dly. That soon after the passing of the said charter of confirmation the sum of two thousand five hundred guineas, part of the said 5,500 guineas, and soon after the passing of the said charter of regulations the further sum of three thousand guineas, other part of the said 5,500 guineas, were, pursuant to the said corrupt contract and agreement, actually received by the said Duke of Leeds or by his agents or servants with his privity and consent.

SECTION B

THE *LETTERS* OF 1710

EDITOR'S INTRODUCTION

A VERY considerable part of the foreign correspondence of the Duke of Leeds during his period of office as Lord Treasurer was published by his own direction in 1710 under the title, *Copies and Extracts of some Letters written to and from the Earl of Danby (now Duke of Leeds) in the Years 1676, 1677, and 1678. With particular Remarks upon some of them.*[1] That the letters thus printed are neither complete nor accurate reproductions of the originals is now fully recognised ; but neither at the moment of their publication nor for long afterwards does their authenticity appear to have been called in question. In the second edition of his *Complete History* Bishop Kennett, whose own accuracy had been seriously challenged by the Duke of Leeds, quotes the collection without comment.[2] Even the Bishop's biographer, while defending his hero against the Duke's criticisms, and declaring that the published correspondence reflects only on its compiler, indulges in no charge of falsification.[3] Hallam, Lingard, and Macaulay, all accept the *Letters* as genuine. The alterations introduced in them were skilfully effected ; the originals were rarely available for comparison ;[4] for at least a century and a half there was no real reason why suspicion should arise.

The first opportunity for the discovery of the truth came with the dispersal of the Leeds Manuscripts in 1869. An examination

---

[1] *Supra*, i. chap. xxii.

[2] *A Complete History of England*, vol. iii., 1719, p. 355. Kennett prints part of Danby's letter of November 22, 1678, as written to Sir William Temple, though it was really written to Sir Leoline Jenkins (*infra*, p. 612).

[3] *Life of Dr. White Kennet*, by the Rev. William Newton, p. 35.

[4] A comparison with Danby's own pamphlet of 1679, however, would have shown serious discrepancies, for the Duke of Leeds in 1710 altered both the letters from Montagu which he had published correctly thirty years earlier (*infra*, pp. 318, 325).

of the letters and drafts which had been in the possession of
the first Duke of Leeds could not fail to show that many of them
had been tampered with. The heavy yet shaky handwriting
which the Duke developed late in life [1] is entirely characteristic,
as different from his earlier handwriting as it is from that of any
of the correspondents with whom he was in communication.
On letter after letter were to be found alterations about the
authorship of which there could be absolutely no doubt.

Nevertheless the discovery was for some time longer delayed.
The great collection of Leeds Manuscripts acquired by the
British Museum was not made available to the public till 1877,
and even thereafter was not as extensively employed by historians as it deserved to be. The smaller collection which
passed into the hands of Mr. Alfred Morrison appears to have
included few striking examples of the Duke's editorial methods,
and the alterations effected do not seem to have attracted the
attention either of Mr. Morrison himself or of his secretary,
Mr. Thibaudeau.[2] In the very small collection, however, which
was purchased first by Dr. Webster and later by Mr. J. Eliot
Hodgkin, were included some unusually striking and important
examples, and to Mr. Hodgkin belongs the credit of having first
realised their significance. His discovery he imparted to Mr.
J. C. Jeaffreson, who edited his manuscripts for the Historical
Manuscripts Commission, and the latter dealt most elaborately
with the matter in the report which was published in 1897.[3]

Unfortunately Mr. Jeaffreson's own editorial methods are by
no means above criticism. The papers which he examined are
now in the British Museum.[4] and a comparison of them with his
published report convicts him not only of many inaccuracies,

---

[1] About 1706 or 1707. Until that time the Duke's handwriting had shown
surprisingly little variation.

[2] The report on the Morrison MSS. issued in 1884 (*Hist. MSS. Com.*, ix. 2,
pp. 406-93) makes no mention of any alterations. Neither does the *Morrison
Catalogue*, edited by A. W. Thibaudeau, the first six volumes of which, dealing
with all the Leeds papers in Mr. Morrison's possession, appeared between 1883
and 1892. Yet there certainly were some alterations. as is shown by the
curious reading given in the *Morrison Catalogue* of the last sentence in Danby's
letter to William of Orange, dated January 23, 1677-8 (*infra*, p. 417). The
failure to record them is unfortunate in view of the fact that many of the
papers concerned have now passed beyond the reach of historians.

[3] *Hist. MSS. Com.*, xv. 2, pp. 185-98.   [4] B.M. Add. MSS. 38849.

but of failure to appreciate properly the most important point of all, the distinction between the changes which the Earl of Danby made in the drafts of his letters as he was drawing them up, and the alterations which he introduced some thirty years later when he was Duke of Leeds. Interleaved with the actual documents are now bound up the transcripts and annotations made by Mr. Hodgkin. These are infinitely more accurate than Mr. Jeaffreson's report ; but in view of that report Mr. Hodgkin considered that they were not worth publishing, and in the elaborate account of his many treasures which appeared in 1902 [1] he devoted only half a page to the Danby papers in his possession.

Even had Mr. Jeaffreson's report been quite reliable, however, it could not be accepted as the last word on the subject, for the survey on which it is based is much too limited in scope to be of great practical value. The nine documents submitted to his examination were a purely fortuitous collection, constituting the merest fragment of a lengthy and varied correspondence. Any conclusions based upon them are necessarily subject to revision in the light of fuller information.[2]

This fuller information has not hitherto been forthcoming. Since 1897, it is true, the foreign correspondence of the Earl of Danby preserved among the Leeds-Godolphin Manuscripts in the British Museum [3] has been more thoroughly examined, and has been found to corroborate in general terms the conclusions of Mr. Jeaffreson's report. But there the matter has been allowed to rest. No serious attempt has been made to determine the precise extent of the alterations introduced by the Duke of Leeds, to reconstruct the correspondence of which he admittedly published only part, or to estimate the value of the ' particular remarks ' with which he accompanied it. Yet the correspondence itself is of supreme importance. During the years which it

---

[1] J. Eliot Hodgkin, *Rariora*.

[2] A striking illustration, by no means favourable to the Duke of Leeds, is provided by Montagu's letter to Danby of January 18, 1678 (*infra*, p. 321). Mr. Jeaffreson relies on a copy of that letter, and points out how far it differs from the version printed in 1710. But before the copy was made a very large part of the original had been cut out, and the actual letter differs much more from the printed version.

[3] B.M. Add. MSS. 28054.

covers the management of foreign affairs, at least as regards France and Holland, was slipping out of the hand of the Secretaries of State, and the letters which these officials were permitted to receive or dispatch were becoming more and more formal in character. Transactions of serious importance were generally entrusted to Danby, with the exception of some few which were concealed even from him. Thus in his letters is to be found much of the real foreign correspondence of the period.

Happily the original letters have to a great extent been preserved, and are available. The only conspicuous exceptions are Danby's letters to Temple, which Swift did not consider it worth while to print, and Danby's letters to Montagu, which were seized and apparently retained by the Council, and cannot now be found.[1] In a number of cases, however, drafts of these letters have survived, or copies of varying degrees of reliability, and with the assistance of these drafts and copies a surprisingly complete reconstruction has been found possible of the entire foreign correspondence carried on by the Lord Treasurer. Considerations of space have absolutely prohibited the printing of this in full ;[2] but an amplified edition of what the Duke of Leeds himself published has proved within practical compass, and has accordingly been made the object of the following pages. Every discoverable letter which passed during the years 1673-9 between Danby on the one side and Ralph Montagu, William of Orange and William Bentinck on the other, has been printed, and all available light has thus been thrown on the main controversies connected with the Treasurer's incursion into the sphere of foreign politics. In the remaining sections of the published *Letters*, and in a supplementary section devoted to Danby's correspondence with Sir Leoline Jenkins, a different principle has had to be observed. All the Treasurer's letters are still printed, but of his correspondents' letters space has been found only for those which the Duke of Leeds himself published, or which are not available in some readily accessible

---

[1] On March 26, 1679, it was ordered by the King in Council that Montagu's papers should be restored to him (P. C. Reg. 67, p. 142), but this presumably applied only to his private papers, for Danby always believed that his letters remained in the hands of the Council.

[2] The complete correspondence runs to well over 200,000 words.

publication.   A large number of letters from Temple and Brisbane have thus been omitted ; [1] but these letters, though
important in themselves, have rarely any very intimate bearing
on the personal fortunes of the Lord Treasurer.

A comparison of this reconstructed correspondence with the
published *Letters* immediately reveals very serious discrepancies;
but it must not be assumed that a mere enumeration of these
will indicate the nature and extent of the editor's falsifications.
The Duke of Leeds had to work as well as he could with the
material which was in his own hands.   That material presumably included all the ' In ' letters in his correspondence ; but
for the ' Out ' letters he had to rely either on the drafts which
it was his custom to preserve for reference, or on copies made by
clerks.   Not merely was the series of drafts and copies in his
possession very far from complete, but a comparison of draft
and letter, where both are available, reveals the fact that the
Lord Treasurer, in writing his letters, did not always adhere
strictly to the wording of his drafts.   It was inevitable, therefore, that the collection of letters which he published should
differ to a considerable extent from the actual correspondence,
and the unavoidable discrepancies were certainly increased by
the negligent manner in which he was served, both by the
copyists whom he employed in the preparation of his collection
and by his printers.

Nevertheless the vast majority of the discrepancies were
certainly due to the Duke himself.   His publication was intended to serve a political object, and so had to be reasonably
short and readable.   He therefore deliberately omitted a large
number of letters which had no immediate bearing on the point
he wished to explain, and even cut out very considerable
sections from many of those he published.   In justification of
this it might be pleaded that both in the title page and in the
body of the book it is made perfectly clear that only some of the
letters, and only extracts from others, are being printed ; but
it is difficult entirely to excuse an editor who gives no indication
what letters are omitted, and who, when a portion of a letter is

---

[1] Many of Temple's letters are printed in his *Works*, and the majority of
Brisbane's in the *Lindsey MSS*.   The remainder, with few exceptions, have
not been printed at all.

cut out, habitually conceals the fact by inserting a few words of his own to fill up the gap.

Yet if the Duke of Leeds had gone no further his proceedings might have served only as an illustration of the unsatisfactory ideas of editorial responsibility which prevailed two centuries ago. Unfortunately he also made a large number of definite alterations in the letters. These alterations have proved very difficult to trace to their source, for they were made in many ways, sometimes on the letter itself, sometimes on a copy, and sometimes, in all probability, by verbal instructions to the printer. Even if all the letters, drafts and copies which passed through the Duke's hands could be gathered together it is thus questionable whether a complete list of his alterations could be drawn up. Scores if not hundreds have been identified ; but in many other cases where the printed text differs from the original the agency of the Duke in effecting the alteration can only be suspected.

It must not be supposed, however, that these changes are entirely, or even largely, of the nature of falsifications. In reality they are of the most diverse character.

(1) A very large number are purely verbal, amounting to no more than corrections of spelling, improvements in grammar, changes in the turn of sentences, or elucidations of points which might not be perfectly clear to the reader.

(2) A few are inspired by private reasons. The name of Lady Danby, for instance, is cut out wherever it occurs.

(3) A number appear to be the result of the same desire for compression as has led to so many omissions. Not infrequently the Duke has included part of one letter in another, with the object, apparently, of securing the publication of expressions favourable to himself, which belonged to letters otherwise not worth publishing at all. Once or twice he has altered the date of a letter by a year, in order that it might suitably be included among those he was publishing. In much the same spirit he has printed one of his own letters to Sir Leoline Jenkins as a letter to Sir William Temple, presumably because he had no room for a separate section devoted to his correspondence with Jenkins, and yet wanted this particular letter to be published.

(4) Many are obviously designed to minimise the Duke's own connection with the negotiations with France, and to cast a veil over their significance in domestic affairs. Stress is laid on the orders given by the King. The part played by the Treasurer is glossed over. References to Parliament are omitted or toned down. It can seldom be said, however, that in this way the actual meaning of a letter has been seriously altered.

(5) A certain number are plain and deliberate falsifications. The simplest of these is the alteration of the word ' Arlington ' to ' Treasurer ' in Montagu's letter of June 21, 1677 ; [1] the most startling, perhaps, the insertion of the note, ' This letter is writ by my order, C.R.,' after the famous letter of March 25, 1678.[2] Even such changes as these, however, have seldom or never led to the insertion of a statement the truth of which would not now be generally admitted.

Of the grosser forms of falsification there are no signs whatever. There is no reason to believe that any single letter is a forgery. Only on one or two occasions has so much even as an entire sentence been fabricated by the Duke. The obvious course of omitting the most incriminating documents has not been taken. While admiring the ingenuity with which the Duke has introduced his changes, in fact, one cannot but wonder at the supreme uselessness of his labours. Had he published his correspondence in its entirety and without alteration it would have produced very much the same general effect.

This point is well illustrated by the ' particular remarks ' which accompany the letters. Had the letters been really of the nature of forgeries the ' remarks ' would have been designed to lay stress on the passages in them which have been altered ; but they very rarely do so. On the whole, in fact, they are extremely disappointing. They add little to the information contained in the letters, and on some points are demonstrably incorrect. The Duke of Leeds himself in 1710 was none too clear about what had happened thirty years earlier.

To devise a method of making plain all the points connected with the *Letters* has not been an easy task. The following principles have been observed throughout :

(1) The introduction, ' particular remarks,' and conclusion

---

[1] *Infra*, p. 267.   [2] *Infra*, p. 349.

are based, not upon the printed version, but upon the original drafts drawn up by the Duke of Leeds.

(2) The letters are based, wherever possible, on the actual letters sent. Failing these, drafts or copies have been utilised. On a few occasions neither letter, draft, nor copy has been found, and the letter has had to be based on the printed version.

(3) The manner in which the Duke of Leeds dealt with each letter has been indicated by the type employed. Letters printed by the Duke appear in ordinary Roman type. Letters or considerable portions of letters not printed by him appear in *italics*. Insertions unquestionably in his handwriting appear in SMALL CAPITALS, with an insertion mark indicating the place they should occupy. Words and phrases struck out by him are underlined with a heavy black rule. Signs employed by him to guide his printers and copyists (⌐, ⊕, ✗, �) are reproduced as exactly as possible. All other discrepancies and points of interest are dealt with in the notes.

(4) The translations printed in the published collection, of the letters from William of Orange and of French quotations in other letters, have been omitted. There is nothing to suggest that the Duke of Leeds was in any way responsible for these. Where printer's errors occur in the letter they appear also in the translation, and the probability therefore is that the translations were provided in the printer's office.

(5) Within each section the letters have been printed in strict chronological order according to their real date, allowance being made for the difference between Old Style and New Style, and ' Out ' letters being placed before ' In ' letters of the same date. This involves a considerable departure from the order in the *Letters*.

(6) While every effort has been made to notice all points of real importance in the published *Letters*, it has not been considered worth while, in comparing the actual letters with the printed version, to aim at precise verbal exactitude. Innumerable small discrepancies in the *Letters* are not noticed at all.

Copies & Extracts

OF SOME

LETTERS

Written to and from

The Earl of DANBY

(now Duke of LEEDS)

IN THE

Years 1676, 1677, and 1678.

With particular

REMARKS

Upon some of them.

Published by his GRACE's Direction.

LONDON:

Printed for John Nicholson at the Queens-Arms
in Little-Britain, 1710.

THE LETTERS OF 1710

AN

INTRODUCTION

TO THE FOLLOWING

LETTERS[1]

SOME of my freinds, who had long ago seene both the letters now published and many more now in my custody from the same persons herein named, have blamed mee for not sooner publishing those I have now done, for the sake of the publick as well as for my owne justification. But besides my owne innocence as to every article of the charge laid against mee in Parliament in December 1678, so many both of Lords and Comons who had then voted against mee (and particularly the Lord Russell and Sir Henry Capell, who was the man that carried up that impeachment to the Lords) haveing [2] ownd to mee theire being led into great mistakes concerning mee, and that they were sorry for itt, and that many others were then undeceived as well as themselves ; besides which the malice of my accusation did so manifestly appeare in that article wherein I was charged to bee popishly affected, that I dare sweare there was not one of my accusers that did then beleeve that article against mee. The Duke of Devon also, when wee were partners in the secrett trust about the Revolution, and who did meete mee and Mr. John Darcy for that purpose att[3] a towne called Whittington in

---

[1] The original draft of this introduction, partly in the handwriting of the Duke of Leeds, is in B.M. Add. MSS. 28044, ff. 3-5. It contains numerous additions and alterations, the majority of which, however, are of only verbal importance. A clerk's copy, in which some further alterations have been made, follows on ff. 7-10. The latter corresponds substantially with the printed introduction, and has been made the basis of the present version, but the Duke's own spelling has been retained in preference to that of the copyist.

[2] Originally ' had ', which gives a better grammatical construction.

[3] The words ' an ale house in ' have been struck out.

Derbyshire, did in the presence of the said Mr. Darcy make a voluntary acknowlegement of the great mistakes hee had been led into about mee, and said that both hee and most others were intirely convinct of theire error. And hee came to Sir Henry Goodricks house in Yorkshire purposely to meete mee theire againe, in order to concert the times and methods by which hee should act att Nottingham (which was to bee his post) and I att York (which was to bee mine) ; and wee agreed that I should first attempt to surprise York, because there was a small garrison with a governor there, whereas Nottingham was but an open towne, and might give an alarme to York if hee should appeare in arms before I had made my attempt upon York ; which was done accordingly, but is mistaken in divers relations of itt. And I am confident that Duke (had hee been now alive) would have thankt nobody for putting his prosecution of mee amongst the glorious actions of his life.

For these reasons, most of which were so notoriously known, I did not think that I had needed any other justification, and did therefore not comply till now with my freinds desires to make these letters publick. But they haveing lett mee see that care hath been taken to make the articles of my impeachment to be printed in a book entitled A Compleat History of England by an unknown authour (but who calls himself An Impartiall Hand),[1] that the charge against mee might remain to posterity ; and many other mercenary scriblers, as the pamphlett called The Monthly Miscellanies, &c., having presumed amongst their other lyeing stories to make some false reflections upon my acting in those times (some of them being taken verbatim from the foresaid Impartiall Hand, and others of theire owne inventing, as those most egregious lies concerning King Charles and the Countess of Northumberland, and the Lord Montagus being att Nottingham att the time of the Revolution, where hee neither then was nor in arms anywhere else in the kingdome, &c.), and my said freinds also telling mee that my sufferring such falsities to be printed and published in

---

[1] Leeds professes throughout this volume that he does not know the author of the *Complete History*, but that he knew him quite well is shown by his own notes upon it in B.M. Add. MSS. 28042, f. 112.

my lifetime without anything being said to contradict them did make some persons who gave no creditt to them hertofore now beginn to doubt whether there might not be some truth in some of those accusations if nothing should be said in my lifetime to expose the falsity of them—I have therefore annexed the following coppies and extracts of such letters as will shew the small part I had (and that but at second hand) in what related to the French money ; as also how farr I was from ever promoteing any French interest ; how infinitely and constantly I was honoured for many yeares with the freindshipp and kindness of the Prince of Orange, and what his opinion was of my accusation in that Parliament ; and how treacherously [1] I was used, as well as the King my master, by Mr. Mountague (notwithstanding the infinite obligations he owns hee had to mee) after I had refused to assist him against Sir William Temple in being Secretary of State, who was as earnestly desirous to be excused from that employment as the other was to procure it at any rate.

As to the concealment of the Popish Plott (which is another article against mee in the said impeachment), I was so farr from concealeing itt that the greatest displeasure King Charles ever shewed against mee was my bringing Titus Oates his informations concerning that Plott before the Parliament ; and as I find it written in some of Sir William Temples Memoirs,[2] so he told mee himselfe, that the King was very angry with mee for it, and that altho I did not beleive it I should find that I had given the Parliament an handle to ruin mee, as well as to disturb all his affairs, and that I would live to repent it. And indeed I have lived to find kings to be true prophetts as well as kings, for I have seen many villanous designs acted under the cover of that Popish Plott, and I have seen many abuses made of the Trieniall Act, about which King William was very much displeased with mee for concurring in it, and used the very same expression which King Charles had done, that I should live to repent it. And I am not afraid to acknowledge that I have repented both, since I have seen such very wrong uses made of them ; and I verily beleive that if I had made myselfe so much a richer man

[1] The *Letters* read ' unworthily.'   [2] Temple, *Works*, i. 480.

then I am by those great rewards which I might by Mr. Mountagues help have had from France, and that I had kept the papers about the Popish Plott from being brought to Parliament, I should not only have escaped theire prosecution [1] (as King Charles foretold) but have acquired the encomiums of those very persons who are now the promoters [2] of slander against mee.

I putt Mr. Mountagues letters and the remarks upon them in the first place, because the principall articles of my impeachment are grounded upon his accusation ; and the rest are to shew how faithfully I acted to the best of my understanding for the interest of my countrey, attested by so many great and undeniable wittnesses, and whose originall letters are now in my custody to prove the following coppies and extracts herewith printed.

[1] Originally ' reproaches.'   [2] Originally ' contrivers.'

THE CONTENTS

MR. MONTAGU'S LETTERS

To the Lord Treasurer.[1]

Paris, January th 8, [16]77.

My Lord,

I had before this time troubled your Lordship had there passed anything since my being heere worth the giving your Lordship a particular account of ; but I presume whatever is of any moment, you have the knowledge of it both from the King himself and at the Comittee of Forreigne Affaires. This therfore is only to return my humble thankes to you for all your favours to me before I came out of England, and for your last to my father in the buisnesse of Gedington Woodes.[2]   I shall

[1] From the autograph letter in Leeds MSS., Packet 10. It is printed, with the date altered by a year, in *Letters*, p. 46, and an entirely different letter, the real date of which is January 8, 1678, is added to it as a postscript (*infra*, p. 309).

[2] The object of the Duke of Leeds in altering the date of this letter was presumably to make the obligation he had conferred on Ralph Montagu's father appear contemporary with the French intrigues. That the obligation, although earlier, was a real one is shown by the following letters from Edward, Lord Montagu, to the Earl of Danby :
My Lord, I see your favors are very extensive to our family. I am sure I pertake of them very much, and my brother in so high a degree by this honorable advance your Lordship hath beene pleased so obliginly to procure him of his Majesty, that you must give mee leave to presume to give your Lordship this interuption by presenting my most humble service and thankes for so fast a freindshipe I heare you were pleased to vouchsafe him, which is never sufficiently to be acknowliged by him, nor in his behalfe by, My Lord, Your most humble and faithfull servant, Edward Mountagu.—Boughton, April 10, 676. (Leeds MSS., Packet 7.)
My Lord, The sense I always had of your greate kindenes to mee and my amily was a greate encouragement to mee to become an humble petitioner to his Majesty, haveing first considered that the thing I desired could not bee poked upon as any encroahment upon the Crownes revenew, for had I apprended it could have beene any prejudice to his Majesty I durst not have ttempted it, haveing merited so little at his hands, though ever readdy to erve him with my life and fortune. I confess his Majestys greate favor in isaforesting Gedington Wood will bee a greate conveynyance and pleasure to

acknowledge the sence I have of them in being as serviceable as anybody soe inconsiderable as I can be to you in all your interests and all your concerns; and I shall thinke myself extreame happy whenever you will be pleased to give me an oportunity of making goode my professions of being intirely your Lordships.

The French King has at last consented to the Marine Treaty, with all the advantages the King our master desires, and I doe not doubt the having it signed and finished before the meeting of the Parlament. I wish it may have soe goode an influence upon them as to dispose them to doe all things that are necessary to put our master at ease in his affaires, and your Lordship more quiet and satisfaction in the greate employment you are in, the continuance of which is wished, with all the truth imaginable, from him whoe is with all respect, My Lord,

Your Lordships most obedient and humble servant,
R. Montagu. [1]

[*To Mr. Montagu*] [2]

8th January, 1676/7.

My Lord,

I returne your Excellency my thanks for the favour of yours of the 8th instant S.N., but can take none of the acknowlegements to myselfe about the businesse of Geddington Woods, for itt came to his Majestie by petition from my Lord your father, and was imediately granted with all the willingnesse imaginable, so as there is not the least thanks due to anybody but the King.

I am extreame glad to find the Marine Treaty so well advanc't by your Excellency, and I would bee glad to renew another which you heretofore mentioned to mee, and gave mee leave to propose to his Majestie concerning my Lord Plymouth. You may remember

my seate, and therefore myselfe and posterity must for ever acknowledge your Lordships aboundant kindenes in it, which though I am never able to requite, yet I shall ever acknowledge myseilfe, Your Lordships most thankefull and humble servant, Edward Mountagu.—Boughton, December 25, 1676. (*Ibid.*)

The reference in the first letter is to the appointment of William Montagu as Chief Baron of the Exchequer. Danby's reply to the second letter is printed in *Buccleuch MSS. at Whitehall*, i. 323.

[1] Endorsed by Danby, ' From Mr. Mountagu, 8th January [16] 77.' To this is added in the handwriting of the Duke of Leeds, '/8. Note his thanks for Geddington.'

[2] From the autograph draft in Leeds MSS., Packet 8.

I then told your Excellency and I still find that the King would rather that match could bee had for my Lord Northumberland, and I perceive hee is informed that the Dutchesse of Cleaveland and your Lady are upon so good tearmes with one another that hee beleeves the motion might perhaps now bee agreable to your Lady, though itt have not been so formerly, and hee has comanded mee as from myselfe to learne your opinion in this particular. But if yett the same difficulties remaine I find his Majestie will looke upon itt as a good service if your Excellency can procure itt for my Lord Plymouth, and I would beg you to returne such an answer to this as you will give mee leave to show the King.

My Lord Plymouth will shortly bee att Paris in his way for England, and I have hinted to him his obligation to your Excellency, though I have not acquainted him with the particular. I know his Lordship will need no recomendation of your Excellencies care whilst hee is att Paris, and if your Excellency have any comands for mee here they shall bee obey'd by, My Lord,

Your Excellencies, &c.,

[Danby] [1]

[*To the Lord Treasurer*] [2]

Paris, March th 1, [16]77.

My Lord,

I should not have bin soe long as I have bin without returning an answer to your Lordships lettar, but that two dayes after I had received it my wife fell extreame ill, and has not till now bin in a condition to speake of any things that must needes concern her soe much as what relates to the marriage of her daughter, my Lady Betty Percy. I shoed her your Lordships lettar, and will tell you as neere as I can her answer, that you may give his Majesty the better an account how this affaire stands, and at the same time of doeing me the goode office of assuring his Majesty of the utmost of my endeavours in it, whenever it shall be a proper and seasonable time to set it on foote.

But as yet my wife sayes she does think it will be very improper

---

[1] Unsigned, but endorsed by Danby, ' Coppy of my letter to Mr. Montague att Paris, 8th January 1676/7.' To this is added in the handwriting of the Duke of Leeds, ' About the match of Lady Ogle to Lord Northumberland.'

[2] From the autograph letter in Leeds MSS., Packet 10.

and very prejudiciable to the interest she ought by nature, and, though
it be given from her by the rigour of the law, dos yet expect to have in
the disposall of her daughter, if she should entertaine any proposition, for it is by that argument of how fitt and just it is that the child
should be of years to choose for herself before she be engaged that she
keepes my old Lady Northumberland from disposing of her as yet
where she would perhaps be miserable and unhappy all her life,
though I find by her lettars to my wife she is extreamly set upon
marriyng her to my Lord Ogle, and sayes that the Duke of Newcastle
has the Kings leave for his pretensions, as she may easily beleive by
the marques of honour his Majesty has conferred upon him since
the death of his father. I find my wife extreame avers too this
match, in which the grandmother can doe noething these two yeares,
the child being but ten yeares old ; and then I beleive there will be
that disagreement betweene the grandmother and mother that it must
naturally come before the King and Councell, and then will be the
time of serving his Majesty, for I make noe doubt but the daughter
will declare for marriyng wher the mother pleases and not where
the grandmother desires, which she has alwaise bin soe positive in,
though she is soe young, that whenever she is with her mother,
though the grandmother be present, she declares she will never
marry but where her mother will have her.

As for what you are please to take notice in your lettar concerning
my wife and my Lady Dutchess of Cleavland being upon goode
terms, it is that which was not hertofore, for they now visitt pretty
often ; but my Lady Dutchesse has never named yet this matter
either to my wife or me. I confesse her uncle, Mr. Ned Villars, did
to me, and rejoiced soe extreamly at theire visiting one another that
I think but for me he would have have had the discretion to have
proposed the match upon theire second meeting ; and I find by him
that all the family doe reckon that the King has engaged himself to
my Lady Dutchess of Cleavland to doe all he can to procure this
match for my Lord Northumberland, whoe himself is already
cunning enough to be enquiring of me after my Lady Betty Percy,
and has taken such an aversion to my Lord Ogle about the report,
that when they meete at my house he is alwaise ready to laugh or
make mouthes at him, soe that the gouvernour now will never scarce
let them meete.

My Lord Plymouth has bin heere some time; I have done him all the service I could in this place. Mr. Cheeke shoed me a lettar from Mr. Bertue by your Lordships directions that there should meete him a lettar of credit; but it not coming time enough I furnished him with credit for five hundred pound. I shall be glad at any time to receive the honour of your Lordships commands, and of any occasion of shoeing with how much truth and respect I am, My Lord,

Your Lordships most obedient and humble servant,

R. Montagu.

To the Lord Treasurer.[1]

Paris, March th 3, [16] 77.

My Lord,

The Count de Bergec, that is lately come from Madrid and is to reside in England as envoye extraordinary, has desired my recommendations to those that were best with the King our master. He pretends to have matters of greate consequence to propose. I thought I could not adress him better then to your Lordship, as a person of noe partie nor faction, nor capable of being biassed by any that is not for the goode of the nation and the master you serve, the continuance of whose favour I wish your Lordship with all the sincerity of one whoe professeth soe much as I doe the being, My Lord,

Your Lordships most faithfull and most obedient servant,

[R. Montagu] [2]

To the Lord Treasurer.[3]

Paris, Aprill th 4, [16]77.

My Lord,

I have taken the liberty to trouble you with this enclosed that if your Lordship thinks it proper after you have reade it you may

---

[1] From the autograph letter in Leeds MSS., Packet 10. It is printed, with the date altered by a year, in *Letters*, p. 66.

[2] Unsigned, but in Montagu's handwriting, and endorsed by Danby, ' From Mr. Montagu, 3rd March, 1677.' To this the Duke of Leeds has added, ' /8. Note, of use.'

[3] From the autograph letter in B.M. Add. MSS. 39757, f. 40, printed in *Morrison Catalogue*, iv. 272.

*shoe it the King or burn it, and be pleased to doe me that justice as
to interpret aright my intentions in it, not to set up for a politician
but to play into your hands a buisnesse of soe much advantage as
this may be to the King, and which I am sure without complement
you will manage better then anybody els.   I think I can never more
really make goode the profession I have made of being most intirely
your servant, and wishing well to all your concerns, then by offering
to you the meanes of doeing those things that may be both for your
owne and the Kings honour, which I shall alwaise doe to the best
of my understanding, and everything endeavour to acquit myself as
becomes one whoe is with soe much truth, My Lord,*

  Your Lordships most obedient and faithfull servant,

          R. Montagu.

[*To the Lord Treasurer*] [1]

         Paris, Aprill th 4, [16]77.
My Lord,

  *I thought it my duty not to omitt this oportunity of giving
you the best account I could of the state of affaires in this Court,
that a person whome the King dos trust soe much, and for your
prudent management of affaires has reason to put that confidence
which he dos in you, might be soe well informed of everything that
from thence you may advise his Majesty in relation to things
abroade to take those measures which may be most for the honour
and advantage of his Crowne and people.*

  *The King and ministers heere were extreamly alarmed at the
adresse of the Parlament, least by it the King our master should be
drawne to favour the Confederates, and let the world see he was not
soe partiall to the French interest as to refuse soe faire an oportunity
of putting a stop to theire greatenesse when it was in his power to
doe it with the concurrence and assistance of his three kingdomes.
How gratefull his Christian Majesty will be to our master for this
signall marque of his freindship he is himself the best judge, but I
dare boldly say that the townes he takes in Flaunders he owes them
more to our master then to his owne army that takes them, for theire
is not one of those townes which you see soe easyly taken that if they*

---

[1] From the autograph letter in B.M. Add. MSS. 39757, f. 42, printed in
Morrison Catalogue, iv. 273.

were encouraged by a declaration of the King for them would not hold out long enough to ruine the best army in Fraunce before they yeelded. I am sure there is not a man in Fraunce, except those French ministers that know the contrary, that doe not conclude that our master for his newtrality has every yeare subsidies to the valew of at least three or foure millions ; I am sure it is worth three times that to the French King. I was the other day discoursing something of this kind with Monsieur Le Tellier, and I demonstrated to him that Cambray, Valenciennes and St. Omers tooke away nine millions of livers from the Spanyards and gave it the French, which he allowed to be true ; and I will be answearable you will find it as true that whenever our master shall think fitt to insist upon it he may have from the French money or moneys worth to put him considerably at ease in his owne affaires.

It is my part, my Lord, to tell you what may be ; but for the advising part I submitt it to those of a better understanding then myself. Only one thing I hope you will not think me impertinent for giving my opinion in. I am sure your Lordship is informed of the difficulties were made at Nimeguen of giving our master the title of mediatour, which I think was very disrespectfull to soe greate a king, and in it his Majesty knowes the French ministers did not behave themselfes soe well as might have bin expected from them. I would therfore end that dispute of being stiled the mediatour, if I were in his Majestys place, and make myself the sole arbitre of the peace, recall all my plenipotentiaries from Nimeguen, and make all the parties concerned send theire ambassadours and treate at London, or els fight dogg fight beare.

The King will by this, if the treaty, as it may doe, last two yeares, save at least fifty thousand that his ambassadours and ministers cost him there, and draw a greate deale of wealth into his owne kingdome, by the expence of soe many forreigne ministers as must attend the treaty at London. I am sure the French will hope to have an advantage by it by the partiality they think the King has for them, and the Confederates will be fooles enough to think they shall find theires by the partiality of the people. I am sure our master will find his a greate many wayes, and particularly in the greate honour and credit it will be to him abroade and at home, and will besides, his Majesty having seene soe much abroade, and having

*much a clearer and exacter knowledge of all the affaires of Christen-
dome then anybody he can employ, from the comissionaires he shall
appoint to treate have soe suddaine and exact an account, that he
may be able to make such a peace as may for many yeares be of
greate advantage to his owne people. I am sure the respectfull
compliance of this sessions of Parlament to his Majestys desires
(the greate share of managing which I doe most heartily congratulate
with your Lordship for) has put him into soe greate consideration
abroade that he may give what law he pleaseth and where he
pleaseth.*

*Your greate wisdome as well as your zeale and affection to his
service I am sure will improove this greate and happy conjuncture
much better then any silly notion of mine, for troubling you with
which I begg your pardon, as alsoe the beleiving me with all
sincerity and truth, My Lord,*

> *Your Lordships most obedient and humble servant,*
>
> *R. Montagu.*

*I beseech your Lordship not to let this be seene at the Committee
of Forreigne Affaires.*

To the Lord Treasurer.[1]

> *Paris, Aprill th 7, [16]77.*

My Lord,

*I have taken the liberty to trouble your Lordship with a long
letter two a dayes agoe, which I hope by this time is come to
your hands. This is only to congratulate with you the the
marque of honour his Majesty I heare has given you.*[2] *I wish your
Lordship may long weare it and the continuance of all other goode
fortune, which I hope you will doe me the justice to beleive, there
being noe man with more truth nor respect then myself, My Lord,*

> *Your Lordships most obedient and humble servant,*
>
> *R. Montagu.*

[1] From the autograph letter in **B.M. Add. MSS.** 39757, f. 44, printed in
Morrison Catalogue, iv. 273.

[2] The Garter.

[To the King] [1]

Paris, June 21, [16]77.

Sir,

I cannott butt thinke itt my duty, whilst I have the honour of being employd or trusted by your Majestie, to give you an account of those things that by the station you have putt mee in I have the opportunity of discovering [2] for your service ; and when you are acquainted with them I do humbly submitt to your prudence and great wisedome to make what use you shall thinke fitt of itt.

That your Majestie may understand mee the better you must call to mind how, when you made a seperate peace with Holland, Monsieur Ruvigny, att that time the King of France his minister in England, was so emporté and passionate upon itt that you were extreamely dissatisfied with him and his proceedings, and att an intertainement made you by my Lord Lindsey att Chelsey you were pleased to call mee to you and comand mee because of my freindship and acquaintance with him to advise him to change his language and behaviour ; that you could not beleeve his master would countenance him in itt ; and that you thought you gave him great marques of your freindship in proceeding no farther and not takeing up the Triple Alliance againe, [3] which from abroad and att home you were pressed to with so much advantage ; and that dureing the war you were joyned with him in the King [3] of France had extreamely advanced his owne interests and none of your Majesties, as hee

---

[1] From a copy in Danby's handwriting in B.M. Add. MSS. 28054, f. 66, endorsed by him, ' Coppy of Embassador Montagus letter to the King of the 21th June 1677 from Paris. Given mee by the King 1st July 1677, and returned by mee to his Majestie 15th July. Concerning old Mr. Ruvigny, &c.' To this endorsement is added in the handwriting of the Duke of Leeds, ' Note this letter particularly. His advice about money and desireing the King to imploy mee in that trust. That till then Lord Arlington was the man imployd in the money affaire.' The actual letter written by Montagu was probably burnt in accordance with the wish he expresses at the end of it, but there is no reason to suspect the copy made by Danby at the time of any serious inaccuracy. The letter is printed in *Letters*, p. 1.

[2] Carelessly printed ' discoursing ' in the *Letters*.

[3] . . . [3] Although only the first two words are actually struck out by the Duke of Leeds, the whole of this is omitted in the *Letters* and the following is substituted, ' that whilst you had been join'd with his master the Crown.'

was obliged to by the treaty. When I delivered him your Majesties message I found him extreamely surprised and frighted, which I improved as much as I could. All hee had to say to mee was that after such great sumes of money as his master had paid in England itt was hard to bee left so. I told him, as for the sumes of money, they were not so great as to regrett the payment of them ; that to my knowlege the Crowne of France paid to the Crowne of Sweden two millions and an halfe for being neuters (for so the Swedes were then), and that your Majestie, who was so great and so powerfull a king, had but three millions of livers for so vast a fleet as you putt to sea, and for some ten thousand of your subjects that you lett passe over into the French service ; that these kind of discourses and reproaches would but exasperate your Majestie ; that I did not know how far that might carry you ; that his best way was to bee discreet and say nothing. I remember his expression, E bien, j'eparneray mes paroles et le Roy mon maistre son argent.

With this I left him, and gave your Majestie an account, without troubling you with these particulars I do now, that I had obeyed your commands to Monsieur Ruvigny. You ordered mee also to give my Lord Arlington an account (who was yett Secretary of State) of what had passed betweene us, which I also did, and told him that though Monsieur de Ruvigny talked very high yett I observed with what I had said to him of the Triple Alliance being taken up againe hee was extreamely frighted, and so much that I was sure, if hee were well managed, the three millions you had during the war might bee continued to you [1] to bee neuter.[1] Hee answered mee that I was out of play and no longer ambassador, and that you would not take itt well, hee was sure, my medling any more in businesse, upon which admonition I lett that sort of discourse fall.

SEE
Some few days after, Monsieur de Ruvigny came to ᴧ mee againe, telling mee that in returne of my kindnesse for haveing advised him so well hee was come to bee advised by mee ; that hee found all your ministers turning against France, and my

[1] . . . [1] These three words are omitted in the *Letters*.

TREASURER

Lord Arlington particularly absolutely in the Prince of Orange
his interests ; that hee was afraid you would bee brought to
joyne with the Confederates and abandon France ; for himselfe
hee was att his witts end and knew not what measures to take
except I would advise him. Whereupon I told him my Lord
Arlington (as hee was pleased to say to mee) was going out of
play, that my Lord Treasurer was the man you now most
trusted, and in my opinion (if your Majestie would accept of itt)
the best way was to offer the continuance of the three millions
during the war [1] for your neutrallity,[1] car dans ce monde on ne
fait rien pour rien.

After this I heard nothing of Monsieur de Ruvigny of three
months, till att last hee came and told mee, Vous m'avez donné
un bon conseil, et le Roy mon maistre vous en est obligé. ⌐ *I
concluded by his discourse that itt was agreed between the two
Crowns the continuance of the three millions, and had all the satisfaction that a true and faithfull servant of your Majesties ought to
have att the advantage you had by itt, without ever discovering to
any person liveing that I had the least knowlege of a secrett that I
thought so important for your service to bee kept private.*⊕ Since
my coming into France this last time I have conversed much
with Monsieur de Ruvigny, who partly with age and partly with
discontent att his ill usage att Court is the most broke that can
bee, and as you will easily beleeve by what I am going to tell
you. For finding him alwaies complaining of his ill usage after
the great and good services hee had done, I flattered his discontent as much as I could to gett out of him the great services
I found hee so much talked of, and att last hee confessed to mee
that when I advised him to offer your Majestie the continuance
of the three millions that hee proposed itt att this Court, that
they consented to itt, only with a recomendation to menager la
bourse du Roy, that hee had done itt so well as to bring your
Majestie to bee contented with an hundred thousand pounds,
that if hee would the King of France would as easily have paid
you three, and notwithstanding this great service they now

[1] . . . [1] These three words are omitted in the *Letters*.

refused to make his son a brigadier or to give him the reversion of his place of Agent pour les Hugenots, worth 1,000 pistolls a yeare. I have seene all the letters writt to him from France about this affaire, and your Majestie may beleeve mee, if Monsieur de Ruvigny had not managed itt in hopes to make his owne fortune by such a service, you had had 300,000 pistolls a yeare whereas now you have but one.

I trouble you, Sir, with all these particulars, that you may the better know your owne power and greatnesse, and consequently sett a greater valew upon itt if you thinke fitt. I am sure the greatnesse of the King of France is supported only by your Majesties connivance att what hee does and the good will Christendome sees you have for him. The advantages hee has by itt, even in point of revenue by his conquests, do amount to five times the summe you have now from him, and though after-games are hard to play I thinke I understand this Court so well, and if you care to have itt done I am confident I could gett you by agreement a million of livers a yeare to bee paid whilst the war shall last, and foure millions six months after the peace shall bee made. I meane, Sir, over and above what you have from France now, and if you approve of my proposition bee pleased to write me five or six lines with your comands and directions, and I doubt not but to give you a good account of itt.

Since I do not know which of your ministers you are most willing to trust, I have taken the boldnesse to give yourselfe this trouble, and if you trust any I had rather itt were my Lord Treasurer, because I thinke hee is the best judge of such an affaire ; and except you shall thinke itt for your service that hee sees this letter, I humbly beg my sister may see itt burnt, because Monsieur de Ruvigny is concerned in itt, whose utter ruine the story I have told you might bee, and your Majestie is so wise and just that I in no manner doubt of your secrecy. I have prepared everything for the execution of your commands in this matter, and if you lay any upon mee itt must bee soone, for the conjuncture makes a great deale, which towards winter may not bee so favourable. Your Majestie will excuse this trouble from the zeale I have for your service.

[R. Montagu]

To Mr. Montagu.[1]

London, July 15th,[2] 1677.

My Lord,

The King has been pleased to shew mee a letter of yours dated the 21th [3] June, and has comanded mee to write you this answer to that part of itt which concernes the money, that hee shall take itt for a good service to gett an addition of a million of livers to bee well paid during the war, and foure millions well secured to bee paid within six months after the peace shall bee made ; but unlesse hee can bee then certaine of the foure millions the addition of one million during the war will not bee enough, itt being impossible with lesse then the valew of two hundred thousand pounds sterling a yeare while the war lasts to support his affaires here, in which hee suffers so much for theire sakes [4] as I confesse in my owne opinion I thinke no money can recompence.[4] His Majestie knows not how to send you any particular instructions as to the management of this

TELL HIM THAT
matter, but trusts intirely to your judgement, since you _∧ <u>say</u> you have prepared everything for the execution of his comands in itt; but hee has comanded mee to give you this caution, that unlesse you see your way clearely through this affaire hee would have you comunicate to him the steps by which you designe to arrive att itt before you putt itt in execution.

His Majestie has directed this to bee sent by an expresse, both for the safety of itt and the quicker returne of your

---

[1] From the autograph draft in B.M. Add. MSS. 28054, f. 70. *Letters*, p. 7.

[2] Originally ' 7th '. For the explanation see *infra*, p. 270, note 3.

[3] Originally ' 21th or 24th '. Danby had apparently some difficulty in making out the date of Montagu's letter, but seems in the end to have decided in favour of ' 21th '. Montagu, however, writes the figure 5 very like the figure 1, and it is possible the real date is the 25th. The letter itself is of no assistance in elucidating the problem, as only Danby's copy survives.

[4] . . . [4] This clause has been crossed out, then ' stet ' has been written, then ' stet ' in turn has been crossed out. Nevertheless the clause appears in the *Letters* with the omission of ' I thinke '. It is difficult to be sure whether the various alterations are contemporary or not. The clause is repeated in Danby's next letter.

answer, being of your opinion that time is not to bee lost in whatever shall bee done.

[Danby] [1]

To Mr. Montagu. [2]

London, 16th [3] July, [16] 77.

My Lord,

I find by your letter to the King of the 21th [4] June, as well as by many other wayes, that I am much obliged to your Excellency for your good opinion ; and I assure you my endeavours shall bee not to diminish itt, but on the contrary to deserve as well as I can of you by my services.

His Majestie is very well satisfied to know those passages you writt him of Monsieur de Ruvigny, but I confesse I wonder to find that his Majestie has not had more then a million of livers a yeare (and that but for one yeare past) from them for whose sakes I am sure hee suffers more then in my opinion any money can recompence, besides that the very receiveing money from them (were itt knowne here) would bee highly prejudiciall to him, because itt would presently bee construed a bribe to keepe off the meeting of Parliament, and in case any agreement shall bee made about money the way of conveighing or remitting itt must bee carefully considered. But so little faith have I in any of theire promises that unlesse you can some way secure what

---

[1] Unsigned, but endorsed by Danby, ' Coppies of two letters to Embassador Montagu of the same date, viz., 15th July [" and 16th," added by the Duke of Leeds] 1677.' This endorsement clearly refers to the following letter as well. To it was added, probably somewhat later, ' These are most materiall letters, and one or both of the originalls were in Mr. Montagus cabinett and remayne sealed up in the Councill, and were read there by Prince Rupert att the opening Mr. Montagus cabinett.' Finally there is added in the handwriting of the Duke of Leeds, ' And my opinion of the French Kings acting with our King.' This endorsement is probably a continuation of the similar endorsement on the next letter.

[2] From the autograph draft in B.M. Add. MSS. 28054, f. 72. A clerk's copy follows on f. 74, on which nearly all of the alterations made by the Duke of Leeds are written. *Letters*, p. 9.

[3] Originally ' 7th ', altered to ' 15th ', and then to ' 16th '. After drafting the previous letter and the greater part of this, Danby fell ill, and did not complete and dispatch them until a week later.

[4] Originally ' 24th '.

ANY BENEFITT FROM THEM.
they promise I shall expect the noise rather then ∧ the benefitt
of theire money.

BY YOURS THAT MR. CHIFFINCH HATH BEEN AND IS   HIS
I perceive ∧ his Majestie intends Mr. Chiffinch to bee ∧ the

-EVER   FROM THENCE
receivor of what ∧ shall bee had ∧ , as hee has been of that small

ALREADY
treasure the King has ∧ received, and I am very glad of itt, being
truly desirous to have as little to do with them in any kind as I
can, unlesse itt were to cudgell them out of that contempt they
have not only for our nation but the very person of the King,
although hee bee so unhappy as not to beleeve itt. I know not
whither I ever gave you any account of haveing shew'd the
King your letter, where you proposed the remove of the plenipotentiaries from Nimeguen to London,[1] wherein I was and am
still of your opinion, because I would have his Majestie change
the figure of mediator into arbitrator. But I feare that for that
reason his Majestie will not do itt, thinkeing himselfe to bee tied
up to such nice points of honour as I durst take the sacrament
would not bee stood upon an houre by the King of France if the
condition of our master were his. I intertain you the longer
upon this subject because I thinke itt our duty by all the meanes
possible to convince the King of this truth, and if you who have
many opportunities of doing itt could send mee some of those
frequent instances, which I am confident there are, of that
Courts despiseing the councells of this, itt might bee a meanes
of saveing us from being ruined for that nation, which I beleeve
designes nothing so much as to bee the ruine of this.

[2] Amongst many other of theire proceedings with us I am
cheifely amazed att theire deniyng to you what they so bare-
facetly act by theire plenipotentiaries att Nimeguen about the
treaty which they call of comerce with Holland, and I suppose

[1] Montagu's letter of April 4, 1677, printed *supra*, p. 262. This extremely
vague sentence must not be taken as implying that the King had actually read
that letter. Probably Danby had mentioned to him this particular point in it.

[2] There is a change in the handwriting at this point which suggests that the
earlier part of the letter was drawn up on July 7, before Danby's illness, and
the later part on July 15 and 16, after his recovery.

that before this time Mr. Secretary Coventry has lett you understand that itt has been taken here for your mistake, as a thing not possible for them to deny which is so publique. I am infinitely desirous to have this matter explaned, and how far you beleeve they are advanced in itt with the Dutch ; and I will freely declare you my opinion, which is either that itt is already all concluded betwixt them _∧^{PRIVATELY}, or that itt stops only upon the Prince of Orange, till hee sees what tearmes hee can have with us, which hee rather desires.

You had received these letters a weeke agoe, but that I have been sick att Sheene and am returned to London but this day. The King would heare from you about the money matter as soone as possibly you can.[1] The Parliament mett this day and is adjourned to the 3rd of December next.[2] [3] I WAS SORRY AT MY COMING TO TOWN TO FIND MY LADY HARVEY GONE, WHO OTHERWISE I INTENDED TO TROUBLE WITH THIS LETTER, BUT HAVE NOW SENT A MAN ON PURPOSE. I AM SO MUCH A STRANGER TO ALL THE FRENCH COUNCELLS THAT I NEITHER KNOW WHY MONSIEUR COURTIN IS REMOVED NOR UPON WHAT MEASURES MONSIEUR BARILLON IS SENT. ONLY I FIND (AND AM NOT AT ALL SORRY FOR IT) THAT I AM LIKE TO HAVE NO MORE OF HIS CONVERSATION THEN I HAVE HAD OF MONSIEUR COURTIN'S. I AM PERFECTLY, MY LORD,

YOUR EXCELLENCIES, ETC.,[3]

[Danby] [4]

---

[1] The following sentence appears at this point in the draft, but is struck out by Danby, ' Tis fitt you should know Monsieur Courtin hath made an offer to give his Majestie 600,000 crowns to bee paid betwixt this time and Christmas next.'

[2] This sentence must have been written on July 16.

[3] . . . [3] All this passage is taken bodily from Danby's letter to Montagu of September 3, 1677. It is added in the clerk's handwriting to the clerk's copy of this letter, but the authority of the Duke of Leeds for the transposition appears on the letter of September 3 (*infra*, p. 285, note 1).

[4] Unsigned. The clerk's copy is endorsed in the clerk's handwriting, ' A copy of my letter to Embassador Montagu of the 16th of July [16]77.' To this is added in the handwriting of the Duke of Leeds, ' Of great importance. My originall of this is in the Councill papers, and was found in Mr. Montagues cabinett. This shows that I did not know till now that the King had received any money from France.'

To Mr. Montagu.[1]

July 18, [1677], Whitehall.

I have directed my Lord Tresurer to tell you my minde in answer to your letter, and would have you follow those directions, so as I have nothing more to add but to thanke you for the industry with which you serve me in the station where you are, and to assure you that I will allwayes be your assured frind.

Charles R.

To the Lord Treasurer.[2]

Paris, August th 4, [16]77.

My Lord,

I am to acknowledge the honour of your Lordships of July th 16, which came to my hands a day agoe, and by the same messenger I will give you an account of the buisnesse you are pleased to recommend to me, which I am in goode hopes may succeede to his Majestyes satisfaction ; and I am sure there shall be noe care on my part wanting that it may doe soe. Besides it is soe necessary and reasonable it should that it would be a very ill usage from this Court if it should faile. I sent Mr. Secretary Coventry a declaration of his Most Christian Majesty, signed by Monsieur de Pompone, which I hope will convince those that beleived the French denying any treaty with Holland without the King our masters participation was a mistake of mine that they themselfs were in the wrong ; but for theire keeping theire word is a thing noe body can expect I should be answerable.

Whenever your Lordship shall have any commands for me heere you shall see noe man is with more truth and respect then myself, My Lord,

Your Lordships most obedient and humble servant,

R. Montagu.

---

[1] Hist. MSS. Com., *Buccleuch MSS. at Montagu House*, i. 418. There can be little doubt of the date of the letter.

[2] From the autograph letter in B.M. Add. MSS. 39757, f. 46, printed in *Morrison Catalogue*, iv. 273.

To the Lord Treasurer.[1]

Paris, August th 7, [16]77.

My Lord,

I am to return you my humble thanks for your kind expressions in your letter. I doe you assure you, my Lord, there is noe servant you have is more entirely then I am interested nor concerned for the continuation of your goode fortune then myself, nor noe man thinks you deserve it better, both for your capacity and prudence in serving the King and the obliginnesse of your nature to everybody els, of which in my owne particular I have had a greater share then I can have deserved from you, and shall esteeme it as a greate addition to your former favours if you please to give me any occasion of letting you see how reall I am in my professions. I cannot write to you very freely this way, because this messenger may be exposed to severall accidents ; but if you please to send me a cipher by some goode oportunity I will alwaise tel you all I know that may be for your Lordships service, whoe am with all respect, My Lord,

Your Lordships most obedient and humble servant,

R. Montagu.

Pray loose noe time, my Lord, in dispatching a messenger to let me know what you have done with Monsieur Courtin. If the King should be gon to Portchmouth your Lordship may send me your orders without loosing to the time you must to heare from his Majesty there.[2]

[*To the Lord Treasurer*] [3]

Paris, August th 7, [16]77.

My Lord,

I could not dispatch this messenger sooner, because tha Monsieur de Pompone desired me to retaine him till he had a answer from Monsieur Courtin, from whome he did hope to hear

---

[1] From the autograph letter in B.M. Add. MSS. 39757, f. 48, printed in *Morrison Catalogue*, iv. 274. *Letters*, p. 12.

[2] Endorsed by Danby, ' From Mr. Montagu, 7th August, [16]77 : note ' ; and by Leeds, ' Complement only.'

[3] From the autograph letter in B.M. Add. MSS. 39757, f. 50, printed in *Morrison Catalogue*, iv. 274.

that the King our master would be satisfyed with the summe of 600,000 crowns which he had offered in his Christian Majestys name to pay during the warr. But knowing of what consequence it is for the King our master in this conjuncture to know what he is to trust to and what measures he may take, I have now dispatched him, though Monsieur Courtins answer is not yet come, and have undertaken to give it for him, that it will be impossible for the King my master to subsist and support his gouvernment with a lesse summe then 200,000 pound sterling whilst the warr shall last, and to commence from the first of August, which was the day I proposed it. And for the reasons your Lordship was pleased to give me I have insisted with his Christian Majesty for the payment of 200,000 pound sterling during the warr rather then any summe six moneths after the peace, considering how hard it is to secure it, and of what greater advantage the encrease of the summe at present will be to our masters affaires, which I hope by the answer his Christian Majesty, after I had proposed it to him and he had considerd of it, sent me by Monsieur de Pompone, will agree to. But I can have noe positive answer till, as I told you, he has againe heard from Monsieur Courtin.

The Court goes the eleventh of this moneth to Fountainbleau, but I will deferr my journey till I heare from your Lordship againe, and receive by you his Majestys commands for the conclusion of this affaire, which presseth soe much and, as I have told them heere, is there buisnesse as much as ours, for as you say very well in your letter, were it not for theire sake our master would not want this nor a greater summe. Monsieur de Pompone in discours with me told me that he hoped if his Christian Majesty made an effort to pay this 200,000 pound sterling a yeare that then our master would not let the Parlament meete. I told him that was not a thing to be mentioned, but must be wholly left to our masters discretion and wisdome to doe as he judged best. You will easily judg, my Lord, that the delay there is in this buisnesse proceedes from Monsieur Courtin his having a mind, as it is [his] duty, to be as goode a husband as he can for his master, and not understanding soe well as you doe the condition of your owne masters affaires. His Majesty neede be in noe paine about this affaire, for upon the return of this messenger or some other, which I desire you will *dispatch me as soone as you can, if it be not already, it will, I am confident, be concluded to his satisfaction, his Christian Majesty being soe ready as he is upon all occasions to make all the returns he can for his firmnesse and freindship to him in this conjuncture.*

I beg your Lordship's goode offices to his Majesty according to the zeale and care you find I have for his service, and the continuance of your favours to me, whoe am with all respect, My Lord,

> *Your Lordships most obedient and humble servant,*
>
> R. Montagu.

You are pleased, my Lord, to order me to give you an account of something in your lettar which I dare not doe by this messenger, because that sometimes a courier may be robbed, and I having noe cipher with your Lordship my lettars may be seene; but I will doe it in foure or five dayes by the Conte de Castell Melior that comes into England.[1]

[To the Lord Treasurer] [2]

Paris, August th 12, [16]77.

My Lord,

Since my last to your Lordship [3] by the expresse you were pleased to send me by the Kings command,[3] I have bin for two dayes at Versailles, expecting his Christian Majestys answer to the demand I made [4] of 200,000 pound sterling to beginn from the first of this August and to continue being paide till the generall peace was concluded, taking it for graunted that Monsieur Courtins answer must be come back, and that it would be conform to [5] what you were commanded by the King to write to me,[5] to insist either upon two millions of livers a

---

[1] Endorsed by Danby, ' From Mr. Montagu, 7th August, [16]77'; and by Leeds, ' Note his remark of what I say.'

[2] From the autograph letter in B.M. Add. MSS. 39757, f. 53, printed in *Morrison Catalogue*, iv. 274. There is also a clerk's copy in B.M. Add. MSS. 28054, f. 81. Many alterations are made in the handwriting of the Duke of Leeds on the copy, but other alterations must have been effected before the copy was made, for it differs in some most important respects from the original, and in these is followed by the version printed in *Letters*, p. 13.

[3] . . . [3] This does not appear in the copy or in the printed *Letters*.

[4] Copy and *Letters* both insert ' by the Kings directions ' at this point.

[5] . . . [5] Instead of this the copy and *Letters* both read ' my orders from the King.'

yeare during the warr and foure millions of livers well secured
six moneths after the peace, or els 200,000 pound sterling during
the warr, [1] without which the King our master could not
support his gouvernment, with all the ill affection that was in
his nation by reason of his partiality to Fraunce.[1]

But Monsieur de Pompone tells me this morning that Monsieur Courtin has agreede this matter with the King my master
and in your Lordships presence, and that his Majesty will be
contented with two million of livers a yeare only during the
warr, which I confesse surprised me extreamly, considering the
necessity of his Majestys condition and the positivenesse of
his commands to me by your Lordship to insist upon 200,000
pound sterling, which I had done very effectually and must have
succeeded in, considering the reasonablenesse of the demand,
except the generosity of the King our masters nature, whoe
values money soe little, has already condescended to the lesser
summe of two millions, in which I am afraide by the end of the
yeare he will find he will fall short of being able to support all
the emergent occasions that may happen, and perhaps France
be a greater sufferer by it then he himself.   Wherefore I have
dispatched this messenger on purpose to acquaint his Majesty
with what is sayde to me heere, which to me seemes different
from the language HEE HELD TO MONSIEUR COURTIN ATT THE TIME YOU
he held to Monsieur Courtin at the time you[2]
writ to me.

As for the caution you were pleased to give me of communicating to his Majesty the steps by which I would arrive at this
affaire, the steps I had made in order to it were soe sure and
infallible that I thought without any greate presumption I
might, as his Majesty gives me leave, relie upon my owne
judgment in it. It is unnecessary to repeate the long lettar of
mine his Majesty shoed your Lordship, and after those passages
of which I give a full account there I adressed myself for a
preparatif to the effecting this affaire in the same place where

---

[1] . . . [1] This does not appear in the copy or the printed Letters.

[2] The Duke of Leeds seems to have been in doubt about this phrase.
After crossing it out and writing it in again he must have altered his mind
once more, for the Letters read 'he told Mr. Courtin at the time you.'

his Majesty may please to remember I did some six yeares past
for the releasing him of an article in the treaty then made with
Fraunce of his raising and maintaining at his owne charges
6,000 foote in the French service, which I very luckelye did,
saving his Majesty, besides the other inconveniencys, above a
hundred thousand pound a yeare for a present of 2,000 louis
d'or, which he gave me leave to make where it was necessary to
insinuate that which effected the buisnesse. I am engaged to
make the same present now, they taking for graunted that they
have extreamly advanced and facilated this affaire, and promised theire assistance and necessary advertissments for the
punctuall payment of the summe agreede on, or any advances
of the payment, if the occasion shall presse. Therfore pray,
my Lord, acquaint his Majesty with this, and know his pleasure,
for I am soe farr engaged in my word and honour that I know not
how to goe back; and in my opinion such a summe is well
bestowed where upon all occasions theire may be soe much
benefitt and advantage reaped.

In the last buisnesse of this nature I had order from my Lord
Arlington to draw bills upon Sir Stephen Fox at two moneths
sight, and make use of my credit heere to take up the money.
Your Lordship must now give me directions whether I shall draw
bills upon Mr. Bertue and take up the money heere, for I am at
a stand what to doe or how to behave myself in this affaire
without your particular direction in it.

I am to begg your pardon, my Lord, and I think shall easilye
obteyne it, if without your knowledg I have rejected[1] some
propositions made to me of greate advantage to your Lordship,
if you would please to use your credit with the King your master
to be contented with a lesse summe then I insisted upon, they
taking for graunted that it was your advise that raised the
market. I tell you the very expression, and my answer was you
served to goode a master and was to goode a servant to receive
any advantage from anybody els, and there could be noething
soe disobliging to you as the thoughts of offering it.

[1] Both the copy and the *Letters* read ' received.'

The Conte de Castell Melior has bin sick, or els you had by this time had a more perfect account then I can give you this way, though I send one a purpose with it, and conclude if the King has not 200,000 pound sterling it is his owne fault, and not mine [1] nor your Lordships, from whome I received as full powers and orders as was necessary to demand it, and [1] begg the continuance of your favour and goode offices to his Majesty, being with all respect, My Lord,

Your Lordships most obedient and humble servant,

R. Montagu.

[2] I have ordered this messenger to keepe private, presuming Mr. Secretary Coventry nor anybody els knowes anything of this affaire, and to be sent back when you please. You will heare of him at my sisters. [2]

To the Lord Treasurer. [3]

Paris, August th 12, [16]77. N.S.

My Lord,

You will see by my lettar that your Lordship is to shoe the King, how the negociation of the money you charged me with is embrassed, either by Monsieur Courtin not representing the necessity of the Kings affaires as he ought to doe, or the Kings easinesse without your consent to condescend to a lesse summe.[4] But Monsieur Courtin writes positively that he has agreede with your Lordship for two million of livers, whereas I had heere insisted upon the 200,000 pound sterling you mentioned, and could not faile having it graunted, except the King himself has gon back from the orders he gave me. I wish the

---

[1] . . . [1] This does not appear in the copy or the *Letters*, in both of which a new sentence begins with ' I beg.'

[2] . . . [2] This postscript does not appear in the copy or the *Letters*. The original letter is endorsed by Danby, ' From Mr. Montagu, 12th August [16]77. Note.' To this the Duke of Leeds has added, ' The offer made to him of great advantage to myselfe. That hee had used to apply to Lord Arlington in these matters. I was to shew this letter to the King.'

[3] From the autograph letter in B.M. Add. MSS. 39757, f. 56, printed in *Morrison Catalogue*, iv. 275. *Letters*, p. 17.

[4] The *Letters* add ' than he commanded me to insist upon.'

King would have let this whole matter bin transacted by soe wise and faithfull a servant as yourself. He would have found the benefitt of it, and either would have had noething or a larger summe then a million of livers a yeare.

I congratulate very heartily with your Lordship that Mr. Chiffinch is to be the French treasurer. [1] That office can never doe you any goode, and may doe you hurt. ᵐ You may be confident of my secrecye about this whole affaire, both for the Kings, your Lordships, and my owne sake, for it would be noe popular nor creditable thing if it were knowne.[1] And[2] not only in this but [2] everything els that can concern your Lordship you shall find me as carefull and faithfull as any servant you have, being with all truth and respect, My Lord,

Your Lordships most obedient and humble servant,

R. Montagu.[3]

To Mr. Montagu.[4]

Wimbledon, 10th August, [16]77.

My Lord,

I send this by the post, only to lett you know that I have received yours of the 12th instant, which came by the expresse you sent. The King is gone to Plymouth, and till his returne I shall bee able to say nothing to such surprizeing matter as your letter imports in every part of itt. For in the first place I never spoke with Monsieur Courtin in my life about that nor any such affaire, till since I received this last letter from you, so that all hee has said was done in my presence is utterly false. In the next place I know nothing of the Kings change of mind in that businesse ; only I know hee has more reason then ever to bee positive in his resolutions. But I know not what to say in itt, because since I received your letter I had some discourse with

---

[1] . . . [1] This does not appear in the *Letters*. The mark inserted by the Duke of Leeds after ' hurt ' suggests that he originally intended to omit the letter from that point onwards, but if so he must have changed his mind.

[2] . . . [2] The *Letters* read ' in this and.'

[3] Endorsed by Danby, ' Mr. Montagus letter, 12th August [16]77.' To this the Duke of Leeds has added, ' Chiffinch to bee the treasurer of the French money ; the Kings owne comand to insist for the sume ; and hee sent a letter of the same date which I was to shew to the King.'

[4] From the autograph draft in B.M. Add. MSS. 28054, f. 83. *Letters*, p. 18.

Monsieur Courtin, who speakes much of the same kind to mee that you had from Monsieur Pompone, the truth of which must remaine till his Majesties returne, and then wee shall both know what wee are to do.

Your Excellency must till then expect also for orders about the man you say is so usefull to you. In the meane time I thinke itt not necessary to send any expresse, but I do give you thanks for makeing that answer you did concerning ⋀ myselfe,
_{ANY ADVANTAGE TO}
who you will find upon all occasions ready to shew that I am, My Lord,

Your Excellencys most faithfull humble servant,

[Danby] [1]

[To the Lord Treasurer] [2]

Paris, August th 28, [16]77.

I received the favour of yours of th 11,[3] and am very glad to find you are not engaged in anything contrary to what you writ to me in your first, and if all parties concerned are unengaged to, and have not given theire words, the buisnesse cannot faile
_{WAS ORDERED}
and in the manner as ⋀ you proposed it to me. And in case that
_{NOT}
the goode nature of our freind has ⋀ condescended to other terms then what they first proposed, I have ordered matters soe, that I am confident my first proposition may succeede, though I confesse what you directed me to doe was much more advantagious, and as affaires stand there is almost an absolute necessity it should be soe.

As for the person that is and has bin soe usefull in this affaire, I beg I may not discontent them, for I will demonstrate to you upon the first oportunity that it was impossible to leave them

---

[1] Endorsed by Danby, 'Coppy of my letter to Mr. Montague, 10th August 1677, in answer to his of the 12th August, N.S.'

[2] From the autograph letter in B.M. Add. MSS. 39757, f. 58, printed in *Morrison Catalogue*, iv. 276. There is a copy in B.M. Add. MSS. 28054, f. 87, on which the Duke of Leeds has made his alterations. *Letters*, p. 20.

[3] Probably a slip for '10', or possibly Danby dated his draft 10th August and sent off the actual letter on the following day. The letter referred to, at any rate, seems to be that on p. 280.

out ; nor can you till this matter be wholly out of doores be without them, but with a very considerable prejudice. I presume soe much upon your kindnesse[1] and justice as to beleive what I say is purely for the goode of those you concern yourself for, and not out of any pitifull advantage to myself.

This comes by my sistar, whoe has a ciphar to know how to send it to you, and as soone as you explaine yourself to me I shall be able to make an end of this whole matter.

[R. Montagu] [2]

[To the Lord Treasurer] [3]

Paris, August th 30, [16]77.

My Lord,

I think I may write to your Lordship three or foure lines safely by this bearer, a gentleman of my Lord Duras, and therfore I will give you in short the true account of the negociation concerning the money to be payde the King our master from hence during the warr.

After what I had writ to the King concerning the passages betweene Monsieur de Ruvigny and myself, I endeavoured to furnish myself with all the arguments to make the buisnesse surely succeede. And in the first place I did, by the meanes of the person I writ to you concerning a gratification, come to the knowledg of those summes that are given to the Duke of Baviere and Hennauvre, both which are much lesse considerable princes, I hope, then our master, and yet the former has at least as considerable a summe privately paide as what I pretended to for our master, and suffers not halfe soe much for his partiality or rather newtrality for Fraunce ; which argument, when I urged, they could not answer but by desiring me to have patience, because they were assured from Monsieur Courtin, and expected another confirmation every day, that our master was and would be contented with two millions of livers, which as I

---

[1] The copy and the *Letters* read 'friendship.'

[2] Unsigned and unaddressed. Endorsed by Danby, ' From Mr. Montagu, 28th August [16]77.' To this the Duke of Leeds has added, ' Note my knowing nothing of Courtins discourse to the King.'

[3] From the autograph letter in B.M. Add. MSS. 39757, f. 60, printed in *Morrison Catalogue*, iv. 276. *Letters*, p. 21.

sent you word, my Lord, Monsieur Pompone assured me the King had condescended to de concert avec le Grand Tresorier (I tell you the very expression).

Notwithstanding I have still opiniatred for 200,000 pound sterling, telling that I had my orders from the King himself, and till I heard from him the matter was agreede I could beleive noebody els, knowing how impossible it was for him to support his gouvernment without it, and how easie for the French king to furnish it, as I demonstrated, by the addition of his revenue by these new conquests, the true knowledg of which I got by the meanes of the same person. And really that very addition comes to very neere six millions, and methinks our King might have three of them, since he is absolutely the occasion of [the] King of Fraunce his enjoying them. You will find alsoe, my Lord, if you agree for two French millions only, that the King will be a looser out of that summe at least 12,000 pound a yeare by theire adresse in the exchange, whereas all that would be sauved, and a goode deale got, if whatever summe be to be paide you agree that it be in pounds sterling.

Pray, my Lord, let me have your directions at large and as soone as you can, for I doe tell you very francly, and I hope the King will pardon me since it is out of zeale for his service, that if he has not 200,000 pound sterling it is his owne fault, and if he has condescended to two millions I can, I am confident, bring on my first proposition of foure millions after the peace. [1] But for that I will communicate to you my way of doeing it, and take your advise in it before I proceede any farther,[1] and I dare flatter myself soe much as to beleive you will approove the steps I have already made towards the effecting it. I goe to-morrow to Fountainbleau, and leave directions behind that any commands of yours may be brought to me, whoe am with all truth and respect, My Lord,

Your Lordships most obedient and humble servant,

R. Montagu.[2]

[1] . . . [1] This does not appear in the *Letters*.

[2] Endorsed by Danby, ' From Mr. Montagu, 30th August [16]77,' and by the Duke of Leeds, ' Hee received his orders about money from the King himselfe, and can have four millions.'

To Mr. Montagu.[1]

London, 3/13 September, 1677.

My Lord,

I have two of yours to acknowlege, one of the 28th August by the post, and another of the 30th by a servant of my Lord Duras, and for your direction itt is necessary that you know the full state of the matter here.

Att the Kings arrivall from Plymouth I found hee had consented (and in the presence of the Duke) to two millions to bee compleated for one yeare ending att Christmas next, but confessed hee had not considered the difference betwixt that and

200,000 pounds, and ∧ ^{SAID} acknowleged that 200,000 l. was the summe <u>I had alwaies told him</u> would bee att least necessary for his service, and which hee had directed <u>by mee</u> that you should insist upon.⊕ <u>I putt him in mind also how much reason hee had</u> <u>to feare the Spaniards falling out with him, and what an</u> <u>additionall charge that must bring, and all for the French Kings</u>

sake ; whereupon ∧ ^{AND I FOUND} hee was troubled that hee had consented to the two millions, and imediately sent for the Duke, whom hee comanded to speake with Monsieur Courtin about itt, and tell him how necessary itt would bee to have 200,000 l. by reason

of ∧ ^{THE} that danger ∧ ^{OF THE SPANIARDS FALLING OUT WITH HIM.} from the Spaniard. But his Highnesse not being able to prevaile upon Monsieur Courtin, nor his Majestie being willing to speake any more upon that subject to him, the result of his Majesties pleasure hath been that hee will speake no more

of this matter ∧ ^{HIMSELFE} to Monsieur Courtin, but does comand that you do still insist upon the summe to bee 200,000 pounds ; but you

∧ ^{ARE TO} <u>may</u> say that you perceive the King did once thinke to have made a shift with two millions, but that now hee finds so great cause to apprehend a breach with Spaine, or att least so much appearance of itt as will necessitate him to bee att more charge

---

[1] From the autograph draft in B.M. Add. MSS. 28054, f. 89. *Letters*, p. 24.

then hee intended in the Westerne Islands, so that hee must needs desire that sume.

Notwithstanding this resolution I beleeve that Monsieur Courtin, who goes from hence in two or three daies, will bee wholly a stranger to itt, and will arrive in your Court confident of our Kings being content with two millions, so that you are to expect that difficulty and to contend with itt as well as you can. If itt should happen that att last no more then two millions can

bee had I am glad to find you ∧ still confident of the foure millions after the peace, which I hope you will keepe in your power to incompasse.⊕ [1] *I was sorry att my coming [2] to towne to find my Lady Harvey gone, who otherwise I intended to have troubled with this letter, but have now sent a man on purpose. I am so much a stranger to all the French councells that I neither know why Monsieur Courtin is removed, nor upon what measures Monsieur Barillion is sent. Only I find (and am not att all sorry for itt) that I am like to have no more of his conversation then I have had of Monsieur Courtins.* I am perfectly, My Lord,

HOWEVER

Your Excellencies, etc.,

[Danby] [3]

To the Lord Treasurer. [4]

Paris, September th 22, [16]77.

My Lord,

 I had the honour of your Lordships of September th 3 which you sent by an expresse, but not time enough to acknowledg it last post. I am this day returning to Fountainbleau, and will endeavour to give you the best account I can of what you recommend

---

[1] This mark, inserted by the Duke of Leeds, appears to be the authority for the transference of the remainder of this letter to Danby's letter of July 16, 1677 (*supra*, p. 270). Apart from the conclusion, ' I am perfectly ' etc., the version of this letter in the printed collection comes to an end at this point.

[2] The word ' yesterday ' has been struck out in the draft.

[3] Endorsed by Danby, ' Coppy of my letter to Mr. Montagu, 3rd September 1677 '; and by the Duke of Leeds, ' Note, of consequence.'

[4] From the autograph letter in B.M. Add. MSS. 39757, f. 62, printed in *Morrison Catalogue*, iv. 276.

to me, which is all I have to trouble you with at present but the
assurances of my being with all respect, My Lord,

Your Lordships most obedient and humble servant,

R. Montagu.

To the Lord Treasurer.[1]

Fountainbleau, September th 25, [16]77.
My Lord,

I am afraide the Duke of Monmouth should be gon from
Paris, by whome I hope this may come safe to your hands, and
therfore I must referr you, not having time to write a longer lettar,
to this enclosed of his Majesty, by which you will see how farr I
have advanced the negociation you ordered me to goe upon by your
last expresse, and I remaine with all respect, My Lord,

Your Lordships most obedient and humble servant,

R. Montagu.[2]

[To the King] [3]

Fountainbleau, September th 25, [16]77.
Sir,

My Lord Treasurer having sent me new orders from your
Majesty to insist still upon a supply of 200,000 pound sterling
till the peace were made, and your lettar commanding me to
observe what orders he should give me,[4] I have in conformitye

---

[1] From the autograph letter in B.M. Add. MSS. 39757, f. 64, printed in
Morrison Catalogue, iv. 276. This letter and the following three present some
difficulties. The date of all four is apparently September 25, although Montagu's ' 5 ' is so like a badly formed ' 1 ' that Danby himself inclined at first to
take the date as September 21. The letters seem to fall into two sets of two.
The first set consists of a short covering letter to Danby, and a long letter to
the King himself, hurriedly dispatched by the Duke of Monmouth. The
second set consists of a short letter addressed to Danby but intended for the
King's perusal, and a long letter meant for Danby alone, sent immediately
afterwards by the post in case the first set should be delayed.

[2] Endorsed by Danby, ' From Mr. Montagu, 21th September [16]77.'

[3] From the autograph letter in B.M. Add. MSS. 39757, f. 69, printed in
Morrison Catalogue, iv. 277. There is a copy in B.M. Add. MSS. 28054, f. 91,
on which the Duke of Leeds has made his alterations. *Letters,* p. 26. This is
apparently the letter calendared under date September 29 in *Hist. MSS. Com.,*
ix. 2, p. 452.

[4] This letter has not been found. Presumably it was of much the same
character as that printed on p. 273 above.

to ∧ <u>that and the</u> last lettar I <u>received from him</u> represented to
the King and ministers heere the necessity of your Majestys
having ∧ <u>that summe</u>, and to help you ∧ of, Sir, of the embarras
you may be in by theire pressing you of having given your word
to Monsieur Courtin to be contented with two millions, I have
turned the matter this way.

The King heere at my arrivall, as he dos to all other ambassadours, gave me notice that whenever I had anything to say to
him I might have the libertye to speake to him ; but he would
desire me to let him know of it beforehand, and communicate to
the minister whose province my buisnesse concerned what I had
to say, for that sometimes ambassadours had surprized him,
and he had given his word in things, which, when he afterwards
weighed and advised with his ministers, he could not without
greate inconveniency keepe. This I told him was your Majestys
case, for if Monsieur Courtin had consulted with my Lord
Treasurer, without whome noe king in the world can tell what
money is necessary to support his affaires, these mistakes would
not have happened, and you would not soe easilye have
condescended to what prooves soe inconvenient to you, your
Majesty not then considering the breach that may happen with
Spayne, the fall of your Customes by the merchants not daring
to ventur to trade, and the encrease of your expence by your
being obliged perhaps to give them convoies ; that it was alsoe
partly my fault by keeping the courier [1] you sent me heere with
positive orders to insist upon 200,000 pound sterling, which I
did, but ought not to have done, though the King heere desired
it, for it exposed your Majesty, whoe is of soe generous a nature
as not to love the discours or dispute of money matters, to the
solicitation of Monsieur Courtin, whoe, as all goode servants are,
must spare theire masters purse as much as they can ; you were
over and above obliged to a greater expence for the security of
your Western Islands. All these things considered I hoped he
would supply you with the summe first insisted on ; ⊕ *your*

---

[1] The copyist has carelessly transcribed this as ' cover ', and is followed by
the *Letters*.

*Majesty being soe exposed as you were for your firmnesse and
freindship to him was a sufficient testimonye how inviolably you
keepe your word, and therfore did imagine you could not be
thought to breake it in this demande ; and that your being in a
condition to support your Crowne and dignity was as much his
Christian Majestys interest now as yours.*⊕

All these arguments of mine neither the King or ministers can
answer. They have onely desired me to stay till they speake
with Monsieur Courtin, whoe is expected in foure or five dayes.
But in the meane time I conclude Monsieur de Barillon will
endeavour to keepe you to the two millions. Therfore, Sir, if
I may be soe bold as to advise you, say only this when he
speakes to you, Je n'ayme point a parler ny a disputer des
affaires d'argent ; je vous remets a mon Grand Tresorier, avec
quy vous prenderes vos mesures, et a quy jay commende
denvoyer mes ordres a mon ambassadeur sur cette affaire. I
am sure my Lord Treasurer has soe goode a reputation abroade
for his abilitie and management of the revenu that when he tells
the necessity of it they will dispute it noe longer, and will be
convinced that it is not to raise the price but for the reall
support of your gouvernment that you are obliged to insist upon
the first demand. [1] ⊕ But for me, Sir, I can only start the
buisnesse, and have not credit enough to conclude it, because
they may think my pressing an officious zeale to doe [2] have the
merit of doeing a goode peice of service, except I am seconded
by one of my Lord Treasurers reputation and abilitie.⊕ You
must alsoe owne, Sir, your having sent me your commands to
presse this affaire ✗ because you doe not care nor doe not think
it fitt to presse these matters yourself.

I keepe the courier [3] heere my Lord Treasurer sent last,
because I hope after Monsieur de Barillon has spoake to your
Majesty and my Lord Treasurer, and he has given them an

AND THAT
account that [1] ⊕ ∧ your Majestys desires are conformable to

---

[1] . . . [1] All this is omitted in the *Letters*. The various marks and deletions
suggest that the Duke of Leeds at first aimed at retaining part of the passage.

[2] The word ' doe ' should have been struck out.

[3] Again transcribed ' cover ' by the copyist.

what I have represented here, ∧ THAT I MAY to give you such an account as may shoe you the zeale that I shall have for your service, whoe am with all duty <u>and respect</u>, Sir,

Your Majestys most faithfull and dutyfull servant,

R. Montagu.[1]

To the Lord Treasurer.[2]

Fountainbleau, September th 25,[3] [16]77.

My Lord,

I have bin heere these two dayes. I found the King and ministers extreamly surprized when I told them the orders I had from the King my master to propose this last affaire againe, and in some suspition as if my orders did rather come from your Lordship then the King. Wherfore I write by the post, least what I write by the Duke of Monmouth should not come soe soone, to give you this notice ; and I hope when Monsieur de Barillon, whome I think they will beleive sooner then they will your Lordship or me, and whoe will have orders to speake to the King our master upon this affaire, shall give them an account that what I have proposed this second time as well as the first was our masters owne desire, as his owne handwriting justifies me in,[4] they will give his Majesty full satisfaction in what he desires. I am with all respect, My Lord,

Your Lordships most obedient and humble servant,

R. Montagu.[5]

[1] Endorsed by Danby, ' Mr. Montagus letter to the King, 25 September 1677 '; and by Leeds, ' His advice alwaies to refer the French ministers to mee, and particularly about the money affaire.'

[2] From the autograph letter in B.M. Add. MSS. 39757, f. 72, printed in *Morrison Catalogue*, iv. 278. *Letters*, p. 29.

[3] Montagu appears to have written ' 22 ' and then altered it to ' 25.' There can be little doubt that the latter is the correct date.

[4] Montagu seems to have obtained autograph letters from the King authorising both his original demand and the renewal of his application (*supra*, pp. 273 and 286, note 4).

[5] Endorsed by Danby, ' From Mr. Montagu, 25th September [16]77. Note.' To this the Duke of Leeds has added, ' the French suspicion of mee, and his order in the Kings owne hand. This is also quoted.'

[To the Lord Treasurer] [1]

Fountainbleau, September th 25, [16]77.

My Lord,

I send you enclosed a lettar such as your Lordship may shoe the King, and in this I take the libertye to give you the best account I can of this moneye affaire ; and out of the respect and service I have for your Lordship I have ordered matters soe, and I think made things soe easie, that you may have the credit and advantage with the King of concluding it. It will alsoe for the time to come play all things of moment and consequence into your hands, and confirm the King more and more in the opinion he has of your abilitye and fidelity in the management of all his affaires.

I had two dayes before I came heither myself, by a lettar that I writ to the person I have mentioned to you as one usefull in this and other affaires, and which I knew would be shoed the King and ministers, prepared them by the orders ‸ I HAD RECEIVED FOR you had sent me to expecting my insisting still upon 200,000 pound sterling, and when I came the King and ministers seemed to be extreamly surprised at it. But I used soe many arguments to them that they had noething to answer but that the King had agreede with Monsieur Courtin for two millions, to which I answered that though the King had in modesty, or not examining the diffir-ence betweene French and English money, consented to such a thing, yet it was wholly without your ‸ LORDSHIPS consent or participa-tion, ‸ AND that you were the person the King trusted in the management of his money ‸ AFFAIRES, ⊕ *that when you undertooke the support of the gouvernment without any Parlament till the end o April it was upon the supposition of a supplye of 200,000 pound sterling, which summe failing all measures were broken, and could not be set right without coming up to the summe first insisted upon*

[1] From the autograph letter in B.M. Add. MSS. 39757, f. 66, printed in *Morrison Catalogue*, iv. 277. There is a copy in B.M. Add. MSS. 28054, f. 93 on which the Duke of Leeds has made his alterations. *Letters*, p. 30.

soe that now I am desired to stay returning any answer till Mon-
sieur Courtin comes, whoe is expected every day.

But I know in the meane time they will write to Monsieur de
Barillon to prevaile with the King to be contented with two millions.
You must therfore keepe up the King only to say to Monsieur
Barillon when he speakes to him this, Je nayme point a parler des
affaires d'argent ; je vous remets a mon Grand Tresorier, avec qui
il faut prendre vos mesures et a quy j'ay commende d'envoyer des
ordres a mon ambassadeur la dessus. And if you tell him againe
that summe is necessary and I have orders to insist upon it, you
will certainly see the buisnesse done, and I shall be more pleased
that you should have the merit with the King of finishing it then
have it myself, for your favour and kindnesse in doeing me goode
offices to the King will be of more advantage to me then any merit
of my owne. The service will be very considerable to the King, for
the peace is not like to be soone made, and some five and fiftye

thousand pound encrease will stop many a gap. ⊕ And besides ∧^WHICH

I would have you doe that which none of the Kings ministers
have yet had the adresse to doe, which is to take an ascendent
over Fraunce, which is next to what you ∧^SAY YOU have a mind to
^WHICH
doe, ∧ that is to cudgell them into a better behaviour and more
respect towards our master. And this is the time of doeing it,
for by this we shall judg of our strength, which as yet we are
ignorant of.

I have not drawne the bills for that money upon you, because
you tell me not to doe it except the affaire succeede. But pray
consider if they had not done theire part when I assure you upon
my first speaking they told me orders were given for providing
200,000 pound, and only stayed to see if Monsieur Courtin could
get anything bated ; and if the King will spoyle the buisnesse
whoe can help it. When I was last in Fraunce the King trusted
me enough, and gave me leave to keepe my word with them,
and found the goode effect of it. If I doe not now they will
think I cheate them, and if I doe for ought I see the King will
think I cheate him ; soe that I have noe very goode time

betweene both, and only out of the desire to doe the King a service. I have still assured them, let what will happen, I will keepe my word, and assure them I am providing the money ; and if I cannot satisfye your Lordship and the King I will pay it out of my allowance and be warier another time, for if you had not writ me word the King trusted wholly to me and to my judgment to bring this about you are sure, my Lord, I would have had your directions and orders in it first. Therfore pray doe not let a mans goode intentions doe him an ill office, for you shall never find anybody that shall have more deference or respect for any orders you shall send me, nor that is with more truth,⊕[1] My Lord,

Your Lordships most obedient and humble servant,

R. Montagu.

Your Lordship may safely acknowledg the receipt of this by foure or five lines by the post, writing in such a manner as you writ before, which if it were opened noebody can make anything of.

⊕ [2] I had forgot to tell you that I find heere Monsieur Courtin negociated this matter of contenting the King with two millions privately at Mr. Chiffings his lodgings, and I conclude without your participation, for Monsieur de Pompone, in the heate he was to convince me the affaire was concluded, shoed me Monsieur Courtins lettar, where he sayes as much, but was sorry after he had shoed it ; soe that by this you may see how they endeavour to surprise the King.[3]

---

[1] This mark was no doubt intended to denote that the printed version should stop here.

[2] Alongside this mark the Duke of Leeds has written, ' add this.' As a result the latter part of the postscript is printed in the *Letters*, but not the earlier part.

[3] Endorsed by Danby, ' From Mr. Montagu, 21 or 25 September [16]77. Of great importance ' ; and by Leeds, ' and shewing both Courtins falsity and my expression of cudgelling them, and not being privy to the discourse betwixt the King and Monsieur Courtin. This is the letter quoted by mee.'

To the Lord Treasurer.[1]

My Lord,   *Paris, October th 12,* [16]*77.*

 This enclosed to his Majesty will give your Lordship an account in what condition this affaire of the money stands, and how it only wants your helping hand to conclude it. I have begged his Majestys leave to come into England for a fortnight, which I hope you will not be against. I shall draw bills upon my cozen Bertue for 2,000 louis dors, which I will when I come give you an account of, with the assurance that noe man is with more truth nor respect then myself, My Lord,

  Your Lordships most obedient and humble servant,

           R. Montagu.

[To the King] [2]

Sir,   Paris, October th 12, [16]77.

 [3] My Lord Treasurer having by another express sent me [3] your Majestys commands to continue the solicitation heere of 200,000 pound to be paide you during the warr, I have omitted noe arguments to make my demand proove effectuall ; but by reason of your Majestys first condescention to the summe of two millions, and Monsieur Courtins arrivall, whoe has confirmed it, I have mett with greater difficulties to bring the King heere to consent to it then perhaps I should otherwaise have done. Yet however I have had soe much reason of my side for what your Majesty desires,[4] that they know not heere what to answer me,[5] *and the buisnesse is brought to this that yesterday, after I had had a long audience and discours about the matter, I was desired to stay for my answer till after Councell, and then Monsieur Pompone*

---

[1] From the autograph letter in B.M. Add. MSS. 39757, f. 75, printed in *Morrison Catalogue*, iv. 278. The exact relationship between this and the three following letters, all of them dated October 12, is not quite certain. Probably this was a covering letter for that to the King, and the remaining letter to the Treasurer was sent with the note to Charles Bertie.

[2] From the autograph letter in B.M. Add. MSS. 39757, f. 79, printed in *Morrison Catalogue*, iv. 279. *Letters*, p. 36. For the many alterations and omissions in the printed version of this letter the Duke of Leeds must be held responsible, but the copy on which he made his changes has not been found.

[3] . . . [3] This appears in the *Letters* as ' Having by another express receiv'd.'

[4] The *Letters* read ' demands.'

[5] In place of the considerable passage which they here omit the *Letters* insert and do therefore delay to give me any answer.'

brought me word, Monsieur de Barillon finira l'affaire avec le Grand Tresorier en Angleterre, soe that you may reckon upon it as done, for I alwaise told you, Sir, that my pressing heere would be looked upon as a superofficious zeale to doe you a goode service, except I had the assistance of one whome you trust soe much in your affaires as you doe my Lord Treasurer, and whose office as well as his ability puts him in a capacity of representing to Monsieur de Barillon, as I have done heere, the reasonablenesse and indispensable necessity of such a supplye.

I have fixed the payments according to the instructions of my Lord Treasurer, which you order me to follow, to beginne from this Michelmas after the rate of 200,000 pound sterling, and to continue till the peace be made ; soe that if they would hold you to the rigour of what Monsieur Courtin proposed there is but a quarters difference, for he owns himself that he agreede but till Christmas next for the two millions of livers, soe that, as I told them heere, the difference is but one quarter, which is some 12,000 pound, a summe very inconsiderable to the King of Fraunce and extreame necessary to your Majesty, without which you cannot sett up your house and family, which you have soe long retrenched, nor have it in the splendour it ought to be upon the arrivall of the Prince of Orenge and soe many of the Confederate ministers, whoe will little regard what you say if they should see your owne affaires in soe ill a condition as they are at home, and which would have bin in as goode as any princes of Christendome did you not for your firmnesse to Fraunce reject all the advantagious offers made you both abroade and at home.

I have not bin mealy-mouthed in this occasion, and have told them plainly that your Majesty understands very well the advantage the Crowne of Fraunce must receive [1] by this warr, both by encrease of power and revenew, and that it was not reasonable, if you did not get your share,[2] you should be a looser, which you must of necessity be, if they did not assist you [3] *to support your gouvernment, as well as employ all theire money to enlarge there owne. Monsieur de Pompone desired to know of me whether, in case his master should agree to pay from*

---

[1] The *Letters* read ' has receiv'd.'   [2] The *Letters* omit ' your share.'

[3] In place of the passage which they here omit the *Letters* insert ' with such a supply at least as you now desired.'

Michelmas next till a peace be concluded the summe of 200,000
pound, you would not promise to have the meeting of your Parla-
ment defferred till then alsoe. I told him my orders went noe farther
then the summe I have insisted upon ; that your Majesty had very
frankly without capitulation put it of till the spring, but I did
conceive you would have it in your power and be free to have it
meete as your owne greate wisdome and occasion should require.

I take the liberty to give you, Sir, this advertisment,[1]
because I found they would have absolutely have concluded the
matter with me heere, if I would have owned that I had power
to have given them your word in that point [1] which Monsieur
de Barillon will now negociate with your Majesty ; and I hope
you will referr him, as I humbly advised before, to my Lord
Treasurer, whoe [I] am sure will conclude it to your advantage
and satisfaction. *And it is in your power, Sir, according as you*
judg the peace to be neerer or farther from concluding, to lett fall the
negociation of encreasing the two millions from Michelmas, and
insist upon a summe to be paide you six moneths after the peace,
for if it is concluded soone the encrease will be of noe advantage to
you. Considering all these reasons I am confident your Majesty
will find your account very well that all is referred to Monsieur
Barillon and the Grand Tresorier, as they desire heere.

I have severall things of moment and advantage to impart to
your Majesty, which I cannot write, and [2] some little domestique affaires of my owne which are in disorder by the death of
a servant that manegeth all my wifes estate. I [2] humbly beg
your Majestys leave to come into England for a fortnight. I
have writ to Mr. Secretary Coventry[3] to ask it of your Majesty,
[4] he being ignorant of the honour I have of giving your Majesty
trouble, for which I humbly beg your pardon,[4] and remaine with
all duty, Sir,

Your most obedient faithfull servant,

R. Montagu.

---

[1] . . . [1] Omitted in the *Letters* and replaced by ' about those matters.'

[2] . . . [2] Omitted in the *Letters*.

[3] Montagu's dispatches to Coventry, of which mention is frequently made
in these letters, are among the Bath MSS. at Longleat, catalogued in *Hist.*
MSS. Com., iv. 245.

[4] . . . [4] Omitted in the *Letters*.

[To the Lord Treasurer] [1]

Paris, October th 12, [16]77.

My Lord,

I hope your Lordship will upon the reading of the Kings lettar be satisfyed with what I have transacted in this affaire of the money, and the reall desire I have by everything that comes in my way to be a little instrumentall in the confirming his Majesty in the opinion he has already of your ability and dexterity in the management of all his affaires. Wherfore I have playde this buisnesse, which was almost spoyled, into your hands, that the ministers here may see the King trusts you as much in his forreigne affaires as in those that relate to your office at home ; and without complement or flattery you will serve him better then any Secretary of State I ever knew him have yet, [2] or Sir William Temple if he were it.[2]

After having had many conferences with the King and ministers I had yesterday this answer from the King, Monsieur de Barillon finira cette affaire avec le Monsieur le Grand Tresorier ; soe that, my Lord, I dare trust you with the little gentleman, whome you neede not be soe tender of as I have bin of the little one lately come back, whoe is extreamly dissatisfyed that his present at coming away was [3] proportioned to his stature.[3] It is a greate presumption in me to advise your Lordship ; but the Kings lettar, without repeating it againe, will shoe you what steps I have made, and by them you will conclude it which way you judg most advantagious.

I have severall things of importance I would communicate to your Lordship, and which I am sure will be of greate service to you to know. I have therfore begged the Kings leave to come over for a fortnight, which I hope you will approove of. When I come, I will begg the favour of waiting on your Lordship before I see anybody, till when I beg the continuance of your

---

[1] From the autograph letter in B.M. Add. MSS. 39757, f. 77, printed in *Morrison Catalogue*, iv. 278. *Letters*, p. 34. The letter is addressed, ' For your Lordship,' which suggests that it was sent under cover of another letter, presumably Montagu's letter to the King or to Charles Bertie.

[2] . . . [2] These words seem to have been added by Montagu as an afterthought.

[3] . . . [3] The *Letters* give ' made proportionable to his small stature.

favours, and the beleife of my being most unfeignedly and with all respect, My Lord,

Your Lordships most obedient and humble servant,

R. Montagu.[1]

[To Mr. Charles Bertie][2]

Paris, October th 12, [16]77.

Sir,

I have a thousand complements to make to you for all the favours upon all occasions I have and doe receive from you. I will deferre my thanks till I have the honour to see you, which I hope may be soone, for I have desired my Lord Treasurer to get me the Kings leave to come over for a fortnight. But pray take noe notice of this, and doe me the justice to beleive me to be with all truth, Deare Cozen,

Your most obedient faithfull servant and kinsman,

R. Montagu.

To the Lord Treasurer.[3]

Paris, November th 3, [16]77.

My Lord,

I am to acknowledge the honour of your Lordships with the Kings leave to come over.[4] After paying my duty to the King there is noething has made me more desirous of the journy then the waiting of your Lordship, which I hope you will give me leave to doe as soone as I arrive. Before I see anybody els I will find out my cozen Charles Bertue, and attend him wherever you will please to appoint I may see you.

I gave your Lordship an account of my negociation concerning

---

[1] Endorsed by Danby, ' 12th October [16]77 ' ; and by Leeds, ' Note his flattery, and the small present made to Monsieur Courtin in recompence of his lie about mee, and his haveing plaid this businesse into my hands.'

[2] From the autograph letter in B.M. Add. MSS. 39757, f. 74, printed in *Morrison Catalogue*, iv. 278. It is addressed, ' For yourself ; ' but there can be no doubt that Bertie is intended.

[3] From the autograph letter in B.M. Add. MSS. 39757, f. 82, printed in *Morrison Catalogue*, iv. 280.

[4] This letter has not been found.

Don Mario Platy [1] *by his owne gentleman he sent. Since I could doe him noe goode office heere, I would be loath to doe him an ill one to soe goode natured and generous a protectour as your Lordship ; but as soone as I have the honour to see you I will give you an account how his affaires stand heere, and assure your Lordship noe man is with more truth nor respect then myself, My Lord,*

Your Lordships most obedient and most humble servant,

R. Montagu.

I shall sett out after to-morrow, and hope to be in six or seaven dayes at London.

[1] This reference is explained by the following letter from Danby to Montagu, the autograph draft of which is preserved in Leeds MSS., Packet 10. Although undated it was probably written in September 1677.

My Lord, His Majestie is earnestly solicited by an unfortunate gentleman (who writes himselfe Prince Dom Mario Plati, and who by his mother is of very great extraction) that his Majestie would vouchsafe to appeare in his behalfe to the King of France. But his actions haveing been very extraordinary, and by the King of France his usage of him his Majestie haveing great reason to feare whither hee bee not very partiall in the relation hee gives of himselfe, will not any further or otherwise concerne himselfe for him then by directing your Excellency to acquainte the King of France that such a person is in England, who thinks hee is only banished from his presence for want of his Majesties being truly informed of his case, and who begs to bee admitted to relate his owne story to the King att the perill of what his Majestie shall thinke fitt to do with him after hearing him himselfe. But if the King do not approve this motion, your Excellency is to urge itt no further then as an act of charity which the King could not deny to a man of quality in distresse, to know whither the King of France would thinke fitt to have him or no. Hee has desired mee to send your Excellency the memorialls hee gives of himselfe, which I have accordingly inclosed for his satisfaction, but without any instruction concerning them from his Majestie ; and hee begs mee to lett you know and pray of your Excellency that when you speake to the King concerning him itt may bee without the knowlege of any of the ministers, because otherwise hee despaires of any good, Monsieur Pompone being greatly his enemy, and hee would have us beleeve that to bee the sole reason why hee cannot arrive att the justice of being heard by the King. The truth is his fate is very extraordinary if his persecution should continue in France, for itt is pursued against him with such violence by the Spanish ministers here that if the laws of this nation did not give him protection hee would quickly bee made an example of theire wrath, and methinks that should plead something in his behalfe in France. His quality is so good and his extreamities so very great that I should bee glad hee might by your favour receive some comfortable answer. I am, My Lord, Your Excellencies most obedient humble servant, [Danby].

The letter is endorsed by Danby, ' To Mr. Montagu about Dom Mario Plati.'

To the Lord Treasurer.[1]

St. Germains, December th 27, [1677].

My Lord,

I am to acknowledg the honour of your Lordships of December th 10 ; [2] *I shall be sure to observe the directions you give me in it. I have not yet seene the King, being but newly arrived heere. My Lord Dunblane will not be at Paris till to-morrow. I had lost soe much time by being stopped at Dover by the contrary winds that I was forced to come away post as soone as I landed. I have had noe other trouble by his company but the being obliged to leave him behind, which I should not have done had not his Majestys service required it. I wish I may be capable of doeing him any service heere, or of shoeing your Lordship with how much truth and respect I am, My Lord,*

Your Lordships most obedient and humble servant,

R. Montagu.

[To the King] [3]

Paris, December th 29, [16]77.

Sir,

According to your commands laide upon me by a lettar I received from my Lord Treasurer, I have writ a lettar to be seene at the Comittee of Forreigne Affaires, and ᴧ will give your Majesty in this the best account I can of the Kings answer to the propositions of peace you commanded me to insist upon.

At my arrivall at St. Germains I went for forme sake to Monsieur de Pompone, whome I found full of expressions of the greate obligations he knew the King his master had to your Majesty, and full of hopes that you would continue them by making use of your greate credit, which by the honour you have done the Prince of Orenge in his mariage you must needes have

---

[1] From the autograph letter in B.M. Add. MSS. 39757, f. 84, printed in *Morrison Catalogue*, iv. 280.

[2] This letter has not been found.

[3] From the autograph letter in B.M. Add. MSS. 39757, f. 88, printed in *Morrison Catalogue*, iv. 280. There is a copy in B.M. Add. MSS. 28054, f. 115, on which the Duke of Leeds has made his alterations. *Letters*, p. 38.

over him, to prevaile with him to recede from such high terms as are proposed. I will not trouble you, Sir, with all I sayde to him, for the conclusion of this whole affaire being solely betweene the King and Monsieur de Louvoy I thought it must be there that I was to lay [1] the greatest stresse.

When I came to Monsieur de Louvoy I found him very impatient to heare what I had to say, and he began with me, asking, Monsieur, apportes vous nous des bonnes nouvelles. I told him I brought noe newes, for I had brought noe other then what my Lord Duras had brought, and I was sure the King my master was soe freindly to his that he would not have sent them a second time if he had not thought them goode. He presently fell upon the suddaine calling of the Parlament, and saide that was the greatest signe that could be of your Majestys intending

TOLD MEE
to declare against them ; ∧ that for Valenciennes, Conde and Tourney, he knew the King his master would make warr a hundred yeare rather then part with them ; if he lost them by warr there was noe dishonour in it, but if he should give them up without defending them his people would reproach him, and all posterity think him the laschest [2] prince in the world for parting with, out of feare, that which was the security of his kingdome and had cost the lifes of soe many brave men to gaine. I told him his master had to greate a reputation in the world to make that an argument for his denying what was now asked, and that perhaps both in his owne nation, as well as in all others and to posterity afterwards, there could not be a greater blemish to his reputation then the not standing to the arbitrage of the King of England for a peace, whoe would never have suffered him to have made such a progresse in Flaunders but upon his having severall times solemnly given his word, both by his ambassadours in England and to me heere, to that effect.

YOUR MAJESTIE
I made use alsoe of all the other arguments you ∧ had furnished me, Sir, with yourself. In conclusion Monsieur de

---

[1] The copyist has carelessly written ' try ', and is followed by the *Letters.*

[2] The copyist has transcribed this ' falsest ', and is followed by the *Letters.*

Louvoy told me that if the calling of the Parlament soe soone was an effect of your Majesty's greate want of money, there was noe summe you could desire that he did not beleive his master, even to the engaging of his jewells, which are to soe vast a value, would not furnish you with, provided you would not let the Parlament draw you into a warr against France, that ^IF^ you could stop theire mouths with ^WOULD PROCURE^ a generall truce for a yeare, and in that time manage the Prince of Orenge soe as to not [1] insist upon these three [2] places, for which your Majesty should be paide for as much as if they ^THOSE PLACES^ were yours and you sold them; that ^YOUR OWNE, AND ALTHOUGH^ such a summe of money as this would be hard to returne, but it should be put into wedges of gold, and soe put into bales of silk and sent over in a yacht; ^AND^ as for my Lord Treasurer, whome ^WHO^ they looked upon as a greate ^CHEIFE^ adviser in this affaire, if I would but doe them the kindnesse heere as to sound him, there is noething they would not give him to make his fortune; it should be given him in diamonds and pearles, that noebody could ever know it, and I myself should not be forgott if I would propose it to him.

I undertooke to answer that my Lord Treasurer was not to be gained for any interest but what he thought to be his masters; ^AND^ as for my proposing any such thing to your Majesty, I durst not doe it, my positive orders being to insist upon the restoring these towns, which would satisfye your Parlament, make the peace, and be of more advantage to your person and Crowne then all the money of Fraunce would be. Monsieur de Louvoy desired he might see me againe after the Kings supper, for he would goe to him and give him an account of all our discours. After supper Monsieur de Louvoy told me he found

---

[1] The copyist writes 'not to', and is followed by the *Letters*.
[2] The word 'three' is omitted in the copy and the *Letters*.

his master resolved not to part with Valenciennes, Conde and
Tourney, and very hardly with Courtrey ; that Charleroy, Aeth
and Audenard, fortified as they were at his charge, made as
goode a bariere as neede be, and if the Prince of Orenge would
fortifie any other places he would be at the expence of it ; that
since I would not propose the matter of money to your Majestye,
Monsieur de Barillon should have order to doe it, and he hoped
you would think you should find your account better by having
your share of those townes that he kept, which you would
have in effect by having the value [1] in money, then by entring
into a warr against a King that will be soe ready to serve you
upon all occasions.   Soe I ended with Monsieur de Louvoy.

Next morning I had an audience of the King in his closet,
where he repeated to me all Monsieur de Louvoy had saide, and
conjured me to represent to your Majesty that the thing in the
world he feared the most was a breach with you,[2] Mais il faut
tout hazarder plustost que de me laisser couper bras et jambes,
que sont les places que lon me demande.   And then he called
for the mapp, and shoed me the consequence it would be, as he
saide, if he parted with them.   Dites, je vous prie, au Roy vostre
maistre que je feray toutes choses a sa consideration hormis ce
que je ne puis faire en honneur et en conscience.

Thus I have given your Majesty a just account of all that
passed betweene me and the ministers.   I beleive Valenciennes,
Conde and Tourney he will not part with ; Courtray I beleive
he will, and perhaps Conde if it be demolished.   If they venter
to engage in a warr, it is upon presumption that the first yeare
you cannot doe them much hurt, and that the second the
Parlament will be weary of the warr ; but I have endeavored
as much as I can to disabuse them of that.   They are mighty
inquisitive whether the Spaniards upon engaging with them [3]
give you up Ostend ; the feare of that allarms them very much.

If your Majesty shall judg it more prudent, if you can bring
the Prince of Orenge to accept of a truce for a yeare, to doe that
rather then enter into a warr before you have taken your

---

[1] The words ' of them ' are here inserted in an unknown handwriting.

[2] Instead of ' you ' the copy gives ' your Majesty.'

[3] The word ' will ' is here inserted in an unknown handwriting.

measures with the Spaniards, the Dutch and your Parlament, and you shall hearken to any propositions of money made to you by the French, I humbly advise it may be with <u>all the</u> secrecy <u>imaginable,</u> and that whatever summe you shall insist upon you would let my Lord Treasurer manage with Monsieur de Barillon and _^ me with the King heere. When I
IN ENGLAND AND BY
know your mind, I know soe much of theirs that I am sure I shall make a better bargain then you can for yourself. This messenger will bring me any commands you shall have to lay upon me, which I shall obey with all care and duty.

<u>I had forgot to tell your Majesty that they make little account of your satisfying the Swedes, soe they can keepe enough for themselfs.</u>

R. Montagu.[1]

To the Lord Treasurer.[2]

Paris, December th 29, [16]77.

My Lord,

I must repeate the same thing over againe to fill up a lettar for your Lordship, having given his Majesty an account, which I presume he will shoe you, of what he is like to trust to from hence. I have as well as I could writ such a lettar to the Secretary as may signifie noething ; I hope you will stand by me if I am censured by the politicians for having noe better a pen. My Lord Dunblane came very well heither on Wensday. As soone as the holy dayes are over I will put him into the best methode I can of learning all is to be learnt heere. If your Lordships designe should be to have him any time heere, noething can breake him of the English company, nor perfect him in the language, but an academie. I have not sent Mr. Friar back with these lettars, because I presume you may have occasion of sending him that brings this immediatly againe, and then Mr. Friar shall bring you an account of any

---

[1] Endorsed by Danby, ' 29 December 1677 ' ; and by Leeds, ' Mr. Montagus letter to the King. The offer of jewells, &c., to mee. The marriage of the Prince of Orange was a month before this letter. His proposall of a truce and money, and to bee managed by mee here and by him in France.'

[2] From the autograph letter in B.M. Add. MSS. 39757, f. 86, printed in *Morrison Catalogue*, iv. 280.

commands you shall send me. And if there were any for your owne particular service, I shall endeavour to acquitt myself with all the truth and respect that becomes, My Lord,

Your Lordships most obedient and humble servant,

R. Montagu.

[To Mr. Montagu] [1]

London, 24 December, 1677.

My Lord,

The French embassador has by a courrier which arrived here yesterday given his Majestie an account of what the King of France has said to your Lordship (which I find the King expected to have received as early by an expresse from yourselfe). The principall part of itt [2] is an offer of a generall suspention of armes for a yeare or fourteen months, and about which you will receive orders how to behave yourselfe from the Secretaries of State. But the King has comanded mee to lett you know from him that as to the manner of acting this businesse with the King of France, hee would not only have you do itt in the most respectfull way that is possible, but to assure him that our master will take the two months respitt of armes (while hee can know the minds of the Confederates as to the generall suspension) as an act of pure kindnesse to himselfe, and that [3] hee will imploy that time <u>even in his Parliament</u> so as may putt neither of them upon a necessity of a rupture, which the gaining of time can only avoide.

For your better understanding of this you must know that upon the embassadors telling the King hee had received powers as well as orders to give a generall suspension, the King answered hee should bee glad of itt, but that depended not upon him but the Confederates, whose minds must first bee knowne upon itt, and in the meane time the King of France might possess himselfe of two or

---

[1] Hist. MSS. Com., *Buccleuch MSS. at Montagu House*, i. 523, from the original letter. The autograph draft, the spelling of which has been followed, is B.M. Add. MSS. 28054, f. 113, and there is a copy *ibid.*, f. 111. A few alterations in the handwriting of the Duke of Leeds appear in the draft and the copy, but the letter in spite of that was not included in the published collection.

[2] Originally ' which ' in the draft. This explains the construction of the latter part of the sentence.

[3] After ' that ' the draft originally had ' although hee cannot ingage himselfe '; but these words were struck out by Danby.

*three townes more in Flanders while that was doing ; so that
unlesse hee would stop his armes in all the Spanish Netherlands
till the King could send to all the Confederates, this would rather
bee a furtherance to theire destruction then theire releife. To which
the embassador replied that hee was ready to send his Majesties
motion to his master, but surely there must bee some inducement
added to his master, or else itt was but askeing him to stay two
months till they who are not yett in a posture of defence might then
be in a good one ; so that hee hoped if the Confederates would not
accept the generall suspension att the end of two months the King
our master would concerne himselfe no further for them. To this
the King answered hee could not be tied by any meanes, but as I
have already writt he would take itt for such a favour as should
oblige him to make all the kind steps in returne that could possibly
consist with his safety, his principal aim being but to assure himselfe of that. Haveing explained the grounds upon which these
orders are given, I am sure you will improve them to our masters
sense much better then I can direct.⊕ ¹*

*As I was writeing this I had the honour of yours of the 17/27
from St. Germaines, when you had not spoken to the King ; and I
had a letter from a servant of my son Dumblans, who was not then
arrived att Paris, by which I perceive that I have already great
obligations to thanke you for on his part. I shall ease you of that
trouble sooner then I intended, haveing by this post sent him orders
to bee att Calais the 11/21th January, where a yatcht shall bee ready
for him, and I do beg of you that you will helpe to gett him out of
Paris, where I am afraid hee will bee willing to loiter if hee can.*

*Pray by the first expresse lett mee know your thoughts fully as to
our publique matters, and whither you beleeve they will suffer itt to
go to a breach upon the proposalls made by my Lord Feversham.
I am, My Lord,*

Your Excellencys [&c],

[Danby] ²

I heare the deere att Abscourt are intended to bee sold, and if true

---

¹ This sign, which appears on the draft, presumably marks the remainder
of the letter for deletion. The copy stops at this point.

² The draft is endorsed by Danby, 'Coppy of my letter to Mr. Montagu,
4th December 1677'; and by Leeds, 'about a suspension of armes.'

I desire that for the storeing of Wimbleton I may have them all att the price others are to give, which will do mee a great favour.

¹ *Pray let me know whether my Lady Cleaveland comes for England, and when.*¹

[To the King] ²

Paris, January th 5, [16]78.

Sir,

I gave your Majesty an account in my last of the King of Fraunce his answer to me concerning the propositions of peace that you commaunded me to insist on ; ⊕ *but considering this criticall conjunctur I thought it my duty rather to give you this second trouble then to omitt the informing of you of anything that should come to my knowledg.*

I have bin for two dayes at St. Germains, and there hearing that the King had given order for a greate part of his equipage to march to-morrow to be ready at Cinquantin the 10 of the moneth, French style, which day it is sayde he will goe into the feild himself, I desired an audience of him, and represented to him of what ill consequence it would be to your Majestys affaires in England, just upon the meeting of your Parlament, the noyse of his attempting anything that should tend to any farther conquest in Flaunders, and how much it must needes hasten the breach of the freindship which your Majesty is soe willing to keepe with him when all the world shall see the little account he makes of your Majestys endeavoring soe goode and soe honourable a work as the peace of Christendome ; and at this time your Majesty had a more particular reason to expect from him the undertaking noething in Flaunders till he had your answer for a generall truce which he empowerd me to offer, and which answer could not come till you had first sent to the Prince of Orenge and knew his mind in it. The King answered me that

---

¹ . . . ¹ This second postscript is not in the draft, but has been added to the letter at the last moment.

² From the autograph letter in B.M. Add. MSS. 39757, f. 92, printed in *Morrison Catalogue*, iv. 281. The copy on which the Duke of Leeds made his alterations is in Leeds MSS., Packet 10. Owing to Danby's mistaken endorsement of the original letter the copy is dated January 1, and this date is repeated in the printed version in *Letters*, p. 43. There is no doubt, however, that the figure on the original letter is a ' 5 '.

he was sure you were too just and too much his freind pour luy lier
les bras, but that if I pleased he would give me his word not to goe
into the feild till the fifteenth of this moneth, by which he hoped to
have an answer whether the generall truce would be accepted of.
I replied that if he would give his word for a moneth, in that time
the answer would come, but for a lesser time it would signifie
noething, and represented to him that perhaps he would doe his
enemies more goode then hurt, for he would allarme England to a
degree that noething but your declaring warr would content them,
which was all the Confederates desired. He then told me that upon
his word till he had your answer of the generall truce that he
would undertake noething that should either dissatisfye your
Majestye or allarme your people, but that he must faire la mine
d'entreprendre quelque chose to have his owne people in a readinesse
and presse the enemies to be willing to a peace. After this I desired
that your Majestys subjects that are in his service might not be sent
into Scicily, as I heard they were, many of them being already in
Provence. To this he promised they should not goe into Scicily, but
whilst they were in his service he might dispose of them where he
pleased without doeing anything contrary to the capitulation. And
soe my audience ended, with greate expressions of the desire he had
of continuing the freindship and kindnesse that is betweene you.

AND ⊕

∧ What measures your Majesty shall take your owne wisdome
will best direct, but I told my Lord Treasurer when you sent
my Lord Duras that you would never bring France to consent
to those terms but by a generall truce first, and in that time if
they saw you resolved to enter into a league against them, and
were prepared for it much better then you are now, rather then
continue the warr I did beleive they might doe it, if in that time
by your freindship you did not leave them some of the towns
you now insist upon to be restord. Now noething but a truce
can stop them, and I beleive Ghant will be the first thing they
will goe upon, and Monts and Ipres follow, all which will not bee
three weekes work. The Chancellour, Monsieur Colbert, and
Monsieur de Pompone are all for the peace I am certaine, and
the King himself not avers ; but Monsieur de Louvoy has such
a mind that the projects that he has laide for this campayne

should goe on, that he is for venturing all rather then be stopped now. Wherfore if your Majesty can obteyne a truce, I dare confidently affirme you will be master of the peace upon terms that will be honourable for the Prince of Orenge and secure for Flaunders, though perhaps not just those you now insist upon, besides the stopping of what will be done this yeare, which in all probability will be more then has bin done all the warr.

As for Tourney, the King tells me it is of the antient domaine of Fraunce and that he cannot part with it ; for Valenciennes, I am told by some that have heard him discours of it, he would easier part with it, and Conde not without demolishing it, for it is now impregnable, and has cost him three millions. But all these are but towne talk, and everybody heere knowes the terms you are like to breake upon. If you had a yeare time, noe doubt, Sir, you might turn matters better then you can in such hast ; and though I did not thinke it proper nor for your service, when I had only your commands to insist upon the restoring the towns above mentioned, to receive or charge myself with any proposition of money, yet I take the liberty to put you in mind, Sir, that if you come not to a breach with Fraunce, you may certainly accommodate your owne affaires ; and it is not reasonable they should goe away with all the advantage of a warr that you have really helpt them soe much in, and inconvenienced yourself soe much by.

I am sure there shall be noething that I shall alwaise study nor wish soe much as what may be for your honour and advantage.[1]

I have writ by the post a lettar to be reade at the Committee of Forreigne Affaires.

R. Montagu.[2]

---

[1] The copy stops here at the foot of a page, only the signature following The version in the *Letters* concludes ' being, Sir, Your Majesty's most dutifu and obedient servant, R. Mountagu.'

[2] The original letter is endorsed by Danby, ' 1st January [16]78.' The Duk of Leeds has altered this to ' [16]77/8. N.S.', and has added, ' To the King ; not his advice about money.' The copy is marked by Leeds ' Not used.' Never theless it was used.

[*To the Lord Treasurer*] [1]

Paris, January th 5, [16]78.

My Lord,

 I have little to trouble your Lordship, having sayde all that can be in the lettar I have writ his Majesty. You will by it judge what measures it will be best for his Majesty to take, if the shortnesse of time will give him leave to take any. They are very much afraid of a warr now, and will I beleive doe many a thing to prevent it ; but if once we declare there feare is over. Your Lordship seemed when I was in England to approve of my notion of truce first, which must if it be agreede upon have the best effect in the world as to the Kings affaires at home by stopping the present progresse of the French and the mouths of the Parlament men, which otherwaise would be outragious.

 You must be pleased to put the King in mind of representing to Monsieur de Barillon the ill consequence [of] his masters undertaking anything suddainly in Flanders. The greate point I think we are to gaine in England is the stopping the King of France this campayne. What els we have to doe I see by the complexion of this Court will be much easier ; but any successe sets them soe high, as that of Phribourgh did, that you know not where to have them, whereas if we can but gaine a yeares time to put ourselfs in order they will thinke of it twice before they fall out with us.

 Whatever resolution the King takes I wish it may have a goode successe, and your Lordship such a share in it as may confirme you more and more in his favour and goode opinion, whoe am with all ruth and respect, My Lord,

  Your Lordships most obedient and humble servant,

      R. Montagu.

To the Lord Treasurer.[2]

Paris, January th 8, [16]78.

My Lord,

 I have just time to tell your Lordship that I have received a letter of the 24 December, English style, from Mr.

[1] From the autograph letter in Leeds MSS., Packet 10.
[2] From the autograph letter in Leeds MSS., Packet 10. It is printed in *Letters*, p. 47, as a postscript to a letter which is there dated January 8, 1678, but the real date of which is January 8, 1677 (*supra*, p. 257).

Secretary, with the Kings order to make instance in his name with his Christian Majesty for a generall truce for a yeare, and the passing his word to attempt nothing in Flanders till the 1 of March. By my two last your Lordship has reason to imagine that I may succeede in these proposalls, and to-morrow I will dispatch an expresse to give his Majesty an account.[1] *If such a complaisance as this from this Court can pacifye the Parlament I doe not doubt but that the complaisance from hence will encrease rather then diminish. You shall very soone be troubled with a longer lettar, and the assurances of my being with all respect, My Lord,*

Your Lordships most obedient and humble servant,

R. *Montagu.*

[To the King] [2]

Paris, January th 10, [16]78.

Sir,

According to your commands given me by a lettar of my Lord Treasurers of December th 24, English style, and another of Mr. Secretary Coventry, I have represented to the King of Fraunce, with all the respect that could be and all the expressions and assurances of kindnesse on your Majestys part and

YOUR MAJESTIES   YOUR KIND CORRESPONDENCE
your ∧ sincere intentions of continuing it ∧, and how upon that account you desire a respitt of armes in the Spanish [3] Neatherlands for two moneths, which you would owne as the greatest

TO WHICH I HAVE YETT NO ANSWER [4]
marque of kindnesse he could give you, ∧ ⌐ *that this desire of yours had noe relation in any manner to favour the Confederates, but purely to your owne affaires at home, which, by the time this complaisance of his would give you, you might manage soe as to*

---

[1] The printed version stops here.

[2] From the autograph letter in B.M. Add. MSS. 39757, f. 95, printed in *Morrison Catalogue*, iv. 282. More than half of this letter appears to have been marked by the Duke of Leeds for excision, and a copy then seems to have been made which is in Leeds MSS., Packet 10. On this copy in turn several alterations were effected by the Duke and a further considerable passage was marked for deletion. The final result appears in *Letters*, p. 48.

[3] The word ' Spanish ' is omitted in the copy and the *Letters*.

[4] These words are added in the copy.

avoide any misunderstanding betweene you, and receive an answer both from Vienna and Madrid to the generall suspension for a yeare.

The King desired me to stay till after councell for his answer, and then he told me that he had considered of what I had proposed to him in your name for not attempting anything in Flanders till the first of March, that his owne ambassadour had given him account alsoe of the same desires, that he was ready to doe all he could for your Majestys satisfaction, but this was soe disadvantagious a proposition to him that he was sure when you understoode it right you would not presse him to it ; but that if you would please in kindnesse to him to put of your Parlament till the last of February theire style, by which time you might have an answer from Spaine and the Emperour, that then he would give you his word, in case he should attaque or take any townes, to restore them againe in the condition he tooke them, as soone as the ratification of the suspension of armes should come, without reckoning them as anything in the treaty of peace and giving back of towns that should be afterwards made. I could not but take the liberty to replie that his Majesty either was not very well informed how your affaires stoode at home, or cared very little how they went, to thinke that the Spaniards would consent to a truce for the rest of the yeare when theire best towns were lost at the beginning, or that your people would be satisfyed that Flaunders could be secured when at a time that all Christendome looked upon theire meeting to be in order to the defense of it and they should be sent away just to give time enough to have it lost ; that I did presume you giving your royall word to employ the time of theire sitting to hinder things from coming to a rupture was worth the staying a little from taking a towne or two, which if there was noe truce, considering how they are defended, he might take when he would, and if there was a truce must be given back, and his men and money spent to noe purpose. This would appeare a practice soe contrary to his conduct that did not use to doe things to noe purpose, that the world would thinke theire was some misterye at the bottom they could not dive into.

But to explaine to you, Sir, the oddnesse of this proposition, which Monsieur de Pompone was ashamed of, Monsieur Colbert vexed at as a thing that may put a stop to the peace, and which I am sure from certaine hands the Chancellour, Monsieur de Louvoys father, has disputed with him all he could, but which Monsieur de Louvoy will if the other ministers cannot stop drive on (because, as I had the honour to tell you in my last, he will have the vanity to let the King see how well he serves him, and how goode projects are laide for the conquest of Flaunders, if you did not stop it, and therfore dos not value the losse of men or money though the townes that shall be taken are to be immediately restored), the King himself told me, when I had by all the reasons I gave him shoed him I did conceive you could not be satisfyed with this answer, or runn the hazard of inconveniencing your affaires at home by discontenting your Parlament by an adjourment to March when they had come from all parts of England, that he did conceive and had reason to beleive (by which I guesse it is from some wrong intelligence he has had out of England) that if you would tell your Parlament that you had an assurance from Fraunce of a generall suspension for a yeare, an assurance alsoe that whatever was taken in Flaunders should be restored upon the publication of the suspension, and therfore you sent them back till that time and would have them then meete to assist you against either party that should not consent to a reasonable peace, he was very confident it could be noe prejudice to your affaires. This is word for word what was saide to me; and perhaps your Majesty will heare this from Monsieur de Barillon sooner then from me, for when I and they send couriers at the same time theirs are first served, which was the reason that you had the proposition of a generall truce from Monsieur Barillon sooner then me, for I neglected noe time in giving you an account. The King telling me he was sending one away to Monsieur de Barillon, I did humbly beg of him to leave out that part of conditioning with your Majesty to put of your Parlament; and mythoughts, by the reasons I gave him and his ministers of the unpracticablenesse of it, that he may have secret orders when he has heard yours and your ministers reasons, which will be better then mine, not to presse you in it. ⌐ 1

⊕ *By all I can judge, and from the most cleare seeing people that I convers with, the King and all the ministers are for a peace,*

---

1 This mark and the similar mark on p. 310 are made by the Duke of Leeds on the original letter, and indicate the part which he at first proposed to omit.

except Monsieur de Louvoy,[1] *and he violently against it ; and noe-thing could have made him for the suspension but the hopes of letting it come to noething by this new odde proposition, or if it dos his function will still continue, for the troopes will be kept up, and fortifications and such things as are in his province must be looked after as if theire were actually a warr. But if once there is a sus-pension Monsieur Colbert and the rest, nay all Fraunce, would be in an uproare rather then engage anew, especially if your Majesty declared against them soe much better provided to doe it then you can now ; and Monsieur Colbert knowes that if there was a warr, and afterwards they condescended to a worse peace then is now offered (as they must doe in time, for the money would faile), Monsieur de Louvoy*[2] *would lay the blame on him, and disgrace him by it.* ⊕[3]

As to the restoring of Conde, Tourney and Valenciennes, I have had severall discourses, and I am sure by people sett on a purpose, that they knew you only insisted upon Tourney out of kindnesse to your nephew the Prince of Orenge ; that if you were as kind to your neice Madames daughter, which they thought you were, you might easier get her a kingdome then him a towne ; that they were not soe farr engaged to marry the Dauphine to Monsieur de Bavieres daughter that they might not, if your Majesty would favour them in the keeping of Tourney, marry your neice to the Dauphine, whose children, that would be your nephews, would have Tourney and all Fraunce besides, and owe it you. I thought it my duty to give you, Sir, this hint, both for the kindnesse I know you have for the memory of your deare sistar, and because if you can by your credit bring the Prince of Orenge to consent it will be, I am sure, more honour to you in the world and more pleasure to make your neice Queene of Fraunce then to get the Spaniards a towne more. Besides the expedient will not be ill to bring you of the termes you have insisted upon, and which I doe veryly beleive if you should presse now you are unprovided the King of

---

[1] The copy, presumably by a slip, gives ' Torcey ' instead of ' Louvoy.'

[2] The copy again gives ' Torcey ' instead of ' Louvoy.'

[3] This mark and the similar mark on p. 312 are made by the Duke of Leeds on the copy, and indicate a further excision which he later decided upon.

Fraunce will engage in a warr rather then consent to ; wheras if there be a suspension of a yeare, which now appeares difficult, there will be many waies to make you agree. I heare some talk of demolishing Conde and giving it back, of slighting Valenciennes and making it a newter towne.⊕ [1]

The report of Steting being taken allarmes them here extreamly, and though the King sayde noething to me of Steting, yet he told me that he could never conclude a peace without the Swedes were satisfyed. I told him if he would please but to put you in a condition of satisfying your people at home he did not [2] of your Majestys kindnesse and intentions of ending the warr as much to his honour and advantage as he could wish.

I beg your Majestys pardon for this imperfect account, and remaine with all duty

R. Montagu.[3]

[To the Lord Treasurer] [4]

Paris, January 10th, [16]78.

My Lord,

Your Lordship will see by the Kings letter the ridiculous proposition that is made of putting off the Parliament, and the restoreing any places that shall be taken in Flanders before a ratification of the suspension of armes shall be delivered. I cannot imagine from whence this resolution should arise, except it be from the opinion they have in this Court (and indeed till now they have had reason enough for it) that they aught to have us do what they please, and never to do anything wee desire. Besides I am confident some of the discontented

---

[1] This mark, made by the Duke of Leeds on the original letter, indicates that he wished the printed version to end at this point.

[2] A word has clearly been omitted here.

[3] The original letter is endorsed by Danby, ' 10th January [16]78 ' ; and by Leeds, ' To the King, N.S., about the marriage of the Kings neice to the Dauphine and his advice about itt.'

[4] From a copy in a clerk's handwriting in Leeds MSS., Packet 10. This is not necessarily the same as the original, which has not been found, but it is much nearer it than the version printed in *Letters*, p. 50. The relation of this letter to the two which follow is not very clear. It seems probable, however, that the first of the three accompanied the letter of the same date to the King, that the second was sent separately by Montagu's secretary, whom it was partly intended to introduce, and that the third was written and dispatched later on the same day.

Parliament men have beene intrigueing with the French am-
MONSIEUR BARILLON
bassador ∧ ; for I saw a letter of his to Monsieur Courtin (which
I beg of your Lordship never to take notice of), where he says,
Quoyque la Cour tourne contre nous, nous nous sauverons
peutestre par la parlement, car ils ne sont pas sy portées pour
la guerre comme on veut faire a croire.   And they beleiveing

WOULD
this here, and that the King cannot do what he will ∧ with his
Parliament, makes them play such tricks here with the King
our master.

As to what your Lordship desires to know, wether they will
breake upon the termes my Lord Duras brought, I do absolutely
conclude they will, rather then agree to them, because they are
so much forwarder and better prepared for a warr then wee,
and conclude wee cannot hurt them the first yeare.   Especially
Monsieur de Louvoy, being so much master as he is, has out of
vanity a mind to shew that his care and conduct can resist all
the world.   But if you can deferr and bring it to a suspension
for a yeare, and have time enough to prepare,[1] the King our
master may the next yeare certainly give them the law, for the
ministers will be so divided betweene warr and peace that it
will quite alter the case.   Your Lordship has so great an influence (by the obligations he has to you and personall esteeme he
has of you) over the Prince of Orange, that I am confident he
will comply to what you shall make him see is the Kings interest,
which I cannot think will bee to enter into a warr so unprepared[2]
as hee is.⊕

*I finde here that they think the King will be contented with the
proposall of putting off the Parliament till the end of February ;
and though I followed your directions of makeing my proposition
with all the sweetness and respect in the world, the King and your
Lordship both (if you do not, as I presume you will not, like the
answer I have sent) must be a litle round with the ambassador ;
and I fancy if the King does not yeild you'le finde he may have
orders not to stand upon that condition of their not restoreing what*

---

[1] The *Letters* read ' prepare for a war.'
[2] The *Letters* read ' unprovided.'

shall be taken before a suspension. Except the Parliament be sent away till the same time, I am of opinion also that they will be very cautious how they do attacque anything in Flanders. At least they will stay for our masters answer to this, or to see two or three days of the opening of the Parliament over.⊕

I wish your Lordship would let me know freely the Kings intentions as to a warr or a peace ; for if it were to a warr, I might perhaps doe him service I dare not venture to name by a letter, and if to a peace, give you some sight of obtaining termes that would be very advantagious. By the return of this messenger I hope for some positive resolution. I am sorry you have taken one of sending for my Lord Dunblane backe, for without compliment I never knew a young man of better disposition nor inclination in my life, and a yeare in this country would improve him, I am sure, much to your satisfaction, which I should esteeme myselfe extreme happy if I could any way contribute to, as of all other occasions of shewing your Lordship that no man is with more sincerity and respect, My Lord,

Your Lordships most obedient and humble servant,

R. Montagu.

⊕ *My Lady Cleaveland intends to come with her children in the beginning of February, and not a litle vexed at the trouble my Lord Arlington puts her to by the journey and takeing her children from their exercises. Mr. May had desired the deere at Abscourt for the King at Windsor. If the King has them not, I have ordered my servant to attend some of yours to let them know they are at your Lordships service.*[1]

To the Lord Treasurer.[2]

Paris, January th 10, [16]78.

My Lord,

I can say little to your Lordship but what I have sayde already in the Kings letter, only that heere they thinke all our propositions unreasonable and theire owne reasonable, and doe

---

[1] Endorsed in the clerk's handwriting, ' 10th January [16]78, N.S. Of very great consequence as to the Parliament.'

[2] From the autograph letter in Leeds MSS., Packet 10.

thinke whilst the Parlament is not sitting they can much better prevaile with the King then when it is, and therfore they lay that stresse upon its being put off till the last of February, theire style, by which time they conclude the newes of the suspension of armes may come, and if it dos you may see by what I have writ the King that some alteration in my Lord Duras his propositions will make the peace. I have writ to Mr. Secretary a lettar for the Forreigne Affaires, and will alwaise observe the caution you gave me of not letting the bottome of the buisnesse be knowne there.

I am sorry your Lordship will have my Lord Dunblane come away soe soone, but I can say nothing against the reason you doe it for, not to have his Majesty loose a vote in Parlament. But a yeare heere would doe him the most goode in the world, for I never knew a more ingenious young man, or one that is better inclined to all things that should make an honest homme. The answer to this lettar will come by Moonday next, [1] and it is now Moonday that is the day he intends to set out, if your Lordship will not repreive him, and you should see noe want of him this sessions. Therfore be pleased, my Lord, to let him have your commands anew by Thursday post if this comes time enough to your hands.

I observed your directions of making these last propositions of the respitt of the King of France his armes till the first of March with all the gentlenesse that could ; [2] but I thinke if his Majesty be a little free with Monsieur de Barillon upon the answer it can doe noe hurt.

He that brings this lettar is a French gentleman, sonne to a rich advocate of the religion. He is now my secretary and as ingenious a man as any in France, and because of his religion intends to settle in England. He is very well versed in affaires, and if you care to aske him any questions can give you a very goode account. I have ordered him to be ready to bring any commands you have for me, whoe am with all respect, My Lord,

Your Lordships most obedient and humble servant,

R. Montagu.

[1] January 7/17.
[2] A word has been omitted here.

To the Lord Treasurer.[1]

St. Germains, January th 10, [16]78.

My Lord,

Remembring by all the discours I had the honour to have with your Lordship in England of the necessity there was as to the King our masters affaires of the meeting of the Parlament, I have againe argued with the King and ministers how hard and unpracticable a condition that was to impose upon him for soe smale a one as the promise of restoring immediately upon a suspension whatever should be taken before the end of February, French style, and which I doubted was not enough to doe the work our master desired. I find more inclination upon what I have sayde in them as to the desisting the pressing the putting of the Parlament, but none as to the giving a promise not to goe into the feild till the first of March, the King of France telling me that it will appeare to the world a greater complaisance of his towards our master the restoring for his sake what they shall see he can take then the forbearing what the enemies would say he could not take. What the resolution will be concerning the releasing the condition of not putting of the Parlament, which I have assured beforehand our master cannot nor will not doe, I cannot know till after councell, when it would be too late to write by the post. But you shall know very soone some other way from him whoe is with all truth and respect, My Lord,

Your Lordships most obedient and humble servant,

R. Montagu.

The discours is now hot againe of the Kings goeing into the feild.[2]

To the Lord Treasurer.[3]

Paris, January th 11, [16]78.

My Lord,

I have not had the honour of any from your Lordship in answer to all those wherein I gave you the best account I could

---

[1] From the autograph letter in Leeds MSS., Packet 10.

[2] Endorsed by Danby, ' 10th January [16]78 ', which the Duke of Leeds has altered to ' 10th January [16]77/8, N.S.' This suggests that Leeds at one time thought of including this letter in the printed collection, and the suggestion is confirmed by the existence of a copy in a clerk's handwriting in Leeds MSS., Packet 10. The copy is substantially the same as the original.

[3] From the autograph letter in B.M. Add. MSS. 38849, f. 121, printed in

of matters heere by the expresses I sent, nor indeede could I expect his Majesty could take any suddaine resolution in matters of soe greate moment.

The occasion of my giving you this trouble is to give you the best light I can into the reasons of Monsieur de Ruvignys sonnes journy into England, whoe will be there perhaps as soone as this lettar. If his fathers age would have permitted it, I beleive they would have sent him ; soe they have chosen the sonne, whoe is to make use of lights his father will give him ; and by the neere relation he has to my Lady Vaughan, whoe is his cozen germain, and the particular freindship which father and sonne have with Mr. William Russell, he is to be introduced into a greate commerce with the malconted members of Parlament, and insinuate what they shall thinke fitt to crosse your measures at Court, if they shall proove disagreable to them heere, whilst Monsieur de Barillon goes on in his smooth civill way. I thought it my duty to his Majesty to give your Lordship this account, though I have not explained this matter soe much in my lettar to the Secretary, wherfore I hope you will let this be seene by none but his Majesty. What I know farther of this or anything els you shall alwaise be acquainted with.

They are heere in greate paine till it be knowne what will become of the Parlament, and doe not stick to say, if that be put of for a moneth, they doubt not of a peace.[1] I am with all respect, My Lord,

Your Lordships most obedient and humble servant,

R. Montagu.[2]

Letters, p. 53, and with omissions in *Hodgkin MSS.*, p. 187. This is the first of the two letters sent by Danby to the House of Commons on December 20, 1678. There are many copies of it (B.M. Add. MSS. 28054, ff. 121-33 ; Leeds MSS., Packet 10), and it was frequently printed at the time of Danby's impeachment.

[1] No authority has been found in the handwriting of the Duke of Leeds for the omission of this sentence from the printed *Letters*, but it can scarcely have been accidental. It is, however, surprising in view of the fact that Danby had himself published a correct version of this letter in 1679.

[2] Endorsed by Danby, ' 11th January [16]78 ' ; to which the Duke of Leeds has added, ' N.S. Of consequence and about young Ruvignys journey into England.'

[*To the Lord Treasurer*] [1]

> *Wensday, 10 at night.   Paris, January th 12, [16]78.*

My Lord,

When I writ to your Lordship this morning [2] I was in greate hopes that I had convinced the King of Fraunce and most of the ministers how unpracticable at this time and how destructive the putting of the Parlament would proove to the King our masters affaires.   But he, having put me of for his last resolution till after the Councell, sent for me and told me he could not desist from desiring to have the Parlament put of till the end of February, without which condition he would not be engaged to restore immediately upon the accepting of a suspension the towns that he should take betwixt this and the end of February.

I will not trouble you with the reasons they pretend to give for this demand of theires (Monsieur de Barillon will have told them you all) nor with what I sayde.   But knowing soe much of the Kings mind, how necessary he judged when I was in England the meeting of the Parlament to be, I thought it my duty if I could to stave of any such condition being mingled with what he is obliged to desire of the King heere as to the giving two moneths respitt to his undertaking in Flaunders.   Therfore I hope the King will support me in what I have done ; and though I could not expect they would declare themselfs till they have an answer from Monsieur Barillon, yet my opinion is, if our master finds it a thing he cannot complye with as to the putting it of till the end of February, they will content themselfs with his Majestys word and promise of coming to noe declaration against Fraunce till the answer of the suspension be come, and stand engaged to restore upon the suspensions being ratifyed whatever they shall take till that time.   But noe mans opinion is infallible, and soe I may be mistaken ; neither dare I advise in this case.   Your Lordship is the best judge whether a warr be advisable now or noe, and whether it is not better if it can be avoided for our master to be a judge as he is now, or to be a party as he must be then ; or if he must be, whether it were not better for

---

[1] From the autograph letter in B.M. Add. MSS. 38849, f. 124, printed in *Hodgkin MSS.*, p. 188.

[2] This letter has not been found.

him to yeeld a little now he is unprepared, and during the yeare of the suspension putt himself in a condition, if he can, of obliging them to the peace heere he has proposed, or if not of ressenting it much better then he can now ; for they will never be soe well prepared, nor we or the Confederates soe unprepared.

I thought it my duty to let his Majesty be as soone as was possibly informed of theire intentions heere, that by that he might guide his owne measures, and as soone as Monsieur de Barillons courier or mine of the 10 brings back the Kings answer to theire proposition (which they seeme mighty dissatisfyed with me for nott approving of, and doubt not but it will be liked in England) we shall see what they will doe ; but till then, though there is allarms of his goeing every day, I beleive the King of Fraunce will not goe into the feild. I have now two couriers at London that attend to bring me any commands that require hast, and I remaine with all respect, My Lord,

Your Lordships most obedient and humble servant,

R. Montagu.

My Lord Dunblane sets out on Teusday next [1] *if he have noe orders to the contrary. If he were consulted I beleive the Parlament should be put of.*

[To the Lord Treasurer] [2]

Paris, January th 18, [16]78.

My Lord,

I heard just now from Calais that two expresses that I sent were both yet there, and could not passe for the contrary winds, which I am extreamly troubled at because of the consequence it is to his Majestys affaires to have bin sooner acquainted with theire resolutions heere.

What resolutions the King our master may take as to the putting

---

[1] January 8/18.

[2] From the autograph letter in B.M. Add. MSS. 39757, f. 99, printed in *Morrison Catalogue*, iv. 283. There is a partial copy in B.M. Add. MSS. 38849, f. 133, on which the Duke of Leeds has made several alterations. It is printed in *Hodgkin MSS.*, p. 191. From this copy is derived the version printed in *Letters*, p. 61.

of the Parlament till the end of February, as this Court desires, or as to letting them meete and follow theire inclination of coming to a breach with Fraunce, I am ignorant of ; but however in case of the worst, and considering how unprovided we are of goode officers in England in case we should have a warr, I thought I could not doe his Majesty a better service then to engage some of the best they have in this country to come and serve him, and I have engaged one of the best they have, whoe is willing to leave Fraunce and end his dayes in our masters service, and I beleive will bring with him severall goode officers as any are in Fraunce, and that are of the religion. The King will guesse whoe I meane, but I will name noebody. He will expect to have the same conditions made goode to him in England, as to his quality and his fortune, as he leaves heere, which is above foure thousand pound a yeare, and the title of a duke for his owne life and an earldome for his eldest sonne, a thousand pound a yeare of the pension when he dies to goe to his eldest sonne, and five hundred to his yongest ; and I have engaged over and above that whether the proposition is accepted or refused that noebody but the King and your Lordship shall ever know of it, not soe much as the Duke of York. This was his injunction to me, and though there should be noe warr at present, but a suspension for a yeare, and the King thinks theire service usefull, they will come and settle presently in England ; and perhaps it will make them heere give better terms in a peace when they shall see our master, if he is not satisfyed, intends to make the warr in goode earnest, which they will never thinke soe much as when they see he has goode officers ready. It is that has given the King of Denmark such advantages over the Suedes, by being at the charge five or six yeare beforehand of paying goode officers. Now I have done my duty I submitt the resolution of this to his Majestys prudence, but I beg the secrecy of it as in honour and justice I am obliged to doe.

⌐ [1] In my first that I writt to his Majesty after my arrivall heere he may please to remember the account I gave him of what proposalls Monsieur de Louvoy made concerning the King

---

[1] This mark was made by the Duke of Leeds on the original letter to indicate that everything before this should be omitted. The copy accordingly begins at this point.

our masters being contented with a greate summe of money for himself, and not to insist upon the restoring of Tourney, Valenciennes and Conde. But I having noe power or instructions to hearken to any such propositions would not enter [1] with him, whereupon he told me next day that Monsieur de Barillon should propose to our master a summe of money to relinquish his insisting in favour of the Confederates for the restoring of those places, since which time I have had twice with me an intimate freind of Monsieur Colberts, with greate professions of respect to the King our master, and saying how reasonable a thing it was that he whoe has suffered soe much in his owne

FREINDSHIP

kingdome for his greate partiality ʌ to the King of Fraunce should share with him in the advantages he has had by the warr, and for his part he would contribute to his being satisfyed all he could ; that he knew Monsieur de Louvoy had flung out some offers of money, but that was only to amuse my master and gaine time, for that Monsieur de Louvoy intended noething more then the continuing the warr, whereas [2] he was desirous of noething more then the peace, as the only thing that could both [3] secure him and the King his master ; that if the King my master would as an expedient for the peace hearken to a greate summe of money, and give me power to treate with him, it should be done with all the secrecy imaginable, and the peace made whether Monsieur de Louvoy would or noe, provided Tourney might reamaine to the King of Fraunce, in consideration of which the King our master should have the honour of making his neice, Madames daughter, Queene of Fraunce ; and for Valenciennes and Conde such expedients as should be secure and honourable for the Spaniards and the Prince of Orenge ; and for the summe of money our master should insist upon for himself, Monsieur Colbert thinks he could make it come easier then Monsieur de Louvoy, whoe must come to him for it first.

You see, my Lord, the jealousie that is now betweene these

[1] The *Letters* read ' enter upon that subject.

[2] The copy gives ' whereof ' but it is not followed by the *Letters*.

[3] Carelessly printed ' best ' in the *Letters*.

two greate ministers. Pray send me the Kings commands and
his directions how he would have it [1] *improoved and turned to
his owne advantage, for without that I dare not nor know not how*

to make any stepp. Only [2] ᵐ ₐ*ᴬᴺᴰ I must take the liberty to give you
this caution, not to enter with Monsieur Barillon upon this matter,
for he is a creatur of Monsieur de Louvoys ; and if you send me
any orders you must not forgett to let me be informed of all Monsieur
de Barillon has saide, that I may be out in noething, for they
keepe all they can from my knowledg heere, beleving me soe
much your Lordships servant that they will not beleive me theire
freind.* ᵐ [2]

*Monsieur de Ruvignys sonne will give your Lordship a lettar
from his father, to beg your countenance and favour whilst he is in
England. I told you in my last* [3] *part of his* [4] *arrant. What there
is more your Lordship will know better then I. As soone as you
can, my Lord, be pleased by a safe hand to let me know hi
Majestys pleasure upon all I have writ. I wish you would send
my Lord Dunblane back soone enough to let it be by him.* [5] *I ar
sure, my Lord, you can never doe anything soe much to his advan
tage as to let him spend a yeare heere, where if I am he may be sur
of the services of him whoe is with all respect,* My Lord,

Your Lordships most obedient and humble servant,

R. Montagu.[6]

---

[1] The version printed in the *Letters* stops at this point, but no authority i
the handwriting of the Duke of Leeds has been found for this.

[2] . . . [2] Against this passage Leeds has written, ' From this mark ᵐ to sai
mark in this letter must bee added att the end of his other letter of the sam
date in Wardours handwriting.' The passage is accordingly included in th
following letter (*infra*, p. 326).

[3] Apparently Montagu's letter of January 11 (*supra*, p. 318).

[4] The copy gives ' my.'

[5] Dumblane apparently was the bearer of this letter.

[6] The original letter is endorsed by Danby, ' 18th January, [16]78 ', to whic
the Duke of Leeds has added, ' N.S. Of consequence and about Marescha
Schomberg.' The copy is endorsed by Leeds, ' Mr. Montagus, 18 Januar
[16]77/8. Not used.' Nevertheless it was used.

To the Lord Treasurer.[1]

Paris, January th 18, [16]78.

My Lord,

Since I sealed up my letter by my Lord Dunblane I have had one with me that is very exactly as can be informed of most things heere, and has told me the reason of Ruvignys journey. His cheife arrant is to let the King know that the King of France did hope he was soe firme to him as not to be lead away by the Grand Tresorier ; he was an ambitious man, and to keepe himself with the people would gratifie theire inclinations by leading his master into an unreasonable warr against France ; that as for money, if he wanted that, he should have what he would from hence. His instructions are, if this dos not take, by the meanes of Will Russell and other discontented people, to give a greate deale of money and crosse all your measures at Court.

When he gives you his fathers letter of recommendation you cannot but [be] very kind to him, since the cheife part of his journey is to doe you soe goode offices. My Lord, if I might be worthy to give my advise, whoe see things upon the place, there could be noething better done then after he has bin two dayes in England for the King to give you order to tell Monsieur Barillon that he knowes Ruvigny has a relation and commerce with people ill-affected to the gouvernment, and would be therfore glad to have him retire. You cannot imagine how it would dampe them heere when they shall see theire little tricks doe not passe upon us ; and old Ruvigny, that values himself upon knowing England, and having saved soe much money as he had by what I told you formerly order to give, has given it them for a maxime, that they must diminish your credit before they can doe any goode. But since theire cheife quarrell to you is the being soe true to your masters interest I am sure he is too just to let them doe you any hurt.

[1] From the autograph letter in B.M. Add. MSS. 28054, f. 136, printed in *Letters*, p. 59. This is the second of the two letters sent by Danby to the House of Commons on December 20, 1678. There are several copies of it B.M. Add. MSS. 28054, ff. 138-47 ; Leeds MSS., Packet 10), and it was frequently printed.

If the King is for a warr, you know what to doe. If he hearkens to theire money, be pleased to let me know what they offer, and I dare answer to get our master as much againe, for Barillons orders are to make the market as low as he can ; [1] AND I MUST TAKE THE LIBERTY TO GIVE YOU THIS CAUTION, NOT TO ENTER WITH MONSIEUR BARILLON UPON THIS MATTER, FOR HE IS A CREATUR OF MONSIEUR DE LOUVOYS. AND IF YOU SEND ME ANY ORDERS, YOU MUST NOT FORGETT TO LET ME BE INFORMED OF ALL MONSIEUR DE BARILLON HAS SAIDE, THAT I MAY BE OUT IN NOETHING, FOR THEY KEEPE ALL THEY CAN FROM MY KNOWLEDG HEERE, BELEVING ME SOE MUCH YOUR LORDSHIPS SERVANT THAT THEY WILL NOT BELEIVE ME THEIRE FREIND. [1]

[R. Montagu] [2]

[*To Mr. Montagu*] [3]

London, 9th January, 1677/8.

My Lord,

I receivd the favour of two of yours by two severall expresses on Munday last, together with one for the King, which I immediately gave him. I did not return you any answer by that post, because I could have then informd you of nothing more then my receipt of them ; but since that time his Majestie has been constantly in Councill twice a day, and is not yett come to a resolution of what hee shall say to Monsieur Barillon, being very unwilling to come to a rupture with France and yett scarce seeing how to avoid it. Hee shewd mee your letter, and as you therein supposed, the DEMAND *Ambassador has quitted the desire* ∧ *of putting off the Parliament,*

[1] . . . [1] This passage is taken bodily from Montagu's other letter of January 18 (*supra*, p. 324 and note 2). To judge from the endorsement of that lette: the first intention of the Duke of Leeds was not to print it, and his idea, n doubt, was to embody this passage in a letter which was to be printed. Wher eventually he decided to print both letters of January 18 he failed to restor the passage to the letter to which it belonged. Yet he had published the second letter correctly in 1679.

[2] Unsigned, because it accompanied the other letter of January 18.

[3] From a clerk's copy in B.M. Add. MSS. 38849, f. 118, printed in *Hodgki MSS.*, p. 186. On this copy the Duke of Leeds has made many alterations, t which effect is given in a second copy in Leeds MSS., Packet 10. In spite o this careful preparation, however, the letter was not included in the publishe collection. The original draft has not been found.

*and offers the suspension provided his Majestie will bee brought to
no declaration against him ; but his Majestie cannot find it
practicable how to keep his Parliament in any sort of order when
the King of France shall at the same time bee in the field and taking
towns. Hee heartily wishes also that hee were in a capacity to doe
so much good to his niece as you speak of ; but the great hast of the
King of France to bee in the field makes almost everything but war
impossible to him, and begins now to turn his trouble for the King
of France's unkindnesse into perfect anger against him, insomuch
that for anything I can guesse I do truly beleeve wee shall goe into
the warre. And for your better satisfaction in that point, I shewd
the King that part of your letter which saies if there should bee war
you could do his Majestie better service then you durst mention
in a letter, and I askd him what I should say to you upon itt.
Whereupon hee commanded mee to tell you hee did beleeve hee
should not bee able to avoide a war, and would by all means have you
informe him what it was you meant.*

You see by all this that <u>wee are</u> ^{THE KING IS}_∧ *not inrichd with those great
offers which have been held forth to* ^{HIM}_∧<u>us,</u> *but on the contrary
(which I think has not been so wise a* ^{I FIND THAT}_∧*part of Monsieur Barrillon
himself) hee has for three weeks past stopt all that was then become
due to* <u>us</u> _∧^{THE KING}, *insomuch that* <u>wee have</u> ^{HEE SAIES HEE HATH}_∧ *receivd but 18,000 l. of the
50,000 l. which should have been paid* ^{HIM}_∧*in December, although
Monsieur Barrillon acknowledgd that 30,000 l. has been in London
above a moneth since. This breach of word for what was already
due by* ^{SOME PRIVATE}_∧*agreement has helpd to exasperate the Kings humour
*_∧^{WHICH I HOPE TO IMPROVE.}<u>and the Duke is as much dissatisfyd as the King.</u>⊕ [1] *You see
likewise that my Lord Dunbarton's regiment and the rest are all to
bee recalled, insomuch that unlesse some balme from heaven bee
applyd to the wound, I doe not see but it must bleed very suddainly.*

[1] . . . [1] These marks are presumably intended to indicate that the intervening
passage should be omitted. It does not appear in the second copy.

I must needs recommend my Lord Dunbarton to your kindnesse, and I should bee glad to hear that you had found some good officer which might bee preferrd to his Majesties service, if there bee occasion ; but in the mean time X 1 *I must return you my humble thanks for your great care and kindnesse to my son Dunblaine, who you have obliged to such a degree as makes him much more desirous to stay with you then look homewards, and I hope hee will bee no lesse desirous to pay you his services then I am, who shall ever bee,*

  Your most faithfull and most humble servant,

           Danby.[2]

[To Mr. Montagu] [3]

       London, 14 January, 1677/8.

My Lord,

  I have nothing to adde as to the publique to what I writt you in my last of the 9th instant ; but I am on my owne account to acknowlege the justice you have done mee to the ministers in that Court, who judge others by themselves ; and though I know I loose a greate deale of reputation with them to bee thought one that will not make my owne fortune upon any tearmes, yett I have the comfort of beleeveing my creditt so bad with them before that itt can hardly bee made worse, and I wish theires were as litle with others here as itt is with mee.

  Upon that part of your letter to the King which speakes of money hee told mee hee should bee glad of theire money, provided the Confederates might have such a peace as would satisfy them, and if things shall att any time come to that passe you need not feare but your advice of secresy will bee taken. The management of itt will also as certainly fall to your share, both for the reasons given by yourselfe to the King, and that I shall very unwillingly enter into a matter which first I beleeve

---

[1] See note on previous page.

[2] Endorsed in the handwriting of the copyist, ' A coppy of my letter to my Lord Ambassador Mountagu, dated the 19/9 January 1677/8.' To this the Duke of Leeds has added, ' O.S.'

[3] From the autograph draft in B.M. Add. MSS. 38849, f. 127, printed in *Hodgkin MSS.*, p. 189. *Letters*, p. 54.

they will not performe, and if they should may perhaps do the King more hurt then good. [1] I observed in the same letter a postscript concerning the Swedes, which shews what honest allies they are, and therefore in my opinion to bee treated as they do others.[1]

I feare your great civility hath created you more trouble with my son Dunblaine then you will owne, but I hope hee may live to pay you his services as I shall ever, who am, &c.,

[Danby] [2]

To the Lord Treasurer.[3]

Paris, January th 26, [16]78.

My Lord,

I am to acknowled the honour of your Lordship of January th 9. What I had to say to his Majesty in case of a warr I did by my lettar by my Lord Dunblane, because I would loose noe time; and I wish I may soone have his Majestys answer upon what I writ.

The reason of my sending this expresse is to give his Majesty an account of his Christian Majesty's resolution of goeing towards Metz, neare Lorraine, with the Queene and Court the next weeke, Thursday sennight being the day set for it. What may be the reason of this journey I cannot well tell, but greate magazines have beene provided all this winter, and in all probability the designes are upon some considerable place, as Treve, Namur, Charlemont and Luxembourgh; and when the project of this was laide, it was upon a supposition that the turning from Flaunders might have kept England quiett; and they thinke theire successe soe sure that that has made theire unwillingnesse to complye with our masters desire of respitting theire armes till the first of March, the unkindnesse of which refusall I have discoursed at large this morning the King, and told him the warr will lie at his doore that would not allow a competent time for a suspension of armes, which in all probability would have ended in a peace.

[1] . . . [1] This passage is omitted in the *Letters*, but no authority for the omission has been found.

[2] Endorsed by Danby, ' Coppy of my letter to Mr. Montagu, 14th January, 1677/8 '; and by Leeds, ' which is very materiall and shews his being the proposer of money to the King.'

[3] From the autograph letter in B.M. Add. MSS. 28054, f. 152.

I will not trouble your Lordship with all he saide, but he yet hopes our master will not declare against him. I know most of his councell are of opinion that yet his ambassadour in England, if things are not already gon to farr, should offer his forbearing the attempting anything till an answer of the cessation can come, and perhaps the Queene and Court goe the journye, that he may with a better grace undertake noething soe soone, and yet not seeme to the world to stop his journey out of any feare or apprehension of a warr with England. You will know from Monsieur Barillon whether I guesse right or noe.

You will see by my lettar to the Secretary what you are like to trust to as to the English troopes heare. The officers, I beleive, will all come, but the number of souldiers, I presume, will be extreamly diminished. I desire I may know his Majestys pleasure as soone as may be, whether I am to follow the Court where they are goeing, or whether I am like to come soone home. I am ready to obey in either, and desirous of all oportunitys of shoeing that I am with all truth and respect, My Lord,

Your Lordships most obedient and humble servant,

R. Montagu.

[To Mr. Montagu] [1]

London, 17 January, 1677/8.

MY LORD,

I did by my Lord Dumbarton write you att large all the intelligence I could then give you, and there has been nothing since worth the returning either of your expresses withall.

My son Dunblain arrived here on Monday last, who delivered mee your letters and acknowleges your very great kindnesse to him, as I am to do both for him and myselfe, who you have

---

[1] From the autograph draft in B.M. Add. MSS. 38849, f. 130, printed in *Hodgkin MSS.*, p. 189. *Letters*, p. 56. This is the first of the two letters produced by Montagu in the House of Commons. There are many copies of it (B.M. Add. MSS. 28054, f. 134; 38849, f. 146; Leeds MSS., Packet 10; Carte MSS. 72, f. 367), and it has frequently been printed. The actual letter has not been found, but it was entered at the time in the Journal of the House of Commons, from which it has been printed in *C.J.*, ix. 559. A comparison of the draft with this version shows few discrepancies, the most significant of which are noted below.

obliged by so many waies.⊕ [1] Your intelligence concerning
Monsieur Ruvigny has not been the least of your favours ; and
hitherto his sons steps have been very suitable to your information, for yesterday hee came to mee with Monsieur Barillon
(haveing given mee his fathers letter the day before) and discourst much upon the confidence his King hath of the firmenesse
of ours to him, of the good opinion his master has of mee, of
his Kings resolution to condescend to anything that is not
infamous to him for the satisfaction of our King, how certainely
our King may depend upon all sorts of assistances and supplys
from his master in case the freindship bee preserved, and in short
went so far as to seeme desirous to have mee understand
(although hee would not directly say itt) that his master might
bee brought to part with Valenciennes and Conde, but never
with Tournay. And the maine of theire drift was to ingage mee
to prevaile with the King to overule [2] the Prince of Orange as to
that towne, and presst the matter upon mee as a thing wherein
they thought I had an interest of my owne with the Prince of
Orange sufficient to perswade him to putt an end to the war by
that meanes.

[3] I answered them (as is most true) that there is nothing I
am so desirous of as peace,[4] but I thought things were gone so
far as itt was only in theire masters [5] power to prevent the war,
and that I would contribute to any possible expedient to that
end, but that they must apply themselves to the King himselfe,
and when itt came to my part I should bee found to contradict
nothing which might bee equall for preservation of the freindship betwixt the two kings.[3] From mee they went imediately
to the King, who tells me theire discourse was the same they

[1] By this mark the Duke of Leeds intended to indicate that the printed
version of the letter should begin at this point, and the copy in Leeds MSS.,
Packet 10, accordingly omits the two preceding sentences. The idea of the
omission, however, was eventually abandoned.

[2] The *Commons Journal* gives ' prevail with.'

[3] . . . [3] This whole passage has been crossed out by the Duke of Leeds in
the copy in Leeds MSS., Packet 10 ; but the omission has not in the end been
proceeded with.

[4] The *Commons Journal* gives ' the peace.'

[5] The *Letters* read, ' his Majesties power ', probably by mistake.

had held with mee ; and att last hee desired that whatever expedient they had to propose to him might bee putt in writeing for him to consider, and thus itt stands att this time.

As to the officer you mention (who the King assures himselfe to bee Schomberg [1]) hee has taken further time to resolve of his answer ; and as to our maine point of war or peace itt will certainely depend upon the King of France his consenting or not to the first propositions, our King being ingaged to oppose any party that shall refuse them ; nor will the time for that consideration bee much longer, since itt will bee impossible but the King must come to some ∧ declaration of his mind ⊕ [2] to
SPEEDY
the Parliament when that meetes.

That which yett makes the hopes of peace lesse probable is that the Duke grows every day lesse inclined to itt, and has created a greater indifferency in the King then I could have imagined, which being added to the French Kings seeming [3] resolutions not to part with Tournay does, I confesse, make mee wholly [3] despaire of any accommodation. Neverthelesse I am assured that one principall cause of this adjournment for thirteen daies has been to see if any expedient for the peace could have been found in that time ; and the effect of the adjournment has [4] been that nobody will now beleeve other then that the peace is [5] concluded by concert betwixt us and France.

[Danby] [6]

I aprove of this letter. C.R. [7]

---

[1] In the *Commons Journal* the word ' Schomberg ' is omitted.

[2] This mark was made by the Duke of Leeds to indicate that the printed version of the letter should stop here. The copy in Leeds MSS., Packet 10, accordingly stops at this point with the words added in the Duke's handwriting, ' in that affaire.' In the end, however, this change was not carried out.

[3] ' Seeming ' and ' wholly ' are omitted in the *Commons Journal*.

[4] The *Commons Journal* reads ' hath hitherto been.'

[5] The *Commons Journal* inserts ' already.'

[6] Endorsed by Danby, ' Coppy of my letter to Mr. Montagu, 17 January 1677/8 ' ; to which Leeds has added, ' Of great importance and was signed by the King himselfe, and is coppied false in Kennetts *History of Charles 2nd*.'

[7] In the handwriting of Charles II. This note is not printed in any form in the *Letters* or in the *Commons Journal*.

To the Lord Treasurer.[1]

Paris, February th 2, [16]78.

My Lord,

I am to acknowledg the honour of your Lordships, by which I see mine by my Lord Dunblane came safe to your hands. I find by your Lordships everything in England hastens to a warr. I am afraide the copye of a paper which I have sent the Secretary, and which Monsieur de Barillon has order to present the King our master with, as a present expedient to hinder matters from coming to the last extremity, will not be sufficient. I made severall objections to it, which I will not trouble you with repeating. They are soe perswaded heere that it will have a goode effect that I would not oppose theire sending it ; but I would have had that article left out concerning our masters making any alliances, because I told them if he had not made them it were very reasonable he should make them. But if this takes effect for the suspension, they promise to be soe reasonable that they doe not doubt of the peace.

I am sure they are very unwilling to a warr with us (I meane the nation), and they are all as backward to it heere as forward to it in England. I am not politician enough to judg which will be the best for our master, but if there is warr I shall have the advantage of waiting of your Lordship the sooner. If theire be peace I hope you will send my Lord Dunblane back, and lay your commands upon me how you will have him disposed, which I shall be very carefull of, as of all things wherein your Lordship shall have any concern, whoe am with all respect, My Lord,

Your Lordships most obedient and humble servant,

R. Montagu.

[To the Lord Treasurer][2]

Paris, February 12th, [16]78.

My Lord,

I have not much to trouble your Lordship with but to give you an account of the effect his Majestys speech has already had in this country. I had it translated into French, and I never saw a

[1] From the autograph letter in B.M. Add. MSS. 28054, f. 156, printed in *Campana de Cavelli*, i. 208.

[2] From a copy in Leeds MSS., Packet 10.

*greater consternation in my life than it makes in people here. I
was with Monsieur de Louvoy this morning, who told me that he
wondered Monsieur de Berrillon had not already given in the
project sent for a suspension, that he hoped that might have
hindred the King our master from coming to so partiall a declaration for the Confederates as he has done in his speech. After that
I have had with me one of Monsieur de Louvoys intimate friends,
who told me that we had taken an ill way with the King of France
to have the towns we asked for (parceque vous y aves demande
le baston haut—that was the expression), that if things were not
carri'd on with to much precipitation, that if there were a suspension and the King had time to come of by degrees, that perhaps
he would sacrafice his owne humour fier and believe the wise
people of his nation that would not councell him to draw so great a
war upon his people, that must cost them so much blood and
treasure for a towne or two.*

*My answer was that our master had trusted to fair words to long,
and from hence forward would goe upon surer grounds. He asked
me whether I would not write this. I said no, that I durst not venter
to give any uncertain advises that might make any alteration in the
King my masters measures. And indeede, my Lord, the King has
now taken the wisest and only way to bring them here to understand
reason in the midst of all the business. My Lord, I know a long
letter must be troublesome, wherefore I will only add the assurances
of my being with all respect, My Lord,*

Your Lordships most obedient and humble servant,

R. Montagu.[1]

[To Mr. Montagu] [2]

London, 11 February, 1677/8.
My Lord,

*Monsieur Ruvigny, who will give you this letter, will also
acquaint you what he has leave to say from our master to his, which
is, that our master will do all he can to preserve the friendship
betwixt the King of France and him, and to show it (though he had*

---

[1] Endorsed by the Duke of Leeds, ' Not used. 12 February, [16]77/9.'

[2] Hist. MSS. Com., *Buccleuch MSS. at Montagu House*, i. 524, from the
original letter.

reason to expect that for his sake the King of France would have consented to the propositions sent by my Lord Feversham), that he will do what he can with the Prince of Orange to get him agree that Charlemont, or some other place of like consequence, may be given to the King of France in lieu of Tournay, and that if he can get the Prince to consent he will make the peace notwithstanding the progress made by the Parliament here towards the war.

He has power also to tell his master that our King will suffer no declaration of war to be against him until he shall have an answer from the King of France upon this matter, provided that he do not besiege any place in the mean time, because our master cannot answer whether he shall be able to resist the importunity of his Parliament, in case they should see him taking of more towns. He is also to acquaint his master that the King has already sent Mr. Godolphin to the Prince of Orange to know his mind, and that he expects the return of Monsieur Ruvigny as soon as is possible.

This matter is transacted with such secresy here that the Secretaries of State themselves know nothing of it, but believe the journey of Godolphin to be to adjust the matter of Ostend betwixt us and the Spaniard ; and Monsieur Ruvigny has taken leave of the King as going to his regiment without any thoughts of returning hither, so that although his Majesty has commanded me to charge you with strict secresy I know there would have been no need of that caution from the nature of the business itself. Whether this will prove any expedient of accommodation I am not at all able to guess, neither on the part of France nor of the Prince. In the mean time we go on with all preparations for war, and the great advances of the French army makes me fear there will not be time to get the peace, though all sides seem inclined to it. I am, My Lord,

Your Excellencys [&c]

Danby.

[To the Lord Treasurer] [1]

Paris, February th 26, [16]78.

My Lord,

The newes being heere that the Spaniards doe intend wholly to comply with the King our master, and my Lord

---

[1] From the autograph letter in Leeds MSS., Packet 10, where there is also a copy in a clerk's handwriting. *Letters*, p. 64.

Dunbarton presuming that they may give up Ostend to his Majesty, has desired me to beg your Lordships goode word in his favour. I know not whoe the King may intend it to, but we have few fitter for it then he, and his leaving all his fortune soe frankly as he dos, out of duty to his master, is a sufficient proofe of his fidelity.⊕ [1]

The Kings affaires goeing soe well as they doe in England, I cannot now think the French will breake with us ; and if they agree to the first propositions sent by my Lord Duras, beleive me they will be sufficiently mortifyed, for I never saw peoples hearts set upon anything soe much as theires upon Conde, Tourney and Valenciennes.⊕ [1] The Prince of Orenge must be mad if he is opiniastre enough not to part with Charlemont, which is, nor will be when there is a peace, of noe other use to the French then a salvo in point of honour to the King of France, whoe sayde he would never agree to my Lord Duras his propositions without he had some other place in exchange for Flaunders.

If the peace be made upon these tearmes, I am sure, considering how the French have fortified it, it is stronger and better able to defend itself then if things were brought to the Pyrenean treaty ; and for England noething can be more honourable, and most particularly to your Lordship, whoe both at home and abroade has the reputation of the cheife instrument that has kept our master soe firme and resolute in this greate affaire, which must end soe much to his honour and advantage. I am sure noe man shall alwaise [2] take a greater share in what concerns your Lordship then myself, nor be with more respect, My Lord,

Your Lordships most obedient and humble servant,

R. Montagu.[3]

---

[1] These marks, made by the Duke of Leeds on the copy, indicate that the passage between them is not to be printed. It does not appear in the *Letters*.

[2] The *Letters* read ' ever.'

[3] Endorsed by Leeds, ' Of consequence as to myselfe as the instrument of the King's firmness.'

[To the Lord Treasurer] [1]

Paris, March th 1, [16]78.

My Lord,

I had the honour of your Lordships by Monsieur de Ruvigny. [2] I hope your Lordship dos me the justice to beleive that I would not make soe ill a return to the obligation I lye under of being trusted soe freely by you as to faile in _∧ <u>ANYTHING</u> the secrecye that is due to matters of so greate importance. ⊕ *But for my owne justification I must needes tell you that Monsieur de Ruvigny arrived at Paris about ten in the morning, and I saw him not till six at night, and by four in the afternoone my Lord Dunbarton came to me and told me all he came about, and I beleive he had it from Madame de Boullion, whome Monsieur de Ruvigny had seene, and she told it to other woemen. But I did all lay in me to perswade my Lord Dunbarton from the truth of what he told me, and since I have heard noething of it, soe you may be pleased to take noe notice of this to Monsieur de Ruvigny at his return.* ⊕ I am not sorry for his _∧ MONSIEUR RUVIGNYS journey into England, for the King and your Lordship have handled him soe well, that he is come back fully possest of the greate power of our master to doe his hurt, as well as of the greate marke of freindship, to be willing yet to make the peace upon the tearmes proposed by my Lord Duras, and wave all the advantages he may reasonably and probably expect by a warr. ^m

Considering the goode disposition of his Parlament, and the ill condition of the Confederates, whoe must of necessity put themselfs under his Majestys protection, the cheife thing that makes me doubt of the peace is the facility the King of France will find in his present undertaking, it being reported heere that there is a very ill and weake garrison in Namur. If that is, the successe is soe certain, and the consequences soe advantagious, that I am afraide he will

---

[1] From the autograph letter in B.M. Add. MSS. 28054, f. 160. The latter half of this letter was marked by the Duke of Leeds for excision, and a copy of the earlier part was then made, which is in Leeds MSS., Packet 10. On this copy the Duke made several further alterations, all of which are embodied in the very abbreviated version of the letter published in *Letters*, p. 65.

[2] Dated February 11, 1677/8, *supra*, p. 334.

*ventur breaking with England, or at least hope, if he takes Namur,
that he may keepe it, if he shall restore Tourney, Conde and Valenciennes, for that towne alone, joyned with Mastrickt, gives him a
vast countrey that will keepe him an army for noething, and cutt of
all communication betweene Flaunders and Germany. But if the
Spaniards have bin wise enough to put a goode garrison that can
make any resistance, I doe not despaire but Monsieur de Ruvigny
may bring back such an answer as may make a peace.*

*Upon yesterday the 28 the King tooke leave of the Queene and
ladys at Stenay, and went himself to Sedan, by which all heere
concluded he will immediately undertake something ; and they say
the Queene is to come back to St. Germains. Monsieur de Ruvigny
went from hence on Sunday morning the 27, and was the 28 with
the King. On the fifth of this moneth he told me he thought to be back
heere, and in three dayes more at London. I am sure the Parlament cannot be soe desirous of a warr as all the world heere is of a
peace. Considering the multitude of buisnesse you must have at
present, I am afraide I may have bin to tedious, wherfore I will
remaine with all respect, My Lord,*

Your Lordships most obedient and humble servant,

R. Montagu.[1]

[*To the Lord Treasurer*] [2]

Paris, March th 5, [16]78.

My Lord,

*I hope you will not thinke it officiousnesse in me, since upon
what you were pleased to write by his Majesty's permission soe
freely to me in your two last, if I give you my opinion what is the
intention of this Court as to a peace, and what they are like to doe
upon this greate successe, which, perhaps before this can come to
your hands, will happen to them by the reducing of Gaunt. I
alwaise did think (and now it falls out soe) that Monsieur de
Louvoy would very hardly loose the meritt, nor let the King of
Fraunce loose the vanity, of some greate action early in the yeare.
They both of them being satisfyed in these two particulars may*

---

[1] Endorsed by Danby, ' From Mr. Montagu, 1st March, 1677/8 '; and by
Leeds, ' Of use to shew how Ruvigny had been handled here.'

[2] From the autograph letter in B.M. Add. MSS. 28054, f. 165.

*perhaps hearken to a peace sooner then before, and will now
infallible offer to restore Gaunt insteade of some of the three places
soe much insisted upon. If Monsieur de Ruvigny be returned, you
will be able to take some measures of what you are like to trust to
from hence. His father dos judge that he will not come by Paris,
but directly from the camp into England, and then he may be with
you by this time. You see, my Lord, in what ill company our
master is like to be engaged in, and how the burthen of the warr will
certainly lye upon him, as well as almost an impossibility, if Gaunt
be taken, of sending any English succours into Flaunders but
what will be lost and the honour of the nation more exposed then it
would be by a peace, which, though it be not soe goode as were to be
wished, yet may be better then a warr which, with soe many ill
circumstances as must accompanye it, cannot be advantagious to
us at this time.*

*When upon my return from England I insisted upon the same
terms that my Lord Duras brought, I found Tourney was what they
would not part with, but that they were more tractable as to Conde
and Valenciennes. I gave you an account alsoe of what offers of
money were made to the King our master, as well as the fortifying
of more places, if the Prince of Orenge thought fitt, at the King of
Fraunce his expences, and an engagement to the King our master
that whatever difference happened betweene Fraunce and Spaine
should be decided in some other part of the world and never in
Flaunders. But now Monsieur de Ruvigny as he passed by did to
me disowne the King of Fraunce his having the least thoughts of
parting with Conde or Valenciennes, though I beleive in discourse
to your Lordship he might intimate the contrary. My humble
opinion therfore is, my Lord, to know positivly the King of Fraunce
his last resolutions as to the terms of a peace, and to looke upon the
Spaniards as children that are opiniastre and know not what is
goode for themselfs.*

*If Monsieur de Ruvigny's answer be not satisfactory, and the
King our master will make any other proposition, if you please to
send me the Kings commands by this bearer (it is but Mr. Secre-
arys sending me an order to goe to Lisle or Cambray to be nearer the
Court upon occasion), I can goe and make it, and it will be much
secreter then anything that passes betweene the two kings by one sent*

on purpose, which alarms all parties concerned, and makes a buisness publick before anything can be concluded in it, besides the jealousies it gives the Parlament.   I am sure, my Lord, noething can be more for our masters service then to be at a certainty in this affaire, which upon discours with the King and Monsieur de Louvoy I doe not doubt but I may be able to give an account of, and shall be very punctuall as well as secret in observing any directions you shall send me.   This bearer, if you please to discours with him, will give you as true a state of the affaires of all kind of this country as any man in it, as I doe the assurances of my being with all respect, My Lord,

   Your Lordships most obedient and humble servant,

           R. Montagu.

I have sent all the newes in the Secretary's letter.[1]

[To the Lord Treasurer] [2]

         Paris, March th 12, [16]78.

My Lord,

 I am sure before this time you have Monsieur de Ruvigny back with you, and by him the propositions of peace that the King of France now makes, which we heare heere are the same he offered before the taking of Gant, with an offer alsoe to restore Gant and what els he shall take.   Whether this be soe or noe I cannot tell, but I am afraide this successe will elevate them extreamly, especially since in England we have only shoed our teeth and cannot bite And be confident they will make the French proverb goode, L'appetit veinte en mangent ; and the more they take the more they will keepe.

 I had orders last post from Mr. Secretary Coventry to furnish Colonel Dunganun and Laniere with fourty dayes pay for both theire regiments, which after the rate of eightpence English and half a crowne a day the hors, and officers pay to, amounts to neer 30,000 French crowns, besides 2,000 pistols I have order to answe for cloaths for Dunganuns regiment.   I have tryed severall banquer in Paris that I used to deale with, and upon the feare of the war

---

[1] Endorsed by Danby, ' Mr. Montagus letter, 5th March, 1677/8 '.   To th the Duke of Leeds has added, ' of France takeing Ghent and his advices to peace.'

[2] From the autograph letter in Leeds MSS., Packet 10.

none of them will advance such a summe, alleadging that they have
all above a moneth agoe, by Monsieur Colberts advise, called home
all the effects they have in England. Soe that if the King is still in
the mind to have this money advanced to Colonel Dunganun and
Laniere, your Lordship must be pleased to receive his Majestys
orders, either for the sending bills of credit or bills of exchange ;
but if upon Monsieur de Ruvignys return things should come to any
accommodation betweene France and England, the money sent for
the bringing of these troopes over will be clearly lost. But his
Majesty knowes best what he intends to doe. I only thought it my
duty to give that hint in case theire were any likelyhoode of a peace.

If you please to call to mind, or, if you have not burnt it, reade
over a lettar I writ your Lordship upon my return out of England,
you will find that the propositions then made were much more
advantagious to the King our master then any, I am afraide, they
will make now. I am sure I shall never alter from the professions
I have made of being with all truth and respect, My Lord,

Your Lordships most obedient and humble servant,

R. Montagu.[1]

[To the Lord Treasurer] [2]

Paris, March th 12, [16]78.

My Lord,

I hope you will not think it impertinently officious to you,
or malicious to the Duke of Buckingam, if being soe really as
I am in all your concerns I give you an account of some things,
which when you know you may make what use of you please.

There came with me into England one Monsieur de la Tolade,
whome I left sick of the goute. He was formerly a great
acquaintance of the Duke of Buckingamm, and being in
England was much with him. You know, my Lord, how freely
he speakes his mind ; and he told this man that he did not doubt
of ruining you, and being better with the King then ever, and
in order to ruine you he had consulted his freinds whether he
had best make up with you or noe, and that he was advised not
to be freinds with you, and therfore desired the King, whoe
offered to make you freinds, not to doe it. Therfore pray let not

---

[1] Endorsed by Danby, ' From Mr. Montagu, March 12, 1677/8.'

[2] From the autograph letter in B.M. Add. MSS. 28054, f. 167. *Letters*, p. 67.

your generosity or goode nature ever prevaile upon you enough ever to trust him, but be upon your guard, for if ever he can doe you a mischeife he will. This same man tells me that young Ruvigny, by orders from the King of Fraunce, has made Monsieur Barillon strike up a league with him, that they meete often privately, and that Monsieur de Barillon is much guided by him. The Duke of Buckingam, I find, reckons that he has the greatest part of the Court for him, and ownes the having a promise of being very soone againe a gentleman of the bedchamber.

I have had from severall hands an overture of reconcilement; if not, I am to be one of the proscribed, and I intend to doe with him what he resolves to doe with your Lordship, that is not make up. And if I might be worthy to advise, were I in your Lordships place I would doe soe to, for I am confident you will find his freindship as troublesome as his ill will can be dangerous. Pray excuse this liberty from one that is soe intirely,

Your Lordships most humble servant,

[R. Montagu] [1]

[To the Lord Treasurer] [2]

Paris, March th 29, [16]78.

My Lord,

I had the honour of your Lordships of March th 14,[3] by which I perceive the French, after theire accustomed manner, doe still endeavour to amuse our master with faire words and promises, only to gaine time for theire owne advantage, and not care what difficultys or inconveniences they runn him upon, soe they doe what they have a mind to doe. ⋔ The King of Fraunce is expected heere the 8 of Aprill, French style, by which time I may heare from your Lordship if you have any commands from his Majesty for me, and I may give you an account better what his intentions are, having it from his owne mouth, then you can have

---

[1] The absence of a signature suggests that this letter was probably sent under cover of the previous letter, which is of the same date. The letters were presumably written at the same time, but Montagu thought it advisable to deal with the purely personal question of Buckingham's intrigues in a separate note. This letter is endorsed by Danby, ' 12 March, [16]77/8 '; and by Leeds, ' D[uke of] Buckinghams designes against mee and his league with Barillion by Ruvigny.'

[2] From the autograph letter in B.M. Add. MSS. 28054, f. 170. *Letters*, p. 76.

[3] This letter has not been found.

from his ministers, whoe most commonly have some reserve, and are alwaise upon the catch with the King our master. I cannot tell how high and unreasonable these successes may have made him ; but the Chancellour, with whome I had lately a greate deale of discours, seemes more enclined to the peace then before the campayne, and he seldome speakes but his sonnes mind. In the humour the Parlament are in methinks the King has but a sad prospect of entring into the warr, and I feare they may grow weary of it before the King of Fraunce can be forced to give back what he offered once to restore, and with particular advantages to the King himself.

I beleive it will be unnecessary for the King to be at the charge of sending over soe much money as fourty dayes pay for Dunganun and Lanieres regiment, for if there were a million of money heere it would be impossible to get the men away all together, and I have upon my owne credit taken up enough to help away Colonel Dunganun and Laniere and some men and officers that come with them. ᵐ *I have alsoe sauved his Majesty 2,000 pistols which Colonel Dunganun had like to have paide for the cloathes, for, finding that he was only engaged for 200 pistols, and the rest was to be paide upon the regiment, I payde only the 200 for which they would have arrested him, and have got the rest of the summe to be paide by Monsieur de Louvoy out of what he owes the regiment, which he will pay the tradesmen, though he would not Dunganun.*

I have drawne a bill upon Mr. Kingdome, as Mr. Secretary told me I might, but it is at usance, for noe merchant will give money for a longer time because of the warr. I hope your Lordship will let it be accepted. The Secretary has an account of those that received the money. If my servant be not come away your Lordship may dispatch him with any commands you have for me, whoe am [1] with all respect, My Lord,

Your Lordships most obedient and humble servant,

R. Montagu.[2]

[1] The *Letters* read ' I am.'

[2] Endorsed by Danby, ' 29 March, [16]78 '; and by Leeds, ' Note a clause about the Parliament and bad prospect for a war. Quere what successes the French had had at this time.'

To Mr. Charles Bertie.[1]

Paris, March th 29, [16]78.

I am out of countenance at all the troubles you are pleased to give yourself in my concernes. I have heard something of what you tell me of the Queenes engagement to my Lady Arlington, but soe many things come betweene the cup and the lip, especially at Court, that till things are done one must never despaire, noe more then I doe of being Secretary of State, if my Lady Danby [2] continues her [2] favour to me and can work of Sir William Temple.

I know for certaine that there is a greate caball to bring in Mr. [3] *Hide, and that Nelly and the Duke of Buckingam are in it purposely that noe freind of my Lord Treasurers may be in the place. And they have engaged Mr. Secretary Coventry by Herry* [3] Savell, whoe writ a lettar last post to my Lady Cleavland, that his fortune depended upon her coming over, for that he had engaged his unkle, [4] the Secretary, for Mr. Hide, upon condition he should have Mr. Hides place of the Robes, which he could never compasse money to buye,[4] except she got the Kings leave for him to sell his bedchamber place, and some additionall money to help. You may let my Lord Treasurer and Lady Danby[5] know this, but it must be kept very secret, for els it would hinder me knowing many things that may be for theire [6] service.

It is not very well in Mr. Savell, whoe has those obligations to my Lord Treasurer, to manage such an affaire underhand. For my part, I care not for the place except I come in with his

---

[1] From the autograph letter in B.M. Add. MSS. 39757, f. 102, printed in *Morrison Catalogue*, iv. 284, and summarised in *Hist. MSS. Com.*, ix. 2, p. 455. There is a copy in a clerk's handwriting in Leeds MSS., Packet 10, which differs from the original in omitting all reference to Lady Danby. The version printed in *Letters*, p. 78, exhibits still more important discrepancies. For none of these has any authority been found in the handwriting of the Duke of Leeds.

[2] Instead of ' my Lady Danby ' and ' her ' the copy reads ' my Lord ' and ' his ', and is followed by the *Letters*.

[3] . . . [3] This passage appears in the copy, but not in the *Letters*.

[4] . . . [4] As regards this passage the copy follows the original, but the *Letters* read instead, ' Secretary Coventry, for his place, but could not compass money to buy it.'

[5] The copy omits ' and Lady Danby ', and is followed by the *Letters*.

[6] The copy gives ' his ', and is followed by the *Letters*.

favour and kindnesse. I have tryed[1] noe other waies to compasse it, neither will I. [2] *Mr. Godolphin, I heare some say, pretends to it to.*[2] Pray put my Lord Treasurer and my Lady Danby[3] in mind of me, with the assurances that they have[4] noe servant truer to them[4] then myself, nor more intirely, Deare Cozen,

Your most faithfull humble servant,

R. Montagu[5]

The proposalls sent to Mr. Montagu, 25th March, 1678, and returned with the alterations.[6]

As to France and Holland :—

All in Europe to be restored.

BETWIXT France and Spaine :—

Charleroy		
Aeth		
Oudenarde		
Conde	*not*[7]	With their baillages, provosts, annexes, &c. TO BEE RESTORED TO SPAINE.[7a]
St. Ghislain	*demolished*	
Gaund		
Ipres	*not*[7]	
Courtray		
Limbourg		
Binche		

All the places in Sicily[8] to be restored to Spaine.[8]

[1] The copy reads ' urged ', but is not followed by the *Letters.*

[2] . . . [2] This passage appears in the copy, but is omitted in the *Letters.*

[3] The copy omits ' and my Lady Danby ', and is followed by the *Letters.*

[4] Copy and *Letters* read ' he has ' and ' him '.

[5] The original letter is endorsed by Danby, ' From Mr. Montagu, 29 March, 1678 ' ; and by Leeds, ' To brother C[harles] Bertie about Montagus being Secretary, &c., and about Mr. Godolphin and Mr. Hyde.'

[6] From the original document in B.M. Add. MSS. 38849, f. 144, printed in *Letters*, p. 70, and *Hodgkin MSS.*, p. 196. The heading here given is Danby's original endorsement. The body of the document is in a clerk's handwriting, but there are additions made by Montagu (shown in *italics*) and also by Danby (shown in SMALL CAPITALS). The proposals, without the alterations, are printed from Williamson's notes in *Cal. S.P. Dom.*, 1678, p. 67.

[7] No reference to these additions is made in the *Letters.*

[8] . . . [8] This passage is crossed out by Montagu, who notes in its place, ' abandoned to the Spaniards already.' The original passage is, however, printed in the *Letters.*

BETWIXT France and Emperor :—

	All places belonging to the Emperor, the Empire, or to any Princes of the Empire, taken by France during this warr, to be
Fribourgh insisted to [be] kept if Philisbourgh be not restored.	restored, particularly Fribourg and all the places in Brisgow.
	Phillipsbourg not to be restored, and the Franche Comté to remayne to the King of France.

Dutchy of Loraine to be restored to the Duke *according to the Pyrenean treaty, or els Thou insteade of Nancy and other advantages that shall satisfye the Duke.*[1]

[To Mr. Montagu] [2]

[London], 25 March, 1678.

[My Lord],

Since my writeing to you by Mr. Brisbon [3] the resolutions have been altered as to the sending you instructions as yett for the proposeing anything to the French King. The particulars which will bee consented to on the part of the Confederates (and of which this is a coppy) will bee comunicated to you by Mr. Secretary Coventry ; but you will have no other direction from him about them, but only thereby to bee inabled to find the pulse of that King (or his ministers att least) against the time that you shall receive orders to make the proposalls to him.

---

[1] Endorsed, ' The proposalls sent to Mr. Montagu, 25th March 1678, for the peace, and returned with the alterations made by him in the margent. These proposalls to bee placed with my remarks on my letter of 25 March [16]78.' Of this endorsement the words ' for the peace ' and all that follows ' alterations ' are in the handwriting of the Duke of Leeds. The remainder is Danby's contemporary endorsement.

[2] From the autograph draft in B.M. Add. MSS. 38849, f. 140, printed in *Hodgkin MSS.*, p. 194. *Letters*, p. 72. This is the second of the two letters produced by Montagu in the House of Commons. There are many copies of it (B.M. Add. MSS. 28054, f. 168 ; 38849, f. 146 ; Carte MSS. 72, f. 369), and it has also been frequently printed. The actual letter has not been found, but it was entered at the time in the Journal of the House of Commons, from which it has been printed in *C.J.*, ix. 560. A comparison of the draft with this version shows that the letter cannot have varied appreciably from the draft.

[3] This letter has not been found.

That you may know from whence the nicety of this affaire proceeds, itt is necessary to informe you that for feare of its being ill resented by the Parliament here the King will not make any proposall at all of peace, unlesse hee shall bee presst to itt by the Confederates. And although by Mr. Godolphin hee is sufficiently informed that they desire the peace upon the tearmes sent you by the Secretary, yett not haveing received that desire formally the Councell will not advise his Majestie to lett his embassador propose that which hee is not formally impowred to make good ; and so by staying for that formall power, which by letter his Majestie is sufficiently authorised to propose, the time will bee lost of effecting the peace, if att all itt can bee had.

To supply this defect therefore, and [1] to prevent the Kings sending againe [1] into Holland before hee knows the mind of France, I am comanded by his Majestie to lett you know that you are to make the propositions inclosed [2] to the King of France, and to tell him that the King will undertake for the seeing them made good on the part of Spaine and Holland in case they shall bee accepted by him. And in your answer you must write the same thing to the Secretary by way only of haveing felt the King's pulse, which you must do to the King as a full answer from the King of France, and such an one as the King may depend upon, whatever that shall bee. For the more dextrous management of this matter the King is advised to shew these propositions to Monsieur Barillon, but not to give him a coppy, so that by the strength of memory itt is expected hee shall write to his master, and by that meanes only are wee to hope for an answer to a matter of this vast importance ; and consequently you may imagine what a satisfaction wee are like to reape from itt when itt comes. I doubt not but by your conduct itt will bee brought to a speedier [3] issue, which is of as great importance as the thing ittselfe, there being no condition worse for his Majestie then his standing unresolved betwixt peace and war.

[1] . . . [1] As first drafted this passage read, ' that so much time may not bee lost as to send againe.'

[2] *Supra*, p. 345.   [3] The *Commons Journal* and the *Letters* give ' speedy.'

I find by Monsieur Barillon that tis like some places, which are dependencies upon greater townes, may bee demanded by the King of France ; but if hee intend the peace (which you will do very well to know his mind fully in), you may justly say you hope hee will neither stand upon one single place (though a fortified one), nor upon any place unfortified which is a dependant upon those which are to bee restored to Spaine. And if anything should bee mentioned [1] about Sicily to remaine in the French hands untill the peace of Sweden were [2] concluded, you are only to say that you are not impowred to say anything upon itt, and you are confident the King has done all hee could to gett the utmost propositions [3] they would consent to. Only you are to say that the King has againe sent about Conde, not being well satisfied that they have not left itt in his power to give or refuse as hee should have found convenient, and hopes still for some good answer.

In case the conditions of the peace shall bee accepted, the King expects to have six millions of livers a yeare for three yeares from the time that this agreement shall bee signed

PROBABLY

betwixt his Majestie and the King of France, because itt will ∧ bee two or three yeares before [4] the Parliament will bee in humor [4] to give him any supplys after the makeing of [5] any peace with France, and the embassador here has alwaies [6] agreed to that sume, but not for so long time. If you find the peace will not bee accepted, you are not to mention the money att all, and all possible care must bee taken to have this whole negotiation as private as is possible, for feare of giveing offence att home, where for the most part wee heare in ten daies after of anything that is comunicated to the French ministers.

I must againe repeate to you that whatever you write upon this subject to the Secretary (to whom you must not mention a

---

[1] The *Commons Journal* gives ' moved.'

[2] The *Commons Journal* gives ' be.'

[3] The *Commons Journal* gives ' conditions.'

[4] . . . [4] Instead of this passage the *Commons Journal* gives ' he can hope to find his Parliament in humour.'

[5] The *Commons Journal* gives ' the having made.'

[6] The *Commons Journal* omits ' alwaies.'

syllable of the money) you must say only as a thing you beleeve they would [1] consent to, if you had power formally to make those propositions.[2] Pray informe yourselfe to the bottome of what is to bee expected from France, and assure them that you beleeve this will bee the last time that you shall receive any propositions of a peace, if these bee rejected (as indeed I beleeve itt will), so that you may take your owne measures as well as the Kings upon itt. [I am,

Your Excellency's most faithfull and obedient servant,

Danby] [3]

I aprove of this letter. C.R.[4]

To the Lord Treasurer.[5]

Paris, Aprill th 9, [16]78.

My Lord,

I had the honour of two of your Lordships by Mr. Brisban,[6] and shall observe the directions given me in them. This day is soe greate a time of devotion that till to-morrow night neither the King nor any of the ministers will be to be seene. I shall loose noe time in giving you as speedy an account as may be and the best I can of theire intentions heere, till when I will give your Lordship noe farther trouble then to assure you that I am with all respect, My Lord,

Your Lordships most obedient and humble servant,

R. Montagu.

---

[1] The *Commons Journal* gives ' will.'

[2] The *Commons Journal* gives ' demands.'

[3] Endorsed by Danby, ' To Mr. Montagu, 25 March 1678 ' ; and by Leeds, ' This is the letter on which I was impeached, and which was signed by the King himselfe for my justification before I would write itt. And lett this bee compared with Montagues letters before as well as after itt. And vide the forreigne ministers discourses upon itt to Sir William Temple in his letter to me of '. The reference is probably to Temple's letter of January 27, 1679, *infra*, p. 508.

[4] In the handwriting of Charles II. This note is not printed in any form in the *Commons Journal*. The *Letters* give, ' This letter is writ by my order, C.R.' No authority for this alteration has been found, but it can hardly have been made by any one but the Duke of Leeds himself.

[5] From the autograph letter in Leeds MSS., Packet 10.

[6] These letters have not been found.

[To the Lord Treasurer] [1]

Paris, Aprill th 11, [16]78.

My Lord,

I have endeavoured to obey his Majestys commands sent me by two of your Lordships with all the speede I could. It will not be my fault if you have an account sooner by Monsieur de Barillon then by me, by whose adresse and management they hope heere to gaine theire point upon the King our master.

I have at two severall times discoursed with the King of Fraunce the project of the peace you sent me. I find as to Conde he reckons upon it as a sure thing, and for Ipres he seemes to be very positive in not restoring it,⊕ *and soe doeth Monsieur de Louvoy and Monsieur de Pompone. And yet by severall circumstances in the conversation which one cannot expresse I doe really beleive Monsieur de Barillon has power to relinquish it, rather then let the warr be declared, if he sees our master dos really resolve the warr upon the refusing it, or has the power of the peace upon the yeelding it ; soe that the townes that will be restored are the enclosed I send with the alterations. I made noe mention of Siccily, because the French have abandoned it ; but I made use of it as an argument to have Conde and Ipres restored, which the French all along valued soe much, to the King our master. And in effect they restore but foure considerable places to the King our master, if they keepe Conde and Ipres and pretend to have Cassell and Popeyreing with Charlemont or Dinan, which Monsieur de Louvoy tells me Monsieur Barillon had already acquainted our master with.⊕*

HIM
I told the ∧ King that our master could not with any honour at home or abroade consent to any other peace then the list you sent me conteyned, only promised his goode offices that Conde might remaine to him, in case he gave him satisfaction to all the other points. His answer to me after two houres discourse, and shoeing me in the map how necessary Ipres was to him, Je vois que nous ne persuaderons pas lun lautre ; j'envoyeray mes

---

[1] From the autograph letter in B.M. Add. MSS. 38849, f. 150, printed in *Hodgkin MSS.*, p. 196. *Letters*, p. 81. There is a copy in a clerk's handwriting in Leeds MSS., Packet 10, on which the Duke of Leeds has made his alterations.

ordres a Barillon sur Ipres et sur des autre choses, don je ne doute point que le Roy vostre maistre ne soit content. This autre chose I believe was the money, of which, according to your Lordships directions, having not such an answer to the peace as I thought would satisfye, I made noe mention $\wedge$; $\oplus$ [1]

ATT ALL

and if what Monsieur de Barillon has to say dos satisfye, and you send me any farther order to insist upon the money, I desire that we may be both in a story. You will please to let me know for how long time he seemed to consent to the payment of six millions ; for in all discourses they seeme, if the peace were made, to promise millions, but you can be sure of noething without coming to a certainty. As for Fribourgh, they pretend not to restore it without Philesbourgh ; but I beleive theire designe is to have Philisbourgh demolished, or else keepe it till the Emperour shall encline Monsieur de Bradenbourgh to be easyer then they think he will be upon the affaires of Sweden, of which they seeme to take greate care.

I did enough explaine to the King how much ours was pressed in point of time, and he will be it yet more if he dos not quickly resolve one way or other ; for by the beginning of May, or the tenth, the King will be againe in the feild. I told the King at parting that if our master was soe freindly as to manage Conde for him, and to be contented with Ipres and Gaunt added to the other places, our nation would be as little satisfyed as if he had left him all Flaunders, and yet here he and his ministers seemed as dissatisfyed as if he had taken all Flaunders from them. For that now is all theire discourse and complaint, only to avoide making that return they should for the obligation they have to him of all theire successe and goode fortune, and which I beleive will not long continue if he falls out in goode earnest with him, which I doe not see how his Majesty can avoide if they can refuse to satisfye him upon soe inconsiderable things as Ipres and Fribourgh, which I cannot beleive them mad or ungratefull enough to doe, if he pleaseth to be very firme and positive with the embassadour. For I have driven it as far as goode manners and respect, which I know the King will alwaise have me keepe, would permitt me to doe. It is impossible to expresse the

---

[1] By this mark the Duke of Leeds apparently intended to indicate the end of the letter as he wished it published. To provide a suitable conclusion, however, a single sentence is taken from what remains (*infra*, p. 352).

*desire everybody has of peace, and I am confident, if there be
a warr, never anything went more against the graine of a whole
nation then it dos heare, as I am afraide it will in England if
there be a peace.*

*I had forgot to tell your Lordship that the first dayes conversation
I had with Monsieur de Louvoy he seemed very inclinable to all the
propositions, provided Conde were relinquished, and proposed that
there might be three people named, one for the King our master,
another for the King of Fraunce, another for the States Generall, to
signe the peace immediately, and then let all the particulars be
examined and made an end at Nimegue, and sometimes be proposed
a cessation of armes. But I told him the condition of my masters
affaires and the temper of the Parlament would admitt of noething
but either peace immediately or warr immediately. Afterwards
there was a long Councell held, and then the King gave me the
answer I send you.*

*Monsieur de Louvoy and the King were both very inquisitive
whether, in case the peace was, the Parlament were like to be
prorogued. To that I saide I knew noething. But I saide all that
was necessary to prepare them in case of a peace to the six millions
for three yeares, which* [1] I thinke is very inconsiderable in com-
paraison of the advantage they have received and the prejudice
our master has suffered for [1] *his firmnesse to theire interest. One
of the greatest men of the Court next the ministers, and that wisheth
the peace, told me before I had received your orders that if Gaunt
and Ipres could make the peace he was sure the King would restore
them ; but that they would chicanne as long as they could for Ipres.
But I concluded with Monsieur de Louvoy that a delatory answer
was worse for the King our master then a deniall of what he
asked.*

*I hope this messenger will have made goode hast, for I have not
lost an houres time since my answer from the King, and I hope his
ambassadour has such orders as will one way or other bring
matters to a conclusion. I beg your Lordships favour to make my*

[1] . . . [1] This passage forms the conclusion of the letter as published by the
Duke of Leeds. It begins, however, ' but I think the sum demanded is,'
and ends, ' suffered for their sakes.' No authority in the handwriting of the
Duke of Leeds has been found for these alterations or for the inclusion of the
passage at all.

excuse to his Majesty for this imperfect account, and to beleive me [1]
with all respect, My Lord,

Your Lordships most obedient and humble servant,

R. Montagu.[2]

To Mr. Charles Bertie.[3]

Paris, Aprill th 11, [16]78.

I received the favour of yours by Mr. Brisban and another by
the post.[4] I am glad to heare there is such a rubb in Sir William
Temples way. Mr. Secretary Coventry consented to me myself
the endeavoring for his place, provided he had ten thousand
pound, which I will lay downe whenever the King gives me his
consent to come in. But I would neither ventur my money nor
give myself the trouble were anybody but my Lord Treasurer
in the favour and credit he is with the King.

I know all men make professions to get theire ends, but my
Lord Treasurer has a very goode pawne for the security of my
firmnesse to him, since besides the tye of kindred and honour I
ventur my owne money, and anybody that did that, and were
at difference with him, would have layde out his money very
ill. I will [5] noe other steps in it that [6] what I have done by my
Lord Treasurer and his family, to whome noebody is a better
wisher nor a more reall servant then myself, and most particularly to you, whome I have alwaise bin soe much obliged to.

Pray let me know my Lord Treasurers pleasure about the
coaches, and present my most humble service to my Lady
Danby and your owne lady.

[R. Montagu] [7]

---

[1] The *Letters* insert ' I am.'

[2] Endorsed by Danby, ' 11th April, [16]78 ' ; and by Leeds, ' Answer to
mine of 25 March, on which I was impeached, and his opinion after that how
inconsiderable that sume was which was desired.'

[3] From the autograph letter in B.M. Add. MSS. 39757, f. 105, printed in
Morrison Catalogue, iv. 285, and summarised in *Hist. MSS. Com.*, ix. 2, p. 455.
Letters, p. 83.

[4] These letters have not been found.

[5] The *Letters* read ' will make.'   [6] The *Letters* read ' than.'

[7] Unsigned. Endorsed by Danby, ' 11th April, [16]78 '; and by Leeds,
' To brother Bertie, and his offer to give 10,000 l. to Secretary Coventry for
his place.'

[To Mr. Montagu] [1]

London, 4th April, 1678.

My Lord,

I can send you nothing from hence that is either new or different from what I writt you last by Mr. Brisbon ; [2] but I am commanded by the King to tell you that hee would have you use all the indeavours you can possible to gett intelligence in all the considerable ports of France (especially Toulon and Brest) of what ships are in those ports, what preparations are or shall bee makeing for shipping in any of them, and as much as can bee gott att any time of what place they are designed for or from what place they come last, as also all other information you can bee able to procure, and to settle such intelligences if possible in case of a war. WHICH I EXPECT.[3] His Majestie is now more particularly concerned to know whither those ships or men are gone who came from Sicily, which wee heare the French have quitted, and whither my Lord Dumbartons regiment bee sent into Catalonia, as is reported here.

Yesterday I received your letter[4] which gave us an account of Mr. Brisbons arrivall with you, and wee are full with expectation of what your next letters will bring, as being the last by which our measures must bee taken. In the meane time wee are prepared to beleeve they will bring nothing but good words and generall tearmes of uncertainety, and by the bringing theire men from Sicily and the ill usage of our troops amongst them wee conclude that att the bottome they intend no peace, or none but such as must leave Flanders in theire power when they please. Our reason for being thus prepared is because Monsieur Barillon did talke such sort of language to the King last night, and acknowleged to have a courrier newly arrived in answer to what hee had writt to his master, which was the substance of what you had to say to him. If itt prove as wee expect, I

---

[1] From the autograph draft in B.M. Add. MSS. 28054, f. 172. *Letters*, p. 79.

[2] This letter has not been found.

[3] This insertion assumes a more emphatic form in the *Letters*, where it reads, ' which I do certainly expect.'

[4] Probably Montagu's letter of April 9 (*supra*, p. 349).

cannot tell whither the war will not bee declared the next weeke, that is att the next meeting of the Parliament.

I am not so well as to write so largely as I would do, and as I will by the next opportunity. I am, My Lord,

Your Excellencies, &c.,

[Danby] [1]

[To the Lord Treasurer] [2]

Paris, Aprill 17th, [16]78.

My Lord,

You were pleased to lay your commands upon mee that I should give you an account, as neere as is possible for mee to guess, of the last tearms they would be brought to consent to here for a present peace. I did in my last give you my opinion that they would insist upon the keeping of Ipres ; but that if the King our master were firme and resolute to have it restored, they would yeald to it, rather then have him close with his Parliament and come to a declaration of war. I have (since another conversation I have had with the King of France) more reason to be confirmed in the same opinion. Far different from what he used to be, hee grew mighty hot and passionate upon the subject of Ipres, rather like one that was angry and displeased that he was obliged to part with a thing he had a mind to keepe then that ∧HEE had seriously and positively resolved to keepe it.

His greate argument was that he was sure that the Spaniards and Hollanders would be glad of the peace, nay, that they had offered it without Ipres or Conde.⊕ *I said they must be glad of any peace, if my master would not concerne himselfe for them ; but that his Majestie was to consider what his owne subjects in England would say, as well as the Confederates, if he made himselfe the*

¹ Endorsed by Danby, ' Coppy of my letter to Mr. Montagu, 4th April, 1678.' To this the Duke of Leeds has added, ' Newes of Sicily being quitted by the French, &c. This of moment, that I expected war ; and note itt is but nine daies after that of 25 March, on which I was impeached.' The words ' that I expected war ' were inserted after the endorsement was written, presumably at the same time as the words ' which I expect ' were inserted in the letter itself.

² From a copy in Leeds MSS., Packet 10. *Letters*, p. 84.

*mediator of a dishonourable peace ; that the restoring of Ipres was
no greate matter if he could prevaile with the Prince of Orange to
relinquish Conde ; that the restoring of Sicily, which was always
valued as a greate article and motive of the peace, being now out of
doors, my master would finde the Spaniards much higher and
stiffer if he were not able to make some better terms for them than
these which were now offered.*⊕ ∧ The King [1] ended with mee,
saying, J'espere que le Roy vostre maistre ne me fera pas la
guerre pour Ipres, et que je le trouveray plus raisonable que
vous.

The next day Monsieur Courtin and one St. Roman (who are
great confidents of Monsieur de Louvoy) were with mee, and
told me of all that had passed betweene the King and mee, and
desired mee that I would not eschauffer (that was the expression) les choses en Angleterre ; que si Monsieur le Grand
Tresaurier vouloit laisser faire Monsieur de Barillon, le Roy
d'Angleterre se relacheroit sur Ipres ; and that I should oblige
the King here a des grandes reconnoisances en mon particulier.
This is the bottom, my Lord, of all I can find out here. If the
King finds the ambassador in England does not satisfy him,
methinks he should be very round (as they say) with him, and
give me such orders to speak here as they may take to be the
last time of asking.⊕

*There is greate talke here of a journey the King of France will
make in the beginning of May. If he does, it will be no journey of
war ; but about that time Madam Montespan is to lye in, and to
hide a thing which everybody knows of the King always makes
some journey, and then he is in retreate. If he goes not into
Flanders he may take the pretence of goeing into Britanny, and
visitt the sea coasts, which will take up a fortnight.*

*If the two kings can close, I find they desire it may be done
quickly, as much as we do in England.*⊕ I will trouble your
Lordship no longer, but remain with all respect, My Lord,

Your Lordships most obedient and humble servant,

R. Montagu.

---

[1] The *Letters* give ' he ' instead of ' the King.'

To the Lord Treasurer.[1]

Paris, Aprill th 26, [16]78.

My Lord,

 I doe not doubt but before this can come to your hands his Majesty will have taken his measures one way or other. However I thought it my duty to send you this enclosed written in cipher,[2] *which my cozen Bartue will incipher for your Lordship, there being a cipher betweene him and Mr. Brisban, whome I could not avoide trusting in this affaire. What newes there is I have writt Mr. Secretary, and will spare your Lordship in this busie time any farther trouble but the assurance of my being with all respect, My Lord,*

 Your Lordships most obedient and humble servant,

R. Montagu.

 I neede not beg of your Lordship to recommend to Mr. Bertue the secret of this affaire.[3]

To the Lord Treasurer.[4]

Paris, May 16, 1678. N.S.

My Lord,

 Here is now nothing worth the giving you an account of, the King being gone away in very good humour, upon the assurance I believe he has of having such a peace from the Dutch as he desires, which has been managed underhand by great presents to those that are not well-wishers to the Prince of Orange.

 I have in order to your last commands endeavoured in case of a war to inform his Majesty both of the number of ships the French are likely to have at sea, as well as the strength of their sea-coast. I have sent two persons, who were both officers, and are cashiered for want of money to make up their companies. They have both served upon the sea-coasts those years that the Dutch came as if they would have made some descent. I have

---

[1] From the autograph letter in Leeds MSS., Packet 10.

[2] The enclosure has not been found.

[3] Endorsed by Leeds, ' Quere for this cipher betwixt Mr. Brisbon and brother Bertie.'

[4] *Letters*, p. 87. Neither the original letter nor any copy has been found.

sent one to all the ports of Normandy and Brittany, the other to Rochel and the river of Charent.

If there is a war, they offer to come and serve upon the fleet, and go wherever the English may think to land, and in that case, I have answered, the King will provide a subsistence as long as they live. In the mean time I have put the King to no farther charge than to pay their expences for them and their servant, each of them for the time they shall be out. I know that they are so exact in all the sea-ports to all strangers that come, that there is no employing any Englishman in this, for he would certainly be taken and used as a spy. Whether those I have employed will be honest I cannot tell, but in these cases it must be ventured. I am with all respect, My Lord,

> Your Lordships most obedient and humble servant,
>
> R. Mountagu.

To the Lord Treasurer.[1]

Paris, June 4, 1678. N.S.

My Lord,

Some people are so unlucky as to have so few friends, that I hope you will not have the worse opinion of me if for that reason I am obliged to recommend myself to your Lordships favour, of which I confess already to have had a greater share than by my services I can pretend to have deserved. What I beg it in now may perhaps put me in a condition of being more useful and serviceable to your Lordship in all your concerns than I can be whilst I remain so insignificant as I am now. When I was in England I took the liberty to propose to your Lordship my coming into Mr. Secretary Coventry's place ; but finding you lay then under some obligation to Sir William Temple, I wholly submitted my pretension to your Lordships pleasure, not caring or believing it was, or is, possible to compass it without your good liking.

I presume the measures Sir William Temple may have given his Majesty of late in the politicks may have a little worked off that engagement which I am sure your favour only made the King think he had to him ; and without flattering you as to

---

[1] *Letters*, p. 88. Neither the original letter nor any copy has been found.

your wisdom, you have shewed yourself too good a Lord Treasurer to advise the King to give ten thousand pounds for Sir William Temple, so that now his chief merit is your Lordships great nicety of your word, which I am sure any strict casuist in honour would in this case absolve you from. Mr. Secretary Coventry is willing to resign to me, if the King will consent ; and I will lay down ten thousand pounds to satisfie him, without the King's being at any charge. I have no friend, nor will make no application in this matter to any person but yourself, to whom I had rather owe it than to anybody living ; and I am sure you can recommend nobody who will always be with more truth and respect, My Lord,

Your Lordships most faithful and humble servant,

R. Mountagu.

[To Mr. Montagu] [1]

London, 27 May, 1678.

I have been longer silent then I would have been, because wee were arrived to no sort of certainety in our condition neither att home nor abroad. But though wee are still in the same state att home, things seeme to bee reduced to such an assurance of peace abroad that our whole businesse now is to gett our affaires well setled here, and itt is no small step to itt that wee are not under so great apprehensions from abroad as wee have been.

This day Monsieur Ruvigny is arrived here with the newes that a cessation is granted till the 6th of August, N.S., and to comence from the 1st of July ; but that in the meane time the French King will do no act of hostility, and that the Dutch have promised a neutrality in case the Allies shall not then consent to the conditions of the peace. This newes, finding the Parliament sitting, has putt them upon warme debates att this instant whither to support the army for some time longer, or to desire of the King that they may bee disbanded imediately ; and they are not yett come to any resolution. If I had a particular cipher with yourselfe, which I will not comitt

---

[1] From the autograph draft in B.M. Add. MSS. 28054, f. 176. This contains one important alteration in the handwriting of the Duke of Leeds. There is also a copy in Leeds MSS., Packet 10, which contains further alterations. In spite of this preparation for publication the letter was not in the end included in the printed collection.

to anybodys else, I should say a great deale more to you, although I could not in that case bee able to informe you of all things relateing to

THE FRENCH

your ∧ Court, because I am assured there have been divers private negotiations betwixt his Majestie and Monsieur Barillon which

OF THE MINISTERS HERE.

have not been comunicated either to myselfe or any other ∧ .

That which was this day required by the King from the House of Commons was that they would provide some further supply for the army, the last being almost expended ; and the House (which is but just risen when I had writt thus far) have in answer to that demand desired by the Secretaries of State to bee informed from his Majestie whither hee would have itt in order to the war or a peace, because the proportion of theire supply must bee suitable to itt. But in theire debates they have shewed all the desire imaginable to a war, although both Spaine and Holland should go out of itt, [1] WHICH I FEARE IS A DESIGNE PROJECTED ATT HOME BY SOME OF THE KINGS ENEMIES AMONGST US, ITT BEING WHAT ENGLAND ALONE COULD NOT SUPPORT.[1]

US

A few daies will now shew ∧ what good wee have to hope for from this session, upon which I thinke will depend a great deale of our future happinesse or misfortune.   In the meane time I desire you will beleeve mee as ever,

Your, &c.,

[Danby] [2]

To the Lord Treasurer.[3]

Paris, July 1, 1678.   N.S.

My Lord,

I am extreamly ashamed that your Lordship should have given yourself the least trouble in the explaining of the reasons why at that time the King did not consent to my coming over.

---

[1] . . . [1] The whole of this passage was added by the Duke of Leeds, but whereas the main part of it was inserted in the draft the words ' some of ' and ' amongst us . . . support ' were added later on the copy.

[2] Endorsed by Danby, ' Coppy of my letter to Mr. Montagu, 27th May, 1678 ' ; and by Leeds, ' Parliament sitting and designes laid to ingage the King in a war, though Spain and Holland should go out of itt.   This was projected by French agents to bring the King into want and destroy my power, and Lady Portsmouth was in this designe.   Memorandum a number of the House of Comons going to compliment her att Whitehall.'

[3] *Letters*, p. 90.   Neither the original letter nor any copy has been found.

If I had had his leave, considering what has fallen out, I should not have made use of it till I had seen this difficulty of surrendring the towns over, one way or other. But I have had too much experience of your Lordships favour and kindness to me to imagine you could be against a thing which I never desired but by your approbation, and in which, I hope, I have carried myself with all the regard and respect imaginable to your Lordship.

I am very unlucky that your Lordships engagements to Sir William Temple are like to deprive me of your protection and assistance in my pretensions, it being a thing in which I am confident his Majesty will be so wholly directed by you in that it will be in vain for me to make the least step in it. If you do not find yourself free enough to recommend me, all I beg of your Lordship is to believe that what will happen it shall not at all alter the professions I have made of being, with all truth and respect, My Lord,

Your Lordships most obedient and humble servant,

R. Mountagu.

Your Lordship will see by my letter to the Secretary the resolutions of this Court to keep the towns till Sweden be satisfied, which makes me not give you the trouble of repeating the same over again.

To the Lord Treasurer.[1]

Paris, July th 1, [16]78.

My Lord,

My Lord Dunbarton is soe allarmed upon the report of his regiment being like to be disbanded that he has sent this bearer on purpose to beg your goode offices to his Majesty, that he will please to interpose by his recommendation to Monsieur Barillon that he himself and a greate bodye of men, that have soe long and soe eminently served the Crowne of Fraunce, may not be absolutely ruined, but that according to theire capitulation, having born the whole brunt of the warr, they may have an honourable subsistance now in time of peace. I have not bin wanting in all the goode offices I have bin capable of doeing them, but the goode fortune that

---

[1] From the autograph letter in B.M. Add. MSS. 28054, f. 178.

has attended this Court of late makes all the recommendations that come from any other not much considered at present.

The Prince of Orenge his envoye brought the newes of the peace being signed by the Dutch and Spaniards. There is yet noe newes of the Emperours consenting to the propositions, for which reason the Mareshal de Crequy has orders to pousse and presse Monsieur de Lorraine very vigoroussly; and the letters that come from the Mareshall this day brought word that the twelf thousand men from Flaunders were arrived at his camp, and that now he thought of beseeiging Renfeild. I expect next post his Majestys leave to come for a few dayes into England, and then I shall acquaint his Majesty with what I dare not doe by letters, and assure your Lordship that noe man is with more respect, My Lord,

> *Your Lordships most obedient and humble servant,*
>
> R. *Montagu.*[1]

To Mr. Charles Bertie.[2]

> *Paris, July th 2, [16]78.*

Deare Cozen,

The constant troubles you receive from me in my affaires needes more excuses then can be made in a lettar. This is to congratulate with you the birth [of] a sonne, and beg of you to make my complements to your lady upon the same occasion. I hope to doe it myself by word of mouth in a few dayes, for since my Lord Treasurer dos not desaproove of my coming, as soone as I have the Kings leave, which I expect next post from Mr. Secretary, I will come away. I beg of you to beleive that noe man is more intirely, Deare Cozen,

> *Your most obedient and humble servant,*
>
> R. *Montagu.*

[To Lady Harvey] [3]

> *Paris, July 5th, 1678.*

I writ to you in so much hast by an expresse of the Secretarys that I had not time to send this enclosed,[4] *which is a coppy of such a kind*

---

[1] Endorsed by Danby, ' 1st July, [16]78 '; and by Leeds, ' This brought the first newes of the peace being signd by the Spaniards and Dutch.'

[2] From the autograph letter in Leeds MSS., Packet 10.

[3] From a copy in a clerk's handwriting in Leeds MSS., Packet 10.

[4] No copy of the enclosure accompanies the copy of the letter.

of letter as the King must write to my wife, which I'me sure must breed the best blood in the world. Hee must do it before I come away from Paris, that shee may not think I had a hand in it ; and the way of doing it is for the King to order my Lord Treasurer to write to her a very civill letter upon the same occasion, and send it inclosed in his, and then let Mr. Bertue send it Mr. Cole to give her.

As soon as you receive this, pray you gett to see my Lord Treasurer, and shew him this coppy, and let him shew it the King, and gett it dispatchd as soon as may bee and before I come from hence. This way is much better then for you to speak with the King. Besides I am so much obligd to my Lord Treasurer that I would have him have all the share that may bee in a thing that will bee so agreable to the King ; and besides my wife will like the businesse the better if my Lord Treasurer is interested in it, because she has so good an opinion of him.

[R. Montagu] [1]

[To Mr. Montagu] [2]

[1st July, 1678]

Here is so sudden a change of all affaires betwixt us and France that I know not whither wee are not nearer a war then ever, att a time when I thought everything had been establisht beyond the possibility of a rupture ; nor do I yett see any expedient that will bee possible. Itt was intended to have sent my Lord Sunderland instructed more fully then could bee done by writeing, but that intention is changed for the present, and I suppose that whatever can bee done in that Court will bee more effectually done by your hand then any other. Sir William Temple is to depart for Holland to-morrow, and theire envoy, Monsieur van Leewe, with him ; and they pretend here that the King of France has made such a breach of faith in this that they shall not dare to trust him hereafter in anything.

I confesse I am not able to comprehend this part of theire policy, but theire dexterity is so great that I alwaies expect theire successe

---

[1] Endorsed by the copyist, ' A coppy of Mr. Montagus letter ' ; and by the Earl of Danby, ' about getting Lady E[lizabeth] Peircy for Lord Northumberland, 5th July [16]78.'

[2] From the autograph draft in B.M. Add. MSS. 28054, f. 180.

in any undertakeing, though the ways to itt seeme never so obscure ;
but yett if you have any light to theire meaning I should bee glad you
would impart some of itt to us.

[*Danby*] [1]

To the Lord Treasurer.[2]

Moonday, nine at night [July 8, 1678].[3]

My Lord,

According to the leave you are please[d] to give me to
trouble you in my concerns, I take the liberty to acquaint you
that Monsieur de Barillon and Ruvigny sayde in some company
(and a man that was there came in kindnesse and told me),
Quoyque Monsieur de Montagu a eschappe la Tour le Roy le
mettera hors du Conseil. There is nothing the King can doe
to me soe bad as that, for it keepes me from coming to Court
surer then anything. Wherfore I beg the continuance of your
Lordships favour to me, and that betweene this and Wensday
you will be pleased to find out by the King if he intends any
such thing. Your Lordships taking me into your protection is
enough to put a stop to it, and to oblige me to all the acknowledgments whereby I may shoe the service and respect I owe
you, whoe am, My Lord,

Your most obedient and humble servant,

R. Montagu.[4]

---

[1] Endorsed by Danby, ' Coppy of my letter to Mr. Montagu without date.'

[2] From the autograph letter in B.M. Add. MSS. 28054, f. 182. *Letters*, p. 92.

[3] The date is mistakenly given in the *Letters* as August 1678. Montagu
reached London on July 3, and was struck off the Council on July 12.

[4] Endorsed by Danby, ' No date, but was the Monday after his arrivall from
France without the Kings leave. Quere brother Bertie when hee arrived att
London.' To this is added by the Duke of Leeds, ' which I think was in
August [16]78. Vide how this agrees with the memoriall given by one Baker
to Mr. Arnold and by Mr. Arnold to me, 7th December, [16]91 ' (*infra*, p. 375).

REMARKS

MADE UPON

MR. MONTAGUES LETTERS

IN THE YEARS 1677 AND 1678[1]

[16]77, June 21th. In his letter to the King he gives him his advice about money, and tells him the advice hee had given to Monsieur Ruvigny to offer the King three millions, and proposes to gett the King a million of livers during the warr, and four millions after the peace shall be made, over and above what the King had then from France, which in that letter he says was three millions a yeare ; and in the same letter hee tells him that Monsieur Ruvigny told him that hee found most of his Majesties ministers to bee against France, but particularly the Lord Treasurer.[2] Hee saies also that he knows not who the King would trust in that affair, but desires that the King would trust mee in it ; that till then he had transacted the money affair with the Lord Arlington, and that if the King did not think fitt to trust mee in it he desires that his sister might see that letter burnt. By all which it appears that this was the first time of my knowing of any transactions about French money,[3] as also that he would not trust the King himselfe with the burning of his letter unless his sister saw it done.

July 15th and 16th. Two of my letters to Mr. Montagu, both which were found in his cabinett, and were read att the Councell

---

[1] B.M. Add. MSS. 28044, f. 22, in a copyist's handwriting, with some alterations and additions in the handwriting of the Duke of Leeds. *Letters*, p. 94.

[2] This is one of the few occasions on which the Duke of Leeds lays stress on his own alterations. The word originally written in the letter is ' Arlington,' not ' Treasurer.'

[3] A complete misstatement.

table by Prince Rupert, and were then sealed up, and are now among the Councell papers ; by which appears that till his aforesaid letter of 21th of June I knew not what had been received from France, nor that Mr. Chiffinch had been the receiver of itt ; and observes that I was for cudgelling them into better measures with England instead of having their money, which I there declare I thought could not make any recompence. And I am glad that the originalls of both my letters are to be found amongst the Councell papers.

[16]77, August 7th. Is compliment only.[1]

August 12th, N.S. Two letters of the same date, but I was to shew but one of them to the King, in which he mentions the propositions made to him of great advantage offered to mee, and he shews the King that it would be his Majesties fault, and not his, if he had not two hundred thousand pounds sterling. And in that of the same date to mee, which I was not to shew to the King, he wishes mee joy of Mr. Chiffinch being the French treasurer.

August 10/20th. My answer to the two letters of 12th August, N.S., where I thank him for the answers he gave to the French ministers about the advantages offered to myselfe.

August 28th. Wherein he only fears the good nature of our friend (meaning the King) to spoil the business of the money.

August 30th. He owns he hath his orders from the King himselfe for 200,000 l., and again repeats it to be the Kings own fault if he have not that summe, but if he has condescended to two millions he is sure he can bring on his first proposition of four millions after the peace.

September 3/13th. Mine in answer to his of 28th and 30th of August.[2]

September 25th, N.S. To the King, wherein he advises his Majestie what to say to the French ambassador about the money, and to refer him to mee.

September 25th. Two letters of the same date, one of which I was to shew to the King, wherein he puts his Majestie in mind that his demands about money had been by his Majesties

---

[1] This line is omitted in the *Letters*.

[2] This paragraph does not appear in the *Letters*.

commands under his own handwriting, but that they suspected in France that the orders had rather come from mee then from the King, because more was demanded then the King had consented to take. And in his other letter of the same date to mee, which I was not to shew to the King, he mentions Monsieur Courtins false representation of my beeing privy to the Kings debates with him about money, and that he came to the knowledge of it by a letter from Monsieur Courtin to Monsieur Pompone, which Monsieur Pompone had shewed him, but was sorrey after he had shewed it ; and there mentions that I have formerly said I would have them cudgelled into a better behaviour, next to which he takes the getting of their money to be the best ascendant over France.

October 12th, N.S. To the King again about the money, and continuing his advice to have the embassador referred to mee.

In his letter of the same date to mee, after his over-great compliments, he thinks to oblige mee by saying he had played this business into my hands, and tells mee how unsatisfyed Monsieur Courtin was returned into France by his ill treatment here and the small present that was made him at his departure from England.

December 29th. To the King, mentioning the great offers of money made to his Majestie, and to make my fortune, and advises that these matters should be managed by me in England and by him in France.

Note that these last offers were made soon after the marriage of the Lady Mary to the Prince of Orange, which was but about six weeks before that letter.

[16]77/8, January 1st. Ownes hee had no instructions but to insist upon the restitution of the townes, and yett tempts the King to accomodate himselfe with money.

January 8th.[1] His thanks for Geddington Woods, &c.

January 10th. To the King about a suspention of armes, and about a proposall of marrying Madame (his sisters daughter) to the Dolphine of France, and his strong perswasions to itt.

Another of the same date to mee, in which he saies he is onfident that some of the discontented Parliament men had

[1] Really January 8, 1677.

been intriegueing with Monsieur Barrillon, and that he had seen a letter of his to Monsieur Courtin to that purpose, who writes that altho' the Court turn against them they hope to save themselves by the Parliament. And he saies further that they beleeving in France that our King cannot do what he would with his Parliament makes them play such tricks as they do with our master, and takes my interest to be so great with the Prince of Orange that I might perswade him if I would not to enter into a warr, so unprovided as the King was at that time.

January 11th. He gives notice of young Monsieur Ruvignys (now Earle of Galloway) journey into England, viz., to converse amongst the discontented Parliament men, and particularly some of his relations in England.

January 14. Mine, to thank him for the justice he did mee in his answer to the French ministers, which he writ to the King in his of the 29th December last ; and I there heartily wish that my master would give as little creditt to anything that comes from that Court as I do, and I assure him that the management of the money affair will be wholly left to him as he desires.

January 17th. Mine, with thanks for his intelligence about Monsieur Ruvigny, and to assure him that the King will oppose any party that shall refuse those conditions for a peace which were sent by my Lord Duras.

January 18th. Informing mee that Ruvignys chief errand was to tell our King that the King of France hoped that he was so firm to him as not to be led away by mee, for the reasons he gives in that letter, but that if I wanted money I should have what I would ; and he saies his instructions are, if this will not do with mee, then to apply to the discontented Parliament men, by money or any other way. Hee also saies that old Ruvigny has given it them for a maxim that they must diminish my credit before they can do any good in England, and further sayth that they keep all they can from his knowledge because they beleeve him to be so much my friend. And att last he ends that letter, saying that if the King hearkens to their money, if he knows what they offer, he dare answer to gett our King as much again. [1]And I cannot here but take notice with some wonder of the House of Commons refuseing to let this letter and another of the 11th ditto be read when I sent them to the House to vindicate myselfe by such manifest proofs how farr I was from being in the French interest.[1]

In another of the same date, viz., 18th January 1677/8, he saith he hath no power or instructions to hearken to any propositions of money, yett advises to go that way by Colbert as before he had done from Louvoy, and there mentions again a match with the Daulphine for the Kings neice.

February 26th, N.S. Where he tells mee that both att home and abroad I have the reputation of having been the chiefe instrument in keeping our King so firm and resolute to the propositions sent by my Lord Duras.

[16]77/8, March 1st. Hee takes notice that Monsieur Ruvigny had been so handleed here, both by the King and myselfe, that he was returned with a very different opinion from what he was in when he went from France.

March 3rd. His opinion of mee, that I was of no party nor faction.

March 12th. His information by one Monsieur de la Tolade of the Duke of Buckinghams not doubting to ruine mee, and that young Ruvigny has orders from the King of France to make Monsieur Barrillon strike up a league with the Duke of Buckingham, and that they meet often privately.

[16]78, March 25th. This is the letter on which I was impeached in Parliament, and to which no Englishman could have taken the least exception, unless it were to that part which relates to the money, and yett as to that part of it, it was only writ in obedience to the Kings command, who signed the instructions of that letter himselfe, as hee might legally do under the limitations therein given. But in the same letter I both writ that if the propositions for the peace, which were then sent to Mr. Montagu, were not accepted, there should be no mention made at all of the money, and what I writ therein as from myselfe, and not from the King, was that I did beleeve that those propositions would be rejected, and that therefore he might take his own measures as well as the Kings upon it. And accordingly that proposall about the money was never made,

---

[1] ... [1] This passage, which is written in at the side, is misplaced in the *Letters*.

nor did the King ever receive a farthing after that, notwithstanding all the assurances Mr. Montagu had so often repeated to him of having att least four millions after any peace should be concluded.   And in his answer to my said letter of 25th March, [16]78 (which is dated the 11th of April, [16]78, N.S.), instead of thinking the Kings demands of six millions of livers to be any crime, he speaks how inconsiderable a summe that demand is in comparison of the advantage they have received and our master hath suffered for their sakes ; and Sir William Temple takes notice in his letter of 27 January, [16]78/9, from the Hague that the foreign ministers there did wonder it should be thought a crime in any minister to gett money for his master from any other prince when he was to do nothing for it but to consent to such a peace as his allies desired.   And yett in the King my masters case, he thought the peace the Confederates made within four months after was so badd a one, that it was never signed by the English plenipotentiaries, which gave the French King a just cause to have refused the King any money if ever it had been demanded.   And yet that clause in my letter was made an article of treason against mee, who am only sorry that the King did not gett the money, altho' Mr. Montagu would have deserved much the greatest thanks for it.

[16]78, March 29th.   Hee represents the sad prospect he thinks our King has of entring into a war in the humour the Parliament then was ; and in a letter of the same date to Mr. Charles Bertie he sollicets that I would work off Sir William Temple from beeing Secretary of State, which he then feared.

Aprill 4th (which is but ten days after the aforesaid letter of 25 of March for which I was accused).   I tell him that I certainly expect the war will be declared the next weeke,[1] insomuch that he knew my opinion that there would be a war (in which case no mention was to be made of money) before he could write mee an answer to my aforesaid letter of 25th of March, to which I did not receive his answer till the 11th of Aprill, which I have quoted before, and wherein he thinks the sume demanded by the King to be so inconsiderable ; and by this letter he saw that it was not to be demanded att all.

---

[1] Again the Duke of Leeds lays stress on one of his own alterations.

April 11th. Besides his letter to mee of that date (which I have quoted) he writes another to Mr. Charles Bertie, wherein he offers tenn thousand pounds for Secretary Coventrys office.

April 17th. Hee saies that Monsieur Courtin, &c., had been with him, and had desired him not to exasperate things betwixt the King of France and our King, and that if I would be quiett, and lett Monsieur Barrillon treat with the King alone, our master would quitt insisting any longer upon their rendition of the town of Ipres.

[16]78, May 16th. It appears by his answer that instead of treating for money he owns that he was pursuing the orders he had received for getting intelligence about their shipping, &c., in all the ports of France in order to a war.

June 4th. Hee writes to mee in a very pressing manner to gett Secretary Coventrys place (giving him 10,000 l. for itt), and makes some reflections upon Sir William Temple to prevent his having it.

July 1st. [1] Hee writ mee two letters, in one of which he writ the first news of the peace being signed by the Spanierds and Dutch without England, and in the other he writes me [1] a civill resentment for his not being made Secretary, and from thence he begins his displeasure against mee. And in the next month he came back into England without the Kings leave, which was the occasion of his cabinett being searched afterwards, upon some intelligence that had been given to the King concerning him by Monsieur Olivecrans, the Sweedish embassador.

August, dated only Monday, nine at night.[2] Beeing come privately to London without the Kings knowledge, and I not suspecting his designs against mee, I did sollicit the King and prevailed with him to let him see him and kiss his hand, which he did accordingly in private by my introduction at an house then called Hampden House, adjoyning to the Cockpitt.

About a month after that time I had severall private informations given mee of his private [3] intrigueing with severall

---

[1] . . . [1] Instead of this passage the *Letters* give, ' He writes me a letter, wherein he expresses.' Apparently the Duke of Leeds intended at first to publish both Montagu's letters of July 1, but in the end determined to publish only one.

[2] Really July 8, 1678.   [3] The *Letters* read ' secret.'

Parliament men, and of the French ambassador Barrillon being alwaies privy to those private negotiations ; and two gentlemen who were then of that Parliament owned to mee that he had shewed them my letter of the 25th of March above two months before he produced it to the Parliament. And there are at this time many living wittnesses of his almost dayly meetings with Monsieur Barrillon att his sister the Lady Harveys house, when I was under the accusation of the Parliament for being in the French interest. And when I sent his two letters, dated the 11th and 18th of January, 1677/8, to the House of Commons to have been read there, I was refused to have that small peice of justice done mee.

Note that in tenn severall letters before 25th of March, 1678 (on which I was accused), viz., June 21th, [16]77 ; August 12, [16]77 ; August 28th, [16]77 ; August 30th, [16]77 ; September 21th, [16]77 ; October 12, [16]77 ; December 29th, [16]77 ; January 1st, [16]77/8 ; January 10, [16]77/8 ; and January 18th, [16]77/8, Mr. Montagu had both proposed and encouraged the King to have money from France, and severall times repeats that it would be the Kings own fault if he had not the summes which had been proposed. So that it was not to be wondered that the King should give mee his orders to write to Mr. Montague to gett the money if he could, and especially when it was not to be demanded without those propositions for a peace were consented to which were sent by the Lord Duras, Mr. Montague having never received any powers nor instructions to treat about a peace but upon the termes of the said propositions sent by the Lord Duras and desired by the Confederates. Insomuch that if the King would have permitted mee to have produced Mr. Montagues letters, the crime of endeavouring to gett money from France (if it could be called a crime under the circumstances aforesaid) would have been laid to Mr. Montagues charge, and not to mee, as I told the King when he offered mee his pardon, but was answered by his Majestie that I owed him more duty than to expose his and his ambassadors letters of private negotiations betwixt him and the King of France, and he was sure I would not bee guilty of such a perfidious baseness to him as Montague had been.

In severall of the aforesaid ten letters, as well as in divers others of his, I have his frequent testimonialls, not only of my constant aversion to the French interest, but of his own having no creditt in that Court, because he was taken to be so much my friend ; that old Ruvigny had told him that hee found most of the ministers in England against France, and particularly the Lord Treasurer, and had fixed itt for a maxime in that Court that they must diminish my creditt before they could do any good in England ; that I was for cudgelling them into better tearms with us, and how ill the French ministers complained they were alwaies treated by mee ; and young Ruvignys journey into England only to hurt mee, so that if Mr. Montague will pass for good evidence I should need no better than himselfe alone to vindicate me, both as to French money and being in the French interest. But I thank God that as to the last I have many more wittnesses, viz., the Prince of Orange, Lord Sunderland, Sir William Temple, and Mr. Brisbane (then agent att Paris), &c., whose letters testifie sufficiently in my behalfe.

Itt is not easy to comprehend how a Parliament should bee brought to vote the matters contained in my letter of 25 March, 1708,[1] to bee treason if I had had no authority for the writing itt (there being nothing illegall in itt) ; and itt is not lesse difficult to conceive how that Parliament should bee thought a pensionary Parliament which was not only so sparing in the supplies they did give, but did not then give those supplies which were necessary, and did appropriate every penny to particular uses upon account ; and that I who was called the promoter and paymaster of those pensions had not power to preserve myselfe from being impeached of treason by those pensioners for what in justice my worst enemies could not have made a misdemeanour.

These are such contradictions in their owne nature that they need no answer ; but I do not wonder that my pleading a pardon and my absenting myselfe for some time might justly make both Parliament and nation beleeve that I thought myselfe guilty of some great crime.

But as I hope I have made appear that I neither needed a

_____
[1] An obvious slip for ' 1678 ', the date given in the *Letters*.

pardon nor to have absented myselfe from tryall, but that I did both in obedience to the Kings commands, so I verely believe the King was so apprihensive that the producing of these letters would have so much heightened the ill humour of that Parliament that the fear of producing them (which I must have done rather than suffer the bill of attainder to pass against mee) was one of the causes of dissolving that Parliament.

I have [1] hereto added an information, which was written to Mr. Charles Bertie out of France by Mr. Brisbane, concerning Mr. Mountagu, and a narrative concerning him given by a gentleman now living to another gentleman who gave it me, and shews Mr. Mountagu's transactions with Monsieur Barillon in October and November 1678. And I desire that these meetings with Monsieur Barillon and the then angry Parliament men may be compared with Mr. Mountagu's letters of the 10th, 11th, and 18th of January in the same year, in every one of which he gives me intelligence of the meetings of the French ambassadors with the discontented Parliament men, to disturb the King's affairs in Parliament and to hurt me, and (as he calls it) to break my measures at Court ; as also to observe that his meetings with Monsieur Barillon, &c., were at the very same time when he made me the instrument of getting the King to excuse his returning into England without the King's leave, whilst he was his Majesties ambassador in France, of all which proceedings of his there are yet divers living witnesses.

MR. BRISBANE'S INFORMATION
TO MR. CHARLES BERTIE,
14 JANUARY, 1679.[2]

Barillons letter to Monsieur Pomponne says Holmes, the first man of England for the sea, and two more are putt out for voting against my Lord Treasurer, and that many of the Kings best friends, constant to him in all other occasions, voted so also.

[1] No complete draft of this last paragraph has been found. It is printed as it appears in the *Letters*.

[2] From a deciphered note among the Lindsey MSS., printed in *Lindsey MSS.*, p. 399. *Letters*, p. 113.

My Lady Cleveland says that Mr. Montagu hath long designd my Lord Treasurers ruine, and would have putt her upon itt. One Puymoran, a great friend of Mr. Montagu, hath a letter from him excusing his proceeding. Hee speaks att Court his reasons, which are no other but that my Lord Treasurer persecuted him, to which I give the lie by what I know.

I am sure there is great joy here for my Lord Treasurers troubles, and nothing will bee spared to break him. I have told you so long agoe.[1]

MEMORANDUMS CONCERNING MR. MONTAGUE,
FROM MR. BAKER,
GIVEN MEE BY MR. ARNOLD, 7 DECEMBER, [16]91.[2]

Mr. Montague having obteyned his second embassey to France, his sister the Lady Harvey, the later end of August 1677, went over to him, and steyed all the winter till Aprill following. Upon her returne she was imediatly visited by the French ambassador, Mounsieur Barrillon, who constantly afterwards made her very frequent visitts allmost every morning. The Parliament then sitting, a great noise was about towne of a bargaine made by somebody for a peace instead of warr with France. In August following [3] Mr. Montague came suddenly and privatly over, and was imediatly mett at his sisters by Mounsieur Barrillon, where they generally were four or five times a weeke privately togeather.

I being at that time a fellow [4] of generall acquaintance about towne, and much in the company of members of Parliament, and affecting much to heare and tell news, and having for about

---

[1] Endorsed by Leeds, ' This of consequence and to bee coppied, and is coppied.'

[2] B.M. Add. MSS. 28044, f. 33, apparently the original narrative, of which this heading is the endorsement. On f. 37 begins a copy, endorsed, ' Information of Mr. Montagues private transactions with Monsieur Barillon in October and November in 1678.' This copy shows some divergences from the original, and some alterations in the handwriting of the Duke of Leeds, which are noted where they have any significance. From it is taken the version printed in *Letters*, p. 114.

[3] Really at the beginning of July (*supra*, p. 364). This statement is probably the reason for the mistaken date attached by the Duke of Leeds to the letter there printed.

[4] The copy and the *Letters* read ' a fellow at that time.'

ten yeares before been very conversant with them, transacting a great deale of business for them both, they sometimes talked freely to me of affaires at Court, &c. Amongst other thinges, when the talke [1] of French money encreased [2] in the towne, I telling her what I heard of it, she freely told me she was clearly for her brother's driving the bargaine, and that she told him soe when she was with him there, for if they wou'd have money, said she, why should not he have some of it as well as anybody else, and a great deale more to that effect, &c.

In the begining of October [16]78, being out of towne, they sent after me in great hast, and tho t'was late at night when I came home, and from a long journey too, yet at a meeting with Mr. Montague in the morning at his sister's they desired me to post away imediatly into Sussex, to Lewis and Greenstead, to try my skill to get him chosen a member of Parliament for Grensted, that was then to sitt the 21 of that month, but if I found noe probability of doing it there, to returne imediatly, for he must gett in somewhere for a member of that House of Commons. I found noe likelyhood of it there, came back, tooke post for Northampton, where he was chosen. I did not know then the meaning of his being soe earnest to be a member of the House of Commons, but often thought on't, because I had heard him upon all occasions talk contemptably of them. But it afterward appeared.

Very freequent counsells were then held 'twixt the two ambassadors and the lady, and all the intellegence I could pick up I brought them, and it was then proposed to me to accept of a penssion of about 100 l. per annum from the French ambassador. I asked what I was to doe for him for't. They told me at first but indifferent things, as the votes of the House as soone as might be (for they were not then printed), and intelligence from the Clerks of the Counsell, &c., and as a premium I had of him thirty guineas by the lady's hand ; but not answering his expectations I saw noe more, for itt went against me to discover anything of moment that was English to the French whom I alwayes hated.

[1] Instead of ' the talke ' the copy and the *Letters* read ' they talked.'

[2] The *Letters* give ' encreasing.'

Upon the noise [1] and heats that were in the House about seizing Mr. Mountagus papers at his house, my Lady Harvey first told me her brother was very much afrayd of being sent to the Tower. I told her I thought not, the Parliament sitting. She replyed my Lord Danby would cause a disolution or prorogation, and he would then be snap't ; and therfore desired me (for she told me they had talked about it, and he also would speak to me) that I would be as quick among all my freinds and companys as possible [2] to make the first discovery if such a thing were intended, and to be alwayes every day about the House, and if I gott the least inckling of it to send for him out, and clap a cloak about him (which I was enjoyn'd not to be without), and carry him away by water into London or where else I thought fitt, he resolving to trust himselfe, his life, and all he had wholy with me before anybody about, or that belonged to himselfe, they being (as she term'd them) all fooles and
WITH [3]
knaves, some of them every day drincking or playing ∧ cards with Danby's people, that if he were not the greatest beast in the world he would not keepe such fellows about him. He himselfe spoak to me to the same purpose, and swore he had noe mind to eate meat of other's dressing where he must either
EATE
∧ poyson or starve.

The Parliament broak up of a Munday morning.[4] He had notice of it, and did not come to the House. I wayted there,
I COULD
got what intelligence ∧ and made what observations I could, and went to him to a house in Fleet Street, where he had withdrawne himselfe. From thence I tooke him into London to a freinds of mine in Lyme Street, where I kept him about two or three and twenty dayes, in which time I privately carried severall of his freinds to him, amongst others Mounsieur Barrillon. The nights being then long and darke, wee went often out to some taverne or private house of my acquaintance,

---

[1] The copy and the *Letters* give ' news.'
[2] The copy and the *Letters* read ' as I could possible.'
[3] The *Letters* read ' at.'
[4] December 30.

where the French ambassador and others of his freinds severall times mett him.

The visitts at that time from the ambassador were very frequent to Lady Harvey, who never failed once a day to bring him the result of them, or what else she had. After he had been thus secretted about ten or twelve dayes, he told me he was resolved if he must be a prisoner it should be at large ; he wou'd goe over sea, and asked me if I could securely hire a vessell on the exchange, and wou'd goe with him. I told him I could, and wou'd wayte on him wherever he pleased. The next day I gave him an account that a stout ship of Dort of 130 tuns should be ready for him in two dayes, a Dutchman master that I knew, and would undertake for him ; which was done, and I caused her fall downe, cleare herselfe at Gravesend, and lye for us in the hether side the Hope.

Having resolved at last (for he was very irresolute and fearefull) that he would goe, and the time, I order'd the master to wayt us with his boats crew at a certaine place below the blockhouses at night. In the morning we tooke coach, and at the halfe-way house to Deptford mett Sir Thomas Armstrong, who wayted for us with another genleman, a grome, and two spare horses, with armes for us two. We gott on board well that evening, imediatly weighed, and stood as farr as we could that tyde. Next day we gott into Margate Road, the wind chop't upon us, and in the night it proved a great storme. We lost our boate adrift about midnight, which frighted him much. In the morning he asked me what I intended to doe with him. I told him we had good anchors and cables, and could ride it out without any kind of danger in the world. He would not, but told me he had rather I would throw him in the sea then keep him there in that condition, for he was very sick. I would have gone away for Holland, for we could have done it, but he would not. Soe we run back that night into Queenborrough Water, where it was very quiett.

He had then a mind to goe ashoar to sleep a night, and in the morning would goe by land to Dover. I promised to secure him thether, but could not there, because I thought he was well known. He had a thousand resolutions. I left him at Canterbury, and in the night rode [1] to Dover, and hired a small boat to put us over to [2] Calais or Bollen, or anywhere on that shoar, which was to have taken us on board the next night at 12 from the beach. I fetch't him from Canterbury at the time, and as we were stepping into the boat were seized by officers that lay in wayt for us, we having been before discovered by one of the boats crew, were made prisoners there about six dayes till orders came from Court. We gave security to a writt of ne exeat regnum, and came for London ; but just at the towns end were frighted againe by a note from his sisters [3] that told him if he were yet at liberty he would doe well to take care and keepe himselfe soe, for resolutions had be[en] taken at Court the night before to make him close prisoner.

This made us leave his coach and servants just at Kent Street end, soe privately that but one or two of them knew of it, and through the gardens I carried him to Reddriffe, crossed the water to Wapping, and by that time he beleived himselfe safe againe. I brought him to Aldgate in the evening, took coach, and went with him to Bloomsbury Square. He sate in the coach whilest I went to my Lord Russells and to his owne house to give his lady an account that he was well and safe. I lodged him that and the Sunday night in Lumbar Street, and on Munday morning he went home, &c. He was suddenly afterward chosen againe at Huntington.

And now all was well againe, the family very quiet, full of joy and good humour. And as an instance thereof I'le not omitt a frolick of Mounsieur Barrillon's, for he was still one amongst them, more then before if possible. It was the next Pope-burning day, he made me promise to shew him the burning of the Pope. I did, and that I would bring him off safe againe. He came with a genleman that spoak English pretty well to the Palsgraves Head tavern at five, where I steyd for him, and carried him within Temple Barr to a freinds house of mine, where he saw all the shew and the great concourse of people, which was very great at that time, to his great amazement, as

[1] The copy and the *Letters* read ' rode that night.'
[2] The copy and the *Letters* read ' att.'
[3] The copy and the *Letters* give ' sister.'

he pretended, and I beleive 'twas soe. I tooke care for a bottle or two of sack for them, and left them about two hours. At my returne he seem'd frighted, being afraid that somebody that had been in the rome had known him, for then he might have been in some danger, for had the mobb had the least intimation of him they had torne him in peeces, and he seem'd to be sensible of it next day ; but it served then for a good jest amongst them.

He wonder'd when I told him no maner of mischeife was done, not soe much as a head broak, but in three or four hours the streets were all quiett as at other times. It would not have been soe in Paris, he said.

THE PRINCE'S LETTERS

[To the Lord Treasurer] [1]

A la Haye, ce 3 Avril, 1674.

Monseigneur,

Estant informé, par Mr. de Reede, non seulement de vôtre civilité envers luy, mais aussi de vos frequentes expressions d'amitié et d'affection pour moy, je ne puis moins faire que de vous en marquer ma reconnoissance, et de vous assurer qu'en toutes occasions je seray toûjours prêts a vous donner de plus réelles marques de l'estime que jay pour vous, et du fond que je fais de vôtre amitié, et sur laquelle je m'appuie si fortement que j'ose me promettre que vous ne refuserez pas a Mr. de Reede (auquel j'ay donné ordre de s'appliquer a vous dans les choses qui regardent mes affaires) tant de vos avis que de vôtre puissante assistance, afin qu'il puisse surmonter toutes les difficultez qu'il pourra rencontrer.[2] Et comme je suis certain que vous luy accorderez cette faveur pour l'amour de moy, j'espere aussi que vous serez persuadé que je suis avec toute sincerité et verité, Monseigneur,

Vôtre affectionné serviteur,

G. H. Prince d'Orange.

[1] It is unfortunate that the original of this, the first letter in the long correspondence between William of Orange and Danby, has not been found. The present version is reprinted from that in *Letters*, p. 124, with such changes only as are necessary to bring punctuation and the use of capitals more into conformity with modern ideas.

[2] One part of the business in which William was hoping for Latimer's assistance is indicated in his letters at this time to the Earl of Ossory, printed in *Correspondentie van Willem III en Bentinck*, part ii., i. 342.

[*To the Prince of Orange*] ¹

30th April, [*16*]*74*. ²

May itt please your Highnesse,

  I do with all humility imaginable acknowlege the great honour of your Highnesse's letter, and do with no lesse joy receive from your Highnesse's owne hand the assurance of being in your Highnesse's good opinion. If any occasion could make mee ³ so happy as to give your Highnesse a testimony suitable to my desires, I am sure my actions would afford no cause to lessen your Highnesse's favour towards mee, and I hope (besides the nearenesse of relation in blood betwixt my master and your Highnesse) the nearenesse of interests will bee so great a consideration on both sides as may give opportunity to such as intend my masters good to make one of the best steps towards itt by promoteing your Highnesse's. And for what service I may bee capable in my owne particular, I beg your Highnesse to beleeve that nobody shall exceed mee, as in truth none can now, in the high esteeme which all the world must acknowlege to bee due to your great meritt. I dare trouble your Highnesse no longer then to declare the great ambition I have to receive any comands from your Highnesse, and to assure your Highnesse they shall bee most readily obey'd with all duty and respect, as becomes,

May itt please your Highnesse,

 Your Highnesse's most obedient and most humble servant,

Latimer.

---

¹ From the autograph letter in S.P. Dom., King William's Chest, 1. No. 3, printed in *Correspondentie van Willem III en Bentinck*, part ii., i. 355. The draft is still preserved in Leeds MSS., Packet 5.

² The letter itself is undated, and Dalrymple, who ought to have recognised the handwriting, was thus betrayed into printing it (App. i. 232) as written by Edward, Lord Latimer, in 1688. The date is obtained from the draft. It seems clear that this letter is the one referred to in Danby's communication of November 9, and that it was not lost as he there suggests (*infra*, p. 383). Sir Walter Vane, to whom he refers, left England for Holland about the end of April with a letter from the Duke of York to the Prince of Orange dated April 29, 1674 (*Cal. S.P. Dom.*, 1673-5, p. 236), and was killed at the battle of Seneff on August 1. See Sir Walter's own letter to the Treasurer, dated May 20, 1674, in *Hist. MSS. Com.*, ix. 2, p. 449; *Morrison Catalogue*, vi. 299.

³ Accidentally omitted in the letter but given in the draft.

[*To the Prince of Orange*] [1]

9th November, 1674.

I presumed by Sir Walter Vane to give your Highnesse my most humble acknowlegements for the great honour I received of a letter from your owne hand, and understood but a few daies before his death that his servant (*to whom my letter was delivered*) had lost itt, so that I have had the misfortune of not being knowne to have paid my duty as I ought to your Highnesse. I hope itt has in some measure been repaired by the favour of Monsieur Rhede and my Lord Ambassador Temple,[2] who have both promised to do mee right in representing to your Highnesse how truly I am devoted to your service, and I beg your Highnesse to bee assured that I could account no action of my life happier then that wherein I could bee able to give your Highnesse a testimony of itt, haveing a valew for your person suitable to its meritt, and duty becomming mee towards a great prince so nearely related to my master.

I hope your Highnesse will pardon my giveing you this trouble by my son, whose ambition to lay himselfe att your Highnesse's feet has been the greatest motive of his journey ; and if I or mine could bee any way usefull to your Highnesse, I should esteeme itt the greatest happinesse that can ever befall,

May itt please your Highnesse,

Your Highnesses most obedient and most humble servant,

Danby.

[1] From the autograph letter in S.P. Dom., King William's Chest, 1. No. 4, printed in *Correspondentie van Willem III en Bentinck*, part ii., i. 525, and summarised in *Cal. S.P. Dom.*, 1673-5, p. 406. The draft of the letter, showing no substantial variation, is in Leeds MSS., Packet 5.

[2] Danby's letter of the same date to Temple is printed *infra*, p. 451. His letter to van Reede, the autograph draft of which is preserved in Leeds MSS., Packet 5, runs as follows :

9th November [16]74—My son being desirous to take this opportunity of seeing Holland, I have commanded him particularly to waite upon your Lordship with the tender of my most humble service, and to beg the favour of your Lordships protection to him during his stay there. I know not whither your Lordship expected my Lord Arlington so soone in those parts, but his journey appeared here to bee very sudden, nor did I heare of Monsieur Odyke's intention of leaveing us when your Lordship was here, but I hope you will send him againe speedily in kindnesse to Monsieur van Beuninghen. I have presumed to trouble his Highnesse with a letter to assure him of my perfect devotion to his service, and I hope your Lordship will give mee your assistance to confirme him in that beleife, to which I have only to adde that if your Lordship please to honour mee with any comands by my son att his returne itt will make my obligations still greater, who am already infinitely desirous of being esteemed, [&c].

[To the Lord Treasurer] [1]

A la Haye, ce 27 Decembre, 1674.

Monsieur,

Ce m'a este bien de la joye de voir par la lettre que vous avez pris la peine de m'escrire par Monsieur vostre fils que je suis dans vostre souvenir, et que vous vuillies m'asseurer de vostre amitie, qui est une des choses du monde que j'estime le plus et tacherez a la meriter. Sur quoy j'ai prie Monsieur vostre fils de vous informer plus particulierement, et d'un affaire qui me touche dans mon particulier.[2] Je vous aurez une tres grande obligation si vous la pouvez obtenir, et tacherez de recognoistre en tous les occasions ou il ira de vostre service. Cependant je vous prie d'estre asseure que quoy qu'il en arrive, je serez tousjours avec la mesme passion, Monsieur,

Vostre tres affectione serviteur,

G. H. Prince d'Orange.

To the Prince of Orange.[3]

London, 2nd February, 1674/5.

I durst not presume to give your Highnesse this trouble till I could att the same time give your Highnesse an account of those comands I had the honour to receive in a letter by my son concerning the money designed by his Majestie for your Highnesse's use. I am now comanded by his Majestie to acquainte your Highnesse with his resolution to leave all the three last payments of the money due by the late treaty of peace with the States intirely to your Highnesse's dispose, although itt bee not only with inconvenience to his affaires, but (as I formerly told Monsieur Rhede) the second payment being wholly assigned to particular persons att that time when hee first acquainted mee with his Majesties intentions in this affaire.

---

[1] *Morrison Catalogue*, vi. 415; *Hist. MSS. Com.*, ix. 2, p. 451, where the date is given, mistakenly, as 1676; *Letters*, p. 126.

[2] The debt due to him from Charles II.

[3] From the autograph draft in Leeds MSS., Packet 6. The greater part of the letter is printed from the autograph original in *Morrison Catalogue*, iii. 114, and shows no substantial variation. The letter is endorsed by William, 'Lettre du Grand Thesorier touchant le payement de ma debte.' The draft is endorsed by Danby, 'Coppy of my letter to the Prince of Orange, 2nd February 1674/5'; and by Leeds, 'In answer to his Highnesses of 27 December [16]74.'

I can assure your Highnesse that I have att no time received his Majesties comands more chearefully in anything then this, but I can as truly informe your Highnesse that I find him most affectionately concern'd in all things that relate to the person of your Highnesse, and when I can bee any instrument in promoteing your Highnesse's service I know I shall bee happy in doing that which is not lesse agreable to my master then itt is suitable to the duty and respect of, [&c.]

Danby.

[To the Lord Treasurer] [1]

A Arnhem, ce 20 Fevrier, 1675.

Monsieur,

Il sera asses facile de vous persuader la joye que j'ay eu de recevoir la lettre que vous avez pris la piene de m'escrire, par laquelle vous me notifies la grace que sa Majesté ma fait, de vouloir me donner des assignations pour le payement de ma debte sur le reste de ce que Messieurs les Estats doivent au roy en conformite du traitté de paix. Et comme je scay que c'est a vous seul que j'ay l'obligation de m'avoir procure cett affaire, je vous en rends beaucoup de grace, et vous en resteres oblige tout le temps de ma vie. Je vous prie, Monsieur, d'avoir la bonte d'adjouter a cette faveur de me faire avoir l'expedition des susdites assignations le plus tost qu'il se poura, et de me conserver en tous occasions vostre amitié, dont je fais un si grand estime, et que je tacheres de meriter en tous les occasions ou il ira de vous temoigner avec combien de passion je suis, Monsieur,

Vostre tres affectioné serviteur,

G. H. Prince d'Orange.

Je prens la liberte de vous envoye icy joint une lettre pour le roy,[2] par laquelle je luy rends mes tres humbles remercimens de la grace qu'il ma fait, que je vous prie d'avoir la bonte de luy donner quand vous le jugerez convenir.

---

[1] From the autograph letter in Leeds MSS., Packet 6. *Letters*, p. 128.
[2] This letter has not been found.

2B

D.L. II.

[To the Prince of Orange] [1]

May itt please your Highnesse,

  Haveing no pretence for giveing your Highnesse this trouble, I should not have presumed to do itt but that my Lord Embassador Temple has given mee confidence to beleeve your Highnesse will not bee offended att my takeing the liberty to tender your Highnesse the humblest of my duty and service, and to assure your Highnesse that I should esteeme itt my greatest happinesse if I could do anything worthy of your Highnesses consideration. My Lord Embassador will bee able to informe your Highnesse att his returne not only how earnestly but how affectionately the King desires a perfect kindnesse and confidence betwixt your Highnesse and himselfe, and I know nothing in this world of which I could ever bee more ambitious then to bee an instrument both in the promoteing and preserveing of itt.

            TEMPLE

I find my Lord Embassador ∧ *so perfectly of my mind in all things which tend to the service of your Highnesse, that I have desired him to give your Highnesse a larger account of my readinesse to obey any comands wherein your Highnesse may thinke mee usefull.* ⌐ [2] *In the meane time I presume to recomend this bearer Colonel Fenwick to your Highnesses protection, who is not only a gentleman both of considerable quality and fortune, but I beleeve will deserve your Highnesses favour by his deportement in your service.* ⌐ [2] *I am with all duty and respect,*

May itt please your Highnesse,

  Your Highnesse's most humble and most obedient servant,

Danby.

London, 15th July, 1675. [3]

---

 [1] From the autograph letter in S.P. Dom., King William's Chest, 1. No. 6 printed in *Correspondentie van Willem III en Bentinck*, part ii., ii. 47, and summarised in *Cal. S.P. Dom.*, 1675-6, p. 217. The draft, preserved in Leeds MSS., Packet 10, has a number of alterations in the handwriting of the Duke of Leeds, to which effect is given in a copy preserved along with the draft. In spite of this preparation for publication, however, the letter is not included in the printed collection.

 [2] . . . [2] These marks indicate that the intervening passage was to be omitted. It does not appear in the copy.

 [3] In the draft the date has been altered by Leeds to [16]78.

[*To the Lord Treasurer*] [1]

A la Haye, ce 10 de Mars, 1676.

Monsieur,

    Comme il vous a pleu d'en user d'une maniere si obligante envers moy dans l'affaire de ma debte, je prens la liberte de vous faire souvenir qu'elle na pas encore son entier accomplissement, n'ayent point les assignations necessaires.   C'est pourquoy je vous prie, Monsieur, d'avoir la bonte de me les faire avoir.   Se sera un surcroi d'obligation que je vous aurez et que j'espere de meriter en vous temoignant en tous occasions avec combien de passion je suis, Monsieur,

           Vostre tres affectione serviteur,

                G. H. Prince d'Orange.

To Viscount Latimer.[2]

Monsieur,

    Je vous ay tres grande obligation de la bonté qui vous porte a vouloir vous employer pour mes interests.   Je vous renvoye ma procure, redressée comme il faut, et vous prie de croire que j'embrasseray avec toute la joye imaginable les occasions qui me fourniront le moyen de vous temoigner ma reconnoissance, et combien je suis, Monsieur,

           Vostre tres affectione serviteur,

                G. H. Prince d'Orange

A la Haye, le 31 de Mars, 1676.

To the Lord Treasurer.[3]

Monsieur,

    Je serois peu reconnoissant si je negligeois de vous remercier de la bonté que vous avez eue, de considerer la recommandation que je vous fis, il y a quelque temps, en faveur d'une bonne femme qui m'a servy de nourrice.[4]   *Le secours que vous luy avez presté à ma*

---

[1] From the autograph letter in Leeds MSS., Packet 7.

[2] From the original letter, in a clerk's handwriting but signed by the Prince, in Leeds MSS., Packet 7.

[3] From the original letter, in a clerk's handwriting but signed by the Prince, in Leeds MSS., Packet 10.

[4] *Cf.* Temple to Danby, March 24, 1676, *infra*, p. 475.

priere luy est venu si a propos que vous pouvez estre asseuré d'avoir fait une charité tres grande, et en mesme temps m'avoir obligé sensiblement. Vous l'avez fait en beaucoup d'autres occurrences de plus de consequence, et pouvez estre persuade, Monsieur, que je n'ay pas de plus grande impatience que de vous pouvoir temoigner que j'en conserve trés bien le souvenir, et souhaitte passionnement les occasions de vous le verifier par des effets, estant parfaitement, Monsieur,

Vostre tres humble et tres affectione serviteur,

G. H. Prince d'Orange.

A la Haye, le 19 Janvier, 1677.

[*To the Lord Treasurer*] [1]

Au Camp d'Ekelo, ce 28ᵉ d'Avril, 1677.

Monsieur,

Je me sens obligé de vous témoigner la joye que j'ay eu d'apprendre que sa Majesté vous a donné la jartiere, et ainsy étant entré dans nôtre ordre j'ay voulleu vous assurer qu'il n'y a auqu'un chevalier avec lequel je souhaitte de tenir une plus estroitte corespondence. Je vous prie, Monsieur, d'être assuré que personne ne prend plus de part que moy aux avantages qui vous arrivent, et qui desire plus d'avoir un peu de part en vôtre amitié, puisque je suis et seray toûjours avec beaucoup de passion, Monsieur,

Vôtre tres affectionné serviteur,

G. P.

[To the Lord Treasurer] [2]

A Lokeren, ce 9 Juin, 1677.

Monsieur,

Ayent creu necessaire en cette conjuncture de temps d'envoyer au Roy une personne sur lequel je me fie, je luy envoye Monsieur de Bentinck, mon chambelan. Et comme je l'ay expressement encharge de s'addresser a vous, Monsieur, et vous communiquer sa commission, je vous prie d'avoir la bonté

---

[1] From the letter in B.M. Add. MSS. 28054, f. 58, in a clerk's handwriting, but probably the original. It is printed in *Correspondentie van Willem III en Bentinck*, part ii., ii. 163.

[2] *Morrison Catalogue*, vi. 416; *Hist. MSS. Com.*, ix. 2, p. 451; *Letters*, p. 130.

de l'assister par vostre puissant credit, et d'estre asseure que
personne au monde ne vous en sera plus recognoissant, et qui
souhaitte plus d'avoir une estroit amitié avec vous que je
tacheres de meriter en tous les occasions ou il ira de vous faire
voir par les effets avec combien de passion je suis, Monsieur,

Vostre tres humble et tres affectionne serviteur,

G. P. d'Orange.

[To the Prince of Orange] [1]

London, 11th June, 1677.

May itt please your Highnesse,

I have received so great honours, both by your Highnesses letter by Monsieur Bentinck and another I had a litle
before from Eckloe, that I can never make acknowlegements
enough for them ; but they have obliged mee to make the best
returnes I am able, which is by devoteing my services in the
strictest manner to your Highnesse.

I hope your Highnesse will find by Monsieur Bentinck that his
reception here has been to your satisfaction, and I confesse I
have not in my life thought anything more fortunate then your
Highnesses sending to the King att this time and in so obligeing
a manner as Monsieur Bentinck hath performed. I hope itt may
have been an happy beginning to a more happy end, which is the
procureing so strict a freindship betwixt the King and your
Highnesse as may not only bee of the greatest contentment to
yourselves but the greatest security in the world against both
your enemies, itt being apparent (besides the nearenesse of
relation in bloud) that the safest and most prudent course which
can bee taken betwixt you is to make your freindships as in-
seperable as your interests are, if rightly considered.

I beg your Highnesse to forgive this high presumption, which
proceeds from so true a zeale to your service, and that you will

---

[1] From the autograph letter in S.P. Dom., King William's Chest, 1. No. 5A,
printed in *Correspondentie van Willem III en Bentinck*, part ii., ii. 178, and
summarised in *Cal. S.P. Dom.*, 1677-8, p. 691. The draft of the letter is in
B.M. Add. MSS. 28054, f. 60. Between the letter, the draft, and the version
printed in *Letters*, p. 132, there is no substantial variation.

beleeve there is no man will do more to his power in the promoteing of itt, with all the duty and respect which becomes,

May itt please your Highnesse,

Your Highnesses most truly obedient servant,

Danby.

To the Lord Treasurer.[1]

De Lokeren, ce 25 Juin, 1677.

Monsieur,

J'ay tant de reconnoissance des graces que vous m'avez
faites, et des civilitez que j'ay receu chez vous, Monsieur, que je
ne puis suffisamment vous en remercier, vous assurant que le
ressentiment m'en demeurera tôujours. La lettre de son Altesse
ci jointe vous fera voir si je vous ay fait justice, en luy faisant
connoistre les services que vous luy avez rendû, et la sincerité
et la franchize dont vous avez uzé envers moy, et de laquelle
vous m'avez promis, Monsieur, que vous voulez être tôujours de
ses amis et favorizer ses interests. Je luy ay fait connoître que
ce qui c'êtoit fait selon les ordres qu'il m'avoit donné êtoit par
vôtre avis et direction. Je m'assure que vous continuerez a
travailler comme vous avez fait utillement a cette affaire, et
puisque je n'ay pû attendre plus longtems en Angleterre que
vous presserez ainsi les choses que le Roy envoye au plustost
quelqu'un ici pour instruire Monsieur le Prince de ses sentiments,
afin que la bonne intelligence que vous avez jugé vousmême qui
commençoit a s'établir, et qui devoit être utille a sa Majeste et
a Monsieur le Prince, ne demeure point dans cet etat, mais
s'augmente de jour a aûtre. Et comme le succes de mon voyage
depend de vous, Monsieur, par le credit que vous avez aupres
du Roy, connoissant la sincerité de vos sentiments, et l'inclination que vous m'avez témoigné pour les interests de Monsieur le
Prince, je ne doute pas que dans peu son Altesse n'en voye les
effets qu'il s'en promet infalliblement. Surtout, Monsieur, ayez
soing que celuy que sa Majesté envoyera soit un homme en qui
vous prenez entiere confiance, et s'il est possible qu'il ne soit pas

---

[1] The original of this letter has not been found. It is printed as it appears in
Letters, p. 134.

entierement inconnu a Monsieur le Prince. Je vous suplie, Monsieur, de croire que personne au monde n'est plus effective-ment que je suis, Monsieur,

> Votre tres humble et tres obeissant serviteur
>
> W. Bentinck.

[To the Lord Treasurer] [1]

A Lokeren, ce 25 Juin, 1677.

Monsieur,

Il n'est pas possible d'avoir plus de joye que je n'ay d'avoir un peu de part en vostre amitié. La franchise avec laquelle vous en avez usé avec Monsieur Bentinck, et les asseur-ances que vous m'en donnes par la lettre obligante qu'il vous a pleu m'escrire, m'en rendent si fortement persuadé que je ne puis vous en témoigne asses ma recognoissance, ny des honneurs que vous lui avez fait. J'espere que vous vouderez bien avoir la bonté de me continuer tousjours vostre amitié, et que vous vouderez faire souvenir sa Majesté de la promesse qu'il a fait a Monsieur Bentinck de m'envoyer quelqu'un de confiance pour m'informer de ses sentiments ; apres quoy j'attenderes avec un impatience extreme, et aussi apres les occasions de vous pouvoir faire voir par les effets la passion avec laquelle je serez toutte ma vie, Monsieur,

> Vostre tres humble et tres affectionne serviteur,
>
> G. Prince d'Orange.

To Monsieur Bentinck. [2]

London, 29 June, 1677.

Sir,

I was unwilling to give you this trouble till I could give you some account of the King's intentions of sending to the Prince, which hee is now resolved to do by Sir William Temple, as one not only well acquainted with the present state of affaires, but so very well known to the Prince of Orange, as hee thinks will bee more acceptable to his Highnesse then any other. In order to itt his

---

[1] *Morrison Catalogue*, vi. 416 ; *Hist. MSS. Com.*, ix. 2, p. 451 ; *Letters*, p. 138.

[2] *Correspondentie van Willem III en Bentinck*, part i., ii. 4.

Majestie has sent an expresse to comand him hither, and everything will bee so ready for his dispatch that hee will not bee staid here about[1] *two daies before hee goes to the Prince. I should have been sorry for this delay, but that I hope itt will bee redeemed by having so good a messinger imploy'd in this negotiation, who I am sure will contribute, as I shall do, all that is in our power to the satisfaction of his Highnesse.*

Att your departure from hence you may remember that you doubted an expression of the Kinge's about the Prince's coming into England, which I told you I was confident his Majestie meant only as to the time of the Parliament's sitting, and upon inquiry since of his Majestie hee did assure mee that was his meaning and nothing else, and gave mee leave to write you word so that no other construction might bee putt upon what hee had said to you. I give you many thanks for the favour of your letter, and the good offices which I perceive by his Highnesses obligeing letter you had done mee. I will not presume to trouble his Highnesse with anything but the humblest of my duty till Sir William Temples waiteing on him, and I will tire your patience no longer then to give you perfect assurance of my being with great esteeme, Sir,

Your most faithfull and most obedient servant,

Danby.

To the Lord Treasurer.[2]

Du quartier de Calken, ce 16 Juillet, 1677.

Monsieur,

Je vous assure qui c'est avec beaucoup de joye que jay reçu celle que vous m'avez fait l'honneur de m'ecrire, me marquant que le Roy a resolû d'envoyer Mr. Temple a son Altesse. Vous pouvez être assuré, Monsieur, qu'il ne pouvoit avoir choisi personne qui luy fût plus agreable, vû la maniere dont son Altesse le considere et la connoissance qu'il a des affaires êtrangeres. Je vous avoüe que nous serons tous consollez de ce petit retardement quand nous vérrons venir Monsieur Temple.

---

[1] ? ' above.'

[2] *Letters*, p. 140. Printed from an imperfect draft, showing many variations from this version, in *Correspondentie van Willem III en Bentinck*, part i., ii. 5.

Monsieur le Prince a été tres ayze de voir dans la vôtre qui l'explication des paroles que sa Majesté m'avoit dittes sur le sujet de son voyage en Angleterre est conforme a ce que vous me dites, Monsieur, a mon depart. Desque la campagne sera finie il yra rendre ses respects au Roy, en observant le tems que le Parlement ne sera point assemblé. Nous avons marché aujourdhuy et avons passé la riviere pres de Dendermonde avec l'armée pour nous aprocher des Alliez.

Vous ne me devez point de compliments, Monsieur, de ce que vous dites avoir vû par la lettre de son Altesse, que je vous ay rendû justice en luy disant la maniere ouverte et obligeante dont vous en avez uzé a son egard, et les civilitez que vous m'avez fait en mon particulier, qui m'obligeront d'être toute ma vie avec beaucoup de sincerité, Monsieur,

Vôtre tres humble et tres obeissant serviteur,

W. Bentinck.

Vous pardonnerez bien, Monsieur, que je mette cette lettre pour Monsieur Temple dans vôtre couvert.[1] Son Altesse vous prie de la bien donner quand il viendra en Angleterre.

[To the Prince of Orange] [2]

May itt please your Highnesse,

Nothing in this world could trouble mee more then that your Highnesse should ever have occasion to beleeve that I were not just in those informations you receive from mee, and therefore itt troubles mee a litle that Sir William Temple is not like to attend your Highnesse as I hoped hee would have done before now. I know the King gives you the reason of itt himselfe, and I can only adde that I am well assured itt proceeds from no abatement of his kindnesse and good intentions towards your Highnesse, but on the contrary an unwillingnesse to speake anything to you as his sense that hee has not a good ground to hope may bee yours, which hee much doubts by reason of a letter of yours to Sir William Temple [1] and conferences with him upon that subject. Besides hee thinks

---

[1] This letter has not been found.

[2] From the autograph letter in S.P. Dom., King William's Chest, i. No. 7, printed in *Correspondentie van Willem III en Bentinck*, part ii., ii. 191, and summarised in *Cal. S.P. Dom.*, 1677-8, p. 284.

this an improper conjuncture to trouble your Highnesse with any-
body but men for that purpose for which hee has comanded my Lord
Plymouth to attend you. His lordship is above all recomendation
from mee, but yett I cannot but do him that justice as to assure your
Highnesse hee will deserve your kindnesse.

I heare your Highnesse has invested Charleroy, and that may
probably draw on some greater action, in which I pray as heartily
both for your glory and successe as any servant you have upon
earth, being with perfect truth,

   May itt please your Highnesse,

    Your Highnesses most obedient servant,

          Danby.

London, 1st August, 1677.

[To the Lord Treasurer] [1]

    Du Camp de Sombref, ce 16 d'Aoust, [16]77.
Monsieur,

  J'ay este bien surpris de voir, par la lettre que Monsieur
Temple a escrite a son Altesse,[2] qu'il ne croyoit pas venir ici.
Le retardement qui estoit arrive au dessein que le Roy a eu
d'envoyer quelqu'un a son Altesse nous avoit fait craindre du
changement aus affaires ; mais je croy que nous avons [3] plus de
subjet de l'apprehender, voyant le voyage de Monsieur Temple
accroché apres que sa Majesté l'a fait venir expres de Nimwege
pour cet effet et a escrit a son Altesse qu'il le lui envoyeroit, que
son Altesse a témoigné a vostre cour la satisfaction qu'il avoit
de ce chois, et que Messieurs les Estats avoit ordonné a Monsieur van Beuningen de declarer la mesme chose de leur part.

  Nos affaires ici prennent un biais a nous faire craindre que
nous n'aurons pas grand avantage cette campagne, et cela a
cause de meschantes mesures que les Espagnols nous font
prendre. Ils nous ont asseuré que les François ne pourroit
mettre une si forte armée en campagne quils ne fussent en estat
avec les troupes des autres Allies de leur faire teste et de couvrir
nostre siege, et cependant nous les avons veus venir a nous avec

---

[1] From the autograph letter in Leeds MSS., Packet 8. Printed in *Letters*, p.
144, and from a very incomplete draft, showing some variations from this
version, in *Correspondentie van Willem III en Bentinck*, part i., ii. 5.

[2] This letter has not been found.   [3] The *Letters* give ' n'avons.'

une armeé aussi forte que les nostres ensemble avant que nos lignes ne fussent a moitié achevées et nous ont obligez de quitter la place que nous allions assieger, sans qu'il nous ait este possible de les combattre, selon le sentiment de tous nos generaus, sans le plus grand desavantage du monde, estant obligé de défiler devant nos cnnemis au travers d'un grand bois qui nous separoit et ou ils estoit en bataille de l'autre costé.

Vous pouvez facilement juger, Monsieur, les choses demeurant cette saison dans l'estat ou elles sont, et que nos ennemis se puissent servir du printemps a venir, comme ils ont fait ces annees precedentes, si il sera temps alors de songer a la seurete des Pais Bas, puisque les François en seront les maitres. La confiance que j'ay en vos bonnes intentions pour des interrets si justes me font esperer que vous travaillerez utilement en cette affaire, ostant les difficultez qui pouvoit empecher la venue de Monsieur Temple. Je vous suplie de me faire la grace de m'en dire vos sentiments et de me croire tousjours, Monsieur,

Vostre tres humble et tres obeissant serviteur,
W. Bentinck.[1]

[To the Lord Treasurcr] [2]

Au Camp de St. Va, ce 23 d'Aoust, 1677.
Monsieur,

Je ne puis vous celer que j'ay été un peu surpris d'apprendre par la lettre qu'il vous a plû de m'ecrire par Monsieur le Comte de Plymouth [3] que sa Majesté ne m'envoyeroit pas Monsieur le Chevalier Temple, ainsy qu'il m'avoit fait esperer, et cela parce qu'il croit que ses sentiments ne seront point conformcs au miens. Je vous puis assurer que je n'en auray jamais d'autre qu'a luy complaire en tout ce qui sera dans mon pouvoir, et si le Roy a encore les mêmes que vous avez temoigné a Monsieur Bentinck que sa Majesté avoit lors qu'il étoit en

---

[1] Endorsed by Leeds, 'Monsieur Bentinck, 16 August [16]77, about Sir William Temple.'

[2] *Letters*, p. 148. Neither the original letter nor any copy has been found, but there is a translation in B.M. Add. MSS. 28054, f. 85 (printed in *Correspondentie van Willem III en Bentinck*, part ii., ii. 196), which differs from that given in the *Letters*.

[3] *Supra*, p. 393.

Angleterre, je croy que les affaires pourroient s'ajuster. Au moins j'y feray mon possible, ainsi j'espere que par vôtre entremise et puissant credit une affaire de cette importance pourroit avoir une bonne et heureuse issue, a quoy je vous prie de travailler, et d'être persuadé de la forte passion avec laquelle je seray toûjours, Monsieur,

Votre tres humble et tres affectionné serviteur,

G. H. Prince d'Orange.

[*To the Prince of Orange*] [1]

27 August, [*1677*].

May itt please your Highnesse,

Mr. Hyde comes to your Highnesse so fully instructed by his Majestie that I have nothing to adde upon that subject saveing that when your Highnesse should thinke itt convenient to discourse with the King yourselfe I should hope to see things brought to a better accomodation by that meanes then any other. I am to returne my most thankfull acknowlegements to your Highnesse for the honour of your last letter, and am not wanting to obey that part of your Highnesses comands which is to use the utmost of my indeavours with my master to bring the great disorders of the world to such an issue as might bee to your Highnesses satisfaction, which nobody can desire more passionately then,

May itt please your Highnesse,

Your Highnesses most devoted and most obedient servant,

Danby.

[*To Monsieur Bentinck*] [2]

London, 27 August, 1677.

I am to acknowledge the honour of yours of the 16th instant, and have done my part in dispatching one to his Highnesse as soone as might bee, who comes so far instructed as will give his Highnesse the knowledge upon what grounds his Majestie thinks fitt to presse the King of France to a peace. By what wee understand on this side the water, his Highnesse is not so well used by the Spaniard or

---

[1] From the autograph letter in S.P. Dom., King William's Chest, vol. 2, printed in *Correspondentie van Willem III en Bentinck*, part ii., ii. 197.

[2] *Correspondentie van Willem III en Bentinck*, part i., ii. 6.

any other of the Confederates as should oblige him to hurt himselfe for any of them, and if the frontiers of Flanders should not bee altogether so large as hee would for theire sakes desire, yett it makes his army att all times more necessary, and the guaranty of my master will bee so strongly tied for the safety of itt, that I have no feare in our daies of seeing France extend his armes any further that way. I find the King extreame desirous to see the Prince, and when itt can bee with his Highnesse's conveniency I do not thinke any thing can contribute so much to a generall accomodation. I shall beg to heare from you as often as you can, and desire you will beleeve that I am with perfect truth, Sir,

> *Your most humble and most obedient servant,*
>
> *Danby.*

[To the Lord Treasurer] [1]

Au Camp de Sognies,[2] ce 18 de Septembre, 1677.

Monsieur,

Puisque sa Majeste m'a fait la grace de me permettre de venir luy faire la reverance en Angleterre, je vais me preparer pour partir en tres peu de temps, et ainsi je ne vous entretienderes pas sur la commission de Monsieur l'Ambassadeur Hyde, qui vous informera de ce que je luy ay dit ; mais je le reserverez jusques a ce que j'aures l'honneur de vous voir, et vous asseure moy-mesme de la veritable passion avec laquelle je suis, Monsieur,

> Vostre tres humble et tres affectioné serviteur,
>
> G. H. Prince d'Orange.[3]

[To the Lord Treasurer] [4]

> *Du Camp de Soignies, ce 18 Septembre,* [1677].

Monsieur,

J'ay receu la lettre que vous m'avez fait l'honneur de m'escrire par Monsieur l'Ambassadeur Hyde, qui est arrive hier ici. Son Altesse a esté un peu surpris d'entendre par la proposition

---

[1] From the autograph letter in Leeds MSS., Packet 8 ; *Letters*, p. 150.

[2] Carelessly printed ' Longuie ' in the *Letters*.

[3] Endorsed by Leeds, ' Prince of Orange, 18 September, [16]77, N.S. About his comeing into England.'

[4] From the autograph letter in Leeds MSS., Packet 8. Printed from a draft, showing only verbal variations from this version, in *Correspondentie van Willem III en Bentinck*, part i., ii. 7.

*qu'il a eu ordre de faire que les sentiments du Roy sont si eloignes
de ce qui m'a paru en Angleterre. Vous pourrez vous souvenir,
Monsieur, que la dificulte la plus grande que vous trouvates estoit
sur la restitution de la Bourgoigne, et asteur sa Majesté fait faire
des propositions selon lesquelles il n'est pas possible d'avoir aucune
seureté pour l'Estat ni pour l'Angleterre mesme, puisque cela ne
peut faire aucune frontiere en ce pais ici.*

*Son Altesse est tres aise de ce que le Roy lui a fait temoigner qu'il
souhaite quil vienne en Angleterre. Il partira dans peu de jours
d'ici pour la Haye, afin di adjuster un peu ses affaires, et de ce
preparer pour aller rendre ces respects au Roy. J'espere qu'a
son arrivee il i trouvera les affaires sur la mesme piet que je les ay
laissez a mon depart, et que j'auray les occasions de vous asseurer,
Monsieur, avec quelle verite et passion je suis, Monsieur,*

> *Vostres tres humble et tres obeissant serviteur,*
>
> W. Bentinck.[1]

[To the Lord Treasurer] [2]

> A Babin, 23 Novembre/3 Decembre,[3] 1677.

Vous aures sans doute appris par la lettre que j'ay escrit
hier au soir au Roy [4] tous les accidents que nous avons eu. J'ay
receu a ce matin les ordres pour retourner a Londres ; mais les
ayant receu icy, je ne les ay peu executer, n'ayent point de
voitures propres pour transporter des femmes. Ainsi je continue mon chemain vers Canterbery, ou j'attenderes les ordres,
lesquels j'espere ne m'obligeront pas de retourner avec les
femmes a Londres, qui seroit une chose tres embarassante. Pour
moy, je serois fort aise d'y faire un tour en poste, de quoy je vous
prie de parler au Roy, et de tacher a luy persuade qu'il ne nous
fasse pas revenir tous, ayent une repugnance extreme de m'em-
barque de nouveau dans la riviere, le pouvant faire aussi com-
modement que je puis a Marguett.

---

[1] Endorsed by Leeds, ' Monsieur Bentinck without date, 18 September [16]77.'

[2] *Morrison Catalogue*, vi. 416 ; *Hist. MSS. Com.*, ix. 2, p. 453 ; *Letters*,
p. 152.

[3] This date, which is obviously correct, is taken from the *Hist. MSS.
Com.* and the *Letters*. The *Morrison Catalogue* by a slip gives the date as
November 3.

[4] This letter has not been found.

Je vous prie d'avoir cette bonte, et d'estre asseure que j'aurez bien de la joye a vous revoir et a vous remercier de nouveau de tous vos bontes. Continues les moy, je vous en conjure, et croiez moy tousjours absolument a vous,

G. H. P[rince d'Orange]

Je vous prie de m'escrire sans ceremonie, comme je faits a present.

To the Prince of Orange.[1]

London, 23 November, 1677.

I received the honour of your Highnesses letter about three houres agoe, and spoke imediately to the King according to your comands. His Majestie told mee hee would write to your Highnesses himselfe, and I found him only concernd for your owne conveniency in what hee had writt concerning your returne to London, and should leave itt intirely to what you should think best.

When I had writt thus far I was sent for to the King, who told mee that my Lady Frances Villers was dead, and that the Duke had spoke to him for one in her place who hee could not refuse, which was my Lady Henrietta Hyde ; but that hee was a litle embarassed whither your Highnesse might not have some objection to her upon that score which made you except against her husbands being embassador in Holland, although hee thought there was a great difference betwixt the unckle and the wife of an unckle, especially since att your desire hee was resolved not to imploy him in Holland; and hee could easely refuse him that imployment, without giveing the Duke any reason why hee did so, but hee could not refuse the Dukes request for my Lady, without giveing that reason which hee knew your Highnesse would not have the Duke to think. Hee therefore comanded mee to acquainte your Highnesse with itt, and that hee does not think itt a matter worth the takeing any notice of, since the effect would bee the putting of some sort of disobligation upon the Duke.

Wee have yett no newes of my Lord Feversham, more then his being att St. Germaines on Sonday, and the King believes hee wil bee here on Sonday next. In the meane time I know Monsieur Barillon has had a currier, who arrived here yesterday att two a

[1] Groen van Prinsterer, *Archives de la Maison d'Orange-Nassau*, 2me série, v. 353, from the original.

clock, and hee said to one that hee feared the answer to my Lord Feversham would not bee so good as wee expected. I gave an account *of this to the King and Duke this morning, as also of an intelligence I have of theire intention to block Ypres untill the season would give leave to invest itt closer, and (to my great admiration) the Duke said very briskly that in case they do not agree to the propositions sent by my Lord Feversham, the King ought to lett the King of France know that unlesse hee would forbear any further conquests in Flanders hee could not hinder England from coming into the war, and I said I hoped they would give mee leave to renew that motion if wee should receive an ill or dilatory answer from France.*

I am extreame sorry the Kings businesse will not permitt my attendance on your Highnesse att Canterbury, and the more because I was so unfortunate as not to kisse your Highnesses hands att your departure from hence ; but I hope I am so happy in your Highnesses beleife of my zeale to your service that I need make no apologies for ceremony, there being nobody alive with greater passion and respect,

Your Highnesses most faithfull and obedient servant,

D[anby]

To the Lord Treasurer [1]

Au bord du Montegu, a la rade de Marguett,
ce 26 Novembre, 1677, a quattres eures.

L'ancre estant deja presque leve vous me pardonneres bienque j'espere que je me referre au porteur, et que je vous prie seulement de me continuer tousjours vostre amitie. Vostre lettre m'a fort rejoui, vous en comprandres facilement la raison. J'espere d'en apprendre bientost plus de particularite. Croiez moy jusques au dernier soupir entierement a vous,

G. H. P[rince d'Orange]

[To the Lord Treasurer] [2]

A Marguett, ce 28 Novembre/8 Decembre, 1677,
a dix eures du matin.

Enfin voicy la troisième fois que nous allons nous embarquer, esperant que ce sera la derniere. C'est pourquoy j'ay

---

[1] *Morrison Catalogue*, vi. 416 ; *Hist. MSS. Com.*, ix. 2, p. 449 ; *Letters*, p. 154.

[2] From the autograph letter in B.M. Add. MSS. 28054, f. 106, printed in *Correspondentie van Willem III en Bentinck*, part ii., ii. 210. *Letters*, p. 156.

voulu vous escrire, affin qu'en partant d'Angleterre je vous puisse remercier pour la derniere fois de tous vos bontes, et vous prier de me les continuer tousjours. J'attenderes avec une grande impatience de savoir la reponse que le Conte de Fevercham apportera, et espere ou qu'elle sera bonne, ou que l'on prendra une bonne resolution, a quoy je vous conjure de tenir la main, et me croire sans reserve a vous.

G. H. P[rince d'Orange]

[To the Lord Treasurer] [1]

A Honslaerdyck, ce 10 Decembre, 1677.

Nonobstant que je nay mis pied a terre que hier, et qu'ainsi je ne puis avoir grand subjet pour vous écrire, je ne m'en ay pû empêcher pour vous renouveller les assurances de mes tres humbles services et la veritable reconnoissance que j'ay de touttes les obligations que je vous ay. A mon arriveé ici j'ay reçu l'agreable nouvelle du siege de St. Gilain, et que toutes nos troupes y marchoient. Si javois crû y arriver a tems je seray reparty tout aussitots pour les joindre. Jattend la poste de Flandres, qui devoit dêja étre arriveé, pour savoir ce que je feray. Si les ennemis prennent la ville je [2] faudra quils la rendent comme les autres, sans quoy il ny a point de paix a faire. x Quand je seray a la Haye je pourray vous en dire d'avantage, mais ⊕ je ne puis être avec plus de passion a vous que je ne suis.

G. H. P[rince d'Orange]

[3] x POUR MOY, JE ME FIE ENTIEREMENT A VOUS, ET SUIS ASSURÉ QUE VOUS NEGLIGERA RIEN POUR LA SEURETE DES DEUX NATIONS AUTANT QU'IL SERA EN VOTRE POUVOIR, ET ⊕ [3]

[1] From a copy in B.M. Add. MSS. 28054, f. 108, printed, not quite correctly, in *Correspondentie van Willem III en Bentinck*, part ii., ii. 210. *Letters*, p. 158.

[2] The *Letters* give ' il.'

[3] . . . [3] This passage is obviously intended to take the place of that crossed out in the letter, as it does in the printed version. If any confirmation is needed it is provided by the endorsement in the handwriting of the Duke of Leeds, ' to bee extracted as within.' The passage inserted is taken from William's letter of December 14 (*infra*, p. 404), and is thus printed twice in the *Letters*.

To the Prince of Orange.[1]

London, 4 December,[2] 1677.

I have a multitude of acknowledgments to make to your Highnesse for your [3] severall letters and honours in them, which your Highness has been pleased to bestow upon mee since your leaveing this place ; and as I have received great satisfaction from them all, so itt has not been the least that by your last from Honslaerdyck [4] I have heard the good newes of both your Highnesses safe arrival in Holland. Wee had received the news of St. Gillin being beseiged before your letter came, and I hope with no ill effect, for itt did so alarme us here (I meane the King and Duke themselves as well as others) that together with the account wee have received from France by my Lord Feversham itt has made us come up to more brisk councills then I dare bee confident your Highness could expect from us, and of which you would have had an account by the sending of Sir William Temple, but that wee stay him in expectation of haveing more to send him with when wee have heard once more from France by Mr. Montagu, who is to depart hence on Thursday morning [5] with orders to presse for a speedy resolution of theire mind.

The summe of the answer to my Lord Feversham (who has acquitted himselfe very well there) has been that the King of France did not expect the King of England would have thought such propositions reasonable, and that hee should thinke itt as reasonable to desire of him that hee should cutt off his legs and then bid him walke ; that to shew his intentions are [6] not to take all Flanders hee would bee willing to consent to a truce for all the Spanish and Holland townes betwixt the Meuse and the sea, as was in the yeare 1668, and that truce to bee for a yeare, or what further convenient time the King should thinke fitt.

---

[1] Groen van Prinsterer, *Archives de la Maison d'Orange-Nassau*, 2me série, v. 357, from the original. The autograph draft is B.M. Add. MSS. 28054, f. 104, and on this is based the version printed in *Correspondentie van Willem III en Bentinck*, part ii., ii. 214. *Letters*, p. 160.

[2] The *Letters*, probably by a slip, give the date as December 8.

[3] Draft and *Letters* read 'the.'

[4] The *Letters* add, ' of November 30/December 10.'

[5] December 6/16.

[6] Draft and *Letters* read ' were.'

What answer his Majestie has returnd to this, Mr. Hyde is directed to communicate to your Highness att large,[1] so that I will not trouble you with the repetition of itt ; butt you may bee fully assured his Majestie will not now go lesse then the seaven townes mentioned to your Highness, and will, as much as yourselfe, expect [2] that if St. Gillain or any other place shall bee taken, since the sending of my Lord Feversham into France, they bee restored, over and above the townes already demanded. And your Highness may judge how much our temper is altered, when the principall end of this expresse is to tell you that the King will joyne with Holland to oblige France to accept the proposalls sent by my Lord Feversham, in case Holland will joyne with him to oblige Spaine to the same in case they shall refuse itt ; and the King will rely upon your Highnesses single engagement for this, without saying anything to the States of itt. Your Highnesse will easily remember how far the King was from coming up to this, when you made severall essaies to have gained itt from him, so that your Highness will give mee leave to say the fault will now lie on your side of the water, if you have not either the peace upon the tearmes proposed or us as deeply ingaged in the war as yourselves. And if I may offer an advise (though itt may bee too early) [3] I thinke itt were not amisse to consider on your parts, as wee shall bee thinking on ours, in what manner the carriyng on of the war might bee best concerted betwixt England and Holland in case of a rupture with France, because the project of itt will do no harme, though itt should never bee executed.

I beleeve your Highness has as litle expected the short adjournment of the Parliament, which proceeds from the same cause, ᵐ [4] and that which I beleeve you lesse expect then all the rest, and which I asure your Highness the truth of, is that the Duke goes as chearefully into these councills as the King.⊕ [4] In short, I have so great confidence in our stedinesse to these

---

[1] *Cf.* Williamson's letter to Hyde, dated December 4, 1677, *infra*, p. 571.

[2] Draft and *Letters* read ' as much expect as yourselfe.'

[3] The passage in brackets is not in the draft and therefore does not appear in the *Letters*.

[4] . . . [4] These signs, inserted by Leeds in the draft, presumably mark the passage between them for deletion. It is omitted in the *Letters*.

resolutions that I can feare nothing but a Spanish obstinacy to make us recoile, which I hope your Highness will take care to prevent ; and I am comanded by his Majestie privately to tell your Highness that hee wishes you could hasten the recall of the Marquis de Burgomaine by speeding the Marquis de Fuentes hitther, whom wee have expected a good while, and who I hope there will bee care taken to instruct, so as to transact in a more satisfactory manner with his Majestie then this has done, and which will certainely [1] bee more usefull to the interests of Spaine. I am, with all possible duty and zeale,

> Your Highnesses most truly obedient servant,
>
> [Danby]

[To the Lord Treasurer] [2]

> A la Haye, ce 14 Decembre, 1677.

Je vous ay mande par ma derniere que St. Gilain estoit assiege. Je suis marri d'estre oblige a vous dire a present que j'ay hier receu la nouvelle de sa prise. Elle a capitule en mesme temps que nostre armee arrivoit pour la secourir ; je n'en scais pas encore d'autre particularite ny la raison de cette capitulation bizare. Vous pouvez croire comme cette nouvelle fatalite me touche, pas pour la perte de la place, que n'est pas d'une si grande importance, mais de la maniere qu'il faut tousjours que la fortune soit si opiniatre contre nous, et que les ennemis, pardessus tous leurs autres advantages, ayent encore celluy-la. Si l'on ne prend bien garde le temps s'ecoulera, et l'on ne saura a quoy s'en tenir. Pour moy, je me fie entierement a vous, et suis asseure que vous negligeres rien pour la seurete des deus nations, autant qu'il sera en vostre pouvoir.

> G. H. P[rince d'Orange]

Un bien nous est pourtant arriver en perdant Saint-Gilain, que nous avons encore mis quattre regiments dans Mons.

---

[1] Draft and *Letters* read 'also.'

[2] *Morrison Catalogue*, vi. 417 ; *Hist. MSS. Com.*, ix. 2, p. 453 ; *Letters*, p. 164.

[To the Lord Treasurer] [1]

A la Haye, ce 21 Decembre, 1677.

J'advoue que vostre lettre du 4/14 du courant ne ma pas moins surpris que rejoui, et comme assurement vous avez eu un grand part a faire prendre ces bonnes resolutions, je crois estre oblige de vous remercier pour l'interest que j'y ay.

Vous apprendres par la reponse que j'ay donne a Monsieur l'Ambassadeur Hyde qu'elle est telle que le Roy le demande, et je vous puis asseurer que je me suis jamais engage dans une affaire avec plus de joye, et dont je suis asseure que je ne serez desadvoue de personne. J'y ay adjoute seulement une pensée, que j'espere que le Roy ne trouvera pas movais que je luy ay fait representer, puisque je n'y ay point d'autre vue que son propre interest, et que je ne pretends pas que cela aye rien de commun avec la reponse que j'ay donne sur la question qu'il ma fait demande. Ce qui me reste a present a souhaiter est que l'on ne se laisse pas amuser, et qui si le Roy de France ne donne une promte et bonne reponse a Monsieur l'Ambassadeur Montegu que l'on vullie executer promtement les resolutions que l'on a pris, puisque la saison estant deja si fort advance, et les affaires dans un si mechant estat au Paiis Bas, il n'y a point de temps a perdre, car si l'on ne prend bien garde l'on ne sera plus en estat de faire la paix n'y une bonne geurre.

C'est ce que je vous prie de bien representer ou il convient. Cependent je ne laires pas de songe comme l'on poura le mieux concerter les operations de geurre pour estre en tous cas prest de les executer, et j'attenderez avec un impatience extreme la venue de Monsieur Temple, affin que l'on puisse une fois savoir a quoy l'on a a se tenir et en suitte regler toutte chose. Selon les ordres du Roy je faires mon possible que le Marquis de Bourgamene soit promtement rapele, et le Marquis de Fuentes envoye en sa place. En ça et en toutt autre chose je serez ravi de faire quelque chose qui puisse plaire au Roy, et luy temoigner le veritable zele que j'ay pour son service, et combien passionement je suis a vous,

G. H. P[rince d'Orange]

[1] From the autograph letter in B.M. Add. MSS. 28054, f. 109, printed in *Correspondentie van Willem III en Bentinck*, part ii., ii. 217. *Letters*, p. 166.

[To the Prince of Orange] [1]

London, 24/31 December,[2] 1677.

The King has sent Mr. Thynne to your Highnesse on a message for which hee had designed Sir William Temple, but that with infinite earnestnesse hee besought his Majestie to excuse him att a time when some inconveniences in his private fortune would have been so great that the King would not putt such an hardship upon him. *I hope Mr. Thynne will performe all that is necessary in itt, which is to gett some such thing perfected as may justify the King to say truly to his Parliament that an alliance is already made betwixt his Majestie and Holland for the preservation of Flanders. The manner of doing this is difficult to us, because both the King and your Highnesse are greately interested to have itt secrett, and wee neither know whither your Secrett Comittee can conclude such a treaty of alliance, nor if itt can do wee know whither your Highnesse will suffer itt to goe to theire knowlege ; so that as you only are judge in this matter the King has left itt totally to your conduct, resolveing to governe himselfe in itt by your advice, and I hope Mr. Thynne is so throughly instructed in this affaire that hee is able to lett you know the Kings mind in most things that can bee demanded upon this occasion.*

Your Highnesse sees wee persevere as stedily as you could desire, and yett I do assure you there is as much done of all kinds from France to shake itt as is possible, and truly itt has all the appearances imaginable of coming to an absolute war. Wee have yett no account from Mr. Montagu more then that hee arrived att Paris late the 17/27 instant and went next day to St. Germaines,[3] but wee know already by Monsieur Barillon that the answer hee will have is that

---

[1] From the autograph letter in S.P. Dom., King William's Chest, 1. No. 8, printed in *Correspondentie van Willem III en Bentinck*, part ii. ii. 218, and summarised in *Cal. S.P. Dom.*, 1677-8, p. 526. *Letters*, p. 170. There is a draft or copy, partly in a clerk's handwriting and partly in Danby's, in B.M. Add. MSS. 28054, f. 119, on which the Duke of Leeds has made his alterations.

[2] The date is written in this way both in the letter and in the copy, but is printed ' December 21/31 ' in the *Letters*. A comparison with Danby's letter of December 24 to Montagu suggests that the first part of this letter was written on December 23, O.S., and the whole completed and dispatched on the following day.

[3] Nevertheless Montagu dates one of his letters to Danby at St. Germains on December 17/27 (*supra*, p. 299).

*they will agree [to] a truce for Flanders, or more generall if the King
pleases, but can never consent to the proposalls by my Lord Feversham in the direct tearmes as they are there demanded ; and I find
the great effort is to keepe Tournay, unlesse they may have some
considerable place in exchange. In the meane time wee heare that
Ypre or Dixmude is by this time invested, and I perceive they make
no doubt of being master of both before they can bee releived.*

*I thinke itt were of importance (but I say this without any
comission) that as soone as might bee the embassadors both oj
Spaine and Holland should present memorialls to the King,
takeing notice of his good offices and endeavours for the peace and
quiett of Christendome, and that haveing so seasonably call'd his
Parliament they hope hee will do something which may contribute
effectually to the safety of itt, and particularly of the Spanish
Netherlands, which are in so imminent danger. And I hope that
particular care shall bee taken to make Monsieur van Beuninghen
declare to all his acquaintance of the Parliament the great satisfaction hee receives in all things which concerne the States and
theire allies.*[1]

When I had writt thus far I was call'd to the King upon the

A COURRIER IS JUST NOW

occasion x [2] ʌ of a courrier newly arrived to the French embassador, which brought him powers to offer a generall suspention of
armes for a yeare or fourteen monthes, and hee told the King
that his master had given Mr. Montagu that answer, that hee
could not accept the propositions, but would give such a suspension if my master pleased. Upon which the King replied
that that was a matter to which hee could not answer without
first knowing the minds of the Confederates, but hee would take
itt well if the King of France would forbeare his armes in the
Spanish Netherlands for two months, in which time hee could
informe himselfe of theire minds as to the generall suspention.
But the embassador said that would only bee to loose time, and
the King replied that without time to find new expedients hee
could not depart from those hee had offered, and the embassa-

---

[1] Up to this point the draft is written in a clerk's handwriting. It is continued in the handwriting of Danby himself.

[2] This sign denotes the place where the printing of the letter is to be
resumed.

dor has said hee will write ; and so the affaire stands att present,
but with all the firmenesse of resolution of the Kings part that
hee will not heare of the peace upon other tearmes. And I must
do the Duke that justice as to assure your Highnesse that
nobody can carry themselves better then hee does through this
whole matter.

I hope your Highnesse needs no repetition of my constant
duty and services to you, being

Your intirely devoted servant,

D[anby]

[To the Lord Treasurer] [1]

De la Haye, ce 7 Janvier, 1678.

Monsieur,

La crainte que j'ay eu de vous interrompre dans des
affaires de plus grande importance m'ont empêché de vous escrire plustost pour vous remercier, Monsieur, de toutes les
civilitez et graces dont vous m'avez comblé durant mon sejour
en Angleterre. Je croy, Monsieur, que vous serez assez facilement
persuadé de la joye que l'on a ici de l'heureus changement des
affaires dans vostre Cour. Je vous asseure aussi que l'on
vous fait justice, et que par la part que tout le monde sait ici que
vous i avez vous vous attirez mille benedictions, pourveu que
les affaires du Pais Bas soit en estat de pouvoir resister aus
ennemis en attendant vostre secours. Il ni avoit que cela qui
put le sauver d'une perte indubitable, soit par la paix ou par la
guerre.

Nous attendons l'issue du voyage de Monsieur de Montaigu
avec baucoup d'impatience. Cependant, Monsieur, vous pouvez
estre asseuré que personne au monde n'est plus effectivement
que je le suis, Monsieur,

Vostre tres humble et tres obeissant serviteur,

W. Bentinck.

[1] From the original letter in Leeds MSS., Packet 10. *Letters*, p. 172.

[To the Lord Treasurer] [1]

A la Haye, ce 10 Janvier, 1678.

Vous aures un conte si exact, tant par Monsieur l'Ambassadeur Hyde que par Monsieur Thinne, de ce qui c'est passe en la conclusion du traitte, dont vous avez envoye le projett, que ce ne seroit que vous importuner par des redites si je vous en informois. Ainsi je n'adjouteres a ce qu'il vous diront que de vous remercier de tout mon coeur d'avoir contribuer si utilement a l'union du Roy et de cett estat apres quoy j'ay tant souhaitte, et de vous prier que le dit traitte, comme il est a present couche, puisse estre ratifie promtement, et les articles qui ne sont point adjuste le puissent estre au plustost a nostre adventage.

Pour consentir a la demolition de Maestright, nous ne le pouvons. Je ne scay pas aussi en avoir parler. Il est bien vrai de l'avoir veu dans la lettre escritte de Monsieur le Secretaire Williamson a Monsieur Hyde, mais pour ne rien contredire je l'ay passe sous silence, n'y ayent rien allors a convenir. Par la redition [2] de Maestright j'ay tousjours compris Limbourg, qui depuis la demolition a tousjours depandu de cette ville, et qui est impossible que les François puissent guarde, estant si eloigne de tous leurs autres conquestes et paiis. Pour les chastelenies dependentes des villes comprises dans le traitte je ne croi pas qu'il y aye auquun difficulte, n'y aussi pour Binch, qui est enclave au millieus du paiis. L'on n'a pas parle de ces particuliarites a cause que l'on n'est jamais entre en traitte, n'y aussi de mes interests particuliers, lesquels je vous recommande de mesme de vouloir en avoir soin, sur quoy je me fie entierement.

Apres quoy je n'ay plus a vous prier que de prendre bien garde que les Francois ne vous amusent pas par des belles esperances ; et ayent aute le masque et donne l'offense comme vous avez fait a present, de ne pas faire les choses a demi ; et que dabord que vous vaires qu'ils ne veulent pas la paix, comme je suis entierement persuade, de vouloir aussitost faire tous vos efforts pour sauver le reste des Paiis Bas, qui sont en grand danger. Vous

---

[1] From the autograph letter in B.M. Add. MSS. 28054, f. 150, printed in *Correspondentie van Willem III en Bentinck*, part ii., ii. 224. *Letters*, p. 178.

[2] The *Letters* read ' reduction.'

avez si bien commence cette grande affaire que je ne doute pas
que vous la paracheveres de mesme, sur quoy je me repose
entierement, et que vous me croires jusques au dernier soupir de
ma vie,

G. H. P[rince d'Orange] [1]

[To the Prince of Orange] [2]

London, 8/18th January, 1677/8.

Your Highnesse will find by the Kings letter, which my
Lord Ossory brings, that hee has yesterday received such an
answer from the King of France as makes him conclude that his
Christian Majestie will no longer defer his march into Flanders ;
nor does hee give us any other then delatory excuses, which hath
much dissatisfied the King,[3] and no lesse the Duke,[3] who is ∧ NOW
wholly disposed for going into the war. But the businesse will
now bee ∧ SO to adjust matters for the war, so [4] as to keepe us in CONTINUE
the same good humor ; and for that end the King does absolutely insist upon haveing Ostend in his hands for recruit of his men
and sending provisions to them, insomuch that wee have severall
times acquainted Marquis de Burgomaine with this demand of
his Majestie, and hee still answers that hee must first know the
mind of the Duc de Villa Hermosa, although hee has had three
weekes time to do itt, and, till that bee consented, the King will
not begin to make leavies of men, but (in that case) intends
only a war by sea or in other places, but not in Flanders. For
what will concerne Holland, the principall businesse will bee to
have the navall preparations very considerable, viz., seventy
capitall ships att least, and in that particular his Majestie expects to bee assured imediately on the part of the States. The

[1] Endorsed by Leeds, ' Prince of Orange, 10th January [16]77/8.'

[2] From the autograph letter in S.P. Dom., King William's Chest, 1. No. 9,
printed in *Correspondentie van Willem III en Bentinck*, part ii., ii. 225, and
summarised in *Cal. S.P. Dom.*, 1677-8, p. 562. The draft, from which the
version printed in *Letters*, p. 174, is derived, is in Leeds MSS., Packet 10. It
differs in some details from the letter actually sent, and also contains a few
alterations in the handwriting of the Duke of Leeds to which effect is given in
the *Letters*.

[3] . . . [3] This does not appear in the draft or in the *Letters*.

[4] The word ' so ' is omitted in the draft and the *Letters*.

rest of the matters which will bee necessary to bee concerted in order to the war your Highness will find his Majestie desires that somebody may bee sent hither to adjust as soone as may bee, where the ministers of the Emperour and of Spaine will also bee impowred to undertake for theire masters.

In my last I acquainted your Highness that the French embassador said hee would write to his master for the respitt of two months from war, while the King might send to all the Confederates to know theire mind about a generall suspention of armes for a yeare ; and the answer to that has been that whatever the King of France shall take betwixt this time and the first of March shall bee all restored, in case the generall suspention shall bee agreed on all hands before the said first of March ; but hee will not agree to stand still two months, because hee saies that is but to loose so much time and then not have the suspention accepted. This expedient the King does not approve; nor will hee, I am confident, any other they can make, unlesse either the Parliament faile him, or that Spaine shall refuse him Ostend during the war and Port Mahon in the Mediterranean, or that Holland shall not furnish a proportionable number of ships with us.

I desire your Highness will please not to take any notice of these propositions from France ; but they have been received so very coldly here that I am confident the French King will thereupon take all his measures for a war with us, and because his Majestie has also writt already to Mr. Montagu to desire the Duke of Munmouths regiment of horse may bee imediately sent over hither under the pretence of some disorders in Scotland. My Lord Dumbarton goes also to-morrow to bring away his regiment, and orders will go in two or three daies more for recalling the rest of his Majesties subjects in that service. Order is also given to the Governour of Gravesend to lett passe any that are going into the service of the States, but his Majestie will not yett have that order made publique.

I wish your Highness could promote the Kings demands from Spayne to gett them dispatcht, because till that bee done there will bee such a backwardnesse on our parts in makeing leavies, &c., as may loose the most necessary time of this yeare for our assistance, besides that I am of opinion they ought to desire us to keepe itt if wee did not demand itt. I suppose there will bee no difficulty made in signing the defensive treaty which is to take place after the war, and itt will bee of use in the Parliament to lett them know that such a treaty is made as well as the present treaty of alliance. I should bee extreame glad to heare your Highnesses opinion in what manner you conceave the war might bee made with most advantage against France, when wee shall come into itt, if this bee not too great a trouble, which I would not putt your Highness to, but with intention to serve you by itt, as will alwaies bee my greatest ambition, being so intirely,

Your Highnesses most obedient and devoted servant,

D[anby]

[*To the Prince of Orange*] [1]

London, 9/19th January, 1677/8.

I had closed my letter of yesterday and was gone to bed when Mr. Thynne arrived with your Highnesses letter,[2] *for which I must returne my humble acknowlegements. Hee has brought back the treaty with some alterations which his Majestie finds necessary to have againe altered, and which I shall not mention, because the whole businesse is sent att large to Mr. Hyde to explaine to your Highness. I will only tell you that the King takes his honour to bee highly concernd not to have itt thought hee knew the mind of Spaine any more then of France before the signing of the treaty, and for what concernes the Emperor hee thinkes himselfe to bee att no certainety att all as the treaty is pennd.*

I beleeve the King intends to respitt the sitting of the Parliament till the treaty is returned, because hee thinks itt would bee rather of ill consequence then good that they should enter upon businesse before hee can assure them of an alliance perfected betwixt England and Holland. I am sorry for this delay att this time, but I hope itt will bee nothing more, for I assure you wee make all the preparations

---

[1] From the autograph letter in S.P. Dom., King William's Chest, 1. No. 10, printed in *Correspondentie van Willem III en Bentinck*, part ii., ii. 227, and summarised in *Cal. S.P. Dom.*, 1677-8, p. 565. There is also a copy in a clerk's handwriting in B.M. Add. MSS. 28054, f. 148.

[2] Dated January 10 (*supra*, p. 409).

*for a war that wee are capable of without the assistance of a Parlia-
ment. Monsieur de Burgomaine has this day desired the King to
send 2,000 men to Ostend, saying that they have not 500 men there,
and therefore that his Majestie will bee master of the place, but that
though hee have power sufficient to give itt hee dares not without
speciall order, insomuch that I beleeve the King will send an envoy
expressly to-morrow to the Duke de Villa Hermosa to know his
mind in itt, which wee shall know about the time of receiveing the
treaty back from Holland. But in the meane time wee shall delay
those leavies which would have given us the liberty of sending three
or four thousand of our old men into those parts for theire present
assistance.*

*Your Highness will find that in the secrett article the King has
been as carefull as you can desire of your particular concernes, and
I have nothing more to adde, but that I am,*

Your Highnesses most truly obedient servant,

D[anby]

[To the Lord Treasurer] [1]

A la Haye, ce 25 Janvier, 1678.
Monsieur le Conte d'Osseri ne faisant que d'arriver tout
presentement que la poste est sur son depart, je ne poures vous
repondre cette fois aus lettres qu'il vous a pleu m'escrire comme
je souhaitterois. Au fait du traitte, je me raporte aux lettres
de Monsieur l'Ambassadeur Hyde, estant extremement marri
que l'on aye si mal compris ou explique mes intentions. J'espere
qu'a present, par l'addition du nouveau article, on sera entierement satisfait ; au moins on le doit estre si l'on va a l'effectif.
Pour mes pensees au reguard de la maniere de faire la guerre,
je vous les faires savoir par le premier courrier. Cependant je
vous prie de bien represente, ou il convient, le danger ou les Pais
Bas sont ; 3,000 ou 4,000 hommes y fairoit a present peut-estre
plus de bien que dix en un mois d'icy. Et pour ceder la ville
d'Oostende durant la guerre, je n'y vois auqu'une difficulte. Je
depescherez demain un expres pour cest effet au Duc de Villa
Hermosa, et s'il y avoit moien de les envoyer la et a Nieuport

[1]*Morrison Catalogue*, vi. 417 ; *Hist. MSS. Com.*, ix. 2, p. 454 ; *Letters*
p. 182.

promtement, ce seroit le plus grand bien du monde. Quandt on veut faire les choses il ne faut jamais les faire a demi.

En peu de jours j'envoyerez quelqu'un entendu au Roy et a Monsieur pour concerter les affaires de l'armement de mer. Je suis tousjours, comme je doits, entierement a vous,

G. H. Prince d'Orange.

Parmi tous ces affaires importantes il faut que je vous escrive d'une qui n'est pas de cette nature ni propre en temps de guerre ; mais il semble que Monsieur Bentinck a voulu suivre l'exemple de son maistre, et va se marrier a Madame Villars. Vous savez l'amitie que j'ay pour luy, et que je prends autant d'interest en ces affaires qu'au miens propres. Ainsi j'espere que vous ne trouveres pas movais que je vous fasse savoir que, comme la personne qu'il va marrie a peu de bien, et que le dot que la Princesse aura n'est pas fort considerable, s'il n'y auroit pas moien que le Roy eut la bonte de l'augmenter, affin que je luy puisse donne l'augmentation. Vous savez que pour moy, quandt on a parle du dot, je n'ay jamais inciste pour l'augmente; mais j'avoue qu'a present se seroit une obligation extreme que je vous aures si vous pouviez me procurer cette grace du Roy, que j'estimerois mille fois plus que s'il estoit fait a moy-mesme. Si vous n'esties autant de mes amis que vous l'estes je n'aures jamais ause en use si famillierement. J'espere que vous n'en serez pas fache et asseurement vous ne pourez faire plaisir a personne qui soit plus effectivement vostre serviteur que Bentinck et moy.

[To the Lord Treasurer] [1]

A la Haye, ce 29 Janvier, 1678.

Puisque vous voules savoir mes pensées de quelle maniere l'Angleterre pouroit agir le plus utilement quandt elle viendra a rompre contre la France, je vous le pourer dire en peu de mots. Il faut qu'elle aye une flotte considerable dans le Canall, et un esquadre asses forte dans la Mediterannée pour empescher leur commerce, et une armée de terre aussi puissante qu'il est possible, ou pour mestre sur la flotte et tacher a faire une

---

[1] From the autograph letter in B.M. Add. MSS. 28054, f. 154, printed in *Correspondentie van Willem III en Bentinck*, part ii., ii. 228. *Letters*, p. 192.

dessente en France, et par la faire une forte divertion, ou l'envoyer au Paiis Bas pour y agir selon que les occasions s'en presenteront. Dans l'estat ou sont les affaires a present, je croi le dernier le plus utile, car sans que l'on fasse un grand effort on aura bien de la piene a sauver le peu de Paiis [1] qui reste. Surtout il est de la derniere importance que le Roy, voyant a present qu'il n'y a plus d'apparance de paix, envoye promtement a Nieuport et Oostende un bon corps de trouppes, a quoy je vous conjure de tenir la main, et de ne pas prendre a movaise part que je vous mande si naivement mes sentiments, qui seront tousjours a vostre egard comme je dois a l'homme du monde auquel j'ay le plus d'obligation.

G. H. P[rince d'Orange] [2]

[To the Prince of Orange] [3]

London, 23 January, 1677/8.

I had the honour of your Highnesses of the 15/25 January the day after the arrivall of the expresse from Holland with the treaty of alliance, of which your Highness had an account yesterday that itt was accepted without any alteration. This day Mr. Godolphin returned from the Duc de Villa Hermosa, who has treated him civilly, but (under the rose to your Highnesse) so very foolishly as to theire owne concernes in Flanders that unlesse some remedy can bee given to itt by your Highnesses influence upon him, I know not whither itt may not change all our measures here, or att least to the sending any force into Flanders. Although the Duc de Villa Hermosa his discourse have been mixt with great folly and greater ignorance (as particularly in his beleife of the port att Neiuport, that itt was capable of receiving a good ship, when the Kings yatchts dare not go in there), yett the King is of opinion (and I said itt this day to the Marquis de Bourgomaine before his Majestie) that

---

[1] The *Letters* read ' Pais Bas.'

[2] Endorsed ' 29 January 1677/8. From the Prince of Orange.' To this the Duke of Leeds has added, ' To bee extracted.'

[3] From the autograph letter in S.P. Dom., King William's Chest, 1. No. 11, printed in *Correspondentie van Willem III en Bentinck*, part ii., ii. 228, and summarised in *Cal. S.P. Dom.*, 1677-8, p. 592. Danby's autograph draft was among the Morrison MSS., and is printed in *Morrison Catalogue*, iii. 115, and summarised in *Hist. MSS. Com.*, ix. 2, p. 454. From the draft is derived the version printed in *Letters*, p. 188.

the Duc de Villa Hermosa is betraied in his councells, or else itt were not possible to do many of the things wee see done, nor to leave undone many of the things which are of such absolute necessity [1] for theire defence. And in this particular of Ostend, itt is most certaine that they have now putt armes into the hands of the burgers and seamen of the towne, whose interest itt is to bee under France and have declared theire willingnesse to bee so, insomuch that I looke upon itt as a garrison kept for France, when they please to come to itt.

This has not only broke our measures as to Flanders, but to the Parliament, who will [2] not att first beleeve it possible [2] that they have refused to lett us putt auxiliaries into Ostend and Neiuport, and will thinke wee have some other designe for those men and ships which were designed to have carried 3,500 men to those places, the men and ships being both ready.   His Majestie was very glad to find that hee had done that which your Highness saies in your letter would have been of more use now then 10,000 men a month hence, and certainely none but madmen could have thought otherwise of itt.   But since they must bee saved against theire wills, or not att all, I thinke itt will bee a principall step towards theire salvation [3] if your Highness can retrive this false measure [4] they have taken [4] by sending some considerable messinger speedily to gett theire error amended in time, for I feare the King will defer the Parliament another weeke upon itt, and a litle time now will loose the whole benefitt of this campagne.

The French embassador now begins to thinke there is no further hopes of peace with England, and the French King has answered that as to the returne of our troops the capitulations shall bee kept, which are not to returne till thirty daies after the war declared betwixt France and England ; and in the meane time hee has ordered the regiment of Douglas to march into Dauphiné. Tis said [5] that the King of France [5] begins his march

---

[1] The draft and the *Letters* read ' so necessary.'
[2] . . . [2] Draft and *Letters* read ' hardly believe.'
[3] So also the draft, but the *Letters* read ' preservation.'
[4] . . . [4] Draft and *Letters* read ' of theirs.'
[5] . . . [5] Draft and *Letters* read ' the French King.'

with his whole Court towards Metz to-morrow, and that his designes are on Treves, Luxembourg, or Charlemont ; but everything is so easy to him on this side, viz., Ypres, Dixmude, Neiuport and Ostend, that tis beleeved there will bee men enough left to take some or most of those places att the same time.

[1] *To that part of your Highnesses letter which concernes Mrs. Villiers the King said itt was a very ill time for him to give money ; but hee did not refuse itt, only said hee would consider of itt, and both in obedience to your Highnesses comands, and to shew the great kindnesse I have for Monsieur Bentinck,*[1] I will not faile to improve the Kings good intentions as much as I can possibly. I am eternally,

Your Highnesses most obedient servant,

D[anby]

The Marquis de Bourgomaine has carried himselfe so very ill in this matter that nothing can bee said worse of itt then hee deserves.

[To the Prince of Orange] [2]

24 January, [1677/8]

I had sealed my letter last night, beleeving the expresse would have been sent away this morning early, but I found hee was staied for the Kings letter, and this day wee have received a pacquett from Madrid, giveing us a discourse betwixt Don Juan and our embassador there, to whom Don Juan has told a long story what offers hee has had from France for the delivering up Flanders, and his resolutions against itt. But wee have been also this day informed by a Spanish merchant that such a secrett treaty is on foot, which I tell your Highness only to have your eye towards them. I cannot but againe beseech your Highnesse to use your utmost indeavours about the matter of Ostend.

D[anby]

[1] . . . [1] In the *Letters* this passage is omitted and ' Whatever happens ' is substituted. In the *Morrison Catalogue* the passage is printed, and ' whatever happens ' is also inserted between ' faile ' and ' to improve.' This looks like a misreading, on the part of the editor, of an alteration made by the Duke of Leeds.

[2] From the autograph letter in S.P. Dom., King William's Chest, vol. 2, printed in *Correspondentie van Willem III en Bentinck*, part ii., ii. 230.

[To the Lord Treasurer] [1]

A la Haye, ce 14 de Fevrier, 1678.

Celle icy n'est a autre fin que de vous recommander fort serieusement d'avoir la bonté d'assister par vostre puissant credit le porteur de celle icy, Monsieur le Baron de Lerinchamp, qui est envoye de la part de Monsieur le Duc de Lorraine au Roy, pour lequel j'ay une si grande amitié que je prans fort a coeur tout ce que luy reguarde. Ainsi vous ne trouverez pas movais que je vous recommande ses interests et la personne de Monsieur de Lerinchamp, qui est tres honest homme et fort de mes amis. Tout ce que vous poures faire tant pour l'un que pour l'autre je vous en aurez une obligation tres grande pardessus toutes les autres que je vous ay.

G. H. P[rince d'Orange]

[To the Lord Treasurer] [2]

De la Haye, ce 16 Febvrier, 1678.

Monsieur,

Je vous asseure que c'est avec toute la joye et la recognoissance imaginable, Monsieur, que j'ay appris de son Altesse les obligantes expressions dont vous vous estes servi sur mon subjet, et de la maniere que vous avez eu la bonté de vous employer dans une affaire qui me reguarde. Je n'ay peu tarder a vous témoigner l'obligation que je vous en ay, Monsieur, vous supliant tres humblement de vouloir continuer dans ces sentiments pour moy, ce qui pourtant n'augmentera rien au respect et a la veneration que j'ay pour vous, puisque je suis deija autant qu'on le peut estre, Monsieur,

Vostre tres humble et tres obeissant serviteur,

W. Bentinck.

[To the Prince of Orange] [3]

London, 8th February, 1677/8.
His Majestie finds such great discouragements, both from the dilatory proceedings of the Parliament and the untoward actings

[1] From the autograph letter in Leeds MSS., Packet 10. *Letters*, p. 200.

[2] From the autograph letter in Leeds MSS., Packet 10. *Letters*, p. 202.

[3] From the autograph letter in S.P. Dom., King William's Chest, 1. No. 12, printed in *Correspondentie van Willem III en Bentinck*, part ii., ii. 234 ; *Cal. S.P. Dom.*, 1677-8, p. 636 ; *Dalrymple*, App., p. 156.

*of the Spaniard with him, that your Highnesse will find by Mr.
Godolphin hee is in hopes of litle good but by a peace ; and I must
confesse our appearances promise litle good by a war.*

*Hee thinkes this peace may bee had by giveing the King of France
some other place for Tournay, and can himselfe thinke only upon
Charlemont as a place the Spaniard may best spare ; but I find
they would rather have Luxembourg or Ypres, and will not to mee
owne lesse then both those places in lieu of Tournay, and I beleeve
his Majestie knows no more then myselfe in this matter.*

*Whatever your Highnesse's opinion may bee of the proposition,
I do assure you there is no cause from itt to feare any alteration in
the King from the measures hee has taken with your Highnesse,
so that when your Highnesse knows the true state of things here, if
you shall not approve the haveing such conditions offered to
France, you may bee confident you will heare no more of them ; but
(as I have formerly writt to your Highnesse) if the King cannot
have Ostend for a port, where to land his men and lay magazines,
you are never to expect any succors of men from us in Flanders.
For my owne part, I know not what either to wish or advise in
this case, on the one hand the nation expecting a war from us, and
yett, on the other, move so slowly toward one that att best wee
cannot expect to have any considerable force in readinesse before
May, and not certaine how long that shall bee supported.*

*I pray God you may advise the best, because I am sure wee shall
go along with you in your fortunes, to which no man wishes more
prosperity then myselfe, who am,*

  Your Highnesses most eternally faithfull servant,

          D[anby]

[To the Lord Treasurer] [1]

     A la Haye, ce 18 Fevrier, 1678.

  Incontinent apres que j'ay receu la lettre du Roy et la
vostre je depesche de nouveau un expres a un envoye que nous
avons a Bruxelles de faire des fortes et nouvelles instances
aupres de Monsieur le Duc de Villa Hermosa pour le faire
resoudre a mestre entre les mains de sa Majeste la ville d'Oostende pendant cette guerre, sur quoy il a resolu d'y accepter les

---

[1] *Morrison Catalogue*, vi. 417 ; *Hist. MSS. Com.*, ix. 2, p. 455 ; *Letter*
p. 194.

trouppes que le Roy y voudra envoyer, ne pouvant se declarer plus loin avant qu'il n'a ordre d'Espagne. Et certainement s'il n'en a point, comme il proteste, je ne voi pas qu'il a peu faire d'avantage ; il en a escrit a sa cour. Cependant j'espere que le Roy envoyera immediatement les trouppes qu'il y avoit destine, puisqu'a present il n'y a qu'une petite difference de formalite, qui en l'essentiel ne signifie rien, puisqu'en effet vous en serez entierement les maistres. C'est pourquoy je vous conjure de faire vostre possible qu'il n'y aye auqu'un obstacle dans une affaire qui est si necessaire pour nous tous.

Je suis bien marri que l'on n'a pas peu encore adjuste le traitte d'alliance, mais il y a des certaines formalites en des republiques que l'on ne peut changer, et qui sont pourtant fort ridicules. J'espere que devant le depart du courrier prochain on la pourra adjuster, si Monsieur l'Ambassadeur n'a des ordres trop precis. Je suis tousjours comme je doy,

G. H. P[rince d'Orange]

[To the Prince of Orange] [1]

London, 9th February, 1677/8.

Since my letter of yesterday (when I thought Mr. Godolphin would have been dispatch[t] the same day) I have reason to beleeve that the proposition about giveing Charlemont or some other place for Tournay will bee accepted in France, and I have not lesse reason to beleeve that the makeing of the peace upon that proposition would bee very fatall to the interests of the King my master att home. I confesse I cannot see but that the consequences must bee ill to your Highnesse also, when the confederacy shall bee thereby broken, and wee perhaps tied to such conditions as may leave us uncapable of giveing you those assistances wee ought to do.[2] Besides the Parliament has now

---

[1] From the autograph letter in S.P. Dom., King William's Chest, 1. No. 13, printed in *Correspondentie van Willem III en Bentinck*, part ii., ii. 235, and summarised in *Cal. S.P. Dom.*, 1677-8, p. 639. Danby's draft in B.M. Add. MSS. 28054, f. 158, forms the basis of the version printed in *Letters*, p. 197. There are a number of unimportant verbal differences between the draft and the letter.

[2] The draft as originally drawn up continues at this point, ' when the French King shall thinke fitt to pick a new quarrell, which hee will never want when hee shall find itt convenient.' These words were crossed out by Danby at the time, and were not included in the letter.

voted 26,000 foot, and 4,000 horse and dragoons, and 90 sayle of men of war, and I am confident will not stop there in case his Majestie will go freely into the war, which yett they all doubt, and not without cause. I will have no reserve to your Highnesse in this matter, and therefore you must know that Monsieur Ruvigny (who has been here about fourteen daies) goes on Monday to the French King with this proposition, and designes to returne hither with an answer about the last of this month (our style), and till that time expects the King my master will make no declaration against him. But his Majestie has promised that only in case they shall attempt no seiges in the meane time, so that this may prove an happy expedient to hinder them so long from makeing any progresse, and may give both you and us so much more time to make our preparations, and att last, unlesse your Highnesse shall consent to this new proposall, the King will not bee ingaged to the French att all.

From what I have now informed your Highnesse, and more that I am not att liberty to say, I hope your Highness will not consent to any alterations of the first propositions by my Lord Feversham ; but if I may offer my advice I would not desire the dispatch of Mr. Godolphin too soone, because the King should not thinke you reject any proposition of his without due consideration. On the other side I cannot wish hee should bee detained above four or five daies, because itt will bee of absolute necessity hee should bee back before the returne of Monsieur de Ruvigny. You see how intirely I trust myselfe in your Highnesses hands, where I can no more doubt of my owne safety then I can of your honour, especially since the designe of all this is for the safety and honour both of my owne master and your Highnesse.

I am sorry to heare by report that the States will not beare the quota of 70 sayle of men of war from 40 guns upwards ; but I hope itt is not true, and I desire the man may bee dispatcht hither whom you intend to adjust those matters, as also that some good account may bee had of the businesse of Ostend. I pray your Highnesse that I may know your sense fully upon what I have writt when Mr. Godolphin returnes, as also that I may then receive a letter to show the King, as well as one in

answer to this. I beg also that your Highness will bee pleased
to burne this letter.

[Danby] [1]

[To the Lord Treasurer] [2]

A la Haye, le 25 de Fevrier, 1678.

*J'advoue que j'ay este un peu surpris de la commission de
Monsieur de Godolphin, et il ne m'avoit pas paru par les resolutions que le Parlement avoient pris et que nous avons eu icy que sa
Majeste avoit lieu de douter qu'il ne seroit assister a suporter les
frais de la geurre comme il est necessaire. Il est difficile a moy a
juger qu'elles pouroient estre les suittes, mais puisque le Roy a
voulu que je luy fisse savoir mon advis je l'ay fait avec la plus
grande ingenuite possible. Si Dieu m'avoit donne plus de
capacite j'aurois peutestre mieux peu juge des evenements. Au
moins j'espere que le Roy aura la bonte de ne m'en pas vouloir
rendre responsable. C'est ce que je vous prie de luy bien representer, et au reste je me raporte a ce que Monsieur de Godolphin
vous dira, et suis tousjours avec la mesme passion et recognoissance,*

G. H. P[rince d'Orange] [3]

[To the Lord Treasurer] [4]

A la Haye, ce 25 de Fevrier, 1678.

Je ne vous puis asses exprime l'obligation que je vous ay
de m'avoir escrit si librement vos sentiments sur la commission
de Monsieur de Godolphin. Je vous asseure en homme d'honneur que personne ne saura jamais rien de cette lettre, et que je
la bruleres selon que vous le desires. Et pour corespondre a
vostre franchise je vous direz naivement tout ce que je scay ou

---

[1] Unsigned. The draft is endorsed by Danby, ' Coppy of my letter to Prince
of Orange.' To this the Duke of Leeds has added, ' The Prince his answer to
this is dated 25th February. This is of very great consequence and desired to
bee burnt.' It will be noticed that in spite of Danby's request and William's
solemn promise the letter was not burnt.

[2] From the autograph letter in Leeds MSS., Packet 10, where there is also a
copy in a clerk's handwriting. This presumably is the letter which was to be
shown to the King.

[3] Endorsed by Leeds, ' Not used.'

[4] From the facsimile reproduction of the autograph letter in *Morrison
Catalogue*, vi. Plate 164 ; *Hist. MSS. Com.*, ix. 2, p. 455 ; *Letters*, p. 204.

pense en cette affaire, par laquelle le Roy ma mis dans un estrange embaras, voulant que je luy donnasse mon advis sur la constitution de son royaume, de laquelle je ne puis avoir [1] une cognoissance si particuliere d'en pouvoir donner [1] un jugement solide, comme il est necessaire dans une affaire de cette importance, et dont on me rendra en quelque maniere responsable si les suites n'en sont pas aussi heureuse que je les souhaitte, et ce qui est pourtant fort incertain. Et si elles ne le sont, je n'en aures pas seulement a repondre de vostre coste, mais icy, ou tout le monde souhaittant la paix avec une passion dereglee m'accuseroit de l'avoir peu avoir et l'avoir neglige, ce qu'ils fairont aussi s'ils savent la commission de Monsieur de Godolphin. Car pour ne vous rien celer, la plus part des Estats accepteroient l'eschange de Charlemont pour Tournay et peutestre viendroient a des conditions encore moindres de paix pour eviter la continuation de la geurre, et ce ne sera pas sans des pienes extremes que l'on les poura engager de continuer a supporter les frais qui sont requis. Pour les Espagnols, je ne scay de quels sentiments ils seroient s'ils estoient fort asseuré qu'en donnant Charlemont l'on auroit la paix sur les conditions cognues, car pour Luxembourg ou Ypre il n'y faut jamais songer.

Nonobstant tout cecy j'ay cru ne pouvoir donner en bonne conscience autre advis que j'ay donne au Roy, puisque je suis entierement persuade qu'elle est conforme a ses interest et ceus de cet estat, et qu'au retour de Monsieur de Ruvigni l'on poura tousjours voir jusques ou la France voudra venir et en suitte prendre ces mesures, puisqu'il est de la plus mechante consequence du monde qu'il songeroit seulement que l'on voulut en auqu'une maniere venir a des conditions de paix moindres que ceus qui ont esté proposes. Et il est certain que si le Roy ne les avoit fait proposer des les commencement les conditions les plus basses ou nous pouvions venir, et qu'au contraire sa Majeste eu demande d'aventage, comme vous savez que j'avois fort souhaite et extrem[em]ent presse, nous aurions deja la paix, ou si la France n'eu veu la grande repugnance qu'il y a a vostre cour pour entrer en geurre et le peu d'envie qu'il y a icy de la

---

[1] . . . [1] This passage does not appear in the *Letters* owing to the carelessness of the copyist or printer, who has omitted a complete line of the original letter.

continuer, ce qui me mest le plus en piene, car sans cela je vous asseure je ne serez pas des sentiments dont je suis.

Je crains aussi fort que la commission de Monsieur de Godolphin ne sera pas tenu secrette, puisque deja icy je ne les ay peu persuader qu'il ne venoit pas parle de paix, mais au contraire de geurre. Apres quoy je n'ay plus a adjouter a ce que je viens de dire que de vous prier de mesme que vous m'avez fait de ne montrer cette lettre a personne, et de la vouloir bruler aussitost que vous l'aurez leu. Je suis comme je dois,

G. H. P[rince d'Orange] [1]

[*To the Lord Treasurer*] [2]

A Malines, ce 5 de Mars, 1678.

Enfin voila les affaires venues a un point que j'avois tousiours apprehande, et que je vous ay si souvant dit et escrit. Il n'est plus dans le pouvoir du Roy de faire faire la paix n'y remettre les affaires qui vont se perdre, dont vous avez esté jusques a present les maistres ; mais quand on laisse eschapper l'occasion il n'y a plus de retour. Vous avez tante Dieu de ne vous estre pas mieus servi des adventages qu'il vous avoit donne, et peutestre avant qu'il ne soit long temps vous en sentires les effets aussi bien que nous. Au moins a present j'espere que l'on ne doutera plus que la France vous a tousjours trompe, et qu'une ville plus ou moins n'a pas empesche la paix d'estre faitte, n'en ayent jamais eu l'intension mais qu'il falloit bien dire quelque chose pour cacher leur dessin. J'advoue que la derniere tromperie qu'ils vienent de vous faire surpasse toutte les autres par le voyage de Monsieur de Ruvignis dans le mesme temps qu'ils marchent pour executer leur dessins.

Les affaires sont dans tel estat icy q'asseurement l'on viendroit a des conditions encore moindres que la proposition de Monsieur de Godolphin, mais il n'y a plus a songer maintenant a la paix, et il faut faire tous ces efforts pour regagner par la continuation de la

[1] Endorsed by Leeds, ' Prince of Orange, 25 February, 1677/8, which hee desires may bee burnt.' Again it will be noticed that the letter was not burnt.

[2] From the autograph letter in B.M. Add. MSS. 38849, f. 137, printed in *Correspondentie van Willem III en Bentinck*, part ii., ii. 237, and *Hodgkin MSS.*, p. 65. As Mr. Hodgkin points out (Add. MSS. 38849, f. 135), it is surprising that the Duke of Leeds did not print this letter, when he printed his reply (*infra*, p. 425), which acknowledges receipt of it.

*geurre ce que l'on ne peut avoir autrement. Les affaires commen-
cent a vous toucher de pres ; je vous prie de ne rien negliger a porter
les choses a ne point perdre de temps a faire tous vos efforts. Vous
vaires par la lettre que j'escris au Roy le veritable estat dans lesquels
les affaires sont icy. En ayent tant sur les bras il n'est impossible
de vous en dire d'aventage. Je me repose aussi entierement sur vos
soins, sachant l'application que vous avez pour le service du Roy,
et l'amitie que vous m'avez tant temoignée, que vous fairez tout ce
qui sera en vostre pouvoir pour moy. Je serez aussi longtemps que
je viveres avec beaucoup de recognoissance entierement a vous.*

G. H. P[rince d'Orange]

[To the Prince of Orange] [1]

London, 4th March, 1677/8.

I have received the honour of your Highnesses letter
from Malines of the 5th instant (new style), and am sorry to
understand by itt the ill posture of that country ; but I must
needs say that the ill conduct of the Spaniards both there and
here has contributed full as much to itt as the good conduct of
the French. They have not only been the cause why succours
have not been sooner sent from hence, but I am sure theire
negotiations here amongst the Parliament men has been a very
great cause of the slow proceedings to give supplys for the
necessary preparations for a war, and there is not yett one Act
in readinesse for any money, either to pay the troops already
raised or to give levy money to those troops which should bee
raised, and for which the comissions have been ready a good
while. However his Majestie will in a day or two give out
comissions for twenty regiments more, and procure money for
the raising of them as well as hee can.

I have inclosed sent your Highness a coppy of Mr. Hydes
OF THE 8TH INSTANT, N.S.[2]
letter to mee ∧ , which has not a litle surprised his Majestie, as
giveing him too just a ground to feare that the States will have
a peace upon any tearmes, and that itt will neither bee in his

---

[1] From the autograph letter in S.P. Dom., King William's Chest, 1. No. 14,
printed in *Correspondentie van Willem III en Bentinck*, part ii., ii. 238, and
Cal. S.P. Dom., 1678, p. 12. The draft of the letter in B.M. Add. MSS. 28054,
f. 162, is the basis of the version in *Letters*, p. 210. One or two alterations
have been made in it by the Duke of Leeds.

[2] *Infra*, p. 576.

power nor yours to hinder itt. For this reason his Majestie thinks itt highly necessary to know your Highnesses opinion in that matter, and desires that you will not flatter yourselfe in itt, being the most fatall mistake both to him and yourselfe which can bee made, if any wrong measure should bee taken of what the States will do in this point. His Majestie has comanded mee att the same time to lett your Highness know that the French embassador has told him that hee has power to signe the treaty sent by my Lord Feversham excepting Tournay, Valenciennes and Condé, and though his Majestie hath refused to propose any such thing as from himselfe, hee thinkes itt fitt you should know what is now offered since the takeing of Ghent; and his Majestie has likewise bid mee acquaint your Highness that the said embassador has assured him that the Popes nuncio did on the part of Spaine offer to quitt Tournay before the seige of Ghent.

This, together with what the Pentioner has said to Mr. Hyde, and his Majesties unprepared condition to give any present considerable assistance to your Highnesse, did move his Majestie to agree to the leaveing Tournay and Valenciennes out of the propositions of the peace, in case your Highness and the Spaniard should desire the peace on those tearmes ; and hee has a beleife that upon them a peace may yett bee had, before they have taken any more places, although they seeme very positive for Condé also. And his Majestie will by no meanes bee any judge of this matter untill hee heares from your Highnesse, being resolved on his part to pursue his late treaty of alliance with the States to the utmost of his power. But in case any of these propositions shall bee found necessary in the present conjuncture of affaires, hee desires by your meanes to know the mind of Spaine as well as of the States, because his Majestie will act nothing that shall not bee according to the desires of both ; and if such a peace shall bee judged more convenient then the continuation of the war, his Majestie does beleeve itt must either bee done speedily, or the tearmes hereafter will bee worse.

If anything of this kind shall bee approved, itt will bee of the utmost importance both to the King and your Highness that itt should bee kept very secrett, and that nothing should appeare but a cessation of armes, whilst the matters bee formally treated and concluded att Nimeguen. [1] Only his Majestie has thought itt necessary that what the French embassador has said to him should bee comunicated by Mr. Godolphin to the Pentioner, both because of the intire confidence your Highnesse hath alwaies expresst to have in him, and that itt comes so neare to what hee has proposed to Mr. Hyde, which hee thinks would bee a great service done both to the States and to your Highnesses interest, which hee is of opinion nothing but a peace can establish.[1] Mr. Godolphin is intrusted with this whole affaire, but his Majestie would have the secrett parts of itt returned only to himselfe, and not to any of the Secretaries of State, but that generall answers may bee returned to the letter your Highness will receive from Secretary Williamson, who your Highness will perceive by Mr. Hydes letter is not made acquainted that Tournay and Valenciennes, or one of them, is the interpretation of the Pentioners [2] expression of ' tant soit peu seure.' * [3]

What his Majestie has done as to the sending of troops to Ostend and Bruges your Highnesse will understand from Mr. Secretary Williamsons letter, so that I have nothing more to trouble you withall, saveing that your Highnesse may fully understand that if anything about the peace shall bee thought convenient, the proposalls for itt must proceed wholly from Spaine and the States to his Majestie, and that hee have no other part in itt then to use his endeavours att theire request to procure such a peace as they shall desire him to gett for them. And in the meane time his Majestie has comanded mee to bid your Highness rest assured that hee doth not nor will not loose one moment in acting all hee can for your assistance. I am, as becomes mee,

Your Highnesses most truly devoted servant,

D[anby] [4]

[1] . . . [1] In the *Letters* this passage is taken bodily from its proper place and inserted at the mark * below.

[2] Carelessly printed ' particular ' in the *Letters*.

[3] This mark is made by Leeds in the draft to indicate the transference referred to in note 1 above.

[4] The draft is endorsed by Danby, ' Coppy of my letter to the Prince of Orange, March 4th, 1677/8.' To this the Duke of Leeds has added, ' Quere Mr. Hydes letter relateing to this,' and later, ' which is of 8th instant, N.S.'

[To the Lord Treasurer] [1]

A Boom, [2] ce 27 Mars, 1678.

Le vent contraire a este cause que Monsieur de Godolphin n'a peu arriver que hier icy. J'ay envoye aussitost a Monsieur le Duc de Villa Hermosa luy donner part de sa commission, affin de savoir ses intentions la-dessus, et pour ne vous point importuner par une longue lettre, je vous dires en peu de mots sa response, que Monsieur de Godolphin vous dira au long, qu'il acceptera les conditions de paix que l'ambassadeur de France a propose au Roi, a savoir, Valencienne et Tournay demeurant a la France et le reste remis a l'Espagne selon le traitte que sa Majeste a fait avec l'Estat. Pour nous, nous fairons de mesme, et ainsi voila la paix faitte, si la France continue a la vouloir sur ce pied, de quoy je doute fort. Il est necessaire de le savoir promtement, et si elle ne se fait point que vous declaries la guerre sans plus de perte de temps.

Je ne vous dires pas les raisons pourquoy nous consentirions a une paix si pernitieuse, ny les movaises suittes qui en pouront resulter, puisque j'ay prie Monsieur de Godolphin de repasser en Angleterre affin de le pouvoir faire mieus que je ne pourois escrire d'affaires d'aussi grande importance. Ainsi je n'adjouteres plus a celle icy, que de vous asseurer que je suis comme tousjours entierement a vous.

G. H. P[rince d'Orange]

[To the Lord Treasurer] [3]

A Anvers, ce 31ᵐ de Mars, 1678.

Depuis le depart de Monsieur de Godolphin il luy est venu hier un expres avec une lettre de Monsieur le Secretaire Williamson, [4] *et comme je croiois qu'il y pouroit avoir des affaires pressées et qui me toucheroit j'ay cru ne faire pas mal d'ouvrir la lettre, laquelle je vous ranvoye icy joint, esperant que le Roy ne le trouvera pas movais. Et puisqu'elle ne contient que ce dont j'ay enchargé*

---

[1] *Morrison Catalogue*, vi. 418 ; *Hist. MSS. Com.*, ix. 2, p. 455 ; *Letters*, p. 214.

[2] Carelessly printed ' Bonn ' in the *Letters*.

[3] From the autograph letter in Leeds MSS., Packet 10, where there is also a copy.

[4] Printed *infra*, p. 603.

Monsieur de Godolphin, je n'ay rien a adjouter a ce que je luy ay dit, sinon que s'il y avoit moien d'avoir encore Tournay ou Valenciennes, se seroit une bonne affaire.

Selon les advis, apres que Ypres s'est rendu le Roy de France est retourne a Paris, et son armée se doit estre separe pour se rafraichir. Ils disent qu'il doit revenir pour le 21 du mois prochain, et puis se remestre en campagne, pendant quel temps je croi qu'il voudra voir ce qui arrivera de la paix. Quoy qu'il puisse arriver, vous me trouverez tousjours sans reserve entierement a vous.

G. H. P[rince d'Orange] [1]

[To the Prince of Orange] [2]

London, 3rd April, 1678.

I am not able to give your Highnesse any account whither those propositions for a peace, which were sent over by Mr. Godolphin, are like to take any effect, because wee have not heard anything from Paris since the Kings arrivall there ; but I am apt to beleeve they will not, because, since the takeing of Ipres, I find by his embassador here that they expect to keepe itt as well as Conde. On the other side I perceive by the last letter I had the honour to receive from your Highnesse that you give yourselfe hopes of saveing Tournay or Valenciennes, so that in my opinion the distance is too great betwixt your expectations to bee reconciled untill some further triall of the war, for which only wee are now prepareing ; and our greatest feares are that Holland will not bee obliged to those strict tearmes of continueing and supporting itt, which wee shall desire to bee assured of when wee shall bee ingaged in itt. In the meane time the King himselfe will not absolutely despaire of the peace, and that hee may bee prepared for itt has sent orders to Mr. Hyde to presse for something in writing both from the Duke de Villa Hermosa and the States, which may expresse theire desire to have him indeavour the getting such a peace.

I suppose your Highnesse is before now enough convinct how earnest the Duke of York is for the war, and how hee is resolved to go over with the army himselfe ; but I feare itt will bee the middle of

---

[1] Endorsed by Leeds, ' Not used.'

[2] From the autograph letter in S.P. Dom., King William's Chest, i. No. 15, printed in *Correspondentie van Willem III en Bentinck*, part ii., ii. 242, and *Cal. S.P. Dom.*, 1678, p. 91.

*June before you can depend upon any use of that army, and I
should bee glad to heare the comfort from your Highnesse that you
did beleeve they could then give life to a game so far spent. I am
sorry I am not in a capacity to bee one of that number that shall have
the honour of attending your Highnesse, there being none who would
do itt with more zeale to your service then*

Your Highnesses most obedient servant,

D[anby]

[To the Prince of Orange] [1]

London, 16 April, 1678.

Wee are so surprised here att the obstructions given by
the States to the generall treaty of alliance betwixt us, the
Emperor, Spaine and them, that itt has putt things amongst us
into greater uncertaineties then ever. And that which amazeth
most is to find them make a difficulty upon the hindring all
traffick with France, when Monsieur van Beuninghen has so
long insisted to gaine itt here, and (as hee saith) by the States
order to assure the King of theire entring into the same obligation, but pretends now not to have the same power when there
is most need of itt. Wee are not able to understand the meaning
of this att a time when my master is so ready to goe into the
utmost alliances against France which any of the Confederates
will come to, and to declare the war whenever those treaties can
bee perfected. But if itt should proceed out of an over-earnest
desire of a peace (which is said here to bee the cause) I am sure
itt is the worst way which can bee taken to have one.

In short I can assure your Highnesse that the fault will not
bee on our part if the war against France bee not pursued to the
utmost, and there hath nothing hindred itt hitherto, nor can
yett, so much as the suffering ourselves to bee still deluded by
France with daily expectations of a peace. And if that expectation could bee driven out of the peoples heads in your country,
itt would quickly bee taken out of ours by the effects which
would soone follow. Wee have received in print the proposi-

[1] From the autograph letter in S.P. Dom., King William's Chest, 1. No. 16,
printed in *Correspondentie van Willem III en Bentinck*, part ii., ii. 243, and
Cal. S.P. Dom., 1678, p. 118. Danby's draft is B.M. Add. MSS. 28054, f. 174.
Letters, p. 217.

tions for a peace made by the French att Nimeguen, which I am glad of, both for the ilnesse of them (which I hope can bee liked by nobody) and for the falsenesse of that part which concerns my master about Sweden, and which hath so exasperated him that hee is resolved to lett the world know the falsenesse of itt.

Mr. Godolphin will acquainte your Highnesse att large what resolutions are taken here with the ministers of the Emperor and Spaine, in case the States will not come up to what wee all desire joyntly, and which ought to bee a secrett, as well to your Highnesse as the States, but that wee are so well assured of your Highnesses being of our mind and not theires in the matter of supporting the war. And therefore in my opinion one principall thing to bee done by your Highnesse (who hath so absolute power upon the Pentioner) is to gett the thoughts of peace out of his mind, so as to make him imploy his time in the States to incourage them to the war, and to lett them see that itt can bee by war only that a tolerable peace is to bee hoped for.

The want of Monsieur van Beuninghen being sufficiently impowred has occasioned an adjournment of the Parliament to the 29th instant. And above all I must confesse that I lament the condition both of my master and your Highnesse, who have more difficulty to save your freinds then you would have to beate your enemies, if our Parliament and your States would do what they ought for the preservation both of themselves and the rest of Christendome ; whereas on the contrary I do verily beleeve they contribute more to the service of the French King, and to his successes, then the best army hee has could do. However, as the case is, the best I can hope will depend upon a cleare and good answer from Holland as to theire conjunction in this quadruple league ; and I doubt not but your Highnesse will putt your utmost helpe to itt, as I shall ever, to shew myselfe

Your Highnesses most truly obedient servant,

Danby.[1]

---

[1] The draft is endorsed by Danby, ' Coppy of my letter to the Prince of Orange, 16 April 1678,' and by the Duke of Leeds, ' Of very great consequence.'

[To the Lord Treasurer] [1]

A la Haye, ce 3 Mai, 1678.

Je ne vous dires rien de la maniere que nous avons adjuste les choses avec Monsieur Churchill, puisqu'il vous en informera. Monsieur Godolphin est arrive hier au soir. Je suis bien marri de n'avoir peu effectuer si promtement ce que le Roy desiroit, et ce qui est si necessaire. Monsieur l'ambassadeur Hyde et luy vous en informeront au long. Je n'ose pas vous en dire d'avantage. J'espere que de vostre coste vous faires ce que vous deves ; pour moi, je ne manquerez jamais du mien, ny d'estre toutte ma vie entierement a vous,

G. H. P[rince d'Orange] [2]

[To the Lord Treasurer] [3]

A la Haye, ce 4 May, 1678.

Monsieur,

Je n'ay pas voulu laisser partir le Sieur de Leeuwen de Leyde, deputé ordinaire a l'assemblée de Messieurs les Estats, et qu'ils ont trouvé a propos dans la conjuncture present d'envoyer en toute diligence au Roy, sans vous le recommander par ce mot, et vous prier de vouloir faciliter en cour les affaires qu'il a en charge. Je croy que vous estes assez persuadé de mon amitié, et de mes bonnes intentions pour vostre service. Il vous en renouvellera pourtant les assurances de ma part, et vous priera de vouloir croire comme une verité fort sincere que je suis, Monsieur,

Vostre tres humble serviteur,

G. H. Prince d'Orange.

[*To the Prince of Orange*] [4]

London, 17 May, 1678.

I am comanded by his Majestie to lett your Highnesse know that hee finds his affaires att home in so ill a posture, and his

---

[1] *Morrison Catalogue*, vi. 418 ; *Hist. MSS. Com.*, ix. 2, p. 455 ; *Letters*, p. 220.

[2] Endorsed by Leeds, ' Prince of Orange ; that hee dares not say more.'

[3] *Letters*, p. 222. Neither the original letter nor any copy has been found.

[4] From the autograph letter in S.P. Dom., King William's Chest, i. No. 17, printed in *Correspondentie van Willem III en Bentinck*, part ii., ii. 247, and *Cal. S.P. Dom.*, 1678, p. 177. There is a copy in a clerk's handwriting in Leeds MSS., Packet 10.

Parliament in so very ill an humor, that hee has not the least hopes of doing anything by his armes for the preservation of Flanders, so that hee desires you will take your measures accordingly, and that your Highnesse would loose no time in shewing your willingnesse to comply with the people of your country for the peace. His Majestie desires also that you will imediately use your indeavours with the Duke de Villa Hermosa to bring him to the acceptance of itt, both to prevent any exchange which may bee made betwixt France and Spaine for Flanders, and that his Majestie may thereby have the better ground for entring into the garrantees which will bee necessary for the preservation of what will remayne to Spaine, and cannot possibly bee saved otherwise ; and his Majestie gives you liberty to undertake for that garrantee as far as you please.

For what may relate to your Highnesses particular concernes, his Majestie has no doubt but they will bee fully preserved to your Highnesse, and hee is only troubled for the interests of the Duke of Lorraine, which hee will do all that lies in his power to remedy by the best offices hee can bee able to performe on his behalfe. I am as I ought to bee.

D[anby]

[To the Lord Treasurer] [1]

Honslaerdyck, ce 7 Juin, 1678.

Je vous aurois repondu par le dernier courier a la lettre que vous m'avez escrit par ordre du Roy du 27 du mois passe, si je n'avois cru qu'il estoit necessaire d'attendre le retour de Monsieur Beverningh avant que d'y repondre. Vous aures veu par la response imprimée que le Roy de France luy a donnée qu'elles son ses intentions.

Il ne me sera pas difficile a suivre le conseil que sa Majeste me donne de ne me point opposer a la paix, puisque je ne puis empescher le torrant qui nous y porte, voyant la desunion qu'il y [a] entre le Roy et son Parlement, et le peu d'assistance que nous avons a attendre de l'Espagne en cas de continuation de guerre. Tout cela ne m'empesche pourtant pas de croire que cette paix est la ruine de toutte l'Europe, surtout de l'Angleterre et de nous qui partiront les premiers, et il n'y a point de doute que la France viendra bientost a

---

[1] *Morrison Catalogue,* vi. 418 ; *Hist. MSS. Com.,* ix. 2, p. 455.

*son but de la monarchie universelle. Il n'y aura point d'alliance
ny de guarantie qui l'empeschera, et selon que je vois icy les affaires
constitues je ne scay si l'on voudra entrer en quoy que ce puisse estre
qui puisse choquer la France a l'avenir, mais demeurer unie avec
elle. Voila ce que l'on gagne par ce bel ouvrage que l'on auroit si
facilement peu empesche.*

*Vous savez que je suis accoutume de dire franchement mes senti-
ments ; je les dits a present aussi, et que sans un miracle du ciel
nous sommes tous perdus. Pour moy, aussi longtemps que je
viveres, je seres inviolablement attache aus interests du Roy, et
avec beaucoup de recognoissance entierement a vous.*

G. H. *Prince d'Orange.*

[To the Lord Treasurer] [1]

A Honslaerdyck, ce 20 de Juin, 1678.

Monsieur l'Ambassadeur Hyde vous informera au long de
mes sentiments sur l'estat present des affaires, et comme il les a
laisse icy. Je l'ay prie de parler au Roy d'une qui me touche en
mon particulier, qui est le payement du premier terme du dot
de ma femme, lequel est echeu il y a plus d'un mois ; et comme
j'ay grand besoin d'argent, j'espere qu'il n'y aura auqu'une
difficulte que je le puisse avoir sans plus de delai. C'est de vous
seul, Monsieur, que j'attens cette faveur, laquelle vous avez eu
la bonte de me promettre en partant d'Angleterre que vous
preniez cette affaire a vostre charge. J'espere donc que j'aures
bientost les effets de vostre promesse, et ce sera un surcroi
d'obligation que je vous aures, et m'engagera de plus en plus
d'estre sans auqu'une reserve absolument a vous,

G. H. Prince d'Orange.

[*To the Lord Treasurer*] [2]

A Honslaerdyck, ce 3 Juillet, 1678.

*Si l'on a jamais eu besoin de vostre credit, c'est dans cette
conjuncture, qui me paroit si favorable de redresser toutte les fautes
que l'on a fait, et remestre les affaires dans l'estat qu'ils doivent*

[1] From the autograph letter in Leeds MSS., Packet 10. *Letters*, p. 224.

[2] From the autograph letter in Leeds MSS., Packet 10, where there is also a
copy.

*estre pour le bien de toutte l'Europe, et particulierement de l'Angle-
terre et de ce paiis. Et comme j'ay informe au long Monsieur de
Godolphin de mes sentiments sur ce subjet, je me refereres entierement a ce qu'il vous dira, et n'y adjouteres que de vous prier tres
instament de faire tous vos effort de ne pas laisse eschapper une
occasion qui me paroit si favorable pour tous les bien intensiones.
Et comme asseurement vous en estes du nombre, je me persuade
aussi que vous n'y negligerez rien ; surquoy je me fie entierement,
et suis et serez tousjours sans reserve a vous.*

G. H. Prince d'Orange.[1]

[To the Prince of Orange] [2]

London, 1st July, 1678.

I am useing all the diligence imaginable to obey your Highnesses comands about that summe which is already due of the
Princesses portion, and I must confesse I did not thinke before I
understood itt by Mr. Hyde that the first payment had become due
till midsummer. But although that cannot bee paid till after the
time itt ought to have been, I do not doubt but wee shall dispatch the
payment of the whole before the time agreed for itt. ⊓

The scœne of things seeme to bee much changed by the
French refuseing of the townes ; and I will not trouble your
Highnesse with a large discourse how wee looke upon itt here,
because Sir William Temple will give your Highnesse that
account very amply. But in short I am confident that, in case
the King of France shall persist to refuse the surrender of the
townes (as hee hath done positively to the Kings embassador
att Paris), itt will wholly depend upon the States what measures
wee shall take here, although without an assurance of theire
maintaining 25 or 30,000 men in Flanders during the war, and
prohibiting the comerce with France, and not makeing peace

---

[1] On a separate slip of paper preserved along with this letter is written in
the handwriting of the Duke of Leeds, ' Quere Lord Godolphin what is meant
by what hee was to informe mee, because I have forgott. This belongs to the
Prince his letter of 3rd July, [16]78.'

[2] From the autograph letter in S.P. Dom., King William's Chest, 1. No. 18,
printed in *Correspondentie van Willem III en Bentinck*, part ii., ii. 259, and
Cal. S.P. Dom., 1678, p. 267. Danby's draft is in Leeds MSS., Packet 10,
and shows several alterations in the handwriting of the Duke of Leeds.
These alterations are embodied in a copy which is also in Leeds MSS., Packet
10. From draft or copy is derived the version printed in *Letters*, p. 226.

but by mutuall consent betwixt England and the States, you will gett us to nothing, and with those assurances I beleeve wee shall goe as far as you can desire.

[1] *I perceive your Highnesse will find Monsieur van Leewe disposed as well as can bee to all those ends you would have promoted, and in all his negotiations here hee has indeavoured to perswade us that hee is as great a promoter of your interests as any man. Your Highnesse may also rest confident that his Royall Highnesse is absolutely for the war.*[1] But nobody here will beleeve itt reasonable for us to ingage (who are out of the war) untill wee can bee assured that you, who are already in itt, shall not abandon us when you thinke fitt, insomuch that I take the whole work to lie in finding how to give us that assurance.

I shall leave all my owne apologies to bee made by Sir William Temple, and am sure hee will bee able to give your Highnesse satisfaction in all points which may have concerned mee in the past negotiations, haveing alwaies been and resolved ever to continue as I ought to your Highnesse,

Danby.

[To the Lord Treasurer] [2]

A Honslaerdyck, ce 26 Juillet, 1678.

Je ne vous informeres pas au long de ce qui c'est passe dans la negotiation de Monsieur l'Ambassadeur Temple, puisque sans doute il le faira plus exactement que je pouvois faire. Je vous dire seulement que tout autre que lieu [3] en ce paiis n'en seroit pas venu a bout, et que la confience que l'on a eu en sa personne a beaucoup contribue a la conclusion d'une chose qui est si importante pour les deus nations.

---

[1] ... [1] This passage does not appear either in the draft or in the *Letters.* Instead the draft reads, ' In the meane time you are to expect our doing all that is possible to persuade the King of France to give up the townes, and to that end my Lord Sunderland is going to Paris in a day or two ; but if hee cannot gett a certaine answer in ten daies hee is to returne, and I beleeve wee shall take that for a refusall.' After the words ' day or two ' the Duke of Leeds has inserted ' to try if hee can prevaile to gett itt done ' ; and before ' refusall ' he has written ' absolute.' The passage is thus printed in the *Letters.* Apparently the resolution to send Sunderland was dropped between the writing of the draft and the writing of the letter, and a change was consequently introduced in the letter for which there is no authority in the draft. The Duke of Leeds was probably acting in good faith in including this passage in the *Letters.*

[2] *Morrison Catalogue*, vi. 419 ; *Letters*, p. 228.

[3] The *Letters* read ' luy.'

Je me suis engage en un point vers l'Estat, que j'espere par vostre bonne conduite l'on ne me faira pas passer pour manteur. C'est que comme dans le traitte il n'est point specifie le jour que le Roy declareroit la guerre, je les ay asseurer que ce seroit immediatement apres l'onsieme du mois d'Aoust, qui est le terme fixe avant lequel il faut que la France se declare sur l'evacuation des villes. Et comme l'on ne peut donner autre sens au traitte, et qu'aussi c'est le butt pourquoy il a este fait, j'espere qu'il n'y aura auqu'une difficulte, ce qui m'a aussi oblige sans scrupule le prendre sur moy. Et si cela venoit a present a manquer, vous jugeres facilement quel prejuditie cela me causeroit icy en mon credit.

Au reste j'ay prie Monsieur l'Ambassadeur de vous representer diverse chose de ma part, a quoy je me refereres, et n'adjouteres a celle icy que de vous asseurer de la veritable passion avec laquelle je suis entierement a vous,

G. H. Prince d'Orange.

[To the Prince of Orange] [1]

London, 12/22 August, 1678.

His Majestie received your Highnesses of the 6/16 [2] with great satisfaction to find that you had gone with so much honour through so great an undertakeing as that att St. Denis, where you incountred so many difficulties. I hope itt is a good omen of what is to follow, and I can assure your Highnesse you will want nothing in which his Majestie can contribute to your good fortune.

The King has been much surprized with the hasty steps the States have made towards the peace, and has sent Mr. Hyde this day into Holland to acquainte them with his sense of itt, which in short is, that the French have not performed theire owne project att Nimiguen in Aprill, and consequently that the treaty betwixt England and Holland which was last ratified is in force, and ought to bee putt in execution. Mr. Hyde is also to lett

---

[1] From the autograph letter in S.P. Dom., King William's Chest, 1. No. 21, printed in *Correspondentie van Willem III en Bentinck*, part ii., ii. 274, and *Cal. S.P. Dom.*, 1678, p. 357. Danby's draft is in B.M. Add. MSS. 28054, f. 190. From it is derived the version printed in *Letters*, p. 232.

[2] Altered in the draft to ' 16/26,' and given thus in the *Letters*.

them know that if they shall do what they ought towards him and Spaine hee will certainely stand by them for the neutrality of Cleves and Juliers, and if they shall bee of his opinion, and declare so, viz., that the French have not complied with theire project of Nimeguen (haveing neither made any due declaration thereof before the 11th of August, and haveing made new demands from Spaine which were not contained in that project), his Majestie will also bee ready on his part imediately to declare the war against France. By this your Highnesse will see that the peace or war will wholly depend upon the resolutions of the States, which I hope your Highnesse will have in your power to influence ; and I am comanded by his Majestie to assure you that hee will do nothing in either but what shall bee by concert [1] with yourselfe.

Wee are not without expectation to heare of a second engagement, where I wish you may have had the assistance of our English batallions which were marching towards you, and of which you may speedily receive additionall recruits if the war continue. But, as his Majestie has already intimated to the States by Mr. Hyde, hee will not draw a war with France upon himselfe only to make an unsafe peace for Holland, and none, or a ruinous one, for Spaine, but will in that case rather withdraw his troops from those countries as fast as hee can. With all the prayers and good wishes for the happinesse and good successe of your Highnesse, I remayne, as I ought to bee,

D[anby] [2]

[To the Lord Treasurer] [3]

A Honslaerdyck, ce 2 de Septembre,[4] 1678.

Depuis mon retour icy j'ay este si fort occupe qu'il m'a este impossible de vous escrire. J'ay receu celle que vous

---

[1] The *Letters* read ' consent.'

[2] The draft is endorsed by Danby, ' Coppy of my letter to the Prince of Orange, 12/22 August 1678,' and by Leeds, ' The Kings message about the peace.'

[3] From the autograph letter in Leeds MSS., Packet 10. *Letters*, p. 234.

[4] In the *Letters* the date is given, probably in good faith, as 1 September. The figure, however, seems to have been written as a ' 1 ' and then altered to a ' 2.' The letter certainly was enclosed in Temple's of September 2 (*infra*, p. 497).

m'avez escrit par ordre du Roy trois jours apres l'arrivée de
Monsieur l'Ambassadeur, qui vous aura informe aussi bien que
Monsieur l'Ambassadeur Temple en quel estat les affaires sont
icy. Je croi qu'en peu de jours nous serons eclaire s'il y aura
geurre ou paix.

Pour mes sentiments, je les ay dit si plainement a Monsieur
l'Ambassadeur Temple, qui m'a dit de vous en avoir informé,
que je ne vous en importuneres pas d'aventage, et ne faires celle
icy plus longue que de vous prier de songer au payement du dot
de ma femme, et d'estre asseure de la passion avec laquelle je
continueres d'estre toutte ma vie entierement a vous,

G. H. Prince d'Orange.

[*To the Prince of Orange*] ¹

London, 30th September, 1678.

*I should not trouble your Highnesse att this time, but that I
am unwilling to lett passe such an opportunity without both presenting my humblest respects to your Highnesse and letting you
know that I am not negligent in my duty of takeing care for your
Highnesses money. I hope speedily to have twenty thousand
pounds in readinesse for your Highnesse, and should bee glad to
receive your comands to whom itt shall bee paid. Your Highnesse knows itt will bee necessary for him you appointe to bee
furnished with an authority to give an acquittance for the money,
and I hope to bee able to comply with your Highnesse[s] expectations
for the remaining twenty thousand pounds, either by the ways
proposed by my Lord Ambassador Temple or such other as may
bee as full to your Highnesses satisfaction.*

*I am sorry I cannot bee so happy as I esteeme those who will now
have the honour of attending your Highnesses, there being no man
more passionately then myselfe,*

Your Highnesses most obedient and most devoted servant,

Danby.

¹ From the autograph letter in S.P. Dom., King William's Chest, I. No. 22,
printed in *Correspondentie van Willem III en Bentinck*, part ii., ii. 282, and
summarised in *Cal. S.P. Dom.*, 1678, p. 435.

[*To the Lord Treasurer*] [1]

A la Haye, ce 8 de Novembre, 1678.

Sans doute Monsieur de Godolphin vous aura montre le pouvoir que je luy ay envoye de recevoir l'argent du dot de ma femme, et comme vous avez eu la bonte de me faire esperer que j'en toucheres a present deus paie, c'est a dire la moitie, j'espere que j'en poures voir bientost les effets, ce qui me sera un surcroi de tous les obligations que je vous ay deja, lesquels je n'oblires jamais, n'y n'en serez point ingrat. J'ay de plus une priere a vous faire pour Sir Gabriel Sylvius, a qui le Roy doit quelque chose, et pour quel subjet il est alle en Angleterre, d'avoir la bonte de le faire payer promtement, affin qu'il puisse revenir icy, ou ma femme a beaucoup besoin de son service. Je vous en serez fort oblige, et vous temoigneres toutte ma vie que je seres sans jamais changer entierement a vous,

G. H. Prince d'Orange. [2]

To the Lord Treasurer. [3]

A la Haye, ce 22 de Novembre, 1678.

Vous m'avez asseuré d'une maniere si obligente que je serois paye en peu de la moitie du dot de ma femme qui est echeu, que je croi que vous ne trouveres pas movais que je vous en renouvelle la memoire, vous priant d'avoir la bonte de m'en faire senti les effets, ayent a present grand besoin d'argent. J'espere donc que vous aures la bonte de donner les ordres necessaires affin que je soie paye promtement. Je suis marri d'estre oblige de vous importune a present de mes affaires particulieres, puisque vous en avez de si facheuses au Parlement, lesquelles je prie Dieu de vouloir faire tourner au bien de la famillie royale et du royaume. Quoy qui puisse arriver je ne changeres jamais d'estre entierement a vous,

G. H. P[rince d'Orange].

---

[1] From the autograph letter in Leeds MSS., Packet 10.
[2] Endorsed by Leeds, ' 8 November, 1678. Prince of Orange.'
[3] From the autograph letter in Leeds MSS., Packet 10. *Letters*, p. 236.

[To the Lord Treasurer] [1]

A la Haye, ce 13 de Janvier, 1679.

Je suis trop de vos amis de n'avoir apris avec un extreme chagrin les mechantes affaires que vos ennemis tachent de vous faire au Parlement. J'espere que vous en sortires a vostre adventage, et j'aures une joye extreme d'estre capable de vous y servir, et en toutte autre occasion ou j'en seres en pouvoir. De toutte les accusations qu'ils font contre vous celle d'estre dans l'interest de la France est la moins vraisemblable,[2] et tous ceus qui vous cognoissent savent asses le contraire s'ils veulent dire la verite. Pour moy j'en suis entierement persuade, et je croi pourtant d'en savoir quelque chose. Enfin vous est subjet a ce que touts les honestes gens sont quelquefois, c'est d'estre accuse a tordt. Je ne vous importuneres plus dans un temps ou vous avez tant d'affaires sur les bras, mais ay cru vous devoir temoigne la part que je prens en tout ce qui vous touche, comme estant sans reserve entierement a vous,

G. H. Prince d'Orange.[3]

To the Prince of Orange.[4]

London, February the 11th, 1678/9.

I should very unwillingly trouble your Highnesse with a letter untill I could write a full satisfaction in the matter of your Highnesses money, but I was earnestly intreated by my Lord Sunderland to recommend him to your Highnesse as one devoted to your service, and since hee has beene desirous of his owne accord to offer it to your Highnesse I hope you may rely upon itt.

When I had begun this letter I received a luckey message from my Lady Temple, which gave a freshe occasion of putting the King in minde of his former intentions to employ my Lord

---

[1] From the autograph letter in B.M. Add. MSS. 28054, f. 198, printed in *Correspondentie van Willem III en Bentinck*, part ii., ii. 289. *Letters*, p. 238.

[2] The *Letters* read simply ' vray.'

[3] Endorsed by Danby, ' Prince of Orange to mee, 13th January 1678/9,' and by Leeds, ' upon my being accused in Parliament.'

[4] From a copy among the Lindsey MSS., printed in *Lindsey MSS.*, p. 401. *Letters*, p. 240. The original letter is not in King William's Chest nor apparently in the archives of the House of Orange-Nassau.

Ambassader Temple as one of his Secretarys of State, and itt
has mett with so good successe that his Majestie has beene
pleased to call him over immediately. And although it bee not a
present revocation from his embassy, yet I hope that will
shortly follow, and his lordship become a more usefull servant
to your Highnesse here then hee can bee in Holland.

I am so tired this day with writing that I would have forborne
my Lord Sunderlands complement till next post, but that I
knew your Highnesse would bee well enough satisfyed with the
neuse concerning Sir William Temple, by whose assistance your
servants will bee very strong in this Courte. You will please to
lett this bee private, because there is nothing yet knowne of it
here. I am,

Your Highnesses most truly obedient servant,

Danby.

REMARKS

ON SOME OF

THE PRINCE'S LETTERS [1]

I have published more of these [2] then was necessary, because
I confess I was willing the world should see how long the correspondence had been betwixt the Prince and myselfe, and how
great testimonialls he had given of my constant adherence to
his service, as also to that of my country, in all the transactions
which had related either to the peace or to the warr with France.
But I do more particularly desire that mine to his Highness of
the 9th of February 1677/8 may be observed, as also his Highnesses of the 25th of the same February in answer to mine of the
9th, both which were desired to be burnt both by the Prince and
mee, because his Highness would not venture to have his known
to the States for fear of displeaseing them, and I durst not let
mine be knowne to the King my master for fear of his displeasure, by which appears the highest degree of trust [3] betwixt
the Prince and myselfe on both sides. [4]

Mine also of the 16th Aprill 1678, and the Princes answer to itt,
which is dated the 3rd May 1678, will shew both the Princes
opinion and mine att that time, that the King of France was
more beholding to the Parliament of England and the States of
Holland for his successes then he was to his owne arms, and as
the Prince desires that his of the 25th February may be burnt

---

[1] B.M. Add. MSS. 28044, f. 45, in a copyist's handwriting, with some alterations in the handwriting of the Duke of Leeds. *Letters*, p. 242.

[2] Instead of ' these ' the *Letters* read ' the Prince's letters.'

[3] The *Letters* read ' personal trust.' The trust appears to have been somewhat misplaced, as neither of the letters referred to was actually burnt.

[4] The *Letters* omit ' on both sides.'

443

for fearing of displeaseing the States, so in this of the 3rd of May he saies that he dares not say more.   And I desire it may be further observed that mine of the 9th of February, which I desired might be burnt (for fear as aforesaid), was but six weeks before my letter of the 25th March,[1] which justifies the differrence betwixt what I writt by the Kings command directed under his owne hand, and what my owne sence of things was at the same time.   But the malicious author who calls himselfe impartiall hath in this, as he doth in most things through his whole *History*, relate whatever he thinks may reflect upon the reputation of anybody whose actions he would blemish, not spareing King Charles the Second himselfe even against the best actions of his life,[2] and magnifying the honesty and actions of some men who were active in the greatest villanies in that reign, and for which their guilt made them flye their country and end their daies out of it.[3]

An instance of this appears by his quotation in that *History*[4] wherein he relates only so much of my letter of the 25th March 1678 as he thinks may have an ill construction, but leaves out the latter end of the said letter, wherein I desire Mr. Mountague to assure them in France that he beleives this will be the last time that he shall receive any propositions of a peace, as I tell him I beleive it will, so that he may take his owne measures as well as the Kings upon it.   But the impartiall author was afraid that this conclusion might qualifie something of the former part of the letter against mee, against whom he is enclined to vent so much mallice (altho I thank God I do not know him) that rather then not shew his spleen he does not only relate an egregious

---

[1] The *Letters* add here, ' on which I was accused, and mine of the 16th of April was not five weeks after the said letter of 25th of March.'

[2] Somewhat more strongly expressed by the Duke of Leeds in his ' Remarks taken out of Dr. Kennets *History of England* '—' Note through his book his constant reflections on King Charles, even on his best actions ' (B.M. Add. MSS. 28042, f. 113).

[3] The reference is obviously to Shaftesbury, whom Leeds mentions several times in his 'Remarks taken out of Dr. Kennets *History of England* '—' Page 289.   Note the expression of Shaftsburys uninterupted good services. . . . Page 284.   Note of Ashley for shutting Exchequer, &c., and yett magnified by Kennett in another place. . . .   His falsitys and mistakes in his book, and his wrong character of Shaftsbury ' (*ibid.*, ff. 112-5).

[4] On p. 368.

lye about Sir Charles Duncombs being saved by my vote, when he was accused in Parliament,[1] but tells what was impossible to be true if I had been his best freind in that House, for as he was discharged but by one vote, so it was equally every mans vote who voted on his side, and is impossible to be any more one lords vote then another, no majority being knowne till the whole House hath been counted. And as I then heard, Sir Charles prevailed with the old Bishop of Gloucester, who was going out of the House, to go in again, which if true helped him to that majority of one vote, and cann yett be no more said to be carryed by the bishops vote then by any other lord of the House who voted on the same side. So that it looks as if that author loved lyeing for lyeing sake, and therefore I hope he is not a divine, as some report him to bee.[2]

I must also desire that particular notice may be taken of the Princes letter of the 13th January 1678/9 upon the occasion of my impeachment,[3] wherein he declares his opinion concerning mee, and that of all the accusations the Parliament could have laid against mee that of being in the interest of France had so little appearance of truth that all those who knew mee did sufficiently know the contrary if they would speak the truth, but saies that I am subject to what all honest men sometimes are in being wrongfully accused, and concludes that letter that

[1] Cf. the note of the Duke of Leeds in his ' Remarks taken out of Dr. Kennets History of England '—' Page 743. Note the affaire of Duncomb, and his false and impossible story about my vote ' (B.M. Add. MSS. 28042, f. 114).

[2] ' Note the selfe-deniyng vote, page 389, and that Kennett would not now comend a Parliament for such a vote, for that hee is constant to his maxime both in Church and State to bee alwaies on the stronger side whatever the doctrine bee ' (ibid., f. 112).

[3] In the preliminary notes on which the completed ' Remarks ' were to be based the Duke of Leeds lays great stress on this letter, with which he associates Temple's letter of January 27, 1679 (B.M. Add. MSS. 28042, f. 112 ; 28044, ff. 1, 2, 12, 14). With the Prince's letter and the Duke's interpretation of it should be compared the views expressed by William in a letter written about the same time to the Earl of Ossory—' Danby . . . son refuge . . . Je sçay de quoy que l'on l'accuse en Angleterre et que je me fairois grand tord auprès du Parlement, si je le caressois fort, mais il me sera bien rude de néglige un homme qui m'a asseurément servi, quandt il a esté en bonne fortune. Mon amitié ne c'est jamais attaché à la bonne ou movaise fortune et je suis si grand ennemi de l'ingratitude, que j'aures bien de la piene à le témoigner à une personne à qui j'ay de l'obligation. Tout ce que j'espère est qu'il ne viendra pas à La Haye ' (Correspondentie van Willem III en Bentinck, part ii., ii. 291).

notwithstanding all this he remains without reserve entirely my freind ; and, as Sir William Temple does often say of his Highness, he was a man of sincerity and not compliment. [1] *And after he was King, upon my recovery from a great sickness, his Majestie writt mee the letter of 21th October 1694 out of Holland, which shews the continuation of his Majesties favour when his time was taken up with affaires of much greater importance.*[1]

[1] . . . [1] This passage is crossed out by the Duke of Leeds and does not appear in the *Letters*.   The letter to which it refers has not been found.

SIR WILLIAM TEMPLE'S LETTERS

TO THE

LORD TREASURER

[To the Lord Treasurer] [1]

Shene, June 7th, [16]74.

My Lord,

I thought to have waited on your Lordship to-day at Windsor, but having been hinderd by an indisposition, and fearing to misse that honor by the suddenness of your journey, I resolved to possess myself of the liberty your Lordship was pleased to allowe mee to trouble you this way when I had anything to bear mee out. I left his Majesty inclind to send an offer of his mediation to the States, which hee had before onely signifyed to the Prince. I thinke if hee continued that resolution, and charged the Dutch ambassadors with such a letter, taking notice that the rise of it came from them (as the King told mee it did from Monsieur van Beuninghen in the drawing roome), it might very possibly make way for some overtures from the States against my coming over, which might perhaps bee made better use of if they arise from them then from us. I hope their ambassadors have by this time had an audience, that soe I may goe over with some instruction grounded upon what they have heer to say, or else that my saying nothing there may bee laid upon their example.

Your Lordship will, as you thinke fitt, either give his Majesty the hinte of thees particulars, or else forgett the trouble of them, but will however pleas to beleeve that wherever I am you may there reckon upon a person that is with very great passion as well as very great reason, My Lord,

Your Lordships most faithfull and most humble servant,

W. Temple.

[1] From the autograph letter in Leeds MSS., Packet 5.

[*To the Lord Treasurer*] [1]

London, June 17, [*16*]*74.*

My Lord,

Though I remember very well what your Lordship pleased to tell mee about the miscarriage of your letter to the Prince of Orange by Sir Walter Vanes servant,[2] yett I thought you had resolved to venture another by mee, which I had hopes to receave before I wente, and I thought your Lordship would give mee leave to putt you this way in minde of it. I have not yett his Majestys letter to the Prince, nor can hope for it till Munday,[3] so as till Tuesday next I am like to bee in the way of your Lordships commands heere. I heare this day the plate is coming into the Jewell House, and will bee all ready for mee within two or three days, so as your Lordship will receave no further trouble in that pointe, nor my journey any delay beyond my necessary attendance upon his Majesties dispatches.

This day brought the news of a defeat given by Mareshall Turenne to some of the Imperiall forces, or rather those drawing together from the severall Circles of the Empire. Monsieur Pompones letter to Monsieur Ruvigny, which I just now read, gives account of about 5 or 600 killd upon the place, as many more taken, and the rest of the horse wholly routed ; but the infantry not beeing in the action onely retired in disorder towards Heidelburgh, where the Duke of Bourneville is drawing them again together, as the Francfort letters say, in order to some new action.

I hope I may rejoyce with your Lordship upon the advantages of health which you proposed by the Bath. The encreases of it can bee, I am sure, by none more desired and to none more necessary then to, My Lord,

Your Lordships most faithfull and most humble servant,

W. Temple.

[*To the Lord Treasurer*] [4]

Hague, July 31, S.N., [*16*]*74.*

My Lord,

Though this scene has yett afforded nothing worth entertaining your Lordship, beyond [the] bare relation which I know

---

[1] From the autograph letter in Leeds MSS., Packet 5.   [2] *Supra*, pp. 382-3.
[3] June 22.   [4] From the autograph letter in Leeds MSS., Packet 5.

you have what share you pleas of from my current dispatches to Mr. Secretary, yett I cannot bee content to live wholly out of your Lordships memory nor without making way to it by some such troubles as thees.

I finde the desire of peace in thees countrys very generall, and indeed the necessity of it very great ; but yett they cannot thinke of making any certaine steps towards it before they see the success of this great conjunction of the confederate armys, from which they expect either a battaile suddenly or a march into France. There is one ingredient more wanting towards it, which is confidence in some mediator, for they doubt both ours and the Suedes partiality, and feare the design is to breake the force of their present confederacys with Germany and Spaine, and when those are once disunited to leave both them and Flanders more at the mercy of France. If the King would have his mediation effectuall hee must endeavor to dispossess the Spaniards of the jealosy they have of us in this pointe, and to satisfye them at bottome that hee will not bee content to see Flanders in a condition of being lost or endangerd.

Having receaved no commands from your Lordship concerning Alderman Backwels pursuit heer, I have given him however my assistance in it just in the manner and degree hee desired, and hee tells mee now hee has been assured in my absence of the day by which hee shall bee satisfyed, which is yett longer then methinks hee had reason to expecte, unles they beleeve it is become a marchants business instead of the Kings.

I cannot but tell your Lordship upon what I finde by my last journey towards the Prince, though without successe, that they are not adventures to bee dealt with in pointe of expence by a person with the character and traine of an ambassador about him, and therefore whatever goes to the Prince while hee is in motion may, I thinke, goe by Sir Gabriel Sylvius, who is there without train or character that is taken notice of, that so I may not bee forced to give your Lordship troubles, or desire provisions that may appear very unreasonable to those who have not been acquainted with journeys, especially through campes, in that character, nor on the other may disappoint his Majesties service by beeing unable to performe them without the advance of such extraordinary supplys as I finde they will require. What his Majesty is pleased to allowe mee in this

*imployment will, I hope, appear to bee for his honor and service,
and I would bee glad not to trouble him for more, as has ever been
my custome ; but since I pretend not to make my fortune by thees
services, I may bee the better allowed to bee afraid of ruining it,
which I was last time so neere, that the confidence of your Lordships protection could onely have engaged mee to venture again.
I hope I shall deserve it, if by nothing else, at least by that passion
wherewith I am, My Lord,*

    Your Lordships most faithfull and most obedient servant,

                                  W. Temple.

To the Lord Treasurer.[1]

                        Hague, October 5, [16]74.

My Lord,

    *I have receaved from my wife, by last post, the knoledge of
your Lordship's favor to mee in the dispatch of my three months'
entertainment, and though it seems onely a point of justice, yett
it is such as I have been so little used to in some of my services
abroad, and the circumstances have been on your Lordship's parte
so obliging, that I consider it just as so much bounty, and am
equally sensible of your Lordship's favor to mee in it, as well as
in all the former concerns of this imployment, which I shall never
live to forgett, whether I live to deserve it or no.*

    *If I knew how farr your Lordship were consent to bee troubled
more immediatly with what passes here, or what use you could
make of a man upon this scene, your Lordship should not fayle
of beeing both informed and obeyed in the way and the degree you
desire yourselfe. Without this knoledge I thinke it becomes mee
best to give your Lordship neither many nor long interruptions
but to content myself with the desires of serving you till the occasions
arrive. I know what parte your Lordship pleases of my dispatches
to the Secretarys are at your mercy, and your Lordship knows
I hope, that you may alwaies dispose of a person that is with so
much reason as well as with so much passion as I am,* [&c.]

                                    W. Temple.[2]

---

[1] *Morrison Catalogue*, vi. 233, from the autograph letter.

[2] A long letter from Temple to Danby, dated The Hague, October 26, S.N.
1674, is printed in Temple, *Works*, ii. 311, from a copy.

[*To Sir William Temple*] [1]

9 *November,* [16]74.

Haveing this opportunity of writeing to your Excellency by my son (whose anxiety and desire to kiss the Prince of Orange his hande has led him to this course), I will make use of itt both to thanke you for the very great favour of your last letter, and to give you the best account I can of this embassy of my Lord Arlington's, under the confidence of that honour I have long been acquainted with in your Excellency. I take it to arise from a letter writt by the Prince of Orange to Monsieur Odyke importing some dissatisfactions in his Highnesse, which are thought both necessary to bee removed, and att the same time to come to a certaine knowledge of his Highnesses mind as well in relation to his personall good understanding with his Majesty as his resolutions as to peace or war. This, itt was believed, could be had by no other means than these two lords, whose acquaintance and interests are so great with his Highnesse, and itt had need to be so, because I heare they are limited to fourteen or sixteen daies for the obtaining of all this knowledge. As they goe without any character, so I believe they have no written instructions, but Monsieur Ruvigny is knowing both to theire journey and businesse, and expects the principall part of itt to be the procuring a speedy peace between those States and his master.

The towne discourse of this matter is that theire businesse is to conclude a match betwixt the Prince and the Duke of York's daughter; but I feare there is little ground for that beleife, though itt is not impossible that the same discourse may be made use of there as well as here, if the noise of itt can turn to any advantage. Whatever the event may bee, I do assure you that Monsieur Odyke valews himselfe no little upon itt, and I beg of your Excellency to have what information you can give mee when my son returnes; and if anything should happen extraordinary before the time of your giving my son any letter, I have commanded him to send back one of his servants with itt. I have bid him also beg the favour of your Excellency to bee presented by you to the Prince, and I doubt not of your kindnesse in doing itt to his best advantage; and in all other

---

[1] *Morrison Catalogue,* vi. 234, note, from an autograph draft.

matters during his stay I have referr'd him wholly to your advice and protection, for which I must beg your pardon.   I have only to add my wife's and my most humble service to my Lady, and to assure your Excellency of my being with great reallity, [*&c.*]

[*Danby*]

To the Lord Treasurer.[1]

Hague, November 23, [16]74.

My Lord,

    Since the last account I gave your Lordship of affairs on this side nothing has happen'd to change the scene.   I can onely observe, upon much conversation with the Prince since his returne, that both his dispositions and opinions looke very resolute towards going on with the warr, or obtaining such a peace as may leave Flanders as well as this state out of danger of any new invasions from France.   Yett hee professes so much duty and service to his Majesty that hee saies if hee may know what scheame of the peace the King proposes to himselfe hee will imploy his endeavors with the State and all their allys to bring it about.   In the mean time hee sitts every day in the Councill of State upon the framing a state of warr for the next yeare, and endeavoring the same fonds for it that was for the last.   What advances may bee made towards the peace or new impressions given his Highnesse when my Lord Chamberlain arrives, whom wee expect every day, I know not, but shall bee extreamly glad hee may succeed in bringing to passe what his Majesty desires or proposes to himself in the present conjuncture, and shall continue to give your Lordship the account of all such motions heere as are considerable enough to beare mee out and make your Lordship any amends for the trouble of them.

    I finde Monsieur Reede (who is much your Lordships servant, or at least makes mee many expressions of it becaus he knows I am so) has possest the Prince that his Majesty has absolutely promist to remit the three payments still due from this state upon the late peace towards the satisfaction of what his Majesty owes the Prince.   Your Lordship best knows what his Majestys intentions or engagements are in this matter.   I onely feare that with the possession has been given both the Prince and the States by

---

[1] *Morrison Catalogue*, vi. 233, from the autograph original; *Hist. MSS. Com.*, ix. 2, p. 449.

this reports of Monsieur Reede there will be difficulties attend those payments. And if either upon this regarde or upon his Majestys intentions they shall bee remitted or assigned to the Prince's payment, I should be glad it may bee done with the best grace that can bee on his Majestys parte, and with such circumstances as may value your Lordships good intentions and service in it towards the Prince, who, by his personall qualitys, cannot fayle if hee lives of making a great figure in the world, and deserving those dispositions your Lordship seemed to have alwaies of obliging him. If Monsieur Reede's reporte of his Majestys promise in this particular should bee ill-grounded, I suppose the best and softest way of handling this matter would bee by proposing the payments to bee divided, and one halfe applyed to the Prince's satisfaction, while the other comes into his Majestys coffers, at least untill by supplys of Parliament the King shall bee better able to remitt or satisfye the whole debt. This I thought might be fitt to represent once for all to your Lordship, whose intentions in this matter I shall pursue the best I can whenever you please to signifye them to mee, as well as obey any other of your commands, as becomes a man that is with so much reason and with so much passion, [&c.]

W. Temple.

[To the Lord Treasurer] [1]

Hague, November 27, S.N., [16]74.

My Lord,

Having by chance heard of my Lord Latimers coming over with the other company from England, and knowing how much care the late ill weather must have left his friends upon this occasion, and how possible it is the letters from Zealand may finde no passage over, I thought your Lordship would not bee unwilling to know from hence that I have just now certain advise of their having landed safe in Zealand on Sunday last,[2] and resolving to parte from thence towards this place to-day, so that if the weather bee not very ill I make no question of their arrivall to-morrow. I have reason to complain that your Lordship has taken no notice of us heer upon this occasion, whereas, the rest of the company having friends of their owne in this place, I take the care of my Lord

---

[1] From the autograph letter in Leeds MSS., Packet 5.   [2] November 15/25.

Latimer and his conveniences to belong of right to my wife if not
to mee ; and so wee shall take it upon us with your Lordships
leave, though it had been kinder to have encharged us with it.

If the Suede attaques the Duke of Brandenburgh, the Prince is
resolved immediatly to goe into the field to his assistance, and a
councill was held yesterday for the forming of an army to that
purpose. I am ever with equall passion and truth, My Lord,

Your Lordships most faithfull and most humble servant,

W. Temple.[1]

[*To the Lord Treasurer*] [2]

Hague, December 10th, S.N., [16]74.

My Lord,

   Since my last of this day sennight I finde nothing advanced
heere that can in the least answer any parte of that noyse and
expectation which this late journey has everywhere raysed. I am
more confirmed in the opinion I then had of what it would ende
in, and yett am certain of what I onely conjecturd before, that there
was nothing of that which your Lordship esteemed to have given
the first rise to it. This weeke has not past without many con-
ferences between his Highnesse and their lordships, but I beleeve
they have runn onely upon generals, and chiefly on those two heads
I mentiond in my last.

   For the pointe of the peace, their lordships have upon all occa-
sions declared they had nothing to say of it, unles they were putt
upon that discourse by his Highnesse or the ministers heere. And
though his Highnesse has thought fitt to say upon what tearms
hee beleevd this state would bee content with it, as the restitution
of Burgundy, slighting of Maestricht, and exchange of some towns
in the Low Countrys which wee had formerly talkt of, yett hee
profest, and I beleeve truely, that it was without any commission
either from the State or their allys ; and on the other side it is not
what they have any reason to imagine France will accept of, upon
the events of the last campania, and the appearances they have of

---

[1] A letter from Temple to Danby, dated The Hague, December 4, S.N., 1674,
is printed, from a copy, in Temple, *Works*, ii. 318, and from the autograph
original in *Morrison Catalogue*, vi. 234.

[2] From the autograph letter in B.M. Add. MSS. 28054, f. 28.

busying the House of Austria by the Suedes and the revolt of Messina before the next beginns. So that upon the whole, though I thinke the peace equally necessary both to France and to thees countrys, yett I esteeme it very difficult, considering the honor of that king and the allyes of this state that must both enter so farr into it ; so that I doubt another campania may overtake all partys before they fall into the right way of avoyding it ; for as to a suspension of armes, tis that the confederates will never admitt, becaus the subsidys paid by Spaine and this state to the Emperor and so many other princes must continue the same in that case as if the warr were still open.

This is the best judgement I can make upon this matter ; and upon the other of this late ambassy hither, or what else wee may call it, I will tell your Lordship in confidence, and begg it may passe so, that the Prince thinks it might very well have beene spared, if there bee no more in it then hee yett sees, and wishes it had been so, and will not bee less satisfyed the sooner it endes ; for besides that hee thinks whatever may bee designd towards the peace by it has been upon concert with France, and that the other motives have been a good deal personall to their lordships, hee apprehends a very ill effect from it to himself, by the mighty suspicions it rayses in all his confederates abroad and in the popular party at home, who will not bee persuaded such persons can bee sente over hither without greater errands, and the less is owned are the more jealous of measures proposed and taken between his Majesty, the French King, and his Highnesse. Upon the whole, and after all the feasts and compliments and play that this business has engaged heere, tis that which the Prince and those in his confidence heere wish were well over ; and I beleeve their lordships would not bee ill pleased that it were so too. But I say not a worde of all this to any but your Lordship, and desire you will accordingly use it.

This morning they went to Amsterdam, and returne not till Friday ;[1] *and my Lord Chamberlain told mee they had sett Munday next*[2] *for their returne, but I cannot beleeve it will bee soon. My Lord Latimer contents himself with the ill entertainments of this place beyond what could bee expected, and is the best*

[1] December 4/14.
[2] December 7/17.

liver that I ever mett with. *Your Lordship will never meet with
any that is more then I am and shall bee ever, My Lord,*

  Your Lordships most faithfull and most humble servant,

                                                W. Temple.

To the Lord Treasurer.[1]

                      Hague, February 19, [16]77 [? 1675]
My Lord,

  I receaved by last post the honor of one from your Lordship,[2]
with an enclosed to the Prince,[3] *which I sente away to him the
same day, and took care to let his Highnesse know at the same
time how much hee owed the happy issue of that affaire of his
money to your Lordship, and that, besides what was due to his
Majesty himself, your Lordship ought alone and justly to have
the thanks of it.* *I have since said the same to Monsieur Reede
and Monsieur Duelcon heere, who will represent it to his Highnesse in the same colors, and I take the Prince to bee so disposed
to receave impressions of this kind in what concerns your Lordship that I doe not at all fear any of another kinde, which you
seem to suspect may have been given him by another hande, for
I may assure your Lordship with greate truthe that all I have ever
heard from his Highnesse since my first discourses with him upon
his returne to this place has been not onely with great esteeme of
your Lordships person but also with much confidence of your
kindeness to him and to his affairs.*

  *For what you were pleased to mention in your last of the greate
secresie wherewith matters were carryed in England that concerned
the good intelligence between his Majesty and the Prince, I am
still of opinion there was nothing of negotiation in that journey
at all answerable to the noyse it raised, or the reflexions have been
made upon it since in all places, nor anything more then what
I mentioned in my letter to your Lordship by my son.* *I am sure
the Prince, since their returne, has assured all the ministers of
the Confederates heer that there was nothing in it but comple-*

---

[1] *Morrison Catalogue*, vi. 239, from the autograph letter. The date is there
given as February 19, 1677, and the same date is given in *Hist. MSS. Com.*,
ix. 2, p. 451. It is clear from the contents of the letter, however, that the real
date is 1675.

[2] This letter has not been found.

[3] Obviously Danby's letter to the Prince of Orange, dated February 2,
1674/5, *supra*, p. 384.

ment ; and little Moulin, that was inquisitive enough upon the first arrivall of those lords, has said often and publickly since that it was too much honor for him that so great persons should make such a winter journey for nothing but to destroy poore Moulin. And yett in that very point I doe not see that they had very great success neither, or that hee is not likely to bee provided for better than either he deserves or could have pretended to in any other country. I am very confident, too, that since their lordships return nothing has past from the Prince to his Majesty but upon the subject of his mediation towards a generall peace, and yett after all I will confess that if anything has escaped your Lordships knowledge there, it may much easyer have escaped mine heer, as having neither intervened at any of their conferences heer with the Prince, nor been acquainted with anything of their letters to him since their returne into Englande. Onely the Pensioner showed me my Lord Chamberlain's to him, wherein there was nothing but civilitys and generall expressions of his Majesty's good dispositions to this state and to him.

It is true that in this country nothing is more strongly and more generally believed then that this business of the Prince being made Duke of Gelderland, which has occasioned so great motions of late in peoples minds heere, was concerted between his Highnesse and those lords, and with great reaches and designs on both sides, and severall persons have beene to sounde mee upon it ; but as I disclaim any knowledge of it with great truth, so I doe with much confidence their lordships having had any parte in it. And yett I am very fallible, and your Lordship will know there, better than I can do heer, whether I am so in this particular. I wish what has been not onely talkt of heer upon this subject, but written over into Englande by marchants of Amsterdam, may not have some ill effects upon the popular beleef there as well as it has had heere, which would be another fruit of that journey as good as those your Lordship formerly mentioned. I knowe the course of that business of Gelderlande is given your Lordship as farr as you desire by Sir Joseph Williamson's from my letters, and his others from hence, which makes mee not trouble you with any particular accounts of it, for fear of abusing too much this liberty your Lordship has pleased to allow mee.

My wife beggs your leave for her humble service heer, both to your Lordship and my Lady, and for her acknowledgements of the great honor you are pleased to doe her son. Your Lordship has a right to him by so many severall titles that I hope you looke upon him as a servant that belongs wholly to you, and that you may wholly dispose of, though my Lord Latimer spoke of his stay there but for two months, when hee was pleased to take him over. I have given your Lordship too long an interruption, for which I begg your pardon, and at the same time your justice in beleeving that as I am with all the reason in the world, so I am with all the passion and truth that can be, My Lord,

Your Lordships most faithfull and most humble servant,

W. Temple.

[*To the Lord Treasurer*] [1]

Hague, February 22, S.N., [16]75.

My Lord,

I gave your Lordship too long a trouble by the last to beginn another now without the occasion given mee by the Prince in the enclosure of this pacquet, which carrys one to his Majesty upon the same subject and therefore by your Lordships hande.[2] From what his Highnesse has written to mee at the same time and in answer to that wherein I gave him the account I receaved from your Lordship of that affaire, I doubt not but you will finde in the Princes letter how little share anybody else is like to have in his acknoledgements or the sense hee professes to have of this service besides your Lordship alone, which is all I shall say upon this occasion.

His Highnesse has refused the Dukedome of Gelders, and thereby avoyded many ill consequences presaged by his best friends if it had beene accepted, and withall showed how little reason people had heer to beleeve that affaire any parte of my Lord Ossorys or my Lord Arlingtons negotiation ; and for my parte I beleeve the other secrets supposed by so many to have been in it may bee no better grounded.

---

[1] From the autograph letter in Leeds MSS., Packet 6.

[2] Temple's letter apparently enclosed William's letter to Danby of February 20 (*supra*, p. 385) with the accompanying letter from William to Charles II.

I know how important to his Majesty and the publick your Lordships time is, and will therefore give you no longer interruption then by the professions of my beeing ever, and as I am sure becomes mee, My Lord,

Your Lordships most obedient and most humble servant,

W. Temple.

[To the Lord Treasurer] [1]

Hague, March 26, S.N., [16]75.

My Lord,

Having by last post receaved the knoledge of his Majestys having named mee for one of his plenipotentiarys to the congress at Nimmeguen, and beeing very sensible of neither having deserved any such honors, nor at all pursued them, I could not but conclude I owe this in the same degree to your Lordship as I did that of my beeing designed to come over last spring upon the businesse of the peace between his Majesty and this state, and consequently that I owe you my acknoledgments upon this occasion, which I make your Lordship the more willingly and the more deservedly, becaus you are not pleased to take any care of letting mee know the obligations I have to you.

Since my last I have mett with nothing heere worth your Lordships trouble, nothing having stirrd beyond the paces made upon his Majestys mediation in the present quarrells. I suppose your Lordship is by this time satisfyed that I was in the right in all my conjectures upon those transactions heere that so much secrett and mystery was made of there. If you are not, I can now assure it you, and by very late and infallible testimonys I have had of it. I am very sorry I have not the honor of a cypher with your Lordship, how little occasion soever I might have of using it, but have commanded my son to say three words to your Lordship in a cypher I finde hee has with his mother, that I thought might bee fit for you to know.

I wish your Lordship all good health and good fortunes, and myself many occasions of expressing the constant passion wherwith I am, My Lord,

Your Lordships most faithfull and most humble servant,

W. Temple.

[1] From the autograph letter in Leeds MSS., Packet 6.

[*To the Lord Treasurer*] [1]

Hague, May 14, S.N., [16]75.

My Lord,

Having not lately either receaved any commands from your Lordship, nor met with anything heere to bear mee out in giving your Lordship any troubles, since I know you have what parte you please in the current dispatches and news which goe of course to the Secretarys hands, I have not given many of thees interruptions to your greater affairs. But upon the letters from England of the 27th past which came yesterday to my hands I could not but tell your Lordship how great a parte I take in all that concerns you, and how ignorant I finde myself growne of our affairs at home by some months residence abroad, for by all I had heard since my coming over till this last pacquet I thought your Lordship had receaved the most generall applauses that could bee given a Lord Treasurer for having found the Exchequer in so ill credit and brought it into so good, and more particularly for having with so much application and success recoverd that branch of it which I take to bee of all others the most important to his Majesty and his kingdomes—I mean what touches the satisfaction of the seamen and the certain charges of the navy.

This made it the greatest surprise to mee in the world to finde your Lordships name in the last journals of the House of Commons, but comforted mee with the hopes that it might have been brought in by your friends on purpose to give you so great and so honorable a marke as the approbation of your conduct by such an assembly or the clearing you from any common aspersions by so great a judicature would certainly prove. That I may hear of such an issue in this affaire are both my wishes and my hopes both for his Majestys honor and your Lordships, and for the satisfaction of your friends who are so farr as I am concerned in all that befals you.

The conferences heer with the Elector of Brandenburgh and Marquis de Grana will ende to-day, and within two or three more at furthest the Prince of Orange will goe into the field ; and I suppose the late talke of congress and treatys will give way for

---

[1] From the autograph letter in Leeds MSS., Packet 6.

some months to the noyse of the campania, the events whereof when they beginn will governe the motions and conditions of any peace that shall follow. In so busy a time as this must bee in England nothing from abroad can be worth attending, and I ought rather to aske your Lordships pardon for thus much trouble then encrease it any ways beyond the professions of my beeing ever, My Lord,

Your Lordships most faithfull and most humble servant,

W. Temple.

[To the Lord Treasurer] [1]

Hague, May 21, S.N., [16]75.

My Lord,

Though your Lordship will have found by my last of this day sennight how great a confidence I then had of your Lordships atchieving your late adventure with the honor and success that has attended it, yett I will confess nothing could have given mee greater satisfaction then the certainty I have since receaved of it by the last English letters. Nor ought your Lordship to value this victory the less, how just soever your cause has been, becaus among so many that have enterd those lists so fewe have come off with the honor you have gaind, or have had the fortune to joyne the good opinion of the people with the favor of the prince.

I should not, however, have troubled your Lordship in the midst of so much business upon this occasion had I not had greater compliments then my owne to make you, the Prince of Orange having upon the first news of it exprest a great deal of satisfaction, and desired mee to assure your Lordship by the first, Qu'il prenoit beaucoup de part a l'honneur qui vous estoit arrivè. His High-nesse wente the same day to the rendesvous of his army, which consists of 42 regiments of foot and about 7,000 horse, so that wee now expect news from the motions of a campania instead of a treaty. I am ever with equall passion and truth, My Lord,

Your Lordships most faithfull and most humble servant,

W. Temple.

[1] From the autograph letter in Leeds MSS., Packet 6.

[*To the Lord Treasurer*] [1]

Hague, June *11*, S.N., [*16*]75.

My Lord,

I *receaved this last pacquet an advice your Lordship was pleased to give mee by my sons hande,*[2] *which I cannot enough acknoledge the favor of, but may very justly say that it was a straine of kindeness more then ever I receaved from any of the Kings ministers in the whole course of my services abroad, and so I esteeme it, and shall never live to forgett it whether I live to deserve it or no. Yett nothing can bee more in my desires, or shall bee more in my endeavors. Though I am pretty well acquainted with the scene heere, yett I shall make the best use I can of the advice your Lordship was pleased to give mee, and to that ende will make a stepp to Amsterdam to-morrow for two or three days, which is the great center of the trade and money of thees countrys, and bee backe againe time enough to receave those commands your Lordship mentions.*

Wee have heer no news at present, but greate expectation from all sides very suddenly. The Prince is upon his march, having joyned a body of the Spanish horse, and if the French have, as is said, besieged Limburgh, will venture the relieving it at the hasard of a battaile. The two old captains upon the Rhine are dodging with one another, and looking for advantages which neither of them is very likely to give, and without which they will, I beleeve, bee both unwilling to come to any decisive action, the losse of a battaile beeing of so great importance to either of them. The Danes are beleeved heere to bee upon their march, which may soone give a beginning to a long warr between those northern kings. God bee thanked our finger is out of this generall flame, and sende our conduct and our humor to bee as good as our fortune, which has already turned the arbitrage of Christendome into his Majestys handes, and in a manner the trade of it into those of his subjects. Your Lordship ought to share in the honor and satisfaction as well as you did in the counsels that have brought this about, and the more for having had no parte in those which have raysed all the difficultys his Majesty has yett mett with in his reigne.

[1] From the autograph letter in Leeds MSS., Packet 6.
[2] This has not been found.

*I begg your Lordships pardon for this interruption of your
greater affairs, which I will not lengthen further then the unfeigned
assurances of my beeing ever with very great passion, as well as
I am sure with very great reason, My Lord,*

Your Lordships most faithfull and most humble servant,

W. Temple.

[*To the Lord Treasurer*] [1]

Hague, August 13, S.N., 1675.

My Lord,

Though I hear this is like to finde your Lordship in a
place [2] where leasure and ease ought to come in for a share in the
good effects upon your health wherein his Majesty and the kingdome as well as your servants are so deeply concerned, yett I could
not fayle of giving your Lordship an account, by the returne of
the yacht, which I esteemed the safest conveyance, how farr I have
gone in two conferences I have had with the Pensioner since my
arrivall. Hee is fallen so farr in with his Majestys thoughts upon
the tearms of the peace as to resolve to represent them to the Prince
with all the advantage hee can, and becaus letters are very dead in
comparison of discourses upon thees occasions hee has already
dispatched an express to aske leave of the Prince that hee may
attend him in Flanders, which hee is resolved to doe immediatly
upon the return of this dispatch, and wee propose three days hence
to bee the longest it can bee delayed. I have given his Majesty this
account in a letter to himself,[3] and entertain Mr. Secretary
Williamson by the pacquet in another upon those matters to which
I was pointed by my instructions, a copy whereof I enclose to your
Lordship.[4]

I sende likewise the best relation I can meet with heer of what
has past in the severall late encounters upon the Rhine, untill the
repassing of the French troops, which are said to bee about 12,000

---

[1] From the autograph letter in Leeds MSS., Packet 6.

[2] Danby was then at Bath.

[3] Printed in Temple, *Works*, ii. 335.

[4] This copy is still preserved in Leeds MSS., Packet 6. The letter is printed
from Temple's copy in Temple, *Works*, ii. 334.

men. *Montecuculi writes to the Emperors minister heer that hee
was passing the bridge at Strasbourgh to follow them, and seems
to promise himself that hee shall possess himself of Saverne and
bee able to take up his winter quarters in Loraine and the Dutchy
or County of Burgundy. The Loraine and Luneburgh troops have
a designe upon Metz, and thereby likewise to enter Loraine if they
succeede, or at least to drawe off a part of the army in Flanders
that way, and thereby give the Prince of Orange occasion of some
attempts in Flanders, where the French army continues yett very
strong.*

*I will not encreas your Lordships trouble beyond the very just
and sensible acknoledgments of so much favor and honor as I
receaved from your Lordship in England, and the unfeigned professions of that constant passion and truth wherewith I am and
shall ever bee, My Lord,*

Your Lordships most faithfull and most humble servant,

W. Temple.

[*To the Lord Treasurer*] [1]

Hague, August 23, S.N., [*16*]*75.*

My Lord,

In pursuit of what I writt to your Lordship by the captain
*of the yacht, the Pensioner receaved orders from the Prince to come
away to him immediatly, telling him that hee would meet him at
Brussels, and that hee expected him with great impatience. Whereupon the Pensioner parted from hence the beginning of this weeke,
but intended not to stay with the Prince above two days at most,
having no other business in truth besides what your Lordship
knows of, though hee had some in showe.*

*Monsieur Bevernings going with him was of another piece, and
designd onely to manage some intelligences in the town of Liege
who grow very weary of the French, and have an intrigue going
secretly in Flanders. So that I beleeve if the Prince undertake
anything suddenly it will bee that, though both the Imperiall and
Spanish ministers, as well as those in the Government heer, are
very earnest with him to attempt nothing that has any hazard in*

---

[1] From the autograph letter in Leeds MSS., Packet 6.

it for the present, but to content himself with keeping the French army in Flanders at a bay, that so they may not sende any very considerable detachements into Alsatia, where the game now plays, and in appearance very successfully for the Confederates. At least if (as both promise themselves) Montecu[cu]li should take Saverne and Haguenow, and the Duke of Lorain Treves, I doe not see what is like to hinder those two armys, either separate or in conjunction, to make some impression upon Loraine, the Franche Comtè, or other skirts of France.

I am assured heer, by some who I thinke doe not deceave mee, that the overtures of a private treaty with this state are renewed with great instance by severall hands, but originally from the Count d'Estrades of Maestricht ; but I beleeve they will keepe the great roade, which they take to bee by his Majestys mediation and in conjunction with their Confœderates as farr as they are tyed up by their treatys.

I sende your Lordship a copy of my secretarys paper of what is current, and should bee glad to know whether you would have it transmitted constantly to any of your servants, as it is to the Secretarys office each post. I am ever with perfect truth and passion, My Lord,

Your Lordships most faithfull and most humble servant,

W. Temple.

[To the Lord Treasurer] [1]

Hague, September 6, S.N., [16]75.

My Lord,

I have by this pacquet given his Majesty an account [2] *of the Princes answer by the Pensioner to those discourses I had with him at my last coming over upon the subject of the peace, by which your Lordship will finde the expectations of the Confœderates to have been something raysed by their late successes and the hopes they have still of greater before the yeare endes. To say the truth, while so great events are still depending between the armys in*

---

[1] From the autograph letter in Leeds MSS., Packet 6.

[2] Printed in Temple, *Works*, ii. 337. The King's reply, dated September 3, 1675, is printed in *Morrison Catalogue*, i. 188, and summarised in *Hist. MSS. Com.*, ix. 2, p. 450.

Alsatia, before Treves and in Flanders, I doe not see how it will bee possible to fixe anything that shall not bee subject to change by the consequences of a battaile or a siege as it may happen upon any of those scenes. All that seems at present in his Majestys hands is to hasten the congress at Nimmeguen so as no parte of the season may bee lost when, the campania ending, new accidents will not bee likely to arise and alter the plan that his Majesty may resolve to propose according to the state of affairs and condition of the partys at that time. This both the Prince and the Pensioner seem very much to desire, and have confidence given them by a Suedish commissary still residing heere that France will make no further difficulty of sending their ambassadors to the place of treaty upon assurance from the Emperor that Prince William shall bee deliverd upon the conclusion of a peace, and this there will bee no scruple of on the Emperors side. In the mean time I finde the Prince is resolved to venture for a share in the honor of this campania before it ends, and will endeavor either to take Charleroy, or by a siege of it to bring the French to a battaile, the event whereof may make great changes in the hopes or pretences of the partys.

Your Lordship will pleas to putt his Majesty in minde of giving order to have the project, or at least the heads, sente mee over of such an alliance as hee intends with this state, which both the Prince and Pensioner wish might bee concluded before the peace ; or if his Majesty thinks not that fitt, yett at least that all might bee adjusted beforehande, so as to bee signed immediatly upon it, for the Pensioner says that upon the French negotiations beginning heer it will bee harde to keepe a party in the state from endeavoring to renewe old measures with France, unles they finde them already taken and their security thereby founde with England.

I venture to sende your Lordship my secretarys paper of what is current heer, that by comparing thees accounts with what you receave from France you may the better ghesse at what has past in the late action. I am ever, with the greatest passion and truth. My Lord,

Your Lordships most faithfull and most humble servant,

W. Temple.

[*To the Lord Treasurer*] [1]

Hague, October 18, S.N., [1675].

My Lord,

 I have not since my last mett with anything heere worth your Lordships trouble, and should have little now to beare mee out, if I were not engaged to it by the acknoledgments of the honor I received lately in one from your Lordship of the 30th past,[2] *which I esteem much the greater from the circumstances of so busy a season on that side, and of so little as your Lordship had to command mee on this. I have taken occasion to give them warning heer of Monsieur van Beuninghen's imploying his talent upon any of his usuall projects when the Parliament meets, and am assured hee shall bee tyed up so shore by express orders from hence as shall restrain his naturall dispositions in this kinde. The Prince of Orange is, I heare, certainly upon his way hither, though hee has left his army with the Duke de Villa Hermosa to keepe the field as long as Count Montecuculi shall thinke fitt to doe so in Germany, for fear of any considerable part of the French army in Flanders beeing drawn that way. They say heer the Prince comes away becaus hee sees there will bee no action; but I doubt, by what has been whisperd a good while, that some discontents between him and the Spaniards may have made him weary of the field sooner then hee thought of.*

 As to what your Lordship pleases to enquire of the resolutions heer as to next summers warre, I doe not finde they are very forward in them, but have their thoughts more turnd upon the negotiations of peace, which they expect this winter, and will presse their Confœderates, I beleeve, very hard to a conclusion of it upon any moderate tearms whenever they meet as a congress. But if the warr lasts they will, I beleeve, rather act as seconds then principalls another yeare, having no other interests to pursue in it besides those of Spaine, who they thinke ought to make greater provisions for defence of Flanders then they have hitherto done, trusting so much in those of the Dutch as to neglect their owne. But on the other side I doe not thinke they will bee drawn separately out of the warr. Nor doe I finde they design any great navall prepara-

---

[1] From the autograph letter in Leeds MSS., Packet 8.

[2] This letter has not been found.

tions, beeing forced to have so many ships out upon the severall convoys of their marchants fleets, besides their squadron now in the Straits under de Ruyter, that wherever they thinke fitt to drawe them together they reckon to bee strong enough for any fleets that France is like to sett out.

All present discourses heer are about a congress, which his Majesty has revived by desiring the severall partys to prepare the passeports necessary, though the pointe of Prince William of Fustenburgh lyes still in the way. But though the expectation of any further action either in Flanders or Germany has been of late given over, yett I am apt to beleeve that upon the Princes leaving the field, and severall regiments of the Spanish forces beeing drawn back neer Anwerp for securing the Pais de Waas, the French may endeavor yett to engage the Duke de Villa Hermosa to a battaile, and perhaps with the more advantage the less hee expects it.

I ought to aske your Lordships pardon for this trouble rather then encreas it further then the constant and sincere professions of my beeing ever, with equall passion and truth, My Lord,

Your Lordships most faithfull and most humble servant,

W. Temple.

[*To the Lord Treasurer*] [1]

Hague, November 1st, S.N., [16]75.

My Lord,

At a season of so much business as I know this must bee I should not have given your Lordship any trouble from hence, had not the Prince desired mee to putt you in minde of the assignations of the money heere (applyed by his Majesty to the payment of his Highnesses debt), without which none of it can bee receaved, though about eight months are now past since the second payment fell due, so as the Prince will bee obliged by your Lordships hastning them over.

I found him at his returne hither much stancher in the business of the peace then even I had known him before, and his thoughts bente upon another campagne, having not satisfyed himself with the parte hee has had in this, which some difference of opinion between him and the Spaniards was occasion of. Hee thinks the

---

[1] From the autograph letter in Leeds MSS., Packet 6.

onely way of carrying on the warr another yeare will bee by acting with two separate armys in Flanders, one of the Spaniards and another of this states, and this hee hopes may bee compast another yeare. Hee beleeves the Lunenburgh and Munster troops will cleare their backs of the Suedes, and bee at liberty to act joyntly with the Duke of Loraine in another army towards Metz, and leave Alsatia to the Imperiall and Circle troops.

But after much discourse of all thees matters and the disappointments may bee found in most of thees reckonings, I finde his Highnesse would bee content to fall in with his Majestys project of the peace and quitt the County of Burgundy, in case France would add Douay and Tournay to the other fowre towns. And hee thinks what has been taken from the Suede of more value then those towns, even to France itself; and to say the truth I know not whether all the new conquests in Flanders would bee so considerable to France as the loss would bee of the Suedes possessions in the Empire, by which they are enabled to give a hande to France in all their quarrels with the House of Austria. I cannot take any good measure of the forces or designs of France, but I should thinke upon the whole (and without breaches among the Confœderates) that their best game were to make a peace, if they can restore Sueden, and not stand upon a town or two more or lesse in Flanders unless they have hopes of conquering all the rest.

This small light I thought might bee fitt to give your Lordship upon the Princes returne, which can onely excuse the encreas of this trouble beyond his Highnesses commands. It shall goe no further then the assurances of that constant passion and truth wherewith I am, My Lord,

Your Lordships most faithfull and most humble servant,

W. Temple.

To the Lord Treasurer.[1]

Hague, December 17th, S.N., [16]75.

My Lord,

I have of late given your Lordship no troubles, not onely in regard of the encreas of so much business drawne upon you by the late session of Parliament, but because nothing has happend

[1] From the autograph letter in Leeds MSS., Packet 6.

upon this scene of late either newe or of importance enough to bear mee out in giving your Lordship thees interruptions.

The dispositions both of the Prince and the state continue the same as to the peace with what I last represented them, those of the state still very earnest to have the peace, but yet so farr concerned in the security of Flanders as not to breake off from their allys unless another campagne forces them to other measures, or they should see such conditions offerd by France as would leave Flanders defensible, for in that case they would, I beleeve, not onely presse Spaine to the utmost but the Prince of Orange too if hee should appear averse from the peace upon such tearms. The Prince saies upon all occasions that hee can add nothing to what hee said at his first coming out of the field upon this subject, and what I then gave your Lordship an account of. Hee saies for his owne parte hee would bee content to make the peace upon what tearms soever the King desires it, but that hee cannot breake from his allys, without some satisfaction and security to them, and I finde his discourses runn much of late upon the necessity of a battaile to decide the tearms of the peace. This is all I can gett from the Prince, unles his Majesty shall thinke fitt to lett him know his minde further upon the last answer hee made upon the subject of the peace to what I was commanded at my coming away to discourse to him as his Majestys thoughts.

I hope Sir Gabriel Sylvius will bee able to goe further with his Highness, whose coming over hither to that purpose was I know in contrivance by my Lord Arlington some months since, and indeed not long after my returne hither ; but the traine hee then laid to bring it about, in another way, would not hitt, and so now Sir Gabriel comes to give his Highnesse the compliments of condoleance, and at the same time to discourse with him from his Majesty upon the business of the peace. I did not thinke it strange the King should thinke last yeare that my Lord Arlington might goe further with the Prince then I could doe, but to thinke Sir Gabriel Sylvius can is to beleeve the Prince knows neither of us, whereas I am very sure hee knows us both very well. Wee expect him heere every day, and I suppose the design is laid that hee may continue heere when I am at Nimmeguen, and fasten some negotiations betweene his Majesty and his Highnesse which shall bee carryed on by his and

*my Lord Arlingtons intervention, which I shall bee extream glad
of, in case they prove of better effect then those that were sett on
foote last yeare by the same hands and with the same intentions.*

*The Prince will take care of hastning the payment of what it
seems is still owing of the first tearme due from this state to the
King, and will depute some person to discharge the Exchequer of
what his Majesty intends to assigne his Highnesse for payment of
his debt, upon which hee hopes your Lordship will order the assignations to bee deliverd to the person so deputed, since without them
hee cannot pretende to any parte of that money from the state,
though parte of it is due so long since.   I aske your Lordships
pardon for so long a trouble, which I shall not encreas beyonde the
sincere professions of my beeing ever with equall passion and truth,*
My Lord,

    Your Lordships most faithfull and most humble servant,

                                    W. Temple.

[To the Lord Treasurer] [1]

                  Hague, December 20th, S.N., [16]75.
My Lord,

    *I have receaved from my son the notice hee had from Sir
Lionel Jenkins of your Lordships refusing to allow mee any equipage money towards my journey to Nimmeguen, in the preparations
whereof upon his Majestys orders I have already laid out a great
deal, and finde a great deal more will bee of absolute necessity to
appear at so great an assembly in any proportion to the ministers
of other princes.   Yett I will not pretend to breake any rules of
his Majestys parsimony by alledging either that my Lord Sunderland had three equipages in one yeare, though hee made but one,
which is very different from having one in two year and making
two, that after so long use of mine it can neither bee fitt for a new
appearance, or thereby fall into the same case with my Lord
Berkeley ; nor will I tell your Lordship how I might rather have
expected an encrease of my common appointment upon my keeping
a family at the Hague while I shall bee at Nimmeguen, nor how
great equipages other ambassadors intend to appear in, so as the
Spaniards heer say the Marquis de Manceras will have twenty
pages and the rest in proportion.*

<hr>

[1] From the autograph letter in Leeds MSS., Packet 6.

If I had money of my owne to make use, I should not bee in any paine ; but that cannot bee expected of [a] man whose father still keeps the estate of the family. Therefore I have onely desired his Majesty to pay mee the money hee still owes mee upon my last embassy, which my Lord Cliffords unkindeness kept mee from receaving then, though the case was thought so hard (beeing not of extraordinarys but my constant entertainment) that hee himself never made difficulty of paying mee the constant interest, so as it will bee so much saved to his Majesty, and so much lost to my little estate, since I reckon upon laying it out upon this occasion, beeing about the same summ I ought now to have receaved for my equipage. I begg your Lordships justice and favor in this necessary dispatch, upon which my orders from the Exchequer for the money are ready to bee deliverd, and no rules will bee broken, but I shall bee ever, My Lord,

Your Lordships most faithfull and most humble servant,

W. Temple.[1]

[To the Lord Treasurer] [2]

Hague, March 10th, S.N., 1676.[3]

My Lord,

Yesterday the Prince of Orange told mee hee heard from Alderman Backwell that nothing wanted towards his assignations expected out of England but sending over a power to discharge the Exchequer ; that hee had been considering to whom to sende it, and having made an acquaintance with my Lord Latimer heere, was resolved to desire the favor of his Lordship to take that trouble upon him ; that before hee wente out of towne to-day hee would sende mee his letters both for your Lordship [4] *and my Lord*

---

[1] A letter from Temple to Danby, dated The Hague, January 17, S.N., 1676, together with an enclosed paper of the same date, is printed in Temple, *Works*, ii. 354-7. The paper is also printed, with one paragraph differently worded, in *Morrison Catalogue*, vi. 235, and summarised in *Hist. MSS. Com.*, ix. 2, p. 450. A further letter from Temple to Danby, dated The Hague, January 24, S.N., 1676, is printed from a copy in Temple, *Works*, ii. 359. The autograph original is in B.M. Add. MSS. 28054, f. 38.

[2] From the autograph letter in Leeds MSS., Packet 8.

[3] Altered by Leeds to ' 1676/7.' This change suggests that the Duke considered the inclusion of the letter in his published collection. The endorsement, also in his handwriting, is " Sir Temple, 10 March, [16]76/7. About the Princes letter of atturney to son Latimer to receive his money."

[4] *Supra*, p. 387.

Latimer [1] *upon this occasion, which hee desired mee to enclose, and to begg your Lordships favor in the dispatch of that matter. This was the best excuse I could make for giving your Lordship an unnecessary trouble, for so I know all mine must bee that are not upon great occasions, since I finde by Mr. Secretary Williamson that your Lordship is troubled with all my dispatches at the Foreign Committee, and I know very well they are none of them worth repeating, though your Lordships time were of less moment to his Majesty and the publique then it is.*

One of my dispatches this post will, I know, fall in your Lordships way, and lett you see in how ill a posture the business of the congress seems at present to stand, which I am very sorry for both upon considerations of the peace and those of his Majestys honor, which is so farr and so publikely engaged in it. For my parte, I see no way out of this wood, at least on this side, and therefore must leave it to better guids. If his Majesty had mett with no better lights then mine, hee had not been so early engaged either in Sir Lionel Jenkins or Mr. Skeltons journey, which had been much better not begun then ended as they are like to bee if France continues peremptory in the refusall of the Lorain passeports.

Thees reflexions make mee thinke it necessary to tell your Lordship that his Majesty will bee often in danger of making false paces in this journey, if hee takes his measures with Monsieur van Beuninghen as a man in the secret, or of the humor and complexion with those who at present wholly influence the government heere. In the other side hee is thought a good deal steeped in another interest, and has made three or foure paces of late so contrary to the intention of those from whom hee receaves his orders that nothing continues him in Englande but an apprehension of his talent beeing troublesome in their assemblys heer.

I aske your Lordships pardon for this interruption, and begg your favor in furnishing mee with some occasions whereby I may expresse the truth of that passion wherewith I am and shall bee ever, My Lord,

Your Lordships most faithfull and most humble servant,

W. Temple.

---

[1] This letter has not been found, but a second letter of March 31 is printed *supra*, p. 387.

[*To Sir William Temple*] [1]

March 14, 1675/6.

I desire not to trouble you with letters when I can putt nothing in them that is worth your reading, and truly here has been very litle of late that I could thinke so. I must therefore rather intertaine you upon that subject you were pleas'd to write some time since, viz., 17th January. S.N., when you sent mee a paper which you had shewed to the Prince of Orange,[2] and desired to know if you had apprehended his meaning right, which hee agreed you had, and that hee had said more to you then hee should do to any other. That paper I then shewed his Majestie, and hee told mee I should in a litle time know what I might say to you upon the contents of itt ; but hee has been pleas'd to putt off that discourse till two daies agoe, and then hee was pleased to say :

1st. That nothing had made him desire the generall peace more then the inclinations hee has to enter into the stricktest freindship with the Prince of Orange, which hee cannot do so effectually till the peace is made.

2nd. That though hee will never advise the Prince in the least degree to faile any of his allies, yett hee thinkes that they who beare almost the whole charge of the war, and can gett nothing but blowes, may bee judge of what the King of Spaine ought to bee content with in order to the security of Flanders, when the States and hee [3] are both concernd itt should remaine under the Crowne of Spaine, so as hee conceaves that hee [3] nor the States ought not to bee suspected in this point to bee partiall to France.

3rd. That the Prince cannot give him a greater testimony of his kindnesse then to lett him see hee truly desires the peace, for that hee cannot bee ignorant how much itt is for his interest, and hee is certaine his Highnesses is no lesse involved ; and hee expresst with some warmth that his nephew should see the effects of the neare relation hee has to him, if hee finds the Prince remember that hee is his unckle, and that one of the cheife reasons which has brought him into some straights is the kindnesse hee had and has for his concernes ; but that the Prince must not forgett that hee was the

---

[1] From the autograph draft in Leeds MSS., Packet 7.

[2] *Supra*, p. 472, note 1.

[3] *i.e.* the Prince of Orange.

principall in this quarrell, and ingaged the King of France in this war.

4. *That hee had long heard of the proposition concerning the King of Spaines marriage with his neice in France, but that that matter would never do upon the conditions mentioned.*

5. *That hee was ever of opinion there should bee a convenient frontiere to Flanders, and hee does not perceive the King of France is unwilling to itt ; but hee does not wonder that Spaine is not forward for peace, when the war is made for them att other peoples charges, and all the venture is on the Prince of Oranges side, for the Prince in his owne particular can gett litle advantage by any successe the next campaigne, and if hee should loose a battle may bee of very ill consequence.*

I was resolved to acquainte you att large with the discourse upon every article, both that you might know as much as I do in this matter, and that you may make the best use of itt betwixt his Majestie and the Prince ; and I have power to lett you know that if you thinke fitt you may acquainte the Prince that this was the contents of the Kings discourse to mee upon that paper. I do not find wee are att all edified by Sir Gabriel Silvius his negotiation, but if hee is to stay there till hee can bring us the secrett of his Highnesses intentions I am satisfied wee shall bee a great while without his company. I beg of you to have my most [1] *acknowlege-ments returned to his Highnesse for the honour of his letters to mee* [2] *and my son, who shall bee diligent in obeying his comands and giving him an account of them, as I shall bee in preserveing with you the good opinion of my being, [&c]*

[Danby]

[To the Lord Treasurer] [3]

Hague, March 24, S.N., 1676.

My Lord,

Yesterday in the midst of dinner the Prince turned to mee of a sudden and told mee hee must needs desire mee to write to your Lordship and sollicite a pension for him. I said in the same manner his Highnesse had chosen the best time that could bee now all others were stopt. The Prince replyed, Well, however, you must

[1] A word is obviously omitted here.   [2] *Supra*, p. 387.
[3] From the autograph letter in Leeds MSS., Packet 8.

needs doe it, and though it bee but for threescore pounds a yeare, yett the King will oblige mee more by it then if hee gave mee a pension of threescore thousand pounds a year for myself. Upon this hee told mee twas for one Mrs. Dyke that the King knewe very well, and who had been his Highnesses dry nurse, and had a pension of 60ls. a yeare ever since his Majestys returne; that though shee bee not likely to live a yeare and hee had sente her over a hundred pounds, yett shee was not to bee comforted upon the stopp of her pension, and therefore hee must needs intercede for her, and should take it extreame kindely that shee might have that satisfaction given her upon his request.

His Highnesse desired I would not fayle to write this post, which I promist, and told him that I was sure the King would take a pleasure in doing it, if it were a thing worth troubling his Majesty; but if your Lordship did not thinke it was so, and that without it you were tyed up to generall rules, yett I knew your Lordship was so much a servant of his Highnesse that upon what hee had said I was confident you would pay a much greater pension yourself rather then make any difficulty upon it. His Highnesse said hee beleevd it, and therefore would make one of his servants write to Mrs. Dyke this post to waite on your Lordship upon this confidence.

I have written this post to Mr. Secretary Williamson at large,[1] and all that can concerne his Majesty to know from hence; and becaus what I have there written does so, I am sure your Lordship will meete with it, and therefore shall not repeat it and thereby needlesly encreas your trouble further then to tell your Lordship that the Prince reckons upon going into the field the 18th of next month, upon concert with the rest of the Confœderates, especially the Emperor, whose army is reckon'd upon taking the field at the same time, and both with resolutions of carrying on the warr this summer by other kinde of paces then they did the last. Upon all the dispositions I can observe on all hands I am apt to beleeve this will bee the bloudyest campagne that has been thees many years in Christendome. I am ever with equall passion and truth, My Lord,

Your Lordships most faithfull and most humble servant,

W. Temple.

---

[1] Temple, *Works*, ii. 385.

[*To the Lord Treasurer*] [1]

Hague, March 27th, S.N., 1676.

My Lord,

Having of late observed his Majestys name and offices to have been engaged by discourses of the foreign ministers about him, especially Monsieur van Beuninghen, in severall occasions wherein I knew they were like to fayle, and finding myself now engaged to imploy them in one wherein I foresee the same success, and wherein I confess I was unwilling, upon that reason, to expose his Majestys honor, which I take to bee concerned in every refusall, I have given Mr. Secretary Williamson this post an account of my carriage in that matter,[2] as well as of some foreign ministers, which I thought necessary both for his Majesty and his chiefe ministers to know. Therefore I have presumed to enclose a copy of that letter to your Lordship,[3] and should bee very glad for my better government heerafter to know your Lordships opinion both of what I have done and what I should have done in such a case.

I doe not trouble your Lordship with my secretarys paper of current news that goes every post, becaus I doe not thinke it worth your interruption ; but if your Lordship would have it sente to any of your servants, after the campagne or treaty beginn and aford more matter, I am sure your Lordship knows that or anything else will bee done upon your Lordships least commande to, My Lord,

Your Lordships most faithfull and most humble servant,

W. Temple.

[To the Lord Treasurer] [4]

Hague, Aprill 23, S.N., 1676.

My Lord,

I could not omitt the kissing your Lordships hands upon my wifes going over, beeing glad of any occasions to preserve myself in your Lordships memory and favor, which I must ever esteem among my best possessions. Yett I know tis idle in mee to trouble your Lordship at this time from a place so barren as

---

[1] From the autograph letter in Leeds MSS., Packet 7.
[2] Printed in Temple, *Works*, ii. 387.
[3] This copy is still preserved along with the letter.
[4] From the autograph letter in Leeds MSS., Packet 7. *Letters*, p. 247.

this now is, and by a hande that will entertaine you of anything that can bee worth your Lordships knowing from hence, though that amounts to no more at present then a commission which shee carrys over with her from a much better hande then mine, and from whom shee has it in charge to entertain no person but your Lordship upon it, the privacy of it beeing very much recomended to her. I shall say nothing more of that nor anything else that may encreas your Lordships trouble unnecessaryly and thereby lessen the reason I am sure you have to beleeve mee as much as any man alive, My Lord,

Your Lordships most faithfull and most humble servant,

W. Temple.[1]

[To the Lord Treasurer] [2]

Nimmeguen, November 6, S.V., 1676.

My Lord,

I finde by my wifes discourses, as well as by many other more materiall testimonys, how infinitely I am obliged to your Lordships favor in all that concerns mee. The lesse I can pretende to deserve it, the more reason I have to acknoledge it, and since your Lordships care of mee alone preserves mee from a certain ruine, to which a man in my condition would bee otherwise exposed by thees imployments, I may say with a great deale of justice and truth that I never receaved anywhere so much kindeness, nor ever owed anywhere so much service, nor could I ever bee more pleased then with the payment of it upon all occasions. I hope my son will helpe mee in making thees returns, who having the advantage of beeing young may live to acquitt some parte of so great a debt. At least I am content hee should endeavor it by so early devoting himself to your Lordships service as I finde hee is inclind of himself to doe, and so intirely as, for ought I see, hee will exclude all his other friends from pretending any right or share in him. I wish your Lordship would make that use of him as to convey any of your

---

[1] Endorsed by Leeds, ' Sir Temple, 23 Aprill, [16]76. A message from the Prince by Lady Temple about Lady Mary.' A further letter from Temple to Danby, preserved in Leeds MSS., Packet 7, and dated The Hague, June 24, S.N., 1676, is printed from a copy in Temple, *Works*, ii. 420.

[2] From the autograph letter in Leeds MSS., Packet 7. *Letters*, p. 249.

commands to mee by his hande, which might bee done that way without your trouble, and methinks in a place that furnishes so many things to all parts of the world there should bee something at one time or other that your Lordship had a minde to, in which I am sure you should have a good factor of mee, whether the King has a good ambassador or no. *

I doe not trouble your Lordship with unnecessary accounts of business from hence, knowing very well you have your share of the long and frequent troubles wee are forced to sende over by our dispatches to the Secretarys of State, and of those particular accounts I sometimes give his Majesty himself, of what either concerns the Prince of Orange or I judge not fitt to fall into our common letters. That of this ordinary having fallen to my share and beeing very long, I am to aske your Lordships pardon for that trouble as well as this, which I cannot ende without the sincere professions of that constant passion and unfeigned truth wherewith I am and shall bee ever, My Lord,

Your Lordships most faithfull and most humble servant,

W. Temple.

[*To the Lord Treasurer*] [1]

Hague, January 5th, 1677.

My Lord,

Though I am very unwilling to give your Lordship any further trouble from my stations heere then what you receave by the constant dispatches to Mr. Secretary Williamson (wherein I know your Lordship has your parte), yett finding the conjunctures abroad at present very nice, as well as very greate, I resolved to enclose to your Lordship a copy of what goes this night to the Secretary's office,[2] that your Lordship may thereby at least gaine some time of considering the matter of it before you meete it of course at the Foreign Committee. All I shall say upon it is that if his Majesty continue the desires hee has alwaies exprest of making the general peace, hee never had so favorable a conjuncture ;

---

[1] *Morrison Catalogue*, vi. 236, from the original letter.
[2] Printed in *Morrison Catalogue*, vi. 236, and in Temple, *Works*, ii. 426.

*and the prevention thereby of a separate peace, which would in-
evitably drawe on the losse of all Flanders and the dependance of
this state upon France, is a consideration to make it even popular
at home, as well as glorious abroad.   I know not what dispositions
his Majesty will meet with either in France or Spaine ; but in
my opinion the hazard of *Flanders on one side, and of a battaile
with the German army on the other, may make them both in a good
measure apprehend the events of next campagne, and the easye fall
into some temper that his Majesty may propose, who I am sure
is so well possest of the whole matter in all its extensions as to bee
able to drawe the scheam of an indifferent peace between the severall
interests with most likelyhood of succeeding, and his opinion as
well as his offices cannot fayle of going very farr in it on both
sides.*

*I will adde only one observation I made of the Pensioner's dis-
course to mee, which I thought not necessary to insert in my letter,
which was that where he complained of our indifference in what
became of Flanders or this state, and said Monsieur van Benninghen had powers to make what alliance soever with his Majesty
should be desired there.   He told me it was my Lord Arlington that
putt Monsieur van Benninghen upon sending for such powers,
and that it was done upon a measure taken beforehande (as the
Pensioner thought) between them two.   I suppose the ground of it
was both that the scheam of a closer alliance between the King and
this state was first drawne up when my Lord Arlington was at the
Hague this time two yeare, and that the thing beeing likely to bee
so very popular in England his Lordship was willing to bee the
author of it.*

*I begg your Lordships pardon for this interruption, which I
shall not lengthen beyond the professions of that hearty passion
and truth wherewith I am and shall ever bee, [&c]*

W. Temple.[1]

---

[1] A letter from Temple to Danby, dated The Hague, January 8, S.N., 1677,
is printed from a copy in Temple, *Works*, ii. 432.   The autograph original is
in B.M. Add. MSS. 28054, f. 46; and on f. 48 follows the copy of Temple's
letter of the same date to Secretary Coventry to which reference is made in
the letter to Danby.

To Sir William Temple.[1]

London, *8th January*, 1676/7.

My Lord,

I returne you my very kind thanks for your letters of the 5th and 8th instant, N.S., and for giveing mee opportunity of considering beforehand your dispatch of that post to Secretary Williamson. Besides my particular satisfaction by itt, I hope itt may have been of good use, for your Excellency will from Mr. Secretary Williamson by this post find yourselfe impowred to give the Prince a firme assurance that so soone as the peace shall bee made the King will enter into a defensive league with the States, and upon tearmes of declareing war against theire enemies in case such enemies appeare to bee the aggressors and that they shall not give the States satisfaction within a competent time to bee allowed.

In the debate of this itt was not thought sufficient that this league should only bee reciprocall, but (if wee could have contrivd the manner of doing itt) the designe was by the offer of this league to have gained some assurance from the States or Prince or both that in the meane time they should have made no seperate peace with anybody else, or att least not without consulting his Majestie in itt before any were concluded, and itt was once intended that this should have been writt. But the result att last was only that they should make no peace whatever which should bee prejudiciall to this intended treaty, so that whatever your Excellency can procure more towards our wishes you will have the meritt of acknowleged to you. In our debates I will informe you also that our humors seeming much more inclinable then heretofore to some faire accomodation with the States, my Lord Arlington began to valew himselfe upon the project hee brought with him when hee came last out of Holland, that being much to the same purpose which is now intended, and told us moreover that they then offred to insert in that treaty the assisting the King against any rebellion att home as well as invasion from abroad, but hee did not know whither they might continue still of that mind. Nor do I know whither anything of this hint will bee given to your Excellency; but if by your prudence itt may bee obtained, itt will bee the better that nothing has been said to you of itt, and methinks the haveing once offred itt should bee an argument of force enough

[1] From the autograph draft in B.M. Add. MSS. 28054, f. 44.

to gett itt now, and I am sure itt will bee highly acceptable to his Majestie.

Upon the whole, your Excellency may bee fully assured that there is nothing wee apprehend so much here as a seperate peace, and the expedient now fallen upon has no end so great as the prevention of itt, if possible; but because this expedient (if approved on all sides) does only secure us from any disadvantageous treaty with our neighbours, and does not remove the danger of Flanders or Sicily, his Majestie has further thoughts of makeing some schœme of a generall peace and proposeing itt. * [1] *If you have this from no other hand I desire your Excellency will say nothing of itt. The particulars of this schœme I do not know, nor thinke has the King yett resolved itt; but I am confident the designe of itt betwixt France and Spaine (which is the maine as to us) will bee the leaveing Burgondy to the King of France, and the restoring Sicily and such townes in Flanders as may leave itt with a good frontier; and all that I beleeve remaines doubtfull with his Majestie is what number of townes and which they should bee.* * [1] *And as I indeavour to give your Excellency all the information I can in these matters, so I beg I may receive your opinion and advice upon them, and particularly wherein I may bee any way serviceable to the Prince in these transactions, which I must needs tell you I do not take Monsieur van Beuninghen att all to designe, no more then my Lord Arlington (whatever either of them may pretend); and I make no doubt of the truth of what the Pensioner told your Excellency of the measures taken betwixt them two, for I am well assured of theire great intimacy here, although to mee van Beuning is alwaies blameing my Lord Arlington, and my Lord Arlington in Councell as constantly accuseing van Beuninghen.*

I have this further to acquainte your Excellency out of my infinite desire to have a perfect kindnesse betwixt the King and the Prince of Orange, that the King takes itt ill that although hee has severall times invited the Prince to a more private and more familiar way of writeing to him, the Prince will never do itt but in such forme as makes the King attribute itt either to his unkindnesse or his being afraid to bee thought upon better tearmes with him. And I had a

---

[1] These marks probably indicate that the part between them was to be omitted. It is impossible to say whether they were originally on the draft or were inserted later by the Duke of Leeds.

particular opportunity of knowing this upon the present occasion, when, asking his Majestie whither hee did not thinke itt would bee more respectfull to the Prince to give him the first knowlege of his Majesties good intentions towards the States before hee comunicated his thoughts to Monsieur van Beuninghen, his Majestie told mee what I have said about his writeing, and further said that hee was confident itt would bee all one to the Princes humor, and accordingly has spoke to van Beuning so much as relates to the seperate peace and the defensive treaty. I hope that in this particular also your Excellency will prove an happy instrument, for where your inclination goes so perfectly as itt does in this, joyned to your abilities, I can never despaire of good successe, no more then I hope you doubt of my being with the greatest sincerity imaginable, My Lord,

Your, &c.,

[Danby] [1]

[To the Lord Treasurer] [2]

Arnhem, January 28, S.N., 1677.

My Lord,

I receaved so much honor by two from your Lordship by the last post, of the 8th and 9th current,[3] that I can never enough acknoledge it, and therefore would not omitt the doing it in some parte by this very post, though my dispatch to the Secretary [4] with all that has passed since between the Prince and mee has not left mee any time to encrease your Lordships present trouble either with any of those particulars nor with the answers necessary to many parts of your Lordships letter. For the first I must therefore referr myself to my letter to the Secretary, for the other to the next post, by which I shall God willing from Nimmeguen entertain your Lordship upon those matters at some leisure, both with the confidence due to your Lordships encouragements in your last letter, and which I shall ever use without any reserve while you please to give me leave, and with the greatest sense in the world of what I owe your Lordship in so many kinds and what I shall ever make it my endeavor to deserve by all the testimonys that can bee of that

---

[1] Unsigned, but endorsed by Danby, ' Coppy of my letter to Sir William Temple in answer to his from the Hague of the 5th January 1676/7.'

[2] From the autograph letter in Leeds MSS., Packet 10.

[3] The letter of the 9th has not been found.

[4] This dispatch is printed in Temple, *Works*, ii. 447.

unfeigned passion and truth wherewith I am and shall bee ever,
My Lord,

    Your Lordships most faithfull and most humble servant,

                              W. Temple.[1]

[To the Lord Treasurer] [2]

            Nimmeguen, Aprill 12th, S.V., [16]77.
My Lord,

    Though I gave your Lordship a long trouble too late to renewe
it again so soon, and I am not apt to interrupt so weighty affairs
as your Lordships with the bare observance of common formes,
yett I could not avoyde at this time falling in with the crowde of
those that I know have given you joy upon your late honor,[3] *becaus*
I am sure there is none among them more concernd then I am in
all that can befall your Lordship of good or ill, and becaus I knew
nothing of this kinde more to bee wished then what has now befallen
you, both as the greatest marke of his Majestys favor and I thinke
(in all circumstances) of the greatest lustre hee could have given
you both at home and abroad.

    I wish your Lordship an encrease of all good fortunes you can
propose to yourself, with a continuance of good health and good
humor, and the generall applause of your master and your servants,
among whom there is none that can bee either with more reason or
with greater passion then I am and shall bee ever, My Lord,

    Your Lordships most faithfull and most humble servant,

                              W. Temple.

[1] Another letter to Danby from Temple at Arnheim is printed in Temple, *Works*, ii. 445, where the date is given as January 25, N.S., 1677. There is, however, a copy in B.M. Add. MSS. 9801, f. 83, which gives the date as January 25, S.V. As the letter clearly comes after Temple's of January 28, N.S., it seems probable that January 25, S.V., is the correct date. The same error occurs in a letter to Danby from Temple at Nimeguen, printed from a copy in Temple, *Works*, ii. 452, under date March 26, S.N., 1677. The autograph original, preserved in B.M. Add. MSS. 28054, f. 56, makes it clear that the date is March 26, S.V., and also gives the following very different version of the concluding paragraph : " I said what I could to satisfye him of his Majestys intentions in the thing ; but hee has a way of falling downright into the bottome of a business and is to bee dealt with no other way that ever I could finde, and onely said that when the Kings thoughts came to bee nearer his hee should bee glad to hear of them, and that hee would write to his Majesty when hee wente into the field, which I should bee glad to know if hee did accordingly."

[2] From the autograph letter in Leeds MSS., Packet 8.

[3] *i.e.* the Garter.

To Sir William Temple. [1]

Sheene, 14 June, [16]77.

My Lord,

His Majestie haveing been pleased to lett mee know that Mr. Secretary Coventry has (by reason of his infirmities) desired that hee may resigne his place into the Kings hands, but with hopes that his Majestie will either bee pleased to compensate him with 10,000 l. (as my Lord Arlington had), or give him leave to nominate a person to his Majestie who will give that summe and is fitly qualified for the imployment, and telling mee that hee had taken time to give an answer to the Secretary, I humbly besought him that hee would bee very circumspect in his choice, and presumed to nominate you to him as one who I was sure was capable of doing his Majestie the best service in that place; but I feared your condition was not such as could spare 10,000 l., nor did I beleeve that the fittest men would bee so willing to lay downe that summe as those whose capacities would bee rather fitted to fill theire purses then the place. The King was pleased to say that hee approved of your Excellency extreame well, and would bee willing to give you some assistance towards itt, but that his condition as to money was so low hee could not do much. I asked if itt was his pleasure I should acquainte you with thus much, and hee gave mee leave, but said itt should only bee as from myselfe till hee saw your answer, which hee bad mee to gett as soone as I could. I thought this matter of such importance as would deserve giveing my cosin the trouble of a journey to discourse you more att large upon itt then could bee well done by a letter, and who will informe you best what ways I conceave I may bee most serviceable to you in my sphœre; and in the meane time his Majestie has been pleas'd to promise that hee will neither treat with any other nor acquainte anybody (even the Duke himselfe) with his intentions concerning you.

My cosin should have been with you before now, but that upon the arrivall of Monsieur Bentinck I was desirous to know his businesse for your better information, and I hope his journey may bee improved for the advantage both of the Prince and our master. As hee came without any character, so I found hee had no comission to

[1] From the autograph draft in B.M. Add. MSS. 28054, f. 62, endorsed by Danby, ' Coppy of my letter to Sir William Temple, 14 June 1677.'

do anything but to give the King great assurances of the Princes kindnesse, and how much hee depended upon his Majestie to bee advised and directed by him in all things which related to the present conjuncture of affaires, assureing himselfe with great confidence that his Majestie would expect nothing from him wherein his honour might bee exposed. The King was very well pleased with this message; and if future steps bee made suitable to itt I shall not doubt to succeed in anything that you or I can desire to the Princes satisfaction, who has added so much to my former obligations by the kindnesses I have received from him by Monsieur Bentinck that hee has tied mee very firmly to his service.

His Highnesse was pleased to command Monsieur Bentinck to know my opinion whither itt might bee seasonable to aske the King leave for his Highnesse to give him a visitt in England when this campagne was ended, because hee had formerly received an ill answer to the like request. But I did incourage him to itt, and hee began with knowing of the Duke whither that request to the King would bee agreeable att this time, to which the Duke gave a very favourable answer, and the King a very kind one, viz., that hee should bee extreame glad to see his nephew, and hoped that by that time theire affaires would bee in such a condition as they might see one another without any inconvenience, which latter words Monsieur Bentinck feared might amount to that which was the last answer upon the same occasion, viz., after the peace was made. But I assured him, and know itt to bee true, that the meaning of that expression was only in relation to the sitting of the Parliament (which is adjourned to the winter), and the King does not thinke itt so convenient for the Prince to bee here in the time of theire sitting.

Although Monsieur Bentinck had no power to speake anything from the Prince concerning a schœme for the peace, yett I found the difficulty of the Princes side would still remaine about Burgundy, and that all other matters would bee easily adjusted. But I informed Monsieur Bentinck that wee found by Monsieur van Beuninghen the difficulty would not bee so great with the States, and therefore the Prince would do well to consider whither the King would not have reason to looke ill upon itt that his mediation should prevaile with the States in things wherein they should meet with

opposition from the Prince. I will tire you no longer att this time ; but you see itt is so criticall a one for acting the greatest concernes of Christendome that I long for your helpe with us here in so eminent a station as that of Secretary of State, wherein not only my inclinations but interest will so far carry mee to your service that you may bee sure there is nothing in my power which I shall not contribute to itt, being by all the waies imaginable desirous to shew that I am,
My Lord,
  Your Excellencies most affectionate and most faithfull servant,
                                                            [Danby]
  My most humble service to my Lady, who I hope will forgive my writeing this in her closett.

To the Lord Treasurer.[1]

                            Nimeguen, June 25, 1677.[2]
My Lord,
        If I pretended to make your Lordship the acknowledgments I owe for the honour and kindness of your last letter, this, I am sure, would be made up of nothing else ; and therefore when [3] I have assured your Lordship that no man could be more obliged than I was by it, nor more sensible than I was upon it,[3] *I shall tell you without more circumstance what my thoughts have amounted to upon the consideration of that proposal you are pleased to make me from the King.*
  His Majesty has always been so gracious to me, but so much more particularly in the opinion of my being capable of serving him in that station your Lordship mentions, that if I were worth that sum, or a greater than what, it seems, Mr. Secretary Coventry expects, I would the readiest in the world lay it down, either upon this occasion, or any other, or upon none at all besides the least signification of his Majesty's pleasure. But in the condition of my fortune, I will assure your Lordship, it were as easie for me to coin it as to find it any other ways, my father living still and keeping the whole estate of the family, and the best husbandry in such employ-

---

[1] Temple, *Works*, ii. 455, from a copy. *Letters*, p. 251.

[2] In Temple's *Works*, though not in the *Letters*, this date is given as S.N. This is almost certainly a mistake for S.V.

[3] In the *Letters* the word ' when ' is omitted, and the sentence is brought to a close with the word ' it.' The greater part of the letter is then cut out.

ments as mine have been reaching no farther than to bring the year about, unless upon the change of them some presents attend it. But if either it should arrive that I should outlive my father, who is very infirm, or that this employment should end with the presents usual to mediators, I shall leave it wholly to his Majesty to command me how to dispose of anything I shall thereby possess. And I am of opinion, upon the general prospect I have into the affairs of Christendom from my station here, that I shall easily see to an end of this employment as soon as this campaign is done, and that within three months after we shall either fall into the war or shall see a peace of one sort or other.

In either of these cases my figure here determines, and shall do so in Holland too if his Majesty gives me leave, and the presents of this last will bring something into my purse, though the other should fail, and go a little way towards what your Lordship proposes. And 'tis possible that in the mean while I may be a little necessary to his Majesty's honour in this very post, where it happens unfortunately that though the wise paces a minister makes may never be worth taking notice of, yet he lies every day in the way of making ill ones, and upon them lies as open both to his Majesty's dishonour and his own as, perhaps, in any employment of the world besides.

Upon Mr. Secretary Coventry's part in such a delay I can say little, but hope his Majesty will be content at the least for so long to keep a good servant instead of hazarding an ill one ; and I think the bargain between my Lord Arlington and Mr. Secretary Williamson depended a great deal longer than this can do, though, as I remember, it was but six thousand pounds that was given between them, and my Lord Arlington gave my Lord St. Albans ten. And if his Majesty should have a mind in the meantime to excuse himself from admitting any other, by saying he is engaged, he may very well do it upon what he was pleased to say to me in the year 1674 after the peace was made, when I made my acknowledgments as well as excuses upon the offer of going ambassador into Spain, that he intended me a better thing, and that though he was then engag'd yet when it fell again I should have it. I do not say this to lay the least hold in the world upon any such promise, but to furnish his Majesty with the excuse of being engag'd, if he should think fit. Otherwise it is a thing I absolutely forget, whenever his Majesty

*does so, and if he finds any other person he thinks fit to bring into
the place.* I shall, however, upon my return from hence, either in
any other station or in none, endeavour the rest of my life to deserve
his Majesty's opinion of being either as good a servant or at least as
good a subject as any he has.

I had a letter this last week from the Prince, wherein he was
pleased to give me some account of Monsieur Bentinck's journey
and return, extremely to his Highness's satisfaction as to all
that passed from his Majesty upon that occasion. As to your
Lordship's part he says these words, Je l'avois particulierement
adressé à Monsieur le Grand Tresorier, qui en a usé d'une
maniere si obligeante et luy a parlé avec tant de franchise que
je ne puis m'en assés louer. If he can succeed in the desires I
know he has, of making a journey into England when the campaign ends, I believe so much of his inclinations towards a peace
(that may in any kind save his honour [1] and the rest of Flanders[1])
that I am confident the King and his Highness, if they meet,
will take their measures together upon that matter and upon
the future conduct of both their allies. [2]

I ask your Lordship's pardon for so long a trouble, which yet
must not end without the repetition of all the most sensible
acknowledgments that can be made you for so much favour as
has obliged me to be for ever, and with as much reason as
passion, My Lord,

Your, &c.,

[W. Temple]

[*To the Lord Treasurer*] [3]

Shene, September, [*1677*]

My Lord,

*I could not returne your Lordship the enclosed without
acknoledging the great honor and confidence of the communication
your Lordship has been pleased to give mee of them, though it seems
I had no need of any new ways to informe mee what their contents
were like to be. I will not fayle, God willing, to wait upon your
Lordship this night in towne before you retire, and before I see
anybody at Courte, and I shall as little fayle all my life to seeke*

---

[1] . . . [1] These five words are omitted in the *Letters.*

[2] The *Letters* read ' affairs.'

[3] From the autograph letter in Leeds MSS., Packet 8.

the occasions of expressing the infinite sense I have of your Lord-
ships finding so many and so sensible way[s] of obliging mee.
I am ever with the greatest reason as well as the greatest passion
and truth, My Lord,

      Your Lordships most faithfull and most humble servant,

                            W. Temple.[1]

[*To the Lord Treasurer*] [2]

              Munday at 2 after noone [*July 1, 1678*].
My Lord,

      When I left Mr. Secretarys office I wente to the Dutch
ambassadors to acquaint them with his Majestys resolutions of
sending mee away to-morrow, or next day at furthest. They
seem'd pleased with it, and said that they had been discoursing
between them of Monsieur van Lewes going at the same time with
mee, *pour donner encore plus de poix a l'affaire ;* that they both
had agreed it would bee necessary, but that Monsieur van Lewe,
not having express leave, could hardly thinke fitt to doe it unless
the King should desire it, but in that case hee would. They
further desird mee that if I were of the same minde I would speake
to the King about it, and engage him in passing that forme. I was
glad wee happend to bee of a minde, and promisd them I would.

      In the rest of their discourse they both fell very hard upon the
conduct of France, and the treating them (the Dutch) *comme les*
plus grands duppes de la terre, and showd mee the Most Christian
Kings letter to the Duke of Lutsenburgh to withdraw his troops
from Brussels, and with his resolution to open the traffique with
Holland immediatly as upon a peace concluded, which letter was
dated the 25, and without the least mention of this new incident or
difficulty, whereas those from Nimmeguen of the 28 declare so
plainly nothing could bee done without inclusion of Sweden. They
told mee further that Monsieur du Cros had newly entertaind them
about the new incident, and told them hee saw no expedient unles
France could bee persuaded to put the Spanish towns into the

---

[1] Two letters from Temple to Danby, dated [Sheen], January 3, [1678], and
Sheen, May 18, 1678, are printed in *Lindsey MSS.*, p. 393, and Temple, *Works*,
ii. 462, respectively.

[2] From the autograph letter in B.M. Add. MSS. 28053, f. 121.

Dutch hands, which they said was still but a project to confirme the peace with Holland, who they knew either would not charge themselves with the defence of them or else would not bee able to defend them.

I have seen his Majesty and Royall Highnesse just now, and acquainted them with all this, and upon the last told them my owne thought rather of his Majesty as mediator to demand this deposition of the towns into his owne hands for the severall reasons I mentiond to your Lordship when I spoke to you of it. Both his Majesty and Royall Highnesse seemed very much to like it, and said they would thinke of it, and I desird them it might goe no further then to your Lordship alone till they and you should digest it together. For my parte I thinke at least it may bee worth so much consideration as for mee to bee instructed to know the Prince his thoughts upon it, as well as upon the whole conduct of this affaire in other particulars. For that of Monsieur van Lewe, his Majesty was very glad of it, and will desire him to goe at the same time with mee.

I begg your Lordship to putt his Majesty in minde of instructing mee either publikely or privately about taking a measure between him and the whole House of Luneburgh in case it must come to a warre. Some money must bee given them, but not to the fifth parte of the value in men. Besides their persons and scituation makes them so considerable in this affaire as to give the King a mighty influence upon all Germany. To-morrow at ten in the morning I returne to towne, and am ever,

Your Lordships most humble servant,

W. T[emple]

To the Lord Treasurer.[1]

Hague, 14th [July], 1678.

My Lord,

Though I am quite tired out with my motions thees two days past, and my long dispatch to Mr. Secretary according to a peremptory clause or two in my instructions, yett I could not but trouble your Lordship and myself with one worde to lett you know that I spoke to the Prince about Mons, and that hee goes away resolved

---

[1] From the autograph letter in Leeds MSS., Packet 10.

to relieve it or to fight ; that though his army bee weake, yett hee thinks Monsieur de Luxemburgh's is not much stronger ; that if Monsieur Schomberg should offer at joyning with him, his High-nesse reckons the Confederate army upon the Meuse may joyne with him ; that hee beleeves Mons may have provisions enough for about a fortnight, and so hee is resolved to putt all upon reliev-ing it.

I send your Lordship a hasty copy of my dispatch to the Secre-tary,[1] *that if it comes first to your hands you may pleas to com-municate it to his Majesty and Royall Highnesse before it comes to the Foreign Committee.*

I have consented to a French gentleman's going over in the yacht, who carrys a letter from Mr. Mountagu to the King [2] *and was brought to mee by a Dutch gentleman in this service and of my acquaintance, who was some time a prisoner in France and came acquainted with this de la Brontiere there, saies all the good that can bee of him, and showed mee this enclosed from Mr. Mountagu to him upon his coming in Holland.*[3] *The man seemes to bee one that use may bee made of, and desiring a passage in the yacht, and a worde of address to one of the Secretarys, I have chosen to give it to your Lordship, because anything of the nature he pretends to must perhaps passe through as few hands as is possible, and your Lordship may please to discourse with him about what hee mentiond to mee of Rochfort. A small pension or imployment may I suppose retaine him till by knowing the man, and seeing occasions abroad, you come to judge whether to use him or no. I am ever, and with as much passion and truth as any man, My Lord,*

Your Lordships most faithfull and most humble servant,

W. Temple.

My son is charged with puting a copy of a short cypher into your Lordships hands.[4]

---

[1] The copy is still preserved along with the letter. The dispatch is printed in Temple, *Works*, ii. 464.

[2] This letter has not been found.

[3] The enclosure is no longer with the letter.

[4] Endorsed by Danby, ' Sir William Temple, 1678, but no month. I find itt to bee July 14.' Another letter from Temple to Danby, dated The Hague, July 20, S.N., 1678, is printed in Temple, *Works*, ii. 469.

[To the Lord Treasurer] [1]

Hague, July 25, 1678.

My Lord,

Though the other letter bee of a staler date,[2] yett upon perusall againe I found some things in it that might yett bee proper enough for your Lordship to know, and so I am content to lett it goe. I shall onely heere give your Lordship joy of this great negotiation atchieved heere under your Lordships ministry, which is by all on this side esteemed a much greater then another upon which I have known some former ministers in Englande value themselves very much, though not very long.

That which may possibly make this the more acceptable to his Majesty is the evidence of so much art and industry, with which the French have of late used all the practises imaginable to gaine this state, upon the beleefe whereof I doubt they have not of late considerd us the more, or used us the better, for I doe not finde that the French ambassadors at Nimeguen tooke any notice of Sir Lionel Jenkins in the delivery of their late memorial there, or that hee came to bee possesst of it otherwise then from the Dutch ambassadors. And since I came over, Monsieur d'Estrades has written severall letters to the towns of Amsterdam, Roterdam, Dort and Leyden, to persuade them that the Prince of Orange and his friends will have no peace; and the Pensioner has surprized an originall letter from Monsieur Lovoy to Monsieur d'Estrades, by which hee bids them tell those of his correspondents in Holland, from whom the last advices came, that in case they gave him no better hee would certainly stopp their pensions. The best on't is, the sore seems to bee broken, and to have runn out, so as to leave the body more healthfull then before; and if God bless the Prince in this one enterprise of Mons, hee will bee greater heer then ever any of his ancestors were.

I suppose one good fruit more may arise from this affaire, which is that I doe not beleeve any man who sees the course of my dispatches can beleeve there is any more tricks in the busi-

---

[1] From the autograph letter in Leeds MSS., Packet 10, printed in *Letters*, p. 253. The version in Temple, *Works*, ii. 472, is taken from a copy.

[2] The letter of July 20, which presumably had been delayed.

ness, nor doe I see why men should bee sicke any longer of that imaginary disease in England after they are cured heere. And if the cure should bee wrought at a time in both places, the world is safe, lett peace or warr goe on ; if not, it may bee lost still, and I know not whether I shall have charity enough to pray God forgive them that prove the occasion of it. How all this is receaved in Courte or country I should bee very glad to know from your Lordship, for after all the compliments made mee heere upon it I am from thence to judge what I may have deserved by the infinite perpetuall trouble and application it has forced mee upon since I came over.

I sende your Lordship a copy enclosed of my dispatch this day to Mr. Secretary, which Mr. Meredith resolves to putt first into your Lordships hande. Whatever other observances you can receave from him I am sure will bee renderd your Lordship there and heer upon this and all other occasions, since hee can have learned nothing else in the house of a person that is, and ever shall bee, with a constant and equal passion and truth, My Lord,

Your Lordships most faithfull and most humble servant,

W. Temple.[1]

[*To the Lord Treasurer*] [2]

Hague, August 5, S.N., 1678.

My Lord,

I have your Lordships by Mr. Meredith, with the enclosed copys and instructions.[3] *I have given Mr. Secretary a large account how the whole thing which his Majesty desires of the Suedish ambassadors had been done before Monsieur de Cros arrivall, which has been signifyd to mee not onely by the Pensioner*

---

[1] Endorsed by Leeds, ' Of very great consequence. Note the joy hee gives mee of this treaty.' Another letter from Temple to Danby, dated The Hague, August 2, S.N., 1678, is printed from a copy in Temple, *Works*, ii. 479. The autograph original is in Leeds MSS., Packet 10, and on it the Duke of Leeds has marked for deletion three large passages, from ' I was the more surprised ' to ' relate to affairs here,' from ' The wise conclude all to be artifice ' to ' In the meantime,' and from ' and now lastly ' to the end. Effect is given to these alterations in a copy, also preserved in Leeds MSS., Packet 10.

[2] From the autograph letter in Leeds MSS., Packet 10, where there is also a copy.

[3] Neither letter, copies nor instructions have been found.

*yesterday, but this afternoon by a letter from the Suedish minister
heer to assure mee that Monsieur de Cros himself had receaved
letters of it heer since his coming, so as there was no doubt of the
Suedes going into the conclusion of the peace. They make as little
heer of the French doing so too, and I am glad to bee by this means
able to assure his Majesty without Monsieur de Cros journey or
mine to Nimeguen that the thing is done to his hande, and it lyes
now wholly in that of France to make the peace without any sort
of difficulty from Sueden.*

*Having been ill thees two days I am so spente with this days
business and dispatches that I am not able to hold up my head
any longer ; but I have sente Mr. Aiglionby my secretary over
express with this dispatch, and particular orders to attende your
Lordship and give you a perfect account of everything that passes
heer, and by whom I begg to receave any commands or any lights
your Lordship pleases to give mee heere. I will trouble you no
further then with the assurance that in all places and conditions
of life or health I am ever, My Lord,*

> *Your Lordships most obedient humble servant,*
>
> *W. Temple.*[1]

[To Sir William Temple] [2]

> London, 12/22 August, 1678.

My Lord,

My family has been so much indisposed, and myselfe also
by the disorder of itt, that I cannot write so largely to you as
otherwise I would do. But that defect will bee sufficiently supplied by Mr. Hyde, who I thinke is fully instructed to satisfy
both you and the States themselves of his Majesties firmnesse to
them and theire interests, if they desert not themselves ; for
the King and his whole Councill are unanimous in theire opinion
that the King of France has not performed his offers att Nimiguen in Aprill, and consequently that the treaty betwixt us and
Holland is in force, and ought to bee putt in execution, of which

---

[1] Another letter from Temple to Danby, dated The Hague, August 16, S.N.,
1678, is printed from a copy in Temple, *Works*, ii. 489. The autograph original
is in Leeds MSS., Packet 10.

[2] From the autograph draft in Leeds MSS., Packet 10. *Letters*, p. 256.

there will bee no failor on our part. You will find that Mr. Hyde is no lesse impowred to give satisfaction about Monsieur du Cros, who was so far from haveing any sort of comission from the King that if the Pentioner will permitt anything to bee proved against him of those private discourses, which you say in your letter of the 16th you had from the Pentioner, his Majestie will make him a publique example for the satisfaction of himselfe as well as the rest of the world.

In pursuance of these resolutions his Majestie has designed more troops still to go over instead of recalling any which are ordered to joyne the Prince of Orange, in case hee receive incouragement to itt from the States; but otherwise hee will call back all hee has there, and not ingage himselfe in a war only to make a base and unsafe peace for Holland, and either none att all or a certaine ruinous one for Spaine. As to the two resolutions which in the end of yours of the 16th you say you thinke the King must come to, viz., the measures with the Prince and the neutrality of Cleves, you will find them fully complied with; and as Mr. Hyde is fully instructed to the latter, so I can assure you of the former, and have comission to give that assurance to the Prince of Orange.

I have forborne saying any of those things you have desired mee concerning yourselfe, beleeving you will bee in better humor, and knowing by my owne experience that wee must beare with a great many wrong paces, to prevent worse which would follow to his Majestie in the hands of such as would pursue theire owne humours, and seeke theire ease att any hazard of our master or his concerns. His Majestie does extreamely wonder that hee has not yett received any account of the particulars upon which the treaty is signed betwixt France and Holland, nor what sort of declaration the French King has made for evacuateing the townes.

[Danby] [1]

[1] Endorsed by Danby, ' Coppy of my letter to Sir William Temple, 12/22 August 1678,' and by Leeds, ' Note, about the peace which was then newly signed betwixt the French and Dutch.' Two letters from Temple to Danby, dated The Hague, August 26, S.N., and August 30, S.N., 1678, are printed from copies in Temple, *Works*, ii. 496, 502. The autograph original of the letter of August 26 is in Leeds MSS., Packet 10.

To the Lord Treasurer.[1]

Hague, September 2, S.N., 1678.

My Lord,

I intended not your Lordship any trouble by this post after so long ones by the two last, but could not fayle giving a cover to the enclosed, which was sente mee from the Prince,[2] who will, I doubt not, himself have given your Lordship an account of the state of this country in answer to what you say of the French thinking themselves secure of them. The Prince said to mee upon it that hee thought them lesse so then they have beene any time this eight months past, and this is not the first or second time I have observd them to play their game in England by saying they are secure of the Dutch, and in Holland by saying they are secure of us.

There was not one towne in all the provinces that stucke to Amsterdam when Monsieur Valkeneer upon Wednesday [3] (when the resolution was resumed of not ratifying without Spaine) would faine have spoyled it by offering some new temper in it, and his Highnesse does not doubt of the States beeing firme in that resolution. I am ever with the greatest passion and truth, My Lord,

Your Lordships most faithfull and humble servant,

W. Temple.[4]

To the Lord Treasurer.[5]

Hague, September 21, S.N., 1678.

My Lord,

I shall need give your Lordship no other trouble upon Mr. Hides going away then to refer his Majesty and your Lordship to

---

[1] From the autograph letter in Leeds MSS., Packet 10. *Letters*, p. 258.

[2] The Prince's letter of the same date, printed *supra*, p. 438.

[3] August 21/31.

[4] A letter from Temple to Danby, dated The Hague, September 20, S.N., 1678, is printed from a copy in Temple, *Works*, ii. 505. The autograph original is in Leeds MSS., Packet 10. On it the Duke of Leeds has marked for deletion the passage from " Your Lordship will have observed " to " business or visits of ceremony " ; and effect is given to his directions in a copy, also preserved in Leeds MSS., Packet 10. The original letter is endorsed by Leeds, ' This is of infinite importance in many particulars, and must bee particularly remarked in my narrative. Of very great consequence [indecipherable] States declaration of theire oweing the restitution of theire townes, &c., to our King.'

[5] From the autograph letter in Leeds MSS., Packet 10.

him for all the lights that you can receave from this place, for besides all the paces of business that have been made heere since his coming over in perfect concert between us (notwithstanding Mr. Secretary Williamsons care to have had it otherwise) wee have discourst over all things that can concerne his Majestys service on this side so fully and with so much confidence, that I am sure I can add nothing to the informations hee will bee able to give you, both more usefully and more agreeably then your Lordship can receave them this way ; so that I have nothing left but to assure your Lordship of my being ever with equall passion and truth, My Lord,

Your Lordships most faithfull and most humble servant,

W. Temple.[1]

To the Lord Treasurer.[2]

Hague, October 28, [16]78.

My Lord,

By my letter this ordinary to Mr. Secretary Williamson your Lordship will see plainely the measures that France has resolved to take heer upon the peace, both with the Prince and the state, their courte to one and neglects to the other, and withall the manner this state hitherto receaves it and resolves to live with his Majesty upon thees occasions.

The French ambassador is very busy in his intrigues with severall of the great towns, especially with that of Amsterdam ; but I doe not yet finde hee gaines any further ground then what I alwaies reckond upon, and acquainted your Lordship with in my former letters concerning Monsieur Valkeneer and the parte hee had taken to act in that towne opposite to the Prince and the other towns of this province. But on the contrary, thees paces of France since the peace, delaying the evacuation of Mastricht, demanding Hassels and the other places of Liege (that may in a manner block up that place), seazing Aix [3] and the Dutchy of Juliers, threatning that of Cleves, Colen, and other places upon the Lower Rhine, give the other provinces, and the

---

[1] A letter from Temple to Danby, dated The Hague, October 7, S.N., 1678, is printed from a copy in Temple, *Works*, ii. 510. The original has not been found.

[2] From the autograph letter in Leeds MSS., Packet 10. *Letters*, p. 260.

[3] Carelessly printed ' Aeth ' in the *Letters*.

towns of this, occasion to speake very harde of those of Amsterdam for pressing the peace so violently and without regard either to the honor of their treatys or the safety of their frontiers, so as I beleeve the ill talent of the other towns of this province against the present goverment [1] of the affairs in Amsterdam will breake out upon the first occasion, and very possibly next session of the States of Holland, upon proposall of his Majestys guarentie and this states to bee given the Spanish peace, if the town of Amsterdam should at all oppose it.

I thought it not amiss to put your Lordship in minde whether for satisfaction of the House of Commons when it meets (if it bee necessary), in pointe of the peace and all transactions on this side since last session, it might bee fit for Mr. Secretary, as in confidence to some of the leading members, to communicate severall of Mr. Hides dispatches and mine, by which it will appeare so plainely how farr his Majesty would have enterd into the warr ; how impossible it was to engage this state in continuing it, if France accomplisht the tearms they had accepted of the peace ; how France still pursues the design of beeing at length master of this country as well as Flanders, by invading the Lower Rhine, the towns whereof are the very keys of thees provinces ; and how they attend onely his Majestys and thees states beeing disarmed, to give them the opportunity of accomplishing it by the weakeness of Spaine and the factions they hope to rayse heer. All which are points that Mr. Hide very perfectly comprehends, and may, I suppose, bee of great use in giving the House himself an account of upon occasion, besides what may bee given (if so thought fit) by any private communication of our dispatches.

I begg your Lordships pardon for this interruption, and your beleefe of my beeing ever with equall passion and truth, My Lord,

Your Lordships most faithfull and most humble servant,

W. Temple. [2]

---

[1] The *Letters* read ' governor.'

[2] Endorsed by Danby, ' From Sir William Temple, 28 October, [16]78.' The Duke of Leeds has altered ' 28 ' to ' 25th.' Temple's figure is not very clear, and it is just possible that 25th is correct.

[*To the Lord Treasurer*] [1]

Hague, November 17, S.N., 1678.

My Lord,

    I could not refuse Monsieur Muller, envoyè from the Dukes of Luneburgh, this address, which hee desird for an entrance into the honor of your Lordships knoledge and favor. All that I shall say upon this occasion, and at a time so busy with your Lordship, is that you will finde him a man of honor and plainness in his proceedings, and whom I have known for thees dozen years in his masters confidence and the secret of his Courte.

    As farr as I understand of his business (besides what your Lordship knows of the invitation his Majesty has given to his journey), I take it to bee this. His masters finde it necessary in the present conjunctures to seeke the appuy (as hee saies) of some great prince. They desire it for many reasons of his Majesty, and so have resolved to make him the first offer, upon such strict alliances as hee thinks both sides may finde their accounts in, his Majesty to have the foure Houses of Lunenburgh upon all conjunctures in his interests, with considerable troops they will alwaies bee masters of, which hee thinks will bee necessary to his Majesty if hee will bee considerd as the Crown of England ought to bee in the affairs of Europe, both Spaine and France having growne to give laws in Christendome by their liaisons in the Empire. But the particular advantages hee proposes thereby to his Majesty is the conservation of Flanders by a greater weight falling into the scale then that of Sweden in the Triple Alliance. What they propose to themselves is first the securing their conquests in Bremen, either by his Majestys offices in the mediation or else by his protection, and next some certaine subsidys in case of forces beeing imployd in a warr, and some small ones I suppose in time of peace upon their keeping up troops to a certain number.

    This as farr as I apprehend is the bottome of his errand, upon which hee discoursed at large to Mr. Hyde when hee was last heer, as well as to mee. In case hee fayls in England hee thinks his masters can have what tearms they will from France, and to that purpose Madame de Chastillon is newly arrived at the Duke of

---

[1] From the autograph letter in Leeds MSS., Packet 10.

*Cells courte, having been already with that of Osnabrug. I aske
your Lordships pardon for this interruption, and your beleefe of
my beeing ever with the greatest truth and passion, My Lord,*
　　　Your Lordships most obedient humble servant,
　　　　　　　　　　　　　　　　　　　　W. Temple.

To Sir William Temple.[1]
　　　　　　　　　　　London, 19 November, 1678.
My Lord,
　　Wee have not only our hands overloaded with businesse,
but with such businesse as wee can neither guesse the event of,
nor foresee when itt will end. I know you are enough fill'd with
the generall newes of plots and contrivances both against the
Kings person and to subvert our religion and government, but
wee are yett so unhappy as not to have evidences so convincing
as I hope they will bee when the conspirators have com'd to
theire trialls. In the meane time there arises debates of very
different natures, and sometimes heates upon them, and such
an one particularly yesterday in the House of Commons as
ended in the comitment of Sir Joseph Williamson to the Tower.
His Majestie has this day spoke to the House of Comons upon that
matter, and did att the same time order Mr. Secretaries release,
which has begott an addresse from that House to the King
shewing the reasons of theire comitting him, and desiring that
his Majestie would please to continue the comitment ; but the
Secretary is att liberty, and how the matter will rest or bee
taken up againe to-morrow must shew.

　　The cheife aime seemes to bee against the Duke, but is
attended with designes also against lesser ones, as myselfe and
others of the Cabinett ; and truly itt is the opinion of very many
that those designes are rather pursued under the cover of the
plott then the plott ittselfe. Amidst these disorders (and which
are more likely to increase then otherwise) wee have an army
and fleet on our hands without any provision either to continue
or disband them ; and for those troops abroad, they must either
starve or bee recalled imediately. And yett the Comons will not
indure to heare of this or any other concerne untill they have

───────────────

[1] From the autograph draft in B.M. Add. MSS. 28054, f. 196. *Letters*
p. 263.

further satisfaction in the matter of the plott. What the consequence of these things will bee abroad wee have not time to thinke, nor almost of what wee should do att home ; but because I could not satisfy myselfe to bee any longer silent, I was resolved to acquainte you with the present state of our affaires.

I was in hopes to have seene you in the House by this time, to have had the helpe of such an able phisitian in so desperate a distemper ; but wee are like to bee deprived of that also by the ingratitude of a corporation to his Majestie and the ill practices of Mr. Montagu to debauche them. Since his coming to the House I have heard more of his ill practices of other kinds, and some of them particularly against yourselfe, which I am hunting as eagerly [1] as I can to find out ; and I heare that Monsieur Olivekrans can tell us some things if hee pleases of Mr. Montagu, which would both spoile his plotts and his seate in Parliament, and which you would do well to informe yourselfe of, if you meete with a fitt occasion.

I write this in such an hurry that you must forgive the faults of itt, but before I end I beg to know whither att last you beleeve the peace will bee concluded ∧ or not. I am

TO THE STATES SATISFACTION

Your, &c.,

[Danby] [2]

To the Lord Treasurer. [3]

Hague, December 6, S.N., 1678.

My Lord,

I was so infinitely obliged by the kindeness and confidence of a letter I had this day the honor of receaving from your Lordship by Mr. Hales that I could not delay the acknoledging it by this post, though to doe that as I ought will, I doubt, bee as harde as to deserve it, and besides, I feare to interrupt your Lordship at a time so busy as this will bee a greater fault then any omission could have been.

---

[1] The *Letters* read ' well.'

[2] Endorsed by Danby, ' Coppy of my letter to Sir W. Temple, 19 November 1678 ' ; and by Leeds, ' Of great moment, but to bee considered.'

[3] From the autograph letter in Leeds MSS., Packet 10. Printed in *Letters*, p. 268 ; and, from a copy, in Temple, *Works*, ii. 515.

I had not before any true prospect of your present scene ; and though your Lordship has given mee so much light, yet it serves rather to represent the sadness of it then to discover any hopes of remedy to such fatall distempers as have been long breeding, and are now so violently broken out in our poore unfortunate nation. God alone can bee the physician, who governs the hearts of princes and the humors of people, for to thinke of advise from any other in so many crosse accidents both at home and abroad as meete to make up this violent crisis is too great a compliment to put upon any man. And if your Lordship could hope for it, in my opinion it ought to bee from yourself, who have the best been able to observe the spring and growth of this distemper, with the dispositions of the bodye, and by that as well as your owne naturall prudence must bee fitter then any-body to make a judgment upon it.

For my owne parte, it would bee more presumption in mee then in any man to offer at it, upon many other regards besides that of the distance I am at and have been so long and so often for a great parte of my life. Nor doe I know one quality to make mee fitt for it, unles it bee not onely as neer and sensible but as unpassiond and uninteressed [1] a concernment in the true good and service of my master and my countrey as any man can have. *And for this reason, and becaus your Lordship has used many times to aske mee so kindely and heare mee so favorably upon smaller occasions, and becaus I take you to bee equally concerned with the publique in this, it shall goe harde but I will finde a way of telling your Lordship by some hande or other, and in very few words, all that I have been able to thinke upon it, which can doe no hurte, becaus you may forgett it as soon as tis done.*

For any accounts of foreign affairs which your Lordship might have expected if I had come over, the whole course of my dispatches since I left England last will better informe anybody then I myself could doe, as having been constant and particular, and thereby containing many things that I have forgott. For the question you are pleased to aske about the peace, I cannot adde one worde to that shorte account your Lordship will meet with in my letter this post to Sir Joseph Williamson, unles it bee that nothing seems to mee at

[1] The *Letters* give ' uninterrupted,' probably by mistake.

present so necessary in the foreign affairs as for his Majesty to dispatch away some minister to Spaine, whose cheife instruction should bee to watch any motion of counsels or negotiations there for the exchange of Flanders, to divert them from any such thoughts by the greatest assurances of his Majesty's resolving to take it into his constant care and protection, and so to represent the state of our present disorders themselves as not to dishearten that Courte in the hopes that his Majesty may yett bee able to performe effectually what hee intends and promises in that matter. I thinke the dispatch of this so much the more necessary becaus I doubt the present minister there may in this conjuncture[1] bee possibly inclined to promote other ends in what concerns that very business of Flanders and any exchange of it.[2]

For Mr. Mountague, I have neither deserved such [3] offices as [4] your Lordship speaks of,[4] nor shall [5] trouble myself about making him such returns. *I am infinitely obliged to your Lordship for the enquirys you say you will make, and shall bee very glad to know my faults from my enemys as well as my friends, becaus which way soever I finde them I shall make the same use of it, which is to mende them. I stande alwais upon the ground of having never done either an unjust or ungentlemanly action in my life, or an unfaithfull one to the service of my master or my country, and whoever may bee persuaded otherwise of mee by whispers or malice I shall leave to their owne opinions till they pleas to make fairer inquirys, and concern myself no further in them nor the consequences, having, I thanke God at hearte, neither hopes to serve nor faults to answer for.*

As to Sir Henry Capell, I should bee very sorry to thinke hee meant ill to the Crowne or the kingdome, becaus I alwaies thought otherwise of him, and cannot reproch myself to have been often deceaved in my friends, and whenever I am, thinke I have not more reason to quarrell with them then with myself for choosing them.

---

[1] The version in Temple's *Works* gives at this point ' be a very ill instrument in such an affair, and.'

[2] No authority in the handwriting of Leeds has been found for the omission of this long passage.

[3] The *Letters* read ' ill ' here.

[4] . . . [4] Instead of this passage the *Letters* give ' he has done me.'

[5] The *Letters* read ' I ' here.

*For his unkindeness to mee I will at least bee as just as I desire
others should bee to mee, which is to hear first what hee saies of it
before I judge.* For any [1] to your Lordship I shall not easily
forgive, becaus I doe not thinke you have deserved it upon any
publique considerations, which are all that should lead him in
his present figure, for if your Lordship has not served his Majesty and the true interest of his Crowns with perfect good
intentions to both, and to the best of your power, you have, I
am sure, deceaved mee, which fewe of my friends, I confess,
have done, and I am confident your Lordship will never bee of
the number. I begg your pardon for this long interruption,
which had not been so if I were with less truth and passion then
I am, My Lord,

Your Lordships most faithfull and most humble servant,

W. Temple.

To Sir William Temple. [2]

8 January, 1678/9.

*You will easily beleeve, by what I doubt not but you have had
from others, that I have been too much imploy'd to give you the
trouble of a letter before this time, and yett there is nothing I can bee
more concern'd for then to have the Prince of Orange rightly
informed both as to what regards the King and myselfe in those
transactions which Mr. Montagu hath so treacherously and falsely
represented to the wounding of the King through my sides. For
that end I have sent you the coppy of that letter which Mr. Montagu
has produced in the House of Commons, both for your own information and to bee made such use of as you shall thinke fitt, and
though itt bee enough for mee that I had his Majesties command
under his hand to write that letter as well as many others to Mr.
Montagu, yett on the King's part itt will appeare that his Majestie
bargained for no peace nor no towne, for if hee would have done that,
I have itt to shew under Mr. Montagu's hand that his Majestie
might have sold townes for as much as they were worth, and the*

---

[1] No authority in the handwriting of the Duke of Leeds has been found for
the omission of this passage. In the *Letters* its place is taken by, ' For what
he has done.'

[2] From the autograph draft among the Lindsey MSS., printed in *Lindsey
MSS.*, p. 397.

money have been sent with secrecy, and offers to have made my fortune what I pleased if I would have been the instrument for them to the King. Instead of which, as I scorned that office, so his Majestie would never heare of any propositions but such as Holland and Spaine should approve, and you will see itt was only in case those propositions which were sent by Secretary Coventry should bee accepted by France that his Majestie would have endeavoured (by the perswasion of Mr. Montagu) to gett money from them, and att a time when hee had all the discouragements imaginable both at home and abroad to make him beleeve that the war would neither bee continued by those who were already engaged in itt, nor have been supported here to any degree that was necessary.

Another thing that troubles mee more then Mr. Montagus accusation of mee is that the distempers here have so blasted all creditts of money that I have not been able to procure for the Prince upon the Act that money which has been so long due to him, and for which I had given my owne promise, as I had received other men's to mee, who never failed mee before ; and I do protest that were I any way able to incompasse itt upon my owne estate, I would have pawned itt before this time to have performed with the Prince. And although I am still in hopes itt will not bee long before I shall gett the money, yett I am ashamed to write to his Highnesse untill I can give him an account of the money being in Mr. Godolphin's hands. I most earnestly beg your kind management of all these matters with the Prince, and that a right information of his Majesties transactions with France may bee given both to the States and to all the foreigne ministers to whom you shall thinke itt necessary.

I am by his Majesties command directed to lett you know by this post that he intends very speedily to give leave to Mr. Secretary Coventry to retire from his imployment, and is desirous to have you there rather then any other ; that although his condition bee so ill that hee has not money for his necessary occasions, yett hee is willing to secure to Secretary Coventry 5,000 l. of the 10,000 l. hee is to have for his place, and will bee hereafter willing to reimburse to yourselfe the latter 5,000 l. if you will lay itt downe ; but that not being able to do the whole for you att present as hee intended, hee supposes you will looke upon this offer of his Majesties as a great mark of his kindnesse and such an one as hee shall not shew to any

other, and therefore expects your answer to itt by the first oppor-
tunity. Haveing delivered his Majesties message pray give mee
leave to offer my owne advice, that you would cheerefully imbrace
his Majesties kindnesse in the manner hee offers itt, and that you
would do itt by a letter to himselfe. I know how readily you may
furnish yourselfe with objections against itt, but I thinke itt would
bee but finding out objections against yourselfe, which I can by no
meanes agree to, being so sincerely and so intirely as I am,

Your, [&c.]

[Danby]

[To the Lord Treasurer] [1]

Hague, January 23, S.N., 1679.

My Lord,

Though I know very well [your] Lordship is too busy to
bee troubled with empty letters, and there passes nothing of
importance to fill one from hence, yett upon the parte your
Lordships name had in the last newspapers and journals from
England I cannot forbeare giving you this trouble, though it
bee onely to assure your Lordship how great a sense I have of
whatever touches you in any kinde, and with how much
impatience I expect the good news of some happy issue out of
thees present distractions in England, wherein I see your Lordship has so sensible a parte, and the consequences whereof are
already felt abroad as well as at home, and will, I feare, bee more
so every day. I can assure your Lordship all men I meete with
heere lament our misfortunes at this time as a concerne of their
owne, and so they esteeme it, considering the condition of this
countrey and of Flanders, without a support from England, and
they thinke [2] the peace of Germany, to bee fallen into much
worse tearms already upon the late ill posture of our affairs. [3]

Your Lordship will finde the Princes sense of it in the enclosed. [4]
I am sure what both his Highnesse and the States expresse of it

---

[1] From the autograph letter among the Lindsey MSS., printed in *Lindsey
MSS.*, p. 399. *Letters*, p. 271.

[2] The *Letters* omit ' they thinke.'   [3] The *Letters* add ' in England.'

[4] The *Letters* add ' from himself.' The reference is to the Prince's letter of
January 13, 1679, printed *supra*, p. 441.

upon all occasions is very great, and particularly of what concerns your Lordship. But I keepe you from beeing so much better entertained that I shall doe it no longer, nor increas this present trouble beyond the assurances of my beeing ever with equall passion and truth, My Lord,

Your Lordships most faithfull and most humble servant,

W. Temple.

[To the Lord Treasurer] [1]

Hague, January 27,[2] S.N., 1679.

My Lord,

I had the honor of one from your Lordship of the 7th,[3] and deferred not upon the receipt thereof [4] to make that use of it heere which you intended, and [5] was indeed in a manner necessary for his Majestys service and justification as well as your Lordships heere.[6] I communicated the first parte of it to some of the States who are in chiefe credit heere, and to the Imperiall and Spanish ministers, who all tooke notice of those clauses in it which showed how great advantages might have been made by bargaining for any towns ; [7] how no conditions were [8] proposed but such as were approved by Spaine and Holland ; and how the thoughts of making any advantages of that itselfe were entertained onely at the persuasions of Mr. Montagu. And in the severall conversations [9] I have had upon this subject heere[10] I may assure your Lordship [11] all was done with the success you desired.[11]

For the Prince, who was gone from Utrecht to Arnhem about the time I receaved your Lordships dispatch, I thought there

[1] From the autograph letter among the Lindsey MSS., printed in *Lindsey MSS.*, p. 399 ; Temple, *Works*, ii. 519 ; *Letters*, p. 273. For the very extensive alterations in this letter no authority in the handwriting of the Duke of Leeds has been found.

[2] In Temple's *Works* the date is given as January 24.

[3] The reference seems to be to Danby's letter of which the draft is dated January 8 (*supra*, p. 505).

[4] The *Letters* omit ' upon the receipt thereof.'

[5] The *Letters* omit ' you intended and.'

[6] The *Letters* omit ' heere,' as does also the version printed in Temple's *Works*.

[7] The *Letters* add ' if the King had pleas'd.'   [8] The *Letters* add ' ever.'

[9] The *Letters* read ' greatest conversation.'   [10] The *Letters* omit ' heere.'

[11] . . . [11] The *Letters* read, ' it was receiv'd here with all the success you could desire.'

could[1] bee no way so good of performing[2] your commands towards his Highnesse as by sending him the letter itself, by which hee would best see how much you were concerned, both in his good opinion and in his particular affaire of the money due to him, which I am sure could not have been by mee so well expressed as in your Lordships one words. You will before this time have been fully satisfyed, by the letter I lately sente you enclosed,[3] how much the Prince was concerned in your parte of what lately happened in England, and how litle reason you had to apprehend any change of his Highnesses opinion in what concerned your Lordship upon that occasion, and I knowe very well that hee writt that letter with kinder intentions[4] then onely of making you a compliment at that time. For the money, hee never said one worde of it to me in severall conversations about those affairs, further then complaining of his owne ill lucke, since hee was sure to have receaved it within fowre or five days, at the time when that trouble was given your Lordship there, which hee reckoned upon as what must certainly delay it till some better settlement in his Majestys affairs, and especially that of the revenue.

Having acquitted myself of the duty I owed your Lordship upon the first parte of your letter, I finde another I owe to his Majesty upon the latter, of which I dispaire of beeing able to acquitt myself as I oughte to doe, *or as the sense of so great a grace and favor justly obliges mee to. The distinction his Majesty is pleased to make between mee and other men, both in esteeming mee fitt for the discharge of so great a trust, and in offering to bee himself at the charge of Mr. Secretary Coventrys retiring from it, is that I am sure that I shall never live to forgett, though I can never hope to deserve,* and therefore must begg of your Lordship to assist mee in making the [5] heartyest and [5] humblest acknowledgments to his Majesty that any servant can make to the best master in the world. [5] After this is done [5] I am very sorry that I must make so true and plaine a confession of myself as I am forced to

---

[1] The *Letters* read ' would.'   [2] The *Letters* read ' to the performing.'
[3] The Prince's letter of January 13, printed *supra*, p. 441.
[4] The *Letters* read ' a kinder intention.'
[5] . . . [5] Omitted in the *Letters*.

doe upon this occasion. If I found myself capable of doing his Majesty the service that would become mee in [1] such a poste,[1] I should esteem it the greatest [2] and indeed the onely [2] happines that could befall mee [2] at this time and [2] in the poore remainders of my life. But the sensible decays I feele of late in myself, and which must increas every day with my age and ill health, make mee absolutely dispaire of acquitting myself as I ought [3] *and would bee necessary for his Majestys service in a poste that requires not onely great abilitys but good health and all the application that can bee, neither of which I can any ways promise either his Majesty or myself. And I may pretend to bee so honest a man as never to make so ill a bargaine for so good a master, which would bee like selling him very deer a horse that I knew to bee old and resty and not at all fitt for the service hee designed him.*[3]

I begg your Lordship to represent this to his Majesty, not as any affected modesty, nor as a Speakers forme of disabling himself when hee is chosen, for your Lordship may [4] pleas to [4] remembei [5] I writt the same thing to you six months agoe,[5] and Mr. Hide knows very well the thoughts of this kinde hee both found and left mee in at his last beeing heere.   [6] *The season I have since past in a place so unkinde to my health has given mee a great deal of reason to continue them, and to thinke myself not at all fitt to enter upon so great and laborious an imployment, or even to continue this longer then the spring, beyond which time I can foresee little use his Majesty can have of mee heere. And whenever hee shall pleas to end it, I doubt not but hee will give mee leave to seeke for a little better health in some better climate, and I am sure shall never finde a better subject, how useles a servant soever I may have been, and that none shall ever make more passionate wishes for his happyness and safety then I shall every day of my life.*[6]

[1] . . . [1] The *Letters* read instead, ' the post of a Secretary of State.'

[2] . . . [2] Omitted in the *Letters*.

[3] . . . [3] Instead of this passage the *Letters* read ' to do in such a station.'

[4] . . . [4] Omitted in the *Letters*.

[5] . . . [5] Omitted in the *Letters* and ' heretofore ' substituted.

[6] . . . [6] Instead of this passage the *Letters* read, ' Besides, my bad state of health makes me hope that his Majesty will give me leave to seek to mend it in some better climate, and especially since your Lordship seems to think of retiring yourself, upon whose assistance I should principally have rely'd.'

[1] I cannot ende this without making your Lordship likewise my particular acknoledgments for your favor and good opinion, which I shall ever esteem among my best possessions. But having had the honor of agreeing so often with you [2] in what wee have talkt of,[2] I cannot but bee confident that if you knew mee as well as I doe myself you would bee perfectly of my minde [3] *in this matter, as I should bee of yours if I found myself indeed what your Lordship is pleased to esteem mee.*[3] That which I hope wee both agree in is the beleefe [4] that you can never meet with a greater and sincerer [5] passion then that wherewith I have been so long and shall bee ever, My Lord,

Your Lordships most faithfull and most humble servant,

W. Temple.

To Sir William Temple.[6]

London, 11th February, 1678/9.

My Lord,

You will by this post receive orders from his Majestie by my Lord Sunderland to come over instead of Sir Leoline Jenkyns ; and that you may know the true cause of itt (which you will not receive from my Lord Sunderland), I had this day an assurance, by my cosin your son from my Lady Temple, and afterwards from her Ladyship, that Sir Joseph Williamson being removed, thereby the chiefe obstacle was taken away which made you onwilling to undertake the Secretarys place with such a partner as might not concur as you desired to the Kings service. Upon this incouragement I resolved to loose no time of tryall how far his Majestie had fixt his resolutions about Sir Leoline, and finding him still willing to prefer you before him, I desired that Sir Leolines order for coming over might bee stopt by this post, and the same direction sent to yourselfe which was given him before, viz., to come over as soone as may bee to his

---

[1] The *Letters* begin, ' In the mean time.'

[2] . . . [2] Instead of this the *Letters* read, ' in most things relating to the publick.'

[3] . . . [3] Instead of this the *Letters* read, ' in what I have said concerning myself, and I cannot deny but I should be of yours, were you not an instrument of so much greater use to the publick than I could be.'

[4] The *Letters* omit ' the beleefe.' [5] The *Letters* read ' more sincere.'

[6] From the autograph draft among the Lindsey MSS., printed in *Lindsey MSS.*, p. 402. *Letters*, p. 281.

Majestie, and that not as a revocation (which may bee better done after you are here) but as a journey in obedience to his Majesties commands.

The inclosed to the Prince [1] was designed (att my Lord Sunderlands request) to have recommended him to his High-
WHO GIVES MEE VERY GREAT
nesse, as <u>I am confident I may do with</u> assurance of his readi-
nesse to serve him ; but [2] since this change has hapned so suddenly, [2] which I am confident will please the Prince as well as itt does mee (and I am sure itt cannot do more), [3] I could not but communicate itt to his Highnesse, although itt will be necessary to keepe itt secrett, because otherwise itt may receive a prejudice you shall know hereafter. And at this instant I dare answer that none in England either know or thinke of itt but your Lady, my Lord Sunderland, your son, and myselfe. I have made my head ache so much with the many letters I have writt this day that I can say no more to you att this time, nor do I know whither that bee sense I have writt. But I know you will easily excuse the faults of, My Lord, [&c.]

[Danby] [4]

I durst use no hand but this to transcribe my letter, [5] and I was not able to do itt myselfe.

To the Lord Treasurer. [6]
Hague, February 21, S.N., 1678/9.
My Lord,
Having since my last had several occasions of discoursing with the Prince upon the subject of your Lordship's last letter, and the account you were pleased to give there both of his Majesty's conduct and your own in those negotiations which were so much talked on of late, his Highness was very full in his

---

[1] Danby's letter of the same date to the Prince, printed *supra*, p. 441.

[2] . . . [2] Instead of this the *Letters* read ' this change has happened since.'

[3] In the *Letters* the passage in brackets is omitted, and the words ' and therefore ' are substituted.

[4] Unsigned, but endorsed by Danby, ' Coppy of my letter to Sir William Temple, 11th February 1678/9. About his being Secretary.'

[5] As the actual letter has not been found it cannot be determined who the transcriber was.

[6] Temple, *Works*, ii. 521, from a copy. *Letters*, p. 277.

expressions of justifying your Lordship upon having done nothing but with his Majesty's order even in writing, and could not talk of Mr. Montagu's part in it without the greatest indignation in the world. For the thing itself, he would say little but that it was past, and so 'twas to no purpose to talk of it ; that nobody had anything left to do since the peace but to play an ill game the best they could, and so he resolved to do here ; but nothing he could now do would signifie much towards the common safety, unless England could grow into a posture of being more united at home and more considered abroad than they seemed likely to be by the present course of our affairs, which he ever talks of with great concernment.

Since the commission I received to go again to Nimeguen, to continue there the figure of his Majesty's mediation upon the recalling of Sir Lyonell Jenkins, he was very inquisitive into the reason of it, which I could not give him, having received barely a commission to act alone in that function, and three lines only from Mr. Secretary Williamson to tell me he had sent it by his Majesty's order. All we could guess was the design of sparing so much money, by ending Mr. Hyde's and Sir Lyonell's embassy now the peace was so near concluded, and continuing mine only for the decency of the mediation till the assembly should break up. And the Prince said upon it that he hoped, however, the King might make some good use of it, and since the peace of the north would certainly be made, now the Emperor's was so, he thought it would be very much better that his Majesty should make it than France, especially that between Brandenburgh and Sweden, and thereby endeavour to draw some dependance of those two princes upon himself after the peace, which he doubted would otherwise fall on France. He said besides that he would think of this matter within two or three days, and tell me, if not write into England, what should occur to him upon it, before I went to Nimeguen ; and that the sooner the peace of the north was now made the better, that France might thereby have no longer a pretext of keeping the seven towns in Cologn, Juliers, and Liege, whereby they are posted so as to awe this country and Flanders and to be ready for any new design upon them.

In this conference, and one before, his Highness desired me to write to your Lordship and put you in mind of his money, concerning which you had expressed so great concernment in your last to me. His Highness said he did not doubt but this sum might be easily advanced upon that Act which provided for it, in case the whole security were not engaged some other ways, which he hoped your Lordship has had the kindness and justice to prevent.

In the midst of your Lordship's great affairs, I know very well I ought to give you as few and as short troubles as I can, and therefore shall not lengthen this beyond the assurances of my being ever, My Lord,

Your Lordships most faithfull and most humble servant,

W. Temple.

[To the Lord Treasurer] [1]

Hague, February 28, S.N., 1679.

My Lord,

I received last Saturday [2] the honor of one from your Lordship of the 11th, which I confess surprised mee more then any I ever received from you, coming not onely after my orders and preparations for Nimeghen, but after my wife had told mee from your Lordship how all that affaire had played, and after I had written to her how infinitely sensible I was of the obligations I had to your Lordship in the whole course of it, and how perfectly I was satisfyed as to myself with the plie it had taken. Time alone must tell if either his Majesty or I have reason to bee satisfyed with the change you have made [3] in that measure, which will depend upon the success of it [4] towards those publique endes I am confident your Lordship aimes at in it, and which none can answer for. I wish to God I could deserve half the honor your Lordship [5] does mee by your [6] good opinion, for

---

[1] From the autograph letter among the Lindsey MSS., printed in *Lindsey MSS.*, p. 402, and, from a copy, in Temple, *Works*, ii. 524. *Letters*, p. 283.

[2] February 15/25.

[3] Temple's *Works* give ' he has since made.'

[4] Temple's *Works* give at this point, ' and of my being of the use designed in so great a post.'

[5] Instead of ' your Lordship ' Temple's *Works* give ' his Majesty.'

[6] Instead of ' your ' Temple's *Works* give ' his.'

I never can the kindeness of your intention (whatever may come of it), though no man can bee more sensible then I am of it.

For the rest, I shall not trouble your Lordship further with any discourses upon that subject, being like to have the honor of waiting on you so soone, for I hope, God willing, to goe aboard the yacht to-morrow or next day [1] if wind and weather suffer mee, and with your Lordships good leave shall make my first stepp into the Cockpitt, where your Lordship will then finde, I am sure,

A most faithfull and most humble servant,

W. Temple.

[1] Temple's *Works* read ' Wednesday.'

REMARKES

UPON SOME OF

SIR WILLIAM TEMPLE'S LETTERS[1]

VIZ. :

Aprill 23rd, [16]76. His letter sent to mee by his Lady with a message to acquaint mee with the Prince of Oranges inclination to propose a match for himselfe to the Lady Mary, and to desire my answer by [2] her Ladyship to divers questions which shee was instructed to inquire of mee in order to that match. And this was the first motion in that affair, and according to the charge of secresy mentioned in that letter it was never communicated to any other person,[3] nor did the King know anything of the Princes thoughts of that matter till May [16]77, when I first tryed how the King would approve of such a proposall ; and it was att least two months after that before I had any hopes of his Majesties allowance of any treaty about it.

November 6th, [16]76. Shews Sir William Temples sincere friendship to me, and with the greatest acknowledgments of his obligations to mee.

July 25th, [16]78. Hee wisheth mee joy of the treaty then concluded by him betwixt England and Hollond under my ministry, by which, as well as by most of his letters, I have his testimony that I was far from beeing in any French interest.

August 12/22, [16]78. Mine shewing the Kings firmness to the last treaty with the States, and his Majesties wonder that he had not been made acquainted with the termes on which the States had made their sepperate peace with France.

---

[1] B.M. Add. MSS. 28044, f. 49, in a clerk's handwriting, with some alterations and additions in the handwriting of the Duke of Leeds. *Letters*, p. 285.

[2] The *Letters* read ' to.'   [3] The words ' but myselfe ' are here crossed out.

January 23th, [16]78/9, and another 27th ditto. Both mentioning how the prosecution of mee in Parliament was looked upon abroad. And there was a letter in that of the 23, from the Prince of Orange of the 13 of said January, which shews his opinion also of that matter, [1] as another of February 21 from Sir William Temple shews what sentiments the Prince had of Mr. Mountagu's part in it.[1]

Itt may also bee observed how many of our letters agree in bemoaning the unfortunate stepps which were then made both in England and Holland contrary to their true interests. And Sir William Temple in his second *Memoirs*, page 332,[2] relates that the States did then owne that the Prince of Orange had made a truer judgment then they had done of the measures both with France and England. And in the same *Memoirs*, page 312 and 313,[3] he gives an account of what answer I gave to himselfe when he asked mee my opinion about the offerrs that were then sent to mee by Mr. Mountague, both about money and the terms which were then proposed from France, and saies my answer to him was that I thought it was the same thing as if it should be proposed to the King to have Windsor put into the French hands, and that I should treat it so. And at the end of the said *Memoirs*, pages 389, 390, 391 and 392,[4] he (who knew all the passages at that time) gives an account who were the cheif managers and at the head of all the designs against mee, viz., the Dutchess of Portsmouth, the Earles of Essex, Sunderland [5] and Shaftsbury, who were joyned with the Duke of Monmouth in the design of my ruin, and it is observable what misfortunes befell [6] the most of them, which I am not willing to repeat.[6]

---

[1] . . . [1] This passage appears only in the *Letters*.

[2] Temple, *Works*, i. 465.   [3] *Ibid.*, p. 459.

[4] *Ibid.*, p. 480.   [5] The *Letters* omit Sunderland.

[6] . . . [6] Instead of this the *Letters* read ' three of them (even whilst I was a prisoner), and the French Lady not long after, who would never forgive me, because she thought me to be the sole cause of obstructing her pension from France, when I was at the same time accused for being the promoter of it.'

LORD SUNDERLAND'S LETTERS

[*To the Lord Treasurer*] [1]

Paris, August the 2, N.S., [1678]

My Lord,

    I came hither on Saterday, [2] *and yesterday being Monday had a private audience at St. Germains, where after a greate deale which his Most Christian Majesty said to justify the sincerity of his intentions (of which I have given an account to Secretary Coventry as well as of what relates to the regiments of Monmouth and Douglas) he told me he hoped I brought some propositions which might facilitate the peace, he affecting no one expedient more then another, and that anything which can secure the satisfaction of Sweden he shall like as well as the keeping of the townes.*

    I told him that the King my master had thought of it very much, and desired it sincerly, but yet found so many difficultys in securing that satisfaction that he could not propose anything in order to it ; that his Most Christian Majesty being the onely support of the interest of Sweden he could much more easily offer an expedient which might satisfy that Crowne, and that I doubted not but that the King my master would agree to anything that was reasonable ; that the time being now expired for the ratification of the private treaty of May the 17/27 I was ordered to demand a prolongation of that time, during which expedients might be thought on to conclude this greate affaire, which was a plaine argument that the King my masters intentions are reall, for if he desired warre it was more convenient for him to make it now then a month hence, all kind of suspension betweene peace and warre being what he was resolved not to suffer, but for some short time which he is willing to sacrifice to the desire he has of obtaining a peace if it is possible. To this his Most Christian Majesty said he could then give me no positive

<hr/>

[1] From the autograph letter in Leeds MSS., Packet 10.
[2] July 20/30.

answer, but he would thinke of it, and that he hoped there would yet be more strict alliances betweene the King my master and him.

I had been with Monsieur de Pompone, as the custome is, before I saw the King ; but finding that what I desired concerning the private treaty was not agreed to so soone as I hoped, I went to him againe to presse it, and to tell him that nothing was so prejudiciall as delays to the King my masters businesse, and that absolutely he could not admit of any. He said he beleived in a few days I should find there would be no greate difficulty in what I desired, but it must be thought of, and that he hoped there might yet be further alliances and important ones betweene the two kings. I told him I should be very glad of it, but that this was necessary to be a foundation to any other, and that I hoped Monsieur de Barrillon might have power at least to finish this at London, which I said because I doe beleive they have a mind to make farther proposals, which may perhaps finish the whole affaire, which that treaty alone can not doe. It is either this or to gaine time, for I know they like the thing itselfe, and were in paine because they had heard no mention made of that treaty, the time being expired.

I doe really beleive they did heere intend to make peace, and that they doe still desire it extreamely, but will never agree to it without a satysfaction for Sweden, from whence the King of Denmarke will suffer no letters to passe, so that if Sweden itselfe should desire to make the peace easyer it can not be knowne but by ships, which are a greate while coming and very uncertainly. This the King told me at St. Germains as a thing never before practiced, and of greate prejudice to the peace. I have left nothing unsaid to let the King and the ministers see plainly that the King my master is absolutely master of the affaires both in England and Holland if he goes into the warre.

My Lord Dunbarton desires your Lordships favour and protection, and I hope you will give it to him. I found my Lady Sussex in the convent of the Port Royal, seeming resolved to obey the King, though something unwillingly. I will at this time entertaine your Lordship no longer, but onely beg of you to thinke no man in the world is so really as I am, My Lord,

 Your most faithfull and most humble servant,

       Sunderland.

[*To the Lord Treasurer*] [1]

Paris, August the 3, S.N., [1678]

My Lord,

     Since I writ to your Lordship by an expresse I sent into England yesterday, nothing has happened heere worth acquainting you with it ; but however, Mr. Brisban going away, I resolved to write, that your Lordship may see I will omit no occasion of doing it. I thinke myselfe obliged also to let you know that he has behaved himselfe very well in this place in all kinds, and perticularly in obeying the Kings orders in relation to my Lady Sussex, who he had managed so well that at my arrivall heere I found her in a convent, full of submission, which was a greate change.

    I beg of your Lordship that you will make use of your credit to prevent things coming to extremitys, at least for a few days, because I doe hope something may be offered worth a short delay. I am and ever shall be, more sincerely then any man in the world, My Lord,

       Your most faithfull and most obedient servant,

                    Sunderland.

[*To the Lord Treasurer*] [2]

Paris, August the 4th, [16]78.

My Lord,

     Last night late his Most Christian Majestie sent to mee to come to him this morning, which I did. He told mee that for the good of the peace the Sweeds had desired him to be less zealous in their behalfe then he had been hitherto, for which reason, and for the sake of the King my master, with whome he did intend an eternall friendship, he had resolved to offer to him by Monsieur de Barillon, and to the assembly at Nimeguen by his ambassadors there, the following conditions :—To deliver up to the Spaniards the townes of Aeth, Oudenard, Courtray, Leuve and St. Ghislain ; that Ghent might be put into the hands of the Dutch for three years, or till Sweede shall be satisfied, to be a guaranty for the nutrality of Spaine during that time ; that Mastricht may be in his owne hands for the same time ; and that St. Dinant, which belongs to

---

[1] From the autograph letter in Leeds MSS., Packet 10.
[2] From a copy in Leeds MSS., Packet 10.

the diocess of Leige and is now in his power, may be secured to France from any pretentions of the Bishop of Leige or any other, or else that Spaine would exchange it with him for Charlemont, which is theirs ; and that till one of the two is done Charleroy may continue in his power.

This his Most Christian Majestie desired mee to lett the King my master know. I cannot guess how his Majestie will approve of these conditions, but I am sure when I came hither the resolution of this Court was never to make any proposalls but only to receive them. I AM WITH GREAT RESPECT, &C.,

[*Sunderland*]

[*To the Lord Treasurer*] [1]

Paris, August the 6, [1678]

My Lord,

Monsieur de Ruvigny delivered to me yesterday the Kings orders and your Lordships letter.[2] *I shall to-morrow morning have an audience of his Most Christian Majesty, in which I will with all the care I can endeavour to procure what the King desires, but I doubt it will be very hard to make peace but on the tearmes proposed last by Monsieur de Barillon, which I acquainted your Lordship with on Thursday,*[3] *after having been at St. Germains. When that dispatch was made, and that the French King spoke to me, he knew by Monsieur de Barillon, whose courier was come, what the King intended to offer, and did certainely make hast to send into England before I could have time to make those propositions heere, which he knew would be so soone.*

One way or other I doubt not but that the peace will be made. It is certainely desired heere extreamely. If his Most Christian Majestys answer to me should be that he can resolve nothing till he hears from England, as I beleive it will, I will send no expresse. Otherwaies I will certainely dispatch one to-morrow. I am with all the respect and truth in the world, My Lord,

Your most faithfull and most obedient servant,

Sunderland.

[1] From the autograph letter in Leeds MSS., Packet 10.
[2] This letter has not been found.
[3] July 25/August 4.

[*To the Lord Sunderland*] [1]

AUGUST
London, 28th July, 1678.

My Lord,

I have divers of your letters to acknowledge, viz., of the
2/12   4/14   N.S.
2nd, 3rd and 4th August, ∧ *which last I received this day, and have
little to say to itt, because all will depend upon the French Kings
answer to what you received by Monsieur de Ruvigny, which could
not be arrived when his Christian Majesty made those propositions
that are contained in your last. I am only to acquaint your Lordship by his Majesties order that hee woud have you do all you can to
procure a certain and speedy answer to the proposals sent by
Monsieur Ruvigny, and to assure both the King and his ministers
that itt will bee impossible for him to offer any other expedient, and
that it will not be in his power after this day sevennight to accept
either those or any other conditions but with the consent of others.* [2]

*I have great hopes that the proposalls by Monsieur de Ruvigny
will procure the peace, because in truth they do more for the security
of Sweden than what is proposed in your letter ; but in the mean
time our preparations for war are every day made with more vigour,
and to that end the Duke of Munmouth is gone this day for Bruges
to put our men there into the best posture hee can to march if the
peace bee not had. And 4,000 horse and dragoons are ordered to bee
imbarqued with all expedition, so that nothing but a timely good
answer from France can prevent the breach, and I find that will not
be expected above a week longer.*

*I doubt not but my Lord Plymouth gives you an account of all
the home affairs, and particularly about all Mr. Montagus
behaviors here. The King takes itt to bee of that absolute importance that hee should know the King of France his mind by this day
sevennight that hee commanded mee to send away this express
to-night. I am with great respect, My Lord, &c.,*

[*Danby*] [3]

---

[1] From a copy in a clerk's handwriting in Leeds MSS., Packet 10 ; apparently prepared for the printer but not used.

[2] Parliament at the moment stood prorogued to August 1.

[3] Endorsed, ' To the Earl of Sunderland, 28 July 1678', with the date
altered by Leeds to ' 28 August/7 September 1678.'

To the Lord Treasurer.[1]

Paris, 10 of August, S.N., [1678]

My Lord,

To follow the instructions I receaved by Monsieur de Ruvigny I went to St. Germains on Saterday.[2] The next morning I saw Monsieur de Pompone, with whom I discoursed at large of all the perticulars of what I had to say, and gave it to him in writing besides. After that I had an audience of the King, who told me that as to the businesse of Lorraine he could not comply with the King my masters desire, and for many reasons he could alter nothing of what he had resolved in that affaire, all which Mr. Mountagu knew, and he supposed had acquainted the King with it. As to the next he could give no positive answer, it being of importance enough to thinke of it, I represented to him the little time there was left. He said in so greate a conjuncture as this was he thought a few dayes more could alter nothing, since both the King my master and he were so well disposed to an agreement.

I have since been able to get no other answer, which I knew before, for they depend very much upon the successe of the propositions sent to Nimeguen and England, and will hardly be brought to make peace upon other tearmes. I am most unfaignedly, My Lord,

Your Lordships most faithfull and most obedient servant,

Sunderland.[3]

If the King will have peace 40.34 : 180 : 70.40.46.47 : 38.20.66.30 : 56.30.20.26.31 : *and mony he must yeild* 135 : 48.52.50.74 : 38.31 : 48.67.62.64 : 74.30.41.46.28 : *to the King of France his offers or* 125 : 131 : 38.40.63 : 50.34.35.31.60.62 : 53.60 :

---

[1] From the autograph letter in Leeds MSS., Packet 10.

[2] July 27/August 6.

[3] Endorsed by Danby, ' 10th August, [16]78. Lord Sunderlands opinion about the peace, &c.'

n e e r e   t h e m,   and   s o   d o i n g
50.30.31.60.31 :   64.38.31.48 :   135 :   62.52 :   28.52.40.50.37 :
I   think   the French Ambassador   m a y
40 :   144 :   201 :   48.20.74 :
s o o n e   c o n c l u d e .
62.52.53.50.30 :   26.53.50.26.46.66.28.30.
My Lord St. Albans has the cypher.[1]

To the Lord Treasurer.[2]

Paris, August 2/12, 1678.

My Lord,

The courier your Lordship dispatch'd from London the
28th of July arrived here on Wednesday morning.[3] The same
day I went to St. Germains, where I represented to his Most
Christian Majesty how impossible it was for the King my master
to accept of any expedient for the peace, without the absolute
restitution of the towns so long in question ; that he thought
what he offered more effectual for the satisfaction of Sweden
than the propositions of his Most Christian Majesty, and therefore he could not doubt but it would have the success he desired ;
that he was ty'd up to a certain time for his final resolution,
and therefore had ordered me to obtain a speedy and positive
answer, which I did desire his Majesty would please to give in a
day or two.

To this his Most Christian Majesty answer'd that he did
certainly believe that the propositions his ambassadors had
made at Nimmeguen would be accepted, and that the peace was
perhaps now signed ; or if any small difficulty remain'd, it
might easily be remov'd by the King my master, which he
doubted not but he would do. I said I was very confident that
Spain and Holland neither could nor would consent to anything
less than the total restitution of the towns, and that tho' the

---

[1] The deciphering has been effected on the letter itself, apparently by a
clerk. The cipher is a very simple one, each letter of the alphabet being represented by one of two or more consecutive two-figure numerals. In addition
certain common words and phrases are represented by purely arbitrary
numerals consisting of three figures.

[2] *Letters*, p. 289. The original letter was among the Webster MSS. (*Hist.
MSS. Com.*, iii. 420), but it was not purchased by Mr. Hodgkin, and cannot
now be traced.

[3] July 31/August 10.

King my master's inclinations were for peace rather than war, he must chuse the latter if the expedient he offered were not accepted, and that I had but a day or two to expect his Most Christian Majesty's resolutions ; to which I was answer'd that every moment news was expected from Nimmeguen, and till then it was unnecessary to think of anything else. So that I came yesterday from St. Germains, resolving to have desir'd an audience again to-morrow, supposing letters might by that time be come from Nimmeguen and a last resolution taken upon them.

But just now, being Friday morning, Monsieur de Pompone came to make me a visit, and told me from the Most Christian King that his Majesty foreseeing some difficulties might arise at Nimmeguen concerning the propositions his ambassadors were to make there (viz., the delivering up the four towns to Spain, Ghent to remain in the hands of the Dutch, and Maestricht in his Most Christian Majesty's), he had sent new orders to them avec d'autres temperaments a fin de lever toutes sortes de difficultées, and that he did not doubt but the peace would be suddenly concluded, if it were not already signed. I told him I believ'd no temperament could prevail with Spain and Holland but the absolute restitution of the towns, nor that neither after a certain time, which either was or would be soon expired. He said again that he thought the peace would be made, and then his Most Christian Majesty depended on the King my master's offers for the satisfaction of Sweden, which must be adjusted. This was the substance of all that pass'd, tho' a great deal more was said on both parts.

I am extremely glad that the offers of Mr. Mountagu were so well understood, which I doubt would scarce have been without your Lordships help. I hope you will always give it on the like occasion, which I question not but will soon offer itself, for he is too unquiet and industrious not to try a thousand ways more of compassing his designs. And tho' you are never so well arm'd against him, he will endeavour to prevail even with you, and not think it impossible to wheedle you to his advantages. When I came from London I had not time to talk to your Lordship of a proposition I once told you was made to my Lady at Chelsea ;

but, my Lord, if my Lady Bristol and my wife say anything of that matter to your Lordship or my Lady, I beg of you not to think it a compliment, but to be sure that on our parts all shall be done to bring a thing we desire so much to a happy conclusion. I am entirely, and with the greatest respect possible, My Lord,

Your Lordships most faithful and most humble servant,

Sunderland.[1]

To the Lord Sunderland.[2]

5/15 August, 1678.

My Lord,

Yesterday his Majesty received news from his ambassador at Nimmeguen that the peace was signed betwixt France and the States ; but they know not the particulars, nor are they come yet to his Majesties knowledge, only he hears that the Spaniard has refused to sign. I received your letter of the 2/12 this day, and am commanded by his Majesty to send back your courier the same day, because his Majesty will have you lose no time in going to his Most Christian Majesty and letting

[1] On the same day Sunderland wrote to the Countess of Danby as follows : Paris, August the 2/12, [1678]—Madame, I set too greate a valew on the favour you were pleased to show me in England not to endeavour all the wayes I can to obtaine the continuance of it, which makes me take the liberty to give you this trouble, to assure your Ladyship that I am and ever will be the same I profest when I waited on you last, and that there's nothing I desire so much as the marriage I first proposed to your Ladyship, and afterwards talked of at Chelsey. It is no complement, and that I am sure you will find if you continue to approve of it. I hoped by this time to have heard news of my Lord Dunblains being in France, but I have yet heard nothing of my Lord Lansdowne, who intended to be heere almost as soone as I arrived. My Lord Threasurer writes me word that he growes every day to like my Lord Plymouth more and more. I hope he has the same good fortune with your Ladyship, and that my Lady Bridget dos not like him lesse for being better acquainted with him. I thinke he can never be more in love then I saw him, though he sayes he is. I am confident everybody that is not preposest with malice, prejudice and ignorance will grow to like him more as they grow to know him better, especially your Ladyship and your family, whom I know he will studdy to please as long as he lives, and will never have greater pleasure then in the being so happy as to succeede in it, which I doe not doubt of. I am with all the sincerity and respect immaginable, Madame, Your most faithfull, most obedient, and humblest servant, Sunderland. (Leeds MSS., Packet 16.)

[2] *Letters*, p. 293. Neither the original letter nor any draft or copy has been found.

him know that the King our master hopes that his Majesty hath suffered all things to return to the same state they were when his Majesty entred with him into the treaty of the 17/27 May ; that the King our master remains of the same mind in all things he then was, and doubts not but his Most Christian Majesty does so too ; and consequently that the same treaty shall subsist in all points. If you shall meet with any difficulty in the confirming of that treaty, you are to press it as a matter wherein the King our master has not justice done in case it shall be refused, first because the lapse of time was not by his Majesties fault, and secondly because it was in consideration of that treaty that his Majesty consented to set the States at liberty from their treaty with him in January last.

You are farther to let his Most Christian Majesty know that this will be a foundation to build those other agreements upon, which may be necessary for the satisfaction of Sweden, and into which the King our master will be then ready to enter with all the willingness his Most Christian Majesty can desire. If his Most Christian Majesty shall enquire whether you are instructed to enter into particulars about such a treaty as may be for the procuring of satisfaction for Sweden, you are to answer that you are not yet instructed as to the particulars of that treaty, but that in general you are to assure his Most Christian Majesty that the King our master is ready to do anything that can be reasonably desired therein, when he shall know his Most Christian Majesties mind upon that matter. I have sent you enclosed the original letter to the King from the Swedish ambassadors, and one of Monsieur Olivecrans to me, of which his Majesty thinks you may make good use by shewing them to the ministers, by which they will be convinc'd of our master's effectual endeavours to get the Swedes consent to the evacuating the towns, and consequently of procuring the peace on those terms.

I had the favour of another letter from your Lordship this day by my Lord Plimouth, who is as much your Lordships friend as is possible ; and I take his friendship to be very valuable, because I think it not easily to be removed. My Lady Sunderland gave herself the trouble of coming hither to-day, and spoke to me about your Lordships money concerns, which I will take care to give her Ladiship a good account of. She was pleased to say very obliging things to me also about my son Dunblan, who should have waited on you by this time, but that he must not be absent from the Parliament. I am with great respect, My Lord,

Your Lordships, &c.,

Danby.

To the Lord Treasurer.[1]

Paris, August 17th, [*1678*]

My Lord,

This letter should have gone by a courrier Monsieur de Pompone dispach'd last night, but that I went yesterday to St. Germaines at the same time that he sent me word of it, and that by the King's order he writ to me to acquaint me with the news of the signing of the peace by the French and Holland ambassadours, and that ours had refused to doe the same, or to suffer it to be done in theire house, which they had offer'd out of respect to the mediatour. This appears in this place a very strange thing, but is thought perticular to the ambassadors owne surprise, without believing it suitable to theire instructions. I desire your Lordship will please to send me directions how to behave myselfe in this matter, as well as in all others upon this change, for unlesse I am commanded the contrary I shall continue to give the friendlyest and best colour to all things that happen that I can.[2]

A few howers after this news from Nimeguen came that of the Prince of Orange's attacquing Monsieur de Luxembourg's. He began it at 12 a clocke, and it lasted till night. It was on Sunday,[3] *and that night Monsieur de Luxembourg retired, but yet it is thought the Prince may againe have attempted something yesterday, if he received no orders from the Hague to the contrary. It was one of the hottest engagements has been in the whole warre, though but a part of the armys were concerned. The French confesse to have lost a great many men and abundance of officers, though none very eminent. They say of the Princes side our countrymen suffered most, but the particulars are not knowne here yet of anything.*

[1] *Morrison Catalogue,* vi. 209; *Hist. MSS. Com.,* ix. 2, p. 456, from the original letter. There is a copy in Leeds MSS., Packet 10.

[2] This passage is crossed out by the Duke of Leeds in the copy.

[3] August 4/14.

*My Lord Dumbarton can obtain nothing from this Court. He
has been more hardly used then anybody. He hopes the King will
consider that, and the zeale he has always showed for his service.
He now sends one of his officers to acquaint his Majesty with his
whole concerne, by whom I send this letter. I am most seriously* [1]
and passionately, My Lord,

> *Your most faithfull and most obedient servant,*
>
> > *Sunderland.*

*There is news come of another advantage the French have had
in Germany, of which I have given Mr. Secretary an account. My
Lord Lansdowne is arrived here very well after a troublesome voyage.* [2]

[*To the Lord Sunderland*] [3]

> *London, 8th August, 1678.*

My Lord,

    *I have nothing to add to my last by your express, but that
finding the peace now agreed betwixt France and Holland (and wee
suppose by this time with Spaine too), his Majestie thinks itt may
be necessary to inform your Lordship that if any exception should
be takein to the moving of his Majesties troops in Flanders towards
the Prince of Orange, it is to be answered that his Majesties orders
to them were not to stir till the 11th of August, N.S., by which time
the peace would either bee concluded (and so they would not move at
all), or they were then to march by vertue of the treaty betwixt
England and Holland, which was then to be in force, and if any of
them did march after that time (which wee do not know), it was
either that the newes of the peace was not comed to them, or it might
perhaps be some of those troops that were to be removed from Newport to Bruges for change of that quarter where so many of our men
fell sick.*

    *Here is yet no care taken with the Secretarie (whos province it is
for embassadors) to gett the privy seales which are necessary for
your money, and without which I cannot pay a shilling to anybody ;
but I have sent to borrow 1,300 l. upon private creditt while your
privy seales are passing, and hope you will have a bill for that
summe this post or next. I am as ever,* [&c.]

> [*Danby*]

---

[1] The copy gives 'sincerely.'   [2] This postscript does not appear in the copy.
[3] From a copy in a clerk's handwriting in Leeds MSS., Packet 10.

To the Lord Treasurer.[1]

Paris, August the 9/19, [16]78.

My Lord,

My courrier arrived heere this morning, and brought me your Lordships letter of the 5 of August, the orders of which shall be obeyd exactly and speedily. To doe so I will goe to St. Germaines this day, which makes me write now, for I cannot have an audience till to-morrow, nor returne soone enough to write by the post which then goes away.

By a courrier my Lord Dunbarton dispach't on Wenesday[2] *I writ to your Lordship and to my Lord St. Albans. I have no other thing to acquaint you with then what I then did, but that the peace was declared betweene the two armys, which I suppose you know more perticularly and sooner from thence then by the way of Paris. I am with more zeale and reality then any man in the world, My Lord,*

Your Lordships most faithfull and most obedient servant,

Sunderland.[3]

To the Lord Sunderland.[4]

London, 12/22 August, 1678.

My Lord,

On Saturday [5] I received your Lordships of the 17th instant, N.S., and the same day his Majesty and the Duke had letters both from the Prince of Orange and Duke of Monmouth, of the 16th from St. Dennis.[6] Yesterday his Majesty had letters from Sir William Temple at the Hague, and from Sir Lionel Jenkins from Nimmeguen ; and although this be the 12/22, we do not yet know the particular conditions on which the peace is

---

[1] From the autograph letter in Leeds MSS., Packet 10.

[2] August 7/17.

[3] Endorsed by the Duke of Leeds, ' Notice of the peace declared betwixt the two armies.'

[4] *Letters,* p. 296. Neither the original letter nor any draft or copy has been found.

[5] August 10/20.

[6] *Cf.* Danby's letter of August 12 to the Prince of Orange (*supra*, p. 437), and the Duke of York's letter of the same date (*Cal. S.P. Dom.*, 1678, p. 357).

signed betwixt France and Holland. Only we hear that as to Spain there are now things demanded by France which were not in the project at Nimmeguen of April ; and if so, the French King does not make good the conditions then promised for evacuating the towns. We perceive also that there are no orders at all given for hostilities to cease, so that things look as if France had done enough only to obstruct the treaty betwixt England and Holland, and yet, for ought we see, the peace as far off as ever. And if after all we can come to no more certain measures with France, his Majesty will be forced to take others, how bad soever they may prove.

For our ambassadors not signing the peace, the French may answer themselves, for without evacuating the towns they had no power to sign anything. And if any new conditions were demanded of Spain, we suppose the Spanish ambassadors have as little power to sign as they, and how is it possible then the towns should be evacuated ?   For my own part, I take all this to be but a new device to keep all the towns but Maestricht, and by that to see if they can perswade Holland to a peace separate from all their allies. And I am able to give you no other advice but to convince the ministers in that Court, if you can, that they must make good the assurances given for evacuating the towns, if they desire the continuance of our friendship. His Majesty has order'd 1,000 l. to be return'd to my Lord Dunbarton, to set him at liberty to come hither, where he will then have better opportunity to sollicite the rest of his business.

[1] The King has resolved to let his troops be with the Prince of Orange, until there be either a cessation of arms or an assurance that the towns shall be evacuated according to the project of Nimmeguen ; but these things you are to keep to yourself.[1]
I am, My Lord,

Your Lordships, &c.,

Danby.

---

[1] . . . [1] This passage is almost certainly an insertion by the Duke of Leeds. It appears to be taken bodily from the cipher copy of instructions to Sunderland which follows.

To the Lord Sunderland.[1]

London, *12 August, 1678.*

I f   t h e y   s h a l l   o f f e r   to
184 :   64.38.30.74 :   62.39.20.46 :   52.34.34.32.60 :   125 :
r e n e w   the treaty o f   t h e   May, *y o u*
60.30.50.30.70 : 106 : 148 : 52.35 : 106 : 17/27 141 : 74.53.66 :
a r e   to   p r e p a r e   and   a g r e e
22.61.33 :   125 :   57.61.32.57.23.61.33 :   135 :   20.37.60.30.32 :
s u c h   a   o n e   with   t h e m,   b u t
63.66.26.39 :   23 :   54.50.30 :   111 :   64.39.32.48 :   25.66.64 :
y o u   a r e   n o t   n o w   to   s i g n e
74.53.66 : 22.60.33 : 51.55.65 : 50.54.70 : 125 : 63.43.37.51.32 :
it   t i l l   y o u   h a v e   f i r s t
133 :   65.42.47.47 :   74.55.66 :   39.21.69.33 :   35.40.60.63.65 :
s e n t   it   h i t h e r   to   bee
62.32.51.64 :   133 :   38.40.64.38.33.60 :   125 :   126 :
a p p r o v e d.   The   King   h a s
22.56.57.60.53.68.33.28 :   106 :   180 :   38.23.62 :
r e s o l v e d   to   l e t   h i s
60.30.62.53.46.69.33.29 :   125 :   46.32.64 :   38.40.63 :
t r o o p s   bee   with   the Prince of Orange
64.60.52.54.56.62 :   126 :   111 :   106 :   185 :
t i l l   a   c e s s a t i o n   o f
65.42.47.47 :   20 :   26.32.66.63.22.64.42.52.50 :   52.34
a r m s,   o r   a n   a s s u r a n c e   that
22.60.48.62 :   52.61 :   23.51 :   21.62.63.66.61.22.50.26.32 :   107 :
the   t o w n s   s h a l l   bee
106 :   64.52.70.51.63 :   62.39.23.46.47 :   126 :
e v a c u a t e d   a c c o r d i n g   to
32.69.23.27.68.20.64.33.29 :   23.26.27.52.60.28.40.50.36 :   125 :
the   p r o j e c t   o f Nimeguen,   b u t
106 :   56.60.54.40.32.26.64 :   52.34 :   169 :   25.68.64 :
t h e s e   t h i n g s   y o u   a r e
64.38.31.62.30 :   64.38.41.50.36.62 :   74.53.66 :   22.61.32 :
to   k e e p e   to   y o u r   s e l f.
125 :   44.30.32.56 :   125 :   64.52.67.60 :   62.30.46.34 :

---

[1] From a copy in a clerk's handwriting in Leeds MSS., Packet 10, endorsed by Danby, ' Coppy of the letter in cipher to my Lord Sunderland, 12/22 August, 1678.'

To the Lord Treasurer.[1]

Paris, August the 12/22, [1678] [2]

My Lord,

Your Lordship had alwayes so ill an opinion of any negotiation in this Court that you will not wonder to find that they change just as they thinke wee may be usefull to them, that being the measure they goe by. *But, my Lord, to let you know this more perticularly, I must acquaint you that on Saterday morning* [3] *I had an audience of his Most Christian Majesty,* X [4] *and expressed to him in the most obliging tearmes I could the greate joy the King my master had to see that worke concluded which had been so long desired, and how glad his Majesty would be to have it brought to perfection by a generall peace, and the freindship secured for the future between him and his Most Christian Majesty, so that nothing might endanger the breach of it ; that all things being now in the condition so long desired, and for which the treaty of May the 17/27 was made, the King my master remained in the same minde he then was, and doubted not but that his Most Christian Majesty did so too, and consequently that the same treaty ought to subsist.*

I was going on, but he interrupted me and said, Pour ce traitté, il est nul. For you know, said he, that the King your master was obliged to furnish the ratification of it by such a time, to recall his troupes from Flanders, and to prorogue the Parlament, none of all which was done, the time being long since past and consequently the treaty voide. I answered him that as to the lapse of time the King my master was not in fault, all the world knowing he did not make the incident which happen'd at Nimeguen about the evacuation of the townes which occasion'd it, and that ever since he had used all the endeavours he could to rectifie that difficulty, and had done it effectually by the meanes of Sweeden, which was very apparent by the letters the Swedish ambassador writ to the King my master. I

---

[1] From the autograph letter in B.M. Add. MSS. 28054, f. 188, printed in *Campana de Cavelli*, i. 220. On this letter the Duke of Leeds has made serious alterations, to which effect is given in a copy preserved in Leeds MSS., Packet 10. On this copy the Duke has then made a few additional alterations. The version in *Letters*, p. 298, shows further divergences from the original.

[2] On the copy Leeds has altered the date to August 17/27, but this change is not followed in the printed *Letters*.

[3] August 10/20.

[4] For the meaning of this mark see the mark further down

said likewise that it was in consideration of the treaty of 17/27 of
May that the King had consented to set the Dutch free from theire
treaty with him of January last, without which they could not have
concluded the peace, and for all these reasons I concluded his Most
Christian Majesty would thinke that that treaty ought to subsist.

He answerd againe he tooke that treaty to be undoubtedly voide,
and that other measures must now be taken in relation to Sweden,
by which a firme alliance might be established betweene the King my
master and himselfe, into which he would enter with joy, desiring
nothing more then there might be alwayes a strict union betweene
them, and that it would be necessary to thinke what my master
would doe towards the furnishing ships or men, and what asistance
he could give either in money or otherwayes to finish this greate
worke. I told him I thought there could be no better foundation to
build those future agreements upon then the confirmation of the
treaty of 17/27 of May, and that according to all sort of justice and
equity it ought to subsist, but could obtaine no other answer.

I went after this to Monsieur de Pompone, and argued it all over
againe at large, and showed him the Swedish letters, and desired
him he would againe represent all these things to his Most Christian
Majesty, and know of him if I could have no other answer to such
just pretensions then what he himselfe had given me already, and
that on Sunday I would goe to St. Germains to know what the King
resolv'd ; which I did doe, and am just now come back, but with

nothing more then before, but that $\overset{3 \text{ AND } 1}{\wedge}$ Monsieur de Pompone said
a greate deale to give me hopes that for the King my masters helpe
to finish what remained to doe in the north greate conditions might
be obtained, but nothing perticular.

I must beg leave to tell your Lordship that since I came
hither I am sure I have past three quarters of my time at St.

---

[1] By the marks x . . . 3 the Duke of Leeds intended to indicate that the
passage between them should be omitted, and that in its place there should
be substituted the brief passage enclosed between similar marks in Sunderland's
letter of September 6/16 (*infra*, p. 540). This was actually done by the copyist
in making his copy. But before the letter was printed the inserted passage was
itself cut out, along with short passages both before and after it, as indicated
by the italics, and the following was substituted : ' The peace being now
agreed betwixt this Court and the States I suppose there will be no occasion
for my continuing much longer here. But in the meantime.' This may possibly
be taken from some letter of Sunderland's which has not survived.

Germains or on the way to it, and that I never was there one minute but upon the Kings businesse, and that I doe not thinke I have omitted anything that could have been done by one in my place. But it is certaine that the difficultys were made at Nimeguen on purpose either to obtaine by our masters helpe that some of the townes might have remained in the power of France, or els to occasion the lapse of time [1] and so save so much money,[1] for the peace has without question been resolved heere a greate while.

The Court is this day gone to Fontainebleau. I intend to follow in a few dayes to be more ready to obey any orders the King shall please to send me. I am intirely and with the greatest respect in the world, My Lord,

Your Lordships most faithfull and most humble servant,

Sunderland.[2]

To the Lord Treasurer.[3]

Paris, August the 17/27, [1678]

My Lord,

I have your Lordships of August the 12/22 with that in cypher. I shall always observe the directions I receave from you. I expect them in answer to the letters I sent by an expresse last Monday.[4] I will not goe to Fontainebleau till he comes backe. Just now the enclosed letter was brought to me from Monsieur de Pompone.[5] I have answerd it according to the instructions your Lordship gave me in one of yours.

[1] . . . [1] These six words are crossed out by Leeds in the copy, but they appear in the *Letters.*

[2] Endorsed by Danby, ' Lord Sunderland, 12/22 August [16]78 '; and by Leeds, ' Of consequence, and shewing the reasons for demands of money and my opinion of France.'

[3] From the autograph letter in Leeds MSS., Packet 10.   [4] August 12/22.

[5] This letter is still preserved along with Sunderland's. It runs :

A Fontainebleau, le 25 Aoust, 1678—Monsieur, Depuis mon arrivée en ce lieu j'ai eu l'honneur de rendre conte au Roy de la visite que vous m'avez fait l'honneur de me rendre avant hier a Paris. Comme je vous temoigné le sentiment dans lequel sa Majeste estoit d'entrer avec le Roy de la Grande Bretagne dans un traitte en faveur du Roy de Suede et dans la discussion [indecipherable] qu'elle pourroit y contribuer, elle ma commande aujourdhuy de scaver de vous sy vous avez un pouvoir pour commencer cette negotiation. Vous jugerez de laquelle on veut perdre aucun temps pour la lier et pour la terminer avecque vous, et pour continuer les liaisons d'amitie sy particuliere qu'elle a avec le Roy vostre maistre. Je suis avec toutte l'estime et la verité possibles, Monsieur, Vostre trez humble et trez, Arnauld de Pomponne.

The armys in Germany furnish no news, nor the ambassadours at Nimeguen, which obliges me to conclude this by assuring your Lordship that I am intirely, My Lord,

Your Lordships most faithfull and most obedient servant,

Sunderland.

The Duke of Buckingham is yet incognito heere, if he is heere.

To the Lord Treasurer.[1]

Paris, September the 1, [1678], S.N.

My Lord,

By the last post I sent your Lordship a letter I had just then receaved from Monsieur de Pompone, in which he desired to know whether or no I had power to treate concerning the satisfaction of Sweden, to which I made answer that I had yet orders onely to assure his Most Christian Majesty that the King my master would willingly agree to any reasonable thing when he knew what was desired of him.

It is thought heere that at Monsieur Bevernings returne to Nimeguen the treaty will be soone concluded betweene France and Spaine. The French pretend they make no new demands, and those places now in question are dependances of the others, always agreed to ; but whether that is so or not I dare say the peace will be made, for I am very confident it is so much resolved heere that they will not breake it for a few vilages. Neither doe I thinke they designed the keeping any townes, beleiving that Holland would never consent to such tearmes ; but they found it more convenient for them to make peace by quitting all then by any other way that was proposed to them.

I resolve not to goe to Fontainebleau till I have an answer to the letter I writ to your Lordship after my last audience at St. Germaines, which I expected before this time. I write now by my Lord Dunbarton, who has certainely been very ill used heere, and I thinke onely because he seemed willing to serve against them, which they did not like, though for his owne King. He depends much upon your Lordships favour. I am most sincerely and intirely, My Lord,

Your most obedient and most humble servant,

Sunderland.

[1] From the autograph letter in Leeds MSS., Packet 10.

To the Lord Sunderland.[1]

Wimbledon, August 26/September 5, 1678.

Yesterday when I was with the King at Windsor I received your Lordships of the 12/22 and 17/27 instant, with one inclosed from Monsieur de Pompone to your Lordship ; and as you tell me in that of the 12/22 that I had always so bad an opinion of that Court that I will believe no good can come from it, so I doubt not but your Lordship must be of the same opinion by the tricks and evasions you meet with from them every day. I shewed both those letters to his Majesty, as also one I received from you by my Lord Dunbarton, wherein you write the answer you return'd to Monsieur de Pompone's letter, which the King approv'd very well.

In your last, by my Lord Dunbarton, your Lordship says you shall not remove to Fountainbleau till you have an answer to that of 12/22, which you had got before now if I had received any instructions for it. But the truth is his Majesty does now expect so little reality from France that he does not much busy his thoughts how to transact with them, being satisfied that if they can propose anything to us which may be for their interest they will not fail to do it themselves, and whatever his Majesty shall propose they will only make use of (as they have done) either to procure delays by it, or to talk of, to the creating jealousies betwixt us and their enemies. For these reasons his Majesty commands me to let your Lordship know that he will propose nothing, but that he would have you give the same good words to the French King that he did you, viz., that his Majesty is still as desirous as ever to preserve a firm friendship with his Most Christian Majesty, and that he would enter with joy into anything which could procure so desirable an end ; that particularly his Majesty is ready to do anything he can for the satisfaction of Sweden, so soon as he may know what his Most Christian Majesty does desire of him for that end, and that he may at the same time know how far his Most Christian Majesty will comply with those demands of his, which will be so abso-

[1] *Letters*, p. 300. Neither the original letter nor any draft or copy has been found.

lutely necessary for him to have, if he expects that our King should be at the expence of giving assistances to Sweden.

In case your Lordship finds them disposed to enter into such measures, his Majesty would have you tell them that you have orders to transmit any proposals about Sweden to his Majesty, and that you dare assure them you can have powers sent you at any time for concluding a treaty in favour of Sweden, if they will by your Lordship send any encouragement for the King to proceed upon it. When your Lordship says this to the ministers, his Majesty would have you at the same time to put them in mind that time will be very precious in this affair, for that perhaps his Majesty may not always be at liberty to enter into those measures he may yet do. I must not omit the King's commands of writing to your Lordship by this post, or otherwise I should scarce have done it now, being very weary, and not very well, but always, My Lord,

Your Lordships, &c.,

Danby.

To the Lord Treasurer.[1]

Fontainebleau, September 6, [*1678*]

My Lord,

I came hither yesterday, and this morning I had occasion to speake to his Most Christian Majesty concerning the Duke of Buckingham, which I did according to the orders I receaved from the King. He assured me he knew nothing of his being in France, nor had not heard it but as a thing talked of at reandome by everybody, but that nobody could give any account of. This I doe beleeve is certainely true, and I doe as much beleive that he has not seene any of the ministers. But he is willing to have it thought he has, and Sir Ellis Leyghton endeavours by all his skill to peswade the world this journey is very misterious ; but I have met with few that have had that opinion of it he wishes.

It is thought the Duke of Lorraine, having past the Rhine, will hazard anything to fight. He must venter a greate deale if he does, for his army is very much weakened. I am with the greatest respect and truth, My Lord,

Your most faithfull and most obedient servant,

Sunderland.[2]

[1] From the autograph letter in B.M. Add. MSS. 28054, f. 192.

[2] Endorsed by Danby, ' 6th September, [16]78, when the Duke of Buckingham was in France with Sir Ellis Leighton privately.'

[*To the Lord Treasurer*] [1]
Fontainebleau, September 9, [*1678*]

My Lord,

The peace is heere thought so sure, that if all parties had signed and ratifyed, it could not be more. If there had been more difficultys, and more townes insisted upon, I beleive all would have beene yeilded to as well as Bovines and Beaumont. They have certainely resolved it a greate while, and those resolutions have been very much quickened by the steps wee have made.

The last letters from Germany make everybody thinke that the Duke of Lorraine will not attempt any greate matter, but part of his army being past the Rhine and being very much weakened by a greate many little losses he has received. I am most intirely,

Your Lordships most faithfull and most obedient servant,

Sunderland.[2]

[*To the Lord Treasurer*] [3]
Fontainbleau, September the 3/13, [*1678*]

My Lord,

I have receaved your Lordships of the 26 of August, and shall exactly obey the Kings orders. By the next post I shall be able to give you an account of them. I beleeve this Court desires enough to treate with the King, but they would made a good bargaine, all the faire words in the world they give. I wish something more might follow, that would advantage his Majestys affaires. I am with all the respect in the world, My Lord,

Your most faithfull and most obedient servant,

Sunderland.[4]

[*To the Lord Treasurer*] [5]
Fontainebleau, September 5/15, [*1678*]

My Lord,

I have so often showed that I desired nothing so much as your Lordships allyance, that you will easily beleive that I doe so

---

[1] From the autograph letter in Leeds MSS., Packet 10.

[2] Endorsed by Danby, ' 9th September [16]78,' and by Leeds, ' The steps made here towards a war hastened the peace with Holland, &c.'

[3] From the autograph letter in Leeds MSS., Packet 10.

[4] Endorsed by Danby, ' 3rd September, [16]78.'

[5] From the autograph letter in Leeds MSS., Packet 10.

still, and that upon the news I receaved of my Lady Sophy's being againe in your power I could not but have new hopes for my sonne. If your Lordship thinkes he can be worthy of her, wee shall esteeme ourselves infinitely happy, and will endeavour all our lives to make her so, and to let you see that you could not place her where she would be more valeued. I hope your Lordship will be favourable to us, and beleive that I am more really then any man in the world, My Lord,

    Your most faithfull and most obedient servant,

        Sunderland.

If any treaty should be made betweene our master and this King, I beleive there must be sent somebody into Sweeden. I thinke if it should be necessary that Harry Savile might be very proper. He is now so sober that I know but that exceptions against his going into that country. Your Lordship knows both his fitnesse and his zeale to your service, which I thinke is all to be considerd in this matter.[1]

To the Lord Treasurer.[2]

    Fontainebleau, September 6/16, [1678]

My Lord,

    Since I writ last I have obeyed the Kings orders I receaved by your Lordships letter of the 26 of August. This Court X[3] WHO ∧ *seemes still very desirous of our helpe for Sweeden, but all I can get from them yet is this, that his Most Christian Majesty does desire the King should declare himselfe for the entire satisfaction of Sweeden, and would know what number of ships and how many men the King will furnish towards the obtaining of it, in case his declaration should not have the effect which they thinke it will, for they say the name of England will make all the Confederates submit; 3 [3] and lastly he desires to know what his Majesty will expect from hence. Monsieur de Pompone asked me if I were not enough instructed to begin to treate. I told him I must first send into England, which*

---

[1] Endorsed by Danby, ' 15 September [16]78. Lord Sunderland about a match of his son to my daughter Sophia.'

[2] From the autograph letter in B.M. Add. MSS. 28054, f. 194.

[3] For the meaning of these marks v. *supra*, p. 534, note.

I would doe by a courrier who would soone be heere againe. They would willingly keepe well with us, but they will begin on a new score, and I feare will not answer the Kings expectation in point of money. The French King does desire that the ships may be fitted and manned for warre, and the men entertained and payed by our master. If the King thinkes fit I should treate about this businesse, I desire your Lordship will let my instructions be so perticular that nothing may be left to me, ᛖ ¹ *for I am not of the humour of those who like a greate power in such cases, for I thinke mine can not be too much limited ; and therefore if you please that a treaty may be drawne up as neere as can be to what the King desires, and sent by this courrier, I will exactly follow it. It will be necessary that the time of the Kings declaring be expressed, and when the ships and men can be ready, and how long employed.*

Monsieur de Barillon has frighted them heere with greate summes, such as they will hardly give. I have prepared them as well as I can by telling them that this is such an allyance as perhaps will not please in England, and consequently the King will be lesse able to be supplyed by his Parlament, and therefore must demand more then otherwaies he would doe. This they seeme to understand and to thinke reasonable, and yet I am affraide they will not give enough. ᛖ ¹ *I have such a comission as is given to all*

BUT

ambassadours. ∧ *I know not whether or no any other powers is necessary. I am with greate respect, My Lord,*

> *Your most faithfull and most humble servant,*
>
>> *Sunderland.²*

To the Lord Treasurer.³

> *Paris, September the 11/21, [1678]*

My Lord,

I came hither on Sunday,⁴ and intend to stay heere till the expresse I sent to your Lordship from Fontainebleau returnes. The Spaniards signing is now expected every day, and reckoned upon as sure, the French having yeilded to all theire demands.

---

¹ . . .¹ The intention of the Duke of Leeds was presumably that the passage between these marks should be omitted.

² Endorsed by Danby, ' 16 September [16]78,' and by Leeds, ' Something about money.'

³ From the autograph letter in Leeds MSS., Packet 10.   ⁴ September 8/18.

The letters from Germany bring news of a thousand horse which came out of Strasbourg being beaten by Monsieur de l'Angallerie. The two army's are neere each other, both strongly entrenched, and so like to continue till the suspension so long talked of be agreed to. I am with all truth and respect, My Lord,

    Your Lordships most faithfull and most obedient servant,

                                   Sunderland.

To the Lord Treasurer. [1]

                         Paris, September the 14/24, [1678]

My Lord,

    I now write to your Lordship to continue as I have done hitherto, that is to let no post day passe without doing it, for I have nothing worth your knowledge to acquaint you with. The armys in Germany are in the same posts they were, that is part of the Duke of Lorraines on this side of the Rhine, very strongly encamp't, and the Mareshall de Crecquy's neere it. It is thought they will expect a suspension or peace without attempting anything. It was thought so sure before that the news of the Spaniards having signed has made no alteration heere.

    I was the other day to see my Lady Sussex, and found her very weary of the monastery. I told her I thought it was a good deale in her owne power to shorten her stay in a place she disliked so much, and that the first step she ought to make was to reconcile herselfe to her mother. She said she was ready to obey the King in that as in all other things, so that if his Majesty cares she should be freinds with my Lady Cleavland, and will let her know it, I make no doubt but she will doe what is fit in order to it. I am most intirely, My Lord,

    Your most faithfull and most obedient servant,

                                     Sunderland.

[To the Lord Sunderland] [2]

                 Wimbleton, 16 [3] *September, [16]78.*

My Lord,

    I am just now returned from Windsor, where his Majestie has been pleased to approve of what I writt your Lordship by the

---

[1] From the autograph letter in Leeds MSS., Packet 10.

[2] From an autograph draft in Leeds MSS., Packet 10.

[3] The figure ' 15 ' has been struck out and ' 16 ' substituted. Probably the draft was begun on September 15 and the letter sent the next day.

last expresse, but saies further that when they have by your Lordship understood in generall what sort of treaty they must come to with his Majestie, if they desire any, hee wishes that his Most Christian Majestie would instruct his embassador here, and impower him to conclude any treaty they intend, and would have your Lordship to acquainte the King that this is his desire.

When you have done this, I perceive his Majestie will bee willing to comply with your Lordships request of returning into England, which I understand only by my Lord St. Alban, but you will desire more formally by a Secretary of State when you would have your revocation. In the meane time upon my Lord St. Albans intimation I have prepared the way for itt, as I shall do for anything within my power which may bee to your Lordships satisfaction, being unfeignedly, My Lord,

Your Lordships, &c.,

[Danby] [1]

To the Lord Treasurer. [2]

Paris, September the 18/28, [1678]

My Lord,

I have receaved your Lordships of the 11 of Septembre, [3] *by which I finde there is not much to be expected from hence as yet, for they will not hearken to anything like what you mention. I will expect heere the next letters, by which your Lordship says I shall be more fully instructed. I have at large writ to my Lord St. Albans concerning the leave I desire to goe into England. He will let you know it, therefore I will onely beg your assistance and assure you it can not prejudice the Kings businesse.*

The Marechall de Bellefonds is recalled to Court, which all the best people are glad of, being extreamely esteemed heere. It furnishes a greate deale of discourse as if it would have consequences of publike importance, but I doe not beleive any such thing is thought of. The affaires in Germany are still as they were. I beleive you will have heard other waies of the death of the Bishop

---

[1] Endorsed by Danby, ' Coppy of my letter to the Earl of Sunderland, 16 September 1678.'

[2] From the autograph letter in Leeds MSS., Packet 10.

[3] This letter has not been found.

of Munster, and that the Bishop of Paderborne succeeds him. I am with the greatest reality in the world, My Lord,

> *Your most faithfull and most obedient servant,*
>
> Sunderland.[1]

[To the Lord Treasurer] [2]

My Lord,

Paris, October the *1,* [*1678*]

Yesterday I receaved the letter your Lordship writ to me at your returne from Windsor,[3] and shall obey your directions, in order to which I am just now going to Fontainebleau. T'is certaine that this Court does desire our helpe for Sweeden, seeing well enough that without it the affaires of the north will prove very difficult, and may in a little time engage all the world in a new warre, which I thinke is not the designe of this place ; but they will heere never be brought to doe anything like what your Lordship mentions to me without being assured of a proportionable assistance from our master. But this is onely my opinion ; by the next post I shall be able to let you know more clearly the sence of his Most Christian Majesty.

I did by the last write a letter to my Lord of St. Albans concerning the desire I had to goe into England, which I suppose he has acquainted your Lordship with, so that I need not repeate what I then writ, but beg of you that you will obtaine the leave I aske in the manner I desire it, which I am sure may be for the Kings service and cannot be against it. I will speake to his Most Christian Majesty that Monsieur de Barillon may be instructed. I am most zealously and sincerely, My Lord,

> *Your most faithfull and most obedient servant,*
>
> Sunderland.

There is no news heere but that the Court returns from Fontainebleau the 10 of this month. It goes first to St. Cloud for five or six dayes, and then to Versailles. Monsieur de Tallart is to be in the Bastille a yeare for challenging the Comte d'Auvergne.[4]

---

[1] Endorsed by Danby, ' 18 September [16]78, in answer to mine of the 11th.'

[2] From the autograph letter in Leeds MSS., Packet 10.

[3] Dated September 16, 1678, *supra*, p. 542.

[4] Endorsed by Danby, ' 1st October [16]78. Lord Sunderlands letter. Perused.'

To the Lord Treasurer.[1]

Paris, October the 8, [1678]

My Lord,

I have let his Most Christian Majesty know with all the care immaginable that it is impossible for the King to make the declaration which is so much desired heere, how much he is courted to enter into the contrary allyance, and have made the proposition your Lordships letters of the 11 and 16 of September [2] directed me to doe ; to which I can obtaine no answer but that the chiefe thing towards the procuring the satisfaction of Sweede is the King's declaring himselfe for it, that his Most Christian Majesty wants neither men nor ships but the countenance of England, and in short that he desires nothing more then such an allyance with my master, [3] *but he can not thinke fit to give much money for a neutrality onely, for so he cals the proposi-*

tion I made ᴀʙᴏᴜᴛ ꜱᴡᴇᴅᴇɴ ∧ *, and he said he had* [3] hoped I would have offerd something which might for ever have assured the good intelligence betweene him and my master, which he so much wished.

I said all that was possible to let him understand that very advantagious propositions were made to the King, that the power of the Prince of Orange was as considerable as ever, that the businesse of Sweeden could never be accomodated if the King should joyne with the Confederates, and severall things to fortify all that, which I am confident he sees very plainely, and doubt not but that he desires extreamely to secure the freindship of our master, and may be brought to doe a greate deale for it, if it were intirely secured. After this I told him that the King desired Monsieur de Barillon might be instructed in this matter, and that I had asked leave to goe into England for a little time, which I hoped to obtaine. He said he should not be sorry that I made such a journey, because he hoped it would contribute to the establishing a correspondence that might be of advantage to my master and to him.

---

[1] From the autograph letter in Leeds MSS., Packet 10. *Letters*, p. 303.

[2] Only the second of these letters has been found.

[3] . . . [3] With the exception of the word ' and ' this whole passage is omitted from the *Letters*. No authority, however, has been found for the omission in the handwriting of the Duke of Leeds.

2M

D.L. II.

This being the state of affaires heere, I beg of your Lordship that you will please to aske leave of the King that I may goe into England for a month or lesse, as he shall thinke fit. I am sure it can not prejudice his businesse, and I hope it may be of some advantage to it, for one can not write a greate many little things which are often important to the greatest. Your Lordship is so unapt to thinke any good can come from hence, that I am afraide of telling you I thinke it may be had, if the King's affaires will permit him to helpe them to a generall peace, for this Court is fix't upon those thoughts, and that can hardly be without the King's assistance, for which they would doe a greate deale, that there might be no warre still depending in the north, which may againe engage the whole world. But I will not any longer detaine your Lordship, hoping soone to have the honour and satisfaction of waiting upon you, and acquainting you with all I know of this matter, and of assuring you that I am most sincerely, My Lord,

> Your most faithfull and most obedient servant,

> > Sunderland.

I thinke it is not necessary for me to say much to perswade you that I am overjoyed that my Lord Plymouth and my Lady Bridget are married, but I can not but tell your Lordship that I am so, and that I beleive as well as hope that nobody concerned in it will ever repent what they contributed towards it.

I was not well at Fontainebleau, which was the occasion of my not writing to your Lordship by the last post.[1]

[*To the Lord Treasurer*][2]

> Paris, the 5/15 of October, [*1678*]

My Lord,

The letters which came yesterday from England give a confused account of a conspiracy that one can not thinke of without horrour. If there are such villains in nature I hope they will find the reward due to them, but I can not thinke there is a man alive that so much as wishes ill to the best of princes. I have received

---

[1] Endorsed by Danby, ‘ Lord Sunderland, October 8, [16]78,’ and by Leeds, ‘ That I will not beleive any good can come from France.’

[2] From the autograph letter in Leeds MSS., Packet 10.

the leave I desired, and have acquainted his Most Christian [Majesty] with it, who told me he hoped my journey would conduce towards the fortifying the freindship betweene my master and him, and that I would soone returne with those assurances. I shall begin my journey this day sennight. I am most intirely,
Your Lordships most faithfull and obedient servant,

Sunderland.

Monsieur de Nouailles writes that the peace is ratifyed at Madrid, but the news is not come any other way. They talke as if Strasbourg would be soone beseiged, but I beleive it is onely talke.[1]

---

[1] Endorsed by Danby, ' Lord Sunderland, 5/15 October [16]78,' and by Leeds, " About his returne and newes of a conspiracy here.'

PARTICULAR REMARKS

ON SOME OF

LORD SUNDERLAND'S LETTERS [1]

They all relate to the negotiations betwixt England and France during that critical time of the treaties of Nimmeguen, which ended in the separate peace betwixt France and Holland, and at last with Spain also. And I have nothing particularly to remark in them, save that in his Lordships of the 2/12 of August he tells me how extreamly glad he was that the offers of Mr. Mountagu had been so well understood, and his repetitions both in his 12/22 of August, 1678, and September 28/October 8, 1678, and several others, that I had so very bad an opinion of all the actings of the French Court that I would never believe any good could come from them.

[1] The draft of these has not been preserved, and they are accordingly printed as they appear in *Letters*, p. 306.

MR. BRISBANE'S LETTERS[1]

[*To the Lord Treasurer*][2]

Paris, 18/28 November, 1676.

My Lord,

I am but just riseing from bed, and indeed not recovered from a strange sort of complicated violent sickness.

Here is inclosed a copie of the Most Christian Kings late ordonnance in favour of our commerce, which I accompany with a true copie of another of the 19th December, 1673.[3] The first, I conjecture, was obtained at the instance of Sir William Lockhart, as this hath been by my Lord Ambassadour. The first was never publickly revocked, as I am informed, but hath been quite abrogated in the practise, as I can justify. I am told it hath been urged often in our causes, and it hath been answered that it was a volontary thing, as indeed I know the Civilians make a notable difference between nuda promissio and that which they call stipulatio. Naturally speaking marks of a particular consideration (these be the words of the ordonnance) or kindnesse oblige the benefactor no longer than he thinks it convenient for him, or that he can find no reason to say his kindnesse is abused. I leave the inferences to your Lordship, and remaine, I'm sure, with great respect and acknowledgement of your favours and very honest intentions, My Lord,

Your Lordships most faithfull and oblidged humble servant,

J. Brisbane.

I'm faint and forced to lye downe upon my bed.

[1] The letters from Brisbane printed in *Lindsey MSS.* are so numerous that they are not individually referred to except for some special reason.

[2] From the original letter in Leeds MSS., Packet 7.

[3] The copy of the ordinance of December 19, 1673, is still preserved along with the letter.

[To the Lord Treasurer] ¹

Paris, 13/23 December, 1676.

My Lord,

Your Lordship hath herewith a copie of my letter this day to Mr. Secretary Coventry, to which I add, with your Lordships leave, ² and I think in pursuance of your commands, ² that the treaty ³ which wee desire, and my Lord Ambassadour presseth ⁴ with much care and application, meets with many difficulties here, and yett the objections that wee heare of are few and weak, ⁵ *onely two.*

The first is that they ought not to bind themselves to secure their ennemies goods in English ships, so long as wee (either for want of such treatys with some nations, or by the inobservation of such treatys where wee have them) doe not secure French goods in our bottoms. This objection was made by the King to my Lord Ambassadour, and the taking of French goods out of some English ships by the Spaniards and Hollanders was all the reason Monsieur Colbert gave me for their silent laying aside the ordonnance of the 29th December 1673 without any warning given. I think this objection is easily answered—that wee offer to give and take the priviledge of free shipping a common advantage to both sides, and ayming principally at an uninterrupted navigation, which can not be if wee bee still vexed with distinguishing our owne from strangers goods; that his Majesty will not require the Most Christian King to make any provision with other princes for the security of English goods in French bottoms, nor to warrant the execution of any such treatys with others when he happens to have them.

The other objection is that our passeports are easily gott, for Hollanders for exemple, and so their ships will enjoy the benifitt of

---

¹ From the autograph letter in B.M. Add. MSS. 28054, f. 40, endorsed by the Duke of Leeds, ' 13/23 December, [16]76. Mr. Brisbane, with materiall things about the Parliament.' The version in *Letters*, p. 308, is widely different, but no authority for the alterations has been found except in the two cases noted below. The principal discrepancies are mentioned in the notes.

² . . . ² Omitted in the *Letters*.   ³ ' Treaty of Commerce ' in the *Letters*.

⁴ ' Has press'd ' in the *Letters*.

⁵ In place of the long passage which is now omitted the *Letters* substitute, ' of which I have given an account to Mr. Secretary, as also of my answers to those objections, so that I will not trouble your Lordship with a repetition of them.'

that treaty. I use to answer to this that I'm sure no nation ever did use so much precaution to prevent this sort of fraud as is now used in England, and that his Majesty will be obliged to any man that shall furnish him with expedients yett more certain to prevent it, and that I'm sure by the numberlesse deceits now used in the ports of France by the officers of the severall Admiralitys and the armateurs they would practise much more of this covering our ennemies if wee had any : that when France entered in such a treaty with Spaine in the yeare 1659 they were nothing so scrupoulous in this matter, the forme of the passport then agreed upon being very slight, the master onely swearing the ship to be French or Spanish, and the passeport to be given by any magistrats of maritime townes : that wee can not learne that France offered to decline the observation of the same treaty the first year of this present warr, though the neighbourhood and liknesse of language between Flanders and Holland afforded them many opportunitys of helping one another with such passeports. In a word, the number of English shipping, the humour of both nations, and the care of our Gouvernment render the suspition more probable on the French side.

However, my Lord, these objections, such as they are, doe hinder (or seem to doe so) the treaty wee desire so justly and so necessarily, in so much that because they are perswaded wee have no such treaty with Spaine, that is to say no article expresly providing that a free ship shall make free goods, they presse that wee must have it with Spaine first, and then wee may have it here. My Lord, this plain enough nothing but a delay,[1] and if they can drive it off till there be something done at Numegue, or till they see our Parliament either prorogued or refusing to supply the King, I venture to tell your Lordship my weak opinion wee shall have no treaty at all.

I must throw myself at your Lordships feet and beg your pardon for yett a further presumption I think myself obldged to use,[2] and which is not without danger to me if you be not carefull and favourable. My Lord, I doe[2] believe this Court is

---

[1] In the *Letters* this reads, ' it is plain enough that they mean nothing but a delay.'

[2] . . . [2] This passage is omitted in the *Letters*, and in its place is substituted, ' which is, that I have reason to.'

persuaded the distrusts of the Parliament are so settled, that upon no termes they will give the King mony, except it be upon such termes as he will not for his honour allow of, no, not (for all the knowne inclinations of the people) [1] if it were to make warr with France ; and particularly that the Parliament will never trust your Lordship with anything they shall give. Monsieur de Ruvigny expressed himself to this whole purpose to me so confidently that he said he would be content to be held infamous if it did not prove so ; and it is naturall enough to believe that so strong a perswasion is gone from him to the other ministers. And truly, my Lord, I make not the least doubt but these jealousies are and will be fomented from hence, because they keep his Majesty and the nation in a condition to be lesse feared, and I will take my oath wee are not loved in France.

None but God can putt in the Parliament a spirit of union and respect to his Majesty, which is the onely thing can render the nation safe, respected, and happy. Yett as the treaty wee are now aiming at looks like one humane meanes to produce that blessed effect, I venture yett further to offer to your Lordship my thoughts about it. Negotiation here will not doe it (I think not at all, and I'm sure not in time to doe good against the Parliament _{SITTS}) ; and therefore if the King would speak of it strongly to Monsieur Courtin and immediatly use him dryly and keep him at some more than ordinary distance, if at the same time
he visited his yards [2] and gave directions for the fitting of _{AND} repairing some ships, [3] if he expressed a resolution to lett the Parliament meet,[3] I should hope some good from these things.

For God's sake, my Lord, pardon me and lett me know from Mr. Bertie how great you think my fault is in venturing at such matters so farr above my capacity and commission, for I am

---

[1] The phrase within the brackets is omitted in the *Letters*.

[2] Instead of ' he visited his yards ' the *Letters* read ' his Majesty would command his yards to be visited.'

[3] . . . [3] Omitted in the *Letters*.

with a perfect sense of your many favours, and an extraordinary[1] and sincere intentions, My Lord,

Your Lordships most humble and most faithfull servant,

Brisbane.

Your Lordship will have another letter from me this day ; I meane a copie of mine to Mr. Secretary, for I durst not lett my clerck copie this, and he knows I use to writ to your Lordship.[2]

To the Lord Treasurer.[3]

Paris, 8th May, 1677, S.N.

My Lord,

It is certainly believed here that Monsieur Courtin is to leave his poste in England, and Monsieur de Brillon to goe in his roome. The reasons given out for it are by some that Monsieur Courtin wants health in England, by others that he can not support the expense of it ; and all agree that it is his owne desire or advice to be recalled. The reasons I imagine for that change are quit different, for he knew both his owne constitution and the expense of the embassy, having made tryall of both before. But, my Lord, there is much discourse here of your Lordships power and influence upon our affaires and of the great success you had this sessions, which even those that did not wish it attribute to your prudence [4] and courage. All hands agree that with these qualities you serve the King so usefully that you must be strongly fixed in his Majestys favour, and that there remaines no hopes of removeing you. Now, my Lord, my conjecture is that Monsieur Courtin from the beginning of his embassy having proposed to himself (perhaps being instructed so to doe) [4] other measures and meanes of succeeding in his

---

[1] ' Extraordinary respect ' in the *Letters*.

[2] The postscript is omitted altogether in the *Letters*. The copy of Brisbane's letter to the Secretary has not been preserved.

[3] From the autograph letter among the Lindsey MSS., printed in *Lindsey MSS.*, p. 381. *Letters*, p. 311.

[4] . . . [4] In the *Letters* this is omitted and the following substituted, ' and are afraid that your serving the King so usefully must fix you so strongly in his Majesty's favour that there will remain no hopes of removing you, and I am sure you can never believe they have any good will for your Lordship, and that being laid down here for a principal of undoubted truth your Lordship may take such measures as you think best to prevent your own harms, as well as the nations. And as to Mr. Courtin, my opinion is that from the beginning of his embassy he having propos'd to himself (and perhaps instructed so to do).'

negotiations than by applications to your Lordship, it is not so easy for him to change his owne measures as it will be for another ambassadour to begin upon new ones. Whether this conjecture be right or wrong will appeare to your Lordship by Monsieur de Barillons cariage when he comes to be employed, and it may be you will perceive something of it by his present journy. As I offer this onely as a conjecture your Lordship will not, I hope, blame me much if I be mistaken in it.

Yesterday morning Monsieur de Luxembourg went from hence early to Condé, where is appointed a rendezvous for the army, though it was spoke of before to be at another place ; and Monsieur de Shomberg tells he must sett out Monday next to meet the King, I beleive at the same place. Monsieur le Comte de St. Geran told me yesterday likewise they expect a great impression of the Confederates from the country of Luxembourg, which (it is reported) the Spaniards have given to the Emperour, though it doth seeme probable the Emperour cannot be much the better for a small country so far from home.

It is reported here likewise that the ajournment of our Parliament to the 21 of May is to be prolonged till October next ; and truly it will not be much amiss to see the success of this campagne over before the King be any more pressed to publick resolutions about the share he is to take in the affaires of our neighbours. It is a hundred to one neither side can be successful but wee may then as well as now cast the ballance. However in the meanetime it hath all the appearance of a glorious, safe and Christian designe for the King to procure and give peace to Christendom, which may be done so as to engage all the parties to be guarantis for the treaty that shall be made. I pray God preserve and direct you, and that the success of all your Lordships undertakings may be answerable to the worthinesses of your intentions.

I waite on Mr. Herbert frequently, whom I find always very commendably employed in study or ingenious conversation or designing. Truly, my Lord, I hope you will have great satisfaction in him, as he has an entire relyance upon your Lordships favour and care of him.
I remaine with perfect respect and gratitude, My Lord,

Your Lordships most humble, most obedient, and

most faithfull servant,   Brisbane.[1]

[1] Endorsed by the Duke of Leeds, ' 8 May, [16]77. Mr. Brisbane. Some part relating to mee.'

[To the Lord Treasurer] [1]

Paris, 25th June, 1677.

My Lord,

I am heartily sorry and in some measure ashamed that my unavoidable applications to our particular claimes doe so wholly swallow up my time that I cannot possibly render myself so usefull in this station by other services as I did hope and earnestly desire to be, as your Lordship did me the favour to think I might. However, I cannot doe even the businesse I am restrained to without making some observations of the genius and thoughts of those that gouverne here, and the opinions they have of us and our inclinations towards them.

They think the King almost at war with the Parliament, and I'm sure would not have them concurring in anything. They think, or say at least, that the personall friendship between our princes is such that our master hath nowhere els so good a security for the support of his prerogative ; and I think and dare say they would be loth upon occasion the defense of it should cost them anything, and God be thanked wee are not like to need their help. One day, or two at most, before wee had the news of the last adresse and adjournment of the Parliament I was with Monsieur de Ruvigny, who is confidently believed here, and with reason, to be the man in France who understands England best. He then told me he believed the Parliament would give the King the 600,000 l., but upon harsh conditions, and appointed administrators of their owne. I replyed [2] they had been of late so sparing in shaking the ministers that probably they would not desire that.[2] He said it was true, I believe, they may not desire it now, parce que Monsieur le Grand Thesorier est de concert avec eux, qu'il leur promet que l'argent sera employé comme ils veulent et qu'ils se fieront peutestre a luy pour une fois ; mais apres cela ils en useront comme je vous dis. The adresse and adjournment have been very gladly received here, and I am asked many questions about it which I can not answer ; but I'm sure they wish all breaches of that

[1] From the autograph letter among the Lindsey MSS., partly printed in *Lindsey MSS.*, p. 384. *Letters*, p. 313.

[2] . . . [2] Instead of this the *Letters* read, ' that probably they would not do so.'

kind wider than ever they will see them if there be a grain of common sense left amongst us.

If your Lordship will give me leave to speak my thoughts concerning that addresse, I think it hard to believe that the feare of the greatnesse of France could be the leading motive to it. *The Romans, a popular state, in feares and extremities of the commonwealth had recourse to a dictator. God and nature, our laws and the right of succession, have given us one, and besides him no other shelter if wee be really afraid and in danger ; and it is an imagination beyond ridiculousnesse to fancy that a prince would chuse to trade and owe to another the support of his authority, when he can so well maintaine it by his owne right and strength.*

It is true he[1] may mistake his measures (and that is all can be said) [2] by useing wrong means to a good end ; but I think truly one instance ought to oblidge us all to reverence his Majestys understanding and counsels, as well as his person and character, which hath not been the work of a day or a yeare but of many. At his restoration he proposed to himself the improvement of trade and navigation, and hath succeeded in it (even before this conjuncture of others warrs) beyond the hopes of those that talked of it seventeen yeares agoe ; and yett I'm sure the meanes that have produced that extraordinary effect have been often blamed by speculative people as not conducing to it. And now the trade of England is at such a height that it is as hard to think it can continue so as it was hard to believe once it would ever rise to it.

Wee doe here confidently think Monsieur de Lorraine hath been to bold in advancing so farr, and that he cannot retire from his post without a check nor keep it but with great difficulty. Wee are every day expecting some action in Lorraine ; Monsieur de Crequi is certainly posted with great advantage and hardly to be removed. The accomptes wee have had of some execution done by the canon on both sides give the advantage to the French, and it is likely enough, because they were then upon the higher ground.

I find many difficulties in the revisions of sentences given against his Majestys subjects, and am afraid they will furnish us matter of

---

[1] The *Letters* read ' the King.'

[2] The clause in brackets is omitted in the *Letters*.

complaint and for a manifestoo, if ever his Majesty have occasion for it. Those of the Councill who are reporters of marine affairs, and whom I have occasion to entertaine about them, doe often insinuate to me their thoughtes as if the King my master would be better pleased if I were slack and complying, and cry up mightily the intimate friendship between the Kings. But truly I have no secret instructions, and if I goe to guesse at the Kings secret thoughts I shall always think he hath a greater interest to protect his marchants than the Most Christian King can have to protect unjustly his privateers, a race of theeves, and ever uselesse and unprofitable to their owne country and destructive to the trade of it. I have written much to Mr. Secretary Coventry about these affaires, and if I thought it worth your Lordships while I would send you copies of my letters and other papers of these matters ; but they are many, troublesome, and full of chicane, so that I think better to forbeare giving you that trouble.

On Thursday last[1] I was with one Monsieur de Bezons, a Counsellor of State, who is intimate with Monsieur de Barillon, and our marine affaires being over he asked me news from England. I told him there was discourse of a progresse of the Kings to Portsmouth and Plimouth, and of the Queen to the Bath. He told me that Monsieur de Barillon was preparing for England, but that he thought he would not go till the end of August. He confirmed me in a conjecture I had formerly about the change of ambassadour in England[2] by saying l'estat present des affaires demandoit d'autres liaisons que celles qu'avoit Monsieur Courtin.

I humbly begg your Lordships pardon for this transgressing upon your leisure (for indeed I have gone further than I ought and then I intended), and wish for your Lordships prosperity as for my owne well being, and remaine, My Lord,

Your Lordships most humble, most faithfull, and
ever obliged servant,

Brisbane.[3]

---

[1] June 21/July 1.

[2] *Cf.* Brisbane's letter of May 8, *supra*, p. 553.

[3] Endorsed by Leeds, ' Mr. Brisbane, 25 June, [16]77. Of consequence.'

[To the Lord Treasurer] [1]

Paris, 27th November, 1677.

My Lord,

On Tuesday last [2] I received a letter from Mr. Secretary Williamson of the 8th [3] of this moneth, old stile, and with it I had two others inclosed, one for the King and the other for Monsieur, both which I delivered with the utmost care and expedition, and both with my owne hand. *The Kings answer was in these words, Je vous remercie de vostre peine, et je la verray. Monsieurs answer was like the Kings, but that he further promised an answer, and told me the King had such another, by which and by what was told me next day by the Mareshall de Grammont,* [4] that the letter I delivered to the King overnight was from the Prince of Orange, [5] I perceive they made no secret of them, *though I did make a secret of from whom they came,* and therefore it is like there was nothing in them but a compliment upon occasion of his Highnesses mariage. It was expected by some here that his Majesty marrying the Princesse of Orange (in the scituation [6] she was in when marryed) would have sent somebody to acquaint this King with the design of it ; *and the speculative people inferre from that omission (as they will reckon it to favour their inference) that this King was sufficiently preacquainted with the matter to dispense with the formality of an envoy ; though on the other hand* [7] it is certain the ministers and those of the Councill I converse with seem to consider that match as a thing done without any communication, counsel, or consent asked or given from this side.

It is, my Lord, a wonderfull care and dexterity that is used here to retrive revenue out of every thing and at every turne. They

[1] From the autograph letter among the Lindsey MSS., printed in *Lindsey MSS.*, p. 387. *Letters*, p. 317.

[2] November 13/23.   [3] The *Letters* read ' third.'

[4] Instead of this omitted passage the *Letters* read ' and the Mareschal de Grammont told me the next day.'

[5] The *Letters* begin a new sentence here.

[6] The *Letters* read ' station.' At the time of her marriage Princess Mary was heiress to the Duke of York, but on November 7 a son, the Duke of Cambridge, had been born to James.

[7] Instead of this omitted passage the *Letters* give, ' But I find, and.'

watch attentively the channels into which the publick expense conveys the money, and from these very channels it is intercepted and brought back to the pond, the Kings tresor, which is the heart of this kingdom, and through which all that blood circulates perpetually, remaining in no greater quantity and for no longer time in the other veines than just enough to give life and motion to the members ; for there is no controle to raising mony by which way soever they please to goe barefaced to it ; and it is a pleasant thing to see how many exactions are disguised like acts of grace to those who are to pay well for them, and how some abatements of taxes are so contrived as to produce an increase of revenue, of all which dexterities I have particular instances. Upon the whole matter, though all sorts of people in this kingdom must of necessity be impoverished in their turnes, yett the unlimited power to create revenue, and the ingenious application that is practised here about that matter, will undoubtedly furnish so many great ressources that it is a vaine hopes in the Confederates to imagine the Most Christian King will faile that way.

If to this consideration of a great and certain revenue one addes the esteem this King is in with his subjects for his personal virtues and love to glory, which they all admire because he is successfull ; the no success of so many powerfull Confederates, who have done nothing this summer, contrary to all appearance ; the abilities and vigilance of his ministers ; the punctual obedience that is payd to all his orders ; his vast armies ; his great numbers of excellent officers exceeding the world besides ; his admirable œconomie for provisions, forrage, artillerie and ammunitions, which he hath in vast quantities ; the neere and absolute dependence of all the considerable subjects (nobility, clergy and officers of justice) upon the Crowne even for their subsistance ; his dreadfull navy, all his owne without borrowing ; the unitednesse of all this strength in one kingdom all of a piece, from the furthest extremities of which a courier in foare days comes to the Court with advices, and in as many more returns with orders ; his great influence upon other Courts ; the facilities his ministers have to intrigue everywhere by their mony, which to often meets with venal souls, and by their language commonly understood, which is no contemptible advantage (and in effect few or none of them need or will daigne to learne

*another, their owne being sufficient to serve all turns)—it seems that
all these layd together renders this power much more formidable than
was that of Charles the Fifth or Philip the Second of Spaine, which
yett raised the jealousy of all Europe against the House of Austria
till it hath been brought low enough now not to be feared. It is true
wee are bound to believe the Spaniards did designe an universall
monarchie, because all the world said so, though they themselves
denied it and gave very plausible reasons for their denial ; and on
the contrary wee must piously believe the French have no such
intention, because they themselves out of modesty deny it, though all
the world besides affirme they have that intention. Whatever the
intentions of either were or are, they may be perhaps impenetrable,
or they may change in time. L'appetit vient en mangeant—one bitt
brings on another.*

*But truly it seemes, if any one will sitt downe and compute
right, and compare the circumstances of power and meanes mentioned before, as the House of Austria had them and used them, and
as the French have them and use them, he will conclude that the
French have the better tooles to work with, and that they have
hitherto gone the righter way to worke to conquest and glory. They
will tell us their friends and neighbours are sufficiently secured by
their affection, sincerity, moderation and desinteressement, as they
call it, and that it is contre la civilité francoise de demander d'autres
seuretez contre les perils que la parole de gens d'honneur. In effect
some people might find some security in that, if the most solemne
treaty of the Pyrenees, which terminated a warr of twenty-five years
very advantageously to France, which was confirmed by the enter-
vieu of both Kings and many protestations, and cemented by a
mariage, if the youth, innocence and beauty (for wee talk much here
of personal tendresses) of the present King of Spaine, and his im-
plicated relations of blood and alliance, had saved him one foot of
ground that the French armes have been able to take and keep.*

*My Lord, I do not take the liberty to writ such things to your
Lordship because I think you need to be putt in mind of your
dangers. I know very well and admire your superior understanding and vigilance, and that you have many better and more reasonable considerations than hundred such as I can furnish you with,
and (which is a happinesse to your country) that all your extra-*

ordinary talents are directed to do good. But as many things evidently just and reasonable need to be helped by number of votes, and that every one makes one, I think it my duty to do the part of an out sentenelle, who is bound to tell what he sees, or what he thinks he sees, though he knows very well that the vigilance of his superiour officers reaches farr beyond his sight. I rely upon your Lordships goodnesse for my pardon and excuse, and remaine with all possible submission and unalterable respect, My Lord,

> Your Lordships most humble, most obliged, and
>> most faithfull servant,
>>> Brisbane.

To the Lord Treasurer.[1]

> *Paris, 4th May, 1678, S.N.*

My Lord,

All that I have now to trouble your Lordship with is this inclosed copie of a letter to Mr. Secretary,[2] *to whom I likewise writ all the particular affaires depending at the Councill of Marine Affaires here, with which I need not trouble your Lordship. I have written the same day a letter to Mr. Bertie concerning some matters of revenue, in which I have been a litle tedious, and repeated what I well remember I had written before, least he should have forgott it. If your Lordship have leisure to call for it, as I think you will not, you will see that I am still confirmed this revenu is not inexhaustible.*

I pray God direct you right, and preserve your Lordship in health and prosperity ; and I remaine with all humble respect and gratefull acknowledgement of your many favours, My Lord,

> *Your Lordships most humble, oblidged and faithfull servant,*
>> *J. Brisbane.*

[To the Lord Treasurer] [3]

> *Paris, 25th June, 1678, S.N.*

My Lord,

Haveing written frequently to Mr. Bertie since I came last hither, I doubt my forbearing to trouble your Lordship with my

---

[1] From the autograph letter in Leeds MSS., Packet 10.
[2] Secretary Coventry. The copy is still preserved along with this note.
[3] From the autograph letter in Leeds MSS., Packet 10.

letters, especially in such a time as you have had, will be found more pardonable than the freedome I now take, though even this doth not want its excuses. Not to mention the general peace which everybody here reckons assured (or at least that the Hollanders will remaine neuters if, by miracle, the peace should happen to faile), I am informed from a good hand, which makes me believe it may be true, that this Court is now in good earnest renewing with Holland their treaty of April 1662, which is a defensive league, and hath in the body of the treaty several advantageous concessions in favour of the Dutch, besides the separate article concerning the 50 sols per tunne, which is now to be inlarged to all their shipping in general, and to the exemption from that whole imposition, where-as in 1662 onely the ships that laded salt in France were exempted, and that for no more than one half of the duty. So necessary they find the commerce to the very subsistance of this kingdom, and so great a blow the obstructing of it would have been.

This conjuncture putts all people here of all conditions in an exstasie. Wee meet with nothing but holding up hands and eyes and crying out, Jesus, quel bonheur pour la France! Que le Roy est heureux, et que l'Angleterre a manqué un grand coup pour se rendre considerable a jamais! The same author I mentioned before told me that upon the conclusion of the peace the Prince of Orange would goe over to England, and spoke of it as if that voyage were not to be altogether voluntary, and as if he were like to find himself uneasy in Holland, which I then did not much reflect upon, till we have since found that the Dutch Gazette speaks of that voyage. One thing I am sure of, that his ennemies wish he may do it suddenly, and doubtlesse his Highnesse will not think fit to leave his post without some extraordinary errand in such times as he is like to see, at least if the prognosticks calculated here and for this meridian prove true.

My Lord, I think you have at present to many great and penible affaires to be able to spend a thought upon me, upon what I shall become, or what part of the Kings service your Lordship will think fitt to recommend me to when my present employment expires. But hopeing that your Lordship is persuaded of my laboriousnesse and perfect fidelity, and thereby prepared to remember me at some time of more leisure, I will onely adde that in conscience I have a

true veneration for your great merite in all senses, and a sincere
affection for your person, and so I remaine, My Lord,
Your Lordships most humble, most oblidged
and most faithfull servant,

J. Brisbane.

[To the Lord Treasurer] [1]

Paris, 9th July, 1678, S.N.

My Lord,

I did yesterday visitt A. R. [Monsieur Courtin], and as it happened found him alone at leisure, [2] and it seemes [2] in an humour to speak freely enough. I adventure to trouble your Lordship with an accompt of that conversation as neere as I can recollect it, being sorry I cannot better entertaine your Lordship, nor make any more profitable use of the freedome you are pleased to allow me.

Concerning the stop to the signing of the peace he says they do not doubt but 38 [Don Emanuel de Lyra] will comply with 55 [the French King] in everything, because no man will dare now to speak of war, the people being esbranlé and made fond of the peace (which was certainly the onely designe of publishing the project and of the letter of the 18th of May), so sure they reckon those measures they take from the humours of people which they think will never agree amongst themselves.

He told me likewise he hoped now all would goe well between 55 [France] and 88 [England], though there have been severall causes of discontent given, which I perceive are not forgotten because he could tell them upon his fingers.

As first, the voyage of 19 [Prince of Orange], which was assented to contrary to pre-ingagements, upon a letter brought by my Lady Temple, and which was not communicated to R. C. [Duke of York] till 88 [King of England] did give it him, and that without the participation or knowledge of 55 [the Franck King] or his ministers. To which I replyed that voyage was so publick, and mentioned in all gazets so long before its execution, and otherwise so impossible to be concealed, that it was not probable anybody would think to make a secret of it.

---

[1] From a copy among the Lindsey MSS. Printed in *Lindsey MSS.*, p. 393. *Letters*, p. 319.

[2] . . . [2] Omitted in the *Letters*.

Secondly, the declaring the mariage next day after a promise made to Monsieur Barillon that it should not be till after the peace. To this I said that if he (A. R.) [Monsieur Courtin] had been upon the place he would never have needed to excuse his owne credulity by alleadging a promise that never was made.

Thirdly, the alliance with Holland and my Lord Duras his message was mentioned and exagerated. And to this I said that most men did find the conditions of peace stipulated in that treaty so advantageous to France that they were persuaded it was done by concert with 55 [the King of France], and nobody can easily believe he is in earnest when he seems to dislike it.

Then he spoke of [1] the calling 2 [the Parliament], and lastly [1] our troops sent into Flanders. And to these points I told him he certainly knew these actions were not onely in themselves reasonable and prudent, but otherwise very consistent with the greatest friendship, and designed in their favour to produce the peace they had so much reason to desire, and which they did so earnestly pursue.

He told me likewise (but I do not remember in which periode of our conversation) that the things 88 [the King of England] desired of 2 [the Parliament] in his last proposition were very reasonable and fitt to be done, but he did believe 2 [the Parliament] was not disposed to lett oo [my Lord Treasurer] have the credit of being instrumental of such an advantage. This is the old string I have found them harping upon ; and to try what he would say I applauded his penetration and knowledge of our affaires, and asked who els he thought would be fitt to promote 88 [the King of Englands] interests. He answered with hums and ha's, and named nobody ; and truly I could name nobody to him. But a while after and upon another occasion he said one of 8 A. [Scotland] seemed to him the most qualified for the ministry of all he had practised, were it not for his passions [2] and those of his consort. [2]

As such conversations never end without compliments on both sides, he was very profuse of them to me, and assured me that Monsieur Colbert and all those of the Councill that I have had to do

---

[1] . . . [1] Omitted in the *Letters.*
[2] . . . [2] Omitted in the *Letters.*

with do highly commend me for many good qualities (of all which I onely owne a litle labour and perfect integrity), and that he could beare me witness that I had with extraordinary successe appaised the quarrels and prevented many disorders which would have arisen about prises and might have created great troubles.   Upon this I took occasion to tell him freely that I wondered much that Monsieur Colbert had never given way to the restitution of anything confiscated before I came hither, especially seeing I had assured him that wee would use so strict and accurate a discerning between the just complaints of our people and those that were fraudolous that he needed not feare to open a doore to numerous and excessive reparations.

He acquiesced to that, and blamed O. B. [Marquis de Seignelay], modestly enough imputing the errours to his youth.   And to be even with him for his commendations I found meanes to extoll his great abilities and his perfect knowledge of forrein affaires and his dexterity in managding them, which rendered him in the opinion of all men the best qualified for the service of L. 8 [Monsieur de Pomponne].   Thereupon he told me a pretty singularity, that he was in passe and in everybodys eye for that employment, but that he lost his opportunity when the last vacancy happened by being at home. For, said he, S. P. [Monsieur le Tellier] persuaded 55 [the French King] to give it to L. 8 [Pomponne], who was then with U. C. [King of Suedeland], and that in the interim 33 [Monsieur Louvois] might exercise the place, which gave him his first entrance into the Councill, where he hath ever since stuck as master as you see.   And L. 8 [Pomponne] will often say merrily that if he had been at home he had never been advanced to the post he hath.

I beg your Lordships pardon for this tedious recapitulation, and wish nothing more earnestly than that I might be furnished with better materials to use more excusably the freedome you allow me.   I remaine with great submission and entire respect, My Lord,

Your Lordships most humble, most oblidged
and faithfull servant,

Brisbane.[1]

---

[1] Endorsed, ' Mr. Brisbanes letter to my Lord Treasurer, July 9th, 1678.' To this Leeds has added, ' which is very remarkable.'

To the Lord Treasurer.[1]

Paris, 16th July, 1678.

My Lord,

I received your Lordships letter of the 3rd instant, old stile,[2] yesternight about nine of the clocke, and have spent so much time in goeing to and againe to meet with and entertaine all the parties mentioned in it that I have not now enough left to give your Lordship an exact accompt of all the steps I have already made. Upon the whole matter I find the person principally concerned [3] expressing much duty, and in general a resolution to obey in all things ; but when I presse the particular order, I am answered that having on the 9th instant, this stile, written to 88 [the King], it is hoped a delay may be allowed till an answer of that letter come to hand, which may reasonably be expected Monday or at furthest Fryday next.[4]

About two houres agoe (it is now almost noon) I wrot to Mr. Bertie a litle note,[5] and have since been with N.B. [Dutchess of Cleveland], who approves hitherto what I have said and endeavoured to do. It is the third time I have been with the same person. That which occasions some difficulty perhaps is that the principall party [3] being now with Z.I. [my Lady Northumberland] there is no meanes of passing by Z.I. [Lady Northumberland], who professeth a designe to advise obedience, and yett I doubt cannot do it so vigourously as if the party were under another roof, because there are some measures of civility that cannot be absolutely waved.[6]

---

[1] From the autograph letter in Leeds MSS., Packet 10.

[2] This letter has not been found.   [3] Lady Sussex.

[4] Monday, July 8/18, or Friday, July 12/22.   [5] Not found.

[6] The attitude of Lady Northumberland is shown by a letter preserved in Leeds MSS., Packet 8, endorsed by Danby, 'Lady Northumberlands letter to Mr. Montagu.' Presumably it was written by Lady Northumberland from Paris to her husband shortly after he had returned to England, and was given by him to Danby when he was endeavouring to make his peace with the Government. It runs :

Since I sealed up my leter Mr. Bridsban has been here to speak with me. His bussinesse was aboute my Lady Sussex, to lett me know that (by order) he was last night to waite upon my Lady Clevland, who he found very possitive about her goeing to Port Royall, and she had the King of her side, and that he thought according to his orders it was fitte for him to perswade her to it, since if she should disobey the King it would be mightily to her prejudice, and it would be thought the advice of others. Soe I told him as for disobeying the King, I thought it was very unfitte for her to doe it, and could I pretend

For the matter of money N.B. [Lady Cleaveland] informes me there are many debts and much squandring, notwithstanding 500 l. which 88 [the King] did lately send hither.

I returne your Lordship my most humble thanks for the latter part of your letter, which concerns myself, and wish I may never draw any reproach upon your Lordships recommendations. If labour and fidelity can deserve the continuance of your favour your Lordship may be at quiet upon that score. I might have something to represent about the employment of 62 [Mr. Perwich], and that some care may be had that I goe no lesse in the esteeme of his Majesty and the countenance may be putt upon me here. But I have hitherto been so bountifully delt with by his Majestys gracious expressions and favourable usages that I hope I need not be anxious about it, especially having the honour and advantage of so noble a patronage and protection as that which your Lordship is pleased to afford me. And therefore with patience and all dutifull respect and thankfullness I remaine, My Lord,

Your Lordships most humble and most faithfull servant,

J. Brisbane.[1]

to advice her (which I did not) I should perswad her to obey him in all things ; but that was not nessesary, for I found her resolutions that ; but since Mr. Mountague was noe more here, and that the poore woman was really ile and taken physicke for her health, I thought it would doe very well if he that were imployed in it would represent that to the King, and that she might make an end of that, since a strange monesterrie where she knew noebody was but a mallincolly place to doe it in ; but that I had nothing to say in it, but that as she was in my hous and I did beleeve her innocent of all was said of you, soe my hous was at her service as long as she thought fitte, provide[d] she lived as she ought to doe in it. Perhapes you may thinke me a little impertinent in troubling you with all this strife, but it is now soe publicke a thing that I thought it not amise to let you know all that passes aboute it, and to receive your orders what I shall doe or say farther in it. Sure there was never a more vexatious bussinesse, but I will say noe more. Pray God send we may meete quickely, Yours for ever.

[1] Endorsed by the Duke of Leeds, ' About Lady Sussex.'

REMARKS

ON SOME OF

MR. BRISBANES PAPERS,

who was a gentleman employed by the King in
the Court of France about marine affairs, and who
was extream well acquainted with the cheif
ministers of France, and did many times give the
best intelligence that was had from that Court.[1]

Most of his letters related to the marine affaires, and to that
treaty with France ; but I have only mentioned such as give an
account of the opinion the ministers of that Court had of the
distrusts betwixt the King of England and his Parliament, and
how much they relyed upon it.[2] And I desire it may be particularly observ'd from Mr. Brisbane's letter of the 25th of June,
1677, how Monsieur de Ruvigny was able to tell what that
Parliament would do in relation to supplies before they did give
the money, and that when they did give it, it was directly under
those restrictions which he had foretold to Mr. Brisbane, which
shews that he was in a much better correspondence with others
than he was with me, as appear'd also afterwards more plainly
by his private negotiations with Mr. Mountagu and others.

I have also added some informations about myself which
were written by him to Mr. Charles Bertie.

[1] B.M. Add. MSS. 28044, f. 53, in a copyist's handwriting, with some
additions in the handwriting of the Duke of Leeds. *Letters*, p. 323.

[2] The version in Add. MSS. 28044 ends here with the following clause, ' and
I have added some informations about myselfe which were written by him to
Mr. Charles Bertie.' The *Letters* are clearly based on an amplified version, and
are followed from this point.

Mr. Brisbane's information to Mr. Bertie, from Paris, July 30, 1678.[1]

Monsieur Courtin told me yesterday that he had shewed the Duke of York that my Lord Treasurer was not respectful to him, when, a resolution being taken to prorogue the Parliament, my Lord Treasurer advised the King to continue it without the knowledge of the Duke. They spare nothing to mischief him.

Thursday last Monsieur Gioe was three hours shut up with Monsieur de Pomponne ; Friday Monsieur de Bonœuil visited me, on purpose, I think, to tell me of it, both designing to give jealousy of him. Yesterday Monsieur Gioe told me it was true, and that it was on no business but former kind acquaintance. I said if he had no business it would be thought otherwise, and I think he should have made his visit public and in company of many. He mistook and was proud of the honour.

Mr. Brisbane's information to Mr. Charles Bertie, from Paris, January 18, 1678/9.[2]

Old Ruvigny visited mee yesterday, told mee my Lord Treasurer was able and bold, that the prorogation is a coup de partie, that hee sowed much money in the House of Commons, but all for himself and not for the King, *and that accusations against my Lord Treasurer had been hissed out of the House of Commons when the next day the same men voted against the King's interest.* This obstinacy to hurt my Lord Treasurer here ought to tye fast honest men to him.

---

[1] Printed from *Lindsey MSS.*, p. 395, where the letter is described, obviously in error, as being written to Danby himself. It is actually in Bertie's handwriting, having presumably been deciphered by him. *Letters*, p. 324.

[2] Autograph note in cipher among the Lindsey MSS., printed in *Lindsey MSS.*, p. 399. *Letters*, p. 325.

MR. HYDE'S LETTERS

To the Lord Treasurer.[1]

Nimmeguen, October the 25th, 1677.

My Lord,

I am so affraid of troubling your Lordship with empty impertinent letters from this place, that it hinders me from paying the duty to your Lordship which your owne commands might in some measure excuse me for. But how little soever there is worth the informing you from hence, I cannot omitt at this time presenting my humble thanks to your Lordship for the order I heare you have been pleased to give for my plate, which was the early and very obliging effect I found of your Lordships returne from New-markett, where I hope that with health and all other satisfaction you enjoyed all the divertizements of that place.

Those that for the present doe cheifly employ us are the meanes for a way for the Suedes ambassadors letters to their King, which is ajusting through such barbarous cold countrys that I thinke the very discourse hath brought the winter upon us sooner then usuall. In the meantime this serves to keep the mediators in breath, till the partys find the effects of the Prince of Orange's journey into England, which they expect will sett them more in good earnest at worke upon the peace. Your Lordship by this time sees a great way into what may be expected of that businesse, in which I wish your Lordship all the successe that your prudence and ability may challenge ; and when you have made it ripe for your servants here you can honour nobody with your commands that with greater zeale and readynesse shall endeavour to obey them then, My Lord,

Your Lordships most obedient and most humble servant,

L. Hyde.

[1] From the autograph letter in B.M. Add. MSS. 28054, f. 95. There is a copy on f. 97, which adds nothing.

To Mr. Hyde.[1]

Whitehall, 4 December, 1677.

My Lord Ambassador,

I had not intended farther to trouble you at present, save onely to have acknowledged the favor of yours of the 22th and 29th, which are come to hand since my last, and to have told you of his Majesties haveing changed his mind as to the time to which the two Houses were to adjourne, by makeing the day, which by the proclamation was to have been the 4th of Aprill, to be now the 15th of the next month; and this I had meant onely by way of news and curiosity for you. But it has pleased his Majestie, considering you will be now found at the Hague, to charge me with a commission of businesse to you, and in order to it to acquaint you that his Majestie haveing prevailed with his Highness the Prince of Orange, some time before he parted hence, to trust his Majestie, under the last confidence of secrecy, with his thoughts as to the conditions his Highness judged the States might finally be content to sitt downe with as to Flanders and those other parts of the Spanish Monarchy in which his Majestie and the States are more nearly concerned, his Highness was pleased to declare himselfe, that without Valenciennes, Tournay and Conde, as well as Charleroy, Aeth, Courtray and Oudenard, he did not conceive Flanders could be in any possibility of defence, and was therefore sure the States could ne're goe lower then that nor could he himselfe ever consent they should.

His Majestie haveing prevailed with the Prince of Orange to trust him with this secret imediately dispatches away my Lord Feversham to the Most Christian King, to know of him under the like secrecy how farr he could be prevailed with to agree to these conditions as to Flanders, adding towards the perfecting of a plan for the generall peace that these conditions being obtained for Flanders, the Franche Comté should remaine to France, Sicily to be finally restored to the Spaniard, and this to be the foot on which matters were to be left between France and Spaine; as to what depends between France and Holland, all to be restored lying in Europe on either side; as to the Emperor, all to stand upon the present foot, or (if it should be insisted on) to have Maestricht slighted on the one side and Philips-

[1] From a copy in B.M. Add. MSS. 28054, f. 99. There is another copy on f. 101. Letters, p. 326.

burg on the other ; and as to Sweden, which would now be the onely considerable interest that according to this scheme would remaine unprovided for, in case any difficulty should arise concerneing the satisfaction to be given to Sweden that might delay the conclusion of the peace, my Lord was to say that, it not being to be hoped for that the generall peace should be made at once, his Majestie would therefore propose to have a truce in these parts till the peace can be adjusted, and if it should be insisted on by the Most Christian King that a truce in these parts will not be a sufficient ground for a satisfaction, in that case the King proposed that in Sicily there should be a truce also, and the Most Christian King to keep those townes he hath in it, as a pawne till a peace should be concluded for Sweden, or if Sicily did not please, then any other place out of Flanders as should be proposed reasonable to the same end.

This was the plan my Lord Feversham carryed with him, upon which haveing tryed the Most Christian Kings mind and returneing on Saturday last with a dry kind of answer, his Majestie found cause to change his mind as to the matter of the adjourment of the Parliament, and instead of the 4th Aprill, to which day by his proclamation he had signified he intended it should adjourne, the King was pleased to order it to be adjourned onely to the 15th of this next month. In which interim, it greatly importing his Majesties affaires to have a finall certainty of the mind of France as to the aforesaid conditions of the peace, ˣ his Majestie hath therefore [1] commanded Mr. Mountague forthwith to returne to Paris, and with utmost instance to presse France anew to accept of the proposition sent by the Earle of Feversham. And because his Majestie would bee prepared to drive this matter to a finall and speedy issue, and that his Majestie foresees the Most Christian King, when pressed afresh by Mr. Mountague in the thing, may not unlikely aske, in case he should on his part accept of the proposition, what security his Majestie can give him that Spaine on their part will accept of it also—in case the thing should possibly come to rest upon this point, his Majestie has thought fitt, after this knowledge given you of what has passed and of the state in which the thing now is, to direct you forthwith upon receipt hereof to addresse yourselfe to the Prince of Orange, and

---

[1] The *Letters* omit ' therefore.'

after you have acquainted his Highness with what has happened in this matter since he parted, the coldnesse of the answer brought by my Lord Feversham, the shortening of the adjournment of the Parliament that has followed upon that, and the dispatch of Mr. Mountague backe to Paris, to acquaint his Highness you have orders from his Majestie to lett him know that if the States will joyne with his Majestie to oblige Spaine, his Majestie will joyne with them to oblige France to accept the conditions sent by my Lord Feversham, in case either should refuse them. And in this the King desires to know clearly how farr he will answer to his Majestie that the States will thus joyne with him, if there be cause for it.

This is a point his Majestie thinkes it will by no meanes be fitt yet to speake of to the States themselves, and therefore his Majestie goes no farther for an answer then to the Prince himselfe, on whose word his Majestie will rely in case his Highness will undertake to answer for the States in the point. His Highness will easely judge how necessary it is for his Majestie to have a speedy and clear answer from his Highness in the point, which you must therefore take care earnestly to sollicite for, and to returne it by the expresse that carryes you this, who is to that end directed to observe your orders as to the time of his stay there and returne backe. I am, &c.,

Your, &c.,

[J. Williamson] [1]

[To the Lord Treasurer] [2]
Hague, January the 16th/26th, 1677/8.
My Lord,

If I thought your Lordship cared for the repetitions of what you may see, if you care for it, in Mr. Secretary's letters, I would oftner take the confidence to trouble your Lordship, but having the misfortune to give so ill an account of the commands I receive I may very well be contented to send it onely to one, and wish that he were not oblidged to communicate it to more.

---

[1] Endorsed by Danby, 'Coppy of Secretary Williamsons letter to Mr. Hyde, 4th December 1677'; and by Leeds, 'This is a principall letter to shew the Kings willingness to press France if hee could bee sure of good assistance from the States.'

[2] From the autograph letter in Leeds MSS., Packet 10.

This expresse who returns now haveing told me that your Lord-ship had done me the honour to remember me by him, I doe with the greater assurance presume to present my most humble thanks to your Lordship. You have the treaty once more returned to you, altered in one of the two points, I hope fully to his Majestys satis-faction. In the other, concerning the Emperour and the Empire, I see it is yett defective of what it came first with out of England, that is to say the particular mention of Philipsbourg and Maestricht. All I can say is that neither the Prince nor the Pen-tionar would endure to hear of the parting with Maestricht againe after it is given them in the very clause before by the words, that all between France and the Low Countrys in Europe was to be restored ; and I must either signe it as it is, or stay till new orders could come out of England, for they would not be moved to consent to that clause wholly as it was first sent over.

I hope at last it is better then it was, and your Lordship will say it had need ; and yet I assure you I had enough to doe to make those I had to deal with here apprehend the reason there was for his Majesty to insist so positively to have the project altered. They would have rather done the same thing in a separate article, and have left the project as it was ; but I had favour enough with the Prince, and with very much adoe, to gett what alterations are made to be inserted in the very treaty. I have nothing more to add to this trouble but to desire your Lordships favourable interpretation of all my errors and faults, and to beg you to vouchsafe your pro-tection, if I be not absolutely unworthy of it, to, My Lord,

Your Lordships most obedient and most humble servant,

L. Hyde.

To Mr. Hyde.[1]

London, 8th February, 1677/8.

My Lord,

I will give you little more trouble than to thank you for the favour of your two letters, because Mr. Godolphin will entertain you fully with all the news of this place. For the business about which he is sent to the Prince, I confess I know not what to advise nor wish, because it would be taken very ill here if we should not under-

---

[1] *Clarendon Correspondence*, i. 5, from the original letter.

take a war upon any terms, and yet at the same time anybody that saw us act would swear that the Parliament were forced to it against their wills, insomuch that nobody can wonder that the King is under great discouragements to think how he shall be supported in a war, when he is voted into it by a small majority upon every division. I shall therefore take upon me in this case rather the office of a divine than a statesman, and pray that all your counsels may be for the best.

Pray do me the favour to represent to me the sense of that country you are in as to their desire of peace or war, for I am satisfied the Spaniards would choose the peace upon any terms rather than the continuance of the war. I beg of you also to do me the honour of presenting my humblest duty to her Highness, and I desire you to believe me most unfeignedly, My Lord,

Your Excellency's most faithful humble servant,

Danby.

[To the Lord Treasurer] [1]

Hague, February the 16th/26th, 1677/8.
My Lord,

Haveing received by Mr. Godolphin the honour of a letter from your Lordship, I take the liberty by the same hands to present my humble thanks to you for it, tho I believe the great businesse you have now upon you would dispose you to forgive me the omission of that duty. I doe not find it is expected I should give any account of the businesse that brought Mr. Godolphin hither, and I am sure it is very needlesse when he is to returne himselfe. I am extremely sensible of the difficultys you are under, haveing been long enough acquainted with the proceedings you are now depending upon to know that when things are carried by a small majority and frequent divisions, tho they may still be carried, it will be with delays ; but that the Prince will not readily comprehend, his sense upon that subject being that in all great assemblys he knows everybody will talke and make a noise, but if the matter can be carried it is no matter for that. To goe on further with any of his Highnesse's thoughts upon this subject would bring upon your Lordship an unnecessary trouble, that of reading what will be better represented to you by word of mouth.

[1] From the autograph letter in Leeds MSS., Packet 10. Hyde's draft is in B.M. Add. MSS. 17016, f. 101.

It would be very hard for me, who am so great a stranger here, to give your Lordship a good account of your commands concerning the sense of this country as to their desires of peace or warr. In generall it is very easy to hear the common cry and dissatisfaction of those that find themselves oppressed with the mighty taxes they lye under, a deliverance from which I believe upon any termes would be accepted by them ; but of the sense of the governours I confesse I am so little informed (and know not how to be better, for perhaps they never speake what they designe and intend in this case) that if I should pretend to give you any account of it, perhaps it might be such as might wholly mislead you, if you should doe me the honour to lett it have any weight with you. When your Lordship hath confessed that you know not what to advise or wish it would be very impertinent in me to pretend to be wiser. I had much rather joyne with your Lordship in the office of a devine then of a statesman, as takeing it to be the easier trade of the two in that I can make my prayers and vows for your Lordships happynesse, and for a blessing upon your endeavours for the good of us all, and in any capacity may with some confidence desire your Lordship to looke upon me as one that is with great respect, My Lord,

   Your Lordships most obedient and most humble servant,

L. Hyde.[1]

[To the Lord Treasurer] [2]

Hague, February the 26th/March the 8th, 1677/8.

My Lord,

Your Lordship will have been informed by a letter the Prince of Orange writt to your Lordship out of Flanders,[3] which the Pentionar Fagel sent you by an expresse, of the desperate condition things were in in that countrey, and that the Spaniards wished for peace upon any termes. And this morning the Pentionar came to me to acquaint me they were as bad in these provinces ; that the consternation even here was so great upon the besiedging of Gant (which they give for gone, and conse-

---

[1] Endorsed by Danby, ' Mr. Hydes letter to mee, 16/26 February, 1677/8.'

[2] From the autograph letter in Leeds MSS., Packet 10. *Letters*, p. 329. There is a somewhat different version in Clarendon MSS. 87, f. 275, printed in the *National Review* for August 1888.

   Printed *supra*, p. 424.

quently Bruges and Bruxelles), that there were designes amongst some of them to submitt themselves to France upon any termes, and that he was afraid it was a torrent too great to be opposed ; that the States of Holland were to meet to-morrow, and that he apprehended he should not be able to hinder them from comeing to such a resolution ; that he would use his utmost industry to prevaile with them to delay it till they could hear out of England in answer to what his expresse carried over, but he owned at the same time that he gives all for gone in Flanders before anything can come from the King to their assistance ; but if his Majesty could procure them any peace, as he said, tant soit peu seure, it would be looked upon as a great service done to the States, and, as he tooke it, for the interest of the Prince of Orange, which was so weakned by the ill successes of this warr that nothing but a peace could establish it. I tooke occasion to desire him to explaine what he meant by that expression, tant soit peu seure, because he had used it twice or thrice ; and he told me that, as he understood, the French had been contented with the termes projected between the King and this state, save Valenchiennes and Tournay, or, said he, it may be one of them. I had rather, sayd he, for my part have Tournay then Valenchiennes, but we are not in a condition to choose.

I have given your Lordship the account of this latter part, concerning these two townes, to yourselfe in particular, and have not mentioned it in my letter to the Secretary, for reasons that your Lordship will easily comprehend. And I thought it lay upon me, as soon as I was able, to give your Lordship a better answer to the letter I had the honour to receive from you by Mr. Godolphin then I could doe then (I mean to your question what I tooke the sense of this country to be as to their desires of peace or warr), by which I hope your Lordship will be persuaded that I did not obey you then for want of good information, and that I am allwaies mindfull of your commands when I am capable of serving you. I remaine with great respect, My Lord,

Your Lordships most obedient and most humble servant,

L. Hyde.[1]

[1] Endorsed by Leeds, ' Note, about the peace.'

[To the Lord Treasurer] [1]

Hague, March the 12/22th, 1677/8.

My Lord,

Mr. Godolphin arrived here yesterday, by whom I received the honour of your Lordships letter of the 5th instant ; [2] and this morning I waited upon him to the Pentionar, where he very fully acquainted him with the termes upon which Monsieur Barillon had owned to have power to signe the peace, and all his Majestys further directions upon that affaire. To which the Pentionar very readily answered that the constitution of their affaires was yett worse then he had ever represented them to me, save that indeed, contrary to his expectation, they had been more patient, and had forborn to make any declarations of their desires of peace upon such termes as should be offered them by France, in expectation of a returne out of England, and that the towne of Amsterdam itselfe, of which he was most apprehensive, had indeed resolved that they would expect a returne out of England to the last repre-sentation of the condition of their affaires, and in the mean time consented to the continuation of the taxes and the new imposition of the two hundredth penny ; but for all this, it was onely in expec-tation to see what his Majesty could doe for them, and that he the Pentionar saw very well that the succors his Majesty was preparing could not be ready neither in point of time nor in proportion to the want they had of them, and that the Emperour on his side could bring nothing considerable into the feild till the month of May, before which time, if the war continued, the French could be master at least of all the great townes. And therefore upon the whole he confessed that he for his part was enclined to accept of the peace ; not but that he said he knew it was a very bad one, and to release both the townes of Valenchiennes and Tournay was very hard, and would give them very little security, and particularly that the Prince had ever reckoned mightily upon Valenchiennes ; but considering there was no probability of recovering out of the desperate condition they were in but by a speedy peace, he should be of opinion to accept

---

[1] From the autograph letter in Leeds MSS., Packet 10, where there is also a copy in a clerk's handwriting. Hyde's draft is in B.M. Add. MSS. 17016, f. 119.

[2] This letter has not been found.

it, not that he would communicate a syllable of it to the States without first acquainting the Prince of Orange with the whole, and expecting his opinion upon it, which he hoped, he said, would be conformable to what he had now said to us, and that he would write his owne opinion very freely to the same purpose ; and added that if the Prince should concurr, which he seemed to have great hopes off, and so it should come to be communicated to the States, he believed it would give a very generall joy to this country ; and he was of opinion that the Duke de Villa Hermosa would be very well content with it. He enlarged very much upon the great importance he tooke it to be to the Prince of Orange's affaires to have a suddaine peace, without which nothing could restore his interests here ; but I thinke I need not at this time repeat all that to your Lordship.

Mr. Godolphin did not faile of very fully representing and repeating to him that if the Prince were of the mind to accept the peace upon these termes, he must make the Spaniards themselves be desirous of it, and that they, together with this state, must make it their desire to the King to procure them the peace upon these termes, without which (that is such a declaration of their desire of it) his Majesty was resolved to support the ullyance made with this state to the uttermost, of which the Pentionar remained fully possessed, and charged himselfe to represent all at large to the Prince by an expresse whom he would dispatch this day before noon to his Highnesse, who would probably arrive much sooner then Mr. Godolphin, who can with no security take any other way then that of the water to gett to his Highnesse. The Pentionar added that in expectation of his Highnesse's consent he would continue the assembly of the States of Holland, who otherwise were to have separated to-morrow or the next day, and that for what concerned the part of this state, for their expressions of their desires of the peace upon these termes, it should be drawne in writing, should be shewed to me, and should be as full as I would propose them to his Majestys satisfaction (which is, by the way, more honour then I desire to take upon me).

I have troubled your Lordship with as full an account as I can recollect of what the Pentionar said, in which perhaps I have been but too particular, considering that Mr. Godolphin may give it you much better,[1] *and might have saved you the trouble of mine. But it was at least fitt for me to acknowledge the honour of your Lordships letter, and at the same time to give you thanks for the confidence you are pleased to putt in me, and to desire your Lordship to continue your favour and protection to me and to reckon me as one that is with great respect, My Lord,*

Your Lordships most obedient and most humble servant,

L. Hyde.[2]

[*To the Lord Treasurer*][3]

Hague, March the 26th/Aprill the 5th, 1678.

My Lord,

I doe not know whether it be absolutely necessary that I give your Lordship this trouble, but for fear it should I venture upon your goodnesse to pardone it, if it should not. It is onely to lett your Lordship know that the Pensionar, haveing since his returne from Antwerp given me an account of what had passed between his Highnesse and him upon the subject of Mr. Godolphin's last journey (of which I need say nothing, because it was no more then what he is gone over to informe you of), added further that the Prince had thought fitt to communicate the subject of that last journey to the Deputys of the States that were then with him, and likewise had acquainted them with his Highnesse's answer, which Mr. Godolphin was returned with; and that he had orders from the Prince to propose in the States that an envoyé extraordinary be sent over to his Majesty to beseech him in their name to gett the peace made upon these termes; but he was first to expect Mr. Godolphins returne back hither, to be sure the termes were consented to in France (which I find both he, the Pentionar, and by him the Prince likewise are doubtfull they will not be, and that the takeing of Ypres may make yett some further alteration); and then that the makeing such a proposition would expose them but too much, if after all the Most Christian King should not consent

---

[1] Godolphin's letter of the same date is printed *infra*, p. 601.

[2] Endorsed by Leeds, ' About the peace.'

[3] From the autograph letter in Leeds MSS., Packet 10, where there is also a copy in a clerk's handwriting. Hyde's draft is in B.M. Add. MSS. 17016, f. 124.

to the peace. So I find the Pentionar is in great expectation of Mr. Godolphin's returne, as that which without further delay will lett them certainly know what they are to trust to, of peace or warr.

This is all I have to trouble your Lordship with, for which I aske your pardone, if it be more then you think necessary, and beg leave to conclude it with the professions of my being with great respect, My Lord,

Your Lordships most obedient and most humble servant,

L. Hyde.[1]

[*To Mr. Hyde*] [2]

[*2nd April, 1678*]

I have yours of the 5th to acknowlege, and not much more to say untill Mr. Godolphin shall come to you, who will give you a better account of all things here. Only I am to lett you know that the particularities of the propositions for the peace which the Prince did send by Mr. Godolphin have not yett been comunicated to the Secretaries of State, so that when they shall bee proposed formally by the Slates (as you will find by the dispatch of Secretary William-son is now expected) itt must bee done so as not to take any notice of haveing mentioned the particulars to his Majestie before that time.

In a letter I received from the Prince [3] *since the returne of Mr. Godolphin his Highness speakes as if hee had some hopes the King might yett save Tournay or Valenciennes, whereas on the contrary itt lookes as if without Conde too the peace were not to bee hoped for, and not certainely with itt, the state of things being changed since Mr. Godolphins going from hence by the takeing of Ipres, which they pretend also to insist upon. But my opinion is that upon the yeilding Conde to them they will restore Ipres.*

But all this is without sufficient ground for anything to be built upon, nor shall wee know anything more certainely untill wee heare from Mr. Montagu, which wee expect about Thursday or Friday

---

[1] Endorsed by Leeds, ' About the peace.'

[2] From the autograph draft in Leeds MSS., Packet 10.

[3] Printed *supra*, p. 428.

next ; and then Mr. Godolphin will be sent to you with all the speed imaginable. I am in so very great hast that I must beg you to excuse this abrupt scrible. I am,

Your, [&c]

[Danby] [1]

[To the Lord Treasurer] [2]

Hague, Aprill the 5th/15th, 1678.

My Lord,

I had a great temptation to write to your Lordship even before I received the honour of your letter of the 2nd, which came to me this afternoon, and it was upon the account of a late dispatch sent to me from Secretary Williamson of the 29th of March by an expresse, by whom haveing not received any commands from your Lordship, I thought your Lordship cared not at that time to receive any further trouble from me. But I confesse to you I was in paine to receive such a commission as that was ; and to be appointed to aske questions againe of the Pentionar, what he meant by tant soit peu seure (which I thought I had asked him before, and had given an account of it to some from whom the Secretary was like to receive his further directions), gave me a little wonder, and putt me in mind of a story I have heard of such as designe to render themselves Capuchins, who in the year of their probation are putt to severall hard tryalls to accustome them cheifly to acts of patience and obedience, and amongst others are directed to plant cabadges with the roots upwards, which tho it seemes contrary to humane reason they must practise in obedience to the commands of their superiors. So I confesse I looked upon that commission to me as such a kind of tryall of my obedience and patience, and with the duty of a Capuchin I endeavoured to obey it, and gave the best account of it I could by the same messenger.

All that comforts me is that I find by the honour of this letter of your Lordships of the 2nd instant that at that time the Secretary of State was not informed of what had been proposed, which was a consideration I had at that time and that gave me the more trouble how I should answer it, in which to avoid speaking out more then

---

[1] Endorsed by Danby, ' Coppy of my letter to Mr. Hyde, 2nd April, 1678,' ; and by Leeds, ' To bee considered.'

[2] From the autograph letter in Leeds MSS., Packet 10.

*I should I tooke the best care I could to explaine no more then
what I found had been allready done in a narrative Mr. Godolphin
had given in of what had passed between the Prince and him, of
which Mr. Secretary sent me the copy. I shall now be carefull to
obey your Lordships commands the best I can, that when the propositions of peace shall come formally to be made by the States it
must be done soe as not to take notice that the particulars had been
mentioned to his Majesty before. But your Lordship may be
pleased to see in my letter of the 2nd to Mr. Secretary the reasons
the Pentionar gave me for the delay of a formall proposition to his
Majesty for a peace upon such termes till they may be assured that
it may be so obtained, which he (the Pentionar) hoped would weigh
with his Majesty ; and my orders at that time being onely to make
the Pensionar fully sensible of what his Majesty expected of that
kind, and to leave it with him to make what use he pleased of it
towards the States and the Prince, and he haveing desired me to
represent backe againe to his Majesty that both he and the States
themselves were fully sensible that the thing ought to be done in
the forme his Majesty expects, and shall be, both in their name and
that of Spayne, but onely desire the King would comply with them
in the point of time, that is not to exact such an addresse from
them till they may be assured they may gett a peace for it, I suppose
I ought not to presse that matter any more till I have fresh commands in answer to my last letter, which gave that account.*

*I have no more to add to this but to aske your Lordships pardone
for giveing you so long a trouble, to present my humble thanks for
this last letter from you, and to desire your Lordship to looke upon
me as one that is with great respect, My Lord,*

Your Lordships most obedient and most humble servant,

L. Hyde.

[To Mr. Hyde] [1]

London, 16 April, 1678.

My Lord,

Besides that my time would not allow mee to say much,
I am sure itt is not necessary, since you will have so good an
informer of all things as Mr. Godolphin.   I shall therefore only

[1] From the autograph draft in Leeds MSS., Packet 10. *Letters*, p. 332.

desire that according to the instructions you will receive by him you will make the Pentioner, and all the forreigne ministers in that place, as sensible as our master is of the unworthynesse and falsenesse of what the French have said of him concerning the Swede, and his undertakeing for the States in theire behalfe ; and that you will indeavour to putt all thoughts of peace out of theire heads (and especially the Pentioners), itt being no longer to bee looked for by them till the French insolence bee a little tamed by a war.

I will trouble you with no more but an assurance of my being,

Your Excellencies most humble and obedient servant,

Danby.[1]

To the Lord Treasurer.[2]

Hague, Aprill the 23rd/May 3, [1678]

My Lord,

I received the honour of your Lordships letter of the 16th by Mr. Godolphin, who had so ill a passage at sea that he got not hither till last night.   And haveing given the Secretary of State as particular an account as my memory would help me with, of all that had passed between us and the Prince and the Pensioner, in pursuance of our instructions, I have not much to adde worth giveing your Lordship the trouble of reading it, onely one particular relating to what you will find in mine to the Secretary of the Prince's private advice how his Majesty should be pleased to answer the envoye extraordinary of this state upon the request he goes to make from hence.   And I am under the strictest promise not to name the body that gives me the information X *I am goeing to acquaint your Lordship with ; but I may assure you it is from a very good hand.*

He would tell me, he said, the particulars of what passed in the Assembly of the States ; that of nineteen votes which compose that Assembly (that is eighteen towns and the nobles, which make one vote more) sixteen of the townes and the nobles, in all seventeen

---

[1] Endorsed by Leeds, ' Of consequence.'

[2] *Morrison Catalogue*, v. 290 ; *Hist. MSS. Com.*, ix. 2, p. 455, from the autograph letter.   *Letters*, p. 333.   There is a copy in a clerk's handwriting in Leeds MSS., Packet 10, on which the Duke of Leeds has made his alterations.

votes, had resolved indeed that, in consideration of the weake and
low condition they were in, his Majesty should be desired to approve
of these conditions of peace for them, but if his Majesty did not,
neither would they accept them ; and that there was thus but two
townes, Haerlem and Amsterdam, that had resolved to accept of the
peace without the consent of his Majesty or Spayne ; but Haerlem
had been gained since to the seventeen, and the six Provinces were
of the same mind with the seventeen votes in Holland. And this he
desired his Majesty might be informed off, as an evidence to him
that if he pleased to answer their messenger shortly and roundly that
he will never consent to such a peace, he may be confident, he said,
this state will continue the warr, and will not abandon his Majesty
in it. And he further adds that he makes little doubt, when his
Majesty shall have so answered and that the argument is taken away
here—Oh, but who knowes but the King is desirous of a peace, and
contented to have it upon these termes—that even the prohibition of
the French trade will follow ; but that is a point not to be gained
while they have any hopes of a peace.

The particulars of the manner of these severall townes voteing is
a great secret, and such a one that the vote that is the subject of
Monsieur van Leven's journey passes for unanimous ; and I am to
beseech his Majesty from this author (of whom I onely say againe
that you may give creditt both to his intelligence and advice) to take
no manner of notice as if he knew anything of the difference there

was among them, ✗ but onely that he ﹍ᴧ would be pleased to

HIS MAJESTIE

answer the messenger roundly as to his businesse, suitable to
what the Prince had desired, and use him in his persone very
civilly and kindly. This further advice I have to give from the
same persone, that if his Majesty would be pleased to lett the
Parliament be acquainted with this proceeding of the States,
and their ungovernable inclinations to a peace, that when his
Majesty expected from them instructions to their ambassador
to conclude a treaty of allyance, instead of it they sent an envoye
to desire a peace upon such ruinous and insupportable conditions, and that his Majesty would be pleased to allow the Parliament to make some declaration of their disapproving such a
conduct, and a contempt of their basenesse and meannesse to

accept of such termes, it would be [1] great use to the setting them right againe in their witts.

I have no more to say of the information, but as to the informer that he made me promise him very solemnly I would not name him ; that besides that if he were discovered it would cost him all, it would render the service the Prince expects from this van Lewen's journey (as a man in whom the contrary party to his Highnesse have entire creditt) wholly ineffectual, if it should come to be known that the answer the King gives proceeds from any intelligence here ; and to that end he desired me not to write it in a letter that was to be produced to any other people. He wished that his Majesty might have the information of it for the direction of his judgment that he may reasonably expect a perfect complyance from this country, if he pleased to declare he would not accept such a peace. And this is the reason I have not said a word of this matter in my letter to the Secretary, tho' I have of the Prince of Orange's advice, which likewise ought to be managed with great secrecy, or else it will certainly doe hurt to the businesse, and may doe to the Prince ; and by this meanes I have putte myselfe againe in the danger of drawing such another businesse upon myselfe as the explanation of the words tant soit peu seure, if your Lordship have not care to divert it from me.

I humbly beg your Lordships pardone for this tedious letter, and desire you to recken me amongst those that are with the greatest respect, My Lord,

Your Lordships most obedient and most humble servant,

L. Hyde. [2]

To the Lord Treasurer. [3]

Hague, Aprill the 30th/May the 10th, 1678.

My Lord,

I hope your Lordship did not take it ill that in my last to you I did not name you the author of the intelligence I then

---

[1] The copy and the *Letters* read ' of great use.'

[2] The letter is endorsed by Leeds, ' Of very great consequence, but to bee very well considered.' This endorsement is repeated in the clerk's handwriting on the copy, where the Duke has added, ' Is used.'

[3] From the autograph letter in Leeds MSS., Packet 10. *Letters*, p. 336. Hyde's draft is in B.M. Add. MSS. 17016, f. 170.

gave you. I had so strictly given my word I would not, that I could not dispense with myselfe in it. But your Lordship might easily imagine from whom I would venture to give you any informations.

Since that time methinks all those assurances are mightily shrunke, for yesterday morning the States of Holland were assembled by five a clocke, and for fear of being concluded in point of time came to a resolution that they for their parts should accept of the conditions of peace offered by the French, and would doe all their endeavours to induce their allys to doe the like, in case they can obtaine prolongation of the time appointed for the accepting of the said conditions, as your Lordship may see more at large in my letter to the Secretary, and the extract of the resolution itselfe of the States which I send likewise enclosed to the Secretary. This very vote the Pensionar told me had been upon debate on Saturday ; but he had then been able to keep them from comeing to a resolution upon it, cheifly by reading to them a letter Monsieur van Beuningen had writt to his masters here, wherein he gave them an account of a particular discourse held by your Lordship to him, wherein your Lordship had said that the King had hopes to gett them a peace upon better termes then those offered by the propositions at Nimmeguen ; and that he haveing asked your Lordship what termes those were, your Lordship had answered him you were not at liberty to tell him the particulars, being yett in hopes to make them better.

Of this I have said nothing in my letter to the Secretary, because it concerned onely what that ambassadour had writt word had passed between your Lordship and him. But I thought it not amisse to give your Lordship the notice of what he (Monsieur van Beuningen) hath writt of it, as I would doe of anything that I thought might doe your Lordship any service, and have nothing more at present to add to your trouble but the professions of being with great respect, My Lord,

Your Lordships most obedient and most humble servant,

L. Hyde.[1]

[1] Endorsed by Leeds, ' About the peace, and what I had said to Monsieur van Beuninghen.'

To the Lord Treasurer.[1]

Hague, May the 10/20th, 1678.

My Lord,

I have nothing to add to the account I have given to the Secretary of State of this long days worke in the Assembly of the States of Holland ; but because the Prince of Orange did more then once repeat to me what his judgment was of what this state would doe in case the King should thinke fitt to refuse againe the conditions of peace offered by the French, and as it seemed to me with an intention his Majesty should take more then ordinary notice of it, I thought it would not be amisse to repeat to your Lordship in particular so much of what you will see likewise in that other dispatch, which is to the same purpose I writt once before in his name at the time Mr. Churchill returned, that if the King will not consent to this peace, but will oblidge the States to make good their treaty and to goe on with his Majesty in the warr, they will then take other measures suitable to that undertakeing. And his Highnesse seemes now to have greater confidence of this his opinion, by his observation of the carriage of the particular townes in all these severall debates, and especially that of Amsterdam, which he takes to be much more moderate then at first. He begins to thinke the Spaniards will consent to the French propositions, the intimation of which by Monsieur Boreel, who is returned from Bruxelles, had made the party here that were earnest for the peace the more instant to have the King pressed a second time to consent to it ; but if his Majesty shall persist, that alone will governe this countrey, and fixe them on a vigorous prosecution of the warr, till a better peace can be obtained. I am with all respect, My Lord,

Your Lordships most obedient and most humble servant,

L. Hyde.

To the Lord Treasurer.[2]

Hague, May the 12/22th, 1678.

My Lord,

To the account I give the Secretary of State by an expresse, of a letter received yesterday by the States from the

---

[1] From the autograph letter in Leeds MSS., Packet 10. Hyde's draft is in B.M. Add. MSS. 17016, f. 194.

[2] From the autograph letter in Leeds MSS., Packet 10. *Letters*, p. 338. Hyde's draft is in B.M. Add. MSS. 17016, f. 197.

French King, I take the liberty to add this trouble to your Lordship, that you may the lesse wonder at me for makeing so suddaine an answer to the Deputys of the States upon the communication of that letter to me. And it is, in as few words as I can, to lett your Lordship know that the Prince, comeing to Monsieur Odyck's house (as soon as the States had resolved to send their Deputys to me) with hopes of finding me there, from whence I was just gone home to receive the Deputys, sent Mr. Godolphin in great hast to me, to tell me what the Deputys were comeing about ; and that if he might ever advise me it should be to give them a short answer, and summoning them upon the performance of their word and treaty with the King ; that the States were not yett come to any resolution amongst themselves; that it might depend in great measure of the answer I and the ministers of the allys should make them ; and that if I should give it to this purpose he had hopes all might goe well.

This earnest recommendation of the Prince's, together with the consideration that it was suitable to the answer the King had given to Monsieur van Lewen, made me take upon me more then perhaps was fitt for me, as your Lordship may see more at large in mine to the Secretary. And when I had done as the Prince had recommended to me, I went to give his Highnesse an account of it, who gave me leave to acquaint your Lordship that he had given me the advice, but desired I would not doe it to anybody whose letter was to be read to any committee of the Counsell, because his Highnesse thought it might be prejudiciall to him if it should come to be knowne againe that he medled in giveing advice upon such occasions. I find by discourse with Monsieur de Lyra last night that he and the rest of the Confederate ministers did in effect give the same answer to the Deputys that I had done, putting them in mind of their treatys ; and yett I thought, even out of what he said himselfe to me, I could see that Spayne would consent to the peace offred by the French.

On Tuesday by the post I may perhaps give your Lordship a further account of what progresse is made in answer of this French letter ; and in the meantime I have nothing at the present more to add, but that I am with great respect, My Lord,

Your Lordships most obedient and most humble servant,

L. Hyde.[1]

To the Lord Treasurer.[2]

Hague, May the 28th/June the 7th, 1678.

My Lord,

I am extremely oblidged to your Lordship for the favour of your letter of the 21th,[3] by which you have been pleased so clearly to informe me of the condition of his Majestys affaires, and of his pleasure concerning my behaviour here, which I shall be sure to conforme to, to the best of my understanding. And accordingly on Saturday last [4] in the evening, when the Deputys of the States came to communicate to me the answer from the French King to Monsieur Beverningk, and desired me in the name of the States to represent to the King that the ill condition of their affaires had made them looke upon the peace as the onely meanes to preserve themselves from ruine, and to desire his Majestys complyance with them in consenting to it, I made no other answer but that I should faithfully represent their desires to his Majesty, and if I received any commands upon it would acquaint them with them.

I suppose your Lordship will find from the Prince of Orange that I have obeyed your commands to him in acquainting him with what you directed me to say to him concerning the separate bargaines the King seemed to be apprehensive of for the exchange of Flanders, for his Highnesse returned me no answer but that he would write particularly of it to your Lordship. And accordingly, while I have been writing this, I have received the enclosed from his Highnesse [5] to be sent your Lordship. X *I know not whether in his letter to you he retaines anything of the complaints he was full of, that the conduct of this peace, which he*

---

[1] Endorsed by Leeds, ' Of use about the peace and Princes leave to tell mee. Note his trust in mee.'

[2] From the autograph letter in Leeds MSS., Packet 10. *Letters*, p. 341. Hyde's draft is in B.M. Add. MSS. 17016, f. 232.

[3] This letter has not been found.   [4] May 25/June 4.

[5] Printed *supra*, p. 433.

hath given over striving any longer in, hath been taken out of his hands, by trusting Monsieur van Lewen so much with it ; but I cannot help saying so much of it to your Lordship that I never saw any man more concerned at anything then his Highnesse was at that part of the management of this businesse.

Upon this occasion of speaking of the Prince I take leave to putt your Lordship in mind that about the time the offensive treaty was concluding here with the States I had at two severall times directions from the Secretary of State to tell the Prince that his Majestys mind and resolution was to insist that his Highnesse's concernes should be provided for in the peace, and was therefore willing to have signed any private article to that purpose if the Prince thought it necessary; to which the Prince appointed me then to returne this answer, with his most humble thanks to his Majesty, that he depended so much upon his Majestys protection that he would by no meanes have any article concerning himselfe, being confident of the effects of his care, when the peace should come to be concluded, without any such engagement. What I now write to your Lordship of this matter is without the least knowledge of his Highnesse. On the contrary, he doth very affectedly decline any mention of himselfe or his interests. But so much as what I have now repeated to you haveing so long agoe pasied thro my hands, I thought it not amisse to say thus much of it to your Lordship, leaving it to your judgment to make what use you please of it, and humbly [1] beg you to believe that I am with all respect, My Lord,

Your Lordships most obedient and most humble servant,

L. Hyde.[2]

To the Lord Treasurer.[3]

Hague, August the 16/26th, 1678.

My Lord,

I have written so long a letter to Mr. Secretary Williamson that I begin now to be affraid it is too particular an account, especially since after all it amounts to little more then that by

---

[1] The version printed in the *Letters* concludes, ' And I have nothing to add but humbly to beg you,' etc. No authority for this has been found in the handwriting of the Duke of Leeds.

[2] Endorsed by Leeds, ' The States desire to his Majestie to consent with them to the conditions of peace offered by France.'

[3] From an autograph draft in B.M. Add. MSS. 17016, f. 264.

Tuesday[1] *it is likely I shall know something more ; and haveing been so particular there, it were but reasonable I should spare your Lordship a new trouble of hearing something more from me by this post. It is onely to add one word to what I have said concerning Monsieur du Cros, which is that the Pensionar named the man to me who gave him that intelligence of the words spoken concerning the Prince of Orange, and says he is liveing at Nimmeguen, in some of the ambassadors familys there, where du Cros said the words. Thus much light the Pensionar was willing to give, to lett the King see he had given him the information upon good grounds, which he wishes may be a meanes to give his Majesty a true character of the man, and to be aware of him. But if any further notice be taken of it, it must be driven home to the author of the intelligence, which can but onely deprive him (the Pensionar) of an usefull correspondent, and perhaps hang a poor man.*

I thought it fitt to give your Lordship this information, because the matter seemes to me in my instructions to be earnestly recommended to a diligent search and enquiry after it, and that your Lordship may be pleased to lett the King know why I cannot arrive at more proofes in it. One thing more I beg I may take the liberty to recommend to your Lordship, and it is from the Pensionar, that great care be taken that whatsoever accounts or advices may be sent from those who serve his Majesty here as comeing from him (the Pensionar), his being the author of them may be managed with great secrecy ; else it is written againe hither from England that the Pensionar had said such and such things to the English ambassador, and whatever Monsieur van Beuningen comes to hear of that kind is not returned with any advantage to the Pensionar. I beg your Lordships pardon for this grave advertisement of mine. It may serve to shew you that I am ready to take any occasion to renew the professions of my being ever with great respect, My Lord,

Your Lordships most obedient and most humble servant,

[L. Hyde]

---

[1] August 20/30.

To the Lord Treasurer.[1]

Hague, August the 20/30th, 1678.

My Lord,

Haveing by the last post and this given Mr. Secretary Williamson as particular an account as I could of all that hath passed here in relation to my commission here, I have very little to trouble your Lordship with, but to beg your favourable interpretation of all my omissions in the execution of his Majestys commands, for which I have made the best justification I can, that it was the Prince of Orange's earnest advice, and submitt all to his Majestys gratious determination. Your Lordship will further give me leave to acquaint you that the journey Monsieur du Cros had made hither, and a letter Monsieur van Beuningen had writt but a weeke before I came over, in which he had sent his masters word that the King approved of their signing the treaty with France, had not at all prepared their minds for the proposition I came to make to them. On the contrary, when they came to hear it, and laid the former passages I have now mentioned and this together, it putt many of them into such jealousys that the King and the Prince of Orange were upon particular designes separate from the interest of the state, that those of Amsterdam, who had not for fifteen days stirrd the sending ambassadors into France, did that very afternoon, after I had communicated my businesse to the States, very violently presse the sending them without delay, and likewise for the ratification of the treaty with France, in which before they had found great faults, and had sufficiently reprooved Monsieur Beverning for signing it.

This for a day or two ran so high that the Prince did not know what to make of it, and wished that my instructions had not gone so farr as they did, but that instead of pressing the States upon the obligation of their treaty with his Majesty, which the King tooke to be of force, they had been onely to this purpose, that the States would not ratifye their treaty with France till Spayne had satisfaction according to the propositions made at Nimmeguen, and in the evacuation of their townes ; that is in plaine termes not to frighten them with the apprehension of falling back into the warr,

[1] From the autograph letter in Leeds MSS., Packet 10. Hyde's draft is in B.M. Add. MSS. 17016, f. 276.

but to keep them up to gett those points of France now, tho they were not done within the terme limited by their treaty with the King, which the Prince from the beginning allwaies told me must be the first step the States could make, whatever they should be brought to after. This temper, which I have sufficiently been a wittnesse of here, may, I hope, dispose your Lordship to thinke I have not done amisse in softning so much of my instructions as the concealing the orders I had to declare his Majesty would withdraw his troops from the Prince of Orange's army hath amounted to.

I should further add to your Lordship that all the forraigne ministers here who have had knowledge of those parts of my instructions that I did communicate to the States (and every one of them now doth know) were all apprehensive que la dose estoit trop forte, according to the terme the Marquis de Grana gave it, and were in great apprehension it would not have had so good an effect as this day hath produced. It is their word that I use, and the Prince of Orange's too, when I call it good, for I cannot tell what his Majestys opinion may be of it, and whether it may at all answer his expectations. I wish heartily it may, and desire your Lordships favour and protection in it to one that is with great truth and respect, My Lord,

Your Lordships most obedient humble servant,

L. Hyde.

To the Lord Treasurer.[1]

Hague, September the 10/20th, 1678.

My Lord,

It is the Prince of Orange's commands that are the occasion of my giveing your Lordship this trouble, who desired me to putt your Lordship in mind of the money due to him for the Princesse's portion, of which there was one payment due before the time that I spoke to your Lordship once allready in this matter, and now there is allmost another, which his Highnesse seemes a little concerned for, and that he doth not heare anything from your Lordship of it. I know nothing more that I can say to your Lordship upon it, but just repeat the Princes desire to your Lordship that

[1] From the autograph letter in Leeds MSS., Packet 10.

he may find the effects of your care and kindnesse to him in this particular, which he very much depends upon ; and your Lordship will find by another debt of his Highnesse's that he hath directed me to recommend to his Majesty, in my letter to the Secretary of State, that the Prince is endeavouring to gett in, or secure at least, all his debts at this time, so that your Lordship will not wonder that when his thoughts are upon that worke your Lordship comes to be sollicited. I have obeyed the Prince's commands, and have no more to add but the professions of my being with great respect, My Lord,

    Your Lordships most obedient and most faithfull humble servant,

L. Hyde.

REMARKS

ON SOME OF

MR. HYDE'S LETTERS [1]

I have mention'd only such of Mr. Hydes letters as relate to the private negotiations betwixt the King my master and the Prince of Orange, most of which the Prince durst not let be knowne to the States, and wherein he trusted nobody in England (besides the King) but myselfe. And in his of April 30th/May 10th he mentions that my discourse to Monsieur van Beuninghen had kept the States from coming to so speedy a resolution about the peace, and that letter of Monsieur van Buninghens about his discourse with me was read to the States on the 29th Aprill 1678, so that my discourse must have been with the embassadour here in England some daies before ; and then I desire it may be observed how that likewise agrees with my so often repeated letter of 25 March, [16]78, on which I was accused, this discourse of mine with the embassadour being within a month at farthest after [2] the said letter, and my discourse with the embassadour made publick to France and all the world so soone after. [2]

For fear of makeing this narrative too large, I have not incerted any letters writt betwixt the Secretaries of State and his Majesties severall embassadours ; [3] but I thought it proper

[1] B.M. Add. MSS. 28044, f. 55, in a copyist's handwriting, with some alterations and additions in the handwriting of the Duke of Leeds. *Letters,* p. 343.

[2] . . . [2] This passage has been substituted by Leeds for the following : ' that foresaid 25th March 1678 to which all my accusations relate, except that which concerns the concealment of the Popish Plott, which I do not think any one man in England did beleive (although they made it one of the articles against mee) and of which I have given a particular account by itselfe.'

[3] These letters, of course, were not in the possession of the Duke of Leeds, although he had copies of one or two of them.

to incert one part of Secretary Williamsons dispatch to Mr. Hyde which is dated the 4th December 1677, which does so fully make appear his Majesties possitive resolutions to joyne with the States to oblige France, if the States will joyn with him to oblige Spain to accept the conditions which were sent by the Lord Feversham, in case either France or Spain should refuse them, and was so forward in this that he offerred to take the Princes word alone for the performance of this resolution if he did but beleive that the States would come up to it.

Note also my respectful treatment of the French in my letter to Mr. Hyde of the 16th of April 1678, which was but twenty days after my so often repeated letter of the 25th of March 1678.[1]

[1] This last paragraph appears only in the *Letters*.

MR. GODOLPHIN'S LETTERS, ETC.

Instructions for Mr. Sidney Godolphin,
8th February, 1677/8.[1]

You are imediately to go to the Prince of Orange, and to represent to him :

1st. That, contrary to my expectations, I find the Parliament very backward in theire proceeding to give mee [2] supplys for the support of a war against France.

2nd. That the steps which have been made towards itt hitherto have been with very great difficulty, and that I have too much reason to bee confident that all I shall bee able to gett att last from them will either bee too litle to maintaine the war, or given so late, and for so short a time, as will not inable mee to do you [3] any good, but may probably putt mee into a dangerous condition both att home and abroad.

3rd. That I have received letters from my resident att Bruxells, who writes that, by the Duc de Villa Hermosa's directions, hee was to lett mee know that the Duke hoped I would conclude a peace upon the best conditions I could gett, for that hee despaired of saveing Flanders by a war, and repeated these desires to him twice.

4th. That although the Marquis de Bourgomaine would not directly owne the saying so much as my resident had writt, yett hee confessed, and does still, that the Duc de Villa Hermosa wishes a peace much rather then the continuance of the war.

5th. That when the Spaniard shall see our backwardnesse, and how litle assistance I shall bee able to give them this yeare (or perhaps att all), and seeing to what extremities they will bee

---

[1] From a copy, or possibly a draft, in Danby's handwriting in Leeds MSS., Packet 10. Printed in *Letters*, p. 346.

[2] The *Letters* insert ' sufficient.'   [3] The *Letters* read ' him.'

reduced by the great preparations made against them, I cannot but beleeve they will either submitt to any seperate peace which shall bee offered by France, or that they will bee no longer able to keepe theire townes from giveing themselves up to the French.

7th.[1] That these considerations have moved mee to send you purposely to acquainte him with this true state of things here, to the end that hee might take his owne measures the more certainely, and that I might receive his opinion what, as the case stands, might bee most adviseable for us both.

8th. That I have reason to thinke (although itt has not been directly proposed to mee) that the propositions for a peace sent by my Lord Feversham would bee accepted, saveing the towne of Tournay, but that, as I will never heare of any alteration without the Prince of Orange his consent to itt, so I have told the French embassador that I would never propose to the Spaniards the quitting of Tournay, because itt opens such a passage into the heart of Flanders. But I desire to know whither, to avoide worse consequences by the war, the Prince might not thinke convenient to lett mee offer Charlemont, or some other place hee may thinke of, for Tournay, if by such an accomodation the peace could bee procured, because I am confident the Duc de Villa Hermosa would bee glad of itt, and I have the same opinion of the States.

9th. You shall give him full assurance that these propositions proceed not in the least from any change or alteration of my resolutions to remaine firme to him and to the treaty I have made with the States, but purely to prevent, by all possible expedients, those greater mischeifes which I feare may befall both him and mee, by my incapacity of assisting him as I would, and the great uncertainety of receiveing either timely or sufficient supplys from my Parliament to do itt.

10th. You may also assure him, in case you shall find any scruple on his part, that the proposall of changeing some place for Tournay is wholly from myselfe, and that I never have received any such proposall from France, nor do know whither any such would bee accepted.

---

[1] The absence of a sixth paragraph is probably due simply to a slip in numbering.

11th. You shall also lett him know that in case a peace cannot bee agreed on, itt will bee impossible for mee to send any troops into Flanders, unlesse I may have the port of Ostend putt into my hands ; and I desire that hee will interest himselfe so far in that matter that I may by him know whither in that case the Spaniard will lett mee have itt or no.

Lastly, you are to remind him how long I have been in expectation of somebody from him to concert the navall preparations and other matters relateing to the war, and I desire that somebody may bee sent over for that purpose with all convenient speed.

You shall comunicate all these instructions to my embassador, Mr. Hyde, but both of you are to pretend your businesse to bee only to give the Prince of Orange an account of your negotiation with the Duc de Villa Hermosa about Ostend.

You are to returne in two daies after your arrivall att the Hague, or where else you shall find the Prince, unlesse hee shall desire your stay for some dayes longer.[1]

Instructions to Mr. Godolphin about the Pentioner Monsieur Fagell, *8th February, 1677/8.*[2]

Besides those instructions you have received from Mr. Secretary Williamson in order to your speaking with the Pentioner Monsieur Fagell you are further to lett him know :

1st. That Monsieur Barillon, the French Kings embassador in this Court, hath (since the seige of Ghent, and when they were assured of itts being taken in a few daies) told his Majestie that hee had powers to signe a treaty of peace upon the propositions sent by his Majestie to the French King by my Lord Feversham (excepting Tournay, Valenciennes and Conde), and upon those conditions to restore Ghent so soone as itt should bee taken.

2. That the said embassador did assure his Majestie that the Popes nuncio had on the part of Spaine offered to quitt Tournay before the seige of Ghent.

---

[1] Endorsed by Danby, ' Quere the use of these according to the notes in the large paper.'

[2] From a draft in Danby's handwriting in Leeds MSS., Packet 10. The endorsement, also in his handwriting, is here given as a heading.

3. That the knowlege of this, together with what the Pentioner had said to my Lord Embassador Hyde, and his Majesties unprepared condition to give a present considerable assistance to the Prince of Orange, had made his Majestie agree to the leaveing Tournay and Valenciennes out of the propositions of the peace in case the Prince of Orange and the Spaniard should desire the peace on those tearmes.

4. That although they insist upon Conde as well as Tournay and Valenciennes, his Majestie does beleeve that the peace may bee had upon the two last without Conde, if the answer bee speedy before they shall have taken other places.

5. That his Majestie will act nothing in this matter but what shall bee by the desires both of Spaine and the States signified to him by the Prince of Orange, his resolutions being to pursue the last treaty of alliance with the States to the utmost unlesse hee shall bee requested by them to do otherwise.

6. That you are directed to say all this to the Prince of Orange, but that his Majestie knowing the intire confidence his Highnesse hath in the Pentioner, and being doubtfull whither his distance from the Prince might not occasion some losse of time in this matter, you were comanded to comunicate itt fully to him.

7. That you are to comunicate all this to Mr. Hyde, his Majesties embassador att the Hague, and to take his assistance along with you in the whole matter.

[To the Lord Treasurer] [1]

Hague, the 12/22th of March, 1677/8.
My Lord,

    I arrived here yesterday, and this morning my Lord Embassadour brought me to the Pensioner, whom I acquainted as well as I could with the termes upon which Monsieur Barillon said he had power to signe the peace, as also such other particulars as I had in comand from his Majesty by the hands of Mr. Secretary Williamson, taking notice especially of his (the Pensioners) discourse of the consternation of their country, and the universall desire of a peace represented to his Majesty by my Lord Embassadour there present, which very representation

[1] From the autograph letter in Leeds MSS., Packet 10. *Letters*, p. 351.

my Lord Embassadour explain'd to him was the occasion of his Majestys commanding me to passe that way, and to acquaint him (out of an apprehension of losing time, and knowing the entire trust and confidence the Prince had in him) with this proposition of the French Embassadours concerning the peace.

He answer'd without any delay that the condition of their affayres was worse now than when he had made that representation of it to my Lord Embassadour, for one instance whereof he said that their actions were fallen since that time almost 20 in the 100 ; that notwithstanding this, those of Amsterdam (whom he had most apprehended) had resolv'd to make another contribution toward the support of the warr, and declin'd the taking (for the present) any hasty measures towards a peace, till they had a return of their representation into England of the extremity to which they were reduced ; that he was sensible that neither the King of England nor any other ally's of theirs were in a condition to send them such considerable and immediate succours as the urgent necessity of their affayres required ; that the Spaniards (as I should find) had not in all Flanders above 4,000 men ; that the Emperors army could not possibly march towards their assistance till May at the soonest ; that the forces of Brandenbourgh and the other ally's were likewise very backward ; and concluding, if the peace were not accepted upon these conditions (ill as they were) the French must presently bee masters of all the great towns in Flanders. He added farther that he took it to bee the interest of the Prince of Orange to make the peace even upon these hard conditions, as he often called them, because that without it he could hardly recover his interest in the country and the affections of the people, which had of late too visibly declin'd towards him.

When I told him that the King my master had hopes (soe that this proposition were suddenly consented to) of getting Conde restor'd, though the French insisted now upon that place as well as Tournay and Valenciennes, he said he would lose no time to send immediately to the Prince to acquaint him with the proposition I had brought, as likewise of his own opinion upon it ; and in the mean time he would not communicate any part of it to the States till he had had the Prince's answer, which he

hoped would bee agreeable to what he had there said to my Lord
Embassadour and me, and to what he was well convinced was
the particular interest of the Prince himselfe ; adding that if
the Prince concurr'd in it, when it should come to bee communicated to the States, there would bee an universall joy in the
whole country, and he beleiv'd the Spaniards would also bee
very well pleas'd with it.

Wee repeated often to him how important it was that this
should appeare to bee done at the instance and desire as well of
Spain as of the States, and he promised that should bee done in
such form as my Lord Embassadour himselfe should think most
expedient. I hope your Lordship will please favourably to impute some part of the confusednesse of this letter to the hurry
I am in, being presently to depart towards Antwerp ; and you
may the better excuse my omissions, since they will bee soe fully
supply'd by my Lord Embassadour. I remayn with all possible
respect, My Lord,

Your Lordships most humble and most obedient servant,

S. Godolphin.

To Mr. Godolphin.[1]

Whitehall, the 17th March, 1677/8.[2]

Sir,

My last to you was of the 12th, by the way of the Hague,
since which I have received the favour of yours of the 10/20 and
12/22, which last brought an account of the state of things as
you found them upon discourse with the Pensioner at your
arrivall at the Hague, and that you were that day parting to
continue your journey to the Prince of Orange, in order to the
informing yourselfe what would be his Highnesses mind and
thoughts upon the violent humour that had discovered itselfe in
Holland for the peace. Wee are now in a day or two to expect,
if the weather allow it, some account of that matter from you,
which you will easily judge it extremely imports his Majesty to
know with all the speed possible.

In the meane time his Majesty goes on with all the vigour and

[1] From the autograph letter in Leeds MSS., Packet 10. *Letters*, p. 355.
[2] Noted on the cover as ' 11 at night.'

diligence possible to perfect his leavyes, and in severall places considerable musters have already been made of those new men. Twenty companyes more of 100 apiece are now passeing over to Flanders, beyond the 2,800 already there, so as nothing is left undone which is in his Majestys power for the reliefe of the common cause. It is true that the King cannot goe so fast as he would in this worke, from the great delays the supply has hitherto mett with in the House. You know how ill a humour you left us in, and I am sorry to tell you the humour has growne and does grow dayly much worse.

The Poll Bill indeed is passed the two Houses, but with the tacked clause of an absolute prohibition of the four or five principall French commodityes of wine, salt, linnen, brandy and paper and silke for three years. The rest of the million, which is by farre the greater part, is yet uncared for by the Commons ; and they give us but very small hopes of their goeing much farther [1] towards the making up the million unlesse the King would first declare the warre, which, by an addresse now before the Lords to joine with us in, wee are goeing to presse him most violently to, whereas you know that's absolutely impossible (and so the King in the first opening of this session told them) till they have first given him this aid. And thus wee are againe fallen into the old circle of the King's askeing to be enabled to act, and their insisting to have him act before they have enabled him, so as, God knowes, things looke but very awkwardly as to a warre, and such a warre as this ought to be.

This it is fitt you should know in the station you are, though at the same time you will remember how wary you are to be in the use you make of these advices. That is, whatever discouradgements his Majesty unhappily meets with in this ill humour of the Parliament, yet still his Majestys resolutions you know are (as they were when you left us) to proceed with the utmost vigour in the execution of his allyance with the States ; and that whatever change fall out to be in things (I meane whatever tendencyes there arise elsewhere towards the peace) his Majesty is perfectly passive in it, and will not by any meanes that it should be thought to arise from his Majesty, or that his Majesty

---

[1] Carelessly printed ' faster ' in the *Letters*.

gives at all into it, otherwise then as in a manner forced to it by
the States and Spaine, which you know was the main point you
are by your instructions directed to steere by in this whole
matter. And that is still to be your great caution, and which
you must above all take care of, although, as I tell you, it be
most true that things looke very awkardly here, I meane in
the ill humour of the House of Commons since you left us.

I pray you let us heare, as often and as early as your conveniency and leisure will allow, of all that passes with you. I
am ever with much truth, Sir,

Your most humble and faithful servant,

J. Williamson.[1]

[To the Lord Treasurer][2]

Hague, the 3rd of May/23rd of Aprill, 1678.

My Lord,

Having written very largely to Mr. Secretary Williamson
I will not trouble your Lordship with the repetition of the Princes
and of the Pensioners discourse to my Lord Embassadour and
mee since my arrivall here, but only tell you in short that the
States are come this day to a resolution of sending an extraordinary
embassadour into England without delay to perswade the King to
accept the conditions of peace proposed by France, and have wholly
declin'd to give a finall answer to those poynts which wee were
commanded by his Majesty to presse them in soe earnestly, or to
admitt of any expedient in lieu of them, till such time as they heare
from England what answer his Majestie shall have been pleased
to make to their desire concerning the peace. And it is the opinion
of the Prince of Orange that it will bee wholly impossible to make
them think of taking any measures for continuing in the warr till
the King shall have absolutely refus'd them his consent to this
peace, and then the Prince thinks they will betake themselves to
the thoughts of going on with the warr, though very unwillingly ;

[1] Endorsed by Danby, ' The Prince of Orange opened this letter and sent itt
to mee, Mr. Godolphin being comd away from the Hague.' Cf. the Prince's
letter of March 31, 1678, printed supra, p. 428.

[2] From the autograph letter in Leeds MSS., Packet 10, where there is also
a copy.

and even when they shall resolve to doe it he gives no great hopes that they should agree to prohibitt the comerce unlesse they bee in some measure forced to it by his Majestie, which the Prince thinks (when they shall have once agreed to goe on with the warr) not only practicable but advisable. He says farther (which sounds very preposterously) that at the same time they agree to carry on the war they must bee oblig'd to retrench part of theyr land forces, and all they hope to maintayne at sea is a squadron of small ships, with which they pretend to guard the North Sea, as they call it, leaving the Channell wholly to the Kings care, and theyr fleet at present in the Mediterranean, as long as the Spaniards shall continue to pay it.

I was going on by degrees to have given your Lordship more trouble than I intended when I began this letter, but my Lord Embassadour coming in just now and acquainting me with a discourse he has newly had with one who desires not to bee named in it, and which will acquaint you with all that can be written to you of any importance from hence, I shall refer your Lordship to his letter, and trouble you no farther at this time but with the assurances of my being, with all possible respect, My Lord,

 Your Lordships most humble and obedient servant,

        S. Godolphin.

The Prince goes to Breda to-morrow with intentions of returning hither in a week if no alarm call him in the meantime to the army.

To the Lord Treasurer.[1]

       Hague, May the 12/22, 1678.

My Lord,

 I have seldome anything to adde from hence to the dispatches of my Lord Embassadour worth troubling your Lordship, or else I should give myselfe the honour of writing to you oftner.

Yesterday in the afternoon there came hither a trumpetter from the French King, with a letter from his master to the States Generall ; and great care was taken that it should not miscarry, for there came a duplicate of it another way within

---

[1] From the autograph letter in Leeds MSS., Packet 10. *Letters*, p. 358.

two houres after, and a third at night by the way of Nimmegen. My Lord Embassadour sends a coppy of it to the Secretary, by which your Lordship will see how fittly it is framed, at least to distract the minds and resolutions of these people here, if not to flatter them into a separate peace. The States assembled to receive it, and after two hours consultation resolv'd to communicate it to their allyes, and desire their advice and councell thereupon.

My Lord Embassadour and I wayting to heare what they had done at Monsieur Odyke's house neare the Court, Monsieur Odyke came out of the Assembly to acquaint my Lord Embassadour that the States were just sending some Deputy's to his house, and desir'd him to goe home and receive them. Presently after he was gone the Prince came thither, and told me he would gladly have spoken to my Lord Embassadour before the Deputy's came to him, but since he was gone he desir'd me to goe to him immediatly, and tell him it was his advice, and he did desire him, when the Deputy's of the States should come to him, that he would putt them in mind of their promises and obligations to the King his master, and presse them in his Majesty's name to make good their allyance with him. The Prince added these words to me, And I hope all will goe well, for they have not yett resolv'd what their answer shall bee.

The Prince desir'd this advice of his might not bee written in any letter to bee shew'd at the Committee of Forreign Affaires, because it might bee prejudiciall to him if it were known here. My Lord Embassadour answer'd the Deputy's accordingly. For his answer I shall refer your Lordship to his owne dispatches, remayning ever with all possible respect, My Lord,

Your Lordships most humble and most obedient servant,

S. Godolphin.

To the Lord Treasurer.[1]

Hague, the 24/14th of May, 1678.

My Lord,

By the joynt dispatch of my Lord Embassadour and me to the Secretary of State your Lordship will see what answer the States of Holland have resolv'd to make to the French King's

---

[1] From the autograph letter in Leeds MSS., Packet 10. *Letters*, p. 361.

letter, as also that they were very unanimous in the answer itselfe, though they differ'd in the manner of sending, some desiring [1] to send Deputy's, others (and they the major part) a letter only ; that the Prince himselfe was of the mind of these latter in the morning, and voted with them ; but that afterwards, when my Lord Embassadour and I were with him, he seem'd to bee much unresolved, and to doubt within himselfe whether it were not better to send Deputy's. The reasons of his irresolution your Lordship will also see in the dispatch to Mr. Secretary, and I need not trouble you with the repetition of them.

But one thing which the Prince said to me alone I think myselfe obliged to acquaint you with. It was this. Speaking of the distractions and the divisions in England at this time, and how the finding them to increase every day in the Parliament was that which did most of all discourage him from struggling any longer against the inclinations of this whole country to the peace, ⌐ *he said that in all this time, when he had advices out of England contradicting one another soe that he knew not what to think, yett he had not heard one word from your Lordship, and that he could not but wonder very much at itt. I had little to say in answer to this, nor did I take upon me to excuse it upon the multiplicity of businesse with which you labour'd at this time ; but I thought it lay upon me to acquaint your Lordship with it, that you might judge yourselfe what was fittest to bee said to him.*

And this indeed was the only occasion of my troubling your Lordship now, for as to the businesse here ⌐ I can adde nothing to what you will see in the dispatch which goes by this post to Mr. Secretary. I remayn with all possible respect, My Lord,

Your Lordships most humble and obedient servant,

S. Godolphin.

---

[1] The *Letters* read ' designing.'

REMARKS

ON SOME OF

MR. GODOLPHIN'S LETTERS AND INSTRUCTIONS [1]

I have inserted the instructions given to Mr. Godolphin upon his being sent into Holland the 8th of February 1677/8, that it may thereby appear how firme the King my master continued to his allyance with the States ; and I have only added [2] four of his letters, and three of them written in March, May and June,[2] 1678, by which will appear the earnest sollicitations of the States to the King my master to gett him to consent with them to the conditions of so badd a peace as he could never be brought to, and that the Prince of Orange himselfe durst not be knowne to say anything against the peace, as bad as it was. And I desire it may be observed that this was within two months after the writeing of my letter of the 25th March 1678 to Mr. Mountague, on which I was accused.

[1] B.M. Add. MSS. 28044, f. 56, in a copyist's handwriting, with some altera-tions and additions in the handwriting of the Duke of Leeds. *Letters*, p. 363.

[2] . . . [2] This passage originally read, ' three of his letters to mee written in May.' In the *Letters* it reads, ' four letters, three of them written by Mr. Godolphin to me in March and May 1678, and one by Mr. Secretary Williamson to Mr. Godolphin in March.' The Duke of Leeds must have altered his intentions more than once as to what exactly he would publishhere.

SIR LEOLINE JENKINS'S LETTERS

[*To the Lord Treasurer*] [1]

Nimeghen, 5 November, [16]78.

My Lord,

Monsieur Olivecrantz, one of the Swedish ambassadors here, giving me a visit yesterday, begun his conversation with the news he had had out of England, of the discoveries made touching the horrid plott against his Majestie. He took out a list, and read it to me, of severall persons design'd for great offices military and civill, and sayd he was sure the dessein was not onely against his Majestie and his kingdomes but against all other Protestant princes and states, and that there was no way to prevent and defeat the effects of it but by making up a generall peace in Christendome with all the speed possible.

Discoursing further, he sayd the desseins of the papists against the Protestant religion in England had been long a brewing, and that he did not know how well the King had been serv'd by Mr. Montague while ambassador lately in France. The reason why he doubted was, he sayd, for that Mr. Montague had had, about a year and a halfe agoe, severall conferences in a private house in Paris, and at late houres in the night, with the Popes nuncio there, and that he (Monsieur Olivecrantz) had this notice from the envoyé of Sweden in France, and that that envoyé had had his information from the master of the house himself where Mr. Montague and the nuncio mett.

He added of himself that the King might have severall occasions to employ his ministers to treat with those of the Pope ; and there was, sayd he, about the time that those conferences were had, a

---

[1] From the original letter in B.M. Add. MSS. 34274, f. 99.

busines of importance that was much talkt of (and much desir'd by Spain), wherein his Majestie had a particular interest. It was that of a marriage between the King of Spain and the King's niece, the Duke of Orleans's daughter. This, he sayd, might be a very just cause (and there might be many more) for his Majestie to employ his ministers to speak with the Pope's nuncio at Paris. But it were fitt, sayd he, that his Majestie in such a conjuncture as this is were mov'd that he may please himself to reflect upon former occasions, and to determine whither these interviews were by his orders or not ; for if they were, his Majestie would not be displeas'd with the mention of them ; if they were not, he concluded they must be of very dangerous consequence. And he profess'd to me he mention'd them to that end, that his Majestie might have hereby an occasion given him to satisfy himself in so important a matter.

Hereupon I told him this notice to me was such that, upon the first hearing of it, it becomes my duty to endeavor to have it layd open before his Majestie. I therefore besought him to tell me the time as particularly as he could, to the end his Majestie may be able to make his reflexions the better upon it ; as also that he would be pleas'd to lett me know if anything of the occasion or subject-matter of those conferences was come to his knowledge. For the occasion or the subject-matter, he said, he knew nothing of it, nor of any other circumstances ; and for the time, he could say no more but that it was about a year and a half agoe in May or June, [16]77. I desir'd him that he would be pleas'd to take the paines to see the dates of those letters whence he had the information, and that I would wayt on him at his house in order to have the precise time. He answerd me that he had not had his information by letters or in writing, but that he would write, and in twelve or fifteen dayes would probably be able to tell me the time more precisely, and it may be something more of the dessein against our religion in England.

From this he passt on to the subject of the peace between Sweden and Brandenburgh, which I do give an accompt of to Mr. Secretary Williamson, and therefore doe not presume to trouble your Lordship with it here. Nor doe I write to Mr. Secretary or to any else of this he sayd touching Mr. Montague, well hoping that he hath done nothing but what he hath good warrant for, and will have your Lordship's protection in. My obligations to him, and to my Lord

Chief Baron,[1] *which are very great and ancient, make me to regrett extremely this mention I am forced to make of a name I so much honour. But then the doeing of it becomeing upon me a duty, a duty indispensable, I cannott do Mr. Montague better right then humbly to putt this concern of his into your Lordships hands, knowing your zeal for our religion and the King's service on the one side, and assuring myself on the other side of the justice and care your Lordship will have for that honourable gentleman.*

If your Lordship shall think fitt to have anything sayd to Monsieur Olivecrantz (who does not seem to treat this busines as if a secret were to be made of it), this bearer hath orders to return as soon as he is dismiss'd by your Lordship. I beseech Allmighty God to preserve his Majestie, and that the same blessed providence that hath still watched over his person may now guide and assist your Lordship and all that labour in the discovering and defeating of that malice of hell that means any hurt to his sacred person or disturbance to his government. I am with a perfect respect, and under the deepest sense of obligation, My Lord,

Your Lordships most humble and most obedient servant,

L. Jenkins.

To Sir Leoline Jenkins.[2]

London, 22 November, 1678.

My Lord,

I am to acknowlege the favour of your Excellencys letter of the 5th instant, and to lett you know that I shew'd itt imediately to his Majestie, who is thereby made very desirous of getting all the information hee can possibly of what is yett but darkly hinted by Monsieur Olivecrantz. You say hee did read to you a list of severall persons designed for great offices, &c. ; but itt is not plaine whether that was a list hee had lately from England, or some other list hee knows of, because hee said hee

---

[1] Ralph Montagu's uncle, William Montagu.

[2] From the autograph draft in B.M. Add. MSS. 34274, f. 102. There is another draft or copy in Leeds MSS., Packet 10, differing in some respects from this, which is endorsed by Leeds, ' To Sir Temple, 22 November [16]78. About Mr. Montagu by Monsieur Olivecrans.' This is printed in *Letters*, p. 266, as a letter to Temple.

was sure the designe was not only against his Majestie and kingdomes but against all other Protestant princes and states, and that the designs of the papists against the Protestant religion in England had been long a brewing.

As to what concernes Mr. Montagu, I perceive his Majestie knows nothing of his conferences with the Popes nuncio ; and for what Monsieur Olivecrantz supposes might have been the occasion of those conferences, viz., a treaty of marriage betwixt the King of Spaine and the Duke of Orleans daughter, his Majestie saies hee never entred into any such treaty, nor ever gave Mr. Montagu any instructions about itt. You say also in your letter that in twelve or fifteen daies Monsieur Olivecrantz would probably bee able both to tell the time more precizely of those conferences,[1] and perhaps something more of the designe against our religion in England, which gives us great impatience till wee heare againe from you of that matter, [2] *being under so great apprehensions of the papists att this time that wee can apply our thoughts to no other businesse, of what importance soever itt bee, either att home or abroad.*[2]

If your Excellency shall judge itt necessary att any time [3] for mee to write to Monsieur Olivecrantz to incourage him in this matter, I have the Kings comand to do itt ; and in the meane time his Majestie would have you to tell him how acceptable a service his Majestie shall esteeme itt if hee can disclose any of those practices which hee has too much reason to feare have been designed both against himselfe and Protestant religion.[4] His Majestie has not thought fitt to lett your letter or the substance of itt bee comunicated to anybody whatever, because hee feares the discourse of itt might hinder so ample a discovery as hee hopes to make by Monsieur Olivecrantz his assistance

[1] The copy in Leeds MSS. and the *Letters* give ' the time of those conferences more precizely.'

[2] . . . [2] This passage is omitted in the copy in Leeds MSS. and in the *Letters*.

[3] The copy in Leeds MSS. and the *Letters* omit ' att any time.'

[4] The copy in Leeds MSS. and the *Letters* conclude at this point, ' and of which hee hopes to make a more ample discovery by Monsieur Olivecrantz's assistance and your care. I am, &c., Danby.—P.S. What Monsieur Olivecrantz shall tell you further of this matter his Majesty would have you send by expresse.'

and your care. I am with great esteeme and all the truth in the world, My Lord,

Your Excellencys, &c.,

[Danby] [1]

If Monsieur Olivecrantz shall tell you anything of importance in this affaire, his Majestie would have itt sent away by an expresse.

[To the Lord Treasurer] [2]

Nimmeghen, 3 December, [16]78.

My Lord,

I receiv'd not till yesterday the honour of your Lordships letter of the 22th past by that most unfortunate servant of mine that came over in his Majesties yacht now lost upon the coast of Holland. The displeasure and the losse that his Majestie will have by that accident doe so afflict me that though his Majestie of his royall goodnesse should not impute to me any share in the occasion of it, yet I shall think myself bound to bemoan so great a disaster, and shall never doe it sufficiently the longest day of my life.

This morning I spoke with Monsieur Olivecrantz, taking occasion to doe it from the use I was to make of your Lordships name to him. He told me he had not yet any further light to give me touching any practice against our religion in England. Onely touching the list of officers that he had read to me, he had receiv'd it, he sayd, from Sir John Legenberg, the Swedish minister in London, and was the same with that which came hither about that time to severall hands, and was afterwards common in the prints. As to the precise time of the conferences between Mr. Montague and the nuncio, he had this to adde, 1. that they were had at the time the French besieged and took Cambray ; 2. that they were had in the house of the Abbé Siri, the same Siri that hath written a Generall History in Italian in severall volumes in quarto ; 3. that there were three conferences between them, had within the space of fifteen dayes or thereabouts.

[1] Endorsed by Danby, " Coppy of my letter to Sir Lionell Jenkyns in answer to his of the 5th of November 1678. Dated the 20th [sic] November, [16]78.

[2] From a fragment of the original letter in B.M. Add. MSS. 34274, f. 104.

The reason why Monsieur Olivecrantz can yet say nothing further of what he had told me he might probably be able to doe within a few dayes is that his correspondent when he writt to him had excus'd himself from entring into any further commerce with him upon this matter untill he were possessd of a good cypher between the ambassador and himself. Monsieur Olivecrantz says he could not but give in to the caution, and that he prepar'd a sufficient cypher accordingly, but lighted not on a safe hand to conveigh it till about eight dayes agoe. When his friend hath the cypher he thinks he may advise him of some particulars that may not be unusefull for his Majestie to know.[1]

[*L. Jenkins*]

To Sir Leoline Jenkins.[2]

Whitehall, 31th December, 1678.

My Lord,

I have been thus long silent because I had nothing to add to my last, wherein I signifyed to you his Majestys comands for the pursueing so farre as you could that intelligence you had given him concerning Mr. Mountague, and I have now only to tell you again that his Majestie is a little impatient till he heares more of that matter, having been as ill used by Mr. Mountague heer as hee was there by his negotiating without his Majestys commission or privity.

His Majestie hath been much prest of late to interest himselfe in the concernes of the Duke of Holsteyn, for whom his Majestie would be very glad to doe any good offices ; but there are so many intricacyes in that affaire that his Majestie finds it very difficult to give any particular instructions in it, but is willing you should shew all readinesse to the doeing him any fitting services and (when his minister shall come to you) to let him know how ready his Majestie shal be to improve any occasion that shall offer its selfe for that Dukes service. I shall trouble you with no more now, but wish you a good new year, and assure you of my being with great truth,

Your Excellencyes most humble and faithfull servant,

[*Danby*]

---

[1] There follow two lines of a new paragraph, so heavily crossed out as to be indecipherable, and the letter then breaks off abruptly at the foot of a page.

[2] From a copy in Leeds MSS., Packet 10.

[To the Lord Treasurer] [1]

Nimeghen, 2 January, [16]78/9.

My Lord,

Since my last of the 5th of the last month [2] *I have lett passe no opportunity to wayt on Monsieur Olivecrantz in order to have from him that further light he had given me some hopes of, as I acquainted your Lordship ; and for a motive to induce him to it, I thought I could not do better then represent to him the great expectation his Majestie is pleased to be in of a good deal of light from him in the present conjuncture.*

His answers were very respectfull towards his Majestie, but it was easy to perceive that there was no comeing into any closer confidence with him in this matter, before hee be first satisfied how Monsieur du Cros came to partake of the informations I had given your Lordship concerning Mr. Montague. He does not now say (I come from speaking with him this very morning) that he hath not yet heard from his friend with whom he hath a correspondence by cypher ; but he says that in his informations he hath nothing that can give any light as to anything of a conspiracie against his Majesties person (whom God in his mercy preserve and blesse), nor does he know anything of the plottings of any of the Kings subjects against the government. He says particularly that he can say no more then he hath sayd (and of that I have allready given your Lordship an accompt) touching Mr. Montague, the person from whom he had his informations being now in Sweden.

All the informations, he says, that may have come to his know-ledge (dont je pourrois avoir connoissance were his words) are concerning the intrigues that the papists in severall parts do carry on against the Protestant religion, and that their dessein was to be putt in execution in England in the first place ; that the dessein was not against England onely, but against all Protestant states, and against Sweden in particular, but that the dessein against England is for the present prevented and disappointed ; that these desseins are layd and managed by the Pope and his Jesuites, but since they cannott be brought about but by force, it is certain there

---

[1] From the autograph letter among the Lindsey MSS., printed in *Lindsey MSS.*, p. 395.

[2] Probably Jenkins's letter of December 3 is here referred to, though the reference may be to his original letter of November 5.

are some secular powers that are to act as the Pope and his Jesuites shall have prepar'd things ; that those powers will act seemingly in favour of the popish religion, but their main end will be to serve their own turnes and to promote their own interests. These powers he did not name, tho' I made it my request he would be pleas'd to be particular in this point, and to lett me have some knowledge whom he meant.

He sayd further that while the powers thus engaged are persuaded that this is yet a secret, they will think of gaineing time to ripen things still for their own ends ; but if they perceive that the thing hath once taken wind, and that the Protestants are in allarme at it, they will ballance no longer, but putt things to a push, which he (the ambassador) looks upon as of infinite consequence to all Protestant states, so to Sweden in particular at this time. For this reason principally, that is for the danger that Sweden would be in if the secret he hath should take wind at this time, he desires to be excus'd from entring into any communication of particulars, most especially from committing anything to writing. He thinks he may be at libertie, after that the conferences we are now in are over, to take a turn for a few dayes into England in order to acquaint his Majestie with all particulars, and to negociate some affaires of the King his master.

This is all he would communicate to me, tho' I offered him all assurances to keep the thing as secret as himself could wish ; but finding him resolv'd not to do it but to his Majestie himself, I desir'd him to consider there might be infinite danger in delayeing the notice of it to his Majestie. His answer was there is none, and that he is sure of it there can be none, the measures against England being now broken.

This is the summe and substance of what I have from Monsieur Olivecrantz. I am afflicted that it is not more particular for his Majesties better information and satisfaction. I beseech God to give his Majestie all lights that are requisite for the safety of his sacred person and for the peace and prosperity of his government. I am with very deep obligations, and with a perfect respect, My Lord,

Your Lordships most humble and most obedient servant,

L. Jenkins.

[*To the Lord Treasurer*] [1]

Nimeghen, *13 January*, [16]78/9.

My Lord,

Upon the receipt of the honour of your Lordships letter of the *31th passt by the last poste I took the first occasion to move Monsieur Olivecrantz anew in his Majesties name, acquainting him with the speciall command I had to doe so, and with the expectation his Majestie is in to have from him of a further light touching Mr. Montague.*

He answer'd me that he had nothing more to say than what he had allready sayd in that businesse ; that the gentleman who gave him the intelligence is now in Sweden ; that it were no such hard matter (now that the house where Mr. Montague had his conferences with the nuncio, as also that the time when he had them, is distinctly pointed out, and that the Abbé Siry is a man so well knowen) to discover more of that intrigue then his (the ambassador's) correspondent, if he were within reach, would be able to say. In fine, my Lord, after many affirmations of his desire to serve his Majestie and to satisfie your Lordship, his conclusion was that he had nothing more to say touching Mr. Montague, and for other matters, which he had hinted to me in generall, as 'tis in my last of the 2nd current, that he reserv'd himself till he should have the honour to wayt on his Majestie.

I am extremely sorry not to be able to draw more informations from this ambassador in a matter so important to his Majestie, but I cannott hope that Monsieur Olivecrantz will open himself further to me in this affaire.

The Duke of Holstein's busines I do attend with all the applications I can possibly. If the peace be made with the Emperor the Swedes shall have an article expresse from the Emperors protection and good offices to that Duke. The Holstein ministers would have the Emperor obliged by treaty, over and above this, to relieve the Duke their master against a sentence given in the Imperiall judicature at Vienna to his prejudice. This sentence gives in costs and dammages to the Duke of Holstein-Pleun, against the Duke of Holstein-Gottorp, to the value of seaven hundred thousand*

---

[1] From the autograph letter among the Lindsey MSS., partly printed in *Lindsey MSS.*, p. 398.

crowns. From this he would be reliev'd either by review or else in an amicable way. The Emperor will agree to neither by way of treaty. The review the Emperor cannott deny, if it was askd in time. For amicable offices, they will be the lesse efficacious if they be stipulated by treaty. I think verily the sentence was not well given, but having been given in a judiciall way the Emperor will not be brought to reverse by treaty.

Thus this matter stands with the Imperialists ; but that Duke will not be relievd to effect unless he have a good treaty with Denmark, and of this I have yet little prospect, the Danish ambassadors having yet enter'd into no manner of negotiation with those of Sweden ; and the treaty of Holstein can be at the best but an appendix to that between the Dane and the Swede.

I shall give your Lordship an accompt of every thing that is to be hoped for in that affaire, together with the assurances of my being with a perfect deep respect, My Lord,

Your Lordships most humble and most obedient servant,

L. Jenkins.

CONCLUSION [1]

Although I intend this narrative only for a vindication of myselfe, and not as a memoire to sett forth any actions of my owne (who have done nothing but my duty), yett haveing a claime which no man can deny (and hath been owned by King William himselfe) of my being the cheife instrument in procureing the match betweene him and his Queene (and for which I have had both theire thanks),[2] and that match haveing been under God the sole meanes not only of saveing both our religion and our laws, but of placeing the crowne upon her present Majestie, I will not suffer that part of my services to bee buried in oblivion.[3] And for the part I acted in pursuance of that duty to my country att the time of the Revolution I have so many liveing witnesses who were my companions in the north att that time that I shall rely on theire report of my behavior there, and doubt not but itt will bee such as will justify my haveing performed with success as much as lay in my power.[4]

---

[1] B.M. Add. MSS. 28044, f. 57, in the handwriting of the Duke of Leeds, endorsed by him, ' This is a draught for a conclusion att the end of the book of letters which is to bee printed.' *Letters*, p. 364.

[2] This passage within brackets is omitted in the *Letters*.

[3] The MS. has a cross here, which seems to suggest that a passage was to be inserted. The *Letters* add at this point, ' altho' I expect no thanks, and especially from some of those who owe their rise and preferment to it.'

[4] The *Letters* have a better ending, ' as much as fell within the compass of my power.'